P9-CEV-167

4. Lo siento.

5. —Con (su) permiso.
—Sí, cómo no.

6. ¡Cuidado!

7. —¡Salud!
—Gracias.

8. ¡Ay!

9. ¡Auxilio, socorro!

# DOS MUNDOS

## EN BREVE

## *Dedication*

This book is lovingly dedicated to Tracy D. Terrell (1943–1991). Tracy left us an enduring legacy: the Natural Approach, a methodology that has had a significant impact on second-language teaching and on the evolution of textbook materials. He also envisioned this book and guided us, the co-authors, to its fruitful completion. Tracy was our inspirational mentor. His ever-generous heart touched many of us—friends, colleagues, teachers, students—in an indelible way. We miss him. And we hope he is proud of our work in this new edition of *Dos mundos*. His kind spirit and brilliant vision infuse every page.

CAPÍTULO 3 **Las actividades y los lugares** 103

**Actividades de comunicación y lecturas** 104
**¿Dónde está?** 104
Lectura Una tarjeta postal desde Madrid 106
**Las actividades diarias** 107
Lectura Los amigos hispanos: Adela Martínez 110
El mundo hispano... imágenes 112
**¿De dónde es usted?** 113
El mundo hispano... su gente 114
Nota cultural Los hispanos en los Estados Unidos 115
**Las actividades del momento** 116
El mundo hispano... en los Estados Unidos 118

**En resumen** 119

**Vocabulario** 120

**Gramática y ejercicios** 123
3.1 Locating People and Objects: **estar** 123
3.2 Discussing Habitual Actions: Present Tense of Regular Verbs 124
3.3 Using Irregular Verbs: **hacer, salir, jugar** 127
3.4 Describing Origin and Location: **ser de / estar en** 128
3.5 Referring to Actions in Progress: Present Progressive 130

CAPÍTULO 4 **La vida diaria y los días feriados** 132

**Actividades de comunicación y lecturas** 133
**Los lugares** 133
Lectura Una tarjeta de Clara: Los lugares en Madrid 136
**Los días feriados y las celebraciones** 137
El mundo hispano... en los Estados Unidos 139
Nota cultural Celebraciones del mes de julio 140
**La rutina diaria** 142
El mundo hispano... su gente 144
**Los estados físicos y anímicos** 144
Lectura «Versos sencillos» de José Martí 147

**En resumen** 148

**Vocabulario** 150

**Gramática y ejercicios** 153
4.1 Talking about Location: **ir** + **a(l); estar** + **en** 153
4.2 Discussing Habitual Actions: Verbs with Stem-Vowel Changes (**ie, ue**) in the Present Tense 154
4.3 Discussing Habitual Actions: Irregular Verbs 156
4.4 Describing Daily Routine: Reflexives 157
4.5 Describing States: **estar** + Adjective 160
4.6 Describing States: **tener** + Noun 161

CAPÍTULO 5 **Las clases y las carreras** 163

**Actividades de comunicación y lecturas** 164
**Las actividades de la clase de español** 164
Las palabras viven El inglés y el español 167
**Las habilidades** 168
Nota cultural Los gestos 169
El mundo hispano... en los Estados Unidos 171
**Las carreras y las actividades del trabajo** 171
El mundo hispano... imágenes 175
El mundo hispano... su gente 175
**Las actividades futuras** 176
Lectura Los amigos hispanos: Adriana Bolini 178

**En resumen** 180

**Vocabulario** 181

**Gramática y ejercicios 183**
5.1 Telling to Whom Something Is Said: Indirect Object Pronouns with Verbs of Informing 183
5.2 Expressing Abilities: **saber** and **poder** + Infinitive 186
5.3 Pointing out People and Objects: Demonstrative Adjectives 187
5.4 Expressing Plans and Desires: **pensar, quisiera, me gustaría, tener ganas de** 189
5.5 Ordering Events: Infinitives after Prepositions 191
5.6 Making Suggestions: *Let's* 192

CAPÍTULO 6 **La residencia 193**

**Actividades de comunicación y lecturas 194**
**La casa, los cuartos y los muebles 194**
**La casa y el vecindario 198**
Nota cultural Las ciudades hispanas 200
El mundo hispano... su gente 201
**Las actividades en casa 202**
Las palabras viven ¡Este pibe labura mucho! 204
Lectura Habla la gata Manchitas 205
**Las actividades con los amigos 207**
El mundo hispano... imágenes 210
El mundo hispano... en los Estados Unidos 210
**Las presentaciones 211**

**En resumen 212**

**Vocabulario 213**

**Gramática y ejercicios 216**
6.1 Making Comparisons of Inequality: **más/menos** 216
6.2 Making Comparisons of Equality: **tan/tanto** 218
6.3 Expressing Obligation and Duty: **tener que, deber, necesitar, hay que, es necesario** 219
6.4 Talking about Past Actions: The Preterite of Regular Verbs (Part 1) 220
6.5 Knowing People, Places, and Facts: **conocer** and **saber** 222
6.6 Referring to People Already Mentioned: Personal Direct Object Pronouns 223

CAPÍTULO 7 **Las experiencias 226**

**Actividades de comunicación y lecturas 227**
**Mis experiencias 227**
El mundo hispano... su gente 230
**Las experiencias con los demás 230**
El mundo hispano... en los Estados Unidos 234
**Hablando del pasado 235**
Lectura Los amigos hispanos: Una carta desde Perú 237
El mundo hispano... imágenes 238
Las palabras viven La cultura incaica en Ecuador 239

**En resumen 239**

**Vocabulario 241**

**Gramática y ejercicios 243**
7.1 Talking about Past Actions: The Preterite of Regular Verbs (Part 2) 243
7.2 Relating More about the Past (Part 1): Verbs with Irregular Preterite Forms 246
7.3 Relating More about the Past (Part 2): Stem-Changing Verbs in the Preterite 249
7.4 Reporting the Past: Indirect Object Pronouns with **decir** 251
7.5 Expressing *ago*: **hacer** + Time 252

**Actividades de comunicación 34**
La familia 34
¿Qué tenemos? 35
Los números (10–100) y la edad 37
Los idiomas y las nacionalidades 38

**En resumen 40**

**Vocabulario 41**

**Gramática y ejercicios 43**
C.1 Expressing Possession: The Verb **tener; de(l)** 43
C.2 Expressing Possession: Possessive Adjectives 44
C.3 Expressing Age: The Verb **tener** 46
C.4 Describing People: Adjectives of Nationality 47
C.5 Talking about Habitual Actions: Present Tense of Regular **-ar** Verbs 48

**Actividades de comunicación y lecturas 51**
**Las fechas y los cumpleaños 51**
Lectura El horóscopo 53
**Datos personales: El teléfono y la dirección 54**
El mundo hispano... su gente 56
El mundo hispano... en los Estados Unidos 56
**La hora 57**
**Las actividades y los deportes 60**
El mundo hispano... imágenes 62
Nota cultural Los deportes 63

**En resumen 65**

**Vocabulario 67**

**Gramática y ejercicios 69**
1.1 Counting: Numbers 100–1000 and Dates 69
1.2 Spelling: The Spanish Alphabet 70
1.3 Talking about Habitual Actions: Present Tense of Regular **-er** and **-ir** Verbs 71
1.4 Asking Questions: Question Formation 72
1.5 Telling Time: Hours and Minutes 74
1.6 Expressing Likes and Dislikes: **gustar** + Infinitive 75

**Actividades de comunicación y lecturas 79**
**Los planes 79**
**Las clases 82**
Lectura Los amigos hispanos: Nora Morales 85
**Las preferencias y los deseos 86**
El mundo hispano... su gente 89
Nota cultural ¡Vamos a pasear! 89
**El tiempo 90**
El mundo hispano... imágenes 92
El mundo hispano... en los Estados Unidos 93

**En resumen 93**

**Vocabulario 95**

**Gramática y ejercicios 97**
2.1 Expressing Future Plans: **ir** + **a** + Infinitive 97
2.2 Sequencing: Ordinal Adjectives 98
2.3 Stating Preferences and Desires: **preferir** and **querer** + Infinitive 99
2.4 Describing the Weather: Common Expressions 101

# Contents

To the Instructor xi
To the Student xxvi

PASO A

## La clase y los estudiantes 1

**Actividades de comunicación 2**
Los mandatos en la clase 2
Los nombres de los compañeros de clase 3
¿Quién es? 4
Los colores y la ropa 5
Los números (0–39) 6
Los saludos 7

**Vocabulario 8**

**Gramática 11**
A.1 Responding to Instructions: Commands 11
A.2 Naming: The Verb **llamarse** 12
A.3 Identifying People and Things: Subject Pronouns and the Verb **ser** 12
A.4 Describing People and Things: Negation 13
A.5 Identifying People and Things: Gender (Part 1) 13
A.6 Describing People's Clothing: The Verb **llevar** 14
A.7 Identifying People and Things: Plural Forms (Part 1) 15

PASO B

## Las descripciones 16

**Actividades de comunicación 17**
Hablando con otros 17
Las cosas en el salón de clase y los números (40–69) 18
El cuerpo humano 20
La descripción de las personas 21

**En resumen 22**

**Vocabulario 23**

**Gramática y ejercicios 25**
B.1 Addressing Others: Informal and Polite *you* (**tú/usted**) 25
B.2 Describing People: More about Subject Pronouns 26
B.3 Identifying People and Things: Gender (Part 2) 27
B.4 Expressing Existence: **hay** 29
B.5 Describing People and Things: Plural Forms (Part 2) 30
B.6 Describing People and Things: Adjective-Noun Agreement 31

# DOS MUNDOS

***Tracy D. Terrell***
Late, University of California, San Diego

***Magdalena Andrade***

***Jeanne Egasse***
Irvine Valley College

***Elías Miguel Muñoz***

# EN BREVE

McGraw-Hill College

Boston Burr Ridge, IL Dubuque, IA Madison, WI New York San Francisco St. Louis
Bangkok Bogotá Caracas Lisbon London Madrid
Mexico City Milan New Delhi Seoul Singapore Sydney Taipei Toronto

*McGraw-Hill College*

*A Division of The McGraw-Hill Companies*

This is an EBI book.

*Dos mundos: En breve*

Copyright © 1999 by The McGraw-Hill Companies, Inc. All rights reserved. Printed in the United States of America. Except as permitted under the United States Copyright Act of 1976, no part of this publication may be reproduced or distributed in any form or by any means, or stored in a database or retrieval system, without the prior written permission of the publisher.

This book is printed on acid-free paper.

5 6 7 8 9 0 VNH VNH 9 3 2 1 0

ISBN 0-07-064549-3 (Student Edition)
ISBN 0-07-064550-7 (Instructor's Edition)

This book was set in Janson by GTS Graphics, Inc.
The editors were Thalia Dorwick, Gregory Trauth, Becka McGuire, and Richard Lange.
The production supervisor was Richard DeVitto.
The art editors were Jane Brundage and Nicole Widmyer.
Illustrations were done by David Bohn, Wayne Clark, Anica Gibson, Rick Hackney, and Sally Richardson.
The maps were done by Lori Heckelman.
The text and cover designer was Juan Vargas, Vargas/Williams/Design.
The photo researcher was Susan Friedman.
Von Hoffmann Press, Inc., was printer and binder.

Because this page cannot legibly accommodate all the copyright notices, page C-1 constitutes an extension of the copyright page.

**Library of Congress Cataloging-in-Publication Data**

Dos mundos : en breve / Tracy D. Terrell . . . [et al.].
p. cm.
English and Spanish.
Includes index.
ISBN 0-07-064549-3 (student ed.). — ISBN 0-07-064550-7 (instructors ed.)
1. Spanish language—Textbooks for foreign speakers—English.
I. Terrell, Tracy D.
PC4129.E5D67 1998 98-24083
468.2′421—dc21 CIP

**http://www.mhcollege.com**

## CAPÍTULO 8 La comida 253

**Actividades de comunicación y lecturas 254**
**Las comidas, las bebidas y la nutrición 254**
Lectura «Oda al tomate» de Pablo Neruda 258
Las palabras viven El idioma de los aztecas 260
**La compra y la preparación de la comida 261**
El mundo hispano... su gente 262
El mundo hispano... imágenes 264
Nota cultural Algunos platillos hispanos 266
Las palabras viven ¡Estoy como agua para chocolate! 268
**Los restaurantes 268**
El mundo hispano... en los Estados Unidos 272

**En resumen 272**

**Vocabulario 274**

**Gramática y ejercicios 277**
8.1 Referring to Objects Already Mentioned: Impersonal Direct Object Pronouns **lo, la, los,** and **las** 277
8.2 More about Expressing Likes: The Verbs **gustar** and **encantar** 279
8.3 Expressing *for, from,* and *to whom:* Prepositions + Pronouns 282
8.4 Making Negative Statements and Questions: *No, never* 283
8.5 Expressing *one* or *you:* The Impersonal **se** 285
8.6 Using Stem-Changing Verbs like **pedir** and **servir:** Present-Tense and Preterite Forms 286

## CAPÍTULO 9 El pasado 289

**Actividades de comunicación y lecturas 290**
**La familia y los parientes 290**
Las palabras viven En México, un *cuate* es un buen amigo 292
Nota cultural Los hispanos hablan de su familia 293
El mundo hispano... imágenes 295
**La niñez 296**
Lectura ¡Así piensan los niños! 299
**La juventud 301**
El mundo hispano... su gente 303
El mundo hispano... en los Estados Unidos 304

**En resumen 305**

**Vocabulario 306**

**Gramática y ejercicios 307**
9.1 Describing Family Relationships: The Reciprocal Reflexive Verbs **parecerse** and **llevarse bien** 307
9.2 Saying What You Used to Do: The Imperfect Tense 309
9.3 Describing the Past: The Imperfect and Preterite of "State" Verbs 311
9.4 Saying What You Were Going to Do: The Imperfect of **ir** + **a** + Infinitive 314

## CAPÍTULO 10 La geografía, el transporte y el medio ambiente 315

**Actividades de comunicación y lecturas 316**
**La geografía y el clima 316**
Lectura «Oda a la tormenta» de Pablo Neruda 319
El mundo hispano... su gente 322
El mundo hispano... imágenes 323
Lectura Un terremoto en Chile 324
**Los medios de transporte y el automóvil 325**
Lectura Iberia, la aerolínea española 328
Nota cultural *Seat:* La asistencia en la carretera 330
**La ecología y el medio ambiente 334**
El mundo hispano... en los Estados Unidos 335
Lectura La visión ideal de Costa Rica 337

**En resumen** 339

**Vocabulario** 342

**Gramática y ejercicios** 344
10.1 Saying What You Have Done: The Present Perfect 344
10.2 Exclaiming: **¡Qué... !, ¡Cuánto/a/os/as... !** 346
10.3 Expressing *by, through,* Destination, and Time: **por** and **para** 347
10.4 Describing Actions: Adverbs 348
10.5 Expressing Reactions: More Verbs like **gustar** 349

CAPÍTULO 11 **Los viajes** 351

**Actividades de comunicación y lecturas** 351
**Los planes de viaje** 352
El mundo hispano... su gente 353
**Buscando sitios y usando planos** 355
Lectura Una tarjeta de Clara: ¡Cuánto me gusta Madrid! 356
**De viaje por los países hispanos** 358
Lectura Los amigos hispanos: Planes para un viaje a México 362
El mundo hispano... imágenes 365
**Los sitios turísticos** 367
El mundo hispano... en los Estados Unidos 368

**En resumen** 369

**Vocabulario** 370

**Gramática y ejercicios** 372
11.1 Giving Instructions: Polite Commands 372
11.2 Softening Commands: The Present Subjunctive Following **querer** and **cuando** 374
11.3 Softening Commands and Expressing Future Doubt: The Present Subjunctive of Irregular Verbs 377
11.4 Talking about Past Actions in Progress: The Imperfect Progressive 380
11.5 Saying What Was Happening: The Imperfect in Contrast to the Preterite 381

**Appendices** A-1

**Spanish-English Vocabulary** V-1

**Index** I-1

# To the Instructor

## A Few Words about *Dos mundos: En breve*

This text is a new, shorter version of the Fourth Edition of ***Dos mundos.*** It is identical to that edition of ***Dos mundos,*** except that the last five chapters have been omitted to create a more compact yet still comprehensive first-year Spanish text that is ideal for programs with fewer than four contact hours a week. References to the omitted chapters from the Fourth Edition have been eliminated from the Student Edition, but such references may still appear in the accompanying supplements. A special ***Dos mundos: En breve*** Instructor's Edition, ***Cuaderno de trabajo,*** and sold Audio Program have been created for use with this Student Edition; all other Fourth Edition supplements are available as well and will "work" with ***Dos mundos: En breve.*** You should feel free to use the materials from Chapters 12–16 in those supplements, as needed.

We suggest the following breakdown for use of ***Dos mundos: En breve*** in different academic settings.

First Semester: **Paso A–Capítulo 5**

Second Semester: **Capítulos 6–11**

First Quarter: **Paso A–Capítulo 3**

Second Quarter: **Capítulos 4–7**

Third Quarter: **Capítulos 8–11**

What follows is the preface for the Fourth Edition of ***Dos mundos*** (the complete text).

Welcome to the Fourth Edition of ***Dos mundos***! We are excited about our new edition, which we believe is our best ever. A revision implies much more than just rewriting a few activities or adding new reading selections or grammar exercises. New editions present opportunities for growth, development, and—most important—improvement. Our guiding principle has always been the advancement of communicative ways of teaching. With each new edition we re-evaluate the theoretical premises on which our methodology is based, and we try to bring in fresh, practical ideas from the field of second-language teaching. And, of course, we listen to you, the instructors who use ***Dos mundos.*** We want to express our gratitude to those of you who sent us comments and suggestions. Feedback from you is a compelling reason to undertake the task of rethinking and rewriting our textbook. Your support is definitely a motivating force. Thank you!

Those of you who have used a previous edition of ***Dos mundos*** know that it is a special kind of text. It offers an exciting alternative to the methodology of most Spanish-language textbooks available today: the Natural Approach. The success of the Third Edition has convinced us that many instructors are eager to try out the Natural Approach in their classrooms. We also know about instructors of other languages who are using this methodology successfully. The encouraging message is that our method allows instructors to do what they have always wanted to do as educators: enjoy their work and help students enjoy the process of acquiring a second language.

Like many of you, we were using the Natural Approach in our classrooms long before there was a name for the method or a textbook like ***Dos mundos.*** Of course, we didn't need a book to teach language communicatively! We taught in a manner that felt right to us, and we were happy to prepare material to supplement whatever textbook we were using. But what a difference it made to have our ideas in printed form, finally!

When we designed the First Edition of ***Dos mundos,*** we were uncertain about some aspects of the textbook, such as how many readings or grammar exercises to include. There was one aspect about which we had no doubts, however: Communication was to be the core of our program. Three editions later, our initial objective hasn't changed. We have placed renewed emphasis on the communicative nature of the oral activities; hence the new section title, **Actividades de comunicación y lecturas**. As in earlier editions, grammar continues to play a secondary role as an aid in the language acquisition process.

## Changes in the Fourth Edition

### Overview: Student Text and Workbook/Laboratory Manual

The Fourth Edition begins with three preliminary chapters (**Pasos A–C**), compared with four in the previous edition. There are still sixteen regular chapters.

The structure of the regular chapters of the student text has not changed; each chapter is still divided into three parts:

**Actividades de comunicación y lecturas** (oral activities and readings)
**Vocabulario** (most new vocabulary from the activities)
**Gramática y ejercicios** (grammar explanations and verification exercises)

The organization and content of the Workbook/Laboratory Manual, the ***Cuaderno de trabajo***, has changed significantly. The new features of the student text and the ***Cuaderno*** are explained in the following sections.

## The Heart of *Dos mundos*: Actividades de comunicación y lecturas

Although the name of this section has changed slightly, most of the **actividades orales** have been preserved from the previous edition. We have updated activities when appropriate, and we have added topics to reflect current student interests whenever possible. We hope that the following additional changes to the **actividades** will enhance the success of ***Dos mundos*** in the classroom.

- **The cast of characters:** While many familiar characters remain, we have updated their "look" and have made some changes to their lifestyles to reflect contemporary Hispanic cultures. (You can read more about the new cast on pages xxiii–xxiv.)
- **Chapter themes:** A new theme for **Capítulo 15**, technology (including computer use and the Internet), focuses on the future. In addition, the last two chapters of the Third Edition have been combined into a single chapter entitled **El mundo y las relaciones sociales**, which offers a more in-depth presentation of Hispanic culture and history.
- **Review:** Beginning in **Paso B**, each **Actividades de comunicación** section now ends with a new section, **En resumen**, which presents one or more cooperative learning or creative writing activities, based on the key vocabulary and grammar of the chapter. Starting in **Paso C**, all **En resumen** sections contain a **Videoteca** activity, based on the new, text-specific video. (You can learn more about the video on pages xxiv–xxv.)
- **Organization of the activities:** All activities now fall under fifteen different rubrics (see page xx). In addition, activities in each thematic section have been sequenced more consistently from input to output, in order to promote comprehension *before* production.
- **Dialogues: Diálogo** and **Diálogo abierto** activities now appear only in the first five chapters.
- **Visuals:** More visually based activities (many with new authentic realia) appear throughout ***Dos mundos***.

## What's New With the Reading Materials?

As some of you have probably noticed, the reading component of ***Dos mundos*** has undergone many changes since the First Edition. Over the editions, we have included more authentic material, such as newspaper articles and ads. We have also tried to feature high-interest fiction and poetry, because many students find those types of reading stimulating and exciting. (We have also found that students are encouraged by the idea that they can read real literature in a foreign language.) When preparing each edition, we reassess all the readings, discarding those that proved too difficult or not engaging enough. Our objective is to provide texts that are interesting and culturally rich, but also accessible to first-year students.

As you flip through the pages of ***Dos mundos***, Fourth Edition, and the ***Cuaderno de trabajo,*** you will recognize all the reading features from the Third Edition. For instance, we continue to teach geography by providing maps that highlight countries and cities mentioned in many reading selections. Here are the basic reading types, all carried over from the previous edition.

- **Lecturas:** readings that showcase the ***Dos mundos*** cast of characters; realia-based material such as newspaper ads and magazine articles
- **Notas culturales:** brief segments on Hispanic culture, with photo illustrations
- **Cuentos:** short fiction by Hispanic writers
- **Poesía:** poetry by the renowned poets José Martí, Pablo Neruda, and Amado Nervo
- **El mundo hispano... su gente:** first-person accounts of life and culture in Spanish-speaking countries, featuring the geography of the Hispanic world
- **El mundo hispano... imágenes:** selections consisting of a photograph and a short narrative that focus on specific areas of the Hispanic world

All of these readings reflect the theme and vocabulary of each chapter. Many of them (marked with a headphones icon) are recorded on the *Book on Tape*, which provides students with extra listening practice. As in previous editions, the **Lecturas, Notas culturales, Cuentos,** and **Poesía** are followed by reading activities. These include **Comprensión,** with innovative formats for checking comprehension; **Ahora... ¡usted!,** with personalized questions; and, in this edition, **Un paso más... ¡a escribir!,** a new writing activity that engages students' creativity.

In response to your requests for pre-reading strategies, we have added **Suggestions for Effective Reading** in the annotated *Instructor's Edition*, in which we discuss techniques such as skimming, scanning, cognate recognition, and using context and cues outside the text to guess at meaning. In addition, most of the reading segments are now preceded by a short synopsis and a brief vocabulary box. Both are intended to function as "advance organizers"; in this way, they provide a preview of the reading to enhance students' comprehension.

The Fourth Edition places even more emphasis on reading and literacy. You will find four new features:

- **El mundo hispano... en los Estados Unidos:** These brief narratives by Hispanics living in the United States include comparisons and contrasts between life in the United States and in their countries or cultures of origin.
- **Las palabras viven:** The phrase *Words are alive* reflects how Spanish is continually changing. In these segments you will find information on various linguistic phenomena such as colloquial expressions and word variations in the Hispanic world. There are also readings about the origin of words, including borrowings from other languages, popular idioms and proverbs, as well as readings on the indigenous languages of Latin America such as Quechua and Nahuatl.
- **¡Reír es vivir!:** We truly believe that laughter can help us live happier and healthier lives, so we created this entertaining feature that tells jokes—**chistes**—and presents humorous exchanges. Read these with your students for the sheer fun of it!
- **En nuestro mundo increíble:** These short sidebars offer interesting or extraordinary facts about the incredible world we live in.

Finally, additional reading material is available for your students through the innovative *Storyteller's Series*, the ***¡A leer!*** easy reader series, and the ***El mundo hispano*** reader (see pages xv–xvi).

## The Handling of Grammar: Gramática y ejercicios

The most substantial change in the main text is the reorganization of grammar in the latter part of the book. Instructors like you told us—and we agree!—that there was too much grammar in those chapters. So we placed the most advanced concepts, along with verification exercises, in a new section of the ***Cuaderno*** called **Expansión gramatical.*** If you have the time and wish to do more grammar, this appendix will be very useful. If you've taught with ***Dos mundos*** before and have found the amount of grammar in the last chapters to be excessive, we hope you will now find the latter part of the book more manageable. Here are some additional changes of note:

- **Explanations:** Grammar explanations are now easier to understand and lend themselves readily to self-study.
- **Margin notes:** More margin notes have been added to give students hints or quick overviews of grammar points. For example, "**ser** = origin; **estar** = location" appears in the margin beside the introduction of **ser** and **estar**.
- **Illustrations:** Many graphics have been included in the grammar sections to provide more visual appeal. More complex grammar concepts are now illustrated with a drawing—**Gramática ilustrada**, depicting a relevant scene—to help students visualize the grammatical structure.
- **Reminders for review:** A new feature, **¿Recuerda?**, reminds students to review previous grammar sections.
- **Functional titles:** All grammar topics now have functional titles. For example, **Talking about Actions in Progress: Present Progressive** tells students how the present progressive is used.
- **Recognizing vs. using:** Some advanced grammar exercises that required production have been replaced by others that require recognition only.
- **Verbs:** Simple presentations of **-ar** and **-er/-ir** verbs are now in **Paso C** and **Capítulo 1,** preceding the introduction of **gustar** + infinitive. The present tense is now re-entered more completely in **Capítulos 2** and **3**.

*In addition, the most important grammar concepts and exercises from **Capítulos 12–16** of the Fourth Edition have been added to this section in the ***Cuaderno de trabajo*** *to accompany* ***Dos mundos: En breve.***

## Major Content and Organization Changes: *Cuaderno de trabajo*

The basic premise of the ***Cuaderno*** has not changed. It is still intended for use primarily outside of the classroom, and it still features oral texts (listening comprehension passages) and readings, as well as grammar exercises and a variety of activities, including a section that focuses on pronunciation and spelling.

In this edition we have attempted to iron out some of the organizational problems that adopters have brought to our attention and to focus on the level of difficulty of the listening passages.

Following is the new structure of each chapter of the ***Cuaderno***, along with a brief explanation of each section.

- **Para empezar:** This new section consists of one or more brief listening activities that serve as a chapter warm-up by focusing on the grammar and vocabulary of previous chapters.
- **Comprensión oral** and **Actividades escritas:** These sections are now *completely coordinated* with the thematic sections of the student text. Each thematic section contains two types of activities:
  **Actividades escritas:** guided, form-focused exercises, followed by more open-ended, personalized writing activities for which there is generally no "right" answer.
  **Comprensión oral:** listening comprehension activities coordinated with the *Audiocassette Program.*
- **¡A repasar!:** This new section contains cumulative listening comprehension activities that focus on the theme of the chapter.
- **¡Adelante!:** This new, final listening comprehension activity challenges students to use their listening skills to grasp meaning in novel contexts. At the same time, it prepares them for the topics, vocabulary, and structures that will be presented in the next chapter. Instructors may prefer to work with this activity in class.
- **Pronunciación y ortografía:** These exercises help students work with the sound and spelling systems of Spanish.
- **Lecturas adicionales:** These optional readings contain the same kinds of advance organizers as those in the student text—a brief synopsis and a vocabulary box—as well as follow-up activities.

- **Videoteca:** In these pre- and post-viewing activities, students work with the content of each chapter's video segment.

In addition to the changes in the ***Cuaderno***, the listening comprehension passages have been thoroughly revised, to promote increased comprehension by reducing the amount of new vocabulary in the listening passages and by systematically re-entering key vocabulary and grammar.

## Components of the Fourth Edition

The Fourth Edition of ***Dos mundos*** offers a complete package of instructional materials for beginning Spanish courses whose primary goal is proficiency in communication skills. These materials are designed to encourage you and your students to interact in Spanish as naturally and as spontaneously as possible. In addition to the student text and the ***Cuaderno de trabajo***, the following materials are available:

- The annotated *Instructor's Edition* contains marginal notes that offer extensive pre-text activities and suggestions for using and expanding materials in the student text. These notes also provide teaching hints and references to the supplementary activities in the *Instructor's Resource Kit*.
- The *Instructor's Manual*, with a general introduction to the Natural Approach and to the types of acquisition activities found in the program, provides step-by-step instructions for how to teach the **Pasos** and **Capítulo 1.** It also offers many pre-text activities designed for use before doing the communicative activities, as well as additional strategies for implementing the Natural Approach.
- The *Instructor's Resource Kit* contains the following supplementary activities and games that correspond to themes in the student text: **TPR, Veinte preguntas, Lotería, Búscalo tú, Entrevista, Actividad de firma, Intercambio, Crucigrama,** and **Encuesta.**
- 100 full-color *Overhead Transparencies* display drawings, color maps, and other items, most of which appear in the student text.
- The *Test Bank* contains listening comprehension (with *Testing Tapes*), reading, vocabulary, and grammar tests for each chapter. It also includes suggestions for testing oral achievement and writing skills.
- The *Audiocassette Program* presents oral texts coordinated with the ***Cuaderno de trabajo*** that support the topics and functions of each chapter of the student text. It also includes pronunciation exercises and vocabulary read on tape.
- The *Tapescript* is a transcript of all recorded materials in the *Audiocassette Program*.
- The optional *Book on Tape* contains recordings of many of the readings in the student text (**Lecturas, Notas culturales, Los amigos hispanos,** and **Las palabras viven**).
- The *Storyteller's Series* offers high-interest fiction (novellas and short stories) designed for advanced-beginning or intermediate students.
- The *McGraw-Hill Electronic Language Tutor* (*MHELT 2.1*), an upgraded software program based on the text's grammar exercises, is available in IBM and Macintosh formats.
- *Spanish Partner:* This computer tutorial, by Monica Morley and Carl Fisher, provides students with additional practice in basic Spanish vocabulary and structures.
- The ***Destinos*** *Video Modules* provide footage from the popular ***Destinos*** television series as well as original footage shot on location. The *Modules* offer high-quality video segments on vocabulary, functional language, situational language, and culture.
- The *McGraw-Hill Video Library of Authentic Spanish Materials* consists of several volumes of video materials. Three different sets of slides showing the Hispanic world are accompanied by discussion questions and activities.
- The *Training Video* demonstrates how to use ***Dos mundos*** and the Natural Approach in a variety of classroom settings.

Adopters familiar with previous editions will be pleased to see the following new components of the ***Dos mundos*** package of ancillary materials:

- The *Picture File* contains 50 thematically arranged, color photographs designed to stimulate conversation in the classroom.

- The ***¡A leer!*** easy reader series features two short readers: ***Barriga llena, corazón contento***, on regional Hispanic cuisines; and ***Cuentos de hadas y leyendas***. These readers, developed to reinforce vocabulary acquisition, can be used as early as the second semester and are intended for use outside the classroom.
- The ***El mundo hispano*** reader features five major regions of the Hispanic world, as well as a section on Hispanics living in the United States.
- The *Video to accompany* ***Dos mundos***, shot on location in Mexico, Spain, Ecuador, and the United States by a nationally recognized and award-winning production company, is coordinated with the **Videoteca** sections of the student text and the **Videoteca** pre- and post-viewing activities in the ***Cuaderno de trabajo***. (See pages xxiv-xxv for more information about the video.)
- The interactive *CD-ROM to accompany* ***Dos mundos***, which incorporates Quicktime™ video with comprehension questions and engaging interactive games, is coordinated with chapters of the student text. (See page xxv for more information about the CD-ROM.)

## Second-Language Acquisition: The Five Hypotheses

The materials in ***Dos mundos*** are based on Tracy D. Terrell's Natural Approach to language instruction, which in turn relies on Stephen D. Krashen's theoretical model of second-language acquisition. That theory consists of five interrelated hypotheses, each of which is mirrored in some way in ***Dos mundos***. Along with Krashen's research, we have included in this Fourth Edition elements from Natural Learning Theory, a model developed by Brian Cambourne that is very supportive of Natural Approach principles.[1]

Many of you will be familiar with the following concepts already. But if you're not, don't feel obliged to memorize them. As you gradually work with ***Dos mundos***, Terrell's and Krashen's ideas will become second nature to you. After outlining the five hypotheses below, we present nine ideas for application of the theory in the foreign-language classroom.

### 1 The Acquisition-Learning Hypothesis

This theory suggests that we have two independent ways of developing language ability: acquisition and learning.

- **Language acquisition** is a subconscious process; that is, we are not aware that it is happening. Once we have acquired a segment of language, we are not usually aware that we possess any new knowledge; the knowledge is stored subconsciously. Research strongly supports the view that adults can acquire language subconsciously, as do children.
- **Language learning** is a conscious process; we are aware that we are learning. When you talk about "rules" and grammar, you are usually talking about learning.

### 2 The Natural Order Hypothesis

This theory states that we acquire parts of a language in a *predictable order*. Some grammatical items, for example, tend to be acquired early while others are acquired late. The natural order appears to be unaffected by deliberate teaching; *we cannot change the natural order by explanation, drills, and exercises.* Indeed, more language acquisition takes place when students are given some responsibility for choosing the themes that interest them, without regard to grammatical acquisition order.

### 3 The Monitor Hypothesis

This hypothesis attempts to explain how acquisition and learning are used. We normally produce language using our acquired linguistic competence. The main function of conscious learning is as *monitor* or *editor*. After we produce language using the acquired system, we sometimes inspect it and

[1] Portions of this section and the next are quoted by permission of Stephen D. Krashen, *Fundamentals of Language Acquisition*, Laredo Publications, 1992; and Brian Cambourne, *The Whole Story, Natural Learning and the Acquisition of Literacy*, Ashton Scholastic, 1994.

use our learned system to correct errors. This self-correction can happen internally before we speak or write, or after we produce a sentence.

### 4 The Input Hypothesis

This concept proposes that we acquire language when we *understand messages* or obtain comprehensible input. Comprehensible input can be aural or written: Reading is an excellent source of comprehensible input. According to the Input Hypothesis, production (talking and writing) is a *result* of language acquisition, not a cause.

### 5 The Affective Filter Hypothesis

This theory suggests that attitudes and feelings do not impact language learning directly but can prevent students from acquiring language from input. If a student is *anxious* or does not perceive the target culture in a positive light, he or she may understand the input but a *psychological block* (the Affective Filter) will prevent acquisition.[2]

## The Natural Approach and *Dos mundos*: From Theory to Action

The principles of the Natural Approach follow from the preceding hypotheses. Our goal is to make the theory work for us in the classroom. Here is how we do it:

### 1 Aiming for Meaning

The primary goal of the Natural Approach classroom is to provide comprehensible aural and written input, the components necessary for language acquisition. These components help students do what Cambourne calls "creating meaning." ***Dos mundos*** helps students create meaning through both acquired and learned knowledge.

| ACQUISITION | LEARNING |
|---|---|
| **Actividades de comunicación** | **Gramática y ejercicios** |
| All readings | **En resumen** |
| **Comprensión oral** | **Actividades escritas** |
| Video segments | **Ejercicios de pronunciación y ortografía** |

The input provided by the instructor during the **Actividades de comunicación** and the input received from reading the **Lecturas** and from listening to the **Comprensión oral** and *Book on Tape* audio texts enable students to create meaning from the new language and contribute to students' acquired knowledge. A grammatical syllabus similar to those in other beginning Spanish textbooks is the basis for the **Gramática y ejercicios** section, but the activities that encourage the acquisition of grammar are spread out over several chapters.

### 2 I'm Listening!

While the ability to produce language is the result of acquisition, comprehension precedes production. Thus, students' ability to use new vocabulary and grammar is directly related to the opportunities they have had to listen to and read that vocabulary and grammar in meaningful and relevant contexts. These meaningful contexts are what Cambourne calls "demonstrations." Students need many demonstrations of meaningful language; then opportunities to express their own meanings must follow.

### 3 Taking Our Time

Because speech emerges in stages, ***Dos mundos*** allows for three stages of language development: comprehension; early speech; and speech emergence.

---

[2]For more detailed information see the section on Natural Approach theory in the *Instructor's Manual*. See also Stephen D. Krashen and Tracy D. Terrell, *The Natural Approach: Language Acquisition in the Classroom*, Prentice Hall, 1983.

The activities in **Paso A** are designed to give students the opportunity to develop initial comprehension ability without being required to speak Spanish. The activities in **Paso B** encourage the transition from comprehension to the ability to respond naturally in single words. By the end of **Paso C** and through **Capítulo 1,** most students are making the first transitional steps from short answers to longer phrases and complete sentences. Students will continue to pass through these same three stages with the new material of each chapter. The vocabulary and structures presented in **Capítulo 1** may not be fully acquired until **Capítulo 5** or later.

The Pre-Text and Additional Activities as well as the Follow-Up and Optional Grammar Activities in the *Instructor's Edition*, the **Actividades de comunicación** and **Lecturas** in the student text, and the **Comprensión oral** in the ***Cuaderno de trabajo*** all provide opportunities for understanding Spanish before production is expected. As students become more fluent listeners and speakers, native speakers and teachers will automatically raise the ante and challenge students' skills with higher-level language. It is this process that helps students continue to acquire higher-level lexicon and grammatical structures.

## 4 We All Make Mistakes

Errors in form are not corrected in classroom activities that are aimed at acquisition. We expect students to make many errors as speech emerges. Cambourne calls student attempts to communicate with others in the new language "approximations." "The willingness to accept approximations," he writes, "is absolutely essential to the processes which accompany language learning."[3] Given sufficient exposure to Spanish, these early errors do not become permanent, nor do they affect students' future language development. We recommend correcting only factual errors and responding naturally to students' communication, expanding only when it feels normal and natural to do so, when the correction or expansion can easily be woven into the conversational thread.

In contrast, students can and should correct their responses to the self-study grammar exercises using the key in the back of the text, and to the **Comprensión oral** and the **Actividades escritas** using the key in the back of the ***Cuaderno de trabajo***.

## 5 Relax and Let It Happen Naturally!

Students acquire language only in a low-anxiety environment and when they are truly engaged with the material. A low-anxiety atmosphere is created when the instructor: 1) provides students with truly interesting, comprehensible input, 2) does not focus excessively on form, and 3) lets students know that acquiring a new language is "doable" and is expected of them. ***Dos mundos*** creates such a positive classroom atmosphere by sparking student interest and encouraging involvement in two sorts of activities: those that relate directly to students and their lives, and those that relate to the Hispanic world. Hence, the **dos mundos** referred to in the title. Input and interaction in these two areas—along with the expectation from the instructor that students will be able to communicate their ideas—create a classroom environment wherein the instructor and students feel comfortable listening and talking to one another.

## 6 It Takes a Community

Group work encourages interaction and creates classroom community. In a Natural Approach classroom, students are encouraged to speak and interact. Group work provides valuable opportunities for students to interact in Spanish during a given class period and helps create a sense of classroom community that facilitates communication.

## 7 Speak Your Mind!

Speaking helps language acquisition indirectly in several ways by encouraging comprehensible input via conversation. Our extensive classroom experience has led us to believe that "learners need both the time and the opportunity to use their immature, developing language skills."[4] Speaking also gives students the positive

[3] Cambourne, page 38.

[4] Cambourne, page 38.

feeling of engaging in real language use. It helps create a sense of community as the instructor and students share opinions and information about themselves.

### 8 A Place for Grammar

Although ***Dos mundos*** focuses on acquisition through oral, listening, and written activities, there are practical reasons for grammar study. Formal knowledge of grammar does not contribute to second-language fluency, but it may help some students edit their written work. For others it can lead to a greater appreciation of the structure of the language and/or be a good introduction to the field of linguistics. Also, some language students derive great satisfaction when they learn about what they are acquiring. Finally, very adept language learners can utilize grammatical knowledge to make the input they hear and read more comprehensible.

### 9 Language With a Purpose

The goal of the Natural Approach is proficiency in communication skills: lis tening, reading, speaking, and writing. Proficiency is defined as the ability to understand and convey information and/or feelings in a particular situation for a particular purpose. Grammatical accuracy is one part of communicative proficiency, but it is not a prerequisite.

## Additional Comments about the Student Materials

Each of the sixteen regular chapters of ***Dos mundos*** opens with the **Actividades de comunicación y lecturas**, which stimulate the acquisition of vocabulary and grammar. The following types of communicative activities are repeated from chapter to chapter. Those in the student text are consistently labeled.

TPR (Total Physical Response) Activities (*Instructor's Edition*)
Student-centered input (*Instructor's Edition*)
Photo-centered input (*Instructor's Edition*)
Definitions (**Definiciones**)
Association activities (**Asociaciones**)
Discussions (**Conversación**)
Realia-based activities (**Del mundo hispano**)
Description of drawings (**Descripción de dibujos**)
Culminating activities (**En resumen**)
Interactions (**Intercambios**)
Narration series (**Narración**)
Dialogues (**Diálogos** and **Diálogos abiertos**)
Identification activities (**Identificaciones**)
Situational dialogues (**Situaciones**)
Personal opinion activities (**Preferencias**)
Interviews (**Entrevistas**)
Polls (**Encuestas**)
Creative writing activities (**Un paso más... ¡a escribir!**; and **¡Dígalo por escrito!**)

The **Vocabulario** list that follows each **Actividades de comunicación y lecturas** section contains most of the new words that have been introduced in the vocabulary displays and activities. Students should recognize these words when they are used in a clear communicative context. Many will also be used actively by students in later chapters as the course progresses.

The readings in ***Dos mundos*** are by no means exhaustive; we recommend that instructors read aloud to students and, when students are ready for independent reading, allow them to select reading material of interest to them. Teachers may find the ***¡A leer!*** series, the ***El mundo hispano*** reader, or the *Storyteller's Series* appropriate for second-, third-, or fourth-semester accompaniment to ***Dos mundos***.

The **Gramática y ejercicios** sections, in the "blue pages," are designed for quick reference and ease of study. (The answer key to the grammar exercises is in Appendix 4.) The purpose of the grammar exercises is for students to verify that they have understood the explanation; we do not believe that students acquire grammar by doing exercises.

Most new topics in the **Actividades de comunicación y lecturas** sections begin with references (marked **Lea Gramática...**) to the pertinent grammar section(s) of the chapter. All activities can be done without previous grammar study; it is desirable to do all **Actividades de comunicación** in a purely communicative way, with both instructor and students focusing on the meaning of what is being said.

## Acknowledgments

A special note of thanks is due to Stephen D. Krashen for his research on second-language acquisition theory. Dr. Krashen continues to give us many valuable insights into creating more natural activities and providing more comprehensible input for students in both listening and reading components.

We are also grateful to Joseph Goebel of The College of New Jersey for his careful, annotated reading of the Third Edition of ***Dos mundos,*** *Instructor's Edition*, and ***Cuaderno de trabajo,*** as well as for his review of manuscript of the Fourth Edition. Dr. Goebel's hands-on experience in the classroom and as a trainer of teaching assistants makes his suggestions invaluable. In addition, we want to thank Dr. Goebel for his creative writing activities that appear in the **En resumen** section of each chapter.

Thanks also go to Professor Brian Cambourne at the University of Wollongong, Australia, for his annotated reading of the *Instructor's Manual* and his many comments that have helped us refine Natural Approach theory for this Fourth Edition.

We would like to thank Karen Christian for her contributions to the first *Instructor's Resource Kit* (with the Third Edition of the text). Heartfelt thanks go to Beatrice Tseng (Irvine Valley College) for her creative redesign of the Fourth Edition of the *Instructor's Resource Kit*, for her tireless search for authentic materials, and for her dedication to detail in tracking the vocabulary of ***Dos mundos***. Polly Hodge (Chapman College) deserves special thanks for her exciting work on reading strategies and techniques, as well as for her **Comprensión oral** activities in the ***Cuaderno***, as does Sally Sefamí for her creative work on the reader on regional cuisines, ***Cocina y comidas hispanas***. Thanks also are in order to Christa Harris and Pennie Nichols-Alem for the **Videoteca** activities they developed. We owe much to our on-call computer expert, Richard Zucker (Irvine Valley College), for his invaluable expertise in keeping our computers going and our programs working for us throughout the revision process.

The authors would also like to express their gratitude to the many members of the language-teaching profession whose valuable suggestions contributed to the preparation of this revised edition. The appearance of their names here does not necessarily constitute an endorsement of the text or the Natural Approach methodology.

Marc Accornero, Mission College

Jeff Adams, Walla Walla Community College

Lucía V. Aranda, Kapiolani Community College

F. M. Arguello, Fayetteville State University

Deborah Baldini, University of Missouri–St. Louis

Linda-Jane C. Barnette, Ball State University

Lisa M. Baudler, Austin Community College

Sue Bertoleit-Valdez, Temple Junior College

Carole Byrd, University of Wisconsin at Oshkosh

Justyna M. Carlson, Southern Vermont College

Michelle Connolly, Community College of Rhode Island

James Crapotta, Barnard College

Isabel Creuch, Prescott College

Jorge H. Cubillos, University of Delaware

Marta DePierris, Mills College/College of Marin

John Dolance, Richland College

Lynda Durham, Casper College

Richard K. Evans, Geneva College

Addison Everett, Dixie College

Augustine Fernández, Paul Quinn College

Marisol Fernández García, Michigan State University

Reyes I. Fidalgo, Bowling Green State University

Emy Fischer, Texas State Technical College

Herschel Frey, University of Pittsburgh

Roseanne Fulcher, Erie Community College

Amalia V. Garzón, Del Mar College

Jeannette Harker, Florida Atlantic University

Laura Huffman, Los Medanos College

Shawna L. Kelly, Tennessee Technical University

Anne Key, Tillamook Bay Community College

Michael Langston, St. Meinrad College

Montserrat Linkletter, Tacoma Community College

Melissa Lockhart, Wake Forest University

Kim MacDonald, Azusa Pacific

Zenaida Madurka, SUNY at Stony Brook

Edward H. Mayer, University of Utah

Olga Mendell, D'Youville College

Karin Melson Meyer, Canisius College

Patricia A. Morrissey, Clatsop Community College

Jeanne Mullaney, Community College of Rhode Island

Nancy Nieman, Santa Monica College

Irma O'Connor, Canisius College

Nanette R. Pascal, Richland College

Teresinka Pereira, Bluffton College

Carole Permar, Marshalltown Community College

Ana M. Piffardi, Eastfield College

Sergio Pizarin, Sullivan County Community College

Antonio Prado, University of Oklahoma

Dawn E. Prince, Iowa State University

Rosemary Sands Ptacek, St. Norbert College

Gus Puleo, Columbia University

Lourdes Ramírez Mallis, Keene State College

Celia V. Ramírez-Owens, Big Bend Community College

Sarah Rath, Green Mountain College

Melvyn C. Resnick, University of Tulsa

P. Harlow Rhoades, East Central College

Catherine Rodgers, Wake Forest University

Ingrid Rogers, Manchester College

Ana Isabel Rueda-García, Texas Christian University

Annette Sánchez, Nashville State Technical Institute

Mireya Scheerer, Cypress College

Terry Sellars, Nashville State Technical Institute

Mary Studer Shea, Napa Valley Community College

Nancy E. Shearer, Cuesta College

William H. Shuford, Lenoir-Rhyne College

Jerry Smartt, Friends University

Celia V. Smith, Lincoln University

Laurel B. Sparks, North Dakota State University

Craig R. Stokes, Grove City College

James R. Swann, Northeast Texas Community College

Paul D. Toth, University of Pittsburgh

Myrna E. A. Vélez, Dartmouth College

Keith Watts, University of New Mexico

Estelita C. Young, Collin County Community College

Many other people participated in the preparation of the Fourth Edition of ***Dos mundos***. We feel deeply indebted to Thalia Dorwick for her care and support. As editor of the First Edition, Thalia gave the text its initial push and continues to be an adviser on all major decisions regarding changes. As our first editor and now as our publisher, she has provided us with countless resources, much-needed guidance, and most importantly, the freedom to write the book we wanted to write.

Our Fourth Edition editor, Becka McGuire, was fantastic! She took our program to a new level of quality and creativity. It was reassuring to work with someone as organized and knowledgeable about the Natural Approach and as professionally enthusiastic as Becka. We also appreciate the support of Gregory Trauth, who managed the project, and Jennifer Valko, who professionally and cheerfully handled so many details of the project.

We would like to acknowledge the sales and marketing support we have received from The McGraw-Hill Companies, and specifically from Margaret Metz and Cristene Burr. We are also very grateful to the following McGraw-Hill staff and associates for their excellent work on this complex project, as well as for their patience and perseverance: Karen Judd, Diane Renda, Francis Owens, Rich DeVitto, Nicole Widmyer, and Richard Lange. Special thanks go to Sally Richardson who, for this Fourth Edition, made it possible for our cast of characters to change with the times by giving them a fresh and contemporary look! In addition, we wish to thank Laura Chastain and Wilfrido Corral for their help with questions of language usage and cultural content in the final manuscript and Charlotte Jackson for her painstaking review of the vocabulary.

And, finally, we would like to thank each other for many years of moving the Natural Approach from idea into print. We hope our contributions continue to be worthwhile.

# To the Instructor and Students

## The *Dos mundos* Cast of Characters, Video, and Interactive Multimedia

Most of the exercises and activites in ***Dos mundos*** are based on the lives of a cast of characters from different parts of the Spanish-speaking world. Here they are, followed by a description of the innovative Video and CD-ROM that accompany the Fourth Edition of ***Dos mundos***.

### Cast of Characters: The Textbook and the *Cuaderno de trabajo*

Two groups of characters appear in exercises and activities throughout the print materials for ***Dos mundos***.

**Los amigos norteamericanos** (North American friends), a group of students at the University of Texas at San Antonio. Although they are all majoring in different subjects, they know each other through Professor Adela Martínez's 8:00 A.M. Spanish class.

**Los amigos hispanos** (Hispanic friends) live in various parts of the Spanish-speaking world. In **México** you will meet Silvia Bustamante and her boyfriend, Ignacio (Nacho) Padilla.

You will also get to know Raúl Saucedo and his family. Raúl lives with his parents in Mexico City but is currently studying at the University of Texas at San Antonio; he knows many of the students in Professor Martínez's class. You will meet Raúl's grandmother, doña María Eulalia González de Saucedo, as well as other members of his extended family: his three older sisters, Estela, Andrea and Paula (who are twins), and their families.

Raúl's sister Estela is married to Ernesto Ramírez. They have three children, Amanda, Guillermo, and Ernestito. Andrea is married to Pedro Ruiz, and they have two young daughters, Marisa and Clarisa. Paula is a single travel agent who lives and works in Mexico City.

The Ramírez children have school friends. Amanda's best friend is Graciela Herrero, whose brother is Diego Herrero. Amanda has a boyfriend, Ramón Gómez, and Graciela's boyfriend is Rafael Quesada.

There are also friends and neighbors of the Ramírez and Ruiz families: don Eduardo Alvar and don Anselmo Olivera; doña Lola Batini; and doña Rosita Silva and her husband, don Ramiro.

In **Puerto Rico** you will meet Carla Espinosa and her friend Rogelio Varela, students at the University of Puerto Rico in Río Piedras. You will also meet Marta Guerrero, a young Mexican woman living in Puerto Rico.

In **España** (Spain) you will accompany an American student, Clara Martin, on her travels. Her friends in Spain are Pilar Álvarez and Pilar's boyfriend, José Estrada.

You will get to know Ricardo Sícora in Caracas, **Venezuela**. He is nineteen years old and has just graduated from high school.

In **Argentina** you will meet Adriana Bolini, a young woman who works for a computer company, and her boyfriend, Víctor Ginarte.

On the radio you will listen to Mayín Durán, who is from **Panamá**. Mayín works as an interviewer and reporter for KSUN, Radio Sol de California, in Los Angeles.

You will meet the Yamasaki family in **Perú**: Susana Yamasaki González and her two sons, Armando and Andrés.

In **Miami** you will meet Professor Rubén Hernández Arenas and his wife, Doctora Virginia Béjar de Hernández.

## The Video

New in the Fourth Edition of ***Dos mundos*** is a two-hour video, filmed on location in Mexico, Ecuador, Spain, and the United States. Each video segment consists of a two- to three-minute vignette that focuses on one of the three groups of featured characters, followed by a brief authentic interview with a Hispanic living in the United States. An introduction to each vignette can be found in the **Videoteca** section of **En resumen** (at the end of the **Actividades de comunicación y lecturas** sections of the textbook). Viewing activities are located in the **Videoteca** sections in the ***Cuaderno de trabajo***.

Here are some of the characters you will meet in the vignettes.

### México

Diego González, an American graduate student living in Mexico City.

Lupe Carrasco, an anthropology student from Mexico City.

Antonio Sifuentes, a graduate student from Mexico City.

### Ecuador

Elisa Velasco, a travel writer from Quito.

José Miguel Martín Velasco (son of Elisa), a university freshman.

Paloma Velasco, José Miguel's cousin, also a university freshman.

### España

Manolo Durán García, a university professor of literature in Sevilla.

Lola Benítez Guzmán, a Spanish professor for American students in Sevilla.

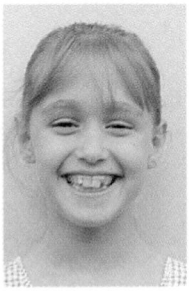

Marta Durán Benítez, their eight-year-old daughter.

## The CD-ROM

Available in both IBM and Macintosh formats, the CD-ROM continues the emphasis on the meaningful use of Spanish that characterizes the ***Dos mundos*** program. Throughout the CD-ROM's innovative and visually appealing activities, students will be able to understand what they are reading or hearing, and exercise critical thinking skills. Many activities focus on the thematic sections of a given chapter. Others introduce students to characters from the video, inviting students to write to them on e-mail or to converse with them. Finally, the CD-ROM format is utilized to make the thematic vocabulary displays interactive. Recording and printing capabilities make the CD-ROM a true four-skills ancillary. The CD-ROM also contains a link to the ***Dos mundos*** web site on the World Wide Web.

## The World Wide Web

Bringing the Spanish-speaking world more directly into the classroom, the ***Dos mundos*** web site provides links to other culturally authentic sites and offers additional activities for each chapter of the text. Available after June 1, 1998, the ***Dos mundos*** web page can be accessed through the McGraw-Hill Spanish web page at: http://www.spanish.mhhe.com

# To the Student

## A Few Words about *Dos mundos: En breve*

This text is a new, shorter version of the Fourth Edition of ***Dos mundos.*** It is identical to that edition of ***Dos mundos,*** except that the last five chapters have been omitted. What follows is the student preface for the Fourth Edition of ***Dos mundos*** (the complete text).

The course you are about to begin is based on a methodology called the Natural Approach. It is designed to help you develop your ability to understand and speak everyday Spanish and to help you learn to read and write in Spanish.

Researchers have distinguished two ways of developing ability in another language: 1) through a subconscious process called *language acquisition*—like "picking up" Spanish while living in Mexico or Spain; and 2) through a conscious process called *language learning,* which has to do with memorizing and applying grammar rules. *Language acquisition* gives us our fluency, much of our accuracy in speaking, and our ability to understand authentic language when we hear it. You know you've acquired a word when it "feels" and sounds right in a given context. *Language learning* is not as useful in oral communication, but it helps us edit our speech and writing. You know you've *learned* a rule when, for example, you can recall it in order to produce the right form of a verb.

The **Actividades de comunicación y lecturas** of ***Dos mundos*** will help you acquire Spanish through listening to your instructor and interacting with your classmates; the **Comprensión oral** sections of the ***Cuaderno de trabajo*** also provide opportunities to practice your listening comprehension skills. The **Gramática y ejercicios** section of the text and many sections of the ***Cuaderno*** will offer opportunities for learning Spanish and for applying the rules you have learned. Our goal in ***Dos mundos*** is to make it possible for you to *acquire* the language, not just *learn* it. Keep in mind that *language acquisition* takes place when we understand messages, that is, when we comprehend what we read or what we hear. The most effective ways for you to improve your Spanish are to listen to it, read it, and interact with native speakers of the language as much as possible!*

Classes that use ***Dos mundos*** provide you with a great deal of language you can understand. Your instructor will always speak Spanish to you and will use gestures, photos, real objects, and sound effects to make himself or herself understood. To get the most out of a class session, you only need to focus on what your instructor is saying, that is, on the *message*. You do not have to think *consciously* about grammar or try to remember all the vocabulary that is being used.

You will also have plenty of opportunities for reading. The more you read, the better your Spanish will become. When you are reading, just pay attention to the message. You don't have to know every word or figure out every grammatical structure in order to understand and enjoy what you read!

You will be speaking a lot of Spanish in the classroom, both with your instructor and with your classmates. And when you speak, you will make mistakes. Don't be overly concerned about these mistakes; they are a natural part of the language-acquisition process. The best way to eliminate your errors is not to worry or think hard about grammar when you talk, but to continue to get more language input through listening, conversation, and reading. In time, your speech will become more accurate.

---

*For a more in-depth understanding of the terms acquisition and learning you may wish to read the To the Instructor section of this preface.

# Getting Acquainted With the Materials

## The Textbook

| | WHAT IS IT? | HOW WILL IT HELP? |
|---|---|---|
| **Actividades de comunicación** | Oral communication activities done in class with your instructor and classmates. | Give you opportunities to listen to and interact in Spanish. |
| **Lecturas**<br>**Notas culturales**<br>**Los amigos hispanos**<br>**Las palabras viven**<br>**El mundo hispano... su gente**<br>**El mundo hispano... imágenes**<br>**El mundo hispano... en los Estados Unidos** | Short readings on interesting topics or topics relevant to the Hispanic world. | Allow you to acquire Spanish and help you learn about the Hispanic world and the Spanish language. |
| **¡Reír es vivir!**<br>**En nuestro mundo increíble** | Very short paragraphs with jokes and interesting facts about the world we live in. | Allow you to read short, interesting texts that are easy to comprehend. |
| **Vocabulario** | A list of the important words from the **Actividades de comunicación.** | For reference or review of vocabulary. |
| **Gramática y ejercicios** | Explanations and examples of grammar rules followed by exercises, at end of each chapter. | For self-study and reference. Refer to grammar to edit your writing. |
| Appendix 1 | Verb charts of regular and irregular verbs in all forms. | Reference. |
| Appendix 2 | Grammar Summary Tables. Summaries of major grammatical points introduced. | Reference. |
| Appendix 3 | Accentuation and Spelling Summary Tables. Summaries of accent and spelling rules. | Reference. |
| Appendix 4 | Answer Key to grammar exercises. | Use to check your answers. |
| Vocabulary | Spanish-English vocabulary. | Reference. |

***Cuaderno de trabajo*** **(Workbook/Lab Manual)**

| | WHAT IS IT? | HOW WILL IT HELP? |
|---|---|---|
| **Para empezar** | Warm-up listening activities that use material from previous chapters. | Help you get started with a new chapter, while reviewing previous ones. |
| **Actividades escritas** | Written activities usually done outside of class. Coordinated with the chapter theme, vocabulary, and grammar. | Allow you to express yourself in writing and let your instructor see your progress. |
| **Comprensión oral** | Listening activities for use outside of class. Most activities have comprehension questions. | Provide you with opportunities to listen to and acquire Spanish outside the classroom. |
| **Ejercicios de pronunciación y ortografía** | Taped pronunciation and spelling exercises. | An introduction to Spanish spelling and pronunciation. |
| **¡A repasar!** | Listening comprehension activity. | Reviews the vocabulary and structures of the chapter. |
| **¡Adelante!** | Chapter-final listening comprehension activity. | Challenges you to understand Spanish in new contexts and prepares you for the next chapter. |
| **Lecturas adicionales** | Additional readings; may be done in class, as homework, or read for pleasure. | Allow you to acquire more Spanish through additional reading. |
| **Videoteca** | Written activities to accompany the **Videoteca** section of the text and the video. | Provide you with opportunities to work with and react to the video segments. |
| **Expansión gramatical** | Additional grammar points along with verification exercises. | For reference or further study. |
| Answer Keys | Answers to the taped **Comprensión oral** and **Ejercicios de ortografía**; answers to some **Actividades escritas** and **Videoteca** activities. | Give you quick feedback on comprehension and written activities. |

## Getting Started with the *Pasos*

Understanding a new language is not difficult once you realize that you can comprehend what someone is saying without knowing every word. *The key to communication is understanding the ideas,* the message the speaker wants to convey.

Several techniques can help you develop good listening comprehension skills. First and most important, *you must guess at meaning!* In order to improve your ability to guess accurately, pay close attention to the context. If someone greets you at 3:00 P.M. by saying **Buenas tardes**, chances are they have said *Good afternoon*, not *Good morning* or *Good evening*. You can make a logical guess about the message being conveyed by focusing on the greeting context and time of day. If someone you don't know says to you, **Hola. Me llamo Roberto**, you can guess from context and from the key word **Roberto** that he is telling you his name.

In class, ask yourself what you think your instructor has said even if you haven't understood most—or any—of the words. What is the most likely thing to have been said in a particular situation? Be logical in your guesses and try to follow along by paying close attention to the flow of the conversation. *Context, gestures, and body language will all help you guess more accurately.*

Another strategy for good guessing is to *listen for key words*. These are the words that carry the basic meaning of the sentence. In the class activities, for example, if your instructor points to a picture and says in Spanish, **¿Tiene el pelo castaño este hombre?** (*Does this man have brown hair?*), you will know from the context and intonation that a question is being asked. By focusing on the key words **pelo** (*hair*), **castaño** (*brown*), and **hombre** (*man*), you will be able to answer the question correctly.

Remember: *you do not need to know grammar rules* to understand much of what your instructor says to you. For example, you wouldn't need to know the words **Tiene**, **el**, or **este** in order to get the gist of the previous question. Nor would you have needed to study verb conjugations. However, if you do not know the meaning of the key vocabulary words, **pelo**, **castaño**, and **hombre**, you will not be able to make good guesses about what is said.

### Vocabulary

Because comprehension depends on your ability to *recognize the meaning of key words* used in the conversations you hear, the preliminary chapters of ***Dos mundos***—the **Pasos**—will help you become familiar with many new words in Spanish, probably several hundred of them. *You should not be concerned about pronouncing these words perfectly;* saying them easily will come with more exposure to spoken Spanish. Your instructor will write all key vocabulary words on the board. You may want to copy them in a vocabulary notebook as they are introduced, for future reference and study. Copy them carefully, but don't worry now about spelling rules. Include English equivalents or small drawings if they help you remember the meaning.

Go over your vocabulary lists frequently: Look at the Spanish and try to *visualize the person* (for words such as *man* or *child*), *the thing* (for words such as *chair* or *pencil*), *a person or thing with particular characteristics* (for words such as *young* or *long*), *or an activity or situation* (for phrases such as *stand up* or *is wearing*). You do not need to memorize these words, but concentrate on recognizing their meaning when you see them and when your instructor uses them in conversation with you in class.

### Classroom Activities

In the preliminary chapter, **Paso** (*Step*) **A,** you will be doing three types of class activities: 1) *TPR*; 2) *descriptions of classmates*; and 3) *descriptions of pictures*.

**TPR** is our version of **Total Physical Response**, a technique developed by Professor James Asher at San Jose State University in Northern California. In TPR activities your instructor gives a command that you act out. This type of activity may seem somewhat childish at first, but if you relax and let your body and mind work together to absorb Spanish, you will be surprised at how quickly and how much you can understand. Remember that you do not have to understand every word your instructor says, only enough to perform the action called for. In TPR, cheating is allowed! If you don't understand a command, sneak a look at your fellow classmates to see what they are doing.

**Descriptions of students:** On various occasions, your instructor will describe students in your class. You should try to remember the name of each of your classmates and identify who is being described. You will begin to recognize the meaning of the Spanish words for colors and clothing, and for some descriptive words such as *tall*, *pretty*, and *new*.

**Descriptions of pictures:** Your instructor will bring many pictures to class and describe the people in them. Your goal is to identify the picture being described.

In addition, just for fun, *you will learn to say a few common phrases of greeting and leave-taking* in Spanish. You will practice these in short dialogues with your classmates. Don't try to memorize the dialogues; just have fun with them. Your pronunciation will not be perfect, but if you are able to communicate successfully with native speakers, then your accent is good enough. Your accent will continue to improve as you listen and interact in Spanish.

# Using *Dos mundos*: Tips for Success

## Actividades de Comunicación

**Concentrate on topic and main idea.**

**Don't try to understand every word.**

**Expand on the activities; don't rush through them.**

During these activities you should concentrate on the topic rather than on the fact that you're learning a foreign language. Remember that you will progress faster when you focus on understanding what is being said or when you are using Spanish to talk about a topic of interest to you. The point of these communicative activities is to develop natural conversations, not just to get through the assignment. Expand on the activity items. Don't rush through them; allow your partner to communicate with you and try to focus on the ideas and content. It isn't even necessary to finish every activity; as long as you are understanding and interacting in Spanish, you will acquire the language.

Some students have reported that it is helpful to look over an activity before doing it in class. Others have suggested that a quick before-class preview of new words makes it easier to participate in the activity. But regardless of which strategy works for you, it is of utmost importance to relax during the communicative activities. Don't worry if you don't understand every word your instructor says; just concentrate on getting the main idea. Nor should you be concerned about making mistakes. You will make fewer mistakes as your listening skills improve, so make every effort to understand. Keep your sentences simple, direct, and to the point. You shouldn't expect to be able to express yourself as well as you do in your native language. And don't worry about your classmates' errors either. Some students will acquire Spanish more rapidly than others, but everyone who perseveres will be successful in the long run. For now, minor grammatical or pronunciation errors do no harm. Always listen to your instructor's feedback when he or she comments on a communicated message or rephrases what a student has said in a more complete and correct manner. This is not done to embarrass anyone, but to give the entire class the chance to hear more Spanish spoken correctly.

**Don't worry about making mistakes.**

**Listen to your instructor's feedback.**

**Speak Spanish; avoid English.**

Finally, speak Spanish; avoid English. If you don't know a particular word in Spanish, try expressing yourself in another way. Use gestures or act things out to get your ideas across. If you can't think of a way to express an idea in Spanish, ask your instructor: **¿Cómo se dice _____ en español?** (*How do you say _____ in Spanish?*). You will find other useful classroom expressions on the inside front cover of your text.

### Lecturas

Reading is a valuable activity that will help you acquire Spanish. There are many reasons to learn to read Spanish. Many of you will want to read signs, advertisements, and menus when you travel in Spanish-speaking countries. Some of you may want to read newspapers, stories, and novels in Spanish for pleasure. Others may want to read research published in Spanish in professional or academic fields.

Whatever your motivation might be for reading in Spanish, you must always try to *focus on the meaning*, that is, to "get into" the context of the story or reading selection. You do not need to know every word to understand a text. There may be a word or two that you will have to look up occasionally, to aid comprehension. But if you find yourself looking up many words in the end vocabulary and translating into English, *you are not reading*. As your ability to comprehend spoken Spanish improves, so will your reading ability, and as reading becomes easier you will, in turn, comprehend more spoken Spanish.

You may want to keep the following techniques in mind as you approach all of the reading materials in ***Dos mundos***:

1. Look at the title, pictures, and any other clues outside the main text for an introduction to what the reading is about.
2. Scan the text for cognates and other familiar words.
3. Skim over the text to get the gist of it without looking up words.
4. Use context to make intelligent guesses about unfamiliar words.
5. Read in Spanish, picturing the story instead of trying to translate it in your mind as you go.

All readings in the main text of ***Dos mundos*** are presented within the **Actividades de comunicación y lecturas** sections. There are also many other readings in the **Lecturas adicionales** sections of the ***Cuaderno de trabajo***. It is a good idea to read as much Spanish as possible. Don't wait for your instructor to assign a particular selection; feel free to explore and enjoy the many **Lecturas** featured in ***Dos mundos***. Try reading Spanish newspapers, comic strips, and magazines as soon as you are able.

### Gramática y ejercicios

The final section of each chapter is a grammar study and reference manual. It is usually difficult to think of grammar rules and apply them correctly while speaking. For this reason, the grammar exercises are meant to be completed at your own pace, at home, in order to allow you time to check the forms of which you are unsure. Your reference tools are the grammar explanations, the Verb Charts, Appendices, and the Answer Key to grammar exercises in Appendix 4. We advise you to use your knowledge of grammar when it does not interfere with communication; for example, when you edit your writing. If you do so, your writing will have a more polished feel. Also, some students find that studying grammar helps them understand classroom activities better.

The beginning of most **Actividades de comunicación y lecturas** sections has a reference note (**Lea** [*Read*] **Gramática...**) that tells you which subsection of grammar in that chapter to read. Keep in mind that grammar exercises teach you *about* Spanish; they do not teach you *Spanish*. Only real comprehension and communicative experiences of the type found in the communication activities and readings will do that.

• • • • • • • • • •

Take advantage of any opportunities you may have outside of class to *interact in and with Spanish:* watch Spanish-language movie videos, find Spanish-language radio and TV programs, read newspapers, talk with native speakers, listen to the **Comprensión oral** and the *Book on Tape*, watch the video, or work with the CD-ROM program to accompany ***Dos mundos***. Remember that your instructor and the text materials can open the door to communicating in Spanish, but you must enter by yourself!

MÉXICO, AMÉRICA CENTRAL Y EL CARIBE
0 800 kilómetros
0 400 millas
N
OCÉANO ATLÁNTICO
OCÉANO PACÍFICO
MAR CARIBE
Golfo de México
Golfo de California
Golfo de Tehuantepec
Golfo de los Mosquitos
Canal de Panamá
Bahía de Campeche
Trópico de Cáncer
ESTADOS UNIDOS
MÉXICO
GUATEMALA
BELICE
HONDURAS
EL SALVADOR
NICARAGUA
COSTA RICA
PANAMÁ
CUBA
JAMAICA
HAITÍ
REPÚBLICA DOMINICANA
PUERTO RICO
ISLAS BAHAMAS
ANTILLAS MENORES
VENEZUELA
COLOMBIA
BRASIL
San Diego
Mexicali
Phoenix
Tijuana
Tucson
Santa Fe
Albuquerque
El Paso
Nogales
Ciudad Juárez
Chihuahua
Baja California
La Paz
Mazatlán
Durango
Monterrey
Nuevo Laredo
San Antonio
Austin
Houston
Dallas
Memphis
Atlanta
Nueva Orleans
San Agustín
Tampa
Miami
Nassau
Río Colorado
Río Misisipí
SIERRA MADRE OCCIDENTAL
SIERRA MADRE ORIENTAL
SIERRA MADRE DEL SUR
Aguascalientes
Guanajuato
Tampico
Puerto Vallarta
Guadalajara
León
México, D.F.
Taxco
Puebla
Veracruz
Manzanillo
Oaxaca
Acapulco
Mérida
Cozumel
Península de Yucatán
Campeche
Belmopan
Guatemala
Tegucigalpa
San Salvador
Managua
San José
Panamá
La Habana
Guantánamo
Santiago de Cuba
Santo Domingo
San Juan
Kingston
Puerto Príncipe
Caracas
Barranquilla
Maracaibo
Mérida
Cartagena
Medellín
Bogotá
Cali

MAR CARIBE
OCÉANO ATLÁNTICO
Maracaibo
Barranquilla
Caracas
PANAMÁ
GUYANA
VENEZUELA
Georgetown
Paramaribo
Cayena
Medellín
Panamá
Río Orinoco
Bogotá
Cali
COLOMBIA
SURINAME
GUAYANA FRANCESA
Quito
Ecuador
ECUADOR
Río Amazonas
Belém
Guayaquil
Manaus
PERÚ
CORDILLERA DE LOS ANDES
BRASIL
Recife
Cuzco
Lima
La Paz
Brasília
Arequipa
BOLIVIA
Sucre
PARAGUAY
Antofagasta
Rio de Janeiro
CHILE
Asunción
Trópico de Capricornio
San Miguel de Tucumán
São Paulo
OCÉANO PACÍFICO
La Serena
Córdoba
Rosario
OCÉANO ATLÁNTICO
URUGUAY
Valparaíso
Santiago
ARGENTINA
Montevideo
Buenos Aires
Concepción
Río de la Plata
Bahía Blanca
N
Puerto Montt
Bariloche
Chiloé
AMÉRICA DEL SUR
Islas Malvinas
0
1500 kilómetros
Estrecho de Magallanes
0
1000 millas
Punta Arenas
Tierra del Fuego
Cabo de Hornos

ESPAÑA
0 200 kilómetros
0 100 millas
N
MAR CANTÁBRICO
Bahía de Vizcaya
FRANCIA
CANTABRIA
San Sebastián
Santander
La Coruña
Oviedo
ASTURIAS
Santiago de Compostela
Bilbao
PAÍS VASCO
LOS PIRINEOS
ANDORRA
Golfo de León
GALICIA
Pamplona
NAVARRA
Vigo
León
Burgos
Logroño
LA RIOJA
CASTILLA-LEÓN
CATALUÑA
Costa Brava
Valladolid
Zaragoza
Lérida
Zamora
ESPAÑA
Río Ebro
Tarragona
Barcelona
Oporto
Río Duero
SIERRA DE GUADARRAMA
ARAGÓN
Segovia
Salamanca
Ávila
MADRID
Guadalajara
PORTUGAL
El Escorial
Madrid
Castellón
Menorca
Mallorca
Río Tajo
Toledo
Cáceres
CASTILLA-LA MANCHA
Valencia
Palma
Lisboa
EXTREMADURA
COMUNIDAD VALENCIANA
Ibiza
ISLAS BALEARES
Ciudad Real
Badajoz
Mérida
Almadén
Albacete
Formentera
Alicante
Río Guadiana
SIERRA MORENA
Murcia
MAR MEDITERRÁNEO
Linares
Río Guadalquivir
MURCIA
Costa Blanca
Córdoba
Jaén
Lorca
Sevilla
ANDALUCÍA
Cartagena
Huelva
SIERRA NEVADA
Granada
Almería
Jerez de la Frontera
Málaga
Golfo de Cádiz
Cádiz
Costa del Sol
OCÉANO ATLÁNTICO
Gibraltar (R.U.)
Tánger
Ceuta (Esp.)
Orán
ISLAS CANARIAS
Santa Cruz de Tenerife
Lanzarote
Fuerte-ventura
La Palma
Tenerife
Las Palmas
Hierro
Gomera
Las Palmas de Gran Canaria
0 200 kilómetros
0 100 millas

# DOS MUNDOS

## EN BREVE

PASO A

# La clase y los estudiantes

**METAS**

In **Paso A** you will learn to understand a good deal of spoken Spanish and get to know your classmates. The listening skills you develop during these first days of class will enhance your ability to understand Spanish and will also make learning to speak Spanish easier.

Ciudad de México, Distrito Federal

**ACTIVIDADES DE COMUNICACIÓN**

Los mandatos en la clase

Los nombres de los compañeros de clase

¿Quién es?

Los colores y la ropa

Los números (0–39)

Los saludos

**GRAMÁTICA**

A.1 Responding to Instructions: Commands

A.2 Naming: The Verb **llamarse**

A.3 Identifying People and Things: Subject Pronouns and the Verb **ser**

A.4 Describing People and Things: Negation

A.5 Identifying People and Things: Gender (Part 1)

A.6 Describing People's Clothing: The Verb **llevar**

A.7 Identifying People and Things: Plural Forms (Part 1)

# Actividades de comunicación

## Los mandatos en la clase

*Lea Gramática A.1.*

### Actividad 1. Identificaciones: Los mandatos

**a.** Dé una vuelta.
**b.** Abra el libro.
**c.** Cierre el libro.
**d.** Camine.
**e.** Saque un bolígrafo.
**f.** Salte.
**g.** Corra.
**h.** Mire hacia arriba.
**i.** Muéstreme el pupitre.

# Los nombres de los compañeros de clase

*Lea Gramática A.2.*

## Actividad 2. Diálogos: Los amigos

—¿Cómo se llama el amigo de _____?
—Se llama _____.

—¿Cómo se llama la amiga de _____?
—Se llama _____.

# ¿Quién es?

*Lea Gramática A.3–A.4.*

## Actividad 3. Asociaciones: Las descripciones de las personas famosas

¿Quién es _____?

1. rubio/a ~ moreno/a
2. alto/a ~ bajo/a
3. guapo/bonita ~ feo/a
4. joven ~ viejo/a
5. delgado/a ~ gordo/a

Roseanne
María Conchita Alonso
Lauren Bacall
Antonio Banderas
Val Kilmer
Sharon Stone
Elijah Wood
Brad Pitt
Barbra Streisand
Michael Jordan
Meryl Streep
Marlon Brando
Danny DeVito
Rosie Pérez

Estudiantes de medicina en la Universidad de Buenos Aires, Argentina

# Los colores y la ropa

*Lea Gramática A.5–A.6.*

## Actividad 4. Asociaciones: Los colores

¿De qué color es _____?

**a.** un automóvil

**b.** una casa

**c.** un lápiz

**d.** una planta

**e.** un gato

**f.** una rosa

**g.** el libro de español

**h.** un perro

**i.** un arco iris

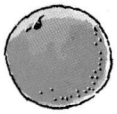

**j.** una naranja

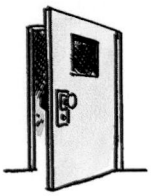

**k.** la puerta

**1.** rojo/a
**2.** amarillo/a
**3.** verde
**4.** color café
**5.** blanco/a
**6.** azul
**7.** morado/a
**8.** anaranjado/a
**9.** ¿ ?

### Actividad 5. Identificaciones: Mis compañeros de clase

Mire a cuatro compañeros de clase. Diga el nombre de cada estudiante, la ropa y el color de la ropa que lleva.

| | NOMBRE | | ROPA | COLOR |
|---|---|---|---|---|
| 1. | *Carmen* | lleva | *una blusa* | *amarilla.* |
| 2. | _____ | lleva | _____ | _____ |
| 3. | _____ | lleva | _____ | _____ |
| 4. | _____ | lleva | _____ | _____ |
| 5. | _____ | lleva | _____ | _____ |

## Los números (0–39)

***Lea Gramática A.7.***

| | | |
|---|---|---|
| 0 cero | 10 diez | 20 veinte |
| 1 uno | 11 once | 21 veintiuno |
| 2 dos | 12 doce | 22 veintidós |
| 3 tres | 13 trece | 23 veintitrés |
| 4 cuatro | 14 catorce | 24 veinticuatro... |
| 5 cinco | 15 quince | 30 treinta |
| 6 seis | 16 dieciséis | 31 treinta y uno |
| 7 siete | 17 diecisiete | 32 treinta y dos |
| 8 ocho | 18 dieciocho | 33 treinta y tres... |
| 9 nueve | 19 diecinueve | 39 treinta y nueve |

### Actividad 6. Identificaciones: ¿Cuántos hay?

Cuente los estudiantes en la clase que...

| LLEVAN | TIENEN |
|---|---|
| _____ pantalones | _____ barba |
| _____ lentes | _____ bigote |
| _____ reloj | _____ el pelo largo |
| _____ blusa | _____ el pelo castaño |
| _____ falda | _____ el pelo rubio |
| _____ botas | _____ los ojos azules |
| _____ aretes | _____ los ojos castaños |

# Los saludos

## Actividad 7. Diálogos: Los saludos

1. Nacho Padilla saluda a Ernesto Ramírez.

   NACHO: Buenos días. ¿Cómo está usted?
   SR. RAMÍREZ: Muy bien, gracias. ¿Y usted?
   NACHO: Muy bien.

2. La señora Silva habla por teléfono con el señor Alvar.

   SRA. SILVA: Señor Alvar, ¿cómo está usted?
   SR. ALVAR: Estoy un poco cansado. ¿Y usted?
   SRA. SILVA: Regular.

3. Amanda habla con doña Lola Batini.

   DOÑA LOLA: Buenas tardes, Amanda.
   AMANDA: Buenas tardes, doña Lola. ¿Cómo está la familia?
   DOÑA LOLA: Bien, gracias.

4. Rogelio Varela presenta a Carla.

   ROGELIO: Marta, ésta es mi amiga Carla.
   CARLA: Mucho gusto.
   MARTA: Igualmente.

5. Un amigo nuevo / Una amiga nueva en la clase de español.

   USTED: _____, éste/ésta es mi amigo/a _____.
   AMIGO/A 1: _____.
   AMIGO/A 2: _____.

La Universidad de Michoacán, México

# Vocabulario

## Los mandatos — Commands

| | |
|---|---|
| **abra(n) (el libro)** | open (the book) |
| **baile(n)** | dance |
| **camine(n)** | walk |
| **cante(n)** | sing |
| **cierre(n)** | close |
| **corra(n)** | run |
| **cuente(n)** | count |
| **dé/den una vuelta** | turn around |
| **diga(n)** | say |
| **escriba(n)** | write |
| **escuche(n)** | listen |
| **hable(n)** | speak |
| **lea(n)** | read |
| **mire(n) (hacia arriba/abajo)** | look (up/down) |
| **muéstre(n)me** | show me |
| **pónga(n)se de pie** | stand up |
| **salte(n)** | jump |
| **saque(n) (un bolígrafo)** | take out (a pen) |
| **siénte(n)se** | sit down |

## Las preguntas y las respuestas
Questions and Answers

| | |
|---|---|
| **¿Cómo está la familia?** | How is your family? |
| **¿Cómo está usted?** | How are you? |
| **(Muy) Bien, gracias.** | (Very) Well, thanks. |
| **Estoy bien/regular.** | I am fine/OK. |
| **Estoy un poco cansado/a.** | I am a little tired. |
| **¿Cómo se llama?** | What is his/her name? |
| **Se llama...** | His/Her name is . . . |
| **¿Cómo se llama usted?** | What is your name? |
| **Me llamo...** | My name is . . . |
| **¿Cuál es su nombre?** | What is your name? |
| **Mi nombre es...** | My name is . . . |
| **¿Cuántos/as... (hay)?** | How many . . . (are there)? |
| **¿De qué color es... ?** | What color is (it) . . . ? |
| **¿Quién (es)? / ¿Quiénes (son)?** | Who (is it)? / Who (are they)? |

## La descripción física
Physical Description

| | |
|---|---|
| **Es...** | He/She (It) is . . . |
| **alto/a** | tall |
| **bajo/a** | short |
| **bonito/a** | pretty |
| **delgado/a** | thin |
| **famoso/a** | famous |
| **feo/a** | ugly |
| **gordo/a** | fat |
| **guapo/a** | handsome |
| **joven** | young |
| **moreno/a** | brown-skinned, dark-skinned |
| **nuevo/a** | new |
| **viejo/a** | old |
| **Tiene...** | He has . . . |
| **barba** | (a) beard |
| **bigote** | (a) moustache |
| **Tiene el pelo...** | His/Her hair is . . . (He/She has . . . hair) |
| **castaño** | brown |
| **corto** | short |
| **lacio** | straight |
| **largo** | long |
| **mediano** | medium (length) |
| **negro** | black |
| **rizado** | curly |
| **rubio** | blond |
| **Tiene los ojos...** | His/Her eyes are . . . (He/She has . . . eyes) |
| **azules** | blue |
| **castaños** | brown |
| **negros** | black |
| **verdes** | green |

## Los colores
Colors

| | |
|---|---|
| **amarillo/a** | yellow |
| **anaranjado/a** | orange |
| **azul** | blue |
| **blanco/a** | white |
| **color café** | brown |
| **gris** | gray |
| **morado/a** | purple |
| **negro/a** | black |
| **rojo/a** | red |
| **rosado/a** | pink |
| **verde** | green |

## La ropa
Clothes

| | |
|---|---|
| **¿Quién lleva... ?** | Who is wearing . . . ? |
| **un abrigo** | coat |
| **las botas** | b |
| **una camisa** | s |
| **una camiseta** | |
| **una chaqueta** | |
| **una corbata** | |
| **una falda** | |
| **los pantalones** | pants |
| **los pantalones cortos** | shorts |
| **un saco** | sports coat |
| **un sombrero** | hat |
| **un suéter** | sweater |
| **un traje** | suit |
| **un vestido** | dress |
| **los zapatos (de tenis)** | (tennis) shoes |

## Las personas
People

| | |
|---|---|
| **el amigo / la amiga** | friend |
| **el compañero / la compañera de clase** | classmate |
| **don** | title of respect used with a man's first name |
| **doña** | title of respect used with a woman's first name |
| **el/la estudiante** | student |
| **la familia** | family |
| **el hombre** | man |
| **el muchacho / la muchacha** | boy, young man / girl, young woman |
| **la mujer** | woman |
| **el niño / la niña** | boy/girl |
| **el profesor / la profesora** | professor |
| **el señor / la señora** | man; Mr. / woman; Mrs. |
| **la señorita** | young lady; Miss |

## Los saludos y las despedidas
Greetings and Goodbyes

| | |
|---|---|
| **Buenos días.** | Good morning. |
| **Buenas tardes.** | Good afternoon. |
| **Buenas noches.** | Good evening. / Good night. |
| **Hasta luego.** | See you later. |
| **Adiós.** | Goodbye. |

## Las presentaciones
Introductions

| | |
|---|---|
| **Ésta es mi amiga...** **Éste es mi amigo...** | This is my friend . . . |
| **Mucho gusto.** | Pleased to meet you. |
| **Igualmente.** | Same here. |

## verbos — Verbs

| | |
|---|---|
| **es** | is |
| **habla (por teléfono)** | speaks (on the telephone) |
| **lleva(n)** | is (are) wearing |
| **presenta** | introduces |
| **saluda** | greets |
| **tiene** | he/she has / you have |
| **tienen** | they have |

## Las cosas — Things

| | |
|---|---|
| **el arco iris** | rainbow |
| **los aretes** | earrings |
| **la casa** | house |
| **el gato** | cat |
| **el lápiz** | pencil |
| **los lentes** | glasses |
| **el libro (de español)** | (Spanish) book |
| **la naranja** | orange |
| **el perro** | dog |
| **la puerta** | door |
| **el pupitre** | desk |
| **el reloj** | watch, clock |

**PALABRAS SEMEJANTES (*Cognates*): el automóvil, la planta, la rosa**

## Palabras del texto — Words from the Text

| | |
|---|---|
| **diga** | say |
| **el español** | Spanish |
| **la gramática** | grammar |
| **los mandatos** | commands |
| **no** | no, not |
| **¿Qué?** | What? |
| **¿Quién(es)?** | Who? |
| **sí** | yes |

**PALABRAS SEMEJANTES: la actividad, las asociaciones, la clase, la comunicación, la descripción, el diálogo, las identificaciones, el modelo**

## Los números — Numbers

| | |
|---|---|
| **cero** | 0 |
| **uno** | 1 |
| **dos** | 2 |
| **tres** | 3 |
| **cuatro** | 4 |
| **cinco** | 5 |
| **seis** | 6 |
| **siete** | 7 |
| **ocho** | 8 |
| **nueve** | 9 |
| **diez** | 10 |
| **once** | 11 |
| **doce** | 12 |
| **trece** | 13 |
| **catorce** | 14 |
| **quince** | 15 |
| **dieciséis** | 16 |
| **diecisiete** | 17 |
| **dieciocho** | 18 |
| **diecinueve** | 19 |
| **veinte** | 20 |
| **veintiuno** | 21 |
| **veintidós** | 22 |
| **veintitrés** | 23 |
| **veinticuatro** | 24 |
| **veinticinco** | 25 |
| **veintiséis** | 26 |
| **veintisiete** | 27 |
| **veintiocho** | 28 |
| **veintinueve** | 29 |
| **treinta** | 30 |
| **treinta y uno** | 31 |
| **treinta y dos** | 32 |
| **treinta y nueve** | 39 |

## Palabras útiles — Useful Words

| | |
|---|---|
| **cada** | each |
| **con** | with |
| **de** | of, from |
| **del (de + el) / de la** | of the |
| **el, la, los, las** | the |
| **en** | in, on |
| **gracias** | thank you; thanks |
| **mi(s)** | my |
| **y** | and |

# Gramática

## Introduction

The **Gramática y ejercicios** sections of this book are written for your use outside of class. They contain grammar explanations and exercises that are presented in nontechnical language, so it should not be necessary to go over all of them in class.

The **Lea Gramática...** notes that begin most new topics in the **Actividades de comunicación y lecturas** sections give the grammar point(s) you should read at that time. Study them carefully, then do the exercises in writing and check your answers in the back of the book. If you have little or no trouble with the exercises, you have probably understood the explanation. Remember: It is not necessary to memorize these grammar rules.

Keep in mind that successful completion of a grammar exercise means only that you have understood the explanation. It does not mean that you have *acquired* the rule. True acquisition comes not from study of grammar but from hearing and reading a great deal of meaningful Spanish. Learning the rules of grammar through study will allow you to use those rules when you have time to stop and think about correctness, as during careful writing.

If you have trouble with an exercise, ask your instructor for assistance. In difficult cases, your instructor will go over the material in class to be sure everyone has understood, but probably won't spend too much time on the explanations, in order to save class time for real communication experiences.

The grammar explanations in **Paso A** contain basic information about Spanish grammar. **Paso A** has no exercises because most of the information will be explained again in subsequent chapters.

## A.1 Responding to Instructions: Commands

Your instructor will give you commands during the Total Physical Response activities, as well as for instructions.*

In English the same form of the verb is used for giving commands, whether to one person (singular) or to more than one person (plural).

> Steve, please stand up.
> Mr. and Mrs. Martínez, please stand up.

Singular commands (to one person) end in **-a** or **-e.** Plural commands (to more than one person) end in **-an** or **-en.**

In Spanish, however, singular commands end in **-a** or **-e,** while plural commands add an **-n.**

| | |
|---|---|
| Esteban, **abra** el libro. | *Steve, open the book.* |
| Alberto y Nora, **saquen** un bolígrafo, por favor. | *Al and Nora, take out a pen, please.* |

*You will learn more about how to give commands in **Gramática 11.1.**

## A.2 Naming: The Verb *llamarse*

To ask someone's name:
**¿Cuál es su nombre?**
or
**¿Cómo se llama usted?**
To tell someone your name:
**Mi nombre es...**
or
**Me llamo...**

The most common way to ask someone's name is to use the verb form **llama** (*call*).

| | |
|---|---|
| —¿Cómo **se llama** usted?* | —*What is your name?* |
| —Nora. | —*Nora.* |

You may answer the question either briefly, by saying your name (as in the preceding example), or in a complete sentence with the pronoun **me** (*myself*) and the verb **llamo** (*I call*).

| | |
|---|---|
| **Me llamo** Nora. | *My name is Nora.* |

To ask what someone else's name is, use the following question-and-answer pattern.

| | |
|---|---|
| —¿Cómo **se llama** el amigo de Nora? | —*What's Nora's friend's name?* |
| —**Se llama** Luis. | —*His name is Luis.* |

Here is another way to ask someone's name.

| | |
|---|---|
| —**¿Cuál es su nombre?** | —*What is your name?* |
| —**Mi nombre es Esteban.** | —*My name is Steve.* |

## A.3 Identifying People and Things: Subject Pronouns and the Verb *ser*

**ser** = *to be* (identification)
**Soy estudiante.** (*I am a student.*)

**A.** Spanish uses the verb **ser** (*to be*) to identify things or people.

| | |
|---|---|
| —¿Qué **es** eso? | —*What is that?* |
| —**Es** un bolígrafo. | —*It's a pen.* |
| —¿Quién **es?** | —*Who is it?* |
| —**Es** Luis. | —*It's Luis.* |

**B.** Personal pronouns are used to refer to a person without mentioning the person's name. Here are some of the most common personal pronouns that can serve as the subject of a sentence, with the corresponding present-tense forms of **ser.** It is not necessary to memorize these pronouns. You will see and hear them again and again.

| | | | |
|---|---|---|---|
| yo | soy | *I* | *am* |
| usted | es | *you (singular)* | *are* |
| él†/ella | es | *he/she* | *is* |
| nosotros/nosotras | somos | *we* | *are* |
| ustedes | son | *you (plural)* | *are* |
| ellos/ellas | son | *they* | *are* |

*Literally, this means *How do you call yourself?*
†The pronoun **él** (*he*) has an accent to distinguish it in writing from the definite article **el** (*the*).

| | |
|---|---|
| yo = *I* | nosotros = *we* (masculine) |
| usted = *you* (singular) | nosotras = *we* (feminine) |
| él = *he* | ustedes = *you* (plural) |
| ella = *she* | ellos = *they* (masculine) |
| | ellas = *they* (feminine) |

| | |
|---|---|
| ¿Usted es profesor? | *Are you a professor?* |

**C.** If is often not necessary in Spanish to use a subject pronoun (**yo, usted, nosotros, ellas,** etc.). The verb itself or the context usually tells you who the subject is.

| | |
|---|---|
| Soy profesor de matemáticas. | *I'm a mathematics professor.* |
| Son estudiantes de la clase de la profesora Martínez. | *They are students in Professor Martínez's class.* |

## A.4 Describing People and Things: Negation

**no** = *not*
To say that something is not true, put **no** in front of the verb.

In a negative sentence in Spanish, the word **no** comes in front of the verb.

| | |
|---|---|
| Ramón **no es** mi novio. Es el novio de Amanda. | *Ramón isn't my boyfriend. He's Amanda's boyfriend.* |

There are no additional words in Spanish corresponding to the English negatives *don't* and *doesn't*.

| | |
|---|---|
| Guillermo **no tiene** el pelo largo ahora. | *Guillermo doesn't have long hair now.* |

## A.5 Identifying People and Things: Gender (Part 1)

Masculine nouns usually end in **-o**.
Feminine nouns usually end in **-a**.

**A.** Nouns (words that represent people or things) in Spanish are classified as either masculine or feminine. Masculine nouns often end in **-o** (**sombrero**); feminine nouns often end in **-a** (**falda**). In addition, words ending in **-ción, -sión,** or **-dad** are also feminine.

| | |
|---|---|
| Madrid es una ciu**dad** bonit**a.** | *Madrid is a pretty city.* |
| La civiliza**ción** maya fue muy avanzad**a.** | *The Mayan civilization was very advanced.* |

But the terms *masculine* and *feminine* are grammatical classifications only; Spanish speakers do not perceive things such as notebooks or doors as being "male" or "female." On the other hand, words that refer to males are usually masculine (**amigo**), and words that refer to females are usually feminine (**amiga**).

| | |
|---|---|
| Esteban es mi **amigo** y Carmen es una **amiga** de él. | *Esteban is my friend and Carmen is a friend of his.* |

These endings can be learned, but are acquired late. Don't worry about them while you are speaking, only when you edit your writing.

**B.** Because Spanish nouns have gender, adjectives (words that describe nouns) *agree* with nouns: They change their endings from **-o** to **-a** according to the gender of the nouns they modify. Notice the two words for *black* in the following examples.

| | |
|---|---|
| Lan tiene el pelo **negro.** | *Lan has black hair.* |
| Luis lleva una chaqueta **negra.** | *Luis is wearing a black jacket.* |

**El** and **la** both mean *the*. **El** is used with masculine nouns and **la** is used with feminine nouns.

**Un** and **una** both mean *a/an*. **Un** is used with masculine nouns and **una** is used with feminine nouns.

**C.** Like English, Spanish has definite articles (*the*) and indefinite articles (*a, an*). Articles in Spanish also change form according to the gender of the nouns they accompany.

| | DEFINITE (*the*) | INDEFINITE (*a, an*) |
|---|---|---|
| ***Masculine*** | **el** suéter | **un** sombrero |
| ***Feminine*** | **la** blusa | **una** chaqueta |

| | |
|---|---|
| Hoy Mónica lleva **un** vestido nuevo. | *Today Mónica is wearing a new dress.* |
| **La** chaqueta de Alberto es azul. | *Al's jacket is blue.* |

## A.6 Describing People's Clothing: The Verb *llevar*

The Spanish verb **llevar** corresponds to the English verb *to wear.*

| | |
|---|---|
| Mónica **lleva** un suéter azul. | *Mónica is wearing a blue sweater.* |

Notice that Spanish verbs change their endings according to the subject of the sentence.

| | |
|---|---|
| Yo **llevo** pantalones grises. Mis amigos **llevan** pantalones negros. | *I'm wearing gray pants. My friends are wearing black pants.* |

Spanish verbs change endings. These endings tell you who is performing the action.

Here are some of the common endings for Spanish verbs.* The subject pronouns are in parentheses because it is not always necessary to use them.

**llevar** = *to wear*

| **llevar** (*to wear*) | | |
|---|---|---|
| (yo) | llev**o** | *I wear* |
| (usted, él/ella) | llev**a** | *you (sing.) wear; he/she wears* |
| (nosotros/as) | llev**amos** | *we wear* |
| (ustedes, ellos/as) | llev**an** | *you (pl.) wear; they wear* |

These endings are used on most Spanish verbs, and you will soon become accustomed to hearing and using them.

**tengo** = *I have*
**tiene** = *he/she has*

In **Paso C** you will see the forms of the verb **tener** (*to have*), which you have also heard in class.

| | |
|---|---|
| La profesora Martínez **tiene** el pelo negro. | *Professor Martínez has black hair.* |
| Yo **tengo** los ojos azules. | *I have blue eyes.* |

*You will learn more about verb endings in **Gramática C.5, 1.3,** and **3.2.**

## A.7 Identifying People and Things: Plural Forms (Part 1)

Almost all plural words in Spanish end with **-s** or **-es**. Articles and adjectives agree with the nouns they modify.

Spanish and English nouns may be singular (**camisa,** *shirt*) or plural (**camisas,** *shirts*). Almost all plural words in Spanish end in **-s** or **-es: blusas** (*blouses*), **pantalones** (*pants*), **suéteres** (*sweaters*), **zapatos** (*shoes*), and so on.* In Spanish, unlike English, articles before plural nouns and adjectives that describe plural nouns must also be plural. Notice the plural ending on the Spanish word for *new* in the following example.

Nora tiene dos **faldas nuevas.** *Nora has two new skirts.*

Here are some singular and plural nouns, accompanied by the corresponding definite articles and adjectives.

| | SINGULAR | PLURAL |
|---|---|---|
| ***Masculine*** | el vestido gris | **los** zapato**s** blanco**s** |
| ***Feminine*** | la chaqueta roja | **las** blusa**s** amarilla**s** |

*You will learn more about how to make nouns and adjectives plural in **Gramática B.5.**

PASO

# B Las descripciones

**METAS**

In **Paso B** you will continue to develop your listening and speaking abilities in Spanish. You will learn more vocabulary with which to describe your immediate environment. You will also get to know your classmates better as you converse with them.

Sevilla, España

**ACTIVIDADES DE COMUNICACIÓN**

Hablando con otros

Las cosas en el salón de clase y los números (40–69)

El cuerpo humano

La descripción de las personas

**EN RESUMEN**

**GRAMÁTICA Y EJERCICIOS**

B.1 Addressing Others: Informal and Polite *you* (**tú/usted**)

B.2 Describing People: More about Subject Pronouns

B.3 Identifying People and Things: Gender (Part 2)

B.4 Expressing Existence: **hay**

B.5 Describing People and Things: Plural Forms (Part 2)

B.6 Describing People and Things: Adjective-Noun Agreement

# Actividades de comunicación

## Hablando con otros

*Lea Gramática B.1–B.2.*

### Actividad 1. Identificaciones: ¿*Tú* o *usted*?

Usted habla con estas personas. ¿Usa **tú** o **usted**?

1. un amigo de la universidad
2. el profesor de matemáticas
3. una niña de diez años
4. un amigo de su papá
5. una señora de treinta y cinco años
6. una recepcionista
7. su doctor
8. su hermano/a

### Actividad 2. Diálogos: ¿Cómo está usted? ¿Cómo estás tú?

El señor Olivera saluda a su joven vecina Amanda.

DON ANSELMO: Hola, Amanda.
AMANDA: Buenos días, señor Olivera. ¿Cómo está usted?
DON ANSELMO: Muy bien, gracias. ¿Cómo está tu mamá?
AMANDA: Ella está bien, gracias.

Amanda saluda a su amiga Graciela.

AMANDA: Buenas tardes, Graciela. ¿Cómo estás?
GRACIELA: Regular. ¿Y tú?
AMANDA: Un poco cansada.

### Actividad 3. Diálogos abiertos: Más saludos

EL ESTUDIANTE NUEVO
E1: Hola, _____. ¿Cómo estás?
E2: _____. ¿Y tú?
E1: _____.
E2: ¿Quién es el chico de pelo _____?
E1: Es un amigo de _____. Se llama _____.

EN LA OFICINA
E1: Buenos días, _____. ¿Cómo está usted?
E2: Estoy _____. ¿Y usted?
E1: _____. ¿Quién es la señorita de pelo _____?
E2: Es _____. Es la secretaria.

## Las cosas en el salón de clase y los números (40–69)

*Lea Gramática B.3–B.4.*

## Actividad 4. Identificaciones: ¿Qué hay en el salón de clase?

MODELOS: En mi clase hay... → *un lápiz viejo.*
En mi clase hay... → *una pizarra blanca.*

| | |
|---|---|
| **1.** un lápiz | **a.** amarillo/a ~ azul ~ color café |
| **2.** una ventana | **b.** moderno/a ~ antiguo/a |
| **3.** una pizarra | **c.** interesante ~ aburrido/a |
| **4.** un reloj | **d.** fácil ~ difícil |
| **5.** un bolígrafo | **e.** blanco/a ~ negro/a |
| **6.** una mesa | **f.** largo/a |
| **7.** un libro | **g.** viejo/a ~ nuevo/a |
| **8.** una puerta | **h.** pequeño/a ~ grande |
| **9.** un mapa | **i.** ¿ ? |
| **10.** un cartel | |

## Actividad 5. Intercambios: El salón de clase

MODELO: E1: ¿Cuántos/as _____ hay en el salón de clase?
E2: Hay _____.

| | |
|---|---|
| **1.** estudiantes | **5.** ventanas |
| **2.** mesas | **6.** paredes |
| **3.** borradores | **7.** puertas |
| **4.** pizarras | **8.** luces |

## Actividad 6. Intercambios: ¿Cuánto cuesta?

MODELO: E1: ¿Cuánto cuesta *la mochila?*
E2: Cuesta *$50.39* (*cincuenta dólares y treinta y nueve centavos*).

| | | |
|---|---|---|
| 40 cuarenta | 50 cincuenta | 60 sesenta |
| 41 cuarenta y uno | 52 cincuenta y dos | 63 sesenta y tres |
| 45 cuarenta y cinco | 58 cincuenta y ocho | 69 sesenta y nueve |

# El cuerpo humano

*Lea Gramática B.5.*

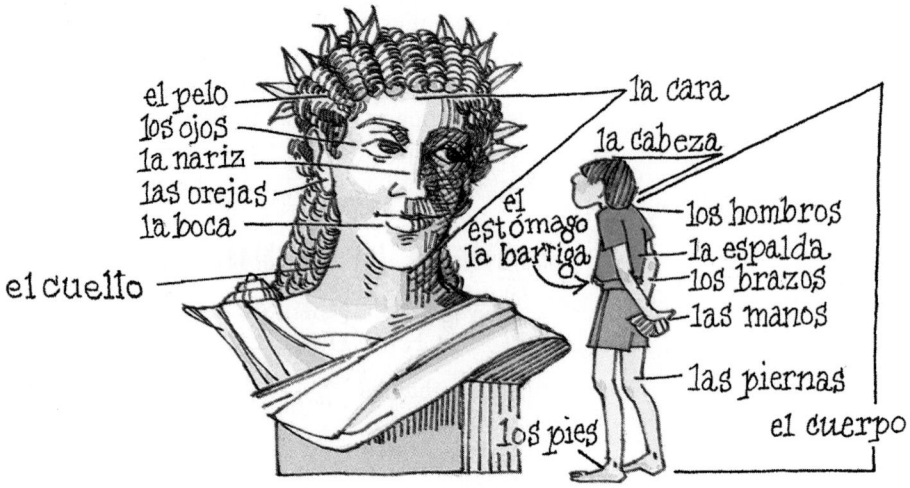


## Actividad 7. Descripción de dibujos: ¿Quién es?

Mire a estas personas. Escuche la descripción que da su profesor(a), y diga cómo se llama la persona.

# La descripción de las personas

*Lea Gramática B.6.*

## Actividad 8. Diálogo: La amiga nueva

ESTEBAN: ¿Cómo es tu amiga nueva, Luis?
LUIS: Es alta, delgada y de pelo castaño. ¡Y muy inteligente!
ESTEBAN: ¿Cómo se llama?
LUIS: Cecilia Teresa.
ESTEBAN: Es un nombre muy bonito.
LUIS: ¡Ella también es una chica muy bonita!
also

## Actividad 9. Diálogo abierto: Los amigos nuevos

E1: ¿Tienes amigos nuevos?
E2: Sí, tengo dos.
E1: ¿Cómo se llaman?
E2: Se llaman _____ y _____ y son muy _____.
E1: ¿Y son _____ también?
E2: ¡Claro que sí! (¡Claro que no!)

## Actividad 10. Intercambios: Mis compañeros y yo

Diga cómo es usted con tres descripciones, dos ciertas y una falsa. Su compañero/a va a decir si cada descripción es cierta o falsa.

MODELO: E1: ¿Cómo eres?
E2: Soy *simpático/a.*
E1: Es cierto.
E2: También soy *materialista.*
E1: ¡No es cierto! (¡Es falso!)
E2: Y soy *trabajador(a).*
E1: Es cierto.

| | | | |
|---|---|---|---|
| agresivo/a | extrovertido/a | introvertido/a | reservado/a |
| antipático/a | filosófico/a | materialista | simpático/a |
| conservador(a) | generoso/a | nervioso/a | tacaño/a |
| considerado/a | idealista | perezoso/a | tímido/a |
| deportista | impulsivo/a | práctico/a | tonto/a |
| entusiasta | inteligente | religioso/a | trabajador(a) |

### EXPRESIONES ÚTILES

¿Es cierto?
Es cierto.
¡No es cierto!
¡Es falso!

## Actividad 11. Entrevista: Mi mejor amigo/a

| ESTUDIANTE 1 | ESTUDIANTE 2 |
|---|---|
| **1.** ¿Cómo se llama tu mejor amigo/a? | Se llama _____. |
| **2.** ¿De qué color tiene los ojos? | Tiene los ojos _____. |
| **3.** ¿Es alto/a, bajo/a o de estatura mediana? | Es _____. |
| **4.** ¿De qué color tiene el pelo? | Tiene el pelo _____. |
| **5.** ¿Tiene bigote/barba? | (No) Tiene _____. |
| **6.** ¿Cómo es? ¿Es simpático/a? ¿tímido/a? ¿trabajador(a)? ¿ ? | Es _____. |

# En resumen

## De todo un poco

**A.** Un mundo ideal

Use su imaginación y complete estas descripciones.

1. El salón de clase ideal es _____ y _____.
2. En el salón de clase ideal hay _____. No hay _____.
3. El amigo / La amiga ideal es _____, _____ y _____.
4. El/La estudiante ideal es _____, _____ y _____.
5. El profesor / La profesora ideal es _____, _____ y _____.

**B.** Su opinión

Exprese su opinión con su compañero/a.

MODELO: E1: La clase de español *es interesante*.
E2: Estoy de acuerdo. La clase de español *es muy interesante* (*no es aburrida*).

### EXPRESIONES ÚTILES

(No) Estoy de acuerdo.

1. La clase de español es (interesante ~ aburrida).
2. Hay muchos estudiantes (inteligentes ~ tontos) en esta clase.
3. El profesor / La profesora de español es (reservado/a ~ entusiasta).
4. El salón de clase es (bonito ~ feo).
5. Yo soy (extrovertido/a ~ tímido/a).

# Vocabulario

## Las cosas en el salón
Things in the Classroom

| | |
|---|---|
| **el borrador** | eraser |
| **el cuaderno** | notebook; workbook |
| **el diccionario** | dictionary |
| **el escritorio** | (teacher's) desk |
| **la luz** | light |
| **la mesa** | table |
| **el papel** | paper |
| **la pared** | wall |
| **el piso** | floor |
| **la pizarra** | (chalk)board |
| **la pluma** | pen (*Mex.*) |
| **la silla** | chair |
| **el techo** | ceiling |
| **la tiza** | chalk |
| **la ventana** | window |

**REPASO** (*Review*)**: el bolígrafo, el lápiz, el libro, la puerta, el pupitre, el reloj, el texto**

## El cuerpo humano
The Human Body

| | |
|---|---|
| **la boca** | mouth |
| **el brazo** | arm |
| **la cabeza** | head |
| **la cara** | face |
| **el cuello** | neck |
| **la espalda** | back |
| **el estómago** | stomach |
| **el hombro** | shoulder |
| **la mano** | hand |
| **la nariz** | nose |
| **la oreja** | ear |
| **el pie / los pies** | foot/feet |
| **la pierna** | leg |

## Las personas

| | |
|---|---|
| **el chico / la chica** | young man / young woman |
| **el hermano / la hermana** | brother/sister |
| **el niño / la niña** | boy/girl |
| **el vecino / la vecina** | neighbor |

**PALABRAS SEMEJANTES** (*Cognates*)**: el doctor / la doctora, la mamá, el papá, el/la recepcionista, el robot, el secretario / la secretaria**

**REPASO: la señorita**

## Las descripciones

| | |
|---|---|
| **¿Cómo es él/ella?** | What is he/she like? |
| **¿Cómo es usted? / ¿Cómo eres tú?** | What are you like? |
| **abierto/a** | open |
| **aburrido/a** | boring; bored |
| **antiguo/a** | antique |
| **antipático/a** | unpleasant |
| **conservador(a)** | conservative |
| **de... años** | . . . years old |
| **de estatura (mediana)** | (medium) height |
| **deportista** | fond of sports |
| **difícil** | difficult |
| **divertido/a** | fun |
| **entusiasta** | enthusiastic |
| **extrovertido/a** | extroverted |
| **fácil** | easy |
| **grande** | big, large |
| **introvertido/a** | introverted |
| **mejor** | best, better |
| **pequeño/a** | small |
| **perezoso/a** | lazy |
| **simpático/a** | nice, pleasant |
| **tacaño/a** | stingy |
| **tímido/a** | shy |
| **tonto/a** | dumb, not too smart |
| **trabajador(a)** | hard-working |

**PALABRAS SEMEJANTES: agresivo/a, artístico/a, considerado/a, generoso/a, filosófico/a, humano/a, ideal, idealista, impulsivo/a, inteligente, interesante, materialista, moderno/a, nervioso/a, práctico/a, religioso/a, reservado/a**

**REPASO: feo/a**

## Los verbos

| | |
|---|---|
| **conteste(n)** | answer |
| **da** | gives |
| **son** | are |
| **soy** | I am |
| **tiene** | has |
| **¿Tienes... ?** | ¿Do you have . . . ? |

## Expresiones útiles — Useful Expressions

| | |
|---|---|
| **Claro que sí/no.** | Of course (not). |
| **¿Cómo estás (tú)?** | How are you? (How do you feel today?) |
| **¿Cuánto cuesta(n)... ?** | How much is (are) . . . ? |
| **Cuesta(n)...** | It costs (They cost) . . . |
| **¿De qué color tiene el pelo / los ojos?** | What color is your/his/her hair / . . . are your/his/her eyes? |
| **de todo un poco** | a bit of everything |
| **Es verdad.** | That's right (true). |
| **Está bien.** | He/She is fine. |
| **(No) Estoy de acuerdo.** | I (do not) agree. |
| **Hola.** | Hello. |

**REPASO: estoy bien, estoy un poco cansado/a**

## Palabras del texto — Words from the Text

| | |
|---|---|
| **cierto/falso** | true/false |
| **el dibujo** | drawing |
| **diga** | say |
| **la entrevista** | interview |
| **hablando** | speaking |
| **intercambios** | interactions |
| **¡Ojo!** | Attention! |
| **en resumen** | to sum up |

**REPASO: el compañero / la compañera**

## Palabras útiles — Useful Words

| | |
|---|---|
| **el cartel** | poster |
| **el centavo** | cent |
| **¿Cuántos/Cuántas... ?** | How many . . . ? |
| **de** | from; of |
| **el, la, los, las** | the |
| **yo, tú, usted, él/ella** | I, you (*inf.*), you (*pol.*), he/she |
| **nosotros/as, ustedes, ellos/ellas** | we, you (*pl.*), they |
| **España** | Spain |
| **hay** | there is / there are |
| **más** | more |
| **la mochila** | backpack |
| **muchos/as** | much; a lot |
| **el mundo** | world |
| **muy** | very |
| **otro/a** | other, another |
| **¿Qué... ?** | What . . . ? |
| **si** | if |
| **su** | his/her/your (*pol.*) |
| **también** | also |
| **tu** | your (*inf.*) |

**PALABRAS SEMEJANTES: el dólar / los dólares, el mapa, las matemáticas, la oficina, la universidad**

**REPASO: con, mi(s)**

## Los números

| | |
|---|---|
| **cuarenta** | forty |
| **cuarenta y uno** | forty-one |
| **cuarenta y cinco** | forty-five |
| **cincuenta** | fifty |
| **cincuenta y uno** | fifty-one |
| **cincuenta y dos** | fifty-two |
| **cincuenta y ocho** | fifty-eight |
| **sesenta** | sixty |
| **sesenta y nueve** | sixty-nine |

# Gramática y ejercicios

## B.1 Addressing Others: Informal and Polite *you* (*tú/usted*)

**A.** English speakers use the pronoun *you* to address a person directly, whether or not they know that person well. In older forms of English, speakers used an informal pronoun—*thou*—among friends, but today *you* is used with everyone.

Spanish has two pronouns that mean *you*, singular: **usted** and **tú.** The polite (*pol.*) pronoun **usted** is appropriate for people you do not know well, such as salespeople, receptionists, and other professionals, and especially for people older than you. The informal (*inf.*) pronoun **tú** is reserved for friends, peers, children, and other people you know well. In some places in Latin America, including Argentina and Central America, speakers use **vos** instead of **tú** as the informal pronoun for *you.* Everyone who uses **vos,** however, also understands **tú.**

Both **tú** and **usted** mean *you* (singular). **Tú** is used with friends and children. **Usted** is used with people you don't know well and people older than you.

In the activities and exercises, **Dos mundos** addresses you with **usted.** You should use **tú** with your classmates. Some instructors address their students with **tú;** others use **usted.**

Use **tú** with your classmates. Use **usted** with your instructor (unless he/she asks you to use **tú**).

| | |
|---|---|
| Soy puertorriqueño. ¿Y **tú?** ¿De dónde eres? | *I'm Puerto Rican. And you? Where are you from?* |
| Soy profesora de español. ¿Y **usted?** ¿Es **usted** estudiante? | *I'm a professor of Spanish. And you? Are you a student?* |

Present-tense verb forms for **tú** always end in **-s.**

**B.** Although both **tú** and **usted** correspond to *you*, the verb forms used with each are different. Present-tense verb forms for **tú** always end with the letter **-s.** Present-tense verb forms for **usted** end in **-a** or **-e** and are always the same as the forms for **él/ella.**

| | |
|---|---|
| ¿Tiene**s** (**tú**) una blusa gris? | *Do you have a gray blouse?* |
| ¿Tiene **usted** un vestido blanco? | *Do you have a white dress?* |

We introduced some forms of the verb **ser** (*to be*) in **Gramática A.3.** The **tú** form of **ser** is **eres;** the **usted** form of **ser** is **es** (the same as the form for **él/ella**).

| | |
|---|---|
| (**Tú**) **Eres** un buen amigo. | *You are a good friend.* |
| **Usted es** muy amable, señora Ramírez. | *You are very nice, Mrs. Ramírez.* |

**C.** Spanish distinguishes between singular *you* (**tú** or **usted**) and plural *you* (**ustedes**). Many American speakers of English make this distinction by saying "you guys" or "you all." The verb forms used with **ustedes** end in the letter **-n** and are the same as those used with the pronoun **ellos/as.**

| | |
|---|---|
| —¿Cómo **están ustedes**? | —*How are you* (*all*)*?* |
| —Bien, gracias. | —*Fine, thanks.* |

The plural of both **tú** and **usted** in Latin America is **ustedes.** In Spain, the plural of **tú** is **vosotros/as** and the plural of **usted** is **ustedes.**

Most speakers of Spanish do not distinguish between informal and polite address in the plural. **Ustedes** is used with everyone. In Spain, however, most speakers prefer to use **vosotros/as** for the informal plural *you* and reserve **ustedes** for the polite plural *you.*

The regional pronouns **vos** and **vosotros/as** do not appear in the exercises and activities of **Dos mundos** because you will learn them quickly if you travel to areas where they are frequently used. The verb forms corresponding to **vosotros/as** are listed with other verb forms and are given in Appendix 1. The verb forms corresponding to **vos** are footnoted in the grammar explanations. In the listening activities of the *Cuaderno de trabajo*, the characters from countries where **vos** and **vosotros/as** are prevalent use those pronouns. This will give you an opportunity to hear **vos** and **vosotros/as** and their accompanying verb forms, even though you will not need to use them yourself.

### Ejercicio 1

Usted habla con estas personas: ¿usa **tú** o **usted**?

1. una amiga de su clase de español
   a. ¿Tiene usted dos clases hoy?
   b. ¿Tienes dos clases hoy?
2. la recepcionista
   a. ¿Cómo estás?
   b. ¿Cómo está usted?
3. un niño
   a. Tú tienes una bicicleta nueva.
   b. Usted tiene una bicicleta nueva.
4. una persona de cuarenta y nueve años
   a. ¿Cómo se llama usted?
   b. ¿Cómo te llamas?
5. un vecino de setenta años
   a. Estoy bien. ¿Y tú?
   b. Estoy bien. ¿Y usted?

## B.2 Describing People: More about Subject Pronouns

**A. Gramática A.3** introduced some of the personal pronouns that can serve as the subject of a sentence. Here is a complete list, using the verb **ser*** as an example.

**ser** = *to be*

| **ser** (*to be*) | | |
|---|---|---|
| (yo) | soy | *I am* |
| (tú) | eres | *you (inf. sing.) are* |
| (usted, él/ella) | es | *you (pol. sing.) are; he/she is* |
| (nosotros/as) | somos | *we are* |
| (vosotros/as) | sois | *you (inf. pl., Spain) are* |
| (ustedes, ellos/as) | son | *you (pl.) are; they are* |

Remember that subject pronouns are optional in Spanish.
**(Yo) Soy estudiante.** (*I'm a student.*)
**(Nosotros) Somos amigos.** (*We're friends.*)

The pronouns are in parentheses to remind you that Spanish verbs are generally used without an expressed subject. In fact, as the chart indicates, Spanish does not have a subject pronoun for *it* or for *they*, referring to things. When subject pronouns *are* used in Spanish, they often express emphasis.

*Recognition: **vos sos**

| | |
|---|---|
| ¿Mi automóvil? Es pequeño. | *My car? It's small.* |
| ¿Las faldas? Son caras. | *The skirts? They're expensive.* |
| Yo soy de Atlanta. | ***I** am from Atlanta.* |

**B.** Subject pronouns may be used by themselves without verbs, either for emphasis or to point someone out.

| | |
|---|---|
| ¿Quién, **yo**? Yo no soy de Texas; soy de Nueva York. | *Who, me? I'm not from Texas; I'm from New York.* |
| —¿Cómo estás? | *—How are you?* |
| —Estoy bien. ¿Y **tú**? | *—I'm fine. And you?* |

**C.** The pronouns **ellos** (*they*), **nosotros** (*we*), and **vosotros** (*you, inf. pl.*) can refer to groups of people that consist of males only or of males and females. On the other hand, **ellas** (*they, fem.*), **nosotras** (*we, fem.*), and **vosotras** (*you, inf. pl. fem.*) can refer only to groups of all females.

| | |
|---|---|
| —¿Y **ellos**? ¿Quiénes son? | *—And those guys (they)? Who are they?* |
| —¿Esteban y Raúl? Son amigos. | *—Esteban and Raúl? They're friends.* |
| —¿Y **ellas**? ¿Son amigas? | *—What about them? Are they friends?* |
| —Sí, Nora y Carmen son compañeras de mi clase de español. | *—Yes, Nora and Carmen are classmates from my Spanish class.* |

## Ejercicio 2

Escoja el pronombre lógico.

MODELO: —Y *ella*, ¿lleva pantalones? →
—¿Quién, Mónica? Lleva una falda azul.

1. —¿_____ es profesor aquí?
   —¿Quién, Raúl? No, es estudiante.
2. —¿_____ son mexicanos?
   —Sí, Silvia y Nacho son mexicanos.
3. —¡Viejos, _____! No, doña María Eulalia y yo somos muy jóvenes.
4. —Señor Ruiz, _____ tiene bigote, ¿verdad?
5. —¿Y _____? ¿Son estudiantes aquí?
   —No, Pilar y Clara son estudiantes en Madrid.

a. ellos
b. usted
c. ellas
d. él
e. nosotros

## B.3 Identifying People and Things: Gender (Part 2)

How can you determine the gender of a noun? The gender of the article and/or adjective that modifies the noun will tell you whether it is masculine or feminine. In addition, the following two simple rules will help you determine the gender of a noun most of the time.

**¿RECUERDA?**

In **Gramática A.5** you learned that Spanish nouns are classified grammatically as either masculine or feminine. The articles change according to grammatical gender and agree with the nouns they modify.

**un** techo = ***a*** *roof*
**una** oficina = ***an*** *office*
**una** universidad = ***a*** *university*
**el** libro = ***the*** *book*
**la** mesa = ***the*** *table*

*Rule 1:* A noun that refers to a male is masculine; a noun that refers to a female is feminine. Sometimes they are a pair distinguished by the endings **-o/-a**; other times they are completely different words.

| | | |
|---|---|---|
| un muchacho | una muchacha | *boy/girl* |
| un niño | una niña | (*male*) *child* / (*female*) *child* |
| un amigo | una amiga | (*male*) *friend* / (*female*) *friend* |
| un hombre | una mujer | *man/woman* |

For some nouns referring to people, the masculine form ends in a consonant and the feminine form adds **-a** to the masculine noun.*

| | | |
|---|---|---|
| un profesor | una profesora | (*male*) *professor* / (*female*) *professor* |
| un señor | una señora | *a man* (*Mr.*) / *a woman* (*Mrs.*) |

Other nouns do not change at all; only the accompanying article changes.

| | |
|---|---|
| un elefante | (*male*) *elephant* |
| una elefante | (*female*) *elephant* |
| un estudiante | (*male*) *student* |
| una estudiante | (*female*) *student* |
| un joven | *young man* |
| una joven | *young woman* |
| un recepcionista | (*male*) *receptionist* |
| una recepcionista | (*female*) *receptionist* |

Nouns that end in **-o** are usually masculine; nouns that end in **-a** are usually feminine.

*Rule 2:* For most nouns that refer to things (rather than to people or animals), the gender is reflected in the last letter of the word. Nouns that end in **-o** are usually grammatically masculine (**un/el cuaderno**), and nouns that end in **-a** are usually grammatically feminine (**una/la puerta**).†

Words that end in **-d** (**una/la universidad**) or in the letter combination **-ión** (**una/la nación**) are also usually feminine.

| MASCULINE: *-o* | FEMININE: *-a* |
|---|---|
| un/el bolígraf**o** | una/la civilizac**ión** |
| un/el cuadern**o** | una/la mes**a** |
| un/el libr**o** | una/la sill**a** |
| un/el tech**o** | una/la universi**dad** |

*This rule includes a few common animals. Some pairs end in **-o/-a;** others end in consonant / consonant + **-a.**

| | | |
|---|---|---|
| un gato | una gata | (*male*) *cat* / (*female*) *cat* |
| un perro | una perra | (*male*) *dog* / (*female*) *dog* |
| un león | una leona | *lion/lioness* |

†Three common exceptions are **la mano** (*hand*), **el día** (*day*), and **el mapa** (*map*).

Don't worry if you can't remember all these rules! Note where they are in this book so you can refer to them when you are editing your writing and when you are unsure of what gender a noun is.

You will develop a *feel* for gender as you listen and read more in Spanish.

Words that refer to things may also end in **-e** or in consonants other than **-d** and **-ión.** Most of these words that you have heard so far are masculine, but some are feminine.

| | | | |
|---|---|---|---|
| un/el borrador | *eraser* | una/la clase | *class* |
| un/el cartel | *poster* | una/la luz | *light* |
| un/el lápiz | *pencil* | | |
| un/el pupitre | *desk* | | |
| un/el reloj | *clock* | | |

## Ejercicio 3

Conteste según el modelo.

MODELO: —¿Es un bolígrafo? (lápiz) →
—No, no es un bolígrafo. Es *un* lápiz.

1. ¿Es una pizarra? (pared)
2. ¿Es una oficina? (salón de clase)
3. ¿Es una silla? (escritorio)
4. ¿Es un borrador? (cuaderno)
5. ¿Es una ventana? (silla)

## Ejercicio 4

Esteban describe diferentes cosas de su universidad. Complete las oraciones con **el** o **la.**

1. _____ estudiante es rubia.
2. _____ profesor de matemáticas es inteligente.
3. _____ clase es buena.
4. _____ reloj es moderno.
5. _____ papel es amarillo.
6. _____ universidad es buena.
7. _____ motocicleta es negra.
8. _____ automóvil es nuevo.
9. _____ plaza es grande.
10. _____ sombrero es nuevo.

## B.4 Expressing Existence: *hay*

**hay = there is / there are**

**Hay** is used with singular or plural nouns.

The verb form **hay** expresses the idea of existence. When used with singular nouns it means *there is;* with plural nouns it means *there are.*

| | |
|---|---|
| —¿Qué **hay** en el salón de clase? | —*What is there in the classroom?* |
| —**Hay** dos puertas y una ventana. | —*There are two doors and a window.* |

Whereas the verb **ser** (*to be*) identifies nouns (see **Gramática A.3**), **hay** simply states their existence.

| | |
|---|---|
| —¿Qué **es**? | —*What is that?* |
| —**Es** un bolígrafo. | —*It's a pen.* |
| —¿Cuántos **hay**? | —*How many are there?* |
| —**Hay** tres. | —*There are three.* |

## Ejercicio 5

**¿RECUERDA?**

In **Gramática A.4** you learned how to make sentences negative.
—Hay perros en el salón de clase.
—No, no hay perros en el salón de clase.

Imagínese qué cosas o personas hay o no hay en el salón de clase de la profesora Martínez.

MODELOS: lápices → Sí, *hay* lápices en el salón de clase.
perros → No, *no hay* perros en el salón de clase.

1. libros en la mesa
2. un reloj en la pared
3. una profesora
4. un automóvil
5. un profesor
6. papeles en los pupitres
7. un bolígrafo en el pupitre de Alberto
8. muchos cuadernos
9. una bicicleta
10. una ventana

## B.5 Describing People and Things: Plural Forms (Part 2)

**A.** Here are the basic rules for forming plurals in Spanish. Words that end in a vowel (**a, e, i, o, u**) form their plural by adding **-s.**

**¿RECUERDA?**

In **Gramática A.7** you learned that both nouns and words that modify nouns (articles and adjectives) may be plural. Plural words usually end in **-s** or **-es.**

| SINGULAR | PLURAL |
|---|---|
| el braz**o** | los braz**os** |
| el oj**o** | los oj**os** |
| el pi**e** | los pi**es** |
| la pierna | las pierna**s** |

Words that end in a consonant add **-es.**

| SINGULAR | PLURAL |
|---|---|
| el borrador | los borrador**es** |
| la pared | las pared**es** |
| el profesor | los profesor**es** |

To form plurals:
Words ending in vowels add **-s;** words ending in consonants add **-es;** words ending in **-z** change to **-c** and add **-es.** In time, you will acquire a feel for the plural formations.

If the consonant at the end of a word is **-z,** it changes to **-c** and adds **-es.**

| SINGULAR | PLURAL |
|---|---|
| el lápi**z** | los lápi**ces** |
| la lu**z** | las lu**ces** |

**B.** Adjectives that describe plural words must also be plural.

| | | | |
|---|---|---|---|
| ojos azul**es** | *blue eyes* | orejas grand**es** | *big ears* |
| brazos larg**os** | *long arms* | pies peque**ños** | *small feet* |

En mi salón de clase hay dos **ventanas grandes, varias sillas viejas,** cinco **pizarras verdes** y diez **luces.**

*In my classroom there are two large windows, several old chairs, five green chalkboards, and ten lights.*

## Ejercicio 6

Marisa y Clarisa tienen muchas cosas. ¡Pero Marisa siempre tiene una y Clarisa dos!

MODELO: Marisa tiene un suéter azul, pero Clarisa tiene dos... → *suéteres azules.*

1. Marisa tiene un par de zapatos, pero Clarisa tiene dos...
2. Marisa tiene un perro nuevo, pero Clarisa tiene dos...
3. Marisa tiene una chaqueta roja, pero Clarisa tiene dos...
4. Marisa tiene un lápiz amarillo, pero Clarisa tiene dos...
5. Marisa tiene una amiga norteamericana, pero Clarisa tiene dos...

## Ejercicio 7

¡Ahora Clarisa tiene una y Marisa tiene dos!

MODELO: Clarisa tiene un sombrero grande, pero Marisa tiene dos... → *sombreros grandes.*

1. Clarisa tiene un cuaderno pequeño, pero Marisa tiene dos...
2. Clarisa tiene un gato negro, pero Marisa tiene dos...
3. Clarisa tiene una fotografía bonita, pero Marisa tiene dos...
4. Clarisa tiene un reloj bonito, pero Marisa tiene dos...
5. Clarisa tiene un libro difícil, pero Marisa tiene dos...
6. Clarisa tiene un amigo divertido, pero Marisa tiene dos...

## B.6 Describing People and Things: Adjective-Noun Agreement

A singular adjective is used to describe a singular noun. A plural adjective is used to describe a plural noun.

**A.** Adjectives must agree in gender and number with the nouns they describe; that is, if the noun is singular and masculine, the adjective must also be singular and masculine. Adjectives that end in **-o** in the masculine form and **-a** in the feminine form will appear in the vocabulary lists in **Dos mundos** like this: **bonito/a.** Such adjectives have four possible forms.

| | SINGULAR | PLURAL |
|---|---|---|
| ***Masculine*** | viej**o** | viej**os** |
| ***Feminine*** | viej**a** | viej**as** |

Carmen lleva un suéter **bonito** y una falda **nueva.**
Mis zapatos de tenis son **viejos.**

*Carmen is wearing a pretty sweater and a new skirt.*
*My tennis shoes are old.*

**B.** Adjectives that end in a consonant,* the vowel **-e,** or the ending **-ista** have only two forms because the masculine and feminine forms are the same.

| | SINGULAR | PLURAL |
|---|---|---|
| ***Masculine/Feminine*** | joven<br>interesante<br>pesimista<br>azul | jóvenes<br>interesantes<br>pesimistas<br>azules |

Luis lleva una camisa **azul** y un sombrero **azul.**
Mi amigo Nacho es **pesimista,** pero mi amiga Silvia es **optimista.**

*Luis is wearing a blue shirt and a blue hat.*
*My friend Nacho is pessimistic, but my friend Silvia is optimistic.*

## Ejercicio 8

Seleccione todas las descripciones posibles.

MODELO: Alberto → *chico, guapo, estudiante*

1. Nora
2. Alberto
3. Esteban y Carmen
4. la profesora Martínez
5. Luis
6. Mónica y Carmen
7. Pablo

a. mujer
b. chico
c. secretaria
d. chica
e. guapo
f. niñas
g. amigos
h. estudiantes
i. estudiante
j. profesor
k. mexicana
l. altas
m. bajo
n. morena
o. rubio

*Adjectives of nationality that end in a consonant are an exception to this, since they (like adjectives that end in **-o/-a**) have four forms: **inglés, inglesa, ingleses, inglesas.** See **Gramática C.4** for more information.

PASO

# Mi familia y mis amigos

**METAS**

In **Paso C** you will discuss your family, things you own, and people's ages. You will also talk about different languages and nationalities.

Texas, Estados Unidos

**ACTIVIDADES DE COMUNICACIÓN**

La familia
¿Qué tenemos?
Los números (10–100) y la edad
Los idiomas y las nacionalidades
**EN RESUMEN**

**GRAMÁTICA Y EJERCICIOS**

C.1 Expressing Possession: The Verb **tener; de(l)**
C.2 Expressing Possession: Possessive Adjectives
C.3 Expressing Age: The Verb **tener**
C.4 Describing People: Adjectives of Nationality
C.5 Talking about Habitual Actions: Present Tense of Regular **-ar** Verbs

# Actividades de comunicación

## La familia

*Lea Gramática C.1.*

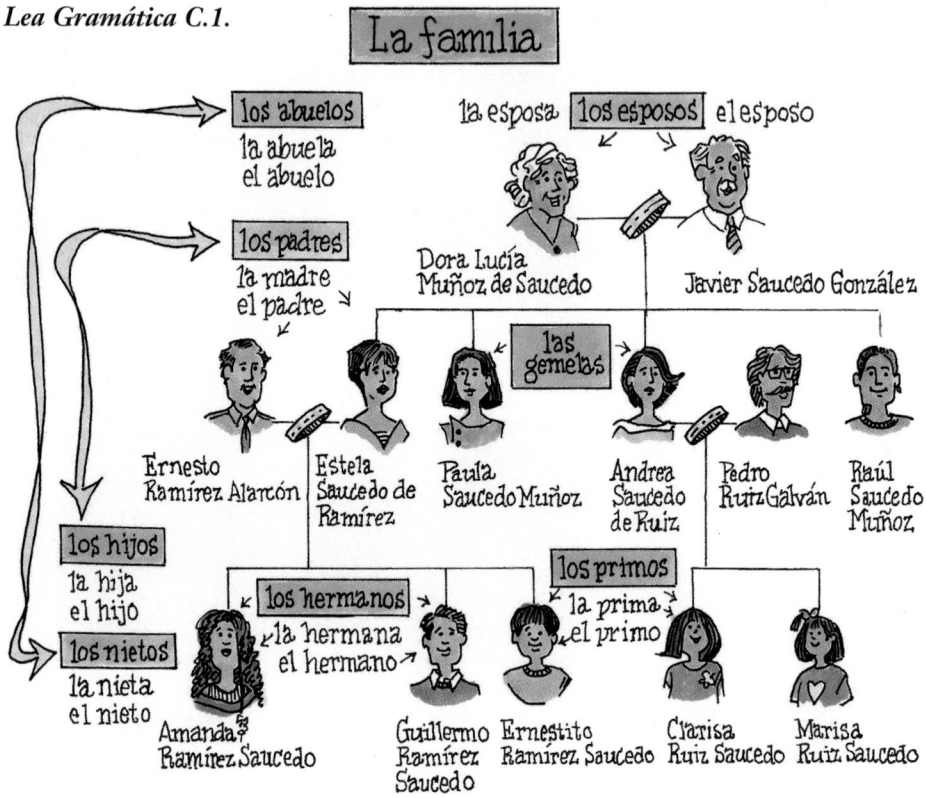


### Actividad 1. Identificaciones: La familia Saucedo (Parte 1)

¿Cierto o falso? Conteste según el dibujo.

1. Dora es la esposa de Javier.
2. Dora y Javier tienen cuatro hijos: tres hijas y un hijo.
3. Estela es soltera.
4. Raúl es casado.
5. Estela, Paula, Andrea y Raúl son hermanos.
6. La esposa de Pedro se llama Paula.
7. Amanda no tiene primos.
8. Dora tiene cinco nietos: tres nietas y dos nietos.
9. Pedro y Raúl son hermanos.
10. Amanda tiene dos hermanas.

## Actividad 2. Intercambios: La familia Saucedo (Parte 2)

Conteste según el dibujo de la página anterior.

MODELOS: E1: ¿Cómo se llama *el hermano de Estela, Paula y Andrea*?
E2: Se llama *Raúl.*

E1: ¿Cuántos *hermanos* tiene *Amanda*?
E2: Tiene *dos.*

## Actividad 3. Diálogo: ¿Quién es?

Don Eduardo Alvar habla con Paula Saucedo.

DON EDUARDO: Perdón, señorita Saucedo. ¿Quién es ese joven?
PAULA SAUCEDO: Su nombre es Jorge Saucedo.
DON EDUARDO: ¿Saucedo? ¿Es su hermano?
PAULA SAUCEDO: No. Su apellido es Saucedo también, pero no es mi hermano. Mi hermano se llama Raúl.

## Actividad 4. Diálogo abierto: Mis hijos

E1: ¿Cómo se llama usted, señor (señora, señorita)?
E2: Me llamo ____.
E1: ¿Es usted casado/a (soltero/a, viudo/a, divorciado/a)?
E2: Soy ____.
E1: ¿Tiene usted hijos?
E2: Sí, tengo ____ hijos y ____ hijas. (No, no tengo hijos.)

## Actividad 5. Entrevista: Mi familia

1. ¿Cómo se llama tu *padre* (madre, hermano/a, abuelo/a)?
   Mi *padre* se llama ____.
2. ¿Cuántos *hermanos* (primos, abuelos, hijos, nietos) tienes?
   Tengo *dos hermanos.* (Tengo *un primo.* Tengo *una nieta.* No tengo *hijos.*)

# ¿Qué tenemos?

***Lea Gramática C.1–C.2.***

Doña Lola tiene un coche nuevo.

Los discos compactos son de Amanda.

Ernestito y su perro Lobo son amigos.

## Actividad 6. Diálogo: El coche de don Eduardo

ERNESTITO: ¿Tiene usted coche, señor Alvar?
DON EDUARDO: Sí, tengo un coche azul, un poco viejo.
ERNESTITO: Yo no tengo coche pero tengo una bicicleta nueva.
DON EDUARDO: Sí, y tu bicicleta es muy bonita.

## Actividad 7. Descripción de dibujos: ¿De quién... ?

1. ¿Quién tiene dos camisas nuevas?
2. ¿Quién tiene dos perros?
3. ¿De quién es el vestido nuevo?
4. ¿Quién tiene una computadora?
5. ¿De quién es el carro nuevo?
6. ¿Quiénes tienen helados?

## Actividad 8. Entrevista: Mi perro y mi carro

1. ¿Tienes perro (gato)?
   Sí, tengo _____. (No, no tengo perro/gato.)
2. ¿Cómo es tu perro (gato)?
   Mi perro (gato) es _____.
3. ¿Tienes carro?
   Sí, tengo _____. (No, no tengo carro. Tengo bicicleta.)
4. ¿Cómo es tu carro (bicicleta)?
   Mi carro (bicicleta) es _____.

# Los números (10–100) y la edad

*Lea Gramática C.3.*

| | |
|---|---|
| 10 diez | 76 setenta y seis |
| 20 veinte | 80 ochenta |
| 30 treinta | 82 ochenta y dos |
| 40 cuarenta | 90 noventa |
| 50 cincuenta | 94 noventa y cuatro |
| 60 sesenta | 100 cien |
| 70 setenta | 110 ciento diez |

## Actividad 9. Diálogos: ¿Cuántos años tienen?

GRACIELA: Amanda, ¿quién es esa niña?
AMANDA: Es mi prima, Clarisa.
GRACIELA: ¿Cuántos años tiene?
AMANDA: Tiene sólo seis años, y es muy inteligente.

DON EDUARDO: Señor Ruiz, ¿cuántos hijos tiene usted?
PEDRO RUIZ: Tengo dos hijas.
DON EDUARDO: ¿Y cuántos años tienen?
PEDRO RUIZ: Bueno, Clarisa tiene seis años y Marisa tiene cuatro.
DON EDUARDO: ¡Sólo dos hijas! ¡Cómo cambia el mundo!

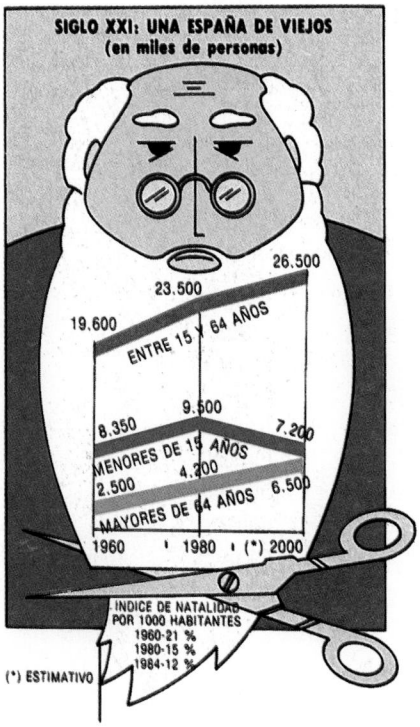


## Actividad 10. Diálogo abierto: ¿Cuántos años tienes?

E1: ¿Cuántos años tienes?
E2: Tengo _____ años.
E1: ¿Tienes hermanos?
E2: Sí, tengo _____ hermanos y _____ hermanas. (No, no tengo hermanos, pero tengo _____.)
E1: ¿Cuántos años tiene tu hermano/a mayor/menor?
E2: Mi hermano/a _____ tiene _____ años.

# Los idiomas y las nacionalidades

*Lea Gramática C.4–C.5.*

Hans Schumann es alemán y habla alemán.

Gina Sfreddo es italiana y habla italiano.

Iara Gomes y Zidia Oliveira son brasileñas y hablan portugués.

Masato Hamasaki y Goro Nishimura son japoneses y hablan japonés.

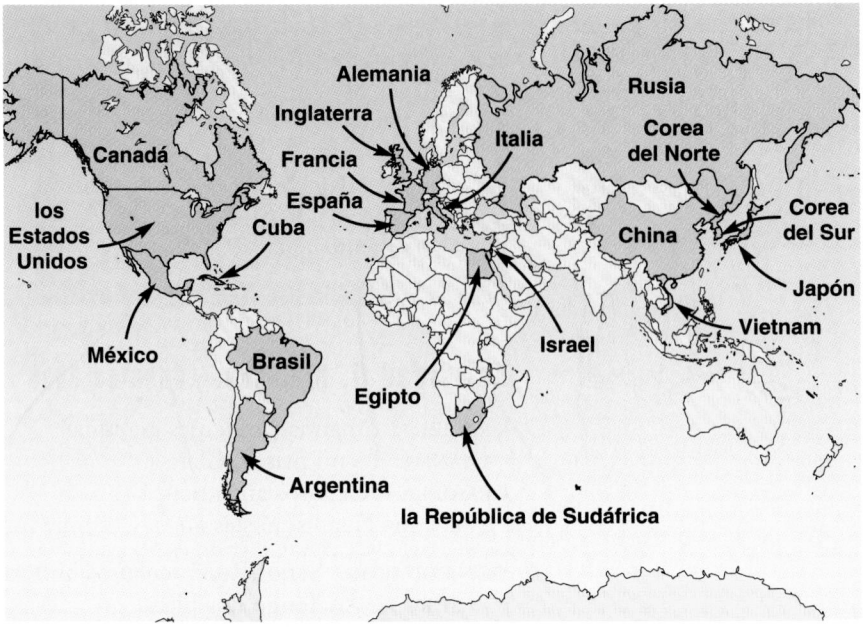


| PAÍS | NACIONALIDAD | IDIOMA(S) |
|---|---|---|
| Alemania | alemán, alemana | alemán |
| Argentina | argentino/a | español |
| Brasil | brasileño/a | portugués |
| Canadá | canadiense | inglés/francés |
| China | chino/a | chino |
| Corea (del Norte / del Sur) | coreano/a | coreano |
| Cuba | cubano/a | español |
| Egipto | egipcio/a | árabe |
| España | español(a) | español |
| los Estados Unidos | (norte)americano/a | inglés |
| Francia | francés, francesa | francés |
| Inglaterra | inglés, inglesa | inglés |
| Israel | israelí | hebreo |
| Italia | italiano/a | italiano |
| Japón | japonés, japonesa | japonés |
| México | mexicano/a | español |

| PAÍS | NACIONALIDAD | IDIOMA(S) |
|---|---|---|
| la República de Sudáfrica | sudafricano/a | afrikaans / lenguas africanas / inglés |
| Rusia | ruso/a | ruso |
| Vietnam | vietnamita | vietnamés |

## Actividad 11. Asociaciones: ¿Qué nacionalidad? ¿Qué idioma?

Diga cuál es la nacionalidad de estas personas y qué idiomas hablan.

MODELO: Gloria Estefan... Cuba →
Gloria Estefan es *cubana* y habla *inglés y español.*

| | PERSONA | PAÍS |
|---|---|---|
| 1. | Nelson Mandela | la República de Sudáfrica |
| 2. | el príncipe Carlos | Inglaterra |
| 3. | Luciano Pavarotti | Italia |
| 4. | Boris Yeltsin | Rusia |
| 5. | Xuxa | Brasil |
| 6. | Hosni Mubarak | Egipto |
| 7. | Gérard Depardieu | Francia |
| 8. | Arantxa Sánchez Vicario | España |
| 9. | Benjamín Netanyahu | Israel |

## Actividad 12. Diálogo abierto: Amigos internacionales

E1: ¿Tienes un amigo *japonés* (una amiga *japonesa*)?
E2: Sí, se llama _____.
E1: ¿Hablas *japonés* o *inglés* con él (ella)?
E2: Hablamos *inglés.* (Normalmente hablamos *inglés,* pero a veces hablamos *japonés.*)

### Actividad 13. Intercambios: En la agencia de viajes

MODELO: CLIENTE: Señorita (Señor, Señora), quiero viajar *a París.*
AGENTE: ¿Habla usted *francés*?
CLIENTE: Sí, hablo *un poco de francés.* (No, no hablo *nada de francés.* / Sí, hablo *francés muy bien.*)

CIUDADES

| | | |
|---|---|---|
| Roma | Madrid | Río de Janeiro |
| Londres | Buenos Aires | Montreal |
| Toronto | Moscú | Berlín |
| Los Ángeles | Pekín | Tokio |

IDIOMAS

| | | |
|---|---|---|
| italiano | ruso | francés |
| inglés | chino | alemán |
| español | portugués | japonés |

**FRASES ÚTILES**

| | | |
|---|---|---|
| un poco de | nada de | muy bien |

# En resumen

## De todo un poco

Entrevista: Su familia y sus amigos

Entreviste a su compañero/a. Tome apuntes y luego comparta la información con la clase.

1. —¿Son norteamericanos tus padres?
   —Sí/No, mis padres son _____.
2. —¿Cuántos años tienen ellos?
   —Mi padre tiene _____ años y mi madre tiene _____ años.
3. —¿Qué idiomas hablan?
   —Mis padres hablan _____. (Mi padre habla _____ y mi madre habla _____.)
4. —¿Cuántos años tienen tus abuelos?
   —Mi abuelo tiene _____ y mi abuela tiene _____. (Mis abuelos están muertos.)
5. —¿Qué idiomas hablan tus abuelos?
   —Hablan _____. (Mi abuelo habla _____ y mi abuela habla _____.)
6. —¿Tienes muchos hermanos?
   —Sí, tengo _____. (No, tengo sólo _____. / No, soy hijo único / hija única.)
7. —¿Cómo se llaman tus hermanos?
   —Mis hermanos se llaman _____ y _____. (Mi hermano/a se llama _____.)

8. —¿Tienes amigos de (*país*)?
   —Sí, tengo amigos (un amigo / una amiga) de ____.
9. —¿Cómo se llaman tus amigos? (¿Cómo se llama tu amigo/a?)
   —Se llaman ____ y ____. (Se llama ____.)
10. —¿Qué idiomas hablan ellos? (¿Qué idiomas habla él/ella?)
    —Hablan ____. (Habla ____.)

**VIDEOTECA**

In this first segment of the *Video to accompany* ***Dos Mundos,*** you will meet two students at **la Universidad Nacional Autónoma de México.** Try to identify where the students are from and how old they are. **Paso C** of the *Cuaderno de trabajo* contains additional activities for you to do after you have seen this video segment.

# Vocabulario

## La familia

| | |
|---|---|
| **el abuelo / la abuela** | grandfather/grandmother |
| **los abuelos** | grandparents |
| **el esposo / la esposa** | husband/wife |
| **el hijo / la hija** | son/daughter |
| **el hijo único / la hija única** | only child (only son / only daughter) |
| **los hijos** | sons (sons and daughters; children) |
| **la madre** | mother |
| **el nieto / la nieta** | grandson/granddaughter |
| **el padre** | father |
| **los padres** | parents |
| **el primo / la prima** | cousin |

## Los países

| | Countries |
|---|---|
| **Alemania** | Germany |
| **Corea del Norte / del Sur** | North/South Korea |
| **(los) Estados Unidos** | United States |
| **Inglaterra** | England |
| **(la) República de Sudáfrica** | South Africa |

**PALABRAS SEMEJANTES: Brasil, Canadá, China, Cuba, Egipto, Francia, Israel, Italia, Japón, México, Rusia, Vietnam**

**REPASO: España**

## Las nacionalidades

| | |
|---|---|
| **alemán/alemana** | German |
| **brasileño/a** | Brazilian |
| **chino/a** | Chinese |
| **coreano/a** | Korean |
| **egipcio/a** | Egyptian |
| **español(a)** | Spanish |
| **francés/francesa** | French |
| **inglés/inglesa** | English |
| **norteamericano/a** | North American |
| **ruso/a** | Russian |
| **sudafricano/a** | South African |
| **vietnamita** | Vietnamese |

**PALABRAS SEMEJANTES: americano/a, árabe, argentino/a, canadiense, cubano/a, israelí, italiano/a, japonés/japonesa, mexicano/a, portugués/portuguesa**

## Los idiomas — Languages

| | |
|---|---|
| **el alemán** | German |
| **el chino** | Chinese |
| **el español** | Spanish |
| **el francés** | French |
| **el hebreo** | Hebrew |
| **el inglés** | English |
| **las lenguas africanas** | African languages |
| **el ruso** | Russian |

**PALABRAS SEMEJANTES: el afrikaans, el árabe, el coreano, el italiano, el japonés, el portugués, el vietnamés**

## Las ciudades — Cities

| | |
|---|---|
| **Londres** | London |
| **Moscú** | Moscow |
| **Pekín** | Beijing |

**PALABRAS SEMEJANTES: Berlín, Buenos Aires, Los Ángeles, Madrid, Montreal, Río de Janeiro, Roma, Tokio, Toronto**

## Los adjetivos

| | |
|---|---|
| **casado/a** | married |
| **divorciado/a** | divorced |
| **mayor** | older |
| **menor** | younger |
| **muerto/a** | dead |
| **soltero/a** | single |
| **viudo/a** | widowed |

## Las personas

| | |
|---|---|
| **el gemelo / la gemela** | twin |
| **la princesa** | princess |
| **el príncipe** | prince |

## Los verbos

| | |
|---|---|
| **quiero** | I want |
| **tener** | to have |
| **viajar** | to travel |

## Expresiones útiles

| | |
|---|---|
| **¡Cómo cambia el mundo!** | How the world changes! |
| **¿Cuántos años tiene(s)?** | How old are you? |
| **Tengo... años.** | I am . . . years old. |
| **¿Cuántos... tiene(s)?** | How many . . . do you have? |
| **¿De quién es/son... ?** | Whose is/are . . . ? |
| **más/menos de** | more/less than |
| **nada de** | nothing; any (at all) |
| **perdón** | pardon me; excuse me |
| **un poco de** | a little |
| **¿Qué tiene(n)... ?** | What do/does . . . have? |
| **¿Quién(es) tiene(n)... ?** | Who has . . . ? |

## Palabras útiles

| | |
|---|---|
| **la agencia de viajes** | travel agency |
| **el apellido** | last name |
| **a veces** | sometimes |
| **la bicicleta** | bicycle |
| **bueno...** | well . . . |
| **el carro / el coche** | car |
| **¿Cuál... ?** | Which . . . ? |
| **la edad** | age |
| **el helado** | ice cream |
| **pero** | but |
| **según** | according to |
| **sólo** | only |

**PALABRAS SEMEJANTES: la computadora, el disco compacto, normalmente**

**REPASO: un poco**

## Palabras y frases del texto

| | |
|---|---|
| **comparta(n)** | share |
| **conteste(n)** | answer |
| **la frase** | phrase, sentence |
| **luego** | then |
| **la página anterior** | preceding page |
| **Tome apuntes.** | Take notes. |

**PALABRAS SEMEJANTES: la información, internacional, la parte**

## Los números

| | |
|---|---|
| **setenta** | seventy |
| **ochenta** | eighty |
| **ochenta y dos** | eighty-two |
| **noventa** | ninety |
| **noventa y cuatro** | ninety-four |
| **cien** | one hundred |
| **ciento diez** | one hundred ten |

# Gramática y ejercicios

## C.1 Expressing Possession: The Verb *tener; de(l)*

Just like English, Spanish has several ways of expressing possession. Unlike English, however, Spanish does not use an apostrophe and *s*.

**tener** = *to have*

**A.** Perhaps the simplest way of expressing possession is to use the verb **tener*** (*to have*). Like the verb **ser, tener** is classified as an irregular verb because of changes in its stem.† The endings that attach to the stem, however, are regular.

**¿RECUERDA?**

In **Gramática A.6** you learned some of the forms of **tener.**

La profesora Martínez **tiene** el pelo negro. Yo **tengo** los ojos azules.

You have also heard and used these forms many times in class.

**tener** (***to have***)

| | | |
|---|---|---|
| (yo) | tengo | *I have* |
| (tú) | tienes | *you (inf. sing.) have* |
| (usted, él/ella) | tiene | *you (pol. sing.) have; he/she has* |
| (nosotros/as) | tenemos | *we have* |
| (vosotros/as) | tenéis | *you (inf. pl., Spain) have* |
| (ustedes, ellos/as) | tienen | *you (pl.) have; they have* |

—Profesora Martínez, ¿**tiene** usted un automóvil nuevo?
—Sí, **tengo** un Toyota verde.

—*Professor Martínez, do you have a new automobile?*
—*Yes, I have a green Toyota.*

English: *'s*
Mike**'s** new car
Sarah**'s** friends
Spanish: **de** + person
el carro nuevo **de Miguel**
los amigos **de Sara**

**B.** The verb **ser** (*to be*) followed by the preposition **de** (*of*) can also be used to express possession. The equivalent of the English word *whose* is **¿de quién?** (literally, *of whom?* or *to whom?*).

—¿**De quién es** el cuaderno?
—**Es de** Carmen.

—*To whom does the notebook belong?*
—*It's Carmen's.*

**de** + **el** = **del**
**de** + **la** remains **de la**

**C.** The preposition **de** (*of*) followed by the masculine article **el** (*the*) contracts to **del** (*of the*).

—¿**De quién es** el bolígrafo?
—**Es del** profesor.

—*Whose pen is this?*
—*It's the professor's.*

The other combinations of **de** + article do not contract: **de la, de los, de las.**

Los zapatos **de la** niña son nuevos.

*The girl's shoes are new.*

---

*Recognition: **vos tenés**
†See **Gramática C.5** for more information on verb stems.

## Ejercicio 1

Diga qué tienen estas personas. Use las formas del verbo **tener**.

MODELO: Luis *tiene* una bicicleta negra.

1. Pablo _____ una chaqueta negra.
2. Esteban y yo _____ un coche viejo.
3. Mónica, tú no _____ el libro de español, ¿verdad?
4. (Yo) _____ dos lápices y un cuaderno sobre mi pupitre.
5. Nora y Alberto no _____ hijos, ¿verdad?

## Ejercicio 2

Diga de quién son estas cosas.

MODELO: Mónica / bolígrafo → El bolígrafo *es de* Mónica.

1. la profesora Martínez / carro

2. Luis / camisa

3. Nora / perro

4. Esteban / lentes

5. Alberto / saco

6. Carmen / bicicleta

## C.2 Expressing Possession: Possessive Adjectives

Possession can be indicated by the following possessive adjectives. The particular adjective you choose depends on the owner, but the adjective itself, like other Spanish adjectives, agrees in number and gender with the word it describes: that is, with the *object owned*, not with the owner.

| SINGULAR OWNER | | PLURAL OWNER | |
|---|---|---|---|
| mi | *my* | nuestro/a | *our* |
| tu* | *your (inf. sing.)* | vuestro/a | *your (inf. pl., Spain)* |
| su | *your (pol. sing.), his/her* | su | *your (pl.); their* |

¿**Mi** hermano? Tiene el pelo negro. — *My brother? He has black hair.*

**Nuestro** carro nuevo es rojo. — *Our new car is red.*

**Nuestra** profesora es Adela Martínez. — *Our professor is Adela Martínez.*

| SINGULAR POSSESSION (PLURAL POSSESSIONS) | | SINGULAR POSSESSION (PLURAL POSSESSIONS) | |
|---|---|---|---|
| mi(s) | *my* | nuestro(s)/a(s) | *our* |
| tu(s) | *your (inf. sing.)* | vuestro(s)/a(s) | *your (inf. pl., Spain)* |
| su(s) | *your (pol. sing.), his/her* | su(s) | *your (pl.); their* |

**Mi** falda es vieja pero **mis** zapatos son nuevos. — *My skirt is old but my shoes are new.*

Clarisa y Marisa tienen una casa grande. **Su** casa es grande. — *Clarisa and Marisa have a big house. Their house is big.*

Raúl, ¿**tus** hermanas son gemelas? — *Raúl, are your sisters twins?*

Clarisa y Marisa tienen dos tías y un tío. **Su** tío se llama Raúl. — *Clarisa and Marisa have two aunts and one uncle. Their uncle's name is Raúl.*

**su** = *his, her, your, their* (one item)
**sus** = *his, her, your, their* (multiple items)

Keep in mind that the pronoun **su(s)** can have various meanings: *your, his, her,* or *their.* The context normally clarifies to whom **su(s)** refers.

Luis no tiene **sus** libros. — *Luis doesn't have his books.*

El señor y la señora Ruiz tienen **su** coche aquí. — *Mr. and Mrs. Ruiz have their car here.*

Generally speaking, use **usted** and **su(s)** when addressing a person by his or her last name.

Señor Ramírez, ¿es **usted** mexicano? ¿Y **sus** padres? — *Mr. Ramírez, are you Mexican? And your parents?*

---

***Tú** (with an accent mark) corresponds to *you;* **tu** (without an accent mark) corresponds to *your.*

Remember that you will acquire much of this material in time as you listen to and read Spanish.

When using a first name to address someone, use **tú** and **tu(s)**.

| | |
|---|---|
| Raúl, **tu** amiga es inglesa pero **tú** y **tus** padres son mexicanos, ¿no? | *Raúl, your friend is English but you and your parents are Mexican, aren't you?* |

## Ejercicio 3

Complete estas oraciones con la forma apropiada del adjetivo posesivo: **mi(s), tu(s), su(s)** o **nuestro(s)/a(s).**

MODELO: Estela, ¿dónde están *tus* hijos?

1. Mi novia no tiene _____ libro de matemáticas.
2. El profesor no tiene _____ botas.
3. No tienes _____ reloj, ¿verdad?
4. No tengo _____ zapatos de tenis.
5. No tenemos _____ cuadernos.
6. —Señores Ruiz, ¿dónde están _____ hijas?
   —_____ hijas, Clarisa y Marisa, están en casa.
7. Guillermo no tiene _____ chaqueta.
8. Estela y Ernesto no tienen _____ automóvil todavía.
9. Graciela, _____ ojos son muy bonitos.
10. No tengo _____ bicicleta aquí.

## Ejercicio 4

Complete los diálogos con la forma apropiada del adjetivo posesivo.

MODELO: RAÚL: ¡Qué inteligente es *tu* amiga!
ALBERTO: Sí, y ella es idealista, también.

1. RAÚL: Silvia, _____ perro, Sultán, es muy inteligente.
   SILVIA: Gracias, Raúl, pero no es _____ perro. Es de Nacho.
2. CLARA: Pilar, ¿tienen un carro _____ padres?
   PILAR: Sí, _____ padres tienen un Seat rojo.
3. JOSÉ: ¿Cómo se llama la novia de Andrés?
   PILAR: _____ novia se llama Ana.
4. ABUELA: Marisa y Clarisa, ¡qué bonitas son _____ faldas! ¿Son nuevas?
   MARISA: Sí, abuelita. Y _____ zapatos son nuevos también.

English: **I am** 24 (years old).
Spanish: **Tengo** 24 (años).

## C.3 Expressing Age: The Verb *tener*

In English, the verb *to be* is used for telling age (*I am 21 years old*), but in Spanish the verb **tener** expresses age. To ask about age, use the question **¿Cuántos años...** ? (*How many years . . . ?*)

| | |
|---|---|
| —Señora Ramírez, **¿cuántos años tiene** usted? | *—Mrs. Ramírez, how old are you?* |
| —**Tengo** treinta y cinco (años). | *—I'm 35 (years old).* |

**¿RECUERDA?**

In **Gramática C.1** you learned the present-tense forms of the verb **tener.** Review them now, if necessary.

## Ejercicio 5

Escriba la edad de estos amigos.

MODELO: Rogelio Varela / 21 → Rogelio Varela *tiene 21 años.*

1. Adriana Bolini / 35
2. Carla Espinosa / 22
3. Rubén Hernández Arenas / 38
4. Susana Yamasaki González / 33
5. doña María Eulalia González de Saucedo / 79
6. yo / _____ años

## Ejercicio 6

Escriba la edad de estas personas.

**¿RECUERDA?**

In **Gramática B.6** you learned that adjectives that end in **-o/-a** have four forms.

roj**o** *masc. sing.*
roj**a** *fem. sing.*
roj**os** *masc. pl.*
roj**as** *fem. pl.*

## C.4 Describing People: Adjectives of Nationality

**A.** Adjectives of nationality that end in **-o/-a,** just like other adjectives that end in **-o/-a,** have four forms.

| | SINGULAR | PLURAL |
|---|---|---|
| ***Masculine*** | chin**o** | chin**os** |
| ***Feminine*** | chin**a** | chin**as** |

Victoria no es **china,** pero habla chino muy bien.

*Victoria is not Chinese, but she speaks Chinese very well.*

**B.** Adjectives of nationality that end in a consonant have four forms also.

| | SINGULAR | PLURAL |
|---|---|---|
| ***Masculine*** | inglé**s*** | ingles**es** |
| ***Feminine*** | ingles**a** | ingles**as** |

John es **inglés,** pero su madre es **española.**

*John is English, but his mother is Spanish.*

*See the *Cuaderno de trabajo*—**Capítulo 2** and Appendix 3—for details on written accent marks.

Do capitalize names of countries in Spanish.
**Colombia**
**Panamá**
**Inglaterra**
Do not capitalize nationalities and languages in Spanish.
**colombiano**
**panameñas**
**español**
**inglés**

**C.** Adjectives of nationality that end in **-e** have only two forms.

| | SINGULAR | PLURAL |
|---|---|---|
| ***Masculine/Feminine*** | canadiens**e** | canadiens**es** |

**D.** Adjectives of nationality and the names of languages are not capitalized in Spanish. Names of countries, however, are capitalized.

## Ejercicio 7

¿De qué nacionalidad son estas personas?

MODELO: el señor Shaoyi He → *Es chino.*

1. _____ la señorita Fernández
2. _____ los señores Watanabe
3. _____ el señor Hartenstein
4. _____ las hermanas Lemieux
5. _____ la señorita Cardinale y la señorita Lomeli
6. _____ la señorita Tang
7. _____ el señor Thatcher

a. alemán/alemana
b. chino/china
c. español/española
d. francés/francesa
e. inglés/inglesa
f. italiano/italiana
g. japonés/japonesa

**¿RECUERDA?**

In Spanish the forms of a verb change to show who is performing the action. You have already seen the forms of **ser** (**Gramática A.3**), **llevar** (**Gramática A.6**), and **tener** (**Gramática C.1**). Now look at the drawings at the bottom of this page and notice the forms of the verb **hablar** (*to speak*).

## C.5 Talking about Habitual Actions: Present Tense of Regular *-ar* Verbs

*infinitive* = verb form ending in **-ar, -er,** or **-ir**

You will not find the conjugated forms of a verb—**hablo, hablas, habla,** and so forth—as main entries in a dictionary. You must know the infinitive in order to look up the verb.

**A.** The verb form listed in the dictionary and in most vocabulary lists is the *infinitive*. In Spanish many infinitives end in **-ar** (**llamar, llevar**), but some end in **-er** (**tener**) or in **-ir** (**vivir**). The forms of the verb are called its *conjugation*. Here is the present-tense conjugation of the regular **-ar** verb **hablar.*** Regular verbs are classified as such because their *stem* (the infinitive minus the ending) remains the same in all forms; the only change is in the endings, which are added to the stem.

*Recognition: **vos hablás**

| hablar (*to speak*) | | |
|---|---|---|
| (yo) | habl**o** | *I speak* |
| (tú) | habl**as** | *you (inf. sing.) speak* |
| (usted, él/ella) | habl**a** | *you (pol. sing.) speak; he/she speaks* |
| (nosotros/as) | habl**amos** | *we speak* |
| (vosotros/as) | habl**áis** | *you (inf. pl., Spain) speak* |
| (ustedes, ellos/as) | habl**an** | *you (pl.) speak; they speak* |

**B.** Remember that Spanish verb endings indicate, in many cases, who or what the subject is, so it is not always necessary to mention the subject explicitly. That is why the pronouns are in parentheses in the preceding table.

| | |
|---|---|
| —¿**Hablas** español? | *—Do you speak Spanish?* |
| —Sí, y **hablo** inglés también. | *—Yes, and I speak English too.* |

These endings take time to acquire. You can understand and communicate with an incomplete knowledge of them, but they are important; make sure you include them when you write.

## Ejercicio 8

Estamos en una fiesta en casa de Esteban. Complete estas oraciones con la forma correcta del verbo **hablar**.

1. Esteban, las dos chicas rubias _____ alemán, ¿verdad?
2. Mónica, ¿_____ francés tu padre?
3. Alberto y Luis no _____ francés.
4. Nora, ¿_____ tú chino?
5. No, yo no _____ chino, pero _____ un poco de japonés.

## Ejercicio 9

¿Qué idiomas hablan estas personas? Complete cada oración con la forma correcta del verbo **hablar** y el idioma apropiado.

1. Susana Yamasaki González es peruana y _____ español y _____.
2. Los señores Ramírez son mexicanos y _____ _____.
3. Li Yuan Tseng y Mei Chang son chinos y _____ _____
4. Kevin Browne y Stephen Craig son ingleses. _____ _____.
5. Talia Meir y Behira Sefamí son israelíes. _____ _____.
6. ¿Eres rusa? Entonces, tú _____ _____.

CAPÍTULO 1

# Los datos personales y las actividades

**METAS**

In **Capítulo 1** you will learn to tell time and give personal information: your address, your phone number, and your birthday. You and your classmates will talk about sports and other leisure-time activities you enjoy.

Torreón, México

**ACTIVIDADES DE COMUNICACIÓN Y LECTURAS**


Las fechas y los cumpleaños

**Lectura** El horóscopo

Datos personales: El teléfono y la dirección

**El mundo hispano...** su gente

**El mundo hispano...** en los Estados Unidos

La hora

Las actividades y los deportes

**El mundo hispano...** imágenes

**Nota cultural** Los deportes

**EN RESUMEN**


**GRAMÁTICA Y EJERCICIOS**


1.1 Counting: Numbers 100–1000 and Dates

1.2 Spelling: The Spanish Alphabet

1.3 Talking about Habitual Actions: Present Tense of Regular **-er** and **-ir** Verbs

1.4 Asking Questions: Question Formation

1.5 Telling Time: Hours and Minutes

1.6 Expressing Likes and Dislikes: **gustar** + Infinitive

# Actividades de comunicación y lecturas

## Las fechas y los cumpleaños

*Lea Gramática 1.1.*

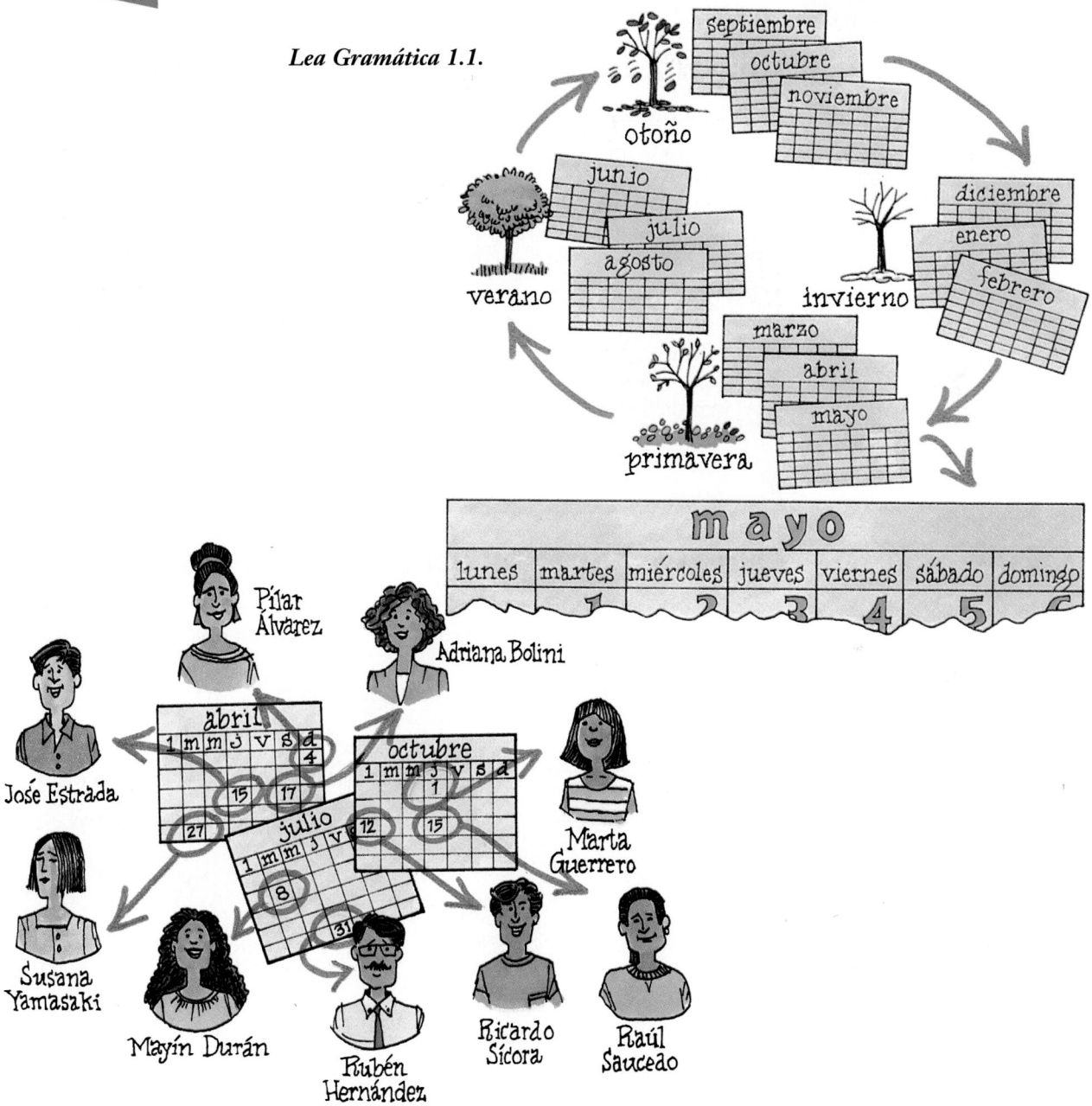

## Actividad 1. Intercambios: El cumpleaños

Hágale preguntas a su compañero/a sobre los dibujos de la página anterior.

MODELOS: E1: ¿Cuándo nació *José Estrada*?
E2: Nació el *15 de abril.*

E1: ¿Quién nació el *15 de octubre*?
E2: *Raúl Saucedo.*

## Actividad 2. Intercambios: Los amigos de Esteban Brown

MODELO: E1: ¿Quién nació el *30 de mayo de 1977*?
E2: *Rogelio Varela.*
E1: ¿Dónde nació?
E2: Nació en *San Juan, Puerto Rico.*

| NOMBRE | LUGAR DE NACIMIENTO | FECHA DE NACIMIENTO |
|---|---|---|
| Raúl Saucedo | Guanajuato, México | 15 de octubre de 1979 |
| Rogelio Varela | San Juan, Puerto Rico | 30 de mayo de 1977 |
| Pilar Álvarez | Madrid, España | 4 de abril de 1976 |
| Ricardo Sícora | Caracas, Venezuela | 12 de octubre de 1979 |
| Carmen Bradley | Corpus Christi, Texas | 23 de junio de 1979 |
| Nora Morales | San Antonio, Texas | 4 de julio de 1973 |

## Actividad 3. Intercambios: ¿Qué quieres para tu cumpleaños?

MODELO: E1: ¿Quieres *un reloj* para tu cumpleaños?
E2: Sí, quiero *un reloj.* (No, no quiero *un reloj,* quiero *una mochila.*)

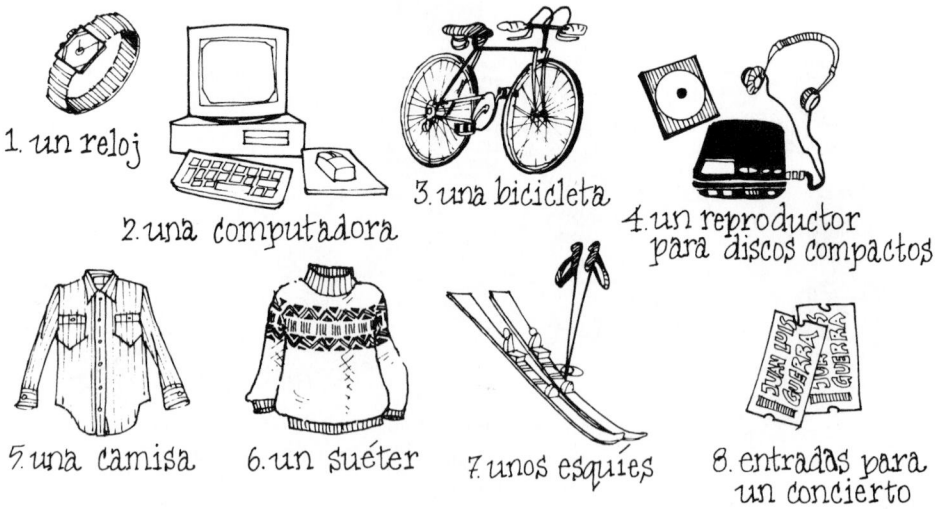

9. un coche

10. una mochila

11. una cámara

12. un televisor

13. discos compactos

14. un equipo de música

# El horóscopo

**VOCABULARIO ÚTIL**

| | |
|---|---|
| todos | *everyone* |
| Lea | *Read* |
| ¡descubra! | *discover!* |
| el sentido | *sense* |

Aquí está el horóscopo, con información para todos. Lea la descripción de su signo y ¡descubra su personalidad!

**CAPRICORNIO** (del 22 de diciembre al 20 de enero): Usted es una persona muy organizada; tiene buen sentido del humor y una personalidad muy atractiva. Su color es el verde claro.

**ACUARIO** (del 21 de enero al 18 de febrero): Usted es una persona elegante y creativa; es un poco idealista y muy independiente. Colores: rosado y blanco.

**PISCIS** (del 19 de febrero al 20 de marzo): Usted es muy independiente y entusiasta. No es una persona idealista, pero sí muy trabajadora. Color: amarillo.

**ARIES** (del 21 de marzo al 19 de abril): Usted tiene una personalidad muy expresiva; es una persona activa, enérgica ¡y un poquito impulsiva! Su color es el rojo brillante.

**TAURO** (del 20 de abril al 20 de mayo): Usted es un poco temperamental. ¡Pero tiene buen sentido del humor! Es una persona muy generosa con sus amigos. Colores: café y negro.

**GÉMINIS** (del 21 de mayo al 20 de junio): Usted es versátil y muy sociable. No es muy sentimental. La familia y los amigos son muy importantes para usted. Su color favorito es el azul.

**CÁNCER** (del 21 de junio al 22 de julio): Usted es una persona romántica y un poco sentimental. Pero también es muy activa y trabajadora. Colores: crema y blanco.

**LEO** (del 23 de julio al 22 de agosto): Usted tiene una personalidad agresiva; es persistente en todas sus actividades. Tiene pocos, pero buenos, amigos. Color: anaranjado.

**VIRGO** (del 23 de agosto al 22 de septiembre): Usted es de carácter serio y práctico. ¡Tiene mucha energía! Es una persona muy selectiva en sus relaciones. Colores: café oscuro y verde.

**LIBRA** (del 23 de septiembre al 22 de octubre): Usted es una persona artística y un poco tímida. Es muy jovial y tiene muchos buenos amigos. Su color favorito: azul.

**ESCORPIÓN** (del 23 de octubre al 22 de noviembre): Usted tiene una personalidad reservada. Es una persona intuitiva, organizada y persistente. Colores: rojo y negro.

**SAGITARIO** (del 23 de noviembre al 21 de diciembre): ¡Usted es muy optimista! Es una persona sociable y sincera. También es idealista y un poco impulsiva. Colores: azul oscuro y violeta o morado.

## Comprensión

Todas las siguientes oraciones son falsas. Cambie las palabras incorrectas para decir la verdad, según la lectura.

MODELO: Capricornio es del *21 de junio al 22 de julio.* →
Capricornio es del *22 de diciembre al 20 de enero.*

1. Libra es del *23 de julio al 22 de agosto.*
2. Las personas del signo Sagitario son *muy pesimistas.*
3. Un hombre del signo Virgo normalmente es *impulsivo.*
4. El signo de una mujer que nació el 25 de marzo es *Piscis.*
5. Si una muchacha es del signo Leo, entonces es *muy tímida.*
6. Los colores del signo Acuario son *el café oscuro y el negro.*
7. Una joven del signo Cáncer es *muy práctica.*
8. Generalmente, las personas del signo Géminis son *aburridas.*
9. Las personas del signo Libra tienen *pocos amigos.*
10. Un joven del signo Escorpión probablemente es *agresivo.*

## Ahora... ¡usted!

1. ¿Le gusta leer el horóscopo? ¿Por qué?
2. ¿Cree usted que el horóscopo dice la verdad?
3. ¿Tiene amigos del mismo signo que usted? ¿Qué aspectos de la personalidad tienen ustedes en común?

### Un paso más... ¡a escribir!

Lea su signo y díganos, ¿es usted así? ¿Qué características de su personalidad *no* se mencionan? Escriba una breve descripción de su signo con más características.

MODELO: Mi signo es _____. ¡Soy muy _____! Soy una persona _____ y _____. También soy _____ y un poco _____. Mi color favorito es el _____.

# Datos personales: El teléfono y la dirección

***Lea Gramática 1.2–1.4.***

**UNIVERSIDAD NACIONAL AUTÓNOMA DE MÉXICO**

Nombre: Ignacio Padilla León
Dirección: Calle Juárez 528, México D.F.
Teléfono: 5-66-57-42
Fecha de Nacimiento: 26-II-77
Sexo: M Edo. Civil: soltero
Ojos: negros Pelo: castaño
Ciudadanía: mexicana
Nº. de Estudiante: 156-87-40-94

**UNIVERSIDAD COMPLUTENSE DE MADRID**

Nombre: Pilar Álvarez Cárdenas
Dirección: Calle Almendras 481, Madrid
Teléfono: 4-71-94-55
Fecha de Nacimiento: 4-IV-76
Sexo: F Edo. Civil: soltera
Ojos: castaños Pelo: castaño
Ciudadanía: española
Nº. de Estudiante: 115-38-95-42

## Actividad 4. Del mundo hispano: El pasaporte

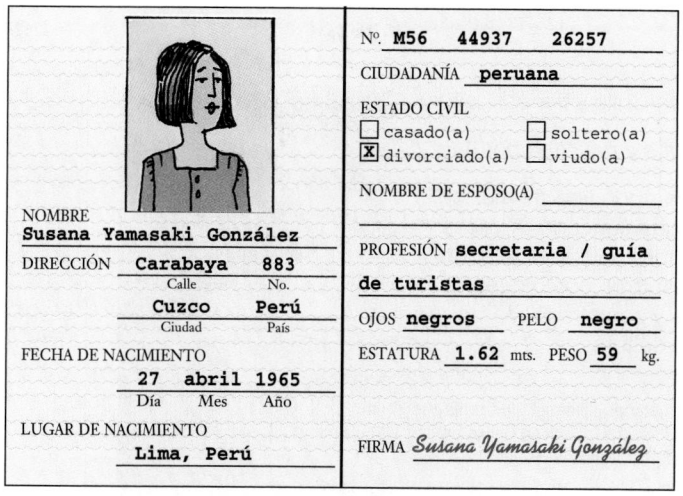

NOMBRE
Susana Yamasaki González

DIRECCIÓN Carabaya 883
Calle No.
Cuzco Perú
Ciudad País

FECHA DE NACIMIENTO
27 abril 1965
Día Mes Año

LUGAR DE NACIMIENTO
Lima, Perú

Nº. M56 44937 26257

CIUDADANÍA peruana

ESTADO CIVIL
☐ casado(a) ☐ soltero(a)
☒ divorciado(a) ☐ viudo(a)

NOMBRE DE ESPOSO(A) _____

PROFESIÓN secretaria / guía de turistas

OJOS negros PELO negro

ESTATURA 1.62 mts. PESO 59 kg.

FIRMA *Susana Yamasaki González*

1. ¿Cómo se llama la señora?
2. ¿Dónde vive?
3. ¿En qué mes nació?
4. ¿Cuál es su estado civil?
5. ¿De qué color tiene los ojos?

## Actividad 5. Intercambios: ¿Cómo se escribe?

Usted habla por teléfono con el operador / la operadora.

MODELO: OPERADOR(A): Su nombre y apellido, por favor.
USTED: *Ted Klamath.*
OPERADOR(A): Perdón, no entendí bien. ¿Cómo se escribe su apellido?
USTED: *Ca-ele-a-eme-a-te-hache.*

OPERADOR(A): Su nombre y apellido, por favor.
USTED: _____.
OPERADOR(A): Perdón, no entendí bien. ¿Cómo se escribe su apellido?
USTED: _____.

## Actividad 6. Diálogo abierto: ¿Dónde vives?

E1: ¿Cómo te llamas?
E2: _____. ¿Y tú?
E1: _____. ¿Dónde vives?
E2: En la calle _____, número _____. ¿Y tú?
E1: Vivo en la calle _____, número _____.
E2: ¿Cuál es tu número de teléfono?
E1: Es el _____. ¿Tienes teléfono tú?
E2: Sí, es el _____.

## EL MUNDO HISPANO... su gente

**A**na Lilia Gaitán es de Chile y tiene 31 años.

*¿Cuáles son sus gustos y pasatiempos?*

Me encanta[1] escuchar todo tipo de música, especialmente la latinoamericana. A veces[2] me gusta leer algún libro de Isabel Allende[3] o artículos de revistas[4] que, por lo general, son muy interesantes y son otra forma de aprender sobre otras culturas.

[1]Me... *I really like* [2]A... *Sometimes* [3]Isabel... *Famous Chilean novelist, author of the novel* La casa de los espíritus (*House of the Spirits*), *published in 1982. The film version was made in 1993.* [4]*magazines*

## EL MUNDO HISPANO... en los Estados Unidos

**E**lizabeth Álvarez nació en los Estados Unidos, de padres mexicanos. Elizabeth tiene 34 años y vive en Perrysburg, Ohio.

*Describa a un buen amigo o a una buena amiga.*

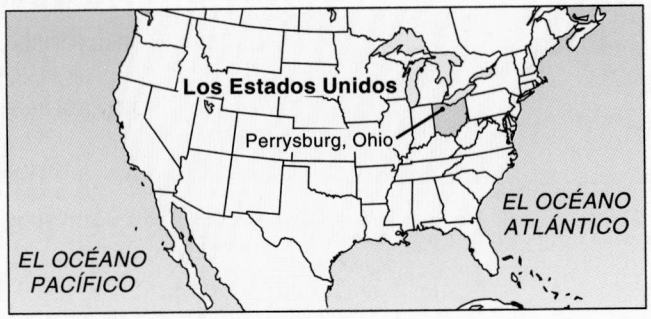


Una buena amiga es una persona que está disponible[1] para escucharte cuando más lo necesitas. Es esa persona que te brinda una amistad[2] sincera y que te acepta tal como eres.[3] Mi buena amiga se llama Juanita García. Vive en Calexico, California. Juanita celebra su cumpleaños el cinco de septiembre. Nos gusta celebrar juntas su cumpleaños cuando se puede,[4] porque yo vivo en otro estado. Lo que más nos gusta hacer cuando estamos juntas es conversar. Hablamos mucho de eventos especiales de nuestra niñez.[5]

[1]*available* [2]te... *offers you a friendship* [3]tal... *just as you are* [4]cuando... *when it's possible* [5]*childhood*

# La hora

*Lea Gramática 1.5.*

## ¿Qué hora es?

Es la una.

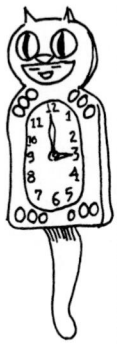

Son las tres.

Son las nueve menos diez.

Es la una y media.

Son las diez menos veinte.

Es mediodía.

Son las once y cuarto.

Es medianoche.

Son las tres menos veinticinco.
(Son las dos y treinta y cinco.)

Son las siete y cinco.

## Actividad 7. Diálogo: ¿Qué hora es?

SRA. SILVA: Perdón, don Anselmo, ¿qué hora tiene?
DON ANSELMO: *Son las siete y cuarto.*
SRA. SILVA: Muchas gracias.

PAULA SAUCEDO: Oye, Ernesto, ¿qué hora tienes?
ERNESTO RAMÍREZ: *Es casi medianoche.*
PAULA SAUCEDO: *¡Ya es tarde!*

## Actividad 8. Intercambios: ¿Qué hora es?

Escuche a su profesor(a). Diga el número del reloj que corresponde a la hora que él/ella dice. Luego, hágale preguntas a su compañero/a según el modelo.

MODELO: E1: ¿Qué hora es?
E2: Es la _____. / Son las _____.

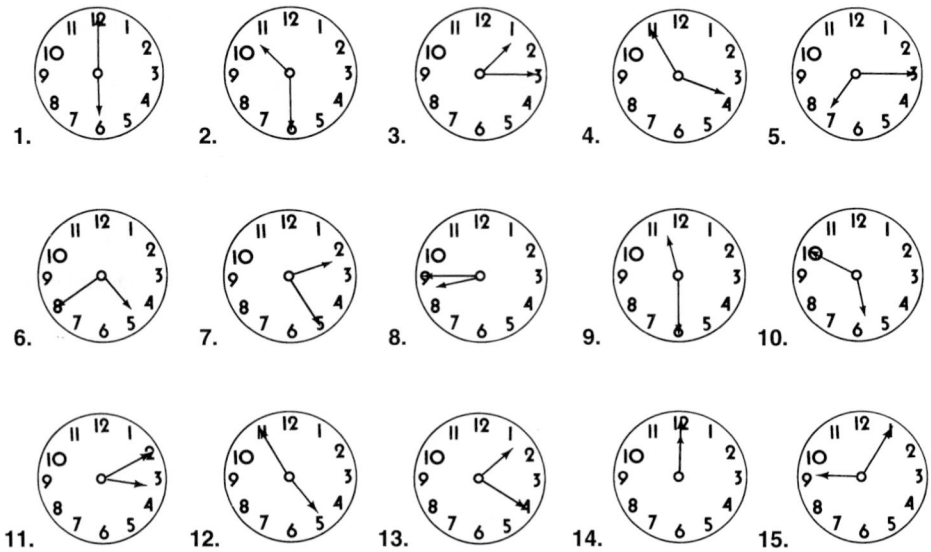

## Actividad 9. Del mundo hispano: Programas de televisión

Hágale preguntas sobre el siguiente horario a un compañero / una compañera.

1. ¿A qué hora es el programa «Treinta minutos»?
2. ¿A qué hora es el «Informativo de la mañana»?
3. ¿En qué canal se presenta el «Festival de cine»?
4. ¿En qué canal se presenta el programa «Hola Raffaella»?
5. ¿Qué canal presenta más programas de deportes?

# Sábado 22 Mayo

| | tve1 | 2 | TELEMADRID |
|---|---|---|---|
| **MAÑANA** | **07. 00 Carta de ajuste.** (Sonido de Radio1, de RNE).<br>**07. 30 Pinnic.** Espacio diario dedicado al público infantil que incluye las siguientes series:<br>– "Los fruittis".<br>–"Mucho cuento".<br>–"Las mil y una Américas".<br>–"Alfred J. Kwak".<br>–"El mundo de Maxie".<br>– "La isla del príncipe".<br>**11. 00 Hola Raffaella.** (Redifusión del programa del pasado jueves, día 20 de mayo).<br>**14. 00 El rescate del talismán.** | **05. 45 Carta de ajuste.**<br>**05. 59 Apertura y presentacón.**<br>**06. 00 El informativo de la mañana.**<br>**09. 25 Testimonio.**<br>**09. 30 Grandes intérpretes.** Orquesta Filarmónica de Arthur Rubinstein.<br>**10. 00 Últimas preguntas.**<br>**10. 30 Jara y sedal.** (Repetición).<br>**11. 00 El mejor deporte.** Espacio deportivo que icluye los siguientes escuentros:<br>– Pelota.<br>– Fútbol sala.<br>– Balonmano. | **08. 30 Baloncesto. NBA.** (Partido sin confirmar al cierre de esta edición).<br>**10. 15 La Liga. Fútbol alemán.** Programa que repasa los encuentros más importantes del fútbol alemán.<br>**12. 00 La liga. Fútbol.** Transmisión del encuentro de fútbol de Segunda División B: Leganés – Atlético de Madrid. Comentarios: Fernando Burgos y Santiago Acedo.<br>**14. 00 Treinta minutos.** Presenta: Jesús López Jordán. |
| **TARDE** | **14. 30 El sábado cocino yo.** Presenta: Karlos Arguiñano.<br>**15. 00 Telediario -1.**<br>**15. 30 Pato aventuras.** (Dibujos animados).<br>**16. 00 Sesión de tarde.** *«Los inconquistables»*. Dir: Cecil B. Demille. Con Gary Cooper, Paulette Goddard, Boris Karloff.<br>**18. 40 Segunda sesión.** *«Blue Bayou»*. Dir: Karen Arthur. Con Alfred Woodard, Mario Van Peebles, Elizabeth Ashley. | – Gimnasia rítmica. (Campeonato de Europa).<br>– Automovilismo. (Entrenamientos del Gran Premio de Mónaco).<br>– Motociclismo. (24 horas de Montjuich).<br>– Baloncesto. (All Star Games. Encuentro: Italia – España).<br>**18. 10 Sala 2.** *«Un reportero bajo sospecha»*. Dir: Miguel Courtois. Con Gerarad Darmon, Anais Jeanneret.<br>**20. 00 El informe del día.** | **14. 30 Telenoticias.**<br>**15. 00 Parker Lewis nunca pierde.**<br>**15. 30 Cine. Una de risa.** *«El divorcio que viene»*. Dir: Pedro Masó. Con José Luis López Vázquez, José Sacristán.<br>**17. 35 Cine. Una de aventuras.** *«La batalla del río Neretva»*. Dir: Velijko Bulajic.<br>**19. 15 La Liga. Fútbol.** – Fútbol previo. Presentador: Javier Reyero. |
| **NOCHE** | **20. 30 Juguemos al Trivial.**<br>**21. 00 Telediario -2.**<br>**21. 30 Informe semanal.**<br>**22. 25 Viéndonos.** Dirección del programa: Martes y Trece. Realización: Pepa Martí Maqueda.<br>**00. 00 Cine de medianoche.** *«El recuperador»*. Dir: Alex Cox. Con Emilio Estevez, Harry Dean Stanton.<br>**01. 40 Deporte noche.**<br>**04. 00 Despedida y cierre.** | **20. 30 La tabla redonda.**<br>**21. 30 Área reservada.** Programa musical presentado por Antonio Fernández<br>**22.20 Festival de cine.** «El ruido y la furia» Dir.: Martin Ritt<br>**00.20 Decálogo 4.** Dir.: Uwe Janson<br>**01.15 Cine Club. gentes de Europa.** *«Los caminos de la supervivencia»* Dir: Krzysztof Kieslowski<br>**03.00 Despedida y cierre.** | – (20.30) Liga española de fútbol: Valencia – Athletic de Bilbao.<br>**22. 15 La gran noche del espectáculo.** Incluye:<br>– Avance informativo.<br>– Entre amigos.<br>**02. 15 Cine. Sala de madrugada.** *«Ángeles sin paraíso»*. Dir: John Cassavetes.<br>**04. 05 Información cultural de la Comunidad de Madrid.** |

# Las actividades y los deportes

***Lea Gramática 1.6.***

## Un fin de semana típico de los Ramírez

A Guillermo y a sus amigos les gusta jugar al fútbol.

A Amanda y a Graciela les gusta jugar al tenis.

A Ernestito le gusta andar en bicicleta.

A Estela le gusta ir de compras.

A Ernesto le gusta leer.

A Amanda le gusta ver su telenovela favorita.

A Ernesto y a Guillermo les gusta ver un partido de béisbol en el estadio.

A los Ramírez les gusta cenar en restaurantes italianos.

### Actividad 10. Intercambios: El fin de semana

MODELOS: E1: ¿A quién le gusta *jugar al basquetbol*?
E2: A *Ricardo Sícora.*

E1: ¿Qué le gusta hacer a *Ricardo los sábados*?
E2: Le gusta *ir al cine.*

| NOMBRE | LOS SÁBADOS LE GUSTA | LOS DOMINGOS LE GUSTA... |
|---|---|---|
| Ricardo Sícora, 18 años<br>Caracas, Venezuela | ir al cine | jugar al basquetbol |
| Adriana Bolini, 35 años<br>Buenos Aires, Argentina | cocinar | jugar al tenis |
| Raúl Saucedo, 19 años<br>México, D.F., México | salir a bailar | ver un partido de fútbol |
| Nacho Padilla, 21 años<br>México, D.F., México | ver la televisión | jugar al voleibol |
| Carla Espinosa, 22 años<br>San Juan, Puerto Rico | ir de compras | ir a la playa |

## Actividad 11. Preferencias: Los gustos

Diga sí o no.

1. Durante las vacaciones me gusta...
   a. viajar.
   b. bailar por la noche.
   c. andar en bicicleta.
   d. dormir todo el día.
2. No me gusta...
   a. nadar en una piscina.
   b. acampar.
   c. jugar en la nieve.
   d. patinar en el hielo.
3. Por la noche, a mis padres les gusta...
   a. ver la televisión.
   b. cenar en restaurantes elegantes.
   c. ir a fiestas.
   d. leer el periódico.
4. A mi profesor(a) de español le gusta...
   a. ir a fiestas.
   b. hacer ejercicio.
   c. cocinar.
   d. llevar ropa elegante.

### Y TÚ, ¿QUÉ DICES?

¡Qué interesante!
¡Qué divertido!
¡Qué aburrido!
¡No lo creo!
A mí sí me gusta.
A mí también me gusta.
A mí no me gusta.
A mí tampoco me gusta.

E1: (A mí) No me gusta acampar.
E2: A mí sí me gusta. (A mí tampoco me gusta.)

## Actividad 12. Entrevista: ¿Qué te gusta hacer?

MODELO: E1: ¿Te gusta *viajar*?
E2: Sí, *me gusta mucho* viajar. (No, *no me gusta* viajar.)

1. ver la televisión
2. cenar en restaurantes
3. pescar
4. bailar en discotecas
5. escribir cartas
6. viajar en carro
7. escuchar música
8. cocinar
9. sacar fotos
10. trabajar

## Actividad 13. Intercambios: Los juegos panamericanos

MODELOS: E1: ¿Qué días hay competición de *baloncesto* (*basquetbol*)?
E2: Del *11 al 21 de marzo, y del 23 al 26.*

E1: ¿Cuándo hay competición de *nado sincronizado* el *13 de marzo*?
E2: Por *la tarde.*

### XII JUEGOS DEPORTIVOS PANAMERICANOS MARZO 1995

PROGRAMA DIARIO DE ACTIVIDADES

| EVENTO | V | S | D | L | M | M | J | V | S | D | L | M | M | J | V | S | D |
|---|---|---|---|---|---|---|---|---|---|---|---|---|---|---|---|---|---|
| | 10 | 11 | 12 | 13 | 14 | 15 | 16 | 17 | 18 | 19 | 20 | 21 | 22 | 23 | 24 | 25 | 26 |
| ACTO DE INAUGURACIÓN | ● | | | | | | | | | | | | | | | | |
| ATLETISMO | | ◐ | ◐ | ◐ | | ◐ | ◐ | | ◐ | ◐ | | | | | | | |
| BALONCESTO | | ◒ | ◒ | ◒ | ◒ | ◒ | ◒ | ◒ | ◒ | ◒ | ◒ | ◒ | | ◒ | ◒ | ◐ | ◐ |
| BALONMANO | | | ◒ | ◒ | ◒ | ◒ | ◒ | | ◒ | ◒ | | | | | | | |
| BÉISBOL | | | ◒ | ◒ | ◒ | ◒ | ◒ | | ◒ | ◒ | ◒ | ◒ | | | ◒ | ◒ | |
| BOXEO | | | | | | ● | ● | ● | ◐ | ● | ● | ● | ● | ● | | ◐ | ◐ |
| CANOA/KAYAK | | ◐ | ◐ | | | | | | | | | | | | | | |
| CICLISMO | | | ◐ | | | ◒ | ◒ | ◒ | ◒ | ◒ | | ◐ | | | | | |
| ECUESTRE | | | | | ◐ | ◐ | ◐ | ◐ | ◐ | | ◐ | | | | | | |
| FÚTBOL | | | ◒ | ◒ | ◒ | ◒ | ◒ | ◒ | | ◒ | | ◒ | | ◒ | | ◒ | |
| GIMNASIA ARTÍSTICA | | ◒ | ◒ | ◒ | ◒ | | ● | ● | ◐ | ◐ | | | | | | | |
| GIMNASIA RÍTMICA | | | | | | | | | | | | | | ● | ● | ◐ | ◐ |
| JUDO | | | | | | | ◐ | ◐ | ◐ | ◐ | | | | | | | |
| LEVANTAMIENTO DE PESAS | | | | ◐ | ◐ | ◐ | ◐ | ● | | | | | | | | | |

| EVENTO | V | S | D | L | M | M | J | V | S | D | L | M | M | J | V | S | D |
|---|---|---|---|---|---|---|---|---|---|---|---|---|---|---|---|---|---|
| | 10 | 11 | 12 | 13 | 14 | 15 | 16 | 17 | 18 | 19 | 20 | 21 | 22 | 23 | 24 | 25 | 26 |
| LUCHA | | | | | ◒ | ◒ | ● | | ◒ | ◒ | ● | | | | | | |
| ACUÁTICOS: CLAVADOS | | ◐ | ◐ | | ◐ | ◐ | | | ◐ | ◐ | | | | | | | |
| ACUÁTICOS: NATACIÓN | | | | | | | | | | | ◐ | ◐ | ◐ | | ◐ | ◐ | ◐ |
| ACUÁTICOS: NADO SINCRONIZADO | | | ◐ | ◐ | ◐ | ◐ | ◐ | ◐ | ◐ | | | | | | | | |
| ACUÁTICOS: POLO ACUÁTICO | | | | | ◐ | ◐ | ◐ | | ◐ | ◐ | ◐ | ◐ | | | | | |
| PATINAJE | | | | | | | | | | | ◒ | ◒ | ◒ | ◒ | ◒ | | |
| TAEKWONDO | | | | | | | | | | | | | ◐ | ◐ | ◐ | ◐ | |
| TENIS | | | | | ◐ | ◐ | ◐ | ◐ | ◐ | ◐ | | ◐ | ◐ | ◐ | ◐ | | |
| TENIS DE MESA | | | | ◒ | ◒ | ◒ | ◒ | ◐ | ◒ | ◒ | ◒ | | | | | | |
| TIRO | | | | | ◐ | ◐ | ◐ | ◐ | ◐ | ◐ | ◐ | | | | | | |
| TIRO CON ARCO | | | | | | ◐ | ◐ | ◐ | ◐ | ◐ | | | | | | | |
| VOLEIBOL | | | | | | | | ◒ | ◒ | ◒ | ◒ | ◒ | ◒ | ◒ | | ◐ | ◐ |
| PELOTA VASCA | | | | ◒ | ◒ | ◒ | ◒ | ◒ | | | | | | | | | |
| CEREMONIA DE CLAUSURA | | | | | | | | | | | | | | | | | ● |

LEYENDA: ● MAÑANA ◐ TARDE ◒ NOCHE

## EL MUNDO HISPANO... imágenes

**U**n deporte muy popular en España es el jai alai, un juego de origen vasco.[1] Las personas que juegan al jai alai necesitan ser ágiles y rápidas. Los dos jugadores de la foto se entrenan para un partido.

[1]*Basque*

NOTA CULTURAL

# Los deportes

Los hispanos practican muchos deportes, pero hay dos que son muy populares. Antes de leer esta Nota cultural, mire las palabras **en negrilla** y descubra rápidamente el nombre de varios deportes importantes.

**VOCABULARIO ÚTIL**

| | |
|---|---|
| Antes de leer | *Before reading* |
| mire | *look at* |
| la natación | *swimming* |
| el ciclismo | *cycle racing* |
| ha ganado | *has won* |
| la carrera Tour-de-France | *Tour-de-France race, a bicycle touring race that covers approximately 2,500 miles (4,000 kilometers) in France and neighboring countries such as Spain.* |
| la Serie Mundial | *World Series (baseball)* |
| De hecho | *In fact* |

A los hispanos les gusta practicar deportes individuales, **el esquí** y **la natación,** por ejemplo. Muchas personas esquían en la Sierra Nevada, que está en España, y también esquían en Chile y Argentina. **El ciclismo** es muy popular en Colombia, México y España. Un ciclista español, Miguel Indurain, ha ganado varias veces la carrera Tour-de-France.

Todas las ciudades hispanas grandes tienen gimnasios donde es posible **nadar, levantar pesas, hacer gimnasia** o **ejercicios aeróbicos** y **jugar al ráquetbol** y **al tenis.** Y hablando del tenis, dos de las mejores tenistas son hispanas: una es una joven argentina que se llama Gabriela Sabatini, y la otra es una española que se llama Arantxa Sánchez Vicario.

Los dos deportes de más popularidad en el mundo hispano son sin duda **el fútbol** y **el béisbol.** (Cuando uno dice «fútbol» en español, habla del *soccer;* lo que en inglés se llama *football,* en español se llama **fútbol norteamericano**). El fútbol es el deporte favorito de los argentinos, los uruguayos y los chilenos, entre otros.

El béisbol, deporte de origen norteamericano, es el que más se juega en los países del Caribe: Puerto Rico, Cuba, Venezuela y la República Dominicana. Muchos caribeños miran la Serie Mundial en la televisión o la escuchan en la radio. ¡El programa tiene un público enorme en esa región!

Uno de los beisbolistas profesionales más jóvenes en los Estados Unidos, Manny Ramírez, nació en la República Dominicana. Pero también en México y otros países de América Latina hay gran entusiasmo por este deporte. De hecho, el famoso jugador profesional de béisbol Fernando Valenzuela es mexicano.

En realidad, la pasión por los deportes es un aspecto esencial del carácter hispano.

## Comprensión

¿Cierto o falso?

1. El fútbol se practica mucho en Chile y Argentina.
2. Es posible esquiar en los gimnasios.
3. Hay muchos jugadores de béisbol en el Caribe.
4. Normalmente, los hispanos no practican deportes individuales.
5. Hay un ciclista español muy famoso.

## Ahora... ¡usted!

1. ¿Le gustan los deportes? ¿Cuáles practica?
2. ¿Hay deportistas famosos que juegan su deporte favorito? ¿Quiénes son? ¿Es usted admirador(a) de esas personas?
3. ¿Cuáles de los deportes mencionados en la Nota cultural le gusta practicar a usted? Indique si le gusta practicarlos mucho, a veces o nunca.

| | MUCHO | A VECES | NUNCA |
|---|---|---|---|
| el béisbol | ☐ | ☐ | ☐ |
| el ciclismo | ☐ | ☐ | ☐ |
| el esquí | ☐ | ☐ | ☐ |
| el fútbol | ☐ | ☐ | ☐ |
| el fútbol norteamericano | ☐ | ☐ | ☐ |
| la natación | ☐ | ☐ | ☐ |
| el ráquetbol | ☐ | ☐ | ☐ |
| el tenis | ☐ | ☐ | ☐ |

### Un paso más... ¡a escribir!

Imagínese que usted es un deportista famoso / una deportista famosa. ¿Cuál es su deporte? ¿Tiene muchos admiradores? ¡Descríbase! Puede incluir una descripción física y también de su personalidad.

Me llamo _____ y juego al _____. Soy muy famoso/a; tengo (*número*) admiradores. Practico este deporte (*frecuencia*). Soy (*descripción física*). ¿Mi personalidad? Pues... soy _____ y _____.

# En resumen

## De todo un poco

**A.** La correspondencia

Estos muchachos y muchachas de México quieren entablar correspondencia con otros muchachos y muchachas. Hágale preguntas a su compañero/a acerca de la información que hay sobre ellos.

MODELOS:
E1: ¿Cuántos años tiene _____?
E2: Tiene _____.

E1: ¿Cuál es la dirección de _____?
E2: Su dirección es _____.

E1: ¿Cuál es el deporte favorito de _____?
E2: Su deporte favorito es el/la _____.

E1: ¿Qué le gusta hacer a _____?
E2: Le gusta _____.

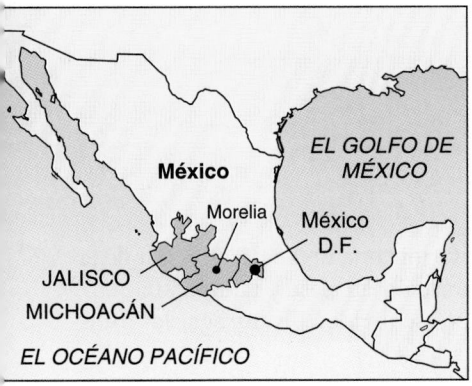


## Y TÚ ¿QUIÉN ERES?

**✏ MIGUEL ÁNGEL OJEDA CEGUEDA (19 años)**
Calz. I. Zaragoza 1111, Col. Agrícola Oriental, México, D.F., C.P. 08500.
Pasatiempos: natación, baloncesto, fútbol americano y ciclismo.

**✏ JOSÉ GUADALUPE AYALA RAMÍREZ (18 años)**
Julio V. Plata 74, Col. Héroe de Nacozari, México, D.F., C.P. 07780.
Pasatiempos: jugar al fútbol y tener amigos por correspondencia.

**✏ LUIS MANUEL GALVÁN O. (20 años)**
Alzate 100, Ozumba, Edo. de México, C.P. 56800.
Pasatiempos: ir a las discos, jugar al basquetbol y leer *Eres*.

**✏ LETICIA VILLANUEVA R. (24 años)**
Ardilla 341, Col. Benito Juárez, Cd. Neza, Edo. de México, D.P. 57000.
Pasatiempos: escuchar música, bailar, pasear y tener amigos.

**✏ MARÍA GUADALUPE E IRMA PRECIADO MENDOZA (16 y 23 años)**
Calle Carretera a Tesistán 1051, Col. Arcos de Zapopan, Zapopan, Jal., C.P. 45130.
Pasatiempos: escuchar música, ver la televisión y leer.

**✏ MARÍA CRUZ RODRÍGUEZ P. (22 años)**
Motolinía 237, Centro, Morelia, Mich., C.P. 58000.
Pasatiempos: ir a la playa, escuchar música y tener muchos amigos.

**Abreviaturas:**

| | | |
|---|---|---|
| Calz.–calzada | C.P.–código postal | Gpe.–Guadalupe |
| Cd.–ciudad | D.F.–Distrito Federal | Jal.–Jalisco |
| Col.–Colonia | Edo.–Estado | Mich.–Michoacán |

**B.** La curiosidad

Trabaje con otros dos o tres estudiantes para escribir por lo menos dos preguntas interesantes para hacerles a estas personas famosas.

1. al presidente de los Estados Unidos
2. a un actor de cine muy guapo
3. a una actriz famosa y bonita
4. a una mujer muy bonita en una fiesta
5. a un hombre muy joven en su clase
6. a su profesor(a) de español

## ¡Dígalo por escrito!

Descripción de personas

De su revista favorita, seleccione una foto que tenga una o más personas y tráigala a clase. Trabajando con un compañero / una compañera, describan cada foto en detalle. ¡Usen su imaginación! Por ejemplo, pueden incluir información sobre los siguientes aspectos de la(s) persona(s) de la foto.

- ¿Cómo se llama?
- ¿De dónde es?
- ¿Dónde vive ahora? ¿Con quién(es) vive?
- ¿Cuántos años tiene?
- ¿Cuál es su fecha de nacimiento? ¿su signo?
- ¿Cómo es?
- ¿Qué ropa lleva?
- ¿Qué hace?
- ¿ ?

Después de la clase, cada uno de ustedes debe escribir una breve descripción de la foto de su compañero/a, basándose en su conversación en clase y también incluyendo todos los otros detalles que puedan. ¡No se olviden de entregar las fotos con las descripciones!

## VIDEOTECA

En este segmento de video, usted va a conocer a dos primos de Ecuador, Paloma y José Miguel. También va a conocer a Gustavo, un amigo de Paloma. Mientras mira el video, escuche bien para distinguir las frases y palabras que ya conoce. Por ejemplo, ¿qué deporte le gusta a Gustavo? ¿Cuál es la fecha del cumpleaños del padre de Paloma? También, trate de apuntar el número de teléfono de Paloma. En el Capítulo 1 del *Cuaderno de trabajo* hay más actividades para hacer después de ver el video.

# Vocabulario

## Los meses del año — Months of the Year

| | |
|---|---|
| **enero** | January |

**PALABRAS SEMEJANTES: febrero, marzo, abril, mayo, junio, julio, agosto, septiembre, octubre, noviembre, diciembre**

## Las estaciones — Seasons

| | |
|---|---|
| **la primavera** | spring |
| **el verano** | summer |
| **el otoño** | fall, autumn |
| **el invierno** | winter |

## Los días de la semana
Days of the Week

| | |
|---|---|
| **(el) lunes** | Monday |
| **(el) martes** | Tuesday |
| **(el) miércoles** | Wednesday |
| **(el) jueves** | Thursday |
| **(el) viernes** | Friday |
| **(el) sábado** | Saturday |
| **(el) domingo** | Sunday |

## ¿Cuándo? — When?

| | |
|---|---|
| **anteayer** | day before yesterday |
| **ayer** | yesterday |
| **durante** | during |
| **hoy** | today |
| **mañana** | tomorrow |
| **la mañana** | morning |
| **pasado mañana** | day after tomorrow |
| **por la mañana/tarde/ noche** | in the morning / afternoon (evening) / at night |

## Los datos personales
Personal Data

| | |
|---|---|
| **la calle** | street |
| **la ciudadanía** | citizenship |
| **el cumpleaños** | birthday |
| **la dirección** | address |
| **¿Dónde vive usted (vives tú)?** | Where do you live? |
| **el estado civil** | marital status |
| **la fecha (de nacimiento)** | date (of birth) |
| **el lugar (de nacimiento)** | place (of birth) |
| **el peso** | weight |

**PALABRAS SEMEJANTES: el pasaporte, el sexo**

**REPASO: el apellido, casado/a, divorciado/a, soltero/a, viudo/a**

## La hora — Time; Hour

| | |
|---|---|
| **¿A qué hora (es)... ?** | At what time (is) . . . ? |
| **(Es) A la(s)...** | (It is) At . . . |
| **la medianoche** | midnight |
| **el mediodía** | noon |
| **¿Qué hora es?** | What time is it? |
| **Es la una y media.** | It is one-thirty. |
| **Son las nueve menos diez (minutos).** | It is ten (minutes) to nine. |
| **Oye, ¿qué hora tienes?** | Hey, what time do you have? |
| **Perdón, ¿qué hora tiene?** | Excuse me, what time do you have? |
| **y cuarto / menos cuarto** | quarter after / quarter till |
| **y media** | half past |

## Los deportes y los juegos
Sports and Games

| | |
|---|---|
| **el basquetbol (baloncesto)** | basketball |
| **el equipo** | team |
| **el esquí** | ski; skiing |
| **el estadio** | stadium |
| **el fútbol** | soccer |
| **el fútbol americano** | football |
| **jugar** | to play |
| **nadar** | to swim |
| **el partido** | game (in sports), match |
| **patinar (en el hielo)** | to skate (on ice) |
| **pescar** | to fish |

**PALABRAS SEMEJANTES: el bate, el béisbol, la competición, el tenis, el voleibol**

## Las actividades

| | |
|---|---|
| **acampar** | to camp (go camping) |
| **andar en bicicleta** | to ride a bicycle |
| **bailar** | to dance |
| **cenar** | to dine, have dinner |

| | |
|---|---|
| **cocinar** | to cook |
| **dormir (todo el día)** | to sleep (all day) |
| **escuchar (música)** | to listen (to music) |
| **escribir (cartas)** | to write (letters) |
| **hacer** | to do; to make |
| **hacer ejercicio** | to exercise |
| **ir** | to go |
| **a fiestas** | to parties |
| **de compras** | shopping |
| **jugar (en la nieve)** | to play (in the snow) |
| **leer (el periódico)** | to read (the newspaper) |
| **sacar fotos** | to take photos |
| **salir (a bailar)** | to go out (dancing) |
| **trabajar** | to work |
| **ver** | to see; to watch |
| **la televisión** | television |
| **una telenovela** | a soap opera |
| **un partido de...** | a . . . game |

**REPASO: hablar por teléfono**

## Los lugares Places

| | |
|---|---|
| **el cine** | movie theater |
| **la piscina** | swimming pool |
| **la playa** | beach |

**PALABRAS SEMEJANTES: la discoteca, el restaurante**

## Los verbos

| | |
|---|---|
| **decir** | to say |
| **dice** | he/she says; you (*pol. sing.*) say |
| **querer** | to want |
| **quieren** | they want |
| **vivir** | to live |
| **vivo** | I live |
| **vives** | you (*inf. sing.*) live |
| **vive** | he/she lives; you (*pol. sing.*) live |

## Palabras y expresiones del texto

| | |
|---|---|
| **¡Dígalo por escrito!** | Say it in writing! |
| **los gustos** | likes (preferences) |
| **Hágale preguntas a...** | Ask . . . questions. |
| **la lectura** | reading (*n.*) |
| **se presenta** | is shown |
| **sobre** | about |
| **trabaje(n)** | work (*command*) |

**PALABRAS SEMEJANTES: corresponde, la nota cultural, la preferencia**

## Palabras útiles

| | |
|---|---|
| **a** | to |
| **casi** | almost |
| **¿Cuándo... ?** | When . . . ? |
| **¿Dónde... ?** | Where . . . ? |
| **del (de + el)** | of the (*required contraction*) |
| **las entradas (para un concierto)** | tickets (for a concert) |
| **el equipo de música** | stereo |
| **este/esta** | this |
| **feliz** | happy |
| **el fin de semana** | weekend |
| **la firma** | signature |
| **el horario** | schedule |
| **para** | for |
| **querido/a** | dear |
| **el reproductor para discos compactos** | CD player |
| **el televisor** | television set |
| **todo/a** | all, every |

**PALABRAS SEMEJANTES: el actor / la actriz, la cámara, el canal, la correspondencia, la curiosidad, elegante, famoso/a, favorito/a, hispano/a, la información, la música, nacional, el operador / la operadora, panamericano/a, el presidente / la presidenta, la profesión, el programa, el teléfono, las vacaciones**

## Expresiones útiles

| | |
|---|---|
| **¿A quién le gusta... ?** | Who likes to . . . ? |
| **¿Cómo te llamas (tú)?** | What is your name? |
| **¿Cómo se escribe... ?** | How do you spell . . . ? |
| **¿Cuándo (¿Dónde) nació?** | When (Where) were you (was he/she) born? |
| **¡Felicidades!** | Congratulations! |
| **¡Feliz cumpleaños!** | Happy birthday! |
| **No entendí bien.** | I didn't understand well. |
| **No lo creo.** | I don't believe it. |
| **Por favor.** | Please. |
| **¡Qué aburrido!** | How boring! |
| **¡Qué divertido!** | How fun! |
| **¡Qué interesante!** | How interesting! |
| **¿Qué le/te/les gusta hacer?** | What do you (*pol. sing. / inf. / pl.*) like to do? |
| **Le gusta...** | He/She likes (You [*pol. sing.*] like) (to) . . . |
| **Les gusta...** | They/You (*pl.*) like (to) . . . |
| **Te gusta...** | You (*inf.*) like (to) . . . |
| **(No) Me gusta...** | I (don't) like (to) . . . |
| **A mí también/tampoco.** | I do too. / I don't either. |
| **Ya es tarde.** | It's late already. |
| **Y tú, ¿qué dices?** | And you? What do you say? |

# Gramática y ejercicios

## 1.1 Counting: Numbers 100–1000 and Dates

**100 = cien**
**101 = ciento uno**
**161 = ciento sesenta y uno**
**doscientos (200) hombres**
**doscientas (200) mujeres**
**quinientos (500) edificios**
**quinientas (500) sillas**

**A.** Here are the hundreds, from 100 to 1000. Note particularly the pronunciation and spelling of 500, 700, and 900. The word for *one hundred* is **cien,** but when combined with other numbers it is usually **ciento(s).** From 200 to 900, there is also a feminine form.

154 ciento cincuenta y cuatro
200 doscientos/as
300 trescientos/as
400 cuatrocientos/as
500 quinientos/as
600 seiscientos/as
700 setecientos/as
800 ochocientos/as
900 novecientos/as
1000 mil

—¿Cuántos estudiantes de España hay en el grupo? ¿Hay **cien**?
—*How many students from Spain are in the group? Are there a hundred?*

—No, hay **ciento cincuenta y cuatro.**
—*No, there are one hundred and fifty-four.*

—¿Cuántas sillas hay?
—Hay **doscientas diez.**
—*How many chairs are there?*
—*There are two hundred and ten.*

**B.** To state a year in Spanish, use **mil** (1000) followed by hundreds in the masculine form (if necessary).

1832 mil ochocientos treinta y dos
1993 mil novecientos noventa y tres
2000 dos mil

### Ejercicio 1

Diga las siguientes fechas.

1. 1876
2. 1588
3. 1775
4. 1991
5. 2000
6. 1945
7. 1011
8. 1929
9. 1615
10. 2025

## 1.2 Spelling: The Spanish Alphabet

| LETTER | NAME | EXAMPLE | LETTER | NAME | EXAMPLE |
|---|---|---|---|---|---|
| a | a | Ana | ñ | eñe | Íñigo |
| b | be, be grande | Bárbara | o | o | Olga |
| c | ce | Celia | p | pe | Pedro |
| d | de | David | q | cu | Quintín |
| e | e | Ernesto | r | ere | Mario |
| f | efe | Franco | rr | erre, doble ere | Roberto |
| g | ge hay | Gerardo | s | ese | Sara |
| h | hache | Hortensia | t | te | Tomás |
| i | i | Isabel | u | u | Úrsula |
| j | jota | Juan | v | uve, ve chica | Vicente |
| k | ca | Kati | w | doble ve, ve doble | Walter |
| l | ele | Laura | x | equis | Ximena |
| m | eme | Miguel | y | i griega | Yolanda |
| n | ene | Nora | z | zeta | Zulema |

Learn how to spell your first and last names in Spanish; that is what you will be expected to spell most frequently.

**A.** Letters are feminine: **la «ele», la «i», la «equis».** The letter combination **ll** (often referred to as **doble ele**) is pronounced like a *y*. The letter combinations **ch, ll,** and **rr** cannot be divided when splitting a word into syllables.*

**B.** **B** and **v** are pronounced identically, so speakers use different devices to differentiate them; the most common is to call one **la be grande** and the other **la ve chica** (or **la b larga** and **la v corta**). Many people say **la be de burro, la ve de vaca** (**b** as in **burro, v** as in **vaca**). The letters **k** and **w** are used mostly in words of foreign origin: **kilo, whisky.**

**C.** Spanish speakers do not normally spell out entire words, but rather tend to refer only to the letters that might cause confusion. For example, if the name is **Rodríguez,** one might ask: **¿Se escribe con *zeta* o con *ese*?** (*Is it written with a* **z** *or with an* **s**?) Common spelling questions asked by most Latin Americans are the following.

| | | | |
|---|---|---|---|
| s, z | ¿Con **ese** o con **zeta**? | y, ll | ¿Con **i griega** o con **doble ele**? |
| c, s | ¿Con **ce** o con **ese**? | g, j | ¿Con **ge** o con **jota**? |
| c, z | ¿Con **ce** o con **zeta**? | v, b | ¿Con **ve chica** o con **be grande**? |

Because the letter **h** is never pronounced in Spanish, a common question is: **¿Con o sin *hache*?** (*With or without* ***h***?)

*Until recently, the letter combinations **ch** and **ll** were considered single units, had separate names (**che** and **elle**), and affected alphabetization (for example, **chico** after **cumpleaños, llamar** after **luna**). You will still see this pattern of alphabetization in many dictionaries and textbooks.

Only with foreign words (or perhaps very unfamiliar Spanish words) do Spanish speakers spell out the entire word.

—¿Cómo se escribe *Dorwick*, por favor?
—Se escribe: **de, o, ere, doble ve, i, ce, ca.**
—Gracias.

## Ejercicio 2

Escoja la respuesta correcta.

MODELO: ¿Cómo se escribe _____apato?
(a.) con zeta
b. con ese

1. ¿Cómo se escribe _____ien?
   **a.** con ce
   **b.** con zeta
2. ¿Cómo se escribe _____aponés?
   **a.** con ge
   **b.** con jota
3. ¿Cómo se escribe nue_____o?
   **a.** con ve chica
   **b.** con be grande
4. ¿Cómo se escribe _____iudad?
   **a.** con ce
   **b.** con ese
5. ¿Cómo se escribe _____amar?
   **a.** con doble ele
   **b.** con i griega (y)
6. ¿Como se escribe _____ermano?
   **a.** con hache
   **b.** sin hache
7. ¿Cómo se escribe amari_____o?
   **a.** con doble ele
   **b.** con i griega (y)
8. ¿Cómo se escribe _____ombre?
   **a.** con hache
   **b.** sin hache
9. ¿Cómo se escribe piza_____a?
   **a.** con ere
   **b.** con erre
10. ¿Cómo se escribe ma_____or?
    **a.** con doble ele
    **b.** con i griega (y)

**¿RECUERDA?**

In **Gramática A.6** you learned that Spanish verbs change endings, letting you know who is performing the action. You saw these endings for regular **-ar** verbs, like **hablar,** in **Gramática C.5.** The verb form that appears in the dictionary and in most vocabulary lists, however, is the *infinitive;* Spanish infinitives always end in **-ar, -er,** or **-ir.** The endings are added to the *stem* (the infinitive minus **-ar, -er,** or **-ir**).

## 1.3 Talking About Habitual Actions: Present Tense of Regular *-er* and *-ir* Verbs

Following are the present-tense conjugations of the regular **-er** and **-ir** verbs **leer** and **vivir.***

| **leer** (***to read***) | | |
|---|---|---|
| (yo) | le**o** | *I read* |
| (tú) | le**es** | *you (inf. sing.) read* |
| (usted, él/ella) | le**e** | *you (pol. sing.) read; he/she reads* |
| (nosotros/as) | le**emos** | *we read* |
| (vosotros/as) | le**éis** | *you (inf. pl., Spain) read* |
| (ustedes, ellos/as) | le**en** | *you (pl.) read; they read* |

*For recognition: **vos leés, vivís**

It takes time to acquire these endings. As you read, listen, and interact more in Spanish, you will be able to use them with greater accuracy.

| **vivir** (***to live***) | | |
|---|---|---|
| (yo) | viv**o** | *I live* |
| (tú) | viv**es** | *you (inf. sing.) live* |
| (usted, él/ella) | viv**e** | *you (pol. sing.) live; he/she lives* |
| (nosotros/as) | viv**imos** | *we live* |
| (vosotros/as) | viv**ís** | *you (inf. pl., Spain) live* |
| (ustedes, ellos/as) | viv**en** | *you (pl.) live; they live* |

Remember that, because Spanish verb endings indicate in many cases who or what the subject is, it is not necessary to use subject pronouns in every sentence.

—¿Dónde vives? —*Where do you live?*
—Vivo en San Juan. —*I live in San Juan.*

## Ejercicio 3

**leer** = *to read*

Complete estas oraciones con la forma correcta del verbo **leer.**

1. Muchos españoles _____ el periódico *El País.*
2. ¿_____ (tú) muchas novelas?
3. Mi amigo _____ la Biblia todos los días.
4. (Yo) _____ libros en español.
5. Profesora, ¿_____ (usted) muchas composiciones?

## Ejercicio 4

**vivir** = *to live*

Complete estas oraciones con la forma correcta del verbo **vivir.**

1. Pablo _____ en Texas.
2. (Nosotros) No _____ en México.
3. Susana y sus hijos _____ en Perú.
4. ¿_____ (vosotros) en España?
5. (Yo) _____ en los Estados Unidos.
6. ¿_____ (ustedes) en Panamá?

**¿RECUERDA?**

As you saw in **Gramática C.5** and **1.3,** Spanish verb endings usually indicate who the subject is, so it is generally not necessary to use subject pronouns (**tú, usted, él/ella, nosotros/as, vosotros/as, ustedes, ellos/as**) in questions.

**¿Tienes (tú) teléfono?**
**¿Dónde vive (ella)?**
**¿Cómo se llaman (ustedes)?**

## 1.4 Asking Questions: Question Formation

You have already seen and heard many questions in Spanish.

¿Cómo se llama usted?
¿Qué hora es?
¿Cuándo nació José?
¿Es alto Guillermo?
¿Habla usted español?
¿Tienen (ustedes) hijos?
¿Eres (tú) extrovertida?
¿Qué tiene Amanda?

**A.** Statements in Spanish are normally formed by using a subject, then the verb, and then any object or description.

Ernestito tiene un perro grande.
subject verb object adjective

Amanda es delgada.
subject verb adjective

Questions, however, are generally formed by placing the subject *after* the verb, with any object or description either following or preceding the subject.

| | | |
|---|---|---|
| STATEMENT: | Ernestito tiene un perro grande. | *Ernestito has a big dog.* |
| QUESTION: | ¿Tiene Ernestito un perro grande? | *Does Ernestito have a big dog?* |
| STATEMENT: | Amanda es delgada. | *Amanda is thin.* |
| QUESTION: | ¿Es delgada Amanda? | *Is Amanda thin?* |
| STATEMENT: | Susana vive en Perú. | *Susana lives in Peru.* |
| QUESTION: | ¿Vive Susana en Perú? | *Does Susana live in Peru?* |
| STATEMENT: | (Tú) Lees muchas novelas. | *You read a lot of novels.* |
| QUESTION: | ¿Lees (tú) muchas novelas? | *Do you read a lot of novels?* |
| STATEMENT: | Ellos hablan árabe. | *They speak Arabic.* |
| QUESTION: | ¿Hablan ellos árabe? | *Do they speak Arabic?* |

Note that in Spanish no additional words, such as *does* or *do*, are needed to turn a statement into a question.

Question words always have a written accent.
**¿Qué?** = *What?*
**¿Cuándo?** = *When?*
**¿Quién(es)?** = *Who?*
**¿De quién?** = *Whose?*
**¿Dónde?** = *Where?*
**¿Cuánto/a/os/as?** = *How much? / How many?*
**¿Cómo?** = *How?; What?*
**¿Cuál(es)?** = *Which?; What?*
**¿Por qué?** = *Why?*

**B.** Sometimes interrogative (question) words like **¿Qué?**, **¿Cuándo?**, **¿(De) Quién?**, **¿Dónde?**, **¿Cuántos?**, **¿Cómo?**, **¿Cuál?**, or **¿Por qué?** are used. These words are placed at the beginning of the question, before the verb.

¿**Cuántos** años tiene Guillermo?
¿**Qué** tiene Ernestito?
¿**Dónde** vive Susana?
¿**De quién** es el coche nuevo?
¿**Cuál** es tu número de teléfono?
¿**Cómo** está usted?
¿**Quién** es ese muchacho?
¿**Cuándo** nació usted?
¿**Por qué** no hablamos inglés en clase?

## Ejercicio 5

Cambie las siguientes oraciones por preguntas.

MODELO: Amanda tiene 14 años. →
*¿Cuántos años tiene Amanda?*

1. Rubén Hernández vive en Florida.
2. Susana habla japonés.
3. Usted se llama Pedro Ruiz.
4. Ernesto y Estela tienen tres hijos.
5. Tú eres estudiante.

## Ejercicio 6

Haga todas las preguntas posibles según los dibujos.

MODELO: →

*¿Estás cansado? / ¿Cómo estás?*

1.

2.

3.

4.

5.

## 1.5 Telling Time: Hours and Minutes

**¿Qué hora es?** = *What time is it?*

1.15: Es la una y cuarto.
2.30: Son las dos y media.
3.25: Son las tres y veinticinco.
5.45: Son las seis menos cuarto.

The phrase **¿Qué hora es?** is often used in Spanish to ask what time it is. Another common question is **¿Qué hora tiene usted?** (*What time do you have?*) In both cases, the answer usually begins with **son.**

| | |
|---|---|
| —¿Qué hora es? | —*What time is it?* |
| —**Son** las tres. | —*It's three o'clock.* |

**Es** (not **son**) is used to tell the time with one o'clock and between one o'clock and two o'clock.

| | |
|---|---|
| —¿**Es** la una? | —*Is it one o'clock?* |
| —No, **es** la una y veinte. | —*No, it's one twenty.* |

Use **y** (*and*) to express minutes after the hour.

| | |
|---|---|
| —¿Son las seis **y** diez? | —*Is it ten after six?* |
| —No, son las seis **y** veinte. | —*No, it's twenty after six.* |

Use **menos** (*less*) or **para** (*to, till*) to express minutes before the hour.

| | |
|---|---|
| Son las siete **menos** veinte. | *It's twenty to seven.* (Literally: *It's seven less twenty.*) |
| Son veinte **para** las siete. | *It's twenty to* (*till*) *seven.* |

Use **cuarto** (*quarter*) and **media** (*half*) for fifteen and thirty minutes, respectively.

| | |
|---|---|
| —¿Qué hora tiene usted? | —*What time do you have?* |
| —Son las tres y **cuarto** (**media**). | —*It's a quarter after* (*half past*) *three.* |

Salvador Dalí, *La persistencia de la memoria*

***a* la una** = ***at*** *one o'clock*
***a* las siete menos cuarto** = ***at*** *six forty-five*

Use **a** to express *when* (*at what time*) an event occurs.

| | |
|---|---|
| **a** la una | *at one o'clock* |
| **a** las cuatro y media | *at four thirty* |
| Tengo clase **a** las nueve. | *I have class at nine.* |

## Ejercicio 7

¿Qué hora es?

MODELOS: 2:20 → *Son las dos y veinte.*
2:40 → *Son las tres menos veinte.*

**1.** 4:20
**2.** 6:15
**3.** 8:13
**4.** 1:10
**5.** 7:07
**6.** 5:30
**7.** 3:00
**8.** 1:49
**9.** 12:30
**10.** 5:15

## 1.6 Expressing Likes and Dislikes: *gustar* + Infinitive

**Gustar** is used to express likes and dislikes.

**Me gusta bailar.** (*I like to dance.*)

**A.** The Spanish verb **gustar** expresses the meaning of English *to like*. From a grammatical point of view, however, it is similar to the English expression *to be pleasing to someone.**

| | |
|---|---|
| **Me gusta** leer. | *I like to read.* (*Reading is pleasing to me.*) |

*You will learn more about the verb **gustar** and similar verbs in **Gramática 8.2.**

**Gustar** is usually used with pronouns that tell *to whom* something is pleasing. Here are the pronoun forms.*

| SINGULAR | | PLURAL | |
|---|---|---|---|
| me | *to me* | nos | *to us* |
| te | *to you (inf. sing.)* | os | *to you (inf. pl., Spain)* |
| le | *to you (pol. sing.); to him/her* | les | *to you (pl.); to them* |

**¿*Te* gusta patinar?**
(*Do you like to skate?*)
**A Ernestito *le* gusta jugar al fútbol.**
(*Ernestito likes to play soccer.*)
**A Estela y a Ernesto *les* gusta ir al cine.**
(*Estela and Ernesto like to go to the movies.*)
***Nos* gusta cocinar.**
(*We like to cook.*)

| | |
|---|---|
| —¿Qué **te** gusta hacer? | —*What do you like to do?* |
| —**Me** gusta aprender cosas nuevas. | —*I like to learn new things.* |
| —¿Qué **les** gusta hacer? | —*What do you like to do?* |
| —**Nos** gusta cocinar. | —*We like to cook.* |

**B.** Since **le gusta** can refer to *you (pol. sing.)*, *him*, or *her*, and **les gusta** can refer to *you (pl.)* or *them*, Spanish speakers often expand the sentence to be more specific. They use phrases with **a** (*to*), such as **a mi papá** (*to my father*), **a Juan** (*to Juan*), or **a los estudiantes** (*to the students*), in addition to using the pronoun **le** or **les**.†

| | |
|---|---|
| **A Carmen le** gusta cantar. | *Carmen likes to sing.* |
| —¿**A usted le** gusta lavar su carro? | —*Do you like to wash your car?* |
| —No, no **me** gusta. | —*No, I don't like to.* |
| —¿**Les** gusta acampar **a Guillermo** y **a Ernestito**? | —*Do Guillermo and Ernestito like to go camping?* |
| —Sí, **les** gusta mucho. | —*Yes, they like to very much.* |

**C.** The verb form that follows **gustar** is an infinitive, such as **hablar** (*to speak*), **leer** (*to read*), or **vivir** (*to live*).

| PRONOUN | + | *gusta* | + | INFINITIVE |
|---|---|---|---|---|
| me | | | | estudiar (*to study*) |
| te | | | | jugar (*to play*) |
| le | + | gusta | + | comer (*to eat*) |
| nos | | | | correr (*to run*) |
| os | | | | competir (*to compete*) |
| les | | | | escribir (*to write*) |

*Recognition: (**A vos**) **Te gusta**
†You will learn more about phrases with **a, le,** and **les** in **Gramática 7.4, 8.2,** and **10.5.**

## Ejercicio 8

¿Qué les gusta hacer a Ernestito y a Guillermo? Complete los diálogos con **me, te, les** o **nos.**

MODELO: AMANDA: Graciela, ¿*te* gusta bailar?
GRACIELA: Sí, *me* gusta mucho bailar.

1. MAESTRA: Ernestito, ¿____ gusta andar en bicicleta?
ERNESTITO: Sí, ____ gusta mucho. Tengo una bici nueva.

2. ERNESTITO: Guillermo, ¿____ gusta jugar al béisbol?
GUILLERMO: No, pero ____ gusta jugar al fútbol.

3. PEDRO: Ernestito y Guillermo, ¿____ gusta escuchar la música rock?
LOS CHICOS: ¡Claro que sí! ____ gusta mucho.

## Ejercicio 9

¿Qué le(s) gusta hacer a las siguientes personas?

1. A Ernestito ____ gusta ____.
2. A Estela (la madre de Ernestito) no ____ gusta ____.
3. A Clarisa y a Marisa (las primas de Ernestito) ____ gusta ____.
4. A Ernestito ____ gusta ____.
5. Al perro ____ gusta ____.
6. A mí ____ gusta ____.

CAPÍTULO 2

# Mis planes y preferencias

**METAS**

In **Capítulo 2** you will discuss your plans for the future and your preferences. You will also talk about your classes and the weather.

Salamanca, España

**ACTIVIDADES DE COMUNICACIÓN Y LECTURAS**

Los planes

Las clases

**Lectura** Los amigos hispanos: Nora Morales

Las preferencias y los deseos

**El mundo hispano**... su gente

**Nota cultural** ¡Vamos a pasear!

El tiempo

**El mundo hispano**... imágenes

**El mundo hispano**... en los Estados Unidos

**EN RESUMEN**

**GRAMÁTICA Y EJERCICIOS**

2.1 Expressing Future Plans: **ir** + **a** + Infinitive

2.2 Sequencing: Ordinal Adjectives

2.3 Stating Preferences and Desires: **preferir** and **querer** + Infinitive

2.4 Describing the Weather: Common Expressions

# Actividades de comunicación y lecturas

## 5 Los planes

*Lea Gramática 2.1.*

### Los planes de Pedro y Andrea para el fin de semana

El viernes por la noche Pedro y Andrea van a ver una película.

También van a bailar en una discoteca.

El sábado Pedro va a lavar el carro.

El sábado por la tarde, Pedro y Andrea van a dar una fiesta.

El domingo por la mañana, los Ruiz van a ir a misa con sus hijas.

Luego van a almorzar en un restaurante.

El domingo por la tarde Pedro va a escribir una carta.

El domingo por la noche Andrea va a escuchar música.

### Actividad 1. Preferencias: Los planes

Diga sí o no. También agregue otra actividad en cada caso.

1. El sábado por la mañana voy a...
   - **a.** reparar mi carro.
   - **b.** pasear por el centro.
   - **c.** dormir.
   - **d.** ¿ ?
2. El viernes por la noche mis padres van a...
   - **a.** salir a cenar.
   - **b.** ver la televisión.
   - **c.** dar una fiesta.
   - **d.** ¿ ?
3. El domingo por la tarde voy a...
   - **a.** limpiar mi cuarto.
   - **b.** practicar algún deporte.
   - **c.** ir al cine.
   - **d.** ¿ ?
4. Durante las vacaciones mis amigos y yo vamos a...
   - **a.** viajar.
   - **b.** descansar.
   - **c.** jugar al tenis.
   - **d.** ¿ ?
5. Este invierno voy a...
   - **a.** esquiar.
   - **b.** estudiar mucho.
   - **c.** patinar en el hielo.
   - **d.** ¿ ?

### Y TÚ, ¿QUÉ DICES?

| | | |
|---|---|---|
| ¡Qué aburrido! | ¿Dónde? | Yo también. |
| ¡Qué divertido! | ¿Con quién? | Yo no. |
| ¡Qué buena idea! | ¿Cuándo? / ¿A qué hora? | |

MODELO: E1: El domingo por la tarde voy a *limpiar mi cuarto.*
E2: *¡Qué aburrido!*

## Actividad 2. Narración: ¿Qué va a hacer Carmen el sábado?

### PALABRAS ÚTILES

primero
luego
después
más tarde
por la mañana
por la tarde
por la noche
finalmente
por último

## Actividad 3. Entrevista: Tus planes

Pregúntele a su compañero/a qué va a hacer en las siguientes ocasiones.

MODELO: E1: ¿Qué vas a hacer *en tu próximo cumpleaños*?
E2: Voy a *salir a cenar con mi familia.*

| OCASIONES | ACTIVIDADES | |
|---|---|---|
| en tu próximo cumpleaños | acampar | viajar |
| hoy, después de clases | ir al cine | salir a cenar |
| esta noche | descansar | estudiar |
| el próximo fin de semana | ir a la playa | nadar en un lago/río |
| durante las próximas vacaciones | trabajar | ir a muchas fiestas |
| el próximo verano | ver la televisión | ir de compras |
| el viernes por la noche | leer un buen libro | |

## Actividad 4. Intercambios: Madrid en el verano

Imagínese que usted está en Madrid en el mes de julio. Mire la lista de actividades posibles y decida qué va a hacer.

MODELO: E1: Voy a *nadar en la piscina.*
E2: ¿Dónde?
E1: En *el Polideportivo de San Blas.*

**Actividades posibles:** jugar al boliche, levantar pesas, nadar, pasear en barca, salir a bailar, salir a cenar, tomar el sol, ver los animales, viajar a la ciudad en tren

### PREGUNTAS Y RESPUESTAS ÚTILES

| | |
|---|---|
| ¿Cuánto cuesta la entrada? | Cuesta *650* pesetas. |
| ¿Dónde está? | Está en *la calle de Alcalá.* |
| ¿A qué hora abren/cierran? | Abren/Cierran a *las 9:00.* |
| ¿A qué hora sale/llega el tren? | Sale/Llega a *las 10:30.* |
| ¿En qué restaurante (piscina, ... )? | En *el Café de Oriente.* |

## Madrid en verano

### Barcas

En los lagos del Retiro y la Casa de Campo y en el río Manzanares, a la altura del puente de Segovia. Desde las 10 de la mañana a la puesta del sol. El precio oscila entre 300 pesetas que cuesta una barca para dos personas y 200 pesetas por persona cuando son tres o más. Paseos de una hora.

### Trenes turísticos

**•Trenes de ida y regreso en el día:**
**«Ciudad de Toledo»** (electrotrén, domingos). Salida de Chamartín a las 9,05 h.; regreso de Toledo a las 19,45 h. Precio: adultos, 1.650 pesetas; niños de cuatro a doce años, 1.200 pesetas.
**«Murallas de Ávila»** (sábados). Salida de Chamartín a las 9,15 h.; regreso de Ávila a las 19,40 h. Precios: adultos, 1.650 pesetas; niños de cuatro a doce años, 1.200 pesetas.

**•Trenes de fin de semana:**
**«Tierras del Cid»** (TER). Salida de Chamartín el sábado a las 8,30 h.; regreso de Burgos a las 17,45 h. **«Ciudad Encantada de Cuenca»** (TER). Salida de Atocha los sábados a las 9,30 h.; regreso de Cuenca, el domingo a las 19 h.

### Parques acuáticos

**Acuópolis.** Toboganes, Rompeolas, Atlantic-Surf, Lago de la Aventura, Poblado del Oeste. Restaurantes, Terrazas, Parking gratuito. Abierto todos los días de 1 a 20 h. Precios: adultos, 1.550 ptas.; menores de catorce años, 1.000 ptas.
**Lagosur.** Km. 9 carretera de Toledo a Leganés (Leganés). Abierto de 11 a 19 h. Precios: adultos, 1.400 ptas. Viernes y sábado abierto también desde las 23 h. hasta la madrugada. Precios: hombres, 1.100 ptas.; mujeres, 700 ptas., con derecho a consumición.

### Boleras

**Bolera Club Stella.** Arlabán, 7. Tel. 231 01 92.
**Bowling Chamartín.** Estación de Chamartín. Tel. 315 71 19.

### Gimnasios

**Gimnasio Ángel López.** Primer Centro Polaris de España. Squash (nueva instalación), karate, gimnasia, pesas, aerobic, gim-jazz, ballet infantil y adulto, baile español y rítmica. Amparo Usera, 14.
**Gimnasio Argüelles.** Karate, squash, aerobic, gimnasia, jazz, culturismo, musculación. Máquinas Polaris. Andrés Mellado, 21-23.

### Piscinas

**Municipales**
Los precios de estas piscinas del Ayuntamiento son de 350 pesetas para los adultos y 150 para los niños. El horario de las piscinas es de 10 a 20 h., ininterrumpidamente.
**Centro. Polideportivo de la Latina** (plaza de la Cebada, 1), una piscina climatizada.
**Ciudad Lineal. Polideportivo de la Concepción** (Virgen del Portillo, s/n.), una piscina climatizada y una olímpica.
**San Blas. Polideportivo de San Blas** (avda. de Hellín, 79), una piscina climatizada, una olímpica, una para nadadores no expertos, una infantil y una piscina de 1.875 metros cuadrados.

### Discotecas al aire libre

**La Fiesta.** Paseo Virgen del Puerto (puente Segovia).
**El Jardín Del Sur. Disco-piscina.** Ctra. Toledo, km. 8. Tels. 688 13 35 y 688 92 83.
**Oh! Madrid. Disco-piscina.** Ctra. Coruña, km. 8,700 (dirección Madrid). Tel. 207 86 97.

### Restaurantes con terraza

**Café Oriente.** Pza. de Oriente, 2. Tels. 241 39 74 y 247 15 64.
**Casa Domingo.** Alcalá, 39. Tel. 276 01 37.
**Casa Mingo.** P°. de la Florida, 2. Tel. 247 79 18.
**Casa Rafa.** Narváez, 68. Tel. 273 10 87.
**Cuarto y Mitad.** Bolivia, 21. Tel. 250 83 84.
**Currito.** Pabellón de Vizcaya de la Feria del Campo. Tel. 464 57 04.

### Zoo

**Casa de Campo.** Tels. 711 98 50/54 16. Metro Batán. Horario apertura, 10 h. Cierre del parque, 21,30 h. Menores de ocho años, 490 pesetas; mayores, 680 pesetas. Pases delfinario: mañana y tarde.

# Las clases

*Lea Gramática 2.2.*

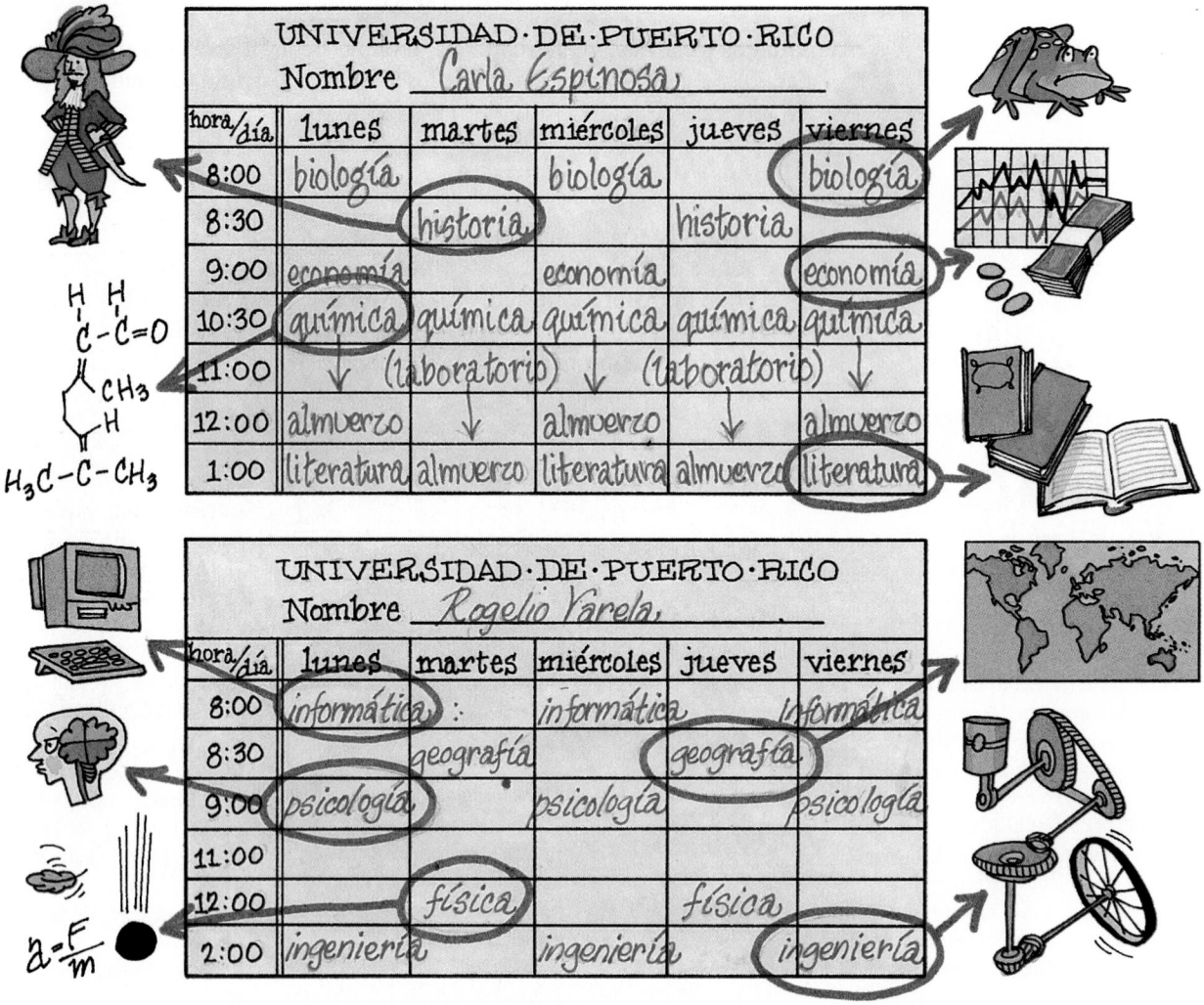

UNIVERSIDAD·DE·PUERTO·RICO
Nombre Carla Espinosa

| hora/día | lunes | martes | miércoles | jueves | viernes |
|---|---|---|---|---|---|
| 8:00 | biología | | biología | | biología |
| 8:30 | | historia | | historia | |
| 9:00 | economía | | economía | | economía |
| 10:30 | química | química | química | química | química |
| 11:00 | ↓ | (laboratorio) ↓ | | (laboratorio) ↓ | |
| 12:00 | almuerzo | ↓ | almuerzo | ↓ | almuerzo |
| 1:00 | literatura | almuerzo | literatura | almuerzo | literatura |

UNIVERSIDAD·DE·PUERTO·RICO
Nombre Rogelio Varela

| hora/día | lunes | martes | miércoles | jueves | viernes |
|---|---|---|---|---|---|
| 8:00 | informática | | informática | | informática |
| 8:30 | | geografía | | geografía | |
| 9:00 | psicología | | psicología | | psicología |
| 11:00 | | | | | |
| 12:00 | | física | | física | |
| 2:00 | ingeniería | | ingeniería | | ingeniería |

## Actividad 5. Diálogo: Las clases

Raúl, un estudiante mexicano, habla de sus clases con Esteban, su amigo norteamericano.

RAÚL: Tengo cuatro clases este semestre.
ESTEBAN: Yo tengo cinco.
RAÚL: ¿Son muy difíciles?
ESTEBAN: Solamente la clase de física es difícil. Las otras son fáciles.
RAÚL: Mi clase de arte es difícil pero muy interesante.
ESTEBAN: No tengo clase de arte, pero sí tengo una clase de sociología que me gusta mucho.

Buscamos la eficiencia a la primera vez, así como el liderazgo de excelencia.

El colegio te incluye las asignaturas de oratoria, cultura empresarial y computación, que son las materias que te darán apoyo, cultura y desarrollo pleno de tu potencial.

**EXÁMENES DE ADMISIÓN:**
18 y 25 de julio y 1 de agosto

**INICIO DE CURSOS:**
1° de septiembre

**H. Escuela Naval Militar 42**
**(casi esquina con Taxqueña)**
**Col. San Francisco Culhuacán**
**(a 1 kilómetro del metro Taxqueña)**

## Actividad 6. Intercambios: Las clases

Ramón tiene muchas clases en su primer año de preparatoria. Pregúntele a su compañero/a cuál es la primera (segunda, tercera, cuarta, etcétera) clase de Ramón, a qué hora es y quién es el profesor / la profesora.

MODELO:
E1: ¿Cuál es la *primera* clase de Ramón?
E2: Su primera clase es la clase de *inglés.*
E1: ¿A qué hora es?
E2: Es a *las 7:45.*
E1: ¿Quién es el profesor o la profesora?
E2: Es *el señor García.*

SAGRADO CORAZÓN

Nombre: Ramón Gómez Año: Primero de preparatoria

| hora | materia | salón de clase | profesor(a) |
|---|---|---|---|
| 7:45→8:30 | inglés | 403 | Manuel García |
| 8:40→9:25 | matemáticas | 207 | Eugenia Ibarra |
| 9:35→10:20 | geografía | 201 | Daniel Contino |
| 10:30→11:05 | alemán | 402 | Alma Morales de Braun |
| 11:05→11:20 | descanso | | |
| 11:30→12:15 | literatura española | 405 | Consuelo Acuña de Ramos |
| 12:25→1:10 | historia de México | 408 | Héctor Magaña M. |
| 1:20→3:20 | almuerzo | | |
| 3:30→4:15 | biología | 214 | Isabel Santizo de Barragán |
| 4:25→5:10 | música | 311 | Víctor Álvarez |

## Actividad 7. Entrevista: Las clases

1. E1: ¿Qué clases tienes este semestre/trimestre?
   E2: Tengo ____, ____ y ____.

2. E1: ¿Cuál es tu clase favorita? ¿A qué hora es?
   E2: Mi clase favorita es la de ____. Es a la(s) ____.

3. E1: ¿Cuál es tu clase más fácil/difícil? ¿A qué hora es?
   E2: Mi clase más fácil/difícil es la de ____. Es a la(s) ____.

## Actividad 8. Del mundo hispano: La Universidad del Valle de México

Éstas son las especialidades más importantes en el México actual. Trabaje con un compañero / una compañera para contestar las preguntas.

**UNIVERSIDAD DEL VALLE DE MEXICO**

| ESPECIALIDADES | CAMPUS: CENTRO – SAN RAFAEL | CENTRO – GUADALUPE INSURGENTES | SUR – SAN ANGEL | SUR – TLALPAN | EDO. MEX. – LOMAS VERDES | QRO. – JURIQUILLA |
|---|---|---|---|---|---|---|
| **AREA ECONOMICO-ADMINISTRATIVA** | | | | | | |
| ADMINISTRACION | | • | • | • | • | |
| ADMINISTRACION DE EMPRESAS TURISTICAS | • | • | | • | • | • |
| CONTADURIA PUBLICA | | • | | • | • | |
| ECONOMIA | • | | | | • | • |
| FINANZAS | | | | | • | • |
| MERCADOTECNIA | | • | | • | • | • |
| RELACIONES INDUSTRIALES | • | | | | • | • |
| RELACIONES PUBLICAS | • | | | | • | • |
| **AREA DE CIENCIAS Y TECNOLOGIA** | | | | | | |
| ECOLOGIA | | | | • | • | |
| INGENIERIA CIVIL | | | | | • | |
| INGENIERIA EN ECOLOGIA | | | | | • | |
| INGENIERIA EN ELECTRONICA Y TELECOMUNICACIONES | | | | | • | |
| INGENIERIA INDUSTRIAL ELECTRICA | | | | • | • | |
| INGENIERIA INDUSTRIAL ELECTRONICA | | | | • | • | |
| INGENIERIA INDUSTRIAL MECANICA | | | | • | • | |
| INGENIERIA INDUSTRIAL QUIMICA | | | | • | • | |
| INGENIERIA INDUSTRIAL EN PRODUCCION | | | | • | • | • |
| SISTEMAS DE COMPUTACION ADMINISTRATIVA | • | | • | • | • | • |
| **AREA DE CIENCIAS SOCIALES** | | | | | | |
| CIENCIAS DE LA COMUNICACION | • | | | • | • | • |
| DERECHO | • | | | • | • | • |
| PEDAGOGIA | | | | • | • | |
| PSICOLOGIA | | | | • | • | |
| **AREA DE ARTE Y HUMANIDADES** | | | | | | |
| ARQUITECTURA | • | | | • | • | • |
| DISEÑO GRAFICO | • | | | • | • | • |

1. ¿Qué campus ofrece todas las especialidades? ¿Cuál ofrece menos especialidades?
2. ¿Cuántos campus ofrecen la especialidad en ingeniería industrial química?
3. Nombren las especialidades más atractivas, en su opinión.
4. ¿Se ofrecen esas especialidades en su universidad? ¿Estudian ustedes alguna de esas especialidades?
5. ¿Cuáles son las especialidades en el área de ciencias sociales?
6. En su opinión, ¿cuáles son las especialidades más importantes en el presente? ¿Por qué?

Estudiantes mexicanos en un laboratorio de biología en México, D.F.

# Los amigos hispanos: Nora Morales

**VOCABULARIO ÚTIL**

| | |
|---|---|
| sobre | *about* |
| la mitad | *half* |
| chistoso | *funny* |
| A veces | *Sometimes* |

Esta lectura es sobre una estudiante mexicoamericana de San Antonio, Texas. Ella habla aquí de su ciudad y de las clases que tiene este semestre.

Las palabras en negrilla son *cognados*, palabras similares en español y en inglés; por ejemplo, **personas** (*persons*). Antes de leer, mire esas palabras para tener una idea general.

Hola, amigos. Me llamo Nora Morales y soy **estudiante de historia** en la Universidad de Texas en San Antonio. Me gusta vivir en San Antonio. Aquí hay muchas **personas** que hablan español, y la **cultura** de esta ciudad tiene gran **influencia hispana.** Caray, pues es **lógico:** ¡la mitad de la **población** de San Antonio es hispana!

Nací el cuatro de **julio** de 1973. Entonces... ¿cuál es mi edad? Soy de estatura mediana; tengo el pelo castaño y los ojos verdes. **Me fascina** la **historia,** especialmente la historia de **México,** porque de allí son mis padres. Y también me gusta mucho el idioma español; este **semestre** tengo una **clase** muy divertida con la **profesora** Martínez.

Tengo también una clase de química y otra de **biología.** En la clase de biología hay un muchacho **mexicano** muy amable y chistoso; se llama Raúl Saucedo. A veces **practico** el español con él y hablamos de México.

## Comprensión

Diga si las siguientes oraciones son ciertas o falsas. Si son falsas, haga las correcciones necesarias.

MODELO: Los padres de Nora son de España. →
*Es falso.* Los padres de Nora son de *México.*

1. Nora nació el Día de la Independencia de los Estados Unidos.
2. Nora habla en español con un amigo norteamericano en la clase de biología.
3. A Nora le gusta mucho su clase de español.
4. Nora es alta y tiene el pelo negro.

## Ahora... ¡usted!

1. ¿Tiene clases que le gustan mucho? ¿Cuáles son sus favoritas?
2. ¿Le gusta su clase de español? ¿Por qué?
3. ¿Cuáles son sus actividades favoritas en la clase de español?

### Un paso más... ¡a escribir!

Describa a su mejor amigo/a. ¿Cuándo nació? ¿Qué edad tiene? ¿Cuáles son sus características físicas? ¿Qué les gusta hacer a ustedes cuando están juntos?

# Las preferencias y los deseos

*Lea Gramática 2.3.*

## Los planes para el sábado

Doña Lola quiere coser.

Guillermo quiere montar a caballo.

El señor Ramírez prefiere nadar.

Doña Rosita quiere ir al parque.

Don Anselmo quiere pescar.

Ramón prefiere andar en motocicleta.

Andrea y Pedro prefieren descansar y charlar.

La familia Ruiz quiere merendar en el parque.

## Actividad 9. Diálogo: Una invitación

ESTEBAN: ¿Te gusta *jugar al tenis*?
LAN: Sí, me gusta mucho.
ESTEBAN: ¿Quieres *jugar al tenis en el parque* el *domingo*?
LAN: ¿A qué hora?
ESTEBAN: A *las once.*
LAN: Perfecto. Nos vemos el *domingo* a *las once.*

## Actividad 10. Intercambios: ¿Cuáles son sus actividades favoritas?

Converse con su compañero/a sobre sus preferencias.

MODELO: E1: ¿Qué prefieres hacer *los lunes a las cuatro de la tarde*?
E2: Prefiero *escribir cartas.*

| HORA Y DÍA | ACTIVIDADES |
|---|---|
| **1.** Los sábados, a las siete de la mañana, prefiero... | **a.** jugar al tenis. |
| **2.** Los viernes, a las ocho de la noche, prefiero... | **b.** cocinar. |
| **3.** Los lunes, a las cuatro de la tarde, prefiero... | **c.** descansar. |
| **4.** Los domingos, a las diez de la mañana, prefiero... | **d.** correr. |
| **5.** Los sábados, a las tres de la tarde, prefiero... | **e.** escribir cartas. |
| | **f.** montar a caballo. |
| | **g.** bailar. |
| | **h.** ver la televisión. |
| | **i.** dormir. |
| | **j.** leer el periódico. |
| | **k.** ¿ ? |

## Actividad 11. Entrevista: Mis actividades favoritas

MODELO: E1: ¿Prefieres *nadar en la piscina o en el mar*?
E2: Prefiero *nadar en el mar.*

**1.** ¿cenar en casa o en un restaurante?
**2.** ¿jugar al boliche o al billar?
**3.** ¿jugar al basquetbol o al fútbol?
**4.** ¿andar en motocicleta o en bicicleta?
**5.** ¿escribir cartas o recibir cartas?
**6.** ¿leer el periódico o ver la televisión?
**7.** ¿lavar el carro o trabajar en el jardín?
**8.** ¿merendar en un parque o comer en casa?
**9.** ¿ir a la playa o a las montañas?
**10.** ¿leer una novela o explorar la red mundial?

## Actividad 12. Del mundo hispano: ¿Qué prefieren hacer los españoles en su tiempo libre?

Converse con un compañero / una compañera sobre la tabla a continuación.

MODELOS: E1: ¿Cuál es la *primera preferencia* de los españoles?
E2: *Pasar tiempo con la familia y los niños.*

E1: En general, ¿los europeos prefieren *recibir visitas* o *escuchar la radio*?
E2: Prefieren *recibir visitas.*

## Actividad 13. Conversación: El perfil del hombre perfecto

Trabajando en grupos, organicen estas descripciones en dos columnas: (1) el macho y (2) el hombre liberado.

- Le gusta ver películas violentas.
- Prefiere jugar al fútbol americano.
- Va a bailar con frecuencia.
- Le gusta jugar al tenis.
- Prefiere montar en motocicleta.
- Le gusta escuchar la música rock.
- Prefiere la música romántica.
- Prefiere manejar un jeep.
- Prefiere salir con los amigos.
- Prefiere llevar ropa deportiva.
- Le gusta mucho salir por la noche.
- Prefiere cenar en familia.
- Siempre quiere llevar vaqueros, botas y chaqueta negra.

Ahora, escriban una lista para describir uno de los siguientes estereotipos de mujer.

1. la mujer tradicional
2. la mujer liberada
3. la mujer perfecta

## EL MUNDO HISPANO... su gente

Cecilia Ortega tiene 24 años y es de España.

*¿Qué le gusta hacer en su tiempo libre?*

Leer me apasiona;[1] prácticamente devoro[2] los libros. Me gustan especialmente las novelas policíacas o de misterio, y las biografías. También voy al cine una vez por semana. Me gustan las películas europeas. En general, detesto las películas violentas y las comedias de chiste fácil,[3] aunque me gustan mucho las comedias inteligentes.

[1]me... *is my passion* [2]*I devour* [3]de... *simplistic*

NOTA CULTURAL

**VOCABULARIO ÚTIL**

| | |
|---|---|
| planificar | *to plan* |
| disfrutar de | *to enjoy* |
| una fuente | *fountain* |
| los bancos | *benches* |
| las damas | *checkers* |

# ¡Vamos a pasear!

En esta Nota cultural se describen dos lugares en las ciudades hispanas donde hay mucha actividad social: las calles y la plaza. La plaza, especialmente, es el lugar que muchos hispanos prefieren para estar con los amigos.

En las calles de las ciudades hispanas siempre hay mucha actividad de todo tipo: hay personas que conversan, que caminan, que van de compras. Los hispanos, en general, prefieren no planificar demasiado su tiempo libre. A muchos les gusta disfrutar del momento presente y hacer las cosas de un modo espontáneo. La gente sale con el pretexto de visitar a un amigo, de comprar algo o para pasear por la plaza.

La plaza está generalmente en el centro de la ciudad. Muchas plazas tienen una fuente, árboles y bancos. En algunos pueblos, la gente juega allí a diferentes juegos como el dominó, las damas o las cartas. Pero a la mayoría de los hispanos les gusta ir a la plaza para sentarse y conversar o simplemente para mirar a las personas que pasan.

¡Me gusta la lluvia en la plaza!

## Comprensión

Complete las siguientes oraciones lógicamente según la Nota cultural. Puede haber más de una respuesta correcta.

1. Generalmente, los hispanos prefieren...
   a. planificar todas sus actividades.
   b. ser espontáneos respecto al tiempo libre.
   c. pensar más en el momento presente.
2. A los hispanos les gusta pasear por...
   a. las calles.
   b. la plaza.
   c. su casa.
3. Normalmente, en la plaza, las personas...
   a. juegan a varios juegos y conversan.
   b. hacen su tarea o trabajan.
   c. se sientan y miran a otras personas.

## Ahora... ¡usted!

1. ¿Tiene esta ciudad un lugar donde la gente puede ir a pasear? ¿Qué lugar es? ¿Qué le gusta hacer a usted allí normalmente?
2. ¿Qué le gusta hacer en su tiempo libre?
3. Generalmente, ¿planifica muy bien sus actividades? ¿Por qué?

### Un paso más... ¡a escribir!

Describa su lugar favorito. ¿Dónde está? ¿Por qué le gusta pasar tiempo allí? ¿Prefiere estar solo/a en ese lugar o con otras personas? ¿Con quién(es) prefiere estar?

# El tiempo

*Lea Gramática 2.4.*

¿Qué tiempo hace?

Hace buen tiempo.

Hace sol.

Hace mucho calor.

Hace mucho frío.

Nieva.

Llueve.

Hace viento.

Hace fresco.

Está nublado.

## Actividad 14. Definiciones: Las estaciones y el clima

Lea estas descripciones y diga qué estación representa cada una: la primavera, el verano, el otoño o el invierno.

sometimes

1. Hace mucho frío y a veces nieva.
2. Llueve mucho, a veces hace viento, nacen muchos animales y hay muchas flores y plantas nuevas.
3. Las clases empiezan y hay árboles de hojas amarillas, anaranjadas y de color café. Es la temporada del fútbol norteamericano.
4. Es la estación de las vacaciones. Hace mucho calor y muchas personas van a nadar al lago o a la piscina.

Ahora, mire el país y los meses y diga qué estación es.

1. España: diciembre, enero, febrero. Es invierno.
2. Chile: diciembre, enero, febrero. Es _____.
3. México: septiembre, octubre, noviembre. Es _____.
4. Perú: septiembre, octubre, noviembre. Es _____.
5. Uruguay: marzo, abril, mayo. Es _____.
6. Argentina: junio, julio, agosto. Es _____.

## Actividad 15. Intercambios: El clima

MODELOS: E1: ¿Cuál va a ser la temperatura *máxima* en *Mexicali mañana*?
E2: Va a ser de *treinta y nueve grados.*

E1: ¿Cuál fue la temperatura *mínima* en *Acapulco ayer*?
E2: Fue de *veinticinco grados.*

**CLIMA**

| CIUDAD | TEMPERATURA DE AYER | | PRONOSTICO | |
|---|---|---|---|---|
| | MAXIMA | MINIMA | MAXIMA | MINIMA |
| DF | 21 | 12 | 22 | 12 |
| Mexicali | 37 | 25 | 39 | 24 |
| Mérida | 34 | 22 | 33 | 23 |
| Toluca | 18 | 8 | 18 | 8 |
| Chihuahua | 33 | 30 | 34 | 19 |
| Monterrey | 34 | 22 | 36 | 22 |
| Guadalajara | 26 | 16 | 25 | 16 |
| Acapulco | 32 | 25 | 32 | 24 |
| Veracruz | 25 | 23 | 29 | 24 |

## Actividad 16. Descripción de dibujos: ¿Qué tiempo hace?

Escuche la descripción de estos dibujos y diga el número del dibujo indicado.

Ahora, hágale preguntas sobre los dibujos a su compañero/a.

MODELO: E1: ¿Qué tiempo hace en el *dibujo número 3*?
E2: *Hace mucho calor.*
E1: ¿Qué estación es?
E2: Es *el verano.*

## EL MUNDO HISPANO... imágenes

**U**na plaza en el Barrio de Santa Cruz, en Sevilla, España. Cuando hace buen tiempo, a los hispanos les gusta ir a la plaza para sentarse, para pasear o para reunirse[1] con los amigos. Sólo cuando hace mucho frío hay muy pocas personas en este lugar.

En la foto vemos a varias personas, algunas alrededor de la fuente[2] y otras que comen en un café. ¡Todo el mundo se reúne en la plaza!

[1]*meet* [2]*fountain*

## EL MUNDO HISPANO... en los Estados Unidos

**S**ofía Panagiotidis tiene 24 años y es de Venezuela. Lleva cinco años en los Estados Unidos y vive en Pensilvania.

*¿Cómo es el clima en su país? ¿Hace mucho frío en el invierno? ¿mucho calor en el verano? Generalmente, ¿llueve mucho o poco? ¿Es muy diferente el clima de su país al de la ciudad donde usted vive ahora? ¿Qué clima le gusta más? ¿Por qué?*

Yo soy de Caracas y el clima allí es muy agradable, nunca hace ni mucho frío ni mucho calor.[1] En general, Venezuela no tiene cuatro estaciones. Sólo hay épocas[2] de lluvia y épocas de sequía.[3] Donde vivo ahora, en el noreste[4] de los Estados Unidos, los inviernos son muy fríos y con mucha nieve, y los veranos son muy calurosos[5] y húmedos. Yo prefiero el clima de Venezuela porque uno no tiene que llevar abrigo cuando hace un poco de frío, y no hay mucha humedad cuando hace un poco de calor. ¡Es como vivir una eterna primavera!

[1]nunca... *it's never too cold nor too hot* [2]*seasons* [3]de... *dry* [4]*northeast* [5]*hot*

# En resumen

## De todo un poco

**A.** La ropa y el clima

MODELO: E1: ¿Qué ropa llevas *cuando hace frío*?
E2: Cuando hace frío *llevo abrigo y botas.*

¿Qué ropa llevas...

1. cuando hace fresco?
2. cuando hace mucho calor?
3. cuando hace viento?
4. cuando nieva?
5. cuando llueve?
6. cuando hace mucho sol?

**B.** ¿Qué actividades asocia usted con el tiempo?

MODELO: E1: ¿Qué te gusta hacer *cuando hace viento*?
E2: Cuando hace viento me gusta *volar una cometa en la playa.*

¿Qué te gusta hacer...

1. cuando hace fresco?
2. cuando hace mucho calor?
3. cuando hace mucho frío?
4. cuando nieva?
5. cuando llueve?
6. cuando hace mucho sol?

**C.** ¡De vacaciones!

Imagínese que usted está de vacaciones. Lea estos pronósticos del tiempo y diga cuáles son sus planes. Luego, invente un pronóstico para la ciudad y el día de su preferencia, y léaselo a la clase para ver cuáles son los planes de sus compañeros.

1. Madrid, 2 de agosto: Va a hacer mucho calor. La temperatura máxima va a ser de 40°C.
2. México, D.F., 22 de julio: Va a hacer fresco y va a estar nublado por la mañana. Va a llover toda la tarde.
3. Los Ángeles, California, 28 de diciembre: Este fin de semana va a nevar en las montañas. Aquí en la ciudad va a hacer mucho frío y va a llover casi todos los días. La temperatura va a bajar a 51°F.
4. ¿ ?

## ¡Dígalo por escrito!

Las actividades de verano

En la página 81 hay una descripción de algunas de las actividades que se puede hacer en Madrid en el verano. Mire esa descripción otra vez y luego trabaje con dos o tres compañeros de clase para comentar algunos de los pasatiempos de verano típicos en su ciudad. Después, trabaje solo/a para escribir una descripción de su ciudad en verano.

## VIDEOTECA

Manolo, Lola y su hija Marta, los personajes de este segmento de video, viven en Sevilla, en la región de España que se llama Andalucía. Lola quiere hacer planes para el fin de semana. ¿Qué tiempo va a hacer? ¿Qué quiere hacer Lola con su familia? En el Capítulo 2 del *Cuaderno de trabajo* hay más actividades para hacer después de ver el video.

# Vocabulario

## Las actividades favoritas

| | |
|---|---|
| **almorzar** | to have lunch |
| **andar en motocicleta/ bicicleta** | to ride a motorcycle/bicycle |
| **caminar** | to walk |
| **charlar** | to chat |
| **comer** | to eat |
| **correr** | to run |
| **coser** | to sew |
| **dar una fiesta** | to give a party |
| **desayunar** | to have breakfast |
| **descansar** | to rest |
| **divertirse** | to have fun |
| **esquiar** | to ski |
| **estudiar** | to study |
| **explorar (la red mundial)** | to explore (the Internet) |
| **ir** | to go |
| **va** | you go; he/she goes |
| **van** | they go |
| **lavar** | to wash |
| **levantar pesas** | to lift weights |
| **limpiar** | to clean |
| **merendar (en el parque)** | to have a picnic (in the park) |
| **montar a caballo** | to ride a horse |
| **pasar tiempo** | to spend time |
| **pasear** | to go for a walk |
| **pasear en barca** | to go for a boat ride |
| **practicar un deporte** | to play a sport |
| **preferir** | to prefer |
| **prefiero** | I prefer |
| **prefiere** | you prefer; he/she prefers |
| **recibir una visita** | to have company |
| **reparar** | to fix |
| **tomar (una siesta)** | to take (a nap) |
| **tomar el sol** | to sunbathe |
| **volar una cometa** | to fly a kite |

## Las materias — School Subjects

| | |
|---|---|
| **la especialidad** | major |
| **la informática** | data processing |
| **la ingeniería** | engineering |
| **la química** | chemistry |

**PALABRAS SEMEJANTES: la antropología, el arte, la biología, las ciencias sociales, el curso, la economía, la física, la geografía, la historia, la literatura, la música, la psicología, la sociología**

**REPASO: el español, el francés, el inglés, las matemáticas**

## El tiempo — The Weather

| | |
|---|---|
| **el clima** | weather; climate |
| **Está nublado.** | It is overcast (cloudy). |
| **el grado** | degree |
| **Hace (muy) buen/mal tiempo.** | The weather is (very) fine/bad. |
| **Hace fresco.** | It's cool. |
| **Hace (mucho) calor.** | It's (very) hot. |
| **Hace (mucho) frío.** | It's (very) cold. |
| **Hace (mucho) sol.** | It's (very) sunny. |
| **Hace (mucho) viento.** | It's (very) windy. |
| **llover** | to rain |
| **Llueve (mucho).** | It rains (a lot). |
| **nevar** | to snow |
| **Nieva (mucho).** | It snows (a lot). |
| **el pronóstico del tiempo** | weather forecast |
| **¿Qué tiempo hace?** | What is the weather like? |

**PALABRAS SEMEJANTES: la temperatura máxima/ mínima**

## ¿Cuándo?

| | |
|---|---|
| **ahora** | now |
| **a la(s)** | at (*time*) |
| **... de la mañana** | . . . in the morning |
| **... de la tarde** | . . . in the afternoon |
| **... de la noche** | . . . in the evening |
| **con frecuencia** | frequently |
| **después** | after |
| **esta noche** | tonight |
| **finalmente** | finally |
| **más tarde** | later |
| **por último** | lastly |
| **siempre** | always |

**REPASO: ¿A qué hora... ?, ayer, anteayer, hoy, luego, mañana, pasado mañana, por la mañana/tarde/noche**

## Los lugares

| | |
|---|---|
| **el centro** | downtown |
| **el jardín** | garden |

| | |
|---|---|
| **el lago** | lake |
| **el mar** | sea |
| **la montaña** | mountain |
| **el parque** | park |
| **la preparatoria** | prep school; high school |
| **el río** | river |

**PALABRAS SEMEJANTES: el campus, el laboratorio**

**REPASO: la playa**

## Los números ordinales
Ordinal Numbers

| | |
|---|---|
| **primer, primero/a** | first |
| **segundo/a** | second |
| **tercer, tercero/a** | third |
| **cuarto/a** | fourth |
| **quinto/a** | fifth |
| **sexto/a** | sixth |
| **séptimo/a** | seventh |
| **octavo/a** | eighth |
| **noveno/a** | ninth |
| **décimo/a** | tenth |

## Las descripciones

| | |
|---|---|
| **actual** | present-day |
| **algún, alguno/a** | some |
| **buen, bueno/a** | good |
| **deportivo/a** | sport related |
| **europeo/a** | European |
| **próximo/a** | next |
| **solo/a** | alone |

**PALABRAS SEMEJANTES: atractivo/a, importante, industrial, liberado/a, macho/a, perfecto/a, romántico/a, tradicional, violento/a**

**REPASO: aburrido/a, interesante**

## Otros verbos útiles Other Useful Verbs

| | |
|---|---|
| **abrir** | to open |
| **bajar** | to go down |
| **cerrar (ie)** | to close |
| **cierran** | they close |
| **contestar** | to answer |
| **empezar (ie)** | to start, begin |
| **llegar** | to arrive |
| **manejar** | to drive |
| **nacer** | to be born |
| **ofrecer** | to offer |
| **recibir** | to receive |
| **ser** | to be |

**REPASO: hablar, leer**

## Los sustantivos Nouns

| | |
|---|---|
| **el almuerzo** | lunch |
| **el árbol** | tree |
| **el billar** | billiards, pool |
| **el boliche** | bowling |
| **el café** | coffee |
| **el descanso** | break |
| **el deseo** | wish |
| **el estereotipo** | stereotype |
| **la(s) flor(es)** | flower(s) |
| **la(s) hoja(s)** | leaf/leaves |
| **la misa** | Mass |
| **los (pantalones) vaqueros** | jeans |
| **el pasatiempo** | hobby |
| **la película** | film, movie |
| **la red mundial** | Internet |
| **la respuesta** | answer |
| **la revista** | magazine |
| **el té** | tea |
| **la temporada** | season |
| **el tiempo libre** | free time |

**PALABRAS SEMEJANTES: el animal, el área, el cereal, el fútbol americano, el grupo, la invitación, la lista, la música rock, la novela, el plan / los planes, las preferencias, el presente, la radio, el semestre, el trimestre**

## Palabras del texto

| | |
|---|---|
| **conversar** | to converse |
| **converse(n)** | converse (*command*) |
| **decidir** | to decide |
| **decida(n)** | decide (*command*) |
| **siguiente** | following |
| **la tabla** | table (graph) |

**PALABRAS SEMEJANTES: asociar, el caso, la columna, la conversación, la definición, describir, inventar, la narración, la ocasión, organizar, la palabra, representar**

## Palabras y expresiones útiles

| | |
|---|---|
| **aquí** | here |
| **en general** | in general |
| **fue** | (it) was |
| **más/menos** | more (most) / less (least) |
| **Nos vemos.** | See you. |
| **por** | by, for |
| **¿Por qué... ?** | Why . . . ? |
| **¡Qué buena idea!** | What a good idea! |
| **solamente** | only |
| **el tren** | train |
| **¿Verdad?** | Isn't that true? |

# Gramática y ejercicios

## 2.1 Expressing Future Plans: *ir* + *a* + Infinitive

**ir** = *to go*
**¿Qué vas a hacer esta noche?** (*What are you going to do tonight?*)
**Voy a estudiar.** (*I'm going to study.*)

The most common way of expressing future plans is to use the verb **ir** (*to go*) plus the preposition **a** (*to*) followed by an infinitive. This construction is commonly referred to as the *informal future*, because Spanish has another future tense, generally reserved for talking about more long-term future plans.*

| | |
|---|---|
| —¿Qué **vas a hacer** mañana? | —*What are you going to do tomorrow?* |
| —**Voy a esquiar.** | —*I am going to ski.* |
| —¿Qué **van a hacer** ustedes este fin de semana? | —*What are you going to do this weekend?* |
| —**Vamos a ir** al cine. | —*We're going to go to the movies.* |
| —¿Qué **van a hacer** Esteban y Alberto después de la clase? | —*What are Steven and Al going to do after class?* |
| —**Van a jugar** al basquetbol. | —*They're going to play basketball.* |

Here are the forms of the irregular verb **ir**.†

| **ir** (*to go*) | | |
|---|---|---|
| (yo) | voy | *I am going* |
| (tú) | vas | *you (inf. sing.) are going* |
| (usted, él/ella) | va | *you (pol. sing.) are going; he/she is going* |
| (nosotros/as) | vamos | *we are going* |
| (vosotros/as) | vais | *you (inf. pl., Spain) are going* |
| (ustedes, ellos/as) | van | *you (pl.) are going; they are going* |

### Ejercicio 1

A continuación tiene usted una conversación sobre los planes de algunos compañeros de clase. Complete las oraciones con las formas correctas del verbo **ir**.

MODELO: Luis *va* a hacer ejercicio en el parque.

1. —¿Qué _____ a hacer tú después de la clase?
   —(Yo) _____ a ir de compras con una amiga.

*See the **Expansión gramatical** in your *Cuaderno de trabajo* for information about the future tense.
†Recognition: **vos vas**

2. —¿Y qué _____ a hacer Esteban y Carmen?
   —Esteban _____ a estudiar y Carmen _____ a trabajar.
3. —¿Y la profesora Martínez? ¿Qué _____ a hacer ella?
   —Creo que _____ a leer la tarea de sus estudiantes, pero nosotros _____a ir al cine.
4. —Pablo, ¿cuándo _____ a estudiar tú?
   —(Yo) _____ a estudiar más tarde, probablemente esta noche.
5. —¿Y tú, Alberto? ¿Cuándo _____ a hacer la tarea para la clase de español?
   —(Yo) _____ a hacer mi tarea mañana por la mañana.

## 2.2 Sequencing: Ordinal Adjectives

**primer, primero/a** = *first*
**segundo/a** = *second*
**tercer, tercero/a** = *third*
**cuarto/a** = *fourth*
**quinto/a** = *fifth*
**sexto/a** = *sixth*
**séptimo/a** = *seventh*
**octavo/a** = *eighth*
**noveno/a** = *ninth*
**décimo/a** = *tenth*

Ordinal adjectives are used to put things and people into a sequence or order. The ordinals in English are *first*, *second*, *third*, *fourth*, and so on. Here are the ordinals from *first* to *tenth* in Spanish.

| | |
|---|---|
| primero/a | sexto/a |
| segundo/a | séptimo/a |
| tercero/a | octavo/a |
| cuarto/a | noveno/a |
| quinto/a | décimo/a |

| | |
|---|---|
| Mi **segunda** clase es difícil. | *My second class is difficult* |

As with **uno** (*one*), the words **primero** and **tercero** drop the final **-o** when used before a masculine singular noun.

| | |
|---|---|
| Estoy en el **primer** (**tercer**) **año.** | *I am in the first* (*third*) *grade.* |

### Ejercicio 2

Conteste las preguntas según el dibujo.

1. ¿Quién es la primera persona*?
2. ¿Quién es la segunda persona?
3. ¿Es Guillermo la quinta?
4. ¿Es Amanda la primera?
5. ¿Es doña Lola la tercera?
6. ¿Quién es la sexta persona?
7. Don Anselmo es la quinta persona, ¿verdad?
8. ¿Quién es el primer hombre?
9. ¿Quién es la segunda mujer?
10. ¿Es don Anselmo el tercer hombre?

*__Persona__ is a feminine word, even when it refers to a man.

**preferir** = *to prefer, would rather*
**querer** = *to want*
**¿Qué quieres hacer ahora?** (*What do you want to do now?*)
**Quiero descansar.** (*I want to rest.*)
**¿Qué prefieres hacer?** (*What do you prefer to do?* [*What would you rather do?*])
**Prefiero comer ahora.** (*I prefer to eat now.*)

## 2.3 Stating Preferences and Desires: *preferir* and *querer* + Infinitive

The verbs **preferir*** (*to prefer, would rather*) and **querer*** (*to want*) are used to express preferences and desires. They are often followed by an infinitive. (Remember that infinitives are the non-conjugated verb forms that end in **-ar, -er,** or **-ir.**)

| | |
|---|---|
| —¿Qué **quieres** hacer este invierno? | —*What do you want to do this winter?* |
| —**Quiero** esquiar. | —*I want to ski.* |
| —¿Qué **prefiere** hacer Pablo? | —*What does Paul prefer to do?* |
| —**Prefiere** viajar. | —*He would rather travel.* |

Note that the **e** of the stem of these verbs changes to **ie**, except in the **nosotros/as** and **vosotros/as** forms.†

| | **querer** (*to want*) | **preferir** (*to prefer*) | |
|---|---|---|---|
| (yo) | quiero | prefiero | *I want/prefer* |
| (tú) | quieres | prefieres | *you (inf. sing.) want/prefer* |
| (usted, él/ella) | quiere | prefiere | *you (pol. sing.) want/prefer; he/she wants/prefers* |
| (nosotros/as) | queremos | preferimos | *we want/prefer* |
| (vosotros/as) | queréis | preferís | *you (inf. pl., Spain) want/prefer* |
| (ustedes, ellos/as) | quieren | prefieren | *you (pl.) want/prefer; they want/prefer* |

### Ejercicio 3

Complete estas oraciones según el modelo.

MODELO: Nora *quiere* patinar, pero Luis *prefiere* jugar al tenis.

1. Yo _____ ir al cine, pero Esteban _____ salir a bailar.
2. Nora _____ver la televisión, pero Alberto _____ ir de compras.
3. Lan _____ pasear por el parque, pero yo _____ dormir todo el día.
4. Nora _____ comer comida china, pero Carmen y Pablo _____ cocinar en casa.
5. Mónica _____ dar una fiesta, pero Alberto _____ bailar en una discoteca.
6. El padre de Esteban _____ acampar, pero yo _____ ir a la playa.
7. Carmen _____ sacar fotos, pero Lan _____ escribir una carta.
8. Luis _____ dibujar, pero yo _____ tocar la guitarra.
9. Mónica y Pablo _____ ir a pasear por el centro, pero yo _____ dormir toda la tarde.
10. Luis y Alberto _____ descansar, pero Esteban _____ leer el periódico.

---

*Recognition: **vos preferís, querés**
†Verbs like **preferir** and **querer** that use more than one stem in their conjugation are known as *irregular verbs.* You will learn more about this type of verb beginning in **Gramática 3.3.**

## Ejercicio 4

¿Qué quieren hacer estas personas? Conteste según el modelo.

MODELO: ¿Qué quiere hacer Guillermo? → *Quiere jugar al basquetbol.*

1. ¿Qué quiere hacer Ernestito?

2. ¿Qué prefiere hacer el señor Ramírez?

3. ¿Qué quieren hacer Estela y Andrea?

4. Luis y Nora, ¿qué prefieren hacer ustedes?

5. ¿Qué prefieren hacer Diego y Rafael?

6. ¿Qué quiere hacer Amanda?

## Ejercicio 5

Escriba los planes y las preferencias de estas personas.

| | PLANES | | PREFERENCIAS/DESEOS |
|---|---|---|---|
| MODELO: Nora | *va a leer* | pero | *prefiere (quiere) dormir.* |

1. Lan

2. Carmen

**3.** Esteban

**4.** Alberto

**5.** Pablo

**6.** Mi compañera

**7.** Yo

## 2.4 Describing the Weather: Common Expressions

Spanish speakers use several verbs to describe weather conditions.

Most Spanish weather expressions use either **hacer** or **haber**.
**Hace frío.** (*It's cold.*)
**Hace calor.** (*It's hot.*)
**Hace buen/mal tiempo.** (*The weather is good/bad.*)
**Hay neblina.** (*It's foggy.*)

But to talk about resultant states, use **estar** + adjective.
**Está nublado.** (*It's cloudy.*)

**Nevar** and **llover** use just the verb.
**Nieva.** (*It's snowing.* [*It snows.*])
**Llueve.** (*It's raining.* [*It rains.*])

**A.** If a weather expression refers to a phenomenon that can be felt (good weather, heat, cold, wind), use **hacer**.

| | |
|---|---|
| —¿Qué tiempo **hace** hoy? | —*What's the weather like today?* |
| —**Hace frío.** | —*It's cold.* |

Other weather expressions with **hacer** are **hace calor** (*it's hot*), **hace buen/mal tiempo** (*the weather is good/bad*), **hace viento** (*it's windy*), **hace sol** (*it's sunny*), and **hace fresco** (*it's cool*).

**B.** If a weather expression refers to a phenomenon that can be seen, use **haber**.

| | |
|---|---|
| —**Hay neblina** por la costa. | —*It's foggy* (*There is fog*) *along the coast.* |
| —**Hay nubes** hoy. | —*It's cloudy* (*There are clouds*) *today.* |

**C.** For resultant states (that is, conditions that result from a specific phenomenon, such as **Hay nubes** or **Hace sol**), use **estar** with the appropriate adjective.

| | |
|---|---|
| —**Está nublado** hoy. | —*It's cloudy today.* |
| —**Está soleado** en las montañas. | —*It's sunny in the mountains.* |

**D.** To talk about rain and snow, use only the corresponding verb (**llover** or **nevar**).

| | |
|---|---|
| —Siempre **llueve** aquí por la tarde. | —*It always rains here in the afternoon.* |
| —**Nieva** mucho en Montana. | —*It snows a lot in Montana.* |

Note in all of these weather expressions that Spanish does not use a pronoun corresponding to English *it*.

## Ejercicio 6

Diga qué tiempo hace.

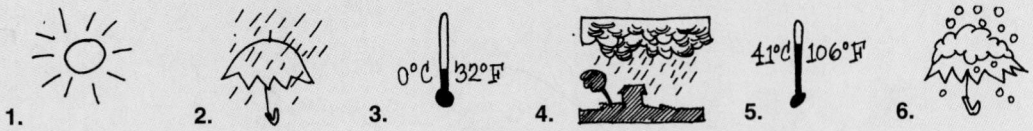


## Ejercicio 7

Diga si son posibles o imposibles estas combinaciones.

1. —¿Hace sol?
   —Sí, y también hace calor.
2. —¿Hace mal tiempo?
   —Sí, y llueve mucho.
3. —¿Hace buen tiempo?
   —Sí, y hace mucho frío.
4. —¿Hace calor?
   —Sí, y también nieva.
5. —¿Hace frío?
   —Sí, y también hace mucho calor.

CAPÍTULO 3

# Las actividades y los lugares

**METAS**

In **Capítulo 3** you will discuss daily activities as well as activities happening at the moment. You will also talk about places on your campus and about where you and others are from.

Tegucigalpa, Honduras

**ACTIVIDADES DE COMUNICACIÓN Y LECTURAS**


¿Dónde está?

**Lectura** Una tarjeta postal desde Madrid

Las actividades diarias

**Lectura** Los amigos hispanos: Adela Martínez

**El mundo hispano...** imágenes

¿De dónde es usted?

**El mundo hispano...** su gente

**Nota cultural** Los hispanos en los Estados Unidos

Las actividades del momento

**El mundo hispano...** en los Estados Unidos

**EN RESUMEN**


**GRAMÁTICA Y EJERCICIOS**


3.1 Locating People and Objects: **estar**

3.2 Talking About Habitual Actions: Present Tense of Regular Verbs

3.3 Using Irregular Verbs: **hacer, salir, jugar**

3.4 Describing Origin and Location: **ser de / estar en**

3.5 Referring to Actions in Progress: Present Progressive

# Actividades de comunicación y lecturas

## ¿Dónde está?

*Lea Gramática 3.1.*

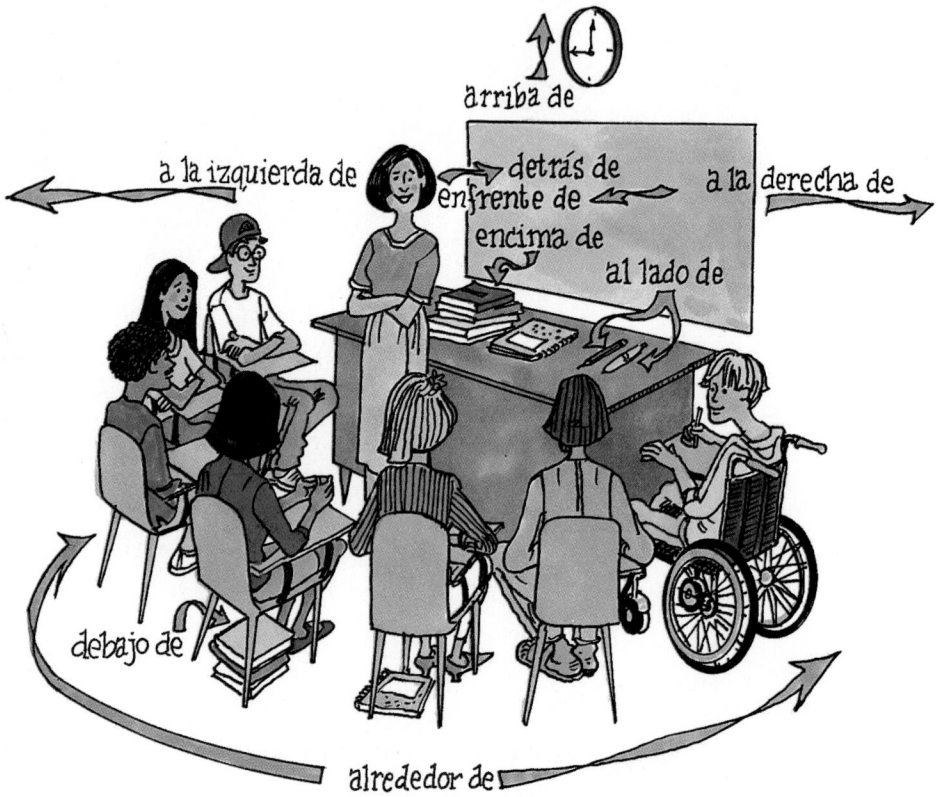


### Actividad 1. Intercambios: La Universidad Estatal del Oriente

Mire el plano de la página siguiente. Escuche mientras su profesor(a) describe dónde están varios edificios. Escriba el nombre del edificio en el espacio en blanco.

**Edificios**: la biblioteca, la cafetería, la Facultad de Ciencias Sociales, la Facultad de Medicina, el gimnasio, el teatro

Ahora, pregúntele a su compañero/a dónde están los edificios en el plano.

MODELOS: E1: ¿Dónde está *el teatro*?
E2: Está *enfrente de la Facultad de Bellas Artes.*

E1: ¿En qué calle está *la cafetería*?
E2: Está en la *avenida de las Rosas, enfrente de la librería.*

LA·UNIVERSIDAD·ESTATAL·DEL·ORIENTE

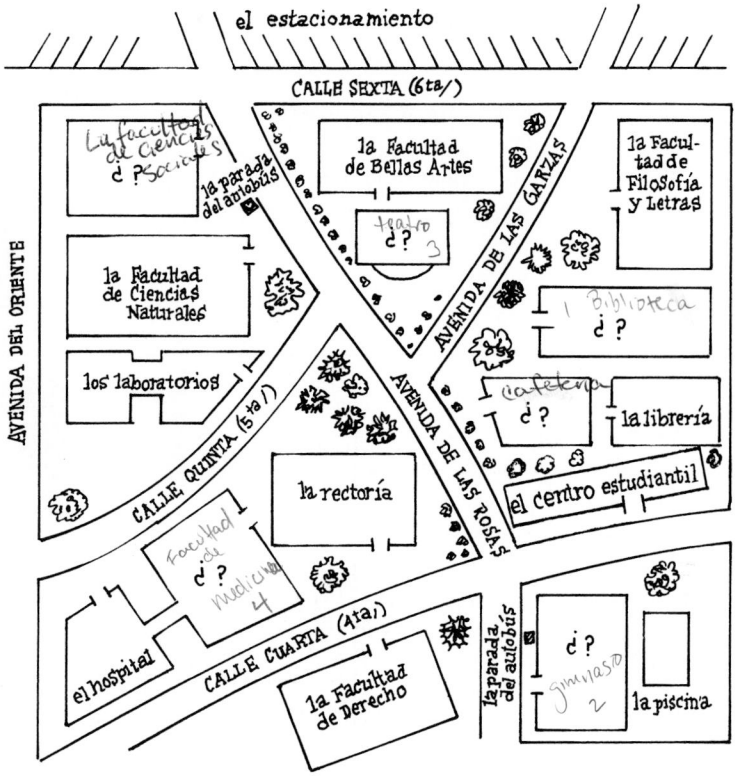


## Actividad 2. Diálogo abierto: Las clases

E1: Hola, _____. ¿Tienes clases hoy?
E2: Sí, tengo _____ y _____.
E1: ¿Dónde?
E2: En el edificio de _____.
E1: ¿Dónde está ese edificio?
E2: Está al lado del / de la _____.

## Actividad 3. Entrevista: En nuestra universidad

Pregúntele a su compañero/a dónde están los siguientes lugares en su universidad. Use **al lado de, enfrente de, detrás de, entre, en el edificio de...**

MODELO: E1: ¿Dónde está *la cafetería*?
E2: Está *detrás de...*

1. la biblioteca
2. el gimnasio
3. la librería
4. el teatro
5. la Facultad de _____
6. ¿ ?

# Una tarjeta postal desde Madrid

**VOCABULARIO ÚTIL**

| | |
|---|---|
| fue | *was* |
| manda | *she sends* |
| Estoy ansiosa por | *I'm looking forward to* |

Clara Martin es una joven norteamericana que ahora estudia en Madrid. El año pasado Clara fue estudiante de la profesora Martínez; gracias a esa clase, ahora Clara habla muy bien el español.

Ésta es la primera tarjeta postal que Clara manda a su profesora. ¡Adela Martínez va a recibir muchas postales más!

Estimada profesora:

¡Por fin estoy en Madrid! Es una ciudad muy grande y tiene mucho más tráfico que San Antonio. Estoy ansiosa por verlo todo. Me gusta mucho el Parque del Retiro. ¡Y el Museo del Prado es impresionante! Esta tarjeta es de la Plaza Mayor, un lugar interesante adonde va mucha gente a tomar café y a conversar. (Es mi lugar favorito.) Bueno, hasta muy pronto.

Un abrazo,

Clara

P.D. ¡Estoy hablando muchísimo español!

MADRID CCP-CHAMARTIN 27 de septiembre 1997 28

12 PTA ESPAÑA

Prof. Adela Martínez
Department of Foreign Languages
University of Texas at San Antonio
San Antonio, TX 78285
USA

Madrid, España

## Comprensión

¿Cierto o falso? Si la oración es falsa, haga las correcciones necesarias.

1. San Antonio tiene menos tráfico que Madrid.
2. Clara va a ver pocos lugares.
3. Clara no practica mucho el español en Madrid.
4. El lugar favorito de Clara es el Museo del Prado.
5. En la Plaza Mayor la gente toma café y conversa.

## Ahora... ¡usted!

1. Cuando usted viaja, ¿les manda tarjetas postales a su familia y amigos? Por lo general, ¿le gusta escribir mucho en las postales o prefiere decir poco?
2. ¿Le gusta recibir tarjetas postales de sus amigos y familiares cuando viajan? ¿Por qué?

## Un paso más... ¡a escribir!

**A.** Imagínese que usted está de vacaciones y que va a mandarle una tarjeta postal a alguna persona. ¿Quién es esa persona? ¿Qué va a decirle? Use la tarjeta de Clara como guía y... ¡escriba!

Querido/a _____:

Por fin estoy en _____. Es un lugar muy _____ y tiene _____. Me gusta mucho _____. Esta tarjeta postal es de _____.

Hasta muy pronto.

Un abrazo,

(*su firma aquí*)

P.D. ¡_____!

**B.** Ahora, léale el texto de su tarjeta postal a su compañero/a, ¡pero no mencione el lugar! Su compañero/a va a tratar de adivinar ese detalle.

# Las actividades diarias

*Lea Gramática 3.2–3.3.*

## Un día típico en la vida de la familia Ramírez

Ernesto lee el periódico todas las mañanas.

Los Ramírez y sus hijos desayunan juntos.

Ernesto sale de la casa a las 8:30.

Amanda y sus hermanos caminan al parque.

Ernesto espera el autobús.

Guillermo juega al fútbol con sus amigos.

Berta limpia la casa.

Estela prepara la cena.

La familia Ramírez cena a las 8:00.

## Actividad 4. Intercambios: Las actividades diarias

MODELOS: E1: ¿Quién *va a misa*?
E2: *Silvia.*

E1: ¿Cuándo *hace ejercicio Mayín*?
E2: *Los viernes por la mañana.*

| | SILVIA BUSTAMANTE MÉXICO, D.F. | ADRIANA BOLINI BUENOS AIRES | MAYÍN DURÁN LOS ÁNGELES |
|---|---|---|---|
| lun., por la mañana | va en metro al trabajo | va en carro a su oficina | va en coche a la estación de radio |
| mié., por la tarde | trabaja en la estación de autobuses | trabaja con una computadora | escribe un reportaje |
| vie., por la mañana | estudia | asiste a una reunión | hace ejercicio en el gimnasio |
| sáb., por la mañana | lleva su ropa a la lavandería | pasea por el parque | lee el periódico |
| dom., por la mañana | va a misa | juega al tenis | ve la televisión |

## Actividad 5. Asociaciones: Las actividades típicas

¿Cuáles son las actividades típicas de estas personas?

1. un profesor / una profesora
2. un hombre / una mujer de negocios
3. una ama de casa
4. un(a) estudiante

**Actividades posibles:** almuerza en un restaurante, charla con un amigo en la cafetería, cocina, habla por teléfono, lee las tareas de los estudiantes, lee una revista, limpia la casa, prepara las lecciones, trabaja en su oficina, va a la biblioteca

## Actividad 6. Narración: Un día en la vida de Carla Espinosa

### PALABRAS ÚTILES

primero
luego
entonces

después
más tarde
¿A qué hora?
A la(s)...

finalmente
por último

## Actividad 7. Preferencias: ¿Con qué frecuencia?

Diga con qué frecuencia usted hace estas actividades durante la semana. Use **siempre, con frecuencia, a veces, varias veces** y **nunca**.

1. Veo la televisión por la noche.
2. Salgo a cenar con amigos.
3. Juego al basquetbol.
4. Voy al cine.
5. Lavo el carro.
6. Hago ejercicio aeróbico.
7. Preparo la cena.
8. Como en el carro.
9. Escucho la radio mientras estudio.
10. Tomo refrescos.

## Actividad 8. Asociaciones: Las actividades de mi familia

En su familia, ¿quién hace las siguientes actividades?

MODELOS: estudia(n) en la universidad →
*Mis hermanos* estudian en la universidad.

trabaja(n) los sábados →
*Nadie* en mi familia trabaja los sábados.

1. sale(n) mucho con sus amigos
2. esquía(n) en el invierno
3. ve(n) la televisión
4. va(n) al cine los fines de semana
5. lee(n) el periódico por la mañana
6. escucha(n) música clásica
7. trabaja(n) los sábados
8. nada(n) en el verano

## Actividad 9. Entrevista: El fin de semana

GENERALMENTE LOS VIERNES POR LA NOCHE...

1. ¿Sales con tus amigos? ¿Vas al cine? ¿Vas a una discoteca o a un club?
2. ¿Trabajas? ¿Hasta qué hora?
3. ¿Cenas en algún restaurante?
4. ¿Lees un libro?
5. ¿Vas a (Das) una fiesta? ¿Dónde? ¿Con quién(es)?

GENERALMENTE LOS SÁBADOS...

6. ¿Practicas algún deporte? ¿Cuál prefieres?
7. ¿Ves la televisión? ¿Qué programas te gustan?
8. ¿Vas de compras? ¿Adónde?
9. ¿Trabajas? ¿Dónde? ¿Cuántas horas?
10. ¿Estudias? ¿Dónde? ¿Con quién(es)?

## Actividad 10. Entrevista: La música

1. ¿Escuchas mucho la radio? ¿Cuándo y dónde? ¿En casa? ¿En el carro? ¿Los fines de semana? ¿Por la mañana?
2. ¿Qué clase de música prefieres? ¿Qué emisora escuchas, generalmente?
3. ¿Cuáles son tus artistas preferidos?
4. ¿Prefieres escuchar la radio o poner discos compactos?

# Los amigos hispanos: Adela Martínez

**VOCABULARIO ÚTIL**

| | |
|---|---|
| la política | *politics* |
| de vez en cuando | *once in a while* |
| me pone | *makes me* |
| le hago la lucha | *I try* |
| estadounidense | *U.S. citizen* |

La profesora Martínez nació en San Antonio, Texas, de padres mexicanos. Ella habla aquí de sus actividades favoritas y de su trabajo de verano en Guanajuato, México. A Adela le gusta conversar con los amigos, montar a caballo, escuchar música, tocar la guitarra y cantar.

¡Hola! Ya saben que soy profesora. Me gusta mucho enseñar español, pero no quiero hablarles solamente de mi trabajo. Voy a contarles, primero, de mis pasatiempos y de las actividades que hago en mi tiempo libre. Uno de mis pasatiempos favoritos es conversar con los amigos en algún café o restaurante. Los temas que más discutimos —¡y siempre con entusiasmo!— son la cultura hispana, la literatura y la política internacional. Pero también hablamos de cosas personales.

De vez en cuando monto a caballo; es un pasatiempo muy divertido. En mi tiempo libre, también escucho música. Creo que tengo un gusto bastante variado: me gusta la música clásica, la folclórica y la popular. Cuando estoy triste, toco la guitarra y canto. ¡La guitarra siempre me pone contenta! A mis estudiantes les fascina escucharme cantar canciones tradicionales como «Cielito lindo». Les confieso que no canto muy bien, pero, como dicen los mexicanos, le hago la lucha.

Durante los veranos enseño español en la ciudad de Guanajuato, México. Guanajuato es la capital del estado del mismo nombre, que está en el centro del país. Es una ciudad pequeña, muy hermosa, de aspecto colonial y con una historia muy interesante. En Guanajuato es fácil llegar a todas partes y la gente es muy amable y amistosa. Es la ciudad ideal para los cursos de verano, creo yo.

Me gustan mucho mis cursos de verano, además, porque llegan a mis clases personas de diferentes países. Normalmente tengo estudiantes árabes, chinos, japoneses, franceses y un gran número de canadienses y estadounidenses. Juntos hacemos excursiones, visitamos los museos y salimos por la noche a bailar. A veces los invito a mi casa a merendar. ¡Cuánto les gusta hablar de México cuando vienen a mi casa!

## Comprensión

Complete los siguientes comentarios. ¡Cuidado! A veces hay más de una respuesta correcta.

1. Cuando la profesora Martínez está triste...
   a. conversa con sus amigos en algún café.
   b. toca la guitarra y canta.
   c. monta a caballo.

2. La profesora viaja a Guanajuato todos los veranos porque...
   a. enseña un curso de español en esa ciudad.
   b. sus padres viven en Guanajuato.
   c. no hay cursos de verano en otras ciudades.

3. A los estudiantes de la profesora Martínez les gusta escucharla cantar porque...
   a. ella tiene una voz de soprano fantástica.
   b. ella sabe cantar canciones mexicanas muy bonitas.
   c. con la música, ellos pueden comprender la cultura de México.

4. A la profesora le gusta tener tiempo libre porque...
   a. entonces sale a cenar con sus amigos.
   b. necesita escribir libros sobre la política mexicana.
   c. detesta su trabajo.

## Ahora... ¡usted!

1. ¿Qué le gusta hacer, generalmente, durante los veranos? ¿estudiar? ¿trabajar? ¿viajar?

2. Compare las actividades de Adela Martínez con las actividades de verano que a usted le gusta hacer.
3. ¿Le gustaría viajar a otro país para estudiar? ¿Adónde le gustaría ir? ¿Por qué?

## Un paso más... ¡a escribir!

Describa la ciudad donde usted nació o la ciudad donde vive ahora. Utilice como guía la descripción de Guanajuato que hace Adela Martínez. Para empezar, ¿es grande o pequeña su ciudad? ¿Cómo se llama? ¿En qué estado del país está? Describa a la gente de allí: ¿es amistosa, indiferente, alegre, amable? Termine su descripción con esta oración: *Mi ciudad es ideal para...*

## EL MUNDO HISPANO... imágenes

En muchas ciudades hispanas, como Guanajuato, México, se conservan los edificios y la arquitectura de la época colonial. Guanajuato es una ciudad muy hermosa. Es famosa en todo el mundo hispano por su Festival de Teatro Cervantino,[1] que se celebra todos los años en octubre.

Un sitio muy interesante —¡y diferente!— en Guanajuato es el Museo del Panteón.[2] Allí se exhíben muchas momias;[3] algunas son del siglo[4] pasado, pero también hay varias más recientes. ¿Cómo es posible esto? Bueno, se dice que la tierra de Guanajuato contiene minerales que conservan intactos los cadáveres. ¡Es algo fantástico!

[1] *Theater festival named after the great Spanish writer Miguel de Cervantes (1547–1616), author of* Don Quijote. [2] *Located on a hilll outside the city, this museum is also known as* El museo de las momias, *the Museum of the Mummies.* [3] *mummies* [4] *century*

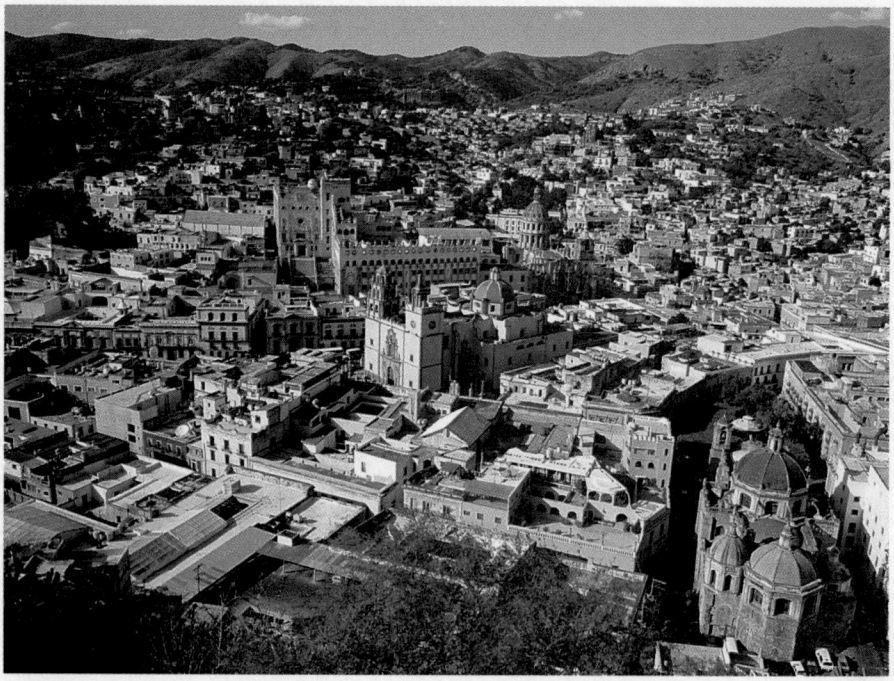

Guanajuato, México

# ¿De dónde es usted?

*Lea Gramática 3.4.*

La presencia hispana en los Estados Unidos es fuerte y se expresa de muchas formas. En la foto, un mural hispano en el distrito de La Misión (*Mission District*) de la ciudad de San Francisco, California.

## Actividad 11. Diálogo: ¿De dónde eres tú?

ROGELIO: Buenos días. Yo soy Rogelio Varela. ¿Cómo te llamas?
MARTA: Me llamo Marta Guerrero. ¿De dónde eres tú?
ROGELIO: Soy de aquí, de San Juan. ¿Y tú?
MARTA: Soy de México, pero vivo en San Juan ahora.

## Actividad 12. Entrevista: ¿De dónde...?

1. E1: ¿De dónde eres?
   E2: Soy de _____.
2. E1: ¿De dónde es tu padre?
   E2: Es de _____.
3. E1: ¿De dónde es tu madre?
   E2: Es de _____.
4. E1: ¿Tienes algún amigo de otro país?
   E2: Sí, tengo un amigo / una amiga de _____.
5. E1: ¿Cómo se llama tu amigo/a?
   E2: Se llama _____.

## EL MUNDO HISPANO... su gente

María Diana Suárez tiene 17 años y es costarricense.

*¿Qué tipo de música le gusta más?*

Escucho todo tipo de música, pero me gusta más el rock en inglés y en español. Mis cantantes favoritos son Luis Miguel[1] y Whitney Houston. Y mis conjuntos[2] favoritos son Green Day y Los Sobraos.[3] Me gusta la música latina —la salsa, el merengue[4]— por su ritmo y su sabor,[5] y porque es nuestra. ¡Amo toda la música!

[1]Luis Miguel es un famoso cantante mexicano que canta canciones románticas. (*In 1994, Luis Miguel recorded "Come Fly With Me" with Frank Sinatra for* Duets II, *Sinatra's second collection of duets with renowned American and international performers.*) [2]grupos musicales [3]Conjunto español; sus alegres canciones son una combinación de rock, música de baile y ritmos flamencos; su disco más popular es *Rumba mola* (1996). [4]La salsa y el merengue son parte de la música tradicional del Caribe. [5]*energy, vitality* (lit., *flavor*)

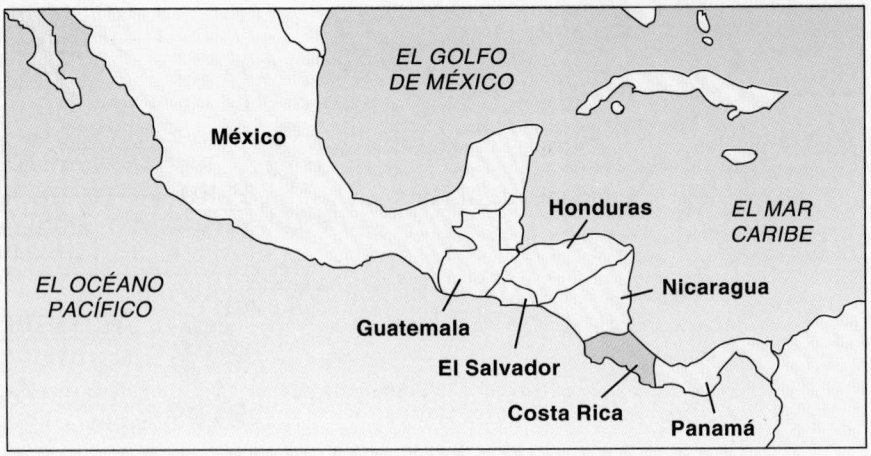

NOTA CULTURAL

**VOCABULARIO ÚTIL**

| | |
|---|---|
| la comunidad | *community* |
| los campos | *fields* |
| se encuentran | *are found* |
| sea cual sea | *whatever might be* |

# Los hispanos en los Estados Unidos

La palabra *Hispanic* se usa con frecuencia para describir a todos los hispanos que viven en los Estados Unidos. Pero dentro de la comunidad hispana hay personas de varios países que forman grupos diferentes, como los mexicoamericanos y los puertorriqueños. En esta lectura se describen estos grupos y otros que también son hispanos.

Jackson Heights, Ciudad de Nueva York

Los hispanos que viven en los Estados Unidos contribuyen de manera importante a la vida cultural y social de este país. Los más famosos trabajan en el mundo artístico —el cine, la música— y en los deportes. Pero también están presentes en otros campos, como la política y la educación, por ejemplo.

Hay hispanos en casi todas las ciudades estadounidenses. Algunos son emigrantes de España, muchos otros de toda América Latina. Los hispanos en los Estados Unidos forman cuatro grandes grupos. Es importante saber cuáles son, pues cada uno tiene una historia interesante y muy particular.

El primer grupo es el de los **mexicoamericanos** o **chicanos**, que viven principalmente en el suroeste, en los estados de California, Nuevo México, Arizona, Texas y Colorado. Dentro de esta población hay descendientes de los primeros exploradores españoles.

El segundo grupo lo forman los **puertorriqueños**, muchos de los cuales viven en Nueva York. Y los **cubanos** forman el tercer grupo; éstos residen en varios estados, pero especialmente en la Florida, Nueva Jersey y California. El cuarto grupo es el de los **centroamericanos**, que se encuentran en California y los estados del este. Por ejemplo, en la ciudad de Takoma Park, Maryland, y en el área de Washington, D.C., hay una comunidad muy grande de **salvadoreños**.

Hay 24 millones de hispanos en los Estados Unidos. Dentro de este enorme grupo, existe una gran variedad de culturas y de historias nacionales. A algunos hispanos les gusta llamarse *Hispanic* o *Hispanic American*; otros usan las palabras *Latino* y *U.S. Latino*; también hay los que prefieren especificar su nacionalidad: salvadoreño, cubano o salvadoreñoamericano y cubanoamericano.

Sea cual sea la palabra preferida, la presencia de esta comunidad —y de cada uno de sus grupos— es cada día más visible y relevante en los Estados Unidos.

## Comprensión

**A.** Diga qué grupo(s) de hispanos predomina(n) en cada ciudad.

| CIUDAD | GRUPO(S) | CIUDAD | GRUPO(S) | CIUDAD | GRUPO(S) |
|---|---|---|---|---|---|
| Houston | _____ | Nueva York | _____ | Los Ángeles | _____ |
| Miami | _____ | Albuquerque | _____ | Takoma Park | _____ |

**B.** ¿Quién habla en cada caso? Indique si es una persona mexicanoamericana (**M**), puertorriqueña (**P**) o cubanoamericana (**C**).

1. _____ Vivo en Nuevo México; mi familia y yo somos descendientes de los primeros colonizadores españoles.
2. _____ Soy bilingüe y vivo en Los Ángeles. Mis padres nacieron en Guadalajara.
3. _____ Soy de una isla que es un estado libre asociado. Me consideran ciudadano de los Estados Unidos.
4. _____ Nací en una isla del Caribe. Ahora vivo con muchos de mis compatriotas en Miami.

## Ahora... ¡usted!

1. ¿Tiene amigos hispanos? ¿Son chicanos o de otros grupos?
2. ¿Cuántos hispanos famosos puede mencionar? ¿De qué países son?

### Un paso más... ¡a escribir!

Usando **Comprensión B** como guía, describa a algunos de sus amigos hispanos. Si no tiene ningún amigo hispano, describa a dos hispanos famosos.

# Las actividades del momento

*Lea Gramática 3.5.*

Son las 5:00 de la tarde y éstas son las actividades de algunos de los vecinos mexicanos.

## Actividad 13. Asociaciones: ¿Acciones extrañas?

El gato está buceando.

El caballo está fumando.

El bebé está levantando pesas.

Diga si estas actividades son extrañas o normales. Después, justifique sus respuestas.

1. una muchacha que está caminando
2. un pez que está nadando
3. un caballo que está fumando
4. un bebé que está llorando
5. una profesora que está masticando tabaco en clase
6. un hombre que está planchando
7. un pájaro que está patinando
8. un perro que está ladrando
9. un gato que está buceando
10. un bebé que está levantando pesas

## Actividad 14. Narración: ¿Qué está haciendo Rogelio?

## Actividad 15. Descripción de dibujos: La hora y las actividades

Diga qué están haciendo las siguientes personas y a qué hora. (Diga la hora usando **menos** o **para**.)

MODELO: Son las ocho menos diez y Guillermo está haciendo su tarea. (Son diez para las ocho... )

**1.** Estela

**2.** Guillermo

**3.** Amanda

**4.** Ernesto

**5.** Berta

**6.** Pedro

## EL MUNDO HISPANO... en los Estados Unidos

Ilia Rolón tiene 25 años y nació en Nueva York, de padres puertorriqueños. Ilia vive en la ciudad de Nueva York.

*¿Qué hace usted para divertirse o descansar?*

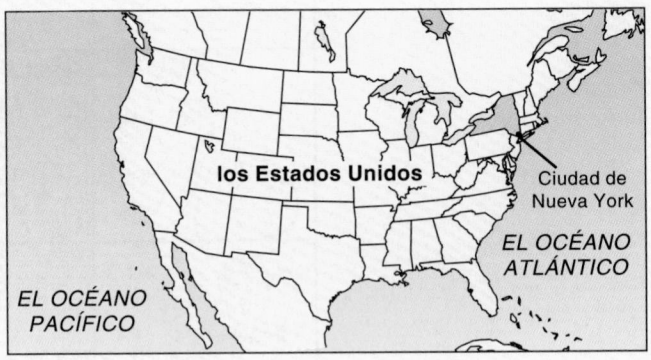


Mi pasatiempo favorito es bailar. Cuando estoy bailando, ¡se me olvida casi todo![1] No me gusta bailar en pareja[2] porque me es difícil coordinar mis pasos con los pasos de mi pareja. Tengo mi propio estilo de baile con influencia latina y africana. A todo el que me ve bailar le impresiona la sensualidad de mi baile. Como puede imaginar, esto a veces causa malentendidos.[3] Pero yo no bailo para impresionar a nadie. El baile me alegra porque me permite una libertad física de la que carezco[4] en mi vida diaria.

[1]¡se... *I forget almost everything!* [2]en... *with a partner* [3]*misunderstandings* [4]*I lack*

# En resumen

## De todo un poco

**A.** Una encuesta sobre las actividades diarias

Diga qué hace usted a estas horas todos los días.

A las 3:00 p.m., _____.
A las 5:00 p.m., _____.
A las 6:30 p.m., _____.
A las 8:00 p.m., _____.
A las 10:00 p.m., _____.
A las 12:00 (medianoche), _____.

Ahora, compare sus actividades con las de varios compañeros. ¿Hacen ustedes las mismas actividades a la misma hora?

MODELO: E1: A las 12:00 *duermo.*
E2: Yo no, yo *estudio.*

Finalmente, hable con varios compañeros para encontrar una persona que haga las mismas actividades que usted, a la misma hora.

**B.** El mapa de Sudamérica: ¿Dónde están estos países?

Trabajen en grupos de cuatro. Una persona debe leer las instrucciones a continuación; las otras tres personas deben seguir las instrucciones y escribir los nombres de los países en el mapa que el profesor / la profesora va a darles.

INSTRUCCIONES

1. Miren Venezuela. Está al norte, *arriba de* Brasil. Brasil es un país muy grande que está *al lado derecho del* mapa, *debajo de* Venezuela.
2. Ahora vamos a Colombia. Está *al lado izquierdo* de Venezuela.
3. Ahora escriban «Ecuador» en el país muy pequeño que está al sur, *debajo de* Colombia y al lado del Océano Pacífico.
4. *Al lado izquierdo de* Brasil, *en medio del* mapa, está Bolivia. Está *lejos del* mar.
5. *Al lado izquierdo de* Brasil y *debajo de* Ecuador y Colombia, escriban «Perú.» Este país está *entre* Brasil, Bolivia y el Océano Pacífico.
6. *Debajo de* Perú, al sur, está Chile. Éste es un país largo y angosto (delgado). Está *al lado del* Océano Pacífico.
7. *Al lado derecho de* Chile está otro país muy grande, Argentina.
8. *Al lado derecho de* Argentina, y *al lado izquierdo del* Océano Atlántico, está Uruguay. Éste es un país muy pequeño.
9. *Arriba de* Argentina, al norte, y *debajo de* Bolivia y Brasil está otro país pequeño, Paraguay. No está *cerca del* mar.

Ahora, revisen su trabajo con el mapa que está en la página 113.

## ¡Dígalo por escrito!

Los pasatiempos y las actividades

Imagínese que usted acaba de recibir una carta de un(a) estudiante de un pueblo pequeño de México. Él/Ella le pregunta: «¿Cómo pasa usted el tiempo libre?» ¿Qué le va a contestar usted? Primero, trabaje con otros dos o tres compañeros de clase para comentar las actividades en que ustedes participan en su tiempo libre y por qué les gustan esas actividades. ¿Las hacen a solas o con otras personas? ¿Con quién(es)? Después, cada uno de ustedes debe escribirle una carta al / a la estudiante, contestando sus preguntas y también incluyendo algunas preguntas que hacerle a él/ella.

## VIDEOTECA

¿Recuerda usted al estudiante Diego González? Es de los Estados Unidos, pero ahora estudia en la Ciudad de México. En este segmento de video, Diego está en la librería y habla con Lupe, una compañera de clase. ¿Qué pasa entre los dos? ¿Cuál es la materia preferida de Diego? ¿Qué tienen en común Lupe y Diego? Al final del segmento, ¿qué planes hacen? En el Capítulo 3 del *Cuaderno de trabajo* hay más actividades para hacer después de ver el video.

# Vocabulario

### ¿Dónde está... ?

| | |
|---|---|
| **a la derecha/izquierda de** | to the right/left of |
| **al lado de** | to the side of |
| **alrededor de** | around |
| **aquí** | here |
| **arriba de** | above; on top of |
| **cerca de** | close to |
| **debajo de** | under |
| **detrás de** | behind |
| **encima de** | on top of |
| **enfrente de** | in front of |
| **en medio de** | in the middle of |
| **entre** | between |
| **lejos de** | far from |
| **al norte/sur** | to the north/south |
| al este | east |
| al ~~oest~~ oeste | west |

### Los lugares en la universidad

| | |
|---|---|
| **la biblioteca** | library |
| **el edificio** | building |
| **el estacionamiento** | parking lot |
| **la Facultad de Bellas Artes** | School of Fine Arts |
| **la Facultad de Ciencias Naturales** | School of Natural Sciences |
| **la Facultad de Ciencias Sociales** | School of Social Sciences |
| **la Facultad de Derecho** | School of Law |
| **la Facultad de Filosofía y Letras** | School of Humanities |
| **la Facultad de Medicina** | School of Medicine |
| **la librería** | bookstore |

| | |
|---|---|
| **la parada del autobús** | bus stop |
| **la rectoría** | office of the president |
| **el teatro** | theater |

**PALABRAS SEMEJANTES: la cafetería, el gimnasio, el hospital**

**REPASO: el laboratorio**

## Los lugares en la ciudad

| | |
|---|---|
| **la avenida** | avenue |
| **la lavandería** | laundromat |
| **la tienda** | store |

## El origen

| | |
|---|---|
| **¿De dónde es usted (eres tú)?** | Where are you from? |
| **Soy de...** | I am from . . . |
| **¿De dónde es... ?** | Where is . . . from? |
| **Es de...** | He/She is from . . . |

## Los países hispanos y las nacionalidades
Hispanic Countries and Nationalities

| | |
|---|---|
| **Bolivia** | **boliviano/a** |
| **Chile** | **chileno/a** |
| **Colombia** | **colombiano/a** |
| **Costa Rica** | **costarricense** |
| **Cuba** | **cubano/a** |
| **Ecuador** | **ecuatoriano/a** |
| **El Salvador** | **salvadoreño/a** |
| **Guatemala** | **guatemalteco/a** |
| **Honduras** | **hondureño/a** |
| **Nicaragua** | **nicaragüense** |
| **Panamá** | **panameño/a** |
| **Paraguay** | **paraguayo/a** |
| **Perú** | **peruano/a** |
| **Puerto Rico** | **puertorriqueño/a** |
| **la República Dominicana** | **dominicano/a** |
| **Uruguay** | **uruguayo/a** |
| **Venezuela** | **venezolano/a** |

**REPASO: Argentina, argentino/a; Brasil, brasileño/a; España, español(a); México, mexicano/a**

## Otros lugares

| | |
|---|---|
| **el Caribe** | Caribbean |
| **Sudamérica** | South America |

**PALABRAS SEMEJANTES: América Central, el Océano Atlántico, el Océano Pacífico, Portugal**

## Los verbos

| | |
|---|---|
| **asistir (a)** | to attend |
| **bucear** | to skin-dive/scuba dive; to snorkle |
| **caminar** | to walk |
| **ducharse** | to take a shower |
| **esperar** | to wait (for) |
| **fumar** | to smoke |
| **ladrar** | to bark |
| **llorar** | to cry |
| **masticar (chicle)** | to chew (gum) |
| **mirar** | to look |
| **planchar** | to iron |
| **poner discos compactos** | to play CDs |
| **recoger** | to gather, pick up |
| **regresar** | to return |
| **tocar la guitarra** | to play the guitar |
| **tomar (el autobús, una clase)** | to take (the bus, a class) |

**PALABRAS SEMEJANTES: preparar, usar**

**REPASO: desayunar, hablar, levantar pesas, manejar, practicar un deporte**

## Las personas

| | |
|---|---|
| **el ama de casa** | housewife |
| **el hombre / la mujer de negocios** | businessman/businesswoman |
| **nadie** | no one, nobody |
| **el novio / la novia** | boyfriend/girlfriend |

**PALABRAS SEMEJANTES: el/la artista, el/la bebé**

## Los sustantivos

| | |
|---|---|
| **la cama** | bed |
| **la cena** | dinner |
| **el metro** | subway |
| **el pájaro** | bird |
| **el pez** | fish |
| **el refresco** | soft drink |
| **el reportaje** | newspaper report, article |
| **la reunión** | meeting |
| **la tarea** | homework |
| **el trabajo** | work |
| **la vida** | life |

**PALABRAS SEMEJANTES: la acción, el autobús, el club, la ensalada, la estación, el tabaco**

**REPASO: el caballo, la misa**

## ¿Cuándo?

| | |
|---|---|
| **a la misma hora** | at the same time |
| **desde (+ *time*)** | since, from |
| **generalmente** | usually; generally |
| **hasta** | until; up to |
| **mientras** | meanwhile |
| **nunca** | never |
| **todos los días** | everyday |
| **varias veces** | several times |

**REPASO: con frecuencia, esta noche, siempre**

## Los adjetivos

| | |
|---|---|
| **diario/a** | daily |
| **ese (edificio)** | that (building) |
| **extraño/a** | strange |
| **juntos/as** | together |
| **preferido/a** | favorite |

**PALABRAS SEMEJANTES: aeróbico/a, clásico/a, normal, posible, típico/a**

## Palabras del texto

| | |
|---|---|
| **comparar** | to compare |
| **deber (debe)** | should |
| **encontrar** | to find |
| **la encuesta** | survey |
| **el espacio en blanco** | blank (space) |
| **el momento** | moment |
| **revisar** | to check; to revise |
| **revise(n)** | check (*command*) |
| **seguir las instrucciones** | to follow directions |
| **varios/as** | several |

## Palabras y expresiones útiles

| | |
|---|---|
| **¿Dónde... ?** | Where . . . ? |
| **la emisora** | radio station |
| **el estado** | state |
| **esto** | this (in general) |
| **el plano** | map (of a room or city) |
| **¿Qué está haciendo... ?** | What are you (is he/she) doing? |
| **Estoy...** | I am . . . |
| **Está...** | He/She is . . . |

**PALABRA SEMEJANTE: la lección**

# Gramática y ejercicios

## 3.1 Locating People and Objects: *estar*

**Estar** is used for location.
**¿Dónde está Susana?** (*Where is Susan?*)
**Está en casa.** (*She's at home.*)

Use the verb **estar*** (*to be*) to locate people and objects.

| | |
|---|---|
| —¿Dónde **está** la profesora Martínez? | —*Where is Professor Martínez?* |
| —**Está** en clase. | —*She's in class.* |
| —Esteban, ¿dónde **está** su libro? | —*Steve, where is your book?* |
| —**Está** en casa. | —*It's at home.* |

Here are the present-tense forms of the irregular verb **estar**.

**estar** = *to be*

| **estar** (***to be***) | | |
|---|---|---|
| (yo) | est**oy** | *I am* |
| (tú) | est**ás** | *you (inf. sing.) are* |
| (usted, él/ella) | est**á** | *you (pol. sing.) are; he/she is*† |
| (nosotros/as) | est**amos** | *we are* |
| (vosotros/as) | est**áis** | *you (inf. pl., Spain) are* |
| (ustedes, ellos/as) | est**án** | *you (pl.) are; they are* |

### Ejercicio 1

Diga dónde están estas personas.

MODELO: Mi hijo *está* en la escuela.

1. Yo _____ en la biblioteca.
2. Luis y Nora _____ en su clase de biología.
3. Tú _____ en la rectoría.
4. Esteban y yo _____ en el edificio de Ciencias Naturales.
5. La profesora Martínez _____ en su oficina.
6. Nora y yo _____ enfrente del hospital.
7. Esteban, ¿_____ detrás del teatro?
8. Profesora Martínez, ¿_____ usted en la librería ahora?
9. Alberto y Pablo _____ en la universidad.
10. Nosotros _____ aquí en la Facultad de Derecho.

---

*Recognition: **vos estás**
†Remember that there is no Spanish equivalent for the English subject pronoun *it*. The third-person verb form conveys the meaning of *it* as well as of *he* or *she*.

## 3.2 Talking About Habitual Actions: Present Tense of Regular Verbs

As you have seen in **Gramática A.6, C.5,** and **1.3,** Spanish verb endings tell us who is performing the action. The subject pronouns (**yo, tú, usted, ella, nosotros,** etc.) are often omitted.

**A.** You already know that the endings of Spanish verbs must correspond to the subject of the sentence: that is, to the person or thing that does the action.

| | |
|---|---|
| —Nora, ¿cuándo estudi**as**? | *—Nora, when do you study?* |
| —Estudi**o** por la mañana. | *—I study in the morning.* |
| —¿Qué hac**en** ustedes los domingos? | *—What do you do on Sundays?* |
| —Visit**amos** a nuestros abuelos. | *—We visit our grandparents.* |

**B.** Most Spanish verbs end in **-ar**. Here are the endings for **-ar** verbs.*

**llegar** = *to arrive*

| **llegar** (***to arrive***) | | |
|---|---|---|
| (yo) | lleg**o** | *I arrive* |
| (tú) | lleg**as** | *you (inf. sing.) arrive* |
| (usted, él/ella) | lleg**a** | *you (pol. sing.) arrive; he/she arrives* |
| (nosotros/as) | lleg**amos** | *we arrive* |
| (vosotros/as) | lleg**áis** | *you (inf. pl., Spain) arrive* |
| (ustedes, ellos/as) | lleg**an** | *you (pl.) arrive; they arrive* |

| | |
|---|---|
| —¿A qué hora lleg**as** a la escuela? | *—What time do you arrive at school?* |
| —Generalmente lleg**o** a las 9:00. | *—Generally I arrive at 9:00.* |

**C.** Verbs that end in **-er** and **-ir** use identical endings, except for the **nosotros/as** and **vosotros/as** forms.†

**comer** = *to eat*

| **comer** (***to eat***) | | |
|---|---|---|
| (yo) | com**o** | *I eat* |
| (tú) | com**es** | *you (inf. sing.) eat* |
| (usted, él/ella) | com**e** | *you (pol. sing.) eat; he/she eats* |
| (nosotros/as) | com**emos** | *we eat* |
| (vosotros/as) | com**éis** | *you (inf. pl., Spain) eat* |
| (ustedes, ellos/as) | com**en** | *you (pl.) eat; they eat* |

*Recognition: **vos llegás**
†Recognition: **vos comés, escribís**

**escribir** = *to write*

| **escribir** (***to write***) | | |
|---|---|---|
| (yo) | escrib**o** | *I write* |
| (tú) | escrib**es** | *you (inf. sing.) write* |
| (usted, él/ella) | escrib**e** | *you (pol. sing.) write; he/she writes* |
| (nosotros/as) | escrib**imos** | *we write* |
| (vosotros/as) | escrib**ís** | *you (inf. pl., Spain) write* |
| (ustedes, ellos/as) | escrib**en** | *you (pl.) write; they write* |

—¿Dónde com**en** al mediodía? — *—Where do you eat at noon?*
—Com**emos** en casa. — *—We eat at home.*

—¿Escrib**es** la tarea a máquina? — *—Do you type the homework?*
—No, escrib**o** los ejercicios a mano. — *—No, I write the exercises by hand.*

These agreement rules take some time to acquire. Think about them when you are editing your writing; don't be overly concerned about them in speech.
Note that the principal difference between **-ar, -er,** and **-ir** verbs are the vowels **a** and **e.**

**D.** The verb form must agree with the subject even when the subject is not explicitly stated. When the subject is expressed, it may be a pronoun, as in the preceding table, or a noun.

**La profesora Martínez** no **habla** francés. — *Professor Martínez does not speak French.*

The subject may also consist of a noun + pronoun. A subject combining a noun or pronoun with **yo** takes the **nosotros/as** form.

**Nora y yo** no **hablamos** italiano. — *Nora and I don't speak Italian.*

A subject combining a noun or pronoun with **tú** or **usted** takes the plural form.

**Alberto y tú hablan** español con Raúl. — *Al and you speak Spanish with Raúl.*

In Central America, Argentina, and Uruguay, **vos** = **tú**.

**E.** Central America, Argentina, and Uruguay use a different subject pronoun—**vos**—and verb form for informal singular address.*

—¿Qué hora ten**és vos**? — *—What time do you have?*
—Tengo las 6:30. — *—I have 6:30.*

—¿Cuándo lleg**ás vos**? — *—When do you arrive?*
—Llego a las 9:00 de la noche. — *—I arrive at 9:00 p.m.*

---

*You may learn more about **vos** forms in the **Expansión gramatical** section of the ***Cuaderno de trabajo***.

## Ejercicio 2

Combine las personas de la lista A con las actividades de la lista B.

MODELO: Mi hermano y yo jugamos al tenis.

| LISTA A | LISTA B |
|---|---|
| **1.** la profesora Martínez | **a.** hacen la tarea para mañana |
| **2.** yo | **b.** maneja un carro nuevo |
| **3.** tú | **c.** jugamos al tenis |
| **4.** mi hermano y yo | **d.** como demasiado |
| **5.** mis compañeros de clase | **e.** habláis español |
| **6.** vosotros | **f.** lees el periódico |

## Ejercicio 3

Éstas son las actividades de Amanda, su familia y sus amigos. Escriba la forma correcta del verbo entre paréntesis.

MODELO: Amanda *llama* a Graciela muy temprano en la mañana. (llamar)

1. Graciela y yo _____ las composiciones juntas. (escribir)
2. Mi novio Ramón _____ ropa muy elegante. (llevar)
3. Mi mamá y yo _____ la casa los sábados. (limpiar)
4. Mis padres _____ juntos por la mañana. (desayunar).
5. Mi hermano Guillermo _____ las tiras cómicas los domingos. (leer)
6. Andrea y Pedro Ruiz _____ juntos al mediodía. (comer)
7. Ernestito _____ mucho en su bicicleta. (montar)
8. (Yo) _____ por teléfono con mi amiga Graciela. (hablar)
9. Amanda, Guillermo y Ernestito _____ a la escuela de lunes a viernes. (asistir)
10. Ramón, Graciela y yo siempre _____ los últimos discos en la radio. (escuchar)

## Ejercicio 4

Imagínese que usted es Amanda. Escriba preguntas según los modelos. Use la forma correcta de **tú**, **usted** o **ustedes**.

MODELOS: Pregúntele a doña Lola si va en metro al trabajo. →
*Doña Lola, ¿va usted en metro al trabajo?*

Pregúntele a Rafael si lee el periódico por la mañana. →
*Rafael, ¿lees el periódico por la mañana?*

1. Pregúntele a su papá si toma mucho café en el trabajo.
2. Pregúntele a Diego si él y sus amigos juegan al béisbol.
3. Pregúnteles a Graciela y a Diego si tienen una computadora.
4. Pregúntele a Raúl si hace ejercicio en un gimnasio.
5. Pregúntele a Pedro Ruiz si trabaja por la noche.
6. Pregúntele a don Eduardo si prepara café por la mañana.
7. Pregúntele a su mamá si cocina por la mañana o por la tarde.
8. Pregúntele a Clarisa si ve la televisión por la noche.
9. Pregúntele a doña Rosita Silva si asiste a misa los domingos.
10. Pregúntele a doña Lola si lava su ropa en casa o en una lavandería.

**¿RECUERDA?**

In **Gramática C.5** you learned that verbs that use only one stem in their conjugations—such as **hablar, comer, vivir**—are regular verbs. Irregular verbs, on the other hand, use more than one stem in their conjugations. You saw the forms of two such irregular verbs, **preferir** and **querer,** in **Gramática 2.3.** Review those forms now, if necessary.

## 3.3 Using Irregular Verbs: *hacer, salir, jugar*

A verb that uses more than one stem in its conjugation is considered irregular. Here are the forms of three common irregular verbs.

**A.** The present tense of **hacer*** (*to do; to make*) uses two stems: **hag-** for the **yo** form and **hac-** for all others.

**hacer** (***to do; to make***)

| | | |
|---|---|---|
| (yo) | hag**o** | *I do* |
| (tú) | hac**es** | *you (inf. sing.) do* |
| (usted, él/ella) | hac**e** | *you (pol. sing.) do; he/she does* |
| (nosotros/as) | hac**emos** | *we do* |
| (vosotros/as) | hac**éis** | *you (inf. pl., Spain) do* |
| (ustedes, ellos/as) | hac**en** | *you (pl.) do; they do* |

**hacer** = *to do; to make*
**(Yo) Hago**. = *I do; I make.*
**(Tú) Haces**. = *You (inf. sing.) do; you make.*
**(Nosotros) Hacemos**. = *We do; we make.*

—¿Qué **haces** después de clases? —*What do you do after school?*
—**Hago** mi tarea. —*I do my homework.*

**B.** The present tense of **salir**† (*to leave; to go out*) uses the stems **salg-** for the **yo** form and **sal-** for all others.

**salir** (***to leave; to go out***)

| | | |
|---|---|---|
| (yo) | salg**o** | *I leave* |
| (tú) | sal**es** | *you (inf. sing.) leave* |
| (usted, él/ella) | sal**e** | *you (pol. sing.) leave; he/she leaves* |
| (nosotros/as) | sal**imos** | *we leave* |
| (vosotros/as) | sal**ís** | *you (inf. pl., Spain) leave* |
| (ustedes, ellos/as) | sal**en** | *you (pl.) leave; they leave* |

**salir** = *to leave; to go out.*
**(Yo) Salgo**. = *I leave; I go out.*
**(Tú) Sales**. = *You (inf. sing.) leave; you go out.*
**(Nosotros) Salimos**. = *We leave; we go out.*

To express a point of departure with **salir**, use the preposition **de**, even if the preposition *from* is not used in English.

—¿A qué hora **sales de** tu casa por la mañana? —*What time do you leave home in the morning?*
—**Salgo** a las 7:30. —*I leave at 7:30.*

*Recognition: **vos hacés**
†Recognition: **vos salís**

**C.** The present tense of the verb **jugar*** (*to play*) uses the stem **jug-** for the infinitive and the **nosotros/as** and **vosotros/as** forms and **jueg-** for all other forms. This verb follows the same pattern as **preferir** and **querer** in **Gramática 2.3.**

**jugar** = *to play*
**(Yo) Juego.** = *I play.*
**(Tú) Juegas.** = *You (inf. sing.) play.*
**(Nosotros) Jugamos.** = *We play.*

| jugar (*to play*) | | |
|---|---|---|
| (yo) | **juego** | *I play* |
| (tú) | **juegas** | *you (inf. sing.) play* |
| (usted, él/ella) | **juega** | *you (pol. sing.) play; he/she plays* |
| (nosotros/as) | jug**amos** | *we play* |
| (vosotros/as) | jug**áis** | *you (inf. pl., Spain) play* |
| (ustedes, ellos/as) | **juegan** | *you (pl.) play; they play* |

Remember that there are two words spelled **juego: el juego** (*the game*) and **(yo) juego** (*I play*).

| | |
|---|---|
| Los sábados **juego** al fútbol con mis amigos. | *Saturdays I play soccer with my friends.* |
| ¡Me gusta mucho ese **juego**! | *I like that game a lot!* |

## Ejercicio 5

Complete las conversaciones con la forma correcta de **hacer**, **salir** o **jugar**.

MODELO: —Luis, ¿cuándo *haces* las tareas?
—*Hago* las tareas por la tarde.

1. —Señor Ramírez, ¿a qué hora _____ usted de casa para su trabajo?
—_____ a las 8:30.
2. —Guillermo, ¿_____ al fútbol por la tarde?
—Sí, _____ después de clases.
3. —Señor Padilla, ¿_____ usted ejercicio todos los días?
—No, _____ ejercicio en el gimnasio solamente los lunes y los miércoles.
4. —Ernesto y Estela, ¿_____ ustedes al tenis?
—Sí, _____ al tenis los sábados.

**¿RECUERDA?**

In **Gramática A.3** you saw how the verb **ser** is used to identify people and things, whereas the verb **estar** is used to locate people and objects (**Gramática 3.1**). Review those verbs and their conjugations now, if necessary.

## 3.4 Describing Origin and Location: *ser de / estar en*

**A.** A form of the verb **ser** (*to be*) followed by **de** (*from, of*) can specify origin. The following questions show you how to ask where someone is from.

| | |
|---|---|
| —¿**De dónde es** Adriana Bolini? | *—Where is Adriana Bolini from?* |
| —**Es de** Buenos Aires. | *—She's from Buenos Aires.* |
| —Raúl, ¿**de dónde eres**? | *—Raúl, where are you from?* |
| —**Soy de** México. | *—I'm from Mexico.* |

*Recognition: **vos jugás**

**ser** = origin; **estar** = location
**¿De dónde es usted?** (*Where are you from?*)
**Soy de Perú**. (*I'm from Peru.*)
**¿Dónde está usted?** (*Where are you?*)
**Estoy aquí, en el patio**. (*I'm here, on the patio.*)

The distinction between **ser** and **estar** takes a while to acquire. Keep listening to and reading Spanish and you will develop a feel for it.

As you know, **ser** can be followed directly by an adjective of nationality (see **Gramática C.4**).

| | |
|---|---|
| —Sr. Ramírez, ¿**es** usted argentino? | —*Mr. Ramírez, are you Argentinean?* |
| —No, **soy** mexicano. | —*No, I'm Mexican.* |

**B.** Remember that two verbs in Spanish correspond to the English verb *to be*. **Ser** is used to tell where someone is from; **estar** is used to express location (see **Gramática 3.1**).

| | |
|---|---|
| Clara **es de** los Estados Unidos, pero este año **está en** España. | *Clara is from the United States, but she's in Spain this year.* |
| Ernesto y Estela **son de** México, pero ahora **están** en Italia. | *Ernesto and Estela are from Mexico, but now they're in Italy.* |

## Ejercicio 6

Diga de dónde son las siguientes personas y dónde están ahora.

MODELO: Adriana es de Argentina, pero ahora está en Washington, D.C.

## 3.5 Referring to Actions in Progress: Present Progressive

The present progressive (**estar** + verb ending in **-ndo**) is used to express actions in progress.
**Estoy leyendo un libro**. (*I am reading a book.*)

To describe an action that is taking place at the moment, Spanish uses a form of **estar** (*to be*) and an **-ndo** (*-ing*) form called a present participle.* This combination is called the *present progressive*.

| estar + -ndo | | |
|---|---|---|
| estoy | + | jugando (*playing*) |
| estás | | caminando (*walking*) |
| está | | fumando (*smoking*) |
| estamos | | escuchando (*listening*) |
| estáis | | escribiendo (*writing*) |
| están | | comiendo (*eating*) |

| | |
|---|---|
| —¿Qué **está haciendo** Paula? | —*What is Paula doing?* |
| —**Está lavando** su carro. | —*She's washing her car.* |
| —Guillermo, ¿qué **estás haciendo**? | —*Guillermo, what are you doing?* |
| —**Estoy escribiendo** una composición. | —*I'm writing a composition.* |

Present participles:
**-ar** verbs: replace **-ar** of infinitive with **-ando**
**-er** and **-ir** verbs: replace **-er/-ir** of infinitive with **-iendo**

The present participle (**-ando, -iendo**) is formed from the infinitive.

| | |
|---|---|
| jug**ar** → jug**ando** | com**er** → com**iendo** |
| habl**ar** → habl**ando** | viv**ir** → viv**iendo** |

When a present participle is irregular, it will be noted as follows: **dormir** (d*u*rmiendo), **leer** (le*y*endo).

| | |
|---|---|
| —¿**Está durmiendo** Ernestito ahora? | —*Is Ernestito sleeping now?* |
| —Sí, está muy cansado. | —*Yes, he's very tired.* |
| —Estela, ¿qué **estás leyendo**? | —*Estela, what are you reading?* |
| —**Estoy leyendo** una novela. | —*I'm reading a novel.* |

### Ejercicio 7

1. ¿Qué está haciendo Guillermo?

2. ¿Qué están haciendo don Eduardo y don Anselmo?

3. ¿Qué está haciendo Amanda?

*Recognition: **vos estás jugando**

**4.** ¿Qué está haciendo la señora Ramírez?

**5.** ¿Qué están haciendo Pedro y Andrea?

**6.** ¿Qué está haciendo Javier Saucedo?

## Ejercicio 8

Don Anselmo tiene curiosidad hoy y le hace muchas preguntas a don Eduardo. Conteste las preguntas que hace don Anselmo.

MODELO: —¿Y Amanda? ¿Va a ver la televisión más tarde?
—No, Amanda ya está *viendo la televisión*.

**1.** —¿Y Raúl? ¿Va a dormir esta noche?
—No, Raúl ya está _____.

**2.** —¿Y Ernestito? ¿Va a jugar con sus amigos esta tarde?
—No, Ernestito ya está _____ con ellos.

**3.** —¿Y doña Lola? ¿Va a leer el periódico más tarde?
—No, doña Lola ya está _____ el periódico.

**4.** —¿Y Estela Ramírez? ¿Va a lavar la ropa mañana?
—No, Estela ya está _____ la ropa.

**5.** —¿Y Guillermo Ramírez? ¿Va a tocar la guitarra esta noche?
—No, Guillermo ya está _____ la guitarra.

CAPÍTULO 4

# La vida diaria y los días feriados

**METAS**

In **Capítulo 4** you will discuss where events take place, daily activities, and how you feel. You will share your family's holiday customs with your classmates and you will also learn about holidays and celebrations in the Hispanic world.

San Antonio, Texas: celebración de La Posada

**ACTIVIDADES DE COMUNICACIÓN Y LECTURAS**


Los lugares

**Lectura** Una tarjeta de Clara: Los lugares en Madrid

Los días feriados y las celebraciones

**El mundo hispano...** en los Estados Unidos

**Nota cultural** Celebraciones del mes de julio

La rutina diaria

**El mundo hispano...** su gente

Los estados físicos y anímicos

**Lectura** «Versos sencillos»

**EN RESUMEN**


**GRAMÁTICA Y EJERCICIOS**


4.1 Talking about Location: **ir** + **a(l); estar** + **en**

4.2 Discussing Habitual Actions: Verbs with Stem-Vowel Changes (**ie, ue**) in the Present Tense

4.3 Discussing Habitual Actions: Irregular Verbs

4.4 Describing Daily Routine: Reflexives

4.5 Describing States: **estar** + Adjective

4.6 Describing States: **tener** + Noun

# Actividades de comunicación y lecturas

## Los lugares

*Lea Gramática 4.1.*

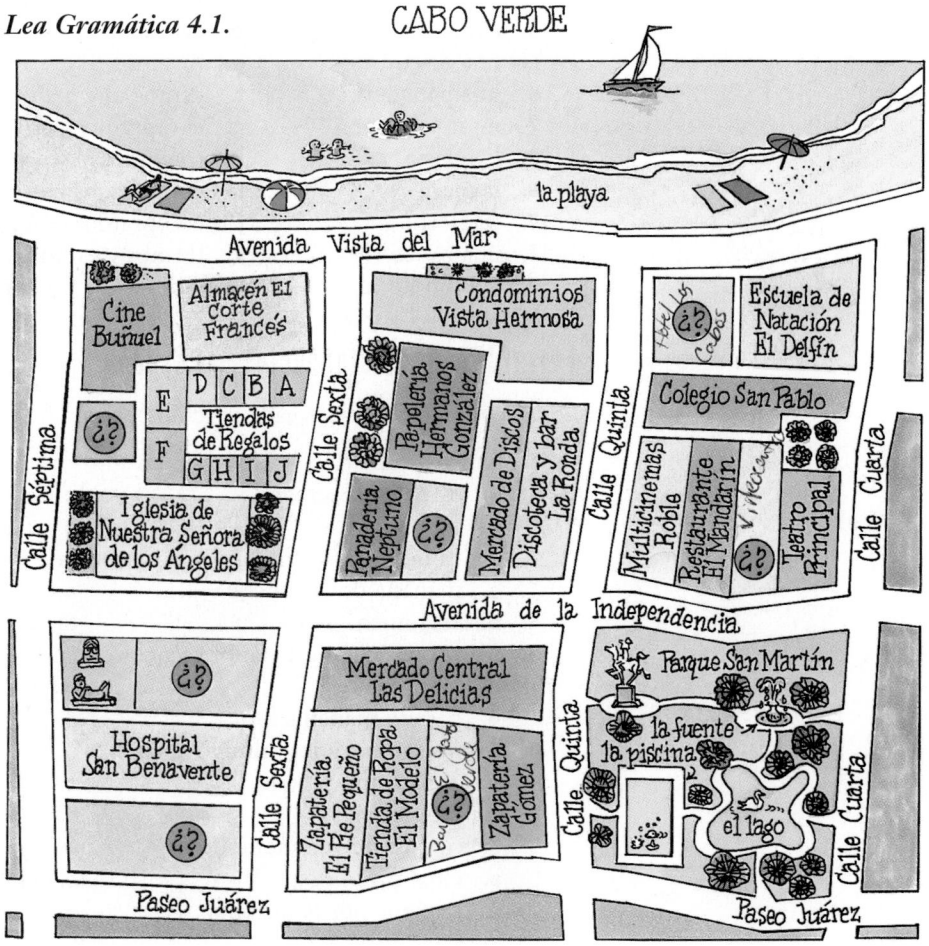


### Actividad 1. Descripción de dibujos: ¿Dónde está?

Escuche a su profesor(a) y escriba el nombre de estos lugares en los cuadros correspondientes.

Videocentro
Hotel Los Cabos
Bar El Gato Verde
Farmacia Cruz Blanca
Café de Paco
Biblioteca Municipal
Museo Nacional

## Actividad 2. Asociaciones: ¿Qué hacemos cuando vamos a estos lugares?

Empareje las actividades a continuación con los lugares apropiados.

MODELOS: el parque →
Cuando vamos al parque, *merendamos con nuestros amigos.*

la papelería →
Cuando vamos a la papelería, *compramos papel, lápices y cuadernos.*

| LUGAR | ACTIVIDAD |
|---|---|
| **1.** el cine | **a.** bailamos |
| **2.** una tienda de ropa | **b.** compramos zapatos |
| **3.** la playa | **c.** vemos las exhibiciones |
| **4.** el mercado | **d.** caminamos y conversamos |
| **5.** una discoteca | **e.** rezamos |
| **6.** una panadería | **f.** vemos una película |
| **7.** un museo | **g.** compramos pan o pasteles |
| **8.** la iglesia | **h.** tomamos el sol y nadamos |
| **9.** la plaza | **i.** compramos vestidos y camisas |
| **10.** un hospital | **j.** compramos comida |
| **11.** una zapatería | **k.** leemos y estudiamos |
| **12.** la biblioteca | **l.** visitamos a un enfermo |

## Actividad 3. Preferencias: ¿Cuándo?

Diga sí o no, o complete cada oración con una frase adecuada.

1. Voy a estudiar en la biblioteca...
   **a.** este fin de semana. **c.** ahora mismo.
   **b.** esta noche. **d.** ¿ ?
2. Voy a ir con mis amigos a una discoteca...
   **a.** mañana por la noche. **c.** el próximo sábado.
   **b.** esta noche. **d.** ¿ ?
3. Mi profesor(a) de español va a comer en un restaurante...
   **a.** hoy. **c.** mañana por la noche.
   **b.** pasado mañana. **d.** ¿ ?
4. Mi novio/a va a ir conmigo al cine...
   **a.** el próximo sábado. **c.** el lunes por la tarde.
   **b.** este viernes. **d.** ¿ ?
5. Voy a salir de vacaciones...
   **a.** el próximo mes. **c.** el próximo fin de semana.
   **b.** mañana por la mañana. **d.** ¿ ?

### Y TÚ, ¿QUÉ DICES?

| | | |
|---|---|---|
| ¿De veras? | Buena idea. | ¡Qué aburrido! |
| ¿De verdad? | Yo también. | ¡Qué lástima! |
| ¡No lo creo! | ¡Qué divertido! | |

MODELO: E1: Voy a estudiar en la biblioteca a las 5:00 de la mañana.
E2: *¡No lo creo!*

## Actividad 4. Intercambios: El cine en Sevilla

Lea esta guía del cine en Sevilla. Luego, hágale preguntas sobre la guía a su compañero/a.

MODELO:
E1: ¿Quieres ir al cine?
E2: Hummm... no sé. ¿Qué película quieres ver?
E1: En el *cine Alameda* ponen *Fenómeno*.
E2: ¿A qué hora?
E1: A *las 12.00, 17.45, 20.15 y 22.45 horas.*
E2: ¿Cuánto cuesta?
E1: *650 pesetas.*
E2: Perfecto.

### Guía del ocio — el cine en Sevilla

***Alameda Multicines 4 salas.***
***Tel. (95) 438 01 56.***

**El Día de la Independencia.** De Roland Emmerich. Con Will Smith y Jeff Goldblum. 15.45, 18.00, 20.15 y 22.30 horas. No recomendada para menores de 18 años. 550 pesetas.

**Las aventuras de Pinocho.** De Steve Barron. Especial para toda la familia. 16.00, 19.00, 22.00 y 0.45 horas. Todos los públicos. 600 pesetas.

**Fenómeno.** De John Turteltaub. Con John Travolta. 12.00, 17.45, 20.15 y 22.45 horas. No recomendada para menores de 18 años. 650 pesetas.

**El hombre de California.** De George Zaloom. 12.30, 17.00, 19.00, 21.00 y 23.00 horas. Todos los públicos. 475 pesetas.

***Azul Multicines 2 salas.***
***Tel. (95) 441 53 09 / La Florida, 15.***

**Los últimos días del Edén.** 18.00, 20.15 y 22.30 horas. No recomendada para menores de 18 años. 500 pesetas.

**Borrador.** De Carles Russell. Con Arnold Schwarzenegger. 17.30, 20.00 y 22.30 horas. No recomendada para menores de 18 años. 650 pesetas.

***Regina***
***Tel. (95) 421 42 12 / Jerónimo Hernández 19.***

**Sensatez y sentimiento.** De Ang Lee. Con Emma Thompson y Hugh Grant. 17.45, 20.15 y 22.45 horas. Todos los públicos. 700 pesetas.

***Rialto Multicines 3 salas.***
***Tel. (95) 425 44 88 / Plaza del Padre Jerónimo de Córdoba, 7.***

**El mundo perdido.** 16.45, 18.45, 20.45 y 22.45 horas. Todos los públicos. 550 pesetas.

**El jorobado (Cuasimodo) de Notre Dame.** Especial infantil. Dibujos animados. 12.30, 17.00, 18.30, 20.00, 21.30 y 23.00 horas. Todos los públicos. 550 pesetas.

**Como agua para chocolate.** De Alfonso Arau. Con Lumi Cavazos y Marco Leonardi. Libreto de Laura Esquivel basado en su novela. 17.00, 19.00, 21.00 y 22.45 horas. No recomendada para menores de 18 años. 600 pesetas.

Madrid: El cine es uno de los pasatiempos favoritos de los españoles. En España se exhiben muchas películas españolas, que hoy tienen una reputación internacional, y películas extranjeras dobladas (*dubbed*) al español.

### Actividad 5. Entrevista: ¿Qué haces tú?

1. ¿Qué te gusta hacer cuando vas a la playa? ¿Te gusta andar en velero?
2. ¿Qué haces cuando estás en una biblioteca? ¿Lees periódicos?
3. ¿Qué haces en un parque? ¿Practicas algún deporte? ¿Cómo se llama tu parque favorito? ¿Caminas mucho allí? ¿Corres? ¿Cuándo?
4. ¿Vas mucho al cine? ¿Adónde vas? ¿Con quién(es)? ¿Qué tipo de películas te gusta? ¿Te gustan las películas de acción?
5. ¿En qué mercado o supermercado compras la comida? ¿Por qué? ¿Está cerca de tu casa? ¿Tiene precios módicos?

# Una tarjeta de Clara: Los lugares en Madrid

Ésta es la segunda tarjeta postal que Clara Martin le manda a la profesora Martínez.

Estimada profesora:

¡Qué divertido es vivir en Madrid! La ciudad es grande, pero es fácil llegar a todos los lugares porque el transporte público es muy bueno. Me gusta mucho ir de compras aquí. Hay dos almacenes muy populares: Galerías Preciados y El Corte Inglés. (Esta postal es de mi almacén favorito.) Pero lo ideal es que cerca de mi apartamento hay de todo: una panadería (¡qué rico es el pan caliente!), un mercado enorme, una plaza muy bonita, un cine, una discoteca... ¡de todo! ¡Hasta la próxima!

Un abrazo,

Clara

MADRID - CCP - CHAMARTIN - 28 - 21 de octubre 1997

Prof. Adela Martínez
Department of Foreign Languages
University of Texas at San Antonio
San Antonio, TX 78285
USA

Madrid: El Corte Inglés es el almacén más grande de España.

## Comprensión

1. ¿Por qué es Madrid un lugar divertido para Clara?
2. ¿Cuál es una de sus actividades favoritas?
3. Mencione los dos almacenes que le gustan a Clara.
4. Según Clara, ¿cuál es el aspecto ideal de Madrid?

## Ahora... ¡usted!

1. ¿Le gusta ir de compras? ¿Por qué? Explique.
2. ¿Va de compras con frecuencia? ¿Adónde va, normalmente?
3. ¿Prefiere ir a los almacenes grandes o a las tiendas pequeñas? ¿Por qué?

### Un paso más... ¡a escribir!

Imagínese que usted va a mandarle una tarjeta postal de su ciudad a un amigo o a una amiga. Mencione sus lugares favoritos en la ciudad donde vive. ¿Cuáles son las actividades más divertidas que hace?

Puede usar el siguiente modelo para escribir la postal.

Querido/a ____:

Aquí tienes una postal de mi ciudad, (*nombre*). Mis lugares favoritos son ____ y ____. En mi ciudad hago varias actividades divertidas. Por ejemplo, me gusta ____, ____ y ____.

Bueno, ¡hasta la próxima!

Un abrazo,

(*firma*)

# Los días feriados y las celebraciones

### Actividad 6. Definiciones: ¿Qué día es?

1. Generalmente hay regalos y un pastel cuando uno celebra su _____.
2. En México se celebra el 16 de septiembre; en Argentina es el 9 de julio; en los Estados Unidos es el 4 de julio. Es el _____.
3. El _____ es un día de fiesta en los Estados Unidos. Las familias se reúnen y preparan una comida abundante.
4. Los hispanos celebran este día más que los norteamericanos. Es el día antes de la Navidad, _____.
5. Es la semana antes del Domingo de Pascua. Las personas religiosas, especialmente en España y en Latinoamérica, asisten a varias ceremonias en las iglesias. Es la _____.
6. Mucha gente le da la bienvenida a este primer día de enero con bailes y fiestas muy alegres. Esperan las 12:00 de la noche con impaciencia. Es el _____.
7. En muchos países hispanos, los niños no reciben regalos el 25 de diciembre. Los reciben el 6 de _____, el Día de _____.
8. El _____ es una fiesta de ocho noches. Cada noche se enciende una vela más, hasta 9. A veces los niños reciben un regalo.

## LAS PALABRAS VIVEN

Hay varios nombres para los días feriados en el mundo hispano. Por ejemplo, en México el Día de la Madre es **el Día de las Madres**. En España, el Día de la Raza es **el Día de la Hispanidad**. En algunos países *Easter* es **la Pascua**, pero también se le llama **las Pascuas**, **la Pascua Florida**, **el domingo de Pascua** o **la Pascua de Resurrección**. Y en muchos países la expresión ¡**Felices Pascuas**! quiere decir lo mismo que ¡**Feliz Navidad**!

### Actividad 7. Entrevista: Las fiestas

¿Qué prefiere usted hacer para celebrar...

1. su cumpleaños?
2. el Día de la Independencia?
3. la Navidad u otro día feriado? (el Jánuca, la Pascua, la Pascua Judía, el Ramadán)
4. su aniversario de boda u otro aniversario importante?
5. el Día de la Madre o el Día del Padre?
6. la Nochevieja o el Año Nuevo?

**Actividades posibles:** celebrar con mis parientes, cenar en casa, comer pastel, dar una fiesta, ir a la playa, ir al cine, ir a un café, ir de compras, merendar en el parque, quedarme en casa, salir a bailar, salir a cenar en un restaurante, ver la televisión

Ahora, entreviste a un compañero / una compañera de clase.

MODELO: E1: ¿Qué prefieres hacer para celebrar *tu cumpleaños*?
E2: Durante el día, prefiero *quedarme en casa* y *ver la televisión*. Por la noche, me gusta *salir a cenar en un restaurante* con mis amigos.

## Actividad 8. Entrevista: Los días feriados

1. ¿Cómo te gusta celebrar tu cumpleaños? ¿Quién hace los preparativos para celebrar tu cumpleaños?
2. ¿Qué haces el Día de Acción de Gracias? ¿Celebras esta fiesta en casa con tu familia o vas a la casa de otros parientes o amigos? ¿Qué comen ustedes?
3. ¿Qué aspecto del Año Nuevo te gusta más? ¿Qué aspecto te gusta menos? ¿Celebras el Año Nuevo con tu familia o con tus amigos? ¿Qué hacen ustedes para celebrarlo?
4. ¿Cómo celebras el Día de la Independencia, con tu familia o con tus amigos? ¿Van a un parque o se quedan en casa? ¿Celebran solos o invitan a otros parientes/amigos? ¿Ven los fuegos artificiales? ¿De dónde los ven, de casa o de un parque? ¿A qué hora vuelves a tu casa?
5. ¿Qué otras fiestas celebras con tu familia o tus amigos? ¿Qué hacen ustedes para celebrar esas fiestas? ¿Dan muchos regalos? ¿Ponen decoraciones en casa?

## EL MUNDO HISPANO... en los Estados Unidos

**Ó**scar M. Ramírez es cubano, tiene 40 años y vive en Miami, Florida. Óscar lleva[1] 30 años en los Estados Unidos.

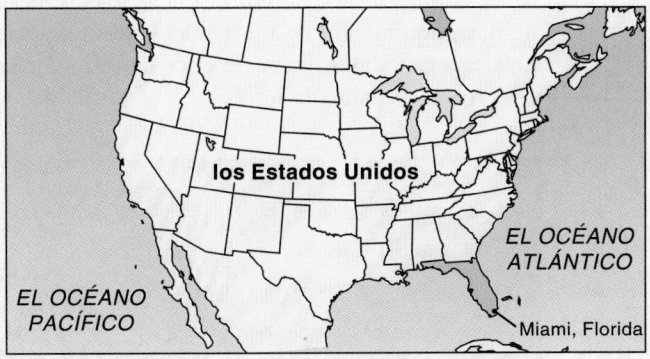


*Describa algunos de los días feriados que usted celebra con su familia.*

El único día feriado que mi familia todavía celebra en los Estados Unidos «a la hispana» es la Nochebuena, el 24 de diciembre. Se celebra dándole a la ocasión todo su significado religioso. La noche es «buena» porque es cuando celebramos el nacimiento del Niño Jesús. Aquí la palabra «buena» quiere decir «santa».

Siempre hay en la sala de la casa un pesebre,[2] con una figurita del Niño Jesús, recién nacido.[3] Están con él su madre, la Virgen María, y su padre en la

[1]*has been* [2]*manger* [3]recién... *just born*

(Continúa)

Tierra, San José. Los rodean una vaca, un burro y muchos pastores con sus ovejas.[4] A todo esto se le llama el «Nacimiento».[5] También están los tres Reyes Magos, que dan al Niño regalos preciosos. Pero los Reyes Magos no se ponen en el Nacimiento hasta[6] el 6 de enero, cuando llegan al pesebre guiados por una estrella,[7] la Estrella de Belén. (En mi país los niños no reciben regalos el 25 de diciembre, sino el 6 de enero.)

Delante del Nacimiento se sirve una gran cena: puerco asado, cidra, uvas, turrones de almendras y nueces[8] de diferentes tipos; se cantan villancicos,[9] y a medianoche todos vamos a misa.[10]

[4]Los... *They are surrounded by a cow, a donkey, and many shepherds with their sheep.*
[5]el... *Nativity scene* [6]*until* [7]guiados... *guided by a star* [8]puerco... *pork roast, cider, grapes, almond nougat, nuts* [9]*Christmas carols* [10]*Mass*

**VOCABULARIO ÚTIL**

| | |
|---|---|
| los artesanos | *craftsmen* |
| la artesanía | *crafts* |
| los toros | *bulls* |
| el pañuelo | *handkerchief* |
| la faja | *waistband* |
| arriesgan la vida | *they risk their lives* |

# Celebraciones del mes de julio

El mes de julio es un mes de fiestas por todo el mundo hispano. Julio es un mes de invierno en algunos países, como en Argentina. Los argentinos celebran con fuegos artificiales la emocionante Fiesta de la nieve en Bariloche. Y México tiene la Fiesta de Uruapan, que se celebra en Michoacán. Puerto Rico ofrece la alegre Feria Artesanal de Barranquitas. En esta feria hay bailes folclóricos, música y canciones. Los artesanos de todo el país llevan sus artesanías para venderlas.

Bariloche, Argentina: Fiesta de la nieve

Michoacán, México: Fiesta de Uruapan

Puerto Rico: Feria Artesanal de Barranquitos

En Pamplona, España, se celebran las Fiestas de San Fermín, que duran una semana. Estas fiestas tienen un espectáculo impresionante. Varias calles de la ciudad se cierran por la mañana y entonces... ¡salen los toros! Muchísimos hombres (dos mil, más o menos) esperan la salida de estos animales. Los hombres van vestidos de blanco, con un pañuelo rojo al cuello y una faja roja a la cintura. Todos corren aproximadamente un kilómetro por las calles... ¡pero corren con los toros! Y algunos arriesgan la vida.

El espectáculo de Pamplona dura sólo cuatro minutos, ¡pero son cuatro minutos de pura emoción!

Pamplona, España: las Fiestas de San Fermín

## Comprensión

Busque la definición correcta. ¡Cuidado! Hay varias respuestas posibles.

1. d las Fiestas de San Fermín
2. b la Fiesta de Uruapan
3. g la Fiesta de la nieve, en Bariloche
4. e la Feria Artesanal de Barranquitas

a. Hay un espectáculo corto, pero impresionante.
b. Se celebra en Michoacán, México.
c. Aquí los artesanos venden su trabajo.
d. Duran siete días.
e. Hay música y bailes.
f. En esta fiesta los hombres corren con los toros.
g. Hay fuegos artificiales.
h. Es una celebración de invierno.

## Ahora... ¡usted!

1. ¿Celebra usted el 4 de Julio, el Día de la Independencia de los Estados Unidos? ¿Cómo celebra este día feriado?
2. ¿En qué otras celebraciones participa usted?
3. ¿Conoce fiestas de otros países que se celebran en julio?
4. Mire las fotos que acompañan la Nota cultural e imagínese que usted está en esas fiestas. ¿Qué ve? ¿Qué está haciendo?

### Un paso más... ¡a escribir!

Usted tiene un amigo o una amiga de otro país. Esta persona quiere saber cuáles son los días feriados que usted celebra. Escríbale una tarjeta postal con una breve descripción de sus fiestas favoritas. ¿Por qué le gustan? ¿Qué hace en estas fiestas? ¿Las celebra con la familia o con amigos?

# La rutina diaria

*Lea Gramática 4.2–4.4.*

## Una mañana en la casa de los Ramírez

Ernesto se afeita. Estela se maquilla. Ernestito se lava los dientes. Amanda se pone la ropa. Guillermo se levanta.

### Actividad 9. Orden lógico: Primero... luego... y después...

Ponga en orden estas actividades. Use las palabras **primero**, **luego** y **después**.

1. **a.** Me seco. **b.** Me lavo los dientes. **c.** Me baño.
2. **a.** Me maquillo. **b.** Me levanto. **c.** Me pongo la ropa.
3. **a.** Me peino. **b.** Me afeito. **c.** Me ducho.
4. **a.** Me baño. **b.** Me levanto. **c.** Me despierto.
5. **a.** Me lavo el pelo. **b.** Me quito la ropa. **c.** Me seco el pelo.
6. **a.** Me lavo los dientes. **b.** Desayuno. **c.** Preparo el desayuno.
7. **a.** Me pongo el pijama. **b.** Me acuesto. **c.** Me quito la ropa.

### Actividad 10. Descripción de dibujos: La rutina

Escuche mientras su profesor(a) describe uno de los dibujos a continuación. Diga el título que corresponde al dibujo.

Un lunes a las 6:30 con la familia Ramírez.

Un jueves a las 6:30 con la familia Ramírez.

Un sábado a las 9:00 de la mañana con los amigos norteamericanos.

Un domingo a las 9:00 de la mañana con los amigos norteamericanos.

Ahora, escoja uno de los dibujos y descríbaselo a un compañero / una compañera de clase. Él/Ella va a decir qué dibujo es.

## Actividad 11. Narración: La rutina de Adriana

**PALABRAS ÚTILES**

primero
luego
después
más tarde
finalmente
por último
a la(s)...
desde la(s)...
hasta la(s)...

## EL MUNDO HISPANO... su gente

Gregorio Merino Díaz tiene 32 años y es de Chile.

*Describa un día típico de su vida.*

Un día típico es un día de trabajo. Soy Inspector General[1] de un colegio particular[2] de Santiago. Para mi esposa y para mí el día comienza a las 6:00 de la mañana, pues vivimos muy lejos de nuestro trabajo. Nos duchamos y luego desayunamos café y tostadas. A las 7:00 nos vamos al trabajo. Tomamos locomoción colectiva.[3] Luego de cuarenta y cinco minutos de viaje, llegamos al colegio; yo voy a mi oficina y mi esposa a la biblioteca, donde trabaja. Por lo general tomamos un café alrededor de[4] las 10:00. Regresamos a casa a las 15 horas, cuando termina la jornada de trabajo.[5]

[1]Inspector... *administrator* [2]colegio... *private school* [3]locomoción... *public transportation* [4]alrededor... *around* [5]jornada... *workday*

### Actividad 12. Entrevista: Preguntas personales

1. ¿Te gusta levantarte temprano o tarde? ¿Quién se levanta primero donde tú vives?
2. ¿Te bañas o te duchas? ¿Cuándo prefieres bañarte? ¿Qué marca de jabón usas?
3. ¿Te afeitas con navaja o con rasuradora eléctrica?
4. ¿Te maquillas todos los días? ¿Te maquillas más cuando sales de noche?
5. ¿Te lavas el pelo todos los días? ¿Qué marca de champú prefieres? ¿Usas un acondicionador? ¿De qué marca es?
6. ¿Te pones perfume/colonia todos los días? ¿Qué marca prefieres?

# Los estados físicos y anímicos

*Lea Gramática 4.5–4.6.*

está contento

están tristes

está enojado

está enferma

está aburrido

está ocupada

está preocupado

tienen hambre

tienen prisa

tiene sueño

tiene sed

tiene calor

tiene frío

tiene miedo

## Actividad 13. Conversación: Las emociones

Diga si usted está de acuerdo o no con las siguientes afirmaciones.

**FRASES ÚTILES**

(No) Estoy de acuerdo.
Depende.

1. Es bueno gritar si uno está enojado.
2. Si uno está deprimido, es mejor comer algo.
3. Si uno tiene frío, es mejor tomar una limonada.
4. Si uno está de mal humor, es buena idea hablar con un buen amigo o un pariente.
5. Si uno está aburrido, es preferible ver la televisión.
6. Si uno tiene prisa y va a llegar tarde a clase, es mejor manejar muy rápido.
7. Es recomendable quedarse en casa cuando uno está enfermo.
8. Si uno tiene miedo, es buena idea comerse las uñas.

## Actividad 14. Preferencias: ¿Qué hace usted en estas situaciones?

1. Cuando estoy triste,...
   a. quiero estar solo/a.
   b. escucho música.
   c. compro ropa nueva.
   d. ¿ ?
2. Cuando estoy contento/a,...
   a. salgo en el carro.
   b. voy de compras.
   c. prefiero estar solo/a.
   d. ¿ ?
3. Cuando estoy cansado/a,...
   a. duermo.
   b. leo.
   c. me baño.
   d. ¿ ?
4. Cuando estoy aburrido/a,...
   a. como.
   b. llamo a mi novio/a o a un amigo / una amiga.
   c. me quedo en casa.
   d. ¿ ?
5. Cuando tengo hambre,...
   a. como hamburguesas.
   b. tomo un vaso de leche.
   c. me lavo los dientes.
   d. ¿ ?
6. Cuando tengo frío,...
   a. me quito la chaqueta.
   b. me baño con agua caliente.
   c. me pongo un suéter.
   d. ¿ ?
7. Cuando tengo calor,...
   a. tomo un refresco.
   b. tomo café caliente.
   c. me ducho.
   d. ¿ ?
8. Cuando tengo prisa,...
   a. camino rápidamente.
   b. tomo el autobús.
   c. doy un paseo.
   d. ¿ ?

### Y TÚ, ¿QUÉ DICES?

| | | |
|---|---|---|
| Sí, yo también. (Sí, a mí también me gusta eso.) | Yo sí. | ¡Excelente idea! |
| Yo tampoco. (A mí tampoco me gusta eso.) | Yo no. | ¡Qué buena idea! |
| | Es mejor. | ¡Ni pensarlo! |
| | Es peor. | ¡Qué ocurrencia! |

## Actividad 15. Asociaciones: Los estados anímicos

¿Qué estado de ánimo asocia usted con las siguientes ocasiones?

1. Es su cumpleaños.
2. Está tomando un examen de español.
3. Es un sábado de primavera. Hace sol y buen tiempo. Usted está en el parque con su perro.
4. Es la Nochevieja.
5. Usted tiene una entrevista para un trabajo en 10 minutos y de pronto recibe una llamada de su abuela.
6. Usted recibe una buena nota en su examen de biología.
7. Encuentra a su perro comiendo su mejor camisa.
8. Su gato está muy enfermo.

## Actividad 16. Entrevista: Soluciones

¿Qué haces cuando estás...

1. deprimido/a?
2. nervioso/a?
3. de buen/mal humor?
4. enamorado/a?

¿Qué haces cuando tienes...

1. frío?
2. sueño?
3. sed?
4. miedo?

# «Versos sencillos» de José Martí (selecciones)

Varios de los *Versos sencillos* de este famoso poeta cubano (1853–1895) son parte de la canción popular «Guantanamera». En las siguientes selecciones, Martí hace una descripción de su personalidad: es un hombre sincero y artístico, a quien le gusta la naturaleza.[1] El poeta también habla de su poesía y de su hijo.

Yo soy un hombre sincero
De donde crece la palma,[2]
Y antes de morirme[3] quiero
Echar[4] mis versos del alma.[5]

Yo vengo de todas partes,
Y hacia[6] todas partes voy:
Arte soy entre[7] las artes.
En los montes,[8] monte soy.

Oigo un suspiro,[9] a través
De[10] las tierras y la mar,
Y no es un suspiro, —es
Que mi hijo va a despertar.

Con los pobres de la tierra
Quiero yo mi suerte[11] echar:
El arroyo[12] de la sierra
Me complace[13] más que el mar.

Todo es hermoso y constante,
Todo es música y razón,
Y todo, como el diamante,
Antes de luz es carbón.[14]

Mi verso es de un verde claro
Y de un carmín encendido:[15]
Mi verso es un ciervo herido[16]
Que busca en el monte amparo.[17]

Camagüey, Cuba: Una de las características del paisaje (*landscape*) cubano es la hermosa palma real (*royal*).

[1]*nature* [2]crece... *the palm tree grows* [3]antes... *before I die* [4]*To cast; To express* [5]*soul* [6]*toward* [7]*among* [8]*forests* [9]*sigh* [10]a... *through* [11]*luck* [12]*brook* [13]Me... *Pleases me* [14]*coal* [15]carmín... *bright crimson* [16]ciervo... *wounded deer* [17]*shelter*

## Comprensión

Escoja las respuestas correctas. ¡Cuidado! Hay más de una posibilidad.

1. ¿Cómo es la personalidad del poeta? Martí es...
   **a.** sincero. **b.** agresivo. **c.** artístico. **d.** como el monte.
   **e.** tímido. **f.** perezoso.
2. ¿De qué color son los versos de José Martí? Son...
   **a.** rojos. **b.** verdes. **c.** amarillos. **d.** negros.
   **e.** de color carmín. **f.** azules.
3. ¿Con qué se relaciona el despertar del hijo de Martí? Con...
   **a.** el llanto. **b.** el suspiro. **c.** la tierra. **d.** el mar.
   **e.** el bosque. **f.** su casa.
4. ¿Qué elementos de la naturaleza menciona el poeta? Martí menciona...
   **a.** la palma. **b.** el arroyo. **c.** el monte. **d.** el árbol.
   **e.** el océano. **f.** el carbón.

## Ahora... ¡usted!

1. ¿Le gusta leer poesía? ¿Por qué? ¿Hay un poeta o una poeta que le guste mucho? ¿Por qué le gusta?
2. ¿Escribe usted poemas u otros tipos de escritura? ¿Cuáles son los temas de su poesía / su escritura en general?

### Un paso más... ¡a escribir!

Use los versos de Martí como guía y escriba un poema para expresar sus propios sentimientos.

Yo soy ____
De donde ____,
Y antes de morirme quiero ____.

Yo vengo de ____
Y hacia ____ voy:
____ soy entre ____
En ____, ____ soy.

# En resumen

## De todo un poco

**A.** ¡Los Reyes Magos vienen mañana!

Mire los dibujos de la siguiente página y ponga en orden las oraciones a continuación para que coincidan con los dibujos.

**a.** 6 Se lavan los dientes.
**b.** 5 Finalmente son las siete y media. Se ponen el pijama.
**c.** 11 Se despiertan a las cinco de la mañana. Tienen miedo de mirar la ventana.
**d.** 9 Se acuestan pero no se duermen. Hablan de los juguetes que esperan recibir.
**e.** 2 Su madre quiere llevarlas al museo y a la biblioteca pero ellas prefieren quedarse en casa.
**f.** 1 Es el cinco de enero. Son las 5:00 de la tarde. Clarisa y Marisa están nerviosas e impacientes.
**g.** 8 Rezan antes de acostarse.
**h.** 12 Corren a la ventana. Ahí están los juguetes que quieren. ¡Qué contentas están!
**i.** 7 Les dicen «Buenas noches» a sus padres con un beso.
**j.** 3 Ponen los zapatos en la ventana y esperan... ¡Los Reyes Magos van a venir mañana muy temprano!
**k.** 10 Por fin se duermen. Sueñan que los Reyes Magos no les traen nada.
**l.** 4 Cenan con sus padres y charlan sobre los juguetes que quieren.

**B.** Entrevista con su profesor(a)

Trabaje con dos o tres estudiantes. Escriban preguntas para entrevistar a su profesor(a). Cada grupo va a escribir ocho buenas preguntas para saber más sobre él/ella. Escriban preguntas sobre su vida en casa, su rutina diaria, sus estados de ánimo, sus actividades favoritas, sus preferencias, cómo celebra los días feriados, etcétera.

MODELOS: ¿A qué hora se levanta usted durante la semana?
¿Qué le gusta hacer después del trabajo?
¿Qué hace usted cuando está aburrido/a?
¿Cómo celebra el Año Nuevo?
¿Qué le gusta hacer los viernes por la noche?

Después, cada grupo debe hacerle sus preguntas al profesor / a la profesora. Tomen apuntes sobre la información para luego escribir una composición sobre él/ella.

## ¡Dígalo por escrito!

Los días feriados

¿Cuál es el día feriado que más le gusta a usted? ¿Por qué? Trabaje con varios compañeros de clase para hablar de sus días feriados favoritos, por qué les gustan esos días y por qué *no* les gustan otros. Luego, en casa, escriba una descripción de su propio día feriado favorito. ¿Cómo lo celebra? ¿Dónde? ¿Con quién(es)? ¿Qué hace usted para prepararse para esa celebración?

## VIDEOTECA

En este segmento de video, la familia Durán, de Sevilla, celebra la primera comunión de Marta. Para muchas familias hispanas, la primera comunión es una ceremonia religiosa muy importante. ¿Quiénes vienen a la ceremonia? ¿Dónde la celebran? En el Capítulo 4 del *Cuaderno de trabajo* hay más actividades para hacer después de ver el video.

# Vocabulario

## Los lugares

| | |
|---|---|
| **abajo** | below |
| **ahí (allí)** | there |
| **el almacén** | department store |
| **el colegio** | private school |
| **la escuela** | school |
| **la iglesia** | church |
| **el mercado** | market |
| **la panadería** | bakery |
| **la papelería** | stationery store |
| **el supermercado** | supermarket |
| **el videocentro** | video store |
| **la zapatería** | shoe store |

**PALABRAS SEMEJANTES: la América Latina (Latinoamérica), el bar, el café, la discoteca, la farmacia, el hotel, el museo, el parque, la plaza**

**REPASO: el cine, el lago, la tienda**

## Los días feriados y las celebraciones
Holidays and Celebrations

| | |
|---|---|
| **el Año Nuevo** | New Year's Day |
| **el Día de Acción de Gracias** | Thanksgiving Day |
| **el Día de las Brujas** witch | Halloween |
| **el Día de los Enamorados** | Valentine's Day |
| **el Día de la Independencia** | Independence Day |
| **el Día de la Madre** | Mother's Day |
| **el Día de los Muertos** | All Souls' Day (November 2nd) |
| **el Día del Padre** | Father's Day |
| **el Día de los Reyes Magos** | Epiphany, Day of the Magi (January 6th) |
| **el día del santo** | saint's day |
| **el Día de Todos los Santos** | All Saints' Day (November 1st) |
| **el Domingo de Pascua** | Easter Sunday |
| **el Jánuca** | Hanukkah |

| | |
|---|---|
| **la(s) Navidad(es)** | Christmas |
| **la Nochebuena** | Christmas Eve |
| **la Nochevieja** | New Year's Eve (December 31st) |
| **la Pascua Judía** | Passover |
| **el Ramadán** | Ramadan |
| **la Semana Santa** | Holy Week |

## La rutina diaria Daily Routine

| | |
|---|---|
| **acostarse (ue)** | to go to bed |
| **me acuesto / se acuesta** | |
| **afeitarse** | to shave |
| **bañarse** | to bathe |
| **despertarse (ie)** | to wake up |
| **me despierto / se despierta** | |
| **dormir (ue)** | to sleep |
| **dormirse (ue)** | to fall asleep |
| **me duermo / se duerme** | |
| **lavarse los dientes** | to brush one's teeth |
| **lavarse el pelo** | to wash one's hair |
| **levantarse** | to get up |
| **maquillarse** | to put on makeup |
| **peinarse** | to comb one's hair |
| **ponerse (perfume / la ropa)** | to put on (perfume/ clothes) |
| **me pongo / se pone** | |
| **quitarse (la ropa)** | to take off (one's clothes) |
| **secarse (el pelo)** | to dry (one's hair) |
| **venir** | to come |
| **vengo/viene** | |
| **volver (ue)** | to return, go back |
| **(vuelvo/vuelve)** | |

**REPASO: almorzar (ue), cenar, ducharse, hacer (hago/hace), ir de compras, manejar**

## Los estados físicos y anímicos
Physical and Mental States

| | |
|---|---|
| **estar...** | to be . . . |
| **alegre** | happy |
| **contento/a** | happy |
| **de buen/mal humor** | in a good/bad mood |
| **deprimido/a** | depressed |
| **enamorado/a** | in love |
| **enfermo/a** | sick |
| **enojado/a** | angry |
| **ocupado/a** | busy |
| **preocupado/a** | worried |
| **triste** | sad |
| **tener...** | to be . . . |
| **calor** | hot |
| **frío** | cold |
| **hambre** | hungry |
| **miedo** | afraid |
| **prisa** | in a hurry |
| **sed** | thirsty |
| **sueño** | sleepy |

**REPASO: (estar) aburrido/a**

## ¿Cuándo?

| | |
|---|---|
| **ahora mismo** | right now |
| **antes de** | before |
| **cuando** | when |
| **de pronto** | suddenly |
| **desde la(s)... hasta la(s)...** | from (*hour*) to (*hour*) |
| **después de** | after |
| **la próxima semana** | next week |
| **tarde** | late |
| **temprano** | early |
| **todos los días** | every day |

**REPASO: ayer, después, hoy, luego, mañana, pasado mañana**

## Los verbos

| | |
|---|---|
| **andar en velero** | to go sailing |
| **aprender** | to learn |
| **beber (un refresco)** | to drink (a soft drink) |
| **comprar** | to buy |
| **dar (doy/da)** | to give |
| **dar la bienvenida** | to welcome |
| **dar un paseo** | to go for a walk |
| **escoger** | to choose |
| **escojo/escoge** | |
| **gritar** | to yell, scream |
| **llamar** | to call (on the phone) |
| **poner** | to put |
| **poner una película** | to show a movie |
| **quedarse (en casa)** | to stay (at home) |
| **reunirse** | to get together |
| **me reúno / se reúne** | |
| **rezar** | to pray |
| **saber** | to know |
| **sé/sabe** | |
| **soñar (ue) (con)** | to dream (about) |
| **traer** | to bring |
| **traigo/trae** | |

**PALABRAS SEMEJANTES: celebrar, coincidir, conversar, corresponder, invitar, visitar**

## Palabras del texto

| | |
|---|---|
| **correspondiente** | corresponding |
| **la oración** | sentence |

## La gente

| | People |
|---|---|
| **el médico** | doctor |
| **el/la paciente** | patient |
| **el pariente / la parienta** | relative |

## Los sustantivos

| | |
|---|---|
| **el acondicionador** | conditioner |
| **el agua** | water |
| **el árbol (de Navidad)** | (Christmas) tree |
| **el beso** | kiss |
| **la boda** | wedding |
| **la colonia** | cologne |
| **la comida** | food |
| **el cuadro** | box, square |
| **el desayuno** | breakfast |
| **los fuegos artificiales** | fireworks |
| **la fuente** | fountain |
| **la guía** | guide; guidebook |
| **el jabón** | soap |
| **el juguete** | toy |
| **la leche** | milk |
| **la llamada** | (telephone) call |
| **la marca** | brand |
| **la natación** | swimming |
| **la navaja** | razor blade |
| **la nota** | note; grade |
| **el pan** | bread |
| **el pastel** | cake |
| **la peseta** | *monetary unit of Spain* |
| **el precio** | price |
| **la rasuradora eléctrica** | electric razor |
| **el regalo** | gift |
| **el tipo** | type |
| **el título** | title |
| **el vaso** | glass |

**PALABRAS SEMEJANTES: la afirmación, el aniversario, el aspecto, la celebración, la ceremonia, el champú, la composición, el condominio, la decoración, la emoción, el examen, la exhibición, la fruta, la hamburguesa, la impaciencia, la limonada, el/la patriota, el pijama, la situación, la solución**

## Los adjetivos

| | |
|---|---|
| **caliente** | hot |
| **hermoso/a** | beautiful |
| **módico/a** | affordable |

**PALABRAS SEMEJANTES: abundante, impaciente, municipal, preferible, recomendable**

## Palabras y expresiones útiles

| | |
|---|---|
| **¿Adónde va usted... ?** | Where do you go . . . ? |
| **algo** | something |
| **conmigo** | with me |
| **depende** | (it) depends |
| **¿De veras? / ¿De verdad?** | Really? |
| **¿Dónde está... ?** | Where is . . . (located)? |
| **es mejor/peor** | it is better/worse |
| **especialmente** | especially |
| **¡Excelente idea!** | Excellent idea! |
| **nada** | nothing |
| **¡Ni pensarlo!** | Don't even think of it! |
| **¡Qué lástima!** | What a pity! |
| **¡Qué ocurrencia!** | What a silly idea! |
| **rápidamente** | quickly, rapidly |
| **rápido** | quick |
| **tampoco** | neither |

# Gramática y ejercicios

**¿RECUERDA?**

Remember from **Gramática 2.1** that the present-tense forms of **ir** are **voy, vas, va, vamos, vais,** and **van.*** These verb forms can mean *going* or simply *go(es)*.

## 4.1 Talking about Location: *ir* + *a(l)*; *estar* + *en*

### Gramática ilustrada

Raúl y Mónica **van al** cine.

Raúl y Mónica **están en** el cine.

**adónde** = *where (to)*
**ir a** = *to go to*
**Voy al cine**. (*I'm going to the movies.*)

**A. ¿Adónde**? ([*To*] *Where*?) is used to ask where someone is going. The verb **ir** (*to go*) followed by the preposition **a** (*to*) is used to express the idea of movement toward a location. Note that **a** + **el** contracts to **al** (*to the*).

| | |
|---|---|
| —**¿Adónde vas**? | —*Where are you going?* |
| —**Voy al** parque. | —*I'm going to the park.* |
| —**¿Adónde van** ustedes los sábados? | —*Where do you go on Saturdays?* |
| —**Vamos al** trabajo y luego **vamos a la** biblioteca para estudiar. | —*We go to work and then we go to the library to study.* |
| —**¿Adónde va** la profesora Martínez? | —*Where's Professor Martínez going?* |
| —**Va a la** universidad. | —*She's going to the university.* |

**Ir a** + infinitive is used to express the future.
**Mañana voy a trabajar**. (*Tomorrow I'm going to work.*)
**este viernes** = *this Friday*
**el próximo viernes** = *next Friday*
**El próximo mes vamos a empezar las clases**. (*Next month we're going to start classes.*)

The expression **ir** + **a** + *location*, used with the following expressions of time, indicates when you are going.

| | | | |
|---|---|---|---|
| este viernes | *this Friday* | el próximo sábado | *next Saturday* |
| este fin de semana | *this weekend* | la próxima semana | *next week* |
| esta primavera | *this spring* | el próximo mes | *next month* |

| | |
|---|---|
| **Vamos a ir al** restaurante El Tecolote **la próxima semana**. | *We're going to go to the Tecolote Restaurant next week.* |

*Recognition: **vos vas**

**¿RECUERDA?**

In **Gramática 3.4** you learned that **estar** + **en** is used to locate people and objects.
—¿Dónde están los niños?
—Están en la escuela.

**B.** The verb **estar** + **en** is used to express the idea of being at a location.

| | |
|---|---|
| —**¿Está** Guillermo **en** la biblioteca? | —*Is Guillermo at the library?* |
| —No, **está en** el gimnasio. | —*No, he's at the gym.* |

## Ejercicio 1

¿Adónde van estas personas? Complete las oraciones con la forma apropiada del verbo **ir** y **al** o **a la**.

MODELO: Usted *va al* parque los domingos.

1. Mis compañeros y yo _____ tienda nueva enfrente de la universidad.
2. Mis hermanos siempre _____ cine los sábados.
3. (Nosotros) _____ supermercado a comprar fruta.
4. La profesora Martínez _____ oficina a trabajar.
5. (Yo) _____ playa a tomar el sol y nadar.
6. (Yo) Siempre _____ biblioteca a leer y estudiar.
7. Esteban y Carmen _____ restaurante chino que hay cerca de aquí para cenar.
8. Luis _____ plaza a pasear con una amiga.
9. (Nosotros) _____ librería a comprar el libro de español.
10. (Tú) _____ trabajo después de las clases.

**¿RECUERDA?**

Recall from **Gramática 2.3** that the verbs **querer** (**quiero, quieres, quiere, queremos, queréis, quieren**) and **preferir** (**prefiero, prefieres, prefiere, preferimos, preferís, prefieren**) use two stems in their present-tense conjugations.* The stem containing the vowel **e** appears only in the infinitive and in the **nosotros/as** and **vosotros/as** forms. The stem containing **ie** occurs in the rest of the forms.

## 4.2 Discussing Habitual Actions: Verbs with Stem-Vowel Changes (*ie*, *ue*) in the Present Tense

**A.** Here is the present tense of several commonly used verbs that follow the same pattern of stem-vowel changes as **querer** and **preferir: cerrar** (*to close*), **pensar** (*to think*), **empezar** (*to begin*), **perder** (*to lose*), and **encender** (*to light*; *to turn on*).†

| | cerrar | pensar | empezar | perder | encender |
|---|---|---|---|---|---|
| (yo) | c**ie**rro | p**ie**nso | emp**ie**zo | p**ie**rdo | enc**ie**ndo |
| (tú) | c**ie**rras | p**ie**nsas | emp**ie**zas | p**ie**rdes | enc**ie**ndes |
| (usted, él/ella) | c**ie**rra | p**ie**nsa | emp**ie**za | p**ie**rde | enc**ie**nde |
| (nosotros/as) | cerramos | pensamos | empezamos | perdemos | encendemos |
| (vosotros/as) | cerráis | pensáis | empezáis | perdéis | encendéis |
| (ustedes, ellos/as) | c**ie**rran | p**ie**nsan | emp**ie**zan | p**ie**rden | enc**ie**nden |

**c*ie*rro** = *I close*
**c*e*rramos** = *we close*
**emp*ie*zo** = *I begin*
**emp*e*zamos** = *we begin*

| | |
|---|---|
| —¿A qué hora **cierran** ustedes la Nochevieja? | —*What time do you close on New Year's Eve?* |
| —**Cerramos** a las 5:00 de la tarde. | —*We close at 5:00 P.M.* |

*Recognition: **vos querés, preferís**
†Recognition: **vos cerrás, pensás, empezás, perdés, encendés**

**¿RECUERDA?**

Recall from **Gramática 3.3** that the verb **jugar*** (*to play*) changes the stem vowel **u** to **ue** in exactly the same way as the verbs listed on page 154 change their stem vowel **e** to **ie.**

—¿**Encienden** ustedes las velas de Jánuca cada año?
—Sí, las **encendemos** por ocho noches seguidas.

—*Do you light Hanukkah candles every year?*
—*Yes, we light them for eight nights in a row.*

**B.** Three other verbs follow the same pattern as **jugar**: **dormir** (*to sleep*), **volver** (*to return, go back*), and **almorzar** (*to have lunch*).*

| | jugar | dormir | volver | almorzar |
|---|---|---|---|---|
| (yo) | **jue**go | **due**rmo | **vue**lvo | alm**ue**rzo |
| (tú) | **jue**gas | **due**rmes | **vue**lves | alm**ue**rzas |
| (usted, él/ella) | **jue**ga | **due**rme | **vue**lve | alm**ue**rza |
| (nosotros/as) | jugamos | dormimos | volvemos | almorzamos |
| (vosotros/as) | jugáis | dormís | volvéis | almorzáis |
| (ustedes, ellos/as) | **jue**gan | **due**rmen | **vue**lven | alm**ue**rzan |

**juego** = *I play*
**jugamos** = *we play*
**vuelvo** = *I return*
**volvemos** = *we return*

These forms may be difficult to remember, but they will feel more natural as you hear and read more Spanish. Therefore, don't try to memorize all this, but do refer to the rules when you edit your writing.

—¿A qué hora **vuelven** a casa después de una fiesta?
—A veces no **volvemos** hasta las 3:00 o 4:00 de la madrugada.

—*What time do you return home after a party?*
—*Sometimes we don't return until 3:00 or 4:00 in the morning.*

## Ejercicio 2

¿Qué hacen usted y sus amigos? Complete estas oraciones con la forma correcta del verbo entre paréntesis.

MODELO: —¿*Cierran* ustedes los ojos en clase? (cerrar) →
—No, no *cerramos* los ojos en clase.

1. —¿____ ustedes en su clase de español? (dormir)
—¡Claro que no! Nunca ____ en clase, porque nos divertimos.
2. —¿____ ustedes en casa o en el trabajo? (almorzar)
—Generalmente ____ en casa con la familia.
3. —¿____ ustedes al trabajo después de almorzar? (volver)
—Sí, ____ a las 2:00.
4. —¿____ ustedes al tenis los fines de semana? (jugar)
—A veces ____, a veces no.
5. —¿____ ustedes mucho al tenis en el invierno? (jugar)
—No, ____ poco porque hace demasiado frío.
6. —¿____ ustedes frecuentemente cuando ____ al basquetbol? (perder, jugar)
—No, casi nunca ____ cuando ____ al basquetbol.
7. —¿____ ustedes ir al cine por la tarde? (preferir)
—No, ____ ir por la mañana con los niños.
8. —¿____ ustedes las vacaciones en mayo o en junio? (empezar)
—Normalmente ____ las vacaciones en junio.

*Recognition: **vos jugás, dormís, volvés, almorzás**

## 4.3 Discussing Habitual Actions: Irregular Verbs

**vengo** = *I come*
**viene** = *he/she comes; you come*
**venimos** = *we come*

**A.** As you know, an irregular verb is one that uses more than one stem to form its conjugation. (In many cases the irregularity is only in the **yo** form.) Here are some common verbs that add a **g** in the **yo** form: **tener** (*to have*), **venir** (*to come*), **salir** (*to leave*; *to go out*), and **poner** (*to put*).*

| | tener | venir | salir | poner |
|---|---|---|---|---|
| (yo) | tengo | vengo | salgo | pongo |
| (tú) | tienes | vienes | sales | pones |
| (usted, él/ella) | tiene | viene | sale | pone |
| (nosotros/as) | tenemos | venimos | salimos | ponemos |
| (vosotros/as) | tenéis | venís | salís | ponéis |
| (ustedes, ellos/as) | tienen | vienen | salen | ponen |

—¿Siempre **viene** usted temprano? —*Do you always come early?*
—Sí, casi siempre **vengo** a las 8:00. —*Yes, I almost always come at 8:00.*

—¿Dónde **pongo** mi ropa? —*Where do I put my clothes?*
—Aquí mismo, encima de esta silla. —*Right here, on this chair.*

**digo** = *I say*
**dice** = *he/she says; you say*
**decimos** = *we say*

**B.** The verbs **traer** (*to bring*) and **oír** (*to hear*) insert **ig** in the **yo** form.† In addition, **oír** adds a **y** in all but the **yo, nosotros/as,** and **vosotros/as** forms. The verbs **hacer** and **decir** change the **c** to **g** in the **yo** form. **Decir** (*to say*, *tell*) also changes the stem vowel **e** to **i** in all but the **nosotros/as** and **vosotros/as** forms.‡

| | traer | oír | hacer | decir |
|---|---|---|---|---|
| (yo) | traigo | oigo | hago | digo |
| (tú) | traes | oyes | haces | dices |
| (usted, él/ella) | trae | oye | hace | dice |
| (nosotros/as) | traemos | oímos | hacemos | decimos |
| (vosotros/as) | traéis | oís | hacéis | decís |
| (ustedes, ellos/as) | traen | oyen | hacen | dicen |

—¿Qué **traes** a las fiestas? —*What do you bring to parties?*
—**Traigo** mis discos compactos y algo de comer. —*I bring my CDs and something to eat.*

—¿No **oyes** un ruido extraño? —*Don't you hear a strange noise?*
—No, no **oigo** nada. —*No, I don't hear anything.*

---

*Recognition: **vos tenés, venís, salís, ponés**
†Recognition: **vos traés, oís**
‡Recognition: **vos hacés, decís**

## Ejercicio 3

Un amigo le hace preguntas sobre su clase de español. Contéstele según el modelo.

MODELO: —Generalmente, ¿vienes temprano a la clase de español?
—Sí, *vengo* temprano todos los días.

1. —¿Traes tu perro a la clase de español?
—¡Claro que no! _____ solamente el libro y el cuaderno.
2. —¿Pones tu libro de español debajo de la mesa?
—No, _____ el libro encima de la mesa.
3. —¿Le dices «Buenos días» en español al profesor / a la profesora?
—¡Qué va! A las 2:00 de la tarde le _____ «Buenas tardes».
4. —¿Oyes música en tu clase?
—Sí, _____ canciones en español, naturalmente.
5. —¿Sales de tu clase a las 3:00?
—No, _____ a las 2:50.
6. —¿Siempre vienes a la clase preparado/a?
—Sí, casi siempre _____ preparado/a.
7. —¿Tienes mucha tarea?
—Sí, _____ tarea todos los días excepto el domingo.
8. —¿Qué haces en tu clase?
—_____ un poco de todo: converso, leo, escribo.

## 4.4. Describing Daily Routine: Reflexives

Actions done to oneself are expressed using reflexive words.
**Me afeito**. (*I shave* [*myself*].)
**Nos ponemos la ropa**. (*We put on our clothes.*)

**A.** In English, pronouns that indicate that the subject of a sentence does something to himself or herself are called *reflexive;* they end in *-self* (*-selves*).

He cut himself.
She looked at herself in the mirror.
Babies often talk to themselves.
We didn't blame ourselves.

Some actions that the subject does to himself or herself are not expressed with reflexive pronouns in English. For example, *I get up at 7:00. I take a bath and then get dressed.* In such sentences, Spanish always uses a reflexive pronoun: **Yo me levanto a las 7:00. Me baño y luego me pongo la ropa**.

**B.** Here is the present tense of the verb **levantarse** (*to get up*) with reflexive pronouns.*

**levantarse** (***to get up***)

| | | |
|---|---|---|
| (yo) | me levanto | *I get up* |
| (tú) | te levantas | *you (inf. sing.) get up* |
| (usted, él/ella) | se levanta | *you (pol. sing.) get up; he/she gets up* |
| (nosotros/as) | nos levantamos | *we get up* |
| (vosotros/as) | os levantáis | *you (inf. pl., Spain) get up* |
| (ustedes, ellos/as) | se levantan | *you (pl.) get up; they get up* |

*Recognition: **vos te levantás**

**C.** Following is a list of verbs with the reflexive pronouns **me** (*myself*) and **se** (*himself*, *herself*, *yourself* [*pol. sing.*]) that you can use to describe your daily routine or that of someone else. Notice that the infinitives with the reflexive pronoun end in **se**.

| | INFINITIVE | |
|---|---|---|
| Me acuesto. / Se acuesta.* | acostarse | *I go to bed. / He/She goes to bed; You (pol. sing.) go to bed.* |
| Me despierto. / Se despierta.† | despertarse | *I wake up. / He/She wakes up; You (pol. sing.) wake up.* |
| Me levanto. / Se levanta. | levantarse | *I get up (out of bed). / He/She gets up; You (pol. sing.) get up.* |
| Me baño. / Se baña. | bañarse | *I take a bath. / He/She takes a bath; You (pol. sing.) take a bath.* |
| Me ducho. / Se ducha. | ducharse | *I take a shower. / He/She takes a shower; You (pol. sing.) take a shower.* |
| Me lavo el pelo. / Se lava el pelo. | lavarse el pelo | *I wash my hair. / He/She washes his/her hair; You (pol. sing.) wash your hair.* |
| Me seco. / Se seca. | secarse | *I dry off. / He/She dries off; You (pol. sing.) dry off.* |
| Me afeito. / Se afeita. | afeitarse | *I shave. / He/She shaves; You (pol. sing.) shave.* |
| Me lavo los dientes. / Se lava los dientes. | lavarse los dientes | *I brush my teeth. / He/She brushes his/her teeth; You (pol. sing.) brush your teeth.* |
| Me peino. / Se peina. | peinarse | *I comb my hair. / He/She combs his/her hair; You (pol. sing.) comb your hair.* |
| Me maquillo. / Se maquilla. | maquillarse | *I put on makeup. / He/She puts on makeup; You (pol. sing.) put on makeup.* |
| Me pongo la ropa. / Se pone la ropa. | ponerse la ropa | *I put on my clothes. / He/She puts on his/her clothes; You (pol. sing.) put on your clothes.* |
| Me quito la ropa. / Se quita la ropa. | quitarse la ropa | *I take off my clothes. / He/She takes off his/her clothes; You (pol. sing.) take off your clothes.* |

| | |
|---|---|
| **Me levanto** temprano y **me ducho** en seguida. Generalmente **me lavo** el pelo. Luego **me seco** y **me peino**. | *I get up early and I take a shower immediately. Generally I wash my hair. Afterward I dry off and I comb my hair.* |
| Alberto **se levanta** tarde. **Se ducha** rápidamente, pero no **se afeita**. **Se pone la ropa** y **se peina**. | *Al gets up late. He showers quickly, but doesn't shave. He dresses and combs his hair.* |

**D.** Reflexive pronouns are normally placed directly before the verb (**me seco**), but they may be attached to infinitives (**secarme**) and present participles (**secándome**).

---

*__Acostarse__ is a stem-changing verb: the stem vowel **o** changes to **ue** in all but the **nosotros/as** and **vosotros/as** forms.

†__Despertarse__ is also a stem-changing verb: the stem vowel **e** changes to **ie** in all but the **nosotros/as** and **vosotros/as** forms.

| | |
|---|---|
| Me gusta **afeitarme** primero y luego **bañarme**. | *I like to shave first and then take a bath.* |
| Ernesto va a **levantarse** y **bañarse** inmediatamente. | *Ernesto is going to get up and take a bath immediately.* |
| —Amanda, ¿qué estás haciendo? | *—Amanda, what are you doing?* |
| —Estoy **lavándome** los dientes. | *—I'm brushing my teeth.* |

## Ejercicio 4

¿Qué oración describe mejor los siguientes dibujos?

1. d

2. b

3. f

4. e

5. c

6. g

7. a

**a.** Él se quita la camisa, pero ella se pone los zapatos.
**b.** Él sale para el trabajo a las 8:00, pero su hijo sale para la escuela a las 8:30.
**c.** Ella lee novelas después de trabajar, pero él prefiere ver la televisión.
**d.** Este joven se ducha por la mañana, pero las niñas prefieren bañarse por la noche.
**e.** Él se afeita la cara, pero su esposa se afeita las piernas.
**f.** A él no le gusta bañarse, pero le gusta bañar al perro.
**g.** Se acuesta a las 11:30 y se levanta a las 6:00.

### Ejercicio 5

Imagínese que su hermanito de tres años le hace estas preguntas tontas. Contéstele correctamente.

MODELO: ¿Te lavas los dientes con jabón? →
No, me lavo los dientes con pasta de dientes.

1. ¿Te bañas antes de las 5:00 de la mañana?
2. ¿Te lavas el pelo con detergente?
3. ¿Te afeitas en la lavandería?
4. ¿Te levantas temprano los domingos?
5. ¿Te quitas la ropa en la universidad?
6. ¿Te peinas en la biblioteca?
7. ¿Te maquillas en la clase de español?
8. ¿Te duchas por la noche?

## 4.5 Describing States: *estar* + Adjective

**Estar** (*to be*) describes a state (how someone is at a particular time).
—¿**Cómo estás**? (*How are you?*)
—**Estoy cansada**. (*I'm tired.*)

Use **estar** (**estoy, estás, está, estamos, estáis, están**) to describe how someone is, or is feeling, at a particular time.

| | |
|---|---|
| —¿Cómo **estás**? | —*How are you?* |
| —**Estoy** un poco deprimido. | —*I'm a bit depressed.* |
| —¿Cómo **está** José Luis hoy? | —*How is José Luis today?* |
| —**Está** enfermo. | —*He's sick.* |
| —¿Cómo **están** ustedes? | —*How are you?* |
| —**Estamos** muy bien, gracias. | —*We are fine, thank you.* |

Remember that **ser** is used to identify or describe the relatively permanent characteristics of someone or something, *not* to tell how that person or thing is (feeling) at a particular moment.

| | |
|---|---|
| Alberto **es alto, delgado, joven y muy guapo**. | *Al is tall, thin, young, and very handsome.* |
| Hoy **está confundido y cansado**. | *Today he's confused and tired.* |

### Ejercicio 6

Describa el estado físico o anímico de estas personas.

MODELOS: Carmen → Carmen *está nerviosa*.
yo → Yo *estoy cansado*.

| | |
|---|---|
| 1. yo | a. está nervioso |
| 2. mi primo | b. están ocupados |
| 3. Luis y yo | c. estoy enojado/a |
| 4. Nora | d. estamos preocupados |
| 5. tú (*f.*) | e. estás contenta |
| 6. Pablo y Mónica | f. está deprimida |

## Ejercicio 7

Mire los dibujos y haga preguntas. Use la forma correcta de **estar** y adjetivos como (**un poco**) **triste**, **ocupado/a**, **cansado/a**, **enojado/a**, **deprimido/a**, **interesado/a en...** , **irritado/a**, **contento/a**, **enamorado/a**, etcétera.

MODELO: ¿Está cansada Graciela?

**¿RECUERDA?**

Recall from **Gramática C.1** the forms of **tener: tengo, tienes, tiene, tenemos, tenéis, tienen.**

## 4.6 Describing States: *tener* + Noun

Some states of being are described in Spanish with the verb **tener** (*to have*), although they correspond to the verb *to be* in English. Common states expressed with **tener** are **tener hambre** (*to be hungry*), **tener sueño** (*to be sleepy*), **tener sed** (*to be thirsty*), **tener prisa** (*to be in a hurry*), **tener frío** (*to be cold*), **tener calor** (*to be hot*), and **tener miedo** (*to be afraid*).

**Tener** + noun is used to describe some states.
**¿Tienes hambre, Yolanda?** (*Are you hungry, Yolanda?*)

| | |
|---|---|
| —Ernesto, ¿cuándo quieres comer? **Tengo** mucha **hambre**. | —*Ernesto, when do you want to eat? I'm very hungry.* |
| —Estela, ¿quieren ir al cine tú y Ernesto esta noche? —No, gracias. **Tenemos** mucho **sueño** y queremos acostarnos. | —*Estela, do you and Ernesto want to go to the movies tonight?* —*No, thanks. We're very sleepy and want to go to bed.* |
| —Guillermo, ¿**tienes sed**? —Sí, **tengo** mucha **sed**. Vamos a tomar algo. | —*Guillermo, are you thirsty?* —*Yes, I'm very thirsty. Let's get something to drink* (*drink something*). |
| —¿Por qué **tiene prisa** Amanda? —Porque su clase empieza a las 8:00. | —*Why is Amanda in a hurry?* —*Because her class begins at 8:00.* |

With the words **calor/frío** (*heat/cold*) and **caliente** (*hot*), several combinations are possible.

To describe people, use **tener** + **calor/frío**.

| | |
|---|---|
| —Nora, ¿tú no **tienes calor**? | *—Nora, aren't you hot?* |
| —No, no **tengo calor**. Me gusta mucho el sol. | *—No, I'm not hot. I love the sun.* |

To describe things, use **estar** + **caliente/frío**.

| | |
|---|---|
| Lan, cuidado. No toques la estufa. **Está** muy **caliente**. | *Lan, be careful. Don't touch the stove. It's very hot.* |

To describe the weather, use **hacer** + **calor/frío**.

| | |
|---|---|
| Ay, Pablo, **hace mucho frío** hoy. Voy a ponerme un abrigo. | *Paul, it's really cold today. I'm going to put on a coat.* |

## Ejercicio 8

Describa el estado de estas personas. Estados posibles: **tener calor**, **frío**, **hambre**, **prisa**, **sed**, **sueño**, **miedo**.

MODELO: (Yo) *Tengo prisa* porque la clase empieza a las 4:00.

1. A mediodía, Mayín _____.
2. Si (tú) _____, ¿por qué no te pones un suéter?
3. (Nosotros) _____ porque la temperatura está a 45°C hoy.
4. A medianoche (yo) _____.
5. Estoy en casa. Son las 8:55 y tengo una clase a las 9:00. (Yo) _____.
6. Hace mucho sol hoy. Guillermo y Ernestito quieren tomar agua fría porque _____.
7. Cuando estoy solo/a de noche, a veces _____.
8. ¿Tienes algo para tomar? (Yo) _____.

## Ejercicio 9

Mire los dibujos. ¿Cuál es la oración que mejor identifica cada dibujo?

MODELO: Tiene sed.

a. Tienen miedo.
b. Tiene prisa.
c. Tiene calor.
e. Hace mucho calor.
f. Nieva hoy.
g. Está enojado.
i. Está preocupado.
j. Está deprimido.
k. Tiene hambre.

1. _____

2. _____

3. _____

4. _____

5. _____

CAPÍTULO 5

# Las clases y las carreras

**METAS**

In **Capítulo 5,** you will discuss classroom activities and your classmates' talents and abilities. You will also talk about careers and recreational plans for the future.

Santiago, República Dominicana: la Universidad de Madre y Maestra

**ACTIVIDADES DE COMUNICACIÓN Y LECTURAS**


Las actividades de la clase de español

**Las palabras viven** El inglés y el español

Las habilidades

**Nota cultural** Los gestos

**El mundo hispano...** en los Estados Unidos

Las carreras y las actividades del trabajo

**El mundo hispano...** imágenes

**El mundo hispano...** su gente

Las actividades futuras

**Lectura** Los amigos hispanos: Adriana Bolini

**EN RESUMEN**


**GRAMÁTICA Y EJERCICIOS**


5.1 Telling to Whom Something Is Said: Indirect Object Pronouns with Verbs of Informing

5.2 Expressing Abilities: **saber** and **poder** + Infinitive

5.3 Pointing out People and Objects: Demonstrative Adjectives

5.4 Expressing Plans and Desires: **pensar, quisiera, me gustaría, tener ganas de**

5.5 Ordering Events: Infinitives after Prepositions

5.6 Making Suggestions: *Let's*

# Actividades de comunicación y lecturas

## Las actividades de la clase de español

*Lea Gramática 5.1.*

Alberto les habla a sus compañeros.

Mónica le escribe una carta a su amigo.

La profesora nos dice «Buenos días».

La profesora nos hace preguntas.

Le contestamos a la profesora.

Nora le lee las Notas culturales a Esteban.

Carmen le hace una pregunta a la profesora Martínez.

La profesora le explica la gramática a Carmen.

## Actividad 1. Encuesta: ¿Con qué frecuencia?

¿Con qué frecuencia hacen ustedes las siguientes actividades en la clase de español?

MODELOS: Escribimos las palabras nuevas en el cuaderno *todos los días*.

*A veces* leemos las Notas culturales.

La profesora *siempre* nos hace preguntas.

### PALABRAS ÚTILES

| | |
|---|---|
| nunca | muchas veces |
| raras veces | siempre |
| a veces | todos los días |

1. Les hablamos a los compañeros de clase.
2. Escribimos las palabras nuevas en el cuaderno.
3. Merendamos en el salón de clase.
4. Contestamos las preguntas del profesor / de la profesora.
5. Escuchamos las opiniones de los compañeros de clase.
6. Jugamos juegos de video.
7. Aprendemos palabras nuevas.
8. Le hacemos preguntas al profesor / a la profesora.
9. Hacemos la tarea en clase.
10. Dormimos una siesta.
11. Le decimos «Buenas noches» al profesor / a la profesora.
12. Les escribimos cartas a los parientes.

## Actividad 2. Preferencias: La clase de español

Aquí hay varias actividades relacionadas con la clase de español. Póngalas en orden, del número 1 (¡Me gusta mucho!) al número 7 (¡No me gusta nada!). Después, compare sus respuestas con las de sus compañeros de clase.

1. En el salón de clase:
   a. 7 tomar exámenes
   b. 3 trabajar en grupos
   c. 4 escuchar al profesor / a la profesora cuando nos habla
   d. 1 hablarles a mis compañeros en español
   e. 6 ver videos
   f. 2 participar en conversaciones
   g. 5 escuchar música hispana o cantar en español

2. Fuera del salón de clase:
   a. 5 estudiar para los exámenes
   b. 2 escribir composiciones
   c. 4 hacer la tarea de gramática
   d. 3 escuchar las cintas de comprensión oral
   e. 1 hablarles a mis amigos hispanos en español
   f. 6 ver la televisión en español
   g. 7 escuchar una emisora de radio hispana

## Actividad 3. Descripción de dibujos: En la universidad

Escuche a su profesor(a) mientras él/ella describe las actividades de los estudiantes norteamericanos. Diga el número del dibujo que corresponde a cada descripción.

1.

2.

3.

4.

Ahora, escoja uno de los dibujos y descríbaselo a su compañero/a. Él/Ella va a decir cuál de los dibujos usted describe.

**ESCUELA DE IDIOMAS "NERJA"**

ESCUELA DE IDIOMAS "NERJA"

***CURSOS DE ESPAÑOL***

**PARA GRUPOS E INDIVIDUALES**
**DURANTE TODO EL AÑO**
**ESTANCIAS DE 2 A 24 SEMANAS**

IALC

**OFRECEMOS PROGRAMAS VARIADOS**
**INTENSIVOS,PROFESORES,NEGOCIOS,EXAMENES OFICIALES**
**ACTIVIDADES CULTURALES Y SOCIALES**
**EXCURSIONES,COCINA,BAILE FLAMENCO,FIESTAS,DEPORTES...**
**ALOJAMIENTOS : FAMILIAS Y APARTAMENTOS.**
**Pídanos información detallada:**

**ESCUELA DE IDIOMAS "NERJA".**
**C/Almirante Ferrandiz 73, Aptado.46.**
**29780 NERJA-MALAGA-ESPAÑA**
**Tfno: 34 5 252 16 87 Fax: 34 5 2 52 21 19**
**E-Mail: idnerja@gandalf.leader.es.**

En la Costa del Sol, en un pueblo andaluz de 15ooo habitantes al lado del mar y rodeado de montañas.A cincuenta minutos del aeropuerto de Málaga.La Escuela está situada en el centro, en una casa típica con amplio jardín.Todo " a unos pasos ".

## Actividad 4. Entrevista: La clase de español

1. ¿Te asigna mucha tarea el profesor / la profesora? ¿Lees todas las lecturas? ¿Dónde escuchas las cintas de comprensión oral: en tu coche, en casa o en el laboratorio de lenguas?
2. ¿Les explicas a tus compañeros cómo hacer la tarea cuando ellos no comprenden las instrucciones del profesor / de la profesora? ¿Te ayudan ellos?
3. ¿A veces llegas tarde a clase? Cuando llegas tarde, ¿qué le dices al profesor / a la profesora?
4. ¿Te gusta cuando el profesor / la profesora te hace una pregunta? ¿Siempre le contestas al profesor / a la profesora en español? ¿Piensas en español cuando hablas español?
5. ¿Te gusta la clase de español? ¿Qué cosas *no* te gusta hacer en la clase?

**LAS PALABRAS VIVEN**

# El inglés y el español

**VOCABULARIO ÚTIL**

| | |
|---|---|
| extranjeras | *foreign* |
| el jonrón | *home run* |
| los préstamos | *borrowed words; lit. loan* |
| pertenecían | *belonged* |
| la pista | *clue; hint* |
| encontrar | *to find* |

La adopción de palabras extranjeras ocurre con frecuencia en todos los idiomas. ¡Es un proceso natural! Por ejemplo, en el idioma español se usan diariamente palabras inglesas. En la comida, **bistec** —que viene de *beef steak*— y **sándwich.** En la ropa, **suéter** y **jeans.** Cuando se habla de deportes, los hispanos juegan al **fútbol,** al **basquetbol,** al **voleibol,** y hacen un **jonrón** o meten un **gol.** Entre los préstamos más recientes están los anglicismos el **estrés** y, del campo de las computadoras, **formatear.**

El inglés también tiene palabras que normalmente se consideran parte del idioma español: por ejemplo, *vista*, *plaza*, *sierra*, *rodeo*, *patio* y *siesta*. Otras palabras inglesas de origen español, un poco modificadas, son *cigar* (**cigarro**) y *lasso* (**lazo**). El inglés también usa palabras de origen indígena que ya forman parte del español que se habla hoy en día: *tamale* (**tamal**), de la lengua náhuatl en México; y *hurricane* (**huracán**) y *barbecue* (**barbacoa**), de la lengua de los indígenas del Caribe.

La influencia del español es muy evidente en los nombres geográficos. *Colorado*, *California*, *Nevada*, *San Francisco*, *San Diego*, *Los Angeles*, *Santa Fe*, *El Paso*, *Amarillo*, *Pueblo* y muchos otros nombres de ciudades y estados norteamericanos son españoles. ¿Sabe usted por qué tienen nombres en español estos lugares? La razón es que muchos de estos sitios pertenecían a México antes de formar parte de los Estados Unidos. Toda la región suroeste era territorio mexicano.

¿Puede usted nombrar otras palabras de origen extranjero que se usan en el inglés? Pista: En el vocabulario de la comida, ¡va a encontrar varias!

# Las habilidades

*Lea Gramática 5.2.*

—Señora Ramírez, ¿sabe usted montar a caballo?
—Sí, y también sé jugar al polo.

—Y sus hijos, ¿saben ellos montar a caballo también?
—No, pero saben patinar.

Ahora mi hijo Guillermo no puede patinar; tiene una pierna fracturada. Sólo puede leer y ver la televisión.

## Actividad 5. Descripción de dibujos: ¿Qué saben hacer estas personas?

Escuche a su profesor(a) mientras él/ella describe los talentos de las siguientes personas. Diga quién es cada persona que describe.

Susana

Estela

Raúl

Doña María Eulalia

Pilar

Nacho

Ricardo

Adriana

## Actividad 6. Orden lógico: Ernestito quiere bañar al perro

Busque el orden correcto de estas oraciones.

_____ ERNESTITO: Mamá, tengo ocho años. ¡Sé bañar a un perro!
_____ ESTELA: Perfecto, pero también vas a...
_____ ESTELA: Bueno, hijo, después de bañarlo, vas a secarlo muy bien.
_____ ERNESTITO: Ya sé, mamá.
_____ ESTELA: Sí, hijo, pero antes de traer al perro, prepara el agua y el jabón.
_____ ERNESTITO: Mamá, mamá, ¿puedo bañar a Lobo?
_____ ERNESTITO: Ya está todo listo, mamá.

## Actividad 7. Entrevistas: ¿Qué sabes hacer? ¿Qué puedes hacer?

LAS HABILIDADES

MODELO: E1: ¿Sabes *esquiar*?
E2: Sí, sé *esquiar*. (No, no sé *esquiar*. / Sí, sé *esquiar un poco*.)

1. patinar en el hielo
2. jugar al basquetbol
3. nadar
4. preparar comida mexicana
5. reparar carros
6. montar en motocicleta
7. bucear
8. hablar otro idioma (¿cuál?)
9. tocar algún instrumento musical (¿cuál?)
10. pintar

EN TU CASA O EN LA RESIDENCIA ESTUDIANTIL

MODELO: E1: ¿Puedes *hacer la tarea en casa* (*en la residencia estudiantil*)?
E2: No, no puedo *hacer la tarea en casa porque hay muchas distracciones*.

1. cenar a la hora que quieras
2. tener animales domésticos donde vives
3. ver la televisión a cualquier hora
4. dormir hasta las 10:00 de la mañana
5. escuchar música y hacer la tarea a la vez

NOTA CULTURAL

# Los gestos

Aunque comunicamos las ideas con palabras, también usamos el cuerpo para la comunicación. Por ejemplo, cuando conocemos a una persona por primera vez, le damos la mano. Y para despedirnos o saludar a alguien también usamos las manos a veces.

(Continúa)

Hay gestos que son universales; hay otros que varían de cultura a cultura. ¡Tenga cuidado! En algunos casos, un gesto que se usa en un país puede crear grandes problemas en otro, porque significa algo diferente.

Aquí tiene usted algunos de los gestos que caracterizan a los hispanos. Éstos son los más usados en España y en América Latina.

**1.** No.

**2.** Quiero comer.

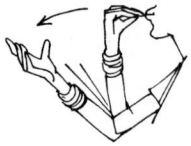

**3.** ¡Excelente!

**4.** furioso/a (enojado/a)

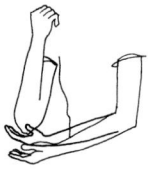

**5.** tacaño/a

**6.** muy amigos

**7.** Un momentito...

**8.** dinero (cuesta mucho)

**9.** ¡Ojo! ¡Tenga cuidado!

## Comprensión

Mire los dibujos y después indique qué gesto se puede usar en las siguientes situaciones.

2 **1.** Un chico tiene mucha hambre.
3 **2.** El profesor está muy contento con la clase.
9 **3.** La recepcionista de una oficina le dice que usted tiene que esperar.
4 **4.** Una muchacha ve a su novio con otra chica.
5 **5.** Un hombre no quiere llevar a su esposa a un restaurante caro.

## Ahora... ¡usted!

1. Haga algunos gestos que caracterizan a los norteamericanos (o a las personas de su país de origen). ¿Qué significan?
2. ¿Conoce algunos gestos similares a los de los hispanos, pero que signifiquen otra cosa? ¿Cómo son y qué significan?

### Un paso más... ¡a escribir!

Escoja una de las situaciones de la actividad de Comprensión y escriba un diálogo corto entre las personas, haciendo referencia a los gestos que hacen cuando hablan. Aquí tiene un ejemplo para la primera situación.

MODELO: HIJO: Papá, tengo mucha hambre.
(*Hace un gesto; pone la mano cerca de la boca y mueve la mano.*)
PAPÁ: Bueno, estoy preparando los sándwiches. Un momentito.
(*Hace un gesto con los dedos.*)
HIJO: ¿Sándwiches? ¡Súper! ¡Excelente!
(*Hace un gesto; se besa los dedos y luego los extiende.*)

## EL MUNDO HISPANO... en los Estados Unidos

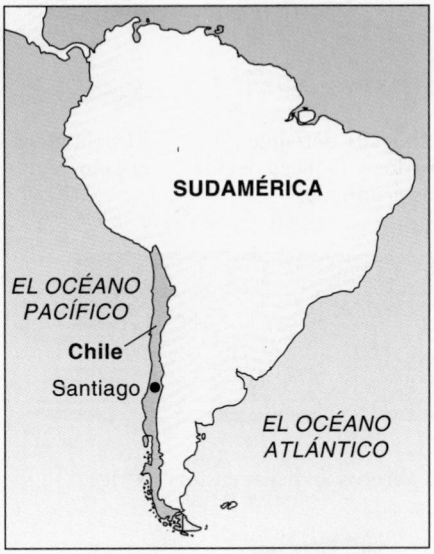


**H**eidi Mercado-Littles tiene 45 años y es chilena. Heidi lleva 20 años en los Estados Unidos y ahora vive en Filadelfia.

*¿Qué cosas sabe usted hacer muy bien? ¿Qué le gustaría poder hacer que no puede hacer ahora? ¿Piensa aprender a hacer eso?*

Muchas de las cosas que hago bien son cosas artísticas. Toco el piano, la guitarra y canto bien. También dibujo y pinto bastante bien. Me gusta trabajar con las manos. Siempre les hago los regalos[1] de cumpleaños a mis niños. Me gustaría aprender a usar una computadora. Espero hacerlo en un futuro cercano.[2]

[1]*presents* [2]*near*

# Las carreras y las actividades del trabajo

***Lea Gramática 5.3.***

El cocinero prepara la comida y el mesero les sirve a los clientes.

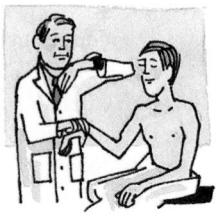

El médico examina a los enfermos.

Los bomberos apagan los incendios.

La cajera recibe el dinero en un banco o en una tienda.

El plomero repara la tubería.

La abogada defiende a los acusados y la jueza decide casos criminales.

El peluquero corta el pelo.

La enfermera cuida a los enfermos.

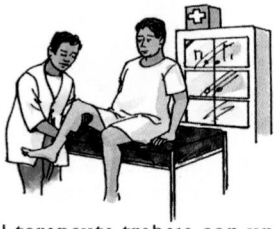

El terapeuta trabaja con un paciente.

Los obreros trabajan en una fábrica.

Esta dependienta habla con una clienta.

Aquella dependienta habla con la supervisora.

Ese dependiente arregla la ropa.

La mecánico repara el automóvil.

## Actividad 8. Asociaciones: ¿Dónde trabaja?

MODELO: Un mecánico trabaja en un taller de reparaciones.

1. f un(a) electricista
2. d un mesero / una mesera
3. j un peluquero / una peluquera
4. b un médico / una doctora
5. k un(a) piloto
6. h un cajero / una cajera
7. n un secretario ejecutivo / una secretaria ejecutiva
8. i un dependiente / una dependienta
9. o un(a) cantante
10. l un profesor / una profesora
11. g un obrero / una obrera industrial
12. m un(a) mecánico
13. e un cocinero / una cocinera
14. c un(a) chofer
15. a un programador / una programadora

a. en un cuarto con muchas computadoras
b. en su consultorio y en un hospital
c. en un autobús
d. en un restaurante
e. en la cocina de un restaurante
f. en la calle o en una casa, con cables eléctricos
g. en una fábrica
h. en un banco
i. en una tienda
j. en una peluquería
k. en un avión
l. en una universidad
m. en un taller de reparaciones
n. en una oficina
o. en un club nocturno

## Actividad 9. Encuesta: Su opinión, por favor

Lea esta lista de profesiones y oficios y marque el más interesante (= 1), el más aburrido (= 2), el más peligroso (= 3), el más necesario (= 4) y el más prestigioso (= 5).

_____ agente de seguros
_____ ama de casa
_____ asistente de médico
_____ (mujer) policía
_____ contador(a)
_____ (mujer) bombero
_____ electricista
_____ gerente
_____ hombre/mujer de negocios
_____ plomero/a
_____ programador(a)
_____ secretario ejecutivo / secretaria ejecutiva
_____ abogado/a
_____ trabajador(a) social

Ahora, compare su opinión con las de sus compañeros y diga por qué usted piensa así.

## Actividad 10. Identificaciones: Un juego

Trate de adivinar la profesión de estas seis personas: los Hurtado (Jaime y Ana), los Pérez (Hugo y Cecilia) y los Salinas (Alejandro y Olivia). Las posibilidades son **doctor(a), dentista, ingeniero/a, maestro/a, secretario/a** y **abogado/a.** Use la siguiente información para encontrar la solución.

1. Ana trabaja en un hospital, pero no es doctora.
2. El esposo de la abogada es ingeniero.
3. La secretaria está casada con un doctor.
4. El esposo de la dentista trabaja en una escuela.
5. Jaime trabaja con enfermeras.
6. Alejandro enseña matemáticas.

## Actividad 11. Entrevistas: Las carreras y el trabajo

LAS CARRERAS

1. ¿Cuál es tu clase favorita en la universidad?
2. ¿Es requisito esa clase para tu especialidad?
3. ¿Qué carrera quieres seguir? ¿Cuántos años tienes que estudiar?
4. ¿Son buenos los sueldos en esa carrera?
5. Después de la graduación, ¿dónde quieres trabajar?

EL TRABAJO

6. ¿Tienes trabajo de jornada completa o de media jornada ahora?
7. ¿Dónde trabajas? ¿Cuánto tiempo tardas en ir de tu casa al trabajo?
8. ¿A qué hora entras al trabajo? ¿A qué hora sales? ¿Te gustan tus horas de trabajo? ¿Por qué? Explica.
9. ¿Qué haces en tu trabajo? ¿Haces actividades diferentes o siempre la misma? De todas las actividades de tu trabajo, ¿cuál te gusta más? ¿Por qué?
10. ¿Cuáles son los aspectos desagradables de tu trabajo? ¿Por qué?

## Actividad 12. Del mundo hispano: ¿Busca empleo?

Conteste las preguntas según la información en estos avisos clasificados.

SE NECESITA cocinero/a con experiencia en comida mexicana. Venga personalmente a la Calle Obregón 838.

BAR «Noche de Ronda» necesita meseras/os para atender mesas. Sueldo y comisión. Si le interesa, favor de llamar al 45-67-94.

SECRETARIA/O con tres años de experiencia. Algo de inglés y que escriba a máquina mínimo 50 ppm, para trabajo estable de oficina cerca del centro. Llame sólo de 5 a 7 P.M. 58-03-49.

GUARDIA h/m. Para trabajo de noche, 4 días a la semana. Llame al 49-05-34.

CHOFER h/m. Con experiencia. Debe hablar inglés. Compañía «Transportes El Blanco» en Coyoacán. 67-45-93.

CARPINTERO h/m. Con experiencia en todo tipo de muebles. Llame de 9–11 A.M. al Sr. Varniz. 80-34-76.

ATENCIÓN: Compañía Hnos. Menéndez necesita varias personas bilingües para sus oficinas en Laredo y Ciudad Juárez. Llame al 56-94-93 o al 93-57-00 desde las 10 hasta las 2.

TALLER DE REPARACIONES busca mecánico con experiencia. Cinco días por semana. Buen sueldo. 56-94-83.

1. ¿Qué tienen que hacer las personas que trabajan en el bar Noche de Ronda?
2. ¿Qué aptitudes necesita tener el/la chofer?
3. Si usted quiere el trabajo de secretario/a, ¿qué experiencia necesita tener?
4. Si usted sabe hacer muebles, ¿a quién tiene que llamar?
5. ¿Qué tiene que saber hacer el cocinero / la cocinera?
6. ¿Es necesario ser hombre para obtener el trabajo de guardia?
7. ¿Qué compañía necesita personas que hablen inglés y español?
8. Si usted sabe reparar coches, ¿a qué número tiene que llamar?

## EL MUNDO HISPANO... imágenes

El sistema escolar en el mundo hispano se divide, por lo general, en cuatro partes: la educación primaria, la secundaria, la preparatoria y la universitaria. La primaria dura seis años. Después, los estudiantes reciben enseñanza preparatoria si quieren seguir estudios universitarios. En la universidad escogen[1] una carrera —Medicina, Filosofía y Letras, Derecho, Ingeniería— y estudian de cuatro a cinco años en la facultad[2] de su elección.

[1]*they choose* [2]*department*

San José, Costa Rica: Estos estudiantes de secundaria participan en un experimento en su clase de química.

Lima, Perú

**¡REÍR ES VIVIR!**

**En la escuela**

Una madre conversa con el maestro de su hijo.
—Maestro, ¿qué tal va mi hijo en la escuela?
—Bueno, pues... ¡como un pez en el agua!
—¿Qué hace?
—Nada.

## EL MUNDO HISPANO... su gente

Su nombre es Erick Mario Braun Santizo y tiene 21 años. Erick es costarricense.

*Háblenos de las profesiones de sus padres.*

Mi padre es técnico en telecomunicaciones y trabaja para el Instituto Costarricense de Electricidad, empresa[1] que también está encargada[2] del servicio telefónico del país. Mi madre es empresaria[3] y tiene su propio negocio;[4] tiene una fábrica procesadora de productos de maíz.

[1]*company* [2]está... *is in charge* [3]*businesswoman* [4]su... *her own business*

# Las actividades futuras

*Lea Gramática 5.4–5.6.*

## Éstos son los planes y los deseos de Pilar Álvarez, José Estrada y Clara Martín.

Estudio informática, porque quisiera ganar mucho dinero.

Después de graduarse, José va a ir de vacaciones a México.

Nos gustaría ir a bailar este viernes por la noche.

Clara piensa quedarse en casa el viernes por la noche. Tiene ganas de descansar.

### Actividad 13. Intercambios: Los planes y los deseos

Escuche a su profesor(a) mientras él/ella describe estos dibujos. Diga quién es la persona en ellos. Ahora, pregúntele a su compañero/a cuáles son los planes y deseos de las siguientes personas. Use **le gustaría, quisiera, piensa** y **antes de** o **después de.**

MODELO: E1: ¿Qué le gustaría hacer a Amanda *después de jugar al tenis?*
E2: Le gustaría *tomar un refresco.*

**1.** Paula

**2.** Guillermo

**3.** Pedro

**4.** Raúl

**5.** doña Lola

**6.** don Eduardo

**7.** doña Rosita

**8.** Ernesto

## Actividad 14. Preferencias: Los planes

Diga sí o no.

1. El sábado por la noche pienso...
   a. salir con los amigos.
   b. ir al cine.
   c. quedarme en casa.
   d. ¿ ?
2. Este fin de semana voy a...
   a. levantarme temprano.
   b. dormir todo el día.
   c. limpiar la casa.
   d. ¿ ?
3. Este fin de semana mi padre tiene ganas de...
   a. acostarse tarde.
   b. trabajar en el jardín.
   c. merendar con la familia.
   d. ¿ ?
4. Durante las vacaciones mis hermanos quisieran...
   a. estudiar.
   b. divertirse mucho.
   c. leer varias novelas policíacas.
   d. ¿ ?
5. El próximo verano a mi amigo/a le gustaría...
   a. trabajar de mesero/a en un restaurante.
   b. viajar a España.
   c. tomar una clase de fotografía.
   d. ¿ ?

### Y TÚ, ¿QUÉ DICES?

| | | |
|---|---|---|
| ¿Dónde? | ¡Qué divertido! | ¿Por qué? |
| ¿Con quién(es)? | Yo también. | ¿Otra vez? |

MODELO: E1: Este fin de semana mi padre tiene ganas de merendar con la familia.
E2: ¿Dónde? ¿En qué parque?

## Actividad 15. Encuesta: ¿Cuáles son sus planes?

1. Mañana, antes de ir a clases,...
2. Hoy, después de clases,...
3. Esta noche, antes de acostarme,...
4. Hoy, después de hacer la tarea,...
5. Antes de salir para el trabajo,...
6. Este fin de semana,...
7. Durante las vacaciones de invierno (verano, primavera),...

a. voy a _____.
b. pienso _____.
c. quisiera _____.
d. me gustaría _____.
e. tengo ganas de _____.

Estudiantes de Derecho en la Universidad de La Habana, Cuba.

## Actividad 16. Intercambios: ¿Qué quieres hacer?

Miren los dibujos a continuación. ¿Qué sugerencias hacen las personas? Inventen su diálogo.

MODELO: E1: ¿Qué quieres hacer?
E2: Vamos a *jugar al voleibol.*

# Los amigos hispanos: Adriana Bolini

**VOCABULARIO ÚTIL**

| | |
|---|---|
| la informática | *data processing* |
| entrena | *she trains* |
| los empleados | *employees* |
| los negocios | *business* |

En esta lectura se describe a una mujer argentina que sabe mucho de computadoras.[1] Ella vive en Buenos Aires.

Adriana Bolini tiene treinta y cinco años y trabaja en el Centro Argentino de Informática. Parte de su trabajo es estudiar los últimos modelos de computadoras y programas de informática que llegan al país. Adriana también entrena a los nuevos empleados del Centro en el uso de algunos programas.

[1]En español se usan las siguientes palabras para *computer*: **computadora** y **computador** (que son traducciones del inglés) en Hispanoamérica; **ordenador,** del francés *ordinateur*, en España.

Para Adriana, su profesión está llena de estímulos. Varias veces al año hace viajes de negocios a Brasil, Venezuela, México y los Estados Unidos. Asiste con frecuencia a exposiciones donde se presentan los últimos avances tecnológicos en el campo de las computadoras. Además del español, Adriana habla italiano —el idioma de sus padres[2]— y también inglés y francés. Le gustaría aprender japonés.

Adriana se divierte cuando puede; sale con sus amigos y va a fiestas, al teatro y al cine. Piensa casarse algún día porque le gustaría tener su propia familia, un esposo e hijos. Pero por el momento, prefiere disfrutar de su independencia y de su trabajo. Por ahora su profesión tiene prioridad en su vida.

[2]Muchos argentinos son de ascendencia italiana.

## Comprensión

Indique si estas actividades de Adriana son negocios (**N**), diversión (**D**) o los dos (**LD**).

1. N Adriana va diariamente al Centro Argentino de Informática.
2. D Sale con sus amigos.
3. N Entrena a otros empleados.
4. LD Viaja a Brasil, Venezuela, México y los Estados Unidos.
5. N Asiste a exposiciones internacionales.
6. LD Usa su computadora personal.
7. D Va al teatro y al cine.
8. LD Habla español, italiano, inglés y francés.

## Ahora... ¡usted!

1. ¿Cree usted que hay más trabajo que diversión en su propia vida? ¿Qué aspectos de su rutina o de sus actividades quisiera cambiar?
2. ¿Usa usted una computadora? ¿Para qué la usa? ¿Cree que es importante hoy día saber usar la computadora? ¿Por qué sí o por qué no?

### Un paso más... ¡a escribir!

Imagínese que su amigo/a es un personaje (*character*) de un libro de texto como *Dos mundos*. ¡Escriba una descripción de ese personaje! Puede usar la lectura como modelo.

(*Nombre*) tiene (*edad*) y trabaja en (*lugar*). Parte de su trabajo es...

# En resumen

## De todo un poco

¿Qué oficio o carrera deben escoger?

Trabajen en grupos de tres para adivinar qué carreras son más apropiadas para las siguientes personas.

1. Juan Limón: Es una persona activa; nunca descansa. Nunca tiene miedo, y le gustaría ser héroe. Sabe manejar muy bien y maneja muy rápido.
2. Guadalupe Morales: Siempre contesta todas las preguntas que le hace la profesora de biología. Sabe mucho del cuerpo humano. No necesita dormir muchas horas. Le gusta ayudar a la gente enferma.
3. Ángela López: Les hace muchas preguntas a los profesores. No es tímida. Siempre quiere hacer presentaciones en clase. Nunca está nerviosa cuando habla en público. Cree que la justicia es muy importante y le gustaría defender a las personas inocentes. Quisiera ser famosa y millonaria.
4. Lilián Torreón: Piensa trabajar en un hospital o en una clínica. Es muy simpática, y sabe bastante sobre el cuerpo humano. También sabe usar las manos para tratar a los deportistas que tienen accidentes.

## ¡Dígalo por escrito!

Descripciones de los compañeros de clase

Trabajando en el mismo grupo, escriban descripciones de dos o tres compañeros para la clase. Hablen de los planes y deseos de la persona, de sus habilidades y de su personalidad. Usen las descripciones de la actividad anterior como modelos. ¡No se olviden de ponerle nombre y apellido(s) a cada persona que describan! Después de escribir las descripciones, escojan a un miembro del grupo para leerlas en voz alta. ¡A ver qué tal adivinan los otros compañeros de clase!

## VIDEOTECA

En este episodio, usted regresa a la Ciudad de México. Lupe Carrasco, la amiga de Diego, busca trabajo. Diego le lee a Lupe los anuncios clasificados. ¿Qué quisiera hacer Lupe? ¿Qué le sugiere Diego? ¿Dónde tiene Lupe la entrevista? ¿Qué le pregunta a Lupe la señora Ibáñez? ¿Por qué son importantes las horas de trabajo? En el Capítulo 5 del *Cuaderno de trabajo* hay más actividades para hacer después de ver este segmento de video.

# Vocabulario

## Las actividades en la clase de español
Activities in Spanish Class

| | |
|---|---|
| **comprender** | to understand |
| **enseñar** | to teach |
| **explicar** | to explain |
| **hacer preguntas** | to ask questions |
| **llegar (tarde / a tiempo)** | to arrive (late / on time) |
| **pensar (ie)** | to think |
| **pensar en** | to think about |

**PALABRA SEMEJANTE: asignar**

**REPASO: aprender**

## Las habilidades
Abilities

| | |
|---|---|
| **poder (ue)** | to be able to |
| **saber** (+ *infin.*) | to know how to (*do something*) |

## Las profesiones y las carreras
Professions and Careers

| | |
|---|---|
| **el abogado / la abogada** | lawyer |
| **el/la agente de seguros** | insurance agent |
| **el bombero / la mujer bombera** | firefighter |
| **el cajero / la cajera** | cashier |
| **el/la cantante** | singer |
| **el/la chofer** | driver |
| **el cocinero / la cocinera** | cook |
| **el contador / la contadora** | accountant |
| **el dependiente / la dependienta** | clerk, salesperson |
| **el/la electricista** | electrician |
| **el enfermero / la enfermera** | nurse |
| **el/la gerente** | manager |
| **el ingeniero / la ingeniera** | engineer |
| **el juez / la jueza** | judge |
| **el maestro / la maestra** | teacher |
| **el médico** | doctor |
| **el mesero / la mesera** | waiter / waitress |
| **el obrero / la obrera (industrial)** | (industrial) worker |
| **el peluquero / la peluquera** | hairdresser |
| **el plomero / la plomera** | plumber |
| **el policía / la mujer policía** | policeman / policewoman |
| **el/la terapeuta** | therapist |
| **el trabajador / la trabajadora social** | social worker |

**PALABRAS SEMEJANTES: el/la asistente, el/la carpintero, el/la dentista, el/la guardia, el/la mecánico, el/la piloto, el programador / la programadora, el secretario (ejecutivo) / la secretaria (ejecutiva), el supervisor / la supervisora**

**REPASO: el doctor / la doctora**

## Los lugares del trabajo
Workplaces

| | |
|---|---|
| **el avión** | (air)plane |
| **el club nocturno** | nightclub |
| **el consultorio** | doctor's office |
| **el empleo** | job |
| **la fábrica** | factory |
| **la peluquería** | beauty parlor |
| **el taller de reparación** | garage |

**PALABRAS SEMEJANTES: el banco, la clínica, la compañía**

## Las actividades del trabajo
Work Activities

| | |
|---|---|
| **apagar (incendios)** | to put out (fires) |
| **arreglar** | to fix |
| **atender (ie) mesas** | to wait on tables |
| **cortar (el pelo)** | to cut (hair) |
| **cuidar (de)** | to take care of |
| **entrar al trabajo** | to start work |
| **escribir a máquina** | to type |
| **ganar dinero** | to earn money |
| **pintar** | to paint |
| **seguir (i) una carrera** | to have a career |
| **servir (i)** | to serve |
| **sirvo/sirve** | |

**PALABRAS SEMEJANTES: defender, examinar**

## Los verbos

| | |
|---|---|
| **ayudar** | to help |
| **buscar** | to look for |
| **cantar** | to sing |
| **creer** | to believe |
| **dibujar** | to draw |
| **divertirse (ie)** | to have fun |
| **escalar montañas** | to go mountain climbing |

| | |
|---|---|
| **hornear** | to bake |
| **necesitar** | to need |
| **obtener** | to obtain |
| **olvidar** | to forget |
| **poner en orden** | to put in order |
| **preguntar** | to ask |
| **sacar buenas/malas notas** | to get good/bad grades |
| **tener que** (+ *infin.*) | to have to (*do something*) |
| **tratar de** (+ *infin.*) | to try to (*do something*) |

**PALABRAS SEMEJANTES: graduarse, marcar, participar**

## Los sustantivos

| | |
|---|---|
| **el acusado / la acusada** | accused (person) |
| **el aviso (comercial)** | commercial |
| **el aviso clasificado** | classified ad |
| **el/la cliente** | customer |
| **la cocina** | kitchen |
| **el dinero** | money |
| **la fotografía** | photography |
| **el incendio** | fire |
| **los juegos de video** | video games |
| **los muebles** | furniture |
| **el oficio** | job, position |
| **el requisito** | requirement |
| **la residencia estudiantil** | (college) dormitory |
| **el sueldo** | salary |
| **la sugerencia** | suggestion |

**PALABRAS SEMEJANTES: el accidente, el animal doméstico, la aptitud, el caso criminal, la comprensión, la distracción, el examen, la experiencia, la graduación, el héroe, el instrumento, la justicia, la novela policíaca, el/la paciente, el plan, la posibilidad, la presentación, el talento, el violín**

## Los adjetivos

| | |
|---|---|
| **desagradable** | unpleasant |
| **(estar) listo/a** | (to be) ready |
| **el mismo / la misma** | the same |
| **peligroso/a** | dangerous |

**PALABRAS SEMEJANTES: activo/a, apropiado/a, bilingüe, correcto/a, diferente, fracturado/a, inocente, millonario/a, musical, necesario/a, prestigioso/a**

## ¿Con qué frecuencia? How Often?

| | |
|---|---|
| **a cualquier hora** | at any time |
| **a la vez** | at the same time |
| **muchas veces** | many times |
| **nunca** | never |
| **otra vez** | again |
| **rara vez** | rarely |

**REPASO: a veces, nunca, ... veces a la / por semana**

## Mi futuro My Future

| | |
|---|---|
| **me (te, le, nos, os, les)** | I (you [*inf. sing.*], you [*pol. sing.*] /he/she, we, you [*inf. pl., Spain*], you [*pl.*]/they) |
| **gustaría** (+ *infin.*) | would like to (*do something*) |
| **pensar (ie)** (+ *infin.*) | to plan to (*do something*) |
| **quisiera** (+ *infin.*) | I (you [*pol. sing.*], he/she) would like to (*do something*) |
| **tener ganas de** (+ *infin.*) | to feel like (*doing something*) |

**REPASO: ir a** (+ *infin.*)**, querer (ie)** (+ *infin.*)

## Palabras y frases del texto
Words and Phrases from the Text

| | |
|---|---|
| **la cinta** | (audio)tape |
| **corresponder** | to correspond |
| **fuera** | outside |
| **el laboratorio de lenguas** | language lab |
| **en voz alta/baja** | in a loud/low voice |

## Palabras y frases útiles

| | |
|---|---|
| **aquel/aquella** | that |
| **así** | this way |
| **este/esta** | this |
| **esto** | this (*in general*) |
| **favor de...** | please . . . |
| **jornada completa** | full time (*work*) |
| **media jornada** | part time (*work*) |
| **porque** | because |
| **vamos a** (+ *infin.*) | let's (*do something*) |
| **ya** | already |

# Gramática y ejercicios

**¿RECUERDA?**

In **Gramática 1.4** you learned to use indirect object pronouns with the verb **gustar** to say to whom something is pleasing. Review that construction now, if necessary.

## 5.1 Telling to Whom Something Is Said: Indirect Object Pronouns with Verbs of Informing

### Gramática ilustrada

Indirect object pronouns: **me, te, le, nos, os, les**

**A.** Indirect object pronouns (**los pronombres de complemento indirecto**) are used with verbs of informing, which tell to whom something is said, told, explained, reported, asked, answered, and so on.*

It takes a good deal of time to acquire these forms. Begin by understanding them and using them to describe pictures.

| | | | |
|---|---|---|---|
| me | *to me* | nos | *to us* |
| te | *to you* (*inf. sing.*) | os | *to you* (*inf. pl., Spain*) |
| le | *to you* (*pol. sing.*); *to him/her* | les | *to you* (*pl.*); *to them* |

*Recognition: The indirect object pronoun for **vos** is **te**.

| | |
|---|---|
| —¿Qué **les explica** la profesora Martínez? | *—What does Professor Martínez explain to you?* |
| —**Nos explica** el significado de las palabras nuevas. | *—She explains the meaning of new words to us.* |
| Amanda ya no **me habla**. | *Amanda doesn't speak to me anymore.* |
| ¡Pobre Ernestito! Su mamá siempre **le dice** que no. | *Poor Ernestito! His mother always says no to him.* |

Indirect object pronouns are placed before the verb or attached to the infinitive.
**Mi novia ya no me habla.** (*My girlfriend doesn't talk to me anymore.*)
**Mi novia ya no quiere hablarme.** (*My girlfriend doesn't want to talk to me anymore.*)

It takes time to acquire these forms. As you read and listen to more Spanish, you will get a feel for these pronouns and how to use them.

**B.** Just like reflexive pronouns, indirect object pronouns are placed before the main verb or attached to infinitives (the **-ar, -er,** or **-ir** form of the verb) and present participles (the **-ndo** form of the verb).

| | |
|---|---|
| —¿Qué **te va** a decir tu papá? | *—What is your father going to say to you?* |
| —No sé qué va a **decirme**. | *—I don't know what he is going to say to me.* |
| Esteban **nos está** leyendo la respuesta.<br>Esteban está **leyéndonos** la respuesta. | *Steve is reading the answer to us.* |

**C.** When using **le** or **les,** it is very common to use a phrase with **a** to specify the person (or thing) involved. Spanish requires the pronoun even when the phrase with **a** is used.

| | |
|---|---|
| —¿**A quién le** escribe Clara la carta? | *—To whom is Clara writing the letter?* |
| —**Le** escribe la carta **a su amiga Norma**. | *—She's writing the letter to her friend Norma.* |
| Yo siempre **le** aviso **a mi jefe** con tiempo si no voy a ir al trabajo. | *I always tell my boss ahead of time if I'm not going to go to work.* |

## Ejercicio 1

Complete las siguientes oraciones basándose en los dibujos. Use **me, te, le, nos** o **les**.

MODELO: Carmen *les* dice «Buenos días» a sus amigas.

**1.** Esteban dice: —_____ contesto a mis compañeros.

**2.** La profesora Martínez _____ explica la lección a los estudiantes.

**3.** Nosotros _____ hacemos muchas preguntas a la profesora.

**4.** Nora _____ lee la Nota cultural a nosotros.

**5.** —Lan, ¿ me dices qué tenemos de tarea?
—Sí, Luis, ahora te digo cuál es la tarea para mañana.

**6.** Carmen les escribe una carta a sus padres.

**7.** le decimos «Adiós» a la profesora, y ella nos dice «Hasta luego».

**8.** —Nora, ¿ me dices la respuesta número 5, por favor?
—Sí, Lan, en un momento te digo todas las respuestas.

## Ejercicio 2

Complete estos diálogos con **me, te, le, nos** o **les**.

**¿RECUERDA?**

In **Gramática 3.3** you learned that a verb that uses more than one stem in its conjugation is considered irregular. Some verbs, like **hacer** (*to do; to make*), use a different stem only in the **yo** form; other verbs, like **jugar** (*to play*), use the different stem in all but the infinitive and the **nosotros/as** and **vosotros/as** forms. Review those conjugations now, if necessary.

## 5.2 Expressing Abilities: *saber* and *poder* + Infinitive

**A.** In the present tense, the verb **saber** (*to know facts, information*)* is irregular only in the **yo** form: **sé, sabes, sabe, sabemos, sabéis, saben.**

| | |
|---|---|
| —¿**Sabes** cuándo va a llegar Alberto? | —*Do you know when Al is going to arrive?* |
| —No, no **sé**. | —*No, I don't know.* |

**Saber** followed by an infinitive means *to know how to do something*. Note that there is no need to include a separate word to convey the English *how to*.

| | |
|---|---|
| —¿**Sabes hablar** francés? | —*Do you know how to speak French?* |
| —No, pero **sé hablar** un poco de árabe. | —*No, but I know how to speak a little Arabic.* |
| —¿Quién **sabe jugar** al ajedrez? | —*Who knows how to play chess?* |
| —Yo **sé jugar** al dominó, pero no al ajedrez. | —*I know how to play dominoes, but not chess.* |

**saber** = *to know facts, information*
**saber** + inf. = *to know how to do something*
**¿Sabes bucear?** (*Do you know how to scuba dive?*)
**No, no sé bucear, pero sé nadar.** (*No, I don't know how to scuba dive, but I know how to swim.*)

**B.** The verb **poder**† followed by an infinitive usually indicates potential (*can, to be able to do something*) or permission (*may*). **Poder** is a stem-changing verb and so uses two stems: **pod-** for the infinitive and the **nosotros/as** and **vosotros/as** forms and **pued-** for all other present-tense forms: **puedo, puedes, puede, podemos, podéis, pueden.**

| | |
|---|---|
| —¿Van a correr una vuelta más Carmen y Nora? | —*Are Carmen and Nora going to run another lap?* |
| —No **pueden**. Ya están cansadas. | —*They can't. They're already tired.* |
| —Guillermo, ¿vas a jugar al fútbol el domingo? | —*Guillermo, are you going to play soccer on Sunday?* |
| —No **puedo**. Tengo un examen el lunes. | —*I can't. I have an exam on Monday.* |

**poder** = *can, to be able to*
**¿Puedes salir esta noche?** (*Can you go out tonight?*)
**No, no puedo; mañana tengo un examen de biología.** (*No, I can't; I have a biology test tomorrow.*)

### Ejercicio 3

¿Qué (no) saben hacer estos vecinos hispanos? Complete las oraciones con la forma apropiada de **saber**.

MODELO: Ernestito dice: «Yo no *sé* mucho de matemáticas.»

1. Doña Lola dice: «Yo sé montar a caballo.»
2. Don Eduardo, ¿Sabe usted hablar italiano?
3. Clarisa y Marisa no saben montar en bicicleta todavía, porque son muy pequeñas.
4. Ernestito le pregunta a Guillermo: «¿Sabes esquiar?»
5. Amanda le dice a Ramón: «Graciela y yo todavía no sabemos manejar.»

*Recognition: **vos sabés**
†Recognition: **vos podés**

## Ejercicio 4

¿Qué (no) pueden hacer estos vecinos hispanos? Complete las oraciones con la forma apropiada de **poder**.

MODELO: Nosotros no *podemos* esperarte hoy después de clase, porque tenemos mucha prisa.

1. Ernestito le pregunta a Guillermo: «¿ puedes ____ salir a jugar conmigo?»
2. Andrea les pregunta a Estela y a Ernesto: «¿ pueden ____ venir a cenar con nosotros mañana?»
3. Silvia no puede ____ salir con Nacho mañana porque va a trabajar.
4. Doña Lola y doña Rosita no pueden ____ ver su programa favorito de televisión mañana porque van a ir de compras.
5. Amanda le pregunta a su mamá: «¿ podemos ____ Graciela y yo ir a la plaza a pasear después de comer?»

## 5.3 Pointing out People and Objects: Demonstrative Adjectives

Demonstrative adjectives are normally used to point out nouns.

| | |
|---|---|
| Quiero terminar **esta lección** primero. | *I want to finish this lesson first.* |
| **Esos** tres **muchachos** quieren ser médicos. | *Those three boys want to be doctors.* |

A demonstrative adjective must agree in gender and number with the noun it modifies.

**este/esta** = *this*
**este libro** = *this book*
**esta fotografía** = *this photo*

**estos/estas** = *these*
**estos cuadernos** = *these notebooks*
**estas tareas** = *these homework assignments*

**ese/esa** = *that*
**ese cartel** = *that poster*
**esa silla** = *that chair*

**esos/esas** = *those*
**esos papeles** = *those papers*
**esas chicas** = *those girls*

| **aquí/acá** (***here***) (***close to the person speaking***) | | | |
|---|---|---|---|
| ***Singular*** | | ***Plural*** | |
| este libro | *this book* | estos pantalones | *these pants* |
| esta señora | *this lady* | estas casas | *these houses* |
| **allí/allá** (***there***) (***at some distance from the person speaking***) | | | |
| ese libro | *that book* | esos pantalones | *those pants* |
| esa señora | *that lady* | esas casas | *those houses* |

| | |
|---|---|
| —Amanda, ¿no te gusta **esta blusa**? | *—Amanda, don't you like this blouse?* |
| —No, prefiero **esa blusa** roja. | *—No, I prefer that red blouse.* |
| —**Estos pantalones** son nuevos. ¿Te gustan? | *—These pants are new. Do you like them?* |

**esto/eso** = *this/that* (*unidentified object*)

Use the demonstrative pronouns **esto** or **eso** when the object has not been identified.

| | |
|---|---|
| —Estela, ¿sabes qué es **esto**? | *—Estela, do you know what this is?* |
| —No, no sé. | *—No, I don't know.* |

**aquel/aquella** = *that*
**aquel edificio** = *that building*
**aquella plaza** = *that plaza*

**aquellos/aquellas** = *those*
**aquellos árboles** = *those trees*
**aquellas puertas** = *those doors*

The demonstratives **aquel, aquellos, aquella,** and **aquellas** indicate that the person or thing pointed out is more distant (generally far away in space or in time from both speakers).

| | |
|---|---|
| —¿Ves **aquella casa**? | *—Do you see that house (over there)?* |
| —¿**Aquella casa** de los árboles grandes? | *—That house with the big trees?* |
| Estudio biología en **este edificio**, y estudio química en **aquel edificio**. | *I study biology in this building, and I study chemistry in that building (over there).* |

## Ejercicio 5

Amanda está hablando con Graciela de su ropa. Complete las oraciones con **este, esta, estos** o **estas.**

MODELO: Me gusta *esta* blusa azul.

1. Esta blusa es mi favorita.
2. Este zapatos son muy viejos.
3. Estos pantalones son nuevos.
4. Estas faldas son bonitas pero un poco viejas.
5. Este suéter es de mi mamá.

## Ejercicio 6

Doña Lola y doña Rosita están en la plaza hablando de sus vecinos. Complete las oraciones con **ese, esa, esos** o **esas.**

MODELO: *Esa* señora es una cocinera magnífica.

1. Esas señoritas trabajan en la oficina con Paula Saucedo.
2. Ese chico es Guillermo, el hijo de Ernesto y Estela Ramírez.
3. Esa muchacha se llama Amanda. Tiene 14 años.
4. Esos señores juegan al ajedrez con don Anselmo.
5. Esos muchachos son compañeros de escuela de Ernestito.

## Ejercicio 7

Imagínese que usted está en una fiesta con Esteban. Él no conoce a muchas personas y por eso le hace a usted las siguientes preguntas. Complete las preguntas de Esteban con formas de **este** o **ese.**

1. ¿Cómo se llama esa señora que está hablando con Nora allí en el rincón?
2. Creo que ese señor que está aquí a la derecha es amigo de tu padre, ¿verdad?
3. ¿Son arquitectos esos dos jóvenes que están allí en la cocina?
4. ¿Se llama Jesús este muchacho que está aquí detrás de nosotros?
5. ¿Cómo se llaman estas muchachas que están sentadas aquí justamente enfrente de nosotros?

## Ejercicio 8

Usted sale a comprar zapatos. ¿Cuáles recomienda? Use formas de **este, ese** y **aquel,** según la distancia entre usted y los dibujos.

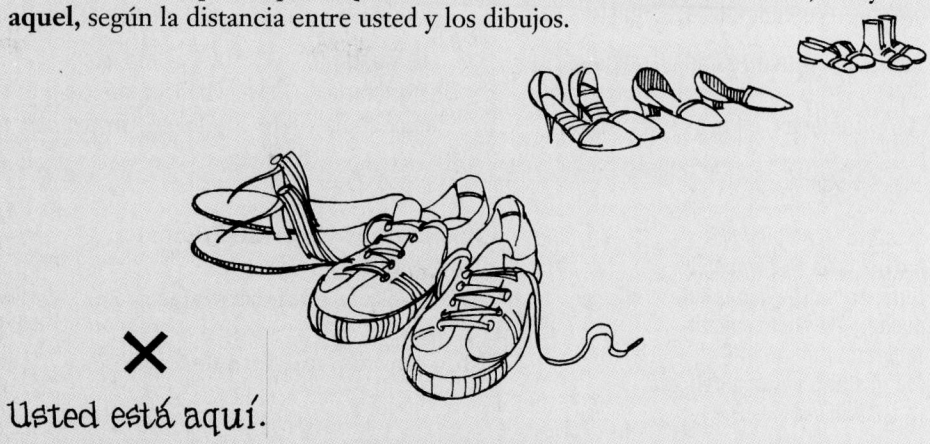


1. estos zapatos son mejores para jugar al tenis.
2. aquellos zapatos son para un señor que trabaja en una oficina.
3. esos zapatos me parecen muy incómodos.
4. esos zapatos son para una mujer que trabaja en una oficina.
5. aquellas botas son para un obrero.
6. Estas sandalias me gustan mucho.

**¿RECUERDA?**

You already know that the verbs **ir** + **a** (see **Gramática 2.1**) and **querer** (see **Gramática 2.3**) followed by infinitives are commonly used to talk about future actions in Spanish.

## 5.4 Expressing Plans and Desires: *pensar, quisiera, me gustaría, tener ganas de*

**A.** The verb **pensar***† (*to think*) followed by an infinitive expresses the idea of *to think about* or *to plan on doing* something. Here are the forms of **pensar (ie)**: **pienso, piensas, piensa, pensamos, pensáis, piensan.**

| | |
|---|---|
| —¿Qué **piensan hacer** ustedes durante las vacaciones? | —*What are you thinking about doing for vacation?* |
| —**Pensamos viajar** a Europa. | —*We're planning on traveling to Europe.* |

**B. Quisiera** and **me (le) gustaría**‡ are also frequently used to indicate future desires, especially those that are speculative. Both forms are equivalent to English *would like*. Neither has a **yo** form ending in **-o**.

**pensar** = *to think*
**pensar** + inf. = *to think about, plan on doing (something)*
**¿Qué piensas hacer después de clases?** (*What are you planning to do after school?*) **Pienso ir a la biblioteca y luego voy a trabajar.** (*I'm planning to go to the library and then I'm going to work.*)

---

*Recognition: **vos pensás**

†When not followed by an infinitive, **pensar (ie)** usually expresses *to think:* **pensar que** (*to think that*), **pensar de** (*to think about, have an opinion of*), **pensar en** (*to think about someone or something, have one's thoughts on*).

| | |
|---|---|
| —¿Qué **piensas del** nuevo plan? | —*What do you think about the new plan?* |
| —**Pienso que** es muy bueno. | —*I think that it's very good.* |
| —Ramón, ¿**piensas** mucho **en** Amanda? | —*Ramón, do you often think about Amanda?* |
| —No, **pienso en** ella solamente de vez en cuando. | —*No, I think about her only from time to time.* |

‡Recognition: **vos quisieras, a vos te gustaría**

| | | | |
|---|---|---|---|
| (yo) | quisiera | me gustaría | *I would like* |
| (tú) | quisieras | te gustaría | *you (inf. sing.) would like* |
| (usted, él/ella) | quisiera | le gustaría | *you (pol. sing.) would like; he/she would like* |
| (nosotros/as) | quisiéramos | nos gustaría | *we would like* |
| (vosotros/as) | quisierais | os gustaría | *you (inf. pl., Spain) would like* |
| (ustedes, ellos/as) | quisieran | les gustaría | *you (pl.) would like; they would like* |

**quisiera** = *I would like*
**me gustaría** = *I would like*
**Quisiera salir a cenar esta noche.** (*I'd like to eat out tonight.*)
**Me gustaría ver una película.** (*I'd like to see a movie.*)

**Quisiéramos viajar** este verano si tenemos tiempo. — *We would like to travel this summer if we have time.*
A mi esposa **le gustaría viajar** a España. — *My wife would like to travel to Spain.*
Estoy cansado; **quisiera descansar** un poco. — *I'm tired; I would like to rest a while.*

**C. Tener ganas de** (*to feel like* [*doing something*]) is also followed by an infinitive.

**tener ganas de** + infinitive = *to feel like* (*doing something*)

**Tenemos ganas de quedarnos** en casa esta noche. — *We feel like staying home tonight.*
**Tengo ganas de salir** a bailar. — *I feel like going out dancing.*

## Ejercicio 9

¿Qué quisieran hacer estos estudiantes el próximo sábado? Escoja la forma correcta: **quisiera, quisieras, quisiéramos** o **quisieran**.

1. Luis quisiera ir al campo a montar a caballo.
2. Carmen y yo quisiéramos ir de compras.
3. Alberto y Pablo quisieran merendar con unas amigas.
4. Mónica, ¿quisieras quedarte en casa a descansar?
5. Esteban dice: «Yo quisiera jugar al tenis.»

## Ejercicio 10

¿Qué les gustaría hacer a Estela Ramírez y a su familia? Escoja la forma correcta del pronombre: **me, te, nos, le** o **les**.

1. A Guillermo le gustaría no tener un examen de matemáticas el viernes.
2. A mis hijos Amanda y Guillermo les gustaría ir al campo a merendar.
3. A mi esposo Ernesto le gustaría ir al cine.
4. A mí me gustaría salir a comer a un buen restaurante.
5. A Andrea y a mí nos gustaría jugar a las cartas el sábado en la noche.

## Ejercicio 11

¿Qué piensan hacer Pilar y sus amigos?

1. El hermano de Pilar piensa quedarse en casa esta noche para estudiar.
2. Clara, ¿piensas tú ir de compras mañana?
3. José y yo pensamos visitar a mis abuelos el sábado.
4. José y Clara piensan ir al Museo del Prado por la tarde.
5. Pilar dice: «Yo pienso hacer mi tarea el domingo por la noche.»

## 5.5 Ordering Events: Infinitives after Prepositions

**A.** When telling a story or relating a sequence of events, speakers use "sequencing" words to let listeners know the order in which the events occur. You have already used many of these sequencing words in the **Narración** activities, for example:

| | | | |
|---|---|---|---|
| primero | *first* | antes | *before* |
| luego | *then* | finalmente | *finally* |
| después | *afterward* | por último | *at last* |
| más tarde | *later (on)* | | |

| | |
|---|---|
| **Primero** me baño y **luego** me cepillo los dientes. **Después,** preparo el desayuno. **Luego** voy al trabajo y trabajo hasta las 6:00 de la tarde. **Finalmente** vuelvo a casa a eso de las 8:00. | *First I take a bath and then I brush my teeth. Afterward, I fix breakfast. Then I go to work and work until 6:00 p.m. Finally I return home about 8:00.* |

**B.** The words **después** and **antes** by themselves express the meanings *after(ward)* and *before*.

| | |
|---|---|
| **Después,** vamos a cenar con Pedro y Andrea Ruiz. | *Afterward, we're going to have dinner with Pedro and Andrea Ruiz.* |

**antes de** + infinitive
**Antes de ducharse, Ramón se afeita.** (*Before showering, Ramón shaves.*)
**después de** + infinitive
**Después de estudiar, vamos a salir a bailar.** (*After studying, we are going out dancing.*)

**C.** The preposition **de** follows **antes** and **después** before a noun or an infinitive. (English uses the *-ing* form instead of the infinitive.) Don't forget to attach any object pronouns to the end of the infinitive.

| | |
|---|---|
| **Antes de acostarme,** quiero terminar la tarea. | *Before going to bed, I want to finish my homework.* |
| Vamos a terminar la tarea **antes de (después de) la comida.** | *We are going to finish our homework before (after) the meal.* |
| **Después de jugar** al béisbol, voy a ir a la playa. | *After playing baseball, I'm going to go to the beach.* |

### Ejercicio 12

¿Qué oración describe mejor cada dibujo?

1. c

2. e

3. d

4. a

5. b

a. Prepara la cena después de trabajar.
b. Limpian la casa antes de salir a jugar.
c. Siempre se lava los dientes después de comer.
d. Después de hacer ejercicio se ducha.
e. Antes de acostarse, apaga la luz.

## Ejercicio 13

Complete las oraciones lógicamente.

1. Nos gusta lavar el coche después de... c
2. El señor Ramírez acostumbra leer el periódico antes de... a
3. Pedro Ruiz dice: «Después de levantarme por la mañana, me gusta... » e
4. Antes de acostarse, es necesario... b
5. Guillermo siempre ayuda a su papá antes de... d

a. desayunar.
b. apagar las luces.
c. almorzar.
d. salir a jugar con sus amigos.
e. salir a pasear.

## Ejercicio 14

Haga una oración lógica con **antes de** o **después de**.

MODELO: terminar la tarea / ver la televisión (nosotros) →
Después de terminar la tarea, vamos a ver la televisión.
(Antes de ver la televisión, vamos a terminar la tarea.)

1. preparar la comida / hacer la compra (Estela)
2. limpiar la casa / invitar a unos amigos (Pedro y Andrea Ruiz)
3. dormir una siesta / ayudar a su papá (Guillermo)
4. correr / bañarse (tú)
5. salir a bailar / ponerse la ropa (nosotros)

## 5.6 Making Suggestions: *Let's*

**¡Vamos a** + infinitive! = *Let's* _____!
**¡Vamos a escuchar música!** (*Let's listen to music!*)
**¡Vámonos!** (*Let's go!*)

To make a suggestion in Spanish, most speakers use the expression **vamos a** + infinitive.

| | |
|---|---|
| No tengo ganas de estudiar esta noche. ¡**Vamos a dar** una fiesta! | *I don't feel like studying tonight. Let's give a party!* |
| No quiero quedarme en casa este fin de semana. ¡**Vamos a salir** a bailar! | *I don't want to stay home this weekend. Let's go out dancing!* |

The use of **nos** makes the **¡vamos!** command more emphatic. When **nos** is added, the **-s** of **vamos** is dropped.

| | |
|---|---|
| **¡Vámonos!** | *Let's go!* (*Let's get going!*) |

## Ejercicio 15

Usted está hablando con unos amigos después de clase. Haga sugerencias usando **vamos a** + infinitivo.

MODELO: Tengo mucha sed. (tomar un refresco) →
¡Vamos a tomar un refresco!

1. Tengo frío.
2. Necesito hacer ejercicio.
3. No tengo comida en casa.
4. Estoy cansado/a.
5. No estoy listo/a para el examen mañana.

a. hacer la compra
b. estudiar esta noche
c. preparar chocolate caliente
d. nadar en la piscina
e. sentarnos debajo de ese árbol

CAPÍTULO 6

# La residencia

**METAS**

In **Capítulo 6,** you will talk about where you live and what you do there. You and your classmates will discuss what you have done recently. You will also learn how to introduce people to each other.

Caracas, Venezuela: una zona residencial

**ACTIVIDADES DE COMUNICACIÓN Y LECTURAS**


La casa, los cuartos y los muebles

La casa y el vecindario

**Nota cultural** Las ciudades hispanas

**El mundo hispano...** su gente

Las actividades en casa

**Las palabras viven** ¡Este pibe labura mucho!

**Lectura** Habla la gata Manchitas

Las actividades con los amigos

**El mundo hispano...** imágenes

**El mundo hispano...** en los Estados Unidos

Las presentaciones

**EN RESUMEN**


**GRAMÁTICA Y EJERCICIOS**


6.1 Making Comparisons of Inequality: **más/menos**

6.2 Making Comparisons of Equality: **tan/tanto**

6.3 Expressing Obligation and Duty: **tener que, deber, necesitar, hay que, es necesario**

6.4 Talking about Past Actions: The Preterite of Regular Verbs (Part 1)

6.5 Knowing People, Places, and Facts: **conocer** and **saber**

6.6 Referring to People Already Mentioned: Personal Direct Object Pronouns

# Actividades de comunicación y lecturas

## La casa, los cuartos y los muebles

*Lea Gramática 6.1.–6.2.*

**Rápida y silenciosamente.**

Calienta o refresca cualquier ambiente.

En calefacción: Ahorra energía gracias a su sistema de control de temperatura y a su rapidez de acción.

En ventilación: Refresca inmediatamente.

**Disfrútelo todo el año.**

## Actividad 1. Encuesta: ¿Qué hay en su casa?

Diga sí o no. Si la respuesta es **no,** explique por qué no.

MODELO: En mi casa hay tres dormitorios. En mi casa no hay cancha de tenis porque no soy rico/a.

1. En mi casa hay...
   a. una cancha de tenis.
   b. tres dormitorios.
   c. una cocina pequeña.
   d. un garaje para dos carros.
   e. un patio detrás de la casa.
   f. ¿ ?
2. En la sala de mi casa hay...
   a. una cama.
   b. un lavabo.
   c. varias lámparas.
   d. muchas plantas.
   e. una alfombra.
   f. ¿ ?
3. En la cocina de mi casa hay...
   a. una estufa.
   b. un lavaplatos.
   c. un refrigerador.
   d. un estante con libros.
   e. un horno de microondas.
   f. ¿ ?
4. En mi cuarto hay...
   a. una cama matrimonial.
   b. una bañera.
   c. un armario.
   d. muchas almohadas.
   e. una cómoda.
   f. ¿ ?

## Actividad 2. Identificaciones: ¿Para qué sirve?

Mire los siguientes objetos y aparatos y diga para qué sirven.

MODELO: Una lámpara sirve para ver y leer de noche.

### FRASES ÚTILES

para apoyar la cabeza cuando uno duerme
para barrer
para calentar la comida rápidamente
para guardar la ropa
para lavarse las manos
para lavarse los dientes
para preparar el té o calentar agua
para secarse
para verse la cara
para ver y leer de noche

1. una lámpara

2. un horno de microondas

3. una almohada

4. una escoba

5. una cómoda

6. un cepillo de dientes

7. una tetera

8. un lavabo

9. un espejo

10. una toalla

## Actividad 3. Intercambios: Los aparatos domésticos

MODELO: E1: ¿Cuál cuesta más, el calentador o la cafetera?
E2: El calentador cuesta más. (El calentador cuesta más que la cafetera.)

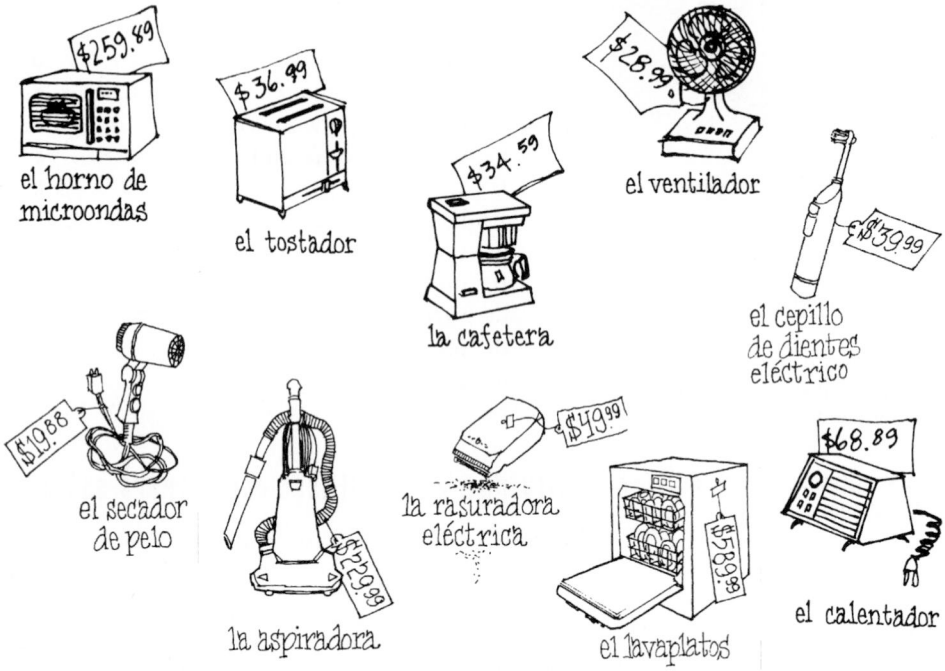


1. ¿Cuál cuesta más, el horno de microondas o la cafetera? ¿el ventilador o el secador de pelo?
2. ¿Cuál cuesta menos, la cafetera o el cepillo de dientes eléctrico? ¿la aspiradora o el tostador?
3. ¿Cuál de estos tres objetos es el más caro: el tostador, la rasuradora eléctrica o la cafetera?
4. ¿Cuál de estas tres cosas es la más cara: el lavaplatos, la rasuradora eléctrica o la aspiradora?
5. ¿Cuál de estas tres cosas cuesta menos: el secador de pelo, el calentador o el cepillo de dientes eléctrico?
6. ¿Cuál cuesta más, el ventilador o el tostador?
7. ¿Cuál cuesta menos, la rasuradora eléctrica o el cepillo de dientes eléctrico?

## Actividad 4. Entrevista: Tu casa

1. ¿Vives en una residencia estudiantil, en un apartamento o en una casa?
2. ¿Vives con otras personas? ¿Cómo son? Si vives solo/a, ¿te gusta? ¿Por qué? Explica.
3. ¿Es grande el lugar donde vives o es pequeño? ¿Es de uno o dos pisos tu casa (apartamento)?
4. ¿Tiene comedor tu casa (apartamento)? ¿Comes allí con frecuencia? Si no, ¿dónde sueles comer?
5. ¿Tienes tu propio dormitorio? ¿O compartes un dormitorio con alguien? ¿Con quién? ¿Qué muebles y aparatos eléctricos hay en tu dormitorio?
6. ¿Tiene patio o terraza tu casa (apartamento)? ¿Cómo es? ¿Hay piscina? ¿Es grande? ¿Nadas allí con frecuencia? ¿Qué otros lugares hay allí para hacer ejercicio?
7. ¿Tu casa (apartamento) tiene garaje para dos coches? ¿Qué hay en tu garaje?
8. De todas las cosas que tienes, ¿cuál te gusta más? ¿Cuál es el aparato más útil que tienes en tu casa (apartamento)?

## LAS PALABRAS VIVEN

**Cuartos y lugares en la casa:** En algunos países **la sala** es también **el living**. Y **el cuarto** es **el dormitorio** en Argentina y varios otros países, **la recámara** en México y **la alcoba** o **la habitación** en España. **La piscina** tiene dos nombres más: **la pileta** en Argentina y **la alberca** en México.

**Algunos aparatos:** En España y varios países **la televisión** es **la tele**. Otras palabras que se usan para **el refrigerador** son **la heladera** en México, **el frigorífero** o **frigorífico** en Argentina y **la nevera** en España.

# La casa y el vecindario

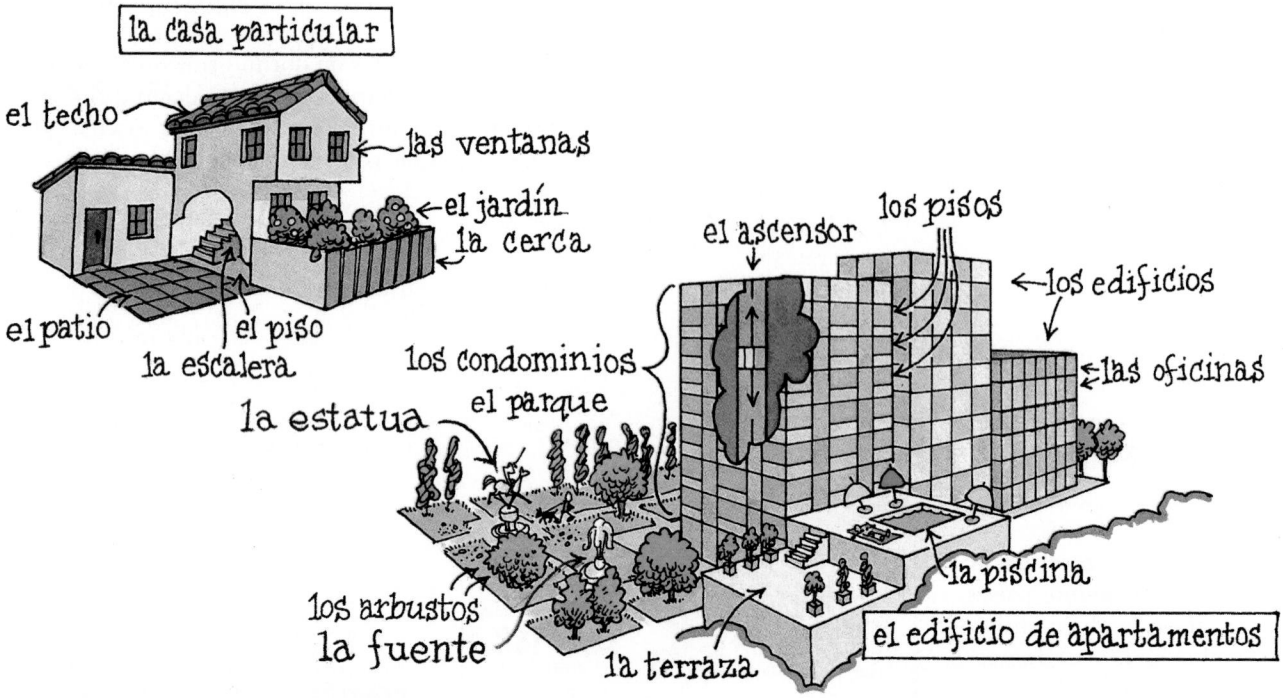


## Actividad 5. Del mundo hispano: Un departamento en México

Imagínese que usted va a pasar tres meses en la Ciudad de México y necesita alquilar un departamento. En el periódico mexicano *La Prensa* encuentra los siguientes anuncios. ¿Cuál le parece mejor? ¿Qué departamento o habitación le gustaría alquilar? ¿Por qué?

**ANUNCIOS**

SE ALQUILA departamento. Dos recámaras. Sala. Comedor. Cocina. Baño. Lugar céntrico. Alquiler módico. Llamar a Luz María Galván. Tel. 6-59-50-69. Calle 12 no. 49, México 22, D.F.

SE ALQUILA departamento amueblado. Dos recámaras. Dos baños. Cocina amplia: estufa, refrigerador, gabinetes grandes y todos los utensilios. Ascensor. Avenida Juárez no. 420, México, D.F.

SE ALQUILA habitación amueblada. Preferible: joven estudiante, callado y serio. Alquiler bajo. Derecho a cocina. Favor de enviar datos personales. Isabel la Católica 96 (centro), México, D.F. Tel. 5-85-72-44.

DEPARTAMENTO Una recámara. Bien decorado. Ventanas grandes. Vista agradable. Cerca de todo transporte. Llamar al 7-79-09-22 o escribir a: Sres. Gallegos, Luis Kuhne no. 755, México 20, D.F.

la casa de los Ramírez:
5 dormitorios
3 baños
1 biblioteca
3 balcones

## Actividad 6. Descripción de dibujos: Comparación de casas

Escuche las preguntas que le hace su profesor(a), y contéstelas según los dibujos que se ven a continuación.

la casa de los Ruiz:
3 dormitorios
2 baños
2 balcones

la casa de los Silva:
2 dormitorios
1 baño

Ahora, hágale preguntas sobre las casas a su compañero/a. (Se puede comparar **baños, dormitorios, puertas, ventanas, balcones, pisos** y **árboles**.)

MODELO: E1: ¿Cuántas *ventanas* tiene la casa de los *Ramírez*?
E2: Tiene *ocho*. Tiene *más que* la casa de los *Ruiz*.
E1: ¿Cuántos *árboles* tiene la casa de los *Silva*?
E2 : Tiene *tres*. Tiene *tantos como* la casa de los *Ruiz*. Tiene *menos que* la casa de los *Ramírez*.

## LAS PALABRAS VIVEN

**El vecindario:** La palabra **vecindad** también se usa con frecuencia en varios sitios. En España, México y otros países, la gente normalmente dice **el barrio** cuando habla de su vecindario. Y en México usan la palabra **colonia** para referirse a los barrios más nuevos de la ciudad.

## Actividad 7. Entrevista: Tu vecindario

1. ¿Vives en un vecindario viejo o nuevo? ¿Te gusta vivir allí? ¿Por qué? Explica.
2. ¿Hay edificios de apartamentos en tu vecindario? ¿condominios?
3. ¿Hay muchos edificios comerciales en tu vecindario?
4. ¿Hay alguna gasolinera cerca de tu casa (apartamento)? ¿Dónde está la más cercana?
5. ¿Cuál es el centro comercial más cercano a tu casa (apartamento)? ¿Vas de compras allí a menudo? ¿Por qué?
6. ¿Llevas tu ropa a la lavandería o tienes lavadora y secadora en tu casa (apartamento)?
7. ¿Hay alguna piscina pública en tu vecindario? ¿Te gusta nadar allí?
8. ¿Hay algún parque en tu vecindario? ¿Vas mucho allí? ¿Qué haces allí?

NOTA CULTURAL

**VOCABULARIO ÚTIL**

| | |
|---|---|
| antiguas | *ancient* |
| reconstruida | *reconstructed* |
| las afueras | *outskirts, suburbs* |
| debido a | *due to* |
| el crecimiento | *growth* |

# Las ciudades hispanas

Aquí tiene una breve descripción de algunas ciudades típicas en el mundo hispano. Entre otras características, son antiguas, grandes y tienen centros de mucha actividad comercial. ¡Visitemos estas ciudades hispanas!

Muchas ciudades hispanas son muy antiguas. Algunas tienen entre trescientos y cuatrocientos años, y en España hay varias que datan del Imperio Romano. En algunas ciudades, la parte más vieja está reconstruida y hoy es un centro de interés turístico, como el Viejo San Juan, la ciudad colonial de Santo Domingo en la República Dominicana y el Quito colonial.

El Viejo San Juan, Puerto Rico

Hay ciudades que se extienden hasta las afueras, debido al gran crecimiento de la población. Algunas zonas son únicamente residenciales, mientras que otras son industriales o comerciales. Pero en la típica ciudad hispana hay más que nada zonas mixtas: calles con casas particulares, apartamentos, tiendas y oficinas. Cartagena, en Colombia, es un buen ejemplo. La zona del centro es un lugar de mucha actividad comercial; allí se encuentran tiendas, oficinas, restaurantes y una gran variedad de negocios.

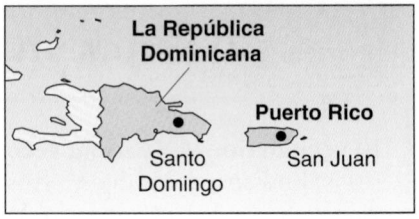

Cartagena, Colombia: El centro de las ciudades hispanas es un lugar de mucha actividad.

El centro de las ciudades hispanas es un lugar lleno de vida donde también residen muchas personas; algunas viven en casas particulares y otras en apartamentos, arriba de los locales comerciales.

Las diferentes zonas de la ciudad generalmente tienen nombres: «Argüelles», «La Loma», «La Villa». En muchos casos, los adultos de la familia trabajan lejos de su casa, pero hacen sus compras en las tiendas de su vecindario y los niños pasan el tiempo allí también, jugando con otros niños.

## Comprensión

Indique si las siguientes descripciones corresponden a las ciudades hispanas (**H**), a las ciudades norteamericanas (**N**) o a las dos (**D**).

1. _____ Son muy viejas.
2. _____ Hay ciudades que datan del Imperio Romano.
3. _____ El centro es muchas veces una zona turística.
4. _____ Hay mucha actividad comercial en el centro.
5. _____ Hay gran cantidad de restaurantes.
6. _____ Muchas personas viven en apartamentos en el centro.
7. _____ Cada área distinta tiene su propio nombre.
8. _____ Se hacen las compras muy cerca de la casa.

## Ahora... ¡usted!

1. ¿Le gusta el vecindario donde vive? ¿Le gustaría vivir en otro vecindario? ¿Por qué?
2. ¿Qué le gusta y qué no le gusta de la ciudad donde vive?
3. ¿Conoce alguna ciudad hispana? ¿Le parece muy diferente de una ciudad norteamericana típica? ¿Qué tienen en común? ¿Qué diferencias hay entre las dos?

### Un paso más... ¡a escribir!

Describa la ciudad donde nació o la ciudad donde vive ahora. Compárela con algunas de las ocho características que aparecen en la actividad de Comprensión.

## EL MUNDO HISPANO... su gente

**S**u nombre es Leticia Recina Pérez y tiene 20 años. Leticia es de Costa Rica.

*Describa su ciudad y su vecindario.*

La ciudad en la que yo vivo se llama Alajuela. A mí me gusta mucho porque todo queda[1] cerca de casa (el supermercado, la zapatería, la carnicería, el parque, la iglesia). Y casi todas las personas nos conocemos.[2]

[1]está [2]todas... *we all know each other*

(Continúa)

El Parque Central, que está enfrente de la Catedral, tiene muchos árboles de mangos, por eso llaman a Alajuela «La Ciudad de los Mangos» y a los alajuelenses «manudos». Las tiendas no son muy grandes, pero podemos conseguir[3] todo lo que necesitamos.

En los jardines de las casas hay árboles frutales (de mango, naranja, mandarina) y algunas flores. Las casas no son muy grandes; unas son muy lindas y lujosas,[4] y hay otras que son muy humildes. Las casas están pegadas unas con otras,[5] ¡pero los vecinos no se pelean[6]!

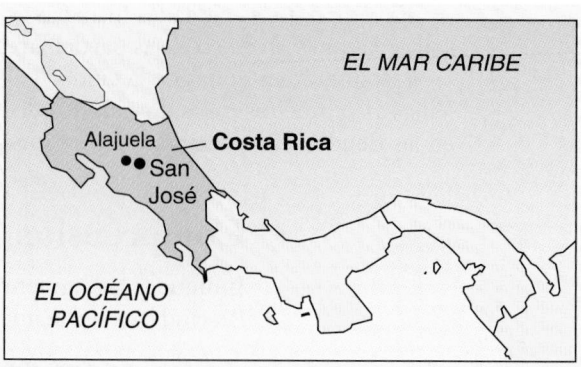


[3]obtener [4]*luxurious* [5]están... *are very close to each other*
[6]se... *argue, fight*

# Las actividades en casa

***Lea Gramática 6.3.***

## Actividad 8. Descripción de dibujos: ¿Qué tiene que hacer?

Escuche a su profesor(a). ¿A cuál de los siguientes dibujos corresponde su descripción?

1. Luis

2. Pablo

3. Mónica Lan

4. Nora

5. Carmen

6. Esteban

### Actividad 9. Descripción de dibujos: ¡El cuarto de Esteban es un desastre!

Con su compañero/a, decidan qué debe hacer Esteban para arreglar su cuarto.

MODELO: Esteban debe recoger la ropa y necesita apagar el televisor. También...

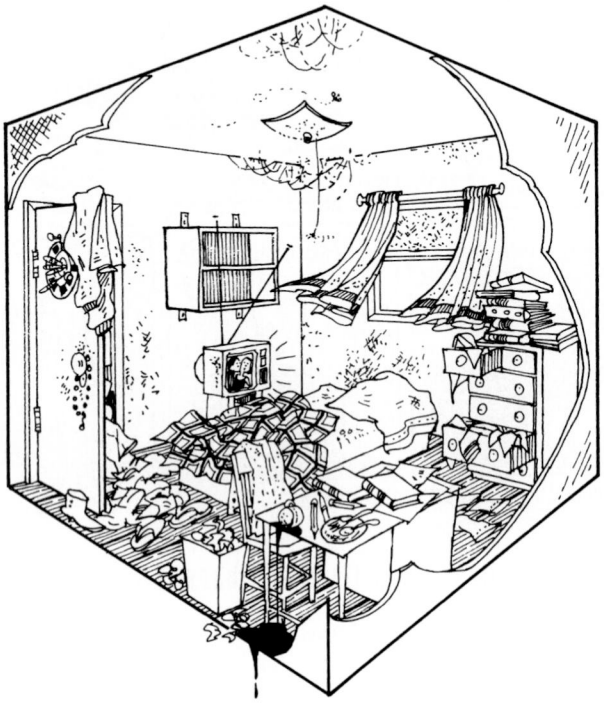

**LAS PALABRAS VIVEN**

**VOCABULARIO ÚTIL**

| | |
|---|---|
| a diario | *every day* |
| mientras | *while* |
| en broma | *jokingly* |

# ¡Este pibe labura mucho!

El idioma italiano tiene gran influencia en el español que se habla en Argentina. En el lenguaje coloquial argentino se usan a diario palabras como **laburar**, que quiere decir **trabajar** y viene de la palabra italiana *lavorare;* también se usa mucho la palabra **pibe**, que viene de *pivetto* y significa **niño**.

Imagínese esta escena en Buenos Aires: un niño está en su casa y su mamá le dice que debe limpiar su cuarto. El hijo no quiere hacerlo; prefiere salir a jugar. Después de muchas protestas, el niño decide hacer el trabajo. Y mientras limpia, lo visitan dos amiguitos. Al verlo tan ocupado, un amiguito le dice al otro, en broma: «¡Este pobre pibe labura mucho!»

En otras palabras: «¡El pobre chico trabaja mucho!»

## Actividad 10. Entrevista: Los quehaceres y las diversiones en casa

1. ¿Quién en tu casa tiene que limpiar el refrigerador, desempolvar, pasar la aspiradora, limpiar el microondas, limpiar los baños?
2. ¿Qué aspecto de tu casa (apartamento) te gusta más? ¿Por qué?
3. ¿Qué te gusta hacer en casa (en tu apartamento)?
4. ¿Pasas mucho tiempo en casa (en tu apartamento) los fines de semana o prefieres salir? ¿Te visitan mucho tus amigos los fines de semana?
5. ¿Das muchas fiestas en tu casa? ¿Qué tienes que hacer antes de la fiesta?

# Habla la gata Manchitas

**VOCABULARIO ÚTIL**

| | |
|---|---|
| las pulgas | *fleas* |
| los amos | *masters* |
| los seres humanos | *human beings* |
| ¡Busca ratones! | *Go look for mice!* |
| ladra | *he barks* |
| las sobras | *leftovers* |
| la lengüita | *little tongue* |

Algunas personas dicen que los animales piensan y que tienen ideas. Pues, en casa de la familia Ramírez vive una gata muy especial. Se llama Manchitas y es un animal muy observador, con opiniones propias. Imagínese que, por un momento fantástico, Manchitas puede hablar. Éstas son sus observaciones...

Estas pulgas, ¡estas pulgas! Aquí estoy en el sofá, muy aburrida. Es que mis amos casi nunca me prestan atención. Sólo los niños de esta familia, Ernestito y Guillermo, juegan conmigo. Y no siempre me gusta jugar con ellos. ¡Esos pequeños seres humanos son muy agresivos! A veces me tratan mal, como un juguete. ¡Ay!

Mis amos, Ernesto y Estela, no saben que soy muy observadora. Ellos probablemente piensan que a mí sólo me gusta comer y dormir. ¡Ay! Los seres humanos no comprenden a los animales, y mucho menos a nosotros, los felinos.

Todos los días mis amos hacen las mismas cosas. Estela, mi ama, se levanta temprano y va a la cocina para tomar esa bebida negra y caliente que ellos toman todas las mañanas, el «café». Después, mi ama llama a mi amo, pero el señor siempre quiere dormir un poco más. Entonces ella abre las cortinas y entra mucha luz en el dormitorio. «¡Qué horror!», grita mi amo. «¡Es mucha luz! ¡No puedo abrir los ojos, Estela!»

Luego mi ama toca a la puerta de su hija Amanda y la muchacha sale de su cuarto. Amanda siempre saluda a su mamá; le dice «¡Buenos días!» La joven de esta familia no tiene problemas en despertarse. ¡Pero Ernestito y Guillermo sí tienen problemas! Estela va a su dormitorio y los despierta. Ellos también quieren dormir más. «¡Vamos, a la escuela!», dice mi ama. Y los dos niños se levantan poco a poco.

Ernesto se baña, se viste, lee el periódico, toma la bebida negra y dice algunas cosas complicadas que yo no comprendo. Mi ama y la señora Berta (que hace trabajos domésticos y también

Mis amos no saben que soy muy observadora...

vive en esta casa) preparan el desayuno de la familia. Todos desayunan juntos casi siempre. (Mmmm. Los seres humanos comen mucho mejor que nosotros los gatos.) Después, Ernesto y sus hijos salen y mi ama se queda en casa.

Estela entonces me lleva afuera, diciendo: «¡Anda, vete, Manchitas! ¡Busca ratones!» Hace frío por la mañana y no me gusta estar afuera; por eso siempre busco un poquito de sol o salto a la ventana. Desde la ventana puedo mirar a mi ama, que está adentro. Ella se baña, se viste, se maquilla, tiende la cama... ¡todos los días lo mismo! Y luego Berta sacude los muebles y pasa la aspiradora. ¡Miau! ¡No me gusta ese aparato!

Mi ama sale con Berta por la tarde. Creo que van al mercado, porque luego regresan con comida. Y yo me quedo en el patio, muy solita. Para divertirme me subo a la cerca. En mi jardín vive Lobo, el perro de Ernestito. Y en la casa de al lado hay un perro que se llama Sultán. Los dos perros saltan y saltan para llegar adonde estoy yo. ¡Ja! No pueden subir; están muy gordos. ¡Y ladran con tanta desesperación! A Ernestito le gusta Sultán; dice que quiere traerlo a vivir con nosotros. Pero ya tiene perro. ¿Dos perros en esta casa? ¡Qué horror!

Por las noches mis amos comen y me dan las sobras. Después de comer, van a visitar a los vecinos o a caminar por el barrio. Los niños miran el objeto de luz, que ellos llaman la «televisión». ¡Cómo les gusta mirar a otros seres humanos en ese objeto!

Por fin, todos se acuestan. Y yo, pues, me doy un buen baño con mi lengüita, y me duermo también en el sofá. Y aquí estoy ahora. ¡Miau! ¡Cuánto detesto estas pulgas!

## Comprensión

¿A quién se refiere cada oración? Diga si se refiere (**a**) al amo, (**b**) al ama, (**c**) a Amanda, (**d**) a Ernestito, (**e**) a Guillermo, (**f**) a Berta, (**g**) a Manchitas o (**h**) a toda la familia. ¡Ojo! A veces hay más de una respuesta.

1. _____ Es muy observadora.
2. _____ Le gusta el perro del vecino.
3. _____ Se levanta temprano.
4. _____ Detesta las pulgas.
5. _____ Pasa la aspiradora.
6. _____ Juega con Manchitas.
7. _____ Le es fácil despertarse.
8. _____ Toma la bebida negra.
9. _____ Mira la televisión.
10. _____ Saluda a su mamá todos los días.
11. _____ Visita a los vecinos.
12. _____ Siempre quiere dormir un poco más.

## Ahora... ¡usted!

1. ¿Le gustan los animales? ¿Por qué sí o por qué no?
2. ¿Tiene usted un animal doméstico? ¿Cómo es? ¿Qué le gusta comer? ¿Tiene una personalidad especial? ¿Hace cosas cómicas a veces? ¡Descríbalo! Si no tienes un animal doméstico, ¿por qué no? ¿Le gustaría tener uno? ¿Qué tipo? Describa lo que para usted es el animal doméstico ideal.
3. ¿Le gusta jugar o pasar mucho tiempo con su animal? ¿Por qué sí o por qué no?

### Un paso más... ¡a escribir!

Imagínese que su animal doméstico puede hablar. (Si no tiene un animal, invente uno.) ¿Cuál es la opinión del animal sobre su condición doméstica? Hágale las siguientes preguntas, y luego escriba un párrafo con sus respuestas.

1. ¿Estás contento/a en tu casa? ¿Por qué sí o por qué no?
2. ¿Te gusta la comida? ¿Qué sueles comer? ¿Y qué prefieres comer?
3. ¿Qué cosas te molestan? ¿las pulgas, por ejemplo?
4. ¿Cómo son tus amos?

# Las actividades con los amigos

*Lea Gramática 6.4.*

1. —¿Limpiaste la casa el sábado?
2. —¿Estudiaste mucho?
3. —¿Saliste a comer en algún restaurante?

1. —¿Vio usted la televisión?
2. —¿Ya escribió los exámenes?
3. —¿Visitó a sus amigos este fin de semana?

## Actividad 11. Encuesta: ¿Qué hice?

Ponga las siguientes actividades en orden cronológico.

**PALABRAS ÚTILES**

| | | |
|---|---|---|
| primero | después | finalmente |
| luego | más tarde | por último |

1. Esta mañana (yo)...
   a. me lavé el pelo.
   b. desayuné.
   c. me desperté.
   d. corrí dos millas.
2. Ayer por la tarde (yo)...
   a. volví a casa.
   b. asistí a una clase.
   c. preparé el almuerzo.
   d. salí para el trabajo.
3. Anoche, antes de acostarme, (yo)...
   a. vi la televisión.
   b. planché una blusa / una camisa.
   c. lavé los platos.
   d. preparé la comida.
4. El sábado pasado (yo)...
   a. invité a unos amigos a cenar.
   b. cené con mis amigos.
   c. limpié la casa.
   d. barrí el patio.

## Actividad 12. Intercambios: El fin de semana

Aquí tiene usted algunas de las actividades del fin de semana pasado de Guillermo, Estela y el señor Alvar. Coméntelas con su compañero/a.

MODELOS: E1: ¿Quién *preparó la comida* (*el viernes*)?
E2: *Estela.*

E1: ¿Cuándo *sacó fotos el señor Alvar*?
E2: *El domingo.*

| NOMBRE | EL VIERNES | EL SÁBADO | EL DOMINGO |
|---|---|---|---|
| Guillermo Ramírez | Bailó en una fiesta.<br>Se acostó tarde. | Se levantó tarde.<br>Limpió su cuarto. | Ayudó a su padre.<br>Salió a pasear. |
| Estela Ramírez | Preparó la comida.<br>Habló por teléfono. | Almorzó con una amiga.<br>Charló con la vecina. | Visitó a su madre.<br>Descansó toda la tarde. |
| el señor Alvar | Escribió una carta.<br>Tocó el piano. | Jugó con sus nietos.<br>Barrió el patio. | Asistió a misa.<br>Sacó unas fotos. |

## Actividad 13. Narración: Un fin de semana de Nora Morales

**PALABRAS ÚTILES**

| | | |
|---|---|---|
| primero | después | finalmente |
| luego | más tarde | por último |

## Actividad 14. Entrevistas: ¿Qué hiciste?

EL FIN DE SEMANA PASADO

1. ¿Limpiaste tu cuarto (tu casa)?
2. ¿Saliste con amigos? ¿Adónde?
3. ¿Comiste en un restaurante? ¿Cuál? ¿Con quién(es)?
4. ¿Practicaste algún deporte? ¿Con quién(es)? ¿Dónde?
5. ¿Fuiste al cine? ¿Qué película viste? ¿Te gustó? ¿Por qué?

ANOCHE

6. ¿Trabajaste? ¿A qué hora volviste a casa?
7. ¿Estudiaste? ¿Qué?
8. ¿Hablaste por teléfono con tus amigos? ¿Escuchaste música?
9. ¿Viste la televisión?
10. ¿A qué hora te acostaste?

ESTA MAÑANA

11. ¿A qué hora te levantaste? ¿Te bañaste?
12. ¿Desayunaste? ¿Qué tomaste?
13. ¿A qué hora saliste para la universidad? ¿A qué hora llegaste?
14. ¿A qué clase asististe primero?
15. ¿Leíste el periódico?

## EL MUNDO HISPANO... imágenes

Las tierras de cultivo son sólo el 2 por ciento del territorio peruano, pero la agricultura es la actividad básica de Perú. Aproximadamente el 60 por ciento de la población se dedica a este trabajo. En Perú se cultivan, entre otros productos, la caña de azúcar, las papas, el maíz y el café.

En algunas partes del país ya tienen métodos modernos de cultivo, pero los campesinos[1] indígenas todavía trabajan de sol a sol, usando métodos tradicionales. En esta foto una pareja de Urubamba está arando[2] la tierra.

Urubamba, Perú: el altiplano (*highlands*)

[1]*peasants* [2]*plowing*

## EL MUNDO HISPANO... en los Estados Unidos

Lety Guerrero Romero tiene 29 años y es de México, D.F. Ahora vive en Wilmington, California, y lleva cuatro años en los Estados Unidos.

*Describa la ciudad o pueblo donde usted se crió. ¿Es muy diferente de la ciudad o pueblo donde vive ahora? Compárelos y contrástelos.*

Nací y me crié en la Ciudad de México, D.F., a la cual quiero y extraño.[1] En la actualidad es una ciudad demasiado poblada. Como visitante, basta[2] estar poco tiempo para no olvidarla. Pero cuando se vive dentro, hay que conocer sus mañas;[3] no es fácil, pero una vez que se logra[4] dominarla y conocerla, es muy difícil dejarla. México es como una ciudad encantada.[5]

Ahora vivo en Wilmington, California, y en mi barrio hay mucha gente hispana. Aquí la vida es más calmada y con menos habitantes. Lo primero que noté aquí fue las distancias que hay de un lugar a otro, y que la mayoría de las personas tiene carro propio. En México todo se encuentra más concentrado y utilizamos más el metro, el camión de pasajeros[6] y los carros de alquiler.[7] ¡En la Ciudad de México la vida se vive mucho más de prisa!

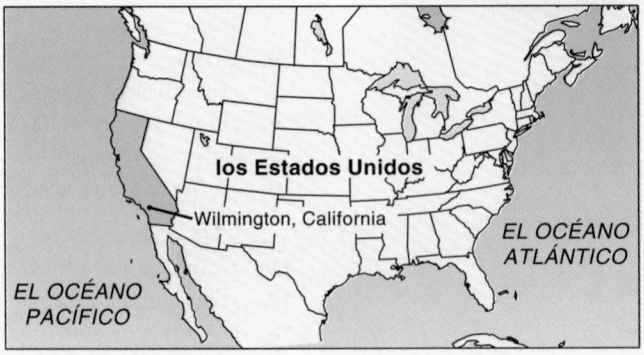


[1]*I miss* [2]*it's enough* [3]secretos [4]una... *once you manage* [5]*enchanted* [6]camión... *bus* (*Mex.*) [7]carros... *taxis*

# Las presentaciones

***Lea Gramática 6.5–6.6.***

ESTEBAN: Mónica, quiero presentarte a mi amigo, Jorge.
MÓNICA: Hola, Jorge, ¿qué tal?
JORGE: ¿Qué tal, Mónica?

ESTELA RAMÍREZ: Señor Luján, quisiera presentarle a mi amiga, la señora Medrano.
SR. LUJÁN: Mucho gusto en conocerla, señora.
SRA. MEDRANO: Igualmente, señor Luján.

DOÑA ROSITA: Señorita Batini, me gustaría presentarle a mi nuevo vecino, el señor Marcos.
LOLA BATINI: Mucho gusto en conocerlo, señor.
SR. MARCOS: Encantado, señorita Batini.

## Actividad 15. Diálogos abiertos: Las presentaciones

Preséntele su nuevo amigo / nueva amiga a otro amigo / otra amiga.

E1: _____, quiero presentarte a mi amigo/a _____. Vive en _____.
E2: Mucho gusto.
E3: _____.

Ahora, preséntele su nuevo amigo / nueva amiga a un amigo / una amiga de su familia.

E1: Sr./Sra./Srta. _____, quiero presentarle a mi amigo/a _____. Es _____.
E2: _____ en conocerlo/la.
E3: _____.

Presente a dos de sus compañeros que no se conocen.

E1: Oye _____, ¿conoces a mi amigo/a _____?
E2: No, no _____ conozco.
E1: _____, te presento a _____. Él/Ella estudia _____ aquí en la universidad.
E2: Mucho gusto, _____.
E3: Igualmente, _____.

### Actividad 16. Entrevista: ¿Conoces tu vecindario?

1. ¿Conoces a los vecinos de la casa (del apartamento) de la izquierda? ¿de la derecha? ¿de enfrente?
2. ¿Sabes el nombre del colegio más cercano a tu casa (apartamento)? ¿Conoces al director / a la directora de ese colegio?
3. ¿Sabes dónde hay un buen restaurante cerca de tu casa (apartamento)?
4. ¿Conoces a los dependientes del supermercado donde haces las compras?
5. ¿Sabes cuánto cuesta un apartamento pequeño en la ciudad o pueblo donde vives?
6. ¿Conoces a alguien que tenga piscina?
7. ¿Sabes cuánto cuesta una casa en tu vecindario?
8. ¿Sabes dónde está el parque _____?

# En resumen

## De todo un poco

**¡REÍR ES VIVIR!**

**Un largo camino**

Ésta es una conversación entre dos niños.
—¿Ves esa lámpara?
—Sí, es una lámpara normal.
—¡No! Es muy especial.
—¿Por qué? ¿Qué tiene de especial?
—Pues... si enciendo esa lámpara y la apunto hacia el planeta Venus, puedes subir hasta el planeta caminando por la luz.
—¡Ja! ¿Crees que soy tonto? ¿Y si a medio camino la apagas?

¿Cómo es tu casa/apartamento?

Trabajando en parejas, hablen de su casa (apartamento), su vecindario y sus obligaciones. Usen esta guía para hablar de su casa (apartamento) y su vecindario.

- descripción de la casa (del apartamento): los cuartos, los muebles, el patio, etcétera
- descripción del vecindario: las escuelas, la biblioteca, las tiendas, la lavandería, la gasolinera, etcétera
- las obligaciones que tiene cada miembro de la familia: lavar, planchar, cocinar, cortar el césped, etcétera

Después de hablar de la casa (del apartamento) y las obligaciones de cada uno de ustedes, hagan comparaciones. ¿Es más grande su casa (apartamento) o la (el) de su compañero/a? ¿Es tan bonito su barrio como el de su compañero/a?

## ¡Dígalo por escrito!

Casa a la venta

Imagínese que usted es agente de bienes raíces. Traiga a la clase una foto o un dibujo de una casa y trate de vendérsela a un compañero / una compañera. Hay que describirle todos los detalles y las ventajas para que compre la casa. Después, escriba un anuncio para una revista de bienes raíces describiendo la casa. Debe incluir en su anuncio una descripción detallada de la casa, los cuartos, los aparatos domésticos que tiene, la vecindad, el precio y, claro, la foto o el dibujo.

### VIDEOTECA

¿Vive usted con su familia, o vive en un apartamento o en una residencia estudiantil? Muchos estudiantes mexicanos viven con su familia, pero otros no. En este segmento de video, Diego va a vivir en el apartamento de su amigo Antonio. ¿Qué pasó esa mañana en la casa de su tía Matilde? ¿Por qué está contento Diego cuando llega al apartamento? ¿Qué muebles hay en su dormitorio? En el Capítulo 6 del *Cuaderno de trabajo* hay más actividades para hacer después de ver el video.

# Vocabulario

## Los cuartos y otras dependencias
Rooms and Other Parts of the House

| | |
|---|---|
| **el ascensor** | elevator |
| **el baño (la sala de baño)** | bathroom |
| **la cerca** | fence |
| **el césped** | grass |
| **la chimenea** | fireplace |
| **el comedor** | dining room |
| **el dormitorio** | bedroom |
| **la escalera** | stairway, stairs |
| **la habitación** | room |
| **la recámara** | bedroom (*Mex.*) |
| **la sala** | living room |

**PALABRAS SEMEJANTES: el balcón, el garaje, el patio, la terraza**

**REPASO: la cocina, el jardín**

## Los muebles y los aparatos eléctricos
Furniture and Electrical Appliances

| | |
|---|---|
| **la alacena** | kitchen cupboard |
| **la alfombra** | carpet |
| **el almohada** | pillow |
| **el aparato (eléctrico)** | (electrical) appliance |
| **el armario** | closet |
| **la aspiradora** | vacuum cleaner |

| | |
|---|---|
| **la bañera** | bathtub |
| **el bote de basura** | trash can |
| **la cafetera** | coffeepot |
| **el calentador** | heater |
| **la cama (matrimonial)** | (master) bed |
| **el cepillo (de dientes)** | (tooth)brush |
| **la cómoda** | chest of drawers |
| **el congelador** | freezer |
| **la cortina** | drapes |
| **el cuadro** | picture (*on a wall*) |
| **la ducha** | shower |
| **la escoba** | broom |
| **el espejo** | mirror |
| **el estante** | shelf |
| **la estufa** | stove, range |
| **el fregadero** | kitchen sink |
| **el gabinete** | cabinet |
| **la gaveta** | drawer |
| **el horno (de microondas)** | (microwave) oven |
| **el inodoro** | toilet |
| **la taza del inodoro** | toilet bowl |
| **el lavabo** | bathroom sink |
| **la lavadora** | washing machine |
| **el lavaplatos** | dishwasher |
| **la mesita** | coffee table |
| **el secador (de pelo)** | hair dryer |
| **la secadora** | (clothes) dryer |
| **el sillón** | easy chair |
| **la tetera** | teapot |
| **la toalla** | towel |
| **el tocador** | dresser |
| **el ventilador** | fan |

**PALABRAS SEMEJANTES: la lámpara, el piano, el plato, el refrigerador, el sofá, el tostador, el utensilio**

**REPASO: los muebles, la rasuradora, la silla, el televisor, el vaso**

## La casa y el vecindario
House and Neighborhood

| | |
|---|---|
| **el arbusto** | bush |
| **la cancha de tenis** | tennis court |
| **la casa particular** | private home |
| **el centro comercial** | shopping center |
| **el departamento** | apartment (*Mex.*) |
| **la estatua** | statue |
| **la gasolinera** | gas station |
| **el vecino de enfrente / de la derecha / de la izquierda** | neighbor across the street / to the right / to the left |

**PALABRAS SEMEJANTES: el apartamento, la vista**

**REPASO: la ciudad, el colegio, el condominio, el edificio, la fuente, la iglesia, el lugar, el parque, la piscina, la plaza, el supermercado, la tienda**

## Los quehaceres domésticos
Household Chores

| | |
|---|---|
| **barrer** | to sweep |
| **calentar (ie)** | to warm up |
| **caliento/calienta** | |
| **dar de comer** | to feed |
| **desempolvar** | to dust |
| **guardar (ropa)** | to put away (clothes) |
| **hacer las compras** | to go grocery shopping |
| **pasar la aspiradora** | to vacuum |
| **regar (ie)** | to water (plants) |
| **riego/riega** | |
| **sacar la basura** | to take out the trash |
| **tender (ie) la cama** | to make the bed |
| **tiendo/tiende** | |

**REPASO: ayudar, cocinar, lavar, limpiar, planchar, sacar fotos, secar**

## Los verbos

| | |
|---|---|
| **alquilar(se)** | to rent; to be rented |
| **se alquila** | |
| **apagar** | to turn off |
| **apoyar** | to support |
| **colgar (ue) (ropa)** | to hang (up) (clothes) |
| **cuelgo/cuelga** | |
| **compartir** | to share |
| **conocer** | to know; to meet |
| **conozco/conoce** | |
| **doblar** | to fold |
| **encender (ie) (la luz)** | to turn on (the light) |
| **enciendo/enciende** | |
| **enviar** | to send |
| **parecer (¿le parece... ?)** | to seem (does it seem . . . to you?) |
| **prender (la luz)** | to turn on (the light) |

**PALABRAS SEMEJANTES: imaginarse (imagínese)**

**REPASO: almorzar (ue), cenar, desayunar**

## Los sustantivos

| | |
|---|---|
| **el alquiler** | rent |
| **el anuncio** | ad |
| **el director / la directora** | (school) principal |

| | |
|---|---|
| **la diversión** | entertainment |
| **el empleado doméstico / la empleada doméstica** | servant |
| **la pareja** | pair; couple |
| **el polvo** | dust |
| **el pueblo** | town |

**PALABRAS SEMEJANTES: la comparación, el desastre, la manera, la milla, el objeto, el transporte**

## Los adjetivos

| | |
|---|---|
| **agradable** | pleasant, nice |
| **amplio/a** | roomy |
| **amueblado/a** | furnished |
| **callado/a** | quiet |
| **caro/a** | expensive |
| **cercano/a** | near, close by |
| **propio/a** | own |
| **rico/a** | rich |
| **serio/a** | serious |

**PALABRAS SEMEJANTES: decorado/a, democrático/a, interior, responsable**

**REPASO: cerca de, módico/a**

## ¿Cuándo? ¿Con qué frecuencia?

| | |
|---|---|
| **a menudo** | often |
| **anoche** | last night |
| **cada semana** | every week |
| **(el mes/año) pasado** | last (month/year) |

**REPASO: ahora, ahora mismo, antes de / después de, ayer, esta noche, hoy, mañana, por la mañana/tarde/noche, una vez (dos/tres/cuatro... veces)**

## Las comparaciones — Comparisons

| | |
|---|---|
| **bueno, mejor, el/la mejor** | good, better, (the) best |
| **malo, peor, el/la peor** | bad, worse, (the) worst |
| **el/la más** (+ *adj.*) | the most (+ *adj.*) |
| **más/menos que (de)** | more/less than |
| **tan... como** | as . . . as |
| **tanto(s)/tanta(s)... como** | as much/many . . . as |

## Las obligaciones — Obligations

| | |
|---|---|
| **es necesario** | it is necessary |
| **hay que** (+ *infin.*) | it is necessary; one has to (*do something*) |

**REPASO: deber** (+ *infin.*), **tener que** (+ *infin.*), **necesitar** (+ *infin.*)

## Las presentaciones — Introductions

| | |
|---|---|
| **Encantado/a.** | Delighted (Pleased) to meet you. |
| **Gusto en conocerlo/la.** | Nice to meet you. |
| **¿Qué tal?** | How's it going? |
| **Quiero presentarle a...** | I want to introduce you to . . . |

**REPASO: igualmente, mucho gusto**

## Palabras y expresiones útiles

| | |
|---|---|
| **alguien** | someone |
| **allí** | there |
| **oye...** | hey . . . |
| **¿Para qué sirve... ?** | What is . . . used for? |

# Gramática y ejercicios

## 6.1 Making Comparisons of Inequality: *más/menos*

### Gramática ilustrada

**más que** = *more than*
**menos que** = *less than*

**A.** Use the words **más... que** (*more . . . than*) and **menos... que** (*less . . . than*) to make unequal comparisons in Spanish. English often uses the ending *-er* (e.g., *taller*) in such comparisons, but Spanish uses **más/menos** + adjective.

| | |
|---|---|
| Guillermo es **más** alto **que** Ramón. | *Guillermo is taller than Ramón.* |
| Graciela es **menos** seria **que** Amanda. | *Graciela is less serious than Amanda.* |
| Yo tengo **más** experiencia **que** Pilar. | *I have more experience than Pilar.* |
| José tiene **menos** tiempo **que** Clara. | *José has less time than Clara.* |

**el más alto** = *the tallest* (*m. sing.*)
**los más altos** = *the tallest* (*m. pl.*)
**la más alta** = *the tallest* (*f. sing.*)
**las más altas** = *the tallest* (*f. pl.*)

**B.** To single out a member of a group as "the most" or "the least," add an article (**el, la, los, las**) to this construction. Note that English often uses the ending *-est*: **el más gordo** (*the fattest*), **las más grandes** (*the biggest ones*), **la más cara** (*the most expensive one*), **el menos útil** (*the least useful*). (Also note that Spanish uses **de** where English uses *of* or *in*.)

| | |
|---|---|
| Adriana es **la más** simpática (**de** las tres que conozco). | *Adriana is the nicest (of the three I know).* |
| Éstas son **las** casas **más** modernas **del** vecindario. | *These are the most modern houses in the neighborhood.* |
| Aquí tiene usted **el** cuarto **más** grande **de** la casa. | *Here you have the largest room in the house.* |

**el/la mejor** = *the best* (*sing.*)
**los/las mejores** = *the best* (*pl.*)
**el/la peor** = *the worst* (*sing.*)
**los/las peores** = *the worst* (*pl.*)

**C.** There are special comparative and superlative forms for **bueno** and **malo**.

| | | | |
|---|---|---|---|
| bueno | mejor | el/la mejor | *good/better/best* |
| malo | peor | el/la peor | *bad/worse/worst* |

| | |
|---|---|
| En mi opinión, la cocina es **el mejor** cuarto de la casa. | *In my opinion, the kitchen is the best room in the house.* |
| No hay nada **peor** que el ruido de los coches cuando uno quiere dormir. | *There is nothing worse than traffic noise when you want to sleep.* |

**mi hermana mayor** = *my older sister*
**mi hermano menor** = *my younger brother*

**D.** The special forms **mayor / el/la mayor** (*older/oldest*) and **menor / el/la menor** (*younger/youngest*) are used to compare ages.

| | |
|---|---|
| Mi hermano **mayor** se llama Jaime y mi hermana **menor** se llama Leticia. | *My older brother is called Jaime, and my younger sister is called Leticia.* |

## Ejercicio 1

Haga comparaciones. Use **más/menos que**.

MODELO: El sofá cuesta $150. El sofá-cama cuesta $500. →
El sofá-cama cuesta *más que* el sofá. (El sofá cuesta *menos que* el sofá-cama.)

1. La mesa pesa 25 kilos. El sillón pesa 48.
2. En mi casa viven ocho personas. En la casa de los vecinos viven cinco.
3. La casa de los López tiene cuatro dormitorios. La casa de los vecinos tiene dos.
4. En el patio de mis abuelos hay tres árboles. En nuestro patio hay cinco.
5. En la casa de los Ruiz hay tres dormitorios. En la casa de los Ramírez hay cuatro.

## Ejercicio 2

Exprese su opinión. Use **mejor**, **peor**, **mayor**, **menor** o **el/la más... de...**

MODELO: el Mercedes Benz; el Jaguar (mejor) →
En mi opinión, el Jaguar es *mejor que* el Mercedes.

1. vivir en el desierto; vivir en el centro de la ciudad (peor)
2. vivir en una casa; vivir en un apartamento (mejor)
3. un ventilador; un horno de microondas; un refrigerador (útil)
4. mi hermano Armando tiene 12 años; mi hermana Irma tiene 10 (mayor)
5. mi sobrino tiene 6 meses; tu sobrina tiene 1 año (menor)
6. un Ferrari que cuesta $85,000; un Rolls Royce que cuesta $200,000; un BMW que cuesta $50,000 (caro)

## 6.2 Making Comparisons of Equality: *tan/tanto*

### Gramática ilustrada

**tan** + adjective + **como** = *as* + adjective + *as*

**A.** When stating that qualities are (or are not) equal or identical (*as pretty as / not as pretty as*), use (**no**) **tan... como**. **Tan** never changes form in comparisons or contrasts of qualities.

| | |
|---|---|
| Marisa es **tan** inteligente **como** Clarisa. | *Marisa is as intelligent as Clarisa.* |
| Ramón **no** es **tan** alto **como** Guillermo. | *Ramón is not as tall as Guillermo.* |

**tanto/a/os/as** + noun + **como** = *as much/many* + noun + *as*

**B.** When equating quantities (*as much/many as*), use **tanto... como**. **Tanto** agrees with the noun that follows: **tanto**, **tanta**, **tantos**, **tantas**.

| | |
|---|---|
| Andrea no tiene **tanto dinero como** Paula. | *Andrea doesn't have as much money as Paula.* |
| Ustedes tienen **tantas tareas como** nosotros. | *You have as many assignments as we do.* |

## Ejercicio 3

Haga comparaciones. Use **tan... como**.

MODELO: El Parque de Chapultepec es muy grande. El Parque Juárez es pequeño. (grande) →
El Parque Juárez no es *tan grande como* el Parque de Chapultepec.

1. La piscina de los señores Montes es muy bonita. La piscina de los señores Lugo es muy bonita también. (bonita)
2. El edificio de la avenida Oriente tiene seis pisos. El edificio nuevo de la avenida del Libertador tiene diez. (alto)
3. La lavandería nueva de la calle Ebro es muy limpia. La lavandería vieja de la avenida Almendros no es muy limpia. (limpia)
4. Los condominios «Princesa» son muy modernos. Los condominios «San Juan» tienen ya once años. (modernos)

## Ejercicio 4

Haga comparaciones. Use **tantos/as... como**.

MODELO: Mi casa tiene dos dormitorios. Su casa tiene cuatro. →
Mi casa no tiene *tantos* dormitorios *como* su casa.

1. La sala de nuestra casa tiene cuatro lámparas. La sala de su casa tiene sólo dos lámparas.
2. La casa de los señores Ramírez tiene ocho cuartos. La casa de los señores Ruiz tiene seis cuartos.
3. La casa de mis padres tiene dos baños. La casa de al lado también tiene dos baños.
4. El patio de doña Lola tiene muchas flores y plantas. El patio de don Anselmo tiene pocas flores y plantas.

**¿RECUERDA?**

You have already seen and used many times the combination of conjugated verb + infinitive: for example, in **Gramática 2.3** (**preferir** and **querer** + infinitive), **5.2** (**saber** and **poder** + infinitive), and **5.4** (**pensar, quisiera, me gustaría,** and **tener ganas de** + infinitive). This is the usual pattern; the other pattern you have learned so far, **estar** + present participle to express actions in progress (**Gramática 3.5**), is an exception to the general rule.

## 6.3 Expressing Obligation and Duty: *tener que, deber, necesitar, hay que, es necesario*

The verbs **tener que** (*to have to*), **deber** (*should, ought to*), and **necesitar** (*to need*) and the impersonal expressions **hay que** (*one must*) and **es necesario** (*it is necessary*) are always followed by infinitives.

| | |
|---|---|
| —¿A qué hora **tenemos que estar** en el teatro? | —*What time do we have to be at the theater?* |
| —A las nueve. **Hay que llegar** un poco antes para recoger los boletos. | —*At 9:00. We have to (One must) get there a little early to pick up the tickets.* |
| —¡Pero **necesito estudiar** más! | —*But I need to study more!* |
| —Está bien, pero **debemos salir** pronto. | —*OK, but we should leave soon.* |

## Ejercicio 5

**¿Qué tienes que hacer este fin de semana?** (*What do you have to do this weekend?*) **Debo estudiar y también necesito lavar el carro y limpiar la casa.** (*I ought to study and I also need to wash the car and clean the house.*)

Esteban cuenta lo que él y sus compañeros de clase tienen que hacer hoy. Complete las oraciones con una forma de **tener que**.

1. Luis _____ trabajar hasta las doce.
2. Carmen y Nora _____ prepararse para un examen de sociología.
3. Yo _____ terminar la tarea para mi clase de matemáticas.
4. Alberto y yo _____ lavar el carro.
5. Mónica, ¿qué _____ hacer tú esta noche?

## Ejercicio 6

**Hay que regar las plantas con frecuencia en el verano.** (*One must* [*We have to*] *water the plants frequently in the summer.*)

Estela Ramírez está hablando de lo que ella y su familia deben hacer mañana. Complete estas oraciones con la forma apropiada de **deber**.

1. Ernesto _____ barrer el patio.
2. Yo _____ limpiar la cocina.
3. Ernestito, tú _____ hacer la tarea para la escuela.
4. Guillermo y Amanda _____ recoger sus libros.
5. Ernesto, tú y yo _____ llevar a los niños al parque a jugar.

# 6.4 Talking About Past Actions: The Preterite of Regular Verbs (Part 1)

### Gramática ilustrada

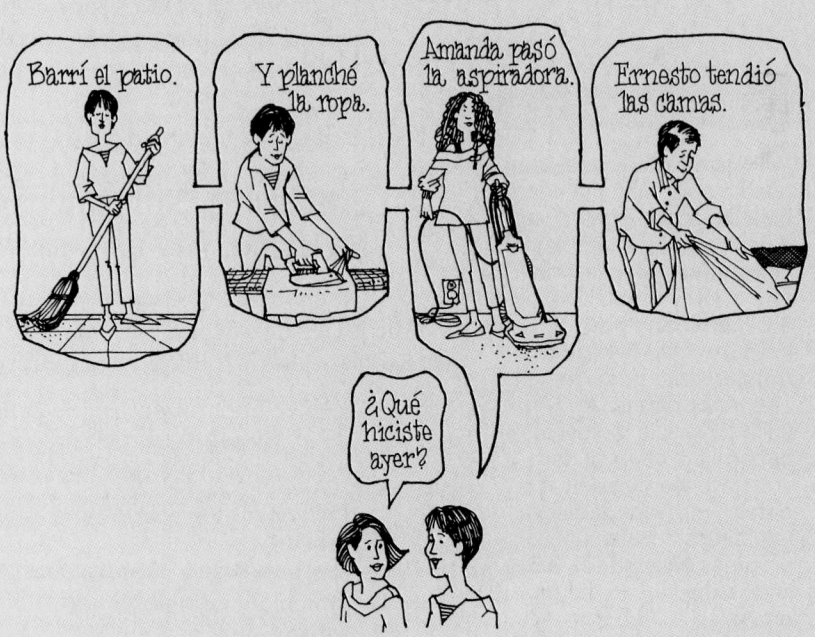

**hablé** = *I spoke*
**comí** = *I ate*
**viví** = *I lived*
**hablaste** = *you (inf. sing.) spoke*
**comiste** = *you (inf. sing.) ate*
**viviste** = *you (inf. sing.) lived*
**habló** = *you (pol. sing.) spoke; he/she spoke*
**comió** = *you (pol. sing.) ate; he/she ate*
**vivió** = *you (pol. sing.) lived; he/she lived*

The Spanish past tense (preterite), like the present tense, is formed by adding a set of endings to the stem. Here are the singular preterite endings of the regular verbs **hablar** (*to speak*), **comer** (*to eat*), and **vivir** (*to live*).*

| | -ar *verbs* | -er *verbs* | -ir *verbs* |
|---|---|---|---|
| (yo) | habl**é** | com**í** | viv**í** |
| (tú) | habl**aste** | com**iste** | viv**iste** |
| (usted, él/ella) | habl**ó** | com**ió** | viv**ió** |

Note the written accent marks. They tell you where to put the stress. Also note that the singular endings for **-er** and **-ir** verbs are the same.

The following are some time expressions that often act as clues to help you recognize the preterite and that you can use to talk about the past.

**anoche, ayer, ayer por la mañana (tarde, noche), anteayer, el lunes (martes, miércoles,** etc.) **pasado, la semana pasada, esta mañana, el mes (año) pasado, ya**

| | |
|---|---|
| **Hablé** con la vecina nueva ayer. | *I spoke with the new neighbor yesterday.* |
| —¿Ya **comiste**?<br>—Sí, **comí** en casa. | *—Did you already eat?*<br>*—Yes, I ate at home.* |

## Ejercicio 7

¿Hizo usted estas actividades ayer? Conteste sí o no.

MODELO: trabajar → Sí, *trabajé* siete horas. (No, *no trabajé*.)

1. comprar un disco compacto
2. comer en un restaurante
3. hablar por teléfono
4. escribir una carta
5. estudiar por cuatro horas
6. abrir la ventana
7. visitar a un amigo / una amiga
8. correr por la mañana
9. tomar un refresco
10. lavar los platos

## Ejercicio 8

Diga si cada una de las personas a continuación hizo las actividades indicadas.

MODELO: Gloria Estefan / cantar en la ducha esta mañana →
Gloria Estefan *cantó* en la ducha esta mañana.

1. mi madre / charlar con el presidente la semana pasada
2. el presidente de México / comer tacos en la calle ayer

---

*The plural endings and many common verbs that are irregular in the preterite are introduced in **Gramática 7.1** and **7.2**.

**¿RECUERDA?**

Spanish uses two different verbs to express the English verb *to know.* You have already seen and practiced the forms of one of these verbs, **saber**, which means *to know facts, information.* When followed by an infinitive, **saber** expresses the idea *to know how to* (*do something*). Return to **Gramática 5.2** to review the verb **saber** in more detail.

3. la profesora de español / salir con Antonio Banderas anoche
4. yo / jugar al tenis con Arantxa Sánchez Vicario ayer a medianoche
5. Fidel Castro / visitar los Estados Unidos el mes pasado

## 6.5 Knowing People, Places, and Facts: *conocer* and *saber*

**A. Conocer** (*to know*) is used in the sense of *to be acquainted* or *familiar with*; it is normally used with people and places. **Saber** (*to know*) is used in the sense of *to know facts, information* or, when followed by an infinitive, *to know how to* (*do something*). Here are the present-tense forms of **conocer*** and **saber.**

| | **conocer** (***to know people, places***) | **saber** (***to know facts, information***) | |
|---|---|---|---|
| (yo) | conozco | sé | *I know* |
| (tú) | conoces | sabes | *you* (*inf. sing.*) *know* |
| (usted, él/ella) | conoce | sabe | *you* (*pol. sing.*) *know; he/she knows* |
| (nosotros/as) | conocemos | sabemos | *we know* |
| (vosotros/as) | conocéis | sabéis | *you* (*inf. pl., Spain*) *know* |
| (ustedes, ellos/as) | conocen | saben | *you* (*pl.*) *know; they know* |

**conocer** = *to know people, places*
**saber** = *to know facts, information*
**saber** + inf. = *to know how to* (*do something*)
***Conozco* a Adriana.** (*I know Adriana.*)
***Sé* que Adriana vive en Buenos Aires.** (*I know that Adriana lives in Buenos Aires.*)

Note that the preposition **a** precedes a direct object noun when that noun is a person. This use of **a** is called the *personal* ***a.***

| | |
|---|---|
| —¿**Conoces a** Carla Espinosa? | *—Do you know Carla Espinosa?* |
| —Sí, y **conozco** también **a** su hermano. | *—Yes, and I also know her brother.* |
| —¿Y **conoces** también **a** su amigo Rogelio? | *—And do you also know her friend Rogelio?* |
| —No, no lo **conozco a** él (no **lo** conozco). | *—No, I don't know him.* |
| —¿**Conoces** muy bien la ciudad de México? | *—Do you know Mexico City well?* |
| —Todavía no. | *—Not yet.* |
| —¿**Sabes** nadar? | *—Do you know how to swim?* |
| —No, no **sé** nadar. | *—No, I don't know how to swim.* |

*Recognition: **vos conocés**

| | |
|---|---|
| —¿**Sabes** dónde está el restaurante? | —*Do you know where the restaurant is?* |
| —No, no **sé**. | —*No, I don't know.* |
| —¿**Sabes** si hay una biblioteca cerca? | —*Do you know if there is a library nearby?* |
| —No, no **sé**. | —*No, I don't know.* |

**conocer** in the preterite = *met* (*for the first time*)

**B.** The preterite of **conocer** (**conocí, conociste, conoció**) expresses the meaning *met* (*for the first time*) in English.

| | |
|---|---|
| **Conocí** a Raúl la semana pasada. | *I met Raúl last week.* |

## Ejercicio 9

—¿Conoce usted a los vecinos que viven enfrente?
—Sí, los conozco muy bien. Su apellido es Ramírez.

El señor Valdés lleva sólo una semana viviendo en el vecindario de San Vicente. Está hablando con su vecino, don Eduardo. Complete con las frases apropiadas las preguntas del señor Valdés.

¿Conoce usted...
¿Sabe usted...

1. a los dueños de la casa de la esquina?
2. a doña Rosita?
3. si hay una farmacia cerca?
4. si hay una alberca (piscina) pública cerca?
5. al director del colegio que está en la esquina?
6. un buen restaurante chino?
7. dónde está el Parque de Colón?
8. si hay una lavandería en el centro comercial El Toro?
9. cuánto cuesta ponerle un techo nuevo a la casa?
10. a la vecina de la casa amarilla?

**¿RECUERDA?**

In **Gramática 5.1** you learned about indirect object pronouns **(los pronombres de complemento indirecto),** which are used with verbs of informing to indicate to whom something is told, reported, said, and so forth. Remember that the indirect object pronouns are **me, te, le, nos, os,** and **les.** Review that section again now, if necessary.

## 6.6 Referring to People Already Mentioned: Personal Direct Object Pronouns

**A.** Personal direct object pronouns **(los pronombres de complemento directo)** are used with verbs such as *to see* (*someone*), *to remember* (*someone*), *to know* (*someone*), *to love* (*someone*), *to take* (*someone somewhere*), *to invite* (*someone*), and so forth. Here are some examples of direct object pronouns in English.

Raúl Saucedo? I don't remember *him*.
Ernestito and his brother and sister? We saw *them* yesterday.
I'm José Estrada. You remember *me*, don't you?

**B.** You already know four of the personal direct object pronouns, because they are the same as the reflexive pronouns and the indirect object pronouns: **me** (*me*), **te** (*you*), **os** (*you; inf. pl., Spain*), and **nos** (*us*).

| | |
|---|---|
| Usted no **me** conoce todavía. Soy Raúl Saucedo. | *You don't know me yet. I'm Raúl Saucedo.* |
| **Te** quiero mucho. | *I love you a lot.* |
| Tú no **nos** recuerdas, ¿verdad? | *You don't remember us, do you?* |

**C.** Four other direct object pronouns are used, according to the gender and number of the person(s) referred to.*

| | | | |
|---|---|---|---|
| lo | *him, you (pol. m. sing.)* | los | *them, you (pl.)* |
| la | *her, you (pol. f. sing.)* | las | *them, you (females only)* |

In the sentence *John saw her*, the word *her* is a direct object pronoun. Direct object pronouns answer the questions *Whom?* or *What?*

In the sentence **Juan la conoce** (*John knows her*), **la** is a direct object pronoun.

—¿**Dónde está *Lan*?**
—**No sé, no *la* veo.**
[***la*** = **Lan**]
(—*Where is* ***Lan?***
—*I don't know, I don't see* ***her.***
[***her*** = *Lan*])
—¿**Conoces a *los Silva?***
—**Sí, *los* conocí ayer.**
[***los*** = **los Silva**]
(—*Do you know* ***the Silvas?***
—*Yes, I met* ***them*** *yesterday.*
[***them*** = *the Silvas*])

| | |
|---|---|
| —¿Conoces a **José Estrada**, el novio de Pilar?<br>—Sí, **lo** conozco. | —*Do you know José Estrada, Pilar's boyfriend?*<br>—*Yes, I know him.* |
| —¿Mi hija Margarita? **La** llevo todos los días a la escuela.<br>—¿No **lo** vi a usted ayer, señor Torres?<br>—Sí, **me** vio en la biblioteca. | —*My daughter Margaret? I take her to school every day.*<br>—*Didn't I see you yesterday, Mr. Torres?*<br>—*Yes, you saw me in the library.* |
| —¿Y tus **parientes**? ¿**Los** ves con frecuencia?<br>—Sí, durante las fiestas, **los** invitamos a casa a cenar con nosotros. | —*And your relatives? Do you see them frequently?*<br>—*Yes, during the holidays we invite them to our house to have dinner with us.* |
| —¿Vas a visitar a tus **hermanas** mañana?<br>—Sí, **las** voy a ver al mediodía. | —*Are you going to visit your sisters tomorrow?*<br>—*Yes, I'm going to see them at noon.* |
| —Mamá, ¿cuándo vas a recoger**nos**?<br>—Paso a recoger**las** a las 2:45. | —*Mom, when are you going to pick us up?*<br>—*I'll pick you up at 2:45.* |

## Ejercicio 10

Complete estos diálogos con los pronombres de complemento directo apropiados.

MODELO: —¿Conoces a Marta Guerrero?
—Sí, *la* conozco.

1. —¿Conocen ustedes a los señores Ramírez?
—Sí, _____ conocemos muy bien.
2. —¿Conoces tú a doña Rosita?
—Sí, _____ conozco un poco.
3. —¿Y a Pedro Ruiz?
—Sí, _____ conozco también.
4. —¿Conoce Estela Ramírez a Silvia y a Nacho?
—Sí, ella _____ conoce un poco.

*Some Spanish speakers from Spain use **le/les** instead of **lo/los** as the direct object pronoun to refer to males.

**5.** —Señor, yo no _____ conozco.
—¿No me conoce? ¡Soy Ernesto Ramírez, su vecino!

**6.** —¿Conoce usted al esposo de Andrea Ruiz?
—No, no _____ conozco.

**7.** —¿Conocen ustedes a la señorita Batini?
—Sí, _____ conocemos muy bien; es amiga de mi madre.

**8.** —¿Conocen los señores Ramírez a los señores Silva?
—Sí, los señores Ramírez _____ conocen muy bien; son vecinos.

**9.** —¿Conoces tú a Guillermo?
—Sí, _____ conozco muy bien; es mi mejor amigo.

**10.** —¿Conoce Amanda a Graciela?
—Sí, _____ conoce muy bien; son muy buenas amigas.

CAPÍTULO 7

# Las experiencias

**METAS**

In **Capítulo 7** you will continue to talk about things that happened in the past: your own experiences and those of others.

Cantabria, España

**ACTIVIDADES DE COMUNICACIÓN Y LECTURAS**


Mis experiencias

**El mundo hispano...** su gente

Las experiencias con los demás

**El mundo hispano...** en los Estados Unidos

Hablando del pasado

**Lectura** Los amigos hispanos: Una carta desde Perú

**El mundo hispano...** imágenes

**Las palabras viven** La cultura incaica en Ecuador

**EN RESUMEN**


**GRAMÁTICA Y EJERCICIOS**


7.1 Talking about Past Actions: The Preterite of Regular Verbs (Part 2)

7.2 Relating More about the Past (Part 1): Verbs with Irregular Preterite Forms

7.3 Relating More about the Past (Part 2): Stem-Changing Verbs in the Preterite

7.4 Reporting the Past: Indirect Object Pronouns with **decir**

7.5 Expressing *ago:* **hacer** + Time

# Actividades de comunicación y lecturas

## Mis experiencias

*Lea Gramática* 7.1–7.2.

**Ayer por la mañana . . .**

Me lavé el pelo.

Desayuné rápidamente.

Salí de la casa.

Asistí a la clase de biología.

Tomé café con algunos amigos.

Escribí un informe para la clase de química.

**Ayer por la tarde...**

Volví a casa a las dos.

Almorcé con mi mamá.

Trabajé por cuatro horas en una tienda de ropa.

**Anoche...**

Cené con mi familia.

Leí un poco antes de acostarme.

Me acosté temprano.

## Actividad 1. Orden lógico: Mis actividades

Ordene lógicamente las siguientes actividades.

_____ Leí una novela.
_____ Me duché.
_____ Me puse el pijama.
_____ Trabajé. / Asistí a clases.
_____ Me acosté.
_____ Hice la tarea.
_____ Cené.
_____ Desayuné.
_____ Salí para el trabajo / la universidad.
_____ Lavé los platos.
_____ Volví a casa.
_____ Me vestí.

## Actividad 2. Narración: La rutina

Complete lógicamente cada secuencia con la actividad que falta.

MODELO: Anoche cené, luego me quité la ropa, *me puse el pijama*, me lavé los dientes y me acosté.

1. Hoy me desperté, me levanté inmediatamente y me duché. Después me sequé y me puse ropa limpia.
2. Anoche llegué del trabajo, me quité la ropa, me puse el pijama, cené y me acosté.
3. Esta mañana me desperté tarde. Me quité rápidamente el pijama, me duché y me sequé. Luego tomé un vaso de leche (no desayuné porque no tuve tiempo) y salí para el trabajo.
4. El sábado pasado fui al cine. Primero me quité la ropa, luego me sequé y me pusa ropa limpia. Un poco más tarde me peiné y me maquillé y, finalmente, salí para el cine con mi novio.
5. El domingo pasado me desperté, desayuné, me duché, me sequé, me vestí y salí de mi casa. Llegué a la cancha de tenis y jugué un partido con Esteban.

Ahora, escriba una secuencia como las anteriores para que la clase diga qué actividad falta.

## Actividad 3. Encuesta: La última vez

¿Cuándo fue la última vez que usted hizo las siguientes actividades?

MODELO: ¿Cuándo habló con su mamá por teléfono? →
*Hablé* con ella *la semana pasada*.

### POSIBILIDADES

esta mañana
ayer
anteayer
anoche
la semana pasada
ayer por la mañana (tarde, noche)
el lunes (martes,... ) pasado
el año pasado

1. ¿Cuándo lavó su carro?
2. ¿Cuándo se bañó?
3. ¿Cuándo se cortó el pelo?
4. ¿Cuándo limpió la casa?
5. ¿Cuándo asistió a clase? ¿a un concierto?
6. ¿Cuándo estudió por más de una hora?
7. ¿Cuándo vio la televisión? ¿una película?
8. ¿Cuándo fue a la playa? ¿al lago? ¿al río?
9. ¿Cuándo fue de compras?
10. ¿Cuándo leyó el periódico? ¿una revista?

## Actividad 4. Narración: El fin de semana de Ricardo Sícora

### PALABRAS ÚTILES

| | | |
|---|---|---|
| primero | luego | más tarde |
| poco después | también | finalmente |

## EL MUNDO HISPANO... su gente

**M**aría del Carmen Méndez tiene 19 años y es española.

*Describa unas vacaciones inolvidables.*[1]

Unas vacaciones inolvidables son las del verano de hace dos años. En junio estuve con mi madre en una residencia de estudiantes en El Escorial,[2] un pueblecito en las montañas. Todo el mes de julio lo pasé en Irlanda, en un pueblo al norte de Dublín. Me pareció un país precioso, ¡y sobre todo verde! Y la gente era toda muy abierta y cantarina.[3] En agosto fui con mi padre a los Pirineos y allí pasamos quince días en un refugio, paseando por el bosque.[4]

Ese verano fui a muchísimos sitios y conocí a mucha gente de mi edad, y todavía me mantengo en contacto con muchos de ellos. Además, ¡descubrí las bellezas[5] que hay por todo el mundo!

[1]*unforgettable* [2]El Escorial es famoso por el monasterio de El Escorial, que fue construido (*was built*) entre los años 1563 y 1584. En el monasterio hay un palacio, una iglesia y un mausoleo donde están enterrados (*buried*) los monarcas españoles. [3]*fond of singing* [4]*forest* [5]*beauty*

# Las experiencias con los demás

***Lea Gramática* 7.3–7.4.**

## Raúl y Esteban fueron a una fiesta ayer.

Se vistieron con cuidado.

Llegaron un poco tarde y les dijeron «¡Disculpen!» a sus amigos.

Bailaron y se divirtieron, pero bebieron mucha cerveza y...

¡Se sintieron mal! Tuvieron que regresar a casa.

Nos pusimos unos vestidos lindos.

Llegamos a la fiesta y nos sirvieron cerveza; no la aceptamos.

No nos quedamos en la fiesta. Preferimos ir a jugar al boliche.

Nos sentimos un poco ridículas con nuestros vestidos de fiesta, pero nos divertimos mucho.

## Actividad 5. Intercambios: El fin de semana de los vecinos

A continuación ustedes tienen una lista de lo que hicieron algunos de los vecinos de Ernesto y Estela durante el fin de semana.

MODELOS: E1: ¿Qué hicieron *los Olivera el viernes*?
E2: Limpiaron la casa.

E1: ¿Quiénes *salieron a cenar el sábado*?
E2: *Los Silva.*

| | LOS OLIVERA | LOS SILVA | LOS RUIZ |
|---|---|---|---|
| el viernes | Limpiaron la casa. | Fueron al cine y vieron *El amor secreto.* | Viajaron a Acapulco con sus hijas. |
| el sábado | Dieron una fiesta y se divirtieron mucho. | Salieron a cenar. | Pasaron el día en la playa. |
| el domingo | Durmieron hasta las once; no hicieron nada. | Asistieron al bautizo del nieto de sus amigos. | Almorzaron en un restaurante elegante. |

## Actividad 6. Narración: Las vacaciones de Rubén y Virginia Hernández

los Hernández
(Rubén y Virginia)

## Actividad 7. Intercambios: Las últimas vacaciones

Pregúntele a su compañero/a qué hicieron las personas en las siguientes fotos.

MODELO: E1: ¿Qué hizo *la familia puertorriqueña*?
E2: *Fueron a la playa, tomaron el sol y nadaron.*

Después, pregúntele a su compañero/a si él/ella hizo las mismas actividades durante sus últimas vacaciones.

MODELO: E1: *¿Fuiste a la playa?*
E2: No, no *fui a la playa*, pero *nadé mucho en la piscina.*

El tenis en México

Una playa en Puerto Rico

El cine en España

De viaje en Argentina

Un restaurante en Sevilla, España

El esquí en Chile

## Actividad 8. Encuesta: ¿Cuándo?

Diga con quién y cuándo hizo usted las actividades de la próxima página. Luego comente sus respuestas con un compañero / una compañera.

MODELO: Fuimos al cine. → *Mi amigo Jorge y yo* fuimos al cine *anoche*.

1. Practicamos un deporte.
2. Esquiamos en las montañas.
3. Dormimos en el campo, al aire libre.
4. Dimos una fiesta.
5. Vimos una película.
6. Bailamos.
7. Nos divertimos muchísimo.
8. Montamos a caballo.
9. Corrimos varios kilómetros.
10. Estudiamos en la biblioteca.

## Y TÚ, ¿QUÉ DICES?

¿Dónde?
¿Cuál?
¡Qué divertido!
¡Qué aburrido!
¿De veras?
¡Qué envidia!

## Actividad 9. Narración: Los héroes y el ladrón

Los dibujos representan una aventura de Guillermo y su hermano Ernestito. Las oraciones a continuación describen cada dibujo. Póngalas en orden según los dibujos.

_____ Guillermo le ató las manos al ladrón y Ernestito llamó a la policía.
_____ Los chicos se pusieron rojos. Pero se sintieron muy bien porque hicieron algo heroico.
_____ Guillermo y Ernestito oyeron unos gritos desesperados.
_____ Corrieron detrás del ladrón.
_____ Miraron por la ventana y vieron a dos hermosas chicas asustadas.
_____ Lo atraparon y le quitaron las bolsas de las chicas.
_____ Ellas les dijeron: «¡Ayúdennos, por favor! ¡Aquel hombre nos robó las bolsas!»
_____ Las chicas les dijeron: «¡Muchísimas gracias!» y les dieron un beso.
_____ El policía arrestó al ladrón.
_____ Salieron y les preguntaron: «¿Qué les pasa?»

## Actividad 10. Entrevista: El domingo pasado

Entreviste a un compañero / una compañera. Hágale preguntas sobre las actividades de un amigo / una amiga, su novio/a o esposo/a o de otro miembro de su familia.

1. ¿Se levantó tarde? ¿A qué hora se levantó?
2. ¿Leyó el periódico? ¿Tomó café o té?
3. ¿Hizo ejercicio? ¿Practicó algún deporte?
4. ¿Asistió a misa? ¿Fue a la iglesia?
5. ¿Dónde almorzó?
6. ¿Salió con algún amigo / alguna amiga? ¿Adónde fueron? ¿Se divirtieron?
7. ¿Trabajó? ¿Dónde? ¿Por cuántas horas?
8. ¿Cenó en casa? ¿Qué hizo después de cenar? ¿Vio la televisión?
9. ¿Estudió? ¿Hizo mucha tarea? ¿Leyó alguna novela?
10. ¿A qué hora se acostó?

## EL MUNDO HISPANO... en los Estados Unidos

Antonio Galván tiene 40 años y es salvadoreño. Antonio vivió por un tiempo en California; ahora reside en Takoma Park, Maryland. Lleva 22 años en los Estados Unidos.

*¿Estuvo alguna vez en una fiesta muy divertida? ¡Descríbala!*

La fiesta que yo no olvido es la de mi amiga Rosita Iraheta. Fue su «Fiesta Rosa», que también la llaman *quinceañera;* Rosita cumplió sus quince años. La fiesta no fue en su casa, sino[1] en la de sus parientes que viven en una mansión en las lomas,[2] con una vista de la ciudad. ¡Fue un fiestón[3]! La música la tocó el conjunto «Los Black Cats», y cantaba Chamba Maldonado. ¡Qué voz! Todo el mundo bailó. Y los enamorados se paseaban[4] por la terraza contemplando la ciudad iluminada, en una noche de brisas tibias inolvidable.

[1]*but rather* [2]en... *on a hill* [3]*huge party* [4]se... *strolled along*

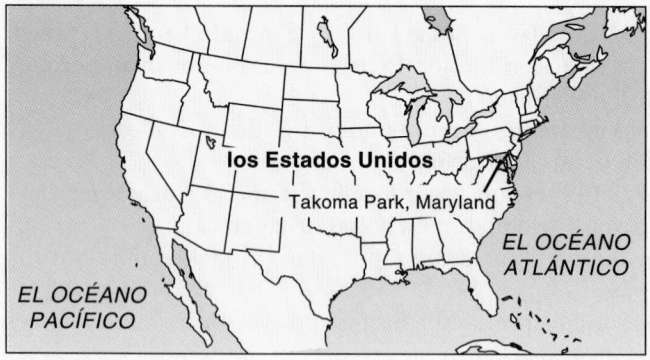

# Hablando del pasado

*Lea Gramática 7.5.*

20,000 a.C.

Los indígenas americanos llegaron al continente desde Asia hace más de 20.000 años.

12 de octubre de 1492

Cristóbal Colón llegó a América hace cinco siglos.

4 de julio de 1776

Thomas Jefferson firmó la Declaración de la Independencia hace más de 200 años.

5 de mayo de 1862

Los mexicanos ganaron la batalla de Puebla hace aproximadamente 140 años.

**¡REÍR ES VIVIR!**

**La carta**

Dos niños conversan.
—¿Qué estás haciendo?
—Estoy escribiendo una carta.
—¿Para quién es?
—Para mí mismo.
—¡¿Para ti?! Hummm... ¿Y qué dice la carta?
—¡No sé! No la he recibido todavía.

## Actividad 11. Asociaciones: Hablando del pasado

Busque las actividades que *no* son lógicas y explique por qué no lo son.

1. Soy Ernesto. Esta mañana me levanté muy tarde.
   a. El despertador no sonó.
   b. Llegué temprano al trabajo.
   c. Desayuné tranquilamente en casa.
   d. Manejé el carro muy rápido, en vez de tomar el autobús, para llegar pronto a la oficina.
2. Hace una semana Ramón fue a acampar en las montañas con su familia.
   a. Su hermano se bañó en el río.
   b. Su hermana bailó toda la noche en una discoteca.
   c. Su papá escaló una montaña.
   d. Su mamá preparó el desayuno.
3. Soy Amanda. Hace dos días fui con algunas amigas a comprar el disco nuevo de Jon Secada.
   a. Tomamos el metro.
   b. No pagamos mucho por el disco.
   c. Compramos un taco en la tienda de discos.
   d. Encontramos otro disco de Enrique Iglesias que nos gustó.
4. Hace un año Estela y Ernesto fueron a Europa.
   a. Visitaron el Museo del Prado en Madrid.
   b. Comieron en restaurantes franceses muy buenos.
   c. Subieron a las pirámides de Teotihuacán.
   d. Cruzaron el canal entre Inglaterra y Francia.

## Actividad 12. Entrevista: Hechos memorables... una entrevista algo indiscreta

MODELO: E1: ¿Cuánto tiempo hace que empezaste a estudiar español? →
E2: Hace *seis meses* que empecé a estudiar español.

1. ¿Cuánto tiempo hace que saliste solo/a con un amigo / una amiga por primera vez?
2. ¿Cuánto tiempo hace que te dieron tu primer beso?
3. ¿Cuánto tiempo hace que te graduaste en la escuela secundaria? ¿que te matriculaste en la universidad?
4. ¿Cuánto tiempo hace que tus padres se casaron? ¿que tú te casaste?
5. ¿Cuánto tiempo hace que nació tu primer hijo / primera hija (primer sobrino / primera sobrina)?
6. ¿Cuánto hace que cumpliste años?
7. ¿Cuánto hace que conociste a tu mejor amigo/a?
8. ¿Cuánto hace que te pusieron una multa por manejar a exceso de velocidad?

# Los amigos hispanos: Una carta desde Perú

**VOCABULARIO ÚTIL**

| | |
|---|---|
| antigua | *ancient* |
| sagrada | *sacred* |
| los indígenas | *natives* |
| entre sí | *among themselves* |
| el paisaje | *landscape* |
| las vueltas | *turns* |
| la ladera | *side of a mountain* |
| la cima | *top* |
| tenían | *they had* |
| la rueda | *wheel* |

En noviembre, Clara Martin viajó a Perú con un grupo de estudiantes españoles. Fue un viaje corto, pero Clara pudo ver las magníficas ruinas de Machu Picchu. La antigua ciudad sagrada de los incas está tan lejos de la civilización que es necesario usar varios medios de transporte para llegar a las ruinas.

En esta carta, Clara le describe a la profesora Martínez la excursión que ella hizo de Cuzco a Machu Picchu.

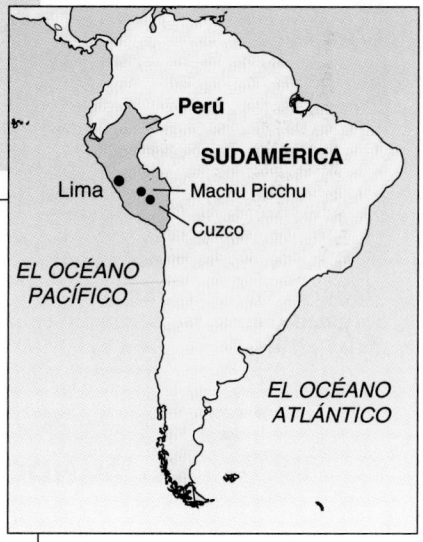


Cuzco, 15 de noviembre

Estimada profesora:

Aquí estoy en Perú. ¡Qué experiencia! Machu Picchu es increíble. Quiero contarle cómo llegamos allí, pues la larga excursión fue parte de la experiencia. Bueno, primero fuimos a Cuzco[1] por avión desde Lima. En el aeropuerto, tomamos un taxi directamente al hotel y allí descansé un poco. Después de una hora, más o menos, salí a pasear por la ciudad con los otros estudiantes. Fuimos al mercado, donde compré un suéter de alpaca muy bonito. Los indígenas de Cuzco hablan quechua[2] entre sí, pero con nosotros hablaron castellano.[3]

A la mañana siguiente, nos encontramos con todos los miembros de la excursión en la estación del tren, para ir a Machu Picchu. En el tren me senté al lado de la ventanilla para ver bien el paisaje. A la salida de Cuzco el tren tiene que subir muchos metros en una distancia muy corta, así que subimos muy despacio. ¡Dimos muchas vueltas por la misma ladera!

El viaje a Machu Picchu duró aproximadamente cuatro horas. Pasamos por valles entre montañas muy verdes. ¡Qué paisajes más bellos! Llegamos a una pequeña estación dentro de un valle profundo. De allí subimos en autobús a la cima de la montaña. Y por fin pudimos admirar las ruinas y una vista panorámica de los Andes. Fue la imagen más impresionante de mi vida. ¿Cómo pudieron construir todo aquello en un lugar tan remoto, tan inaccesible? ¿Cómo llevaron las piedras hasta allá arriba? ¡Si todavía no conocían la rueda!

Comimos en el hotel que está en la cima de la montaña, al lado de las ruinas. Luego bajé en el autobús con los estudiantes y demás miembros de la excursión. Ya casi de noche abordamos el tren para el viaje de regreso a Cuzco.

Como puede ver, profesora, mi viaje a Machu Picchu fue estupendo. Hasta mi próxima carta o tarjeta.

Un abrazo,

Clara

[1]Cuzco es la antigua capital de Perú; Lima es la capital hoy en día.
[2]El quechua es el idioma de los incas que se habla en Perú y Bolivia.
[3]En algunos países, como Argentina y Colombia, se usa la palabra **castellano** más que **español**. La palabra viene de **Castilla**, la región de España donde se originó el idioma.

Machu Picchu, Perú: En el Templo del Sol puede admirarse el tamaño enorme de las piedras.

## Comprensión

Busque el orden correcto.

_____ Clara compró un suéter.
_____ En el tren, Clara se sentó al lado de la ventanilla.
_____ Salió a pasear con otros estudiantes.
_____ Vio las ruinas impresionantes de Machu Picchu.
_____ Bajó en autobús con los demás.
_____ Subió a la cima de la montaña en autobús.
_____ Llegó a Cuzco.

### Un paso más... ¡a escribir!

Clara usó varios medios de transporte para llegar a Machu Picchu: el avión, el taxi, el tren y el autobús. ¿Conoce usted un lugar muy escondido, como Machu Picchu, al cual sea difícil llegar? Si no conoce un lugar así, ¡imagíneselo! ¿Dónde está? ¿Qué medios de transporte se usan para llegar allá? ¿Qué aspectos de interés tiene ese lugar? ¿Cómo son sus habitantes?

## EL MUNDO HISPANO... imágenes

«Subimos en autobús a la cima de la montaña. Y por fin pudimos admirar las ruinas y una vista panorámica de los Andes. Fue la imagen más impresionante de mi vida. ¿Cómo pudieron construir todo aquello en un lugar tan remoto, tan inaccesible? ¿Cómo llevaron las piedras hasta allá arriba?»

Machu Picchu, Perú

**LAS PALABRAS VIVEN**

**VOCABULARIO ÚTIL**

| | |
|---|---|
| incaica | *Incan* |
| la ciudad andina | *Andean city* |
| bordadas | *embroidered* |
| aunque | *although* |
| la cruda | *hangover (Mex.)* |
| en vez de | *instead of* |

# La cultura incaica en Ecuador

La cultura incaica es muy visible en Ecuador. Uno puede ver personas con trajes típicos de esa cultura en todas las ciudades del país. El grupo del área de la ciudad andina Otavalo es uno de los más notables. Las mujeres llevan faldas azul oscuro y hermosas blusas bordadas. Los hombres se ponen pantalones muy blancos y ponchos azules.

La presencia indígena es vital en la sociedad ecuatoriana, y se nota especialmente en el idioma. Se estima que el 30 por ciento de la población de Ecuador es monolingüe: habla solamente la lengua quechua. Y aproximadamente una tercera parte de la población es bilingüe; es decir, que habla español y quechua.

El mercado de Otavalo, Ecuador

Muchas palabras quechuas se usan diariamente en Ecuador. Estas palabras forman parte del español que se habla en ese país. Por ejemplo, *wawa* (se pronuncia *guagua*), que quiere decir **bebé**; *achachay*, que significa **tengo frío**; y *chuchaqui*, que es una **cruda**. Uno de los casos más interesantes es la palabra *ñaña*, que significa **hermana**. Esta palabra se usa tanto, que ahora muchos ecuatorianos dicen *ñaño* en vez de **hermano**. ¡Pero en la lengua quechua la palabra *ñaño* no existe!

## En resumen

### De todo un poco

¿Quién lo hizo?

Diga cuál de las personas que aparecen en la próxima página se relaciona con cada hecho histórico.

a. Neil Armstrong
b. Julio César
c. Hernán Cortés
d. Maximiliano de Habsburgo
e. Michael Johnson
f. Charles Lindbergh
g. Leonardo da Vinci
h. George Wáshington

1. _____ Cortó un árbol y dijo la verdad. Dijo: «Fui yo. No puedo decir una mentira.» Fue el primer presidente de los Estados Unidos.
2. _____ Conquistó a los aztecas hace aproximadamente 480 años. Quemó sus barcos para no regresar a España.
3. _____ Dijo: «Vine, vi y vencí» («*Vini, vidi, vici*» en latín.) Fue emperador de Roma hace muchos años... más de mil quinientos... casi dos mil.
4. _____ Pintó la *Gioconda* (la *Mona Lisa*) en Italia hace más de quinientos años.
5. _____ Es norteamericano; fue el primer hombre que caminó en la luna (hace aproximadamente treinta años).
6. _____ Ganó dos medallas de oro en las Olimpíadas de Atlanta en 1996: una en la carrera de los 200 metros y otra en la carrera de los 400 metros.
7. _____ Hizo el primer vuelo transatlántico. Cruzó el océano Atlántico en el «Espíritu de San Luis» en 1927, hace aproximadamente setenta años.
8. _____ Fue emperador de México hace más de cien años (de 1864 a 1867).

Ahora, trabajando en grupos, preparen dos o tres descripciones como las anteriores para sus compañeros.

## ¡Dígalo por escrito!

¡Soy inocente!

Debido a un error de identidad, la policía sospecha que usted participó en un robo que ocurrió durante el fin de semana pasado. Trabaje con un compañero / una compañera para hablar del asunto (su compañero/a es el policía / la mujer policía). Explíquele exactamente lo que usted hizo el fin de semana pasado (el sábado y/o el domingo). ¿A qué hora lo hizo? ¿Con quién estuvo, y dónde? Después del interrogatorio, escriba su declaración. Su compañero/a también debe escribir una declaración sobre los hechos del asunto y decir si en su juicio usted está diciendo la verdad o si está mintiendo.

## VIDEOTECA

Usted ya sabe algo de José Miguel y Paloma, los dos primos de Ecuador. En este episodio, Paloma le cuenta a José Miguel qué le pasó el fin de semana pasado. ¡Parece que fue un fin de semana muy interesante! Escuche bien y, utilizando las formas del pretérito, apunte tres de las cosas que hizo Paloma y dos más que hicieron Gustavo y Margarita. ¿Alguna vez le ocurrió a usted algo parecido? En el Capítulo 7 del *Cuaderno de trabajo* hay más actividades para hacer después de ver el video.

# Vocabulario

## La naturaleza — Nature

| | |
|---|---|
| **la luna** | moon |
| **la ola** | wave |
| **el oso** | bear |
| **la palmera** | palm tree |

**REPASO: el río, el sol**

## Los lugares — Places

| | |
|---|---|
| **el aire libre** | outdoors |
| **la alberca** | swimming pool (*Mex.*) |
| **el campo** | country(side) |
| **la escuela secundaria** | high school |
| **el (jardín) zoológico** | zoo |

**PALABRAS SEMEJANTES: Asia, el continente, la pirámide**

## Los verbos en el pasado (irregulares)
Verbs in the Past (Irregular)

| | |
|---|---|
| **almorzar (ue)**<br>**almorcé/almorzó** | to have lunch |
| **buscar**<br>**busqué/buscó** | to look for |
| **cruzar**<br>**crucé/cruzó** | to cross |
| **dar (un beso)**<br>**di/dio** | to give (a kiss) |
| **decir**<br>**dije/dijo** | to say; to tell |
| **dormir (ue, u)**<br>**dormí/durmió** | to sleep |
| **empezar**<br>**empecé/empezó** | to start |
| **estar**<br>**estuve/estuvo** | to be |
| **hacer**<br>**hice/hizo** | to do; to make |
| **ir**<br>**fui/fue** | to go |
| **jugar (ue)**<br>**jugué/jugó** | to play |
| **leer**<br>**leí/leyó** | to read |
| **llegar**<br>**llegué/llegó** | to arrive |
| **oír**<br>**oí/oyó** | to hear |
| **ponerse rojo / a**<br>**me puse/se puso...** | to blush |
| **preferir (ie, i)**<br>**preferí/prefirió** | to prefer |
| **querer (ie)**<br>**quise/quiso** | to want |
| **secarse**<br>**me sequé / se secó** | to dry |
| **sentirse (ie, i) (bien/mal)**<br>**me sentí / se sintió** | to feel (good/bad, ill) |
| **ser**<br>**fui/fue** | to be |
| **servir (i)**<br>**serví/sirvió** | to serve |
| **tener**<br>**tuve/tuvo** | to have |
| **traer**<br>**traje/trajo** | to bring |
| **venir**<br>**vine/vino** | to come |
| **vestirse (i)**<br>**me vestí / se vistió** | to get dressed |

## Más verbos

| | |
|---|---|
| **atar** | to tie |
| **atrapar** | to trap |
| **casarse** | to get married |
| **cumplir años** | to have a birthday |
| **estacionar** | to park |
| **firmar** | to sign |
| **ganar** | to win; to earn |
| **hospedarse** | to stay (*at a hotel*) |
| **pagar** | to pay |
| **pasar el día** | to spend the day |
| **quemar** | to burn |
| **robar** | to steal |
| **saludar** | to greet |
| **sonar (ue)** | to ring; to go off (*alarm*) |
| **subir** | to go up |

**PALABRAS SEMEJANTES: aceptar, arrestar, completar, contar**

## Otros sustantivos

| | |
|---|---|
| **la arena** | sand |
| **el barco** | ship |
| **la batalla** | battle |
| **la cerveza** | beer |
| **el exceso de velocidad** | speeding |
| **el grito** | shout, scream |
| **el hecho** | event |
| **el informe** | report |
| **el ladrón / la ladrona** | thief |
| **la medalla de oro** | gold medal |
| **la mentira** | lie |
| **la multa** | traffic ticket |
| **la policía** | police (force) |
| **el siglo** | century |
| **el traje de baño** | bathing suit |
| **el vuelo** | flight |

**PALABRAS SEMEJANTES: la aventura, la declaración, el emperador / la emperatriz, el kilómetro, el latín** (*idioma*)**, las Olimpíadas, el palacio, la posibilidad, el secreto, la secuencia, el taco**

## Los adjetivos

| | |
|---|---|
| **asustado/a** | frightened |
| **limpio/a** | clean |
| **lindo/a** | pretty |

**PALABRAS SEMEJANTES: azteca, desesperado/a, heroico/a, histórico/a, indígena, indiscreto/a, lógico/a, memorable, ridículo/a, transatlántico/a**

## Los adverbios

| | |
|---|---|
| **con cuidado** | carefully |
| **muchísimo** | very much |
| **poco después** | a little later |
| **pronto** | soon |
| **un rato** | a while |

**PALABRAS SEMEJANTES: aproximadamente, inmediatamente, lógicamente, tranquilamente**

## Palabras y expresiones útiles

| | |
|---|---|
| **¡Auxilio!** | Help! |
| **¿Cuánto tiempo hace que... ?** | How long has it been since . . . ? |
| **Hace...** (+ *time*) **que** | It has been (+ *time*) since |
| **Hace más de...** | It has been more than (+ *time*) |
| **disculpe** | excuse me |
| **lo que** | that which; what |
| **los demás** | the rest, others |
| **¡Qué envidia!** | What luck! (Lucky dog!) |
| **¿Qué pasa?** | What's wrong? |
| **¿Qué pasó?** | What happened? |

# Gramática y ejercicios

**¿RECUERDA?**

In **Gramática 6.4** you learned that the past tense (preterite) is formed by adding a set of endings to the verb stem. There are only two sets of endings for regular verbs: one for **-ar** verbs and one for **-er/-ir** verbs. Review that section briefly, if necessary.

## 7.1 Talking about Past Actions: The Preterite of Regular Verbs (Part 2)

### Gramática ilustrada

Singular preterite forms:

| **-ar** | **-er/-ir** |
|---|---|
| -é | -í |
| -aste | -iste |
| -ó | -ió |

Plural preterite forms:

| **-ar** | **-er/-ir** |
|---|---|
| -amos | -imos |
| -asteis | -isteis |
| -aron | -ieron |

**A.** You have already seen and used the singular preterite forms of regular verbs many times. Here is the complete set of preterite forms, singular and plural.*

| | **hablar** | **comer** | **escribir** |
|---|---|---|---|
| (yo) | habl**é** | com**í** | escrib**í** |
| (tú) | habl**aste** | com**iste** | escrib**iste** |
| (usted, él/ella) | habl**ó** | com**ió** | escrib**ió** |
| (nosotros/as) | habl**amos** | com**imos** | escrib**imos** |
| (vosotros/as) | habl**asteis** | com**isteis** | escrib**isteis** |
| (ustedes, ellos/as) | habl**aron** | com**ieron** | escrib**ieron** |

Note the following details about the difference between present and preterite forms.

- In regular preterite forms, the stress is always on the final syllable of the **yo** and **usted**, **él/ella** forms.

  Generalmente me levanto a las ocho, pero ayer **me levanté** a la siete.

  *Usually I get up at 8:00, but yesterday I got up at 7:00.*

- **Tú** forms in the preterite do not end in **-s**.

  Normalmente me llamas por la noche, pero anoche no me **llamaste**.

  *Normally you call me at night, but last night you didn't call me.*

- Though both present and preterite third-person plural forms end in **-n**, it is always **-ron** in the preterite.

  Por lo general mis padres **salen** poco, pero la semana pasada **salieron** cinco veces.

  *Usually my parents go out very little, but last week they went out five times.*

- Notice that the present and preterite **nosotros/as** forms are different in **-er** verbs.

  Por lo general **comemos** un poco de carne, pero ayer no **comimos** ninguna.

  *Usually we eat a little meat, but yesterday we didn't eat any.*

  In **-ar** and **-ir** verbs, however, the **nosotros/as** form is the same in the preterite and the present tense (**hablamos**, **escribimos**). The context clarifies whether the speaker intends the present tense or the preterite.

  Ayer **salimos** para la universidad un poco tarde, pero mañana **salimos** temprano.

  *Yesterday we left for the university a little late, but tomorrow we're leaving early.*

---

*Recognition: **vos hablaste**, **comiste**, **escribiste**

**B.** If the stem of an **-er/-ir** verb ends in a vowel (**le-er**), the **i** of the **-ió** and **-ieron** endings changes to **y** in the preterite.

**leer**: leí, leíste, le**y**ó, leímos, leísteis, le**y**eron
**oír**: oí, oíste, o**y**ó, oímos, oísteis, o**y**eron

Yo **leí** el libro pero Esteban no lo **leyó**. — *I read the book, but Esteban didn't read it.*

**buscar: busqué/buscó**

**llegar: llegué/llegó**
**jugar: jugué/jugó**

**empezar: empecé/empezó**
**almorzar: almorcé/almorzó**

Don't try to remember all of this. Refer to this information when you are writing. In time you will acquire much of it through listening and reading.

**C.** Regular verbs that end in **-car**, **-gar**, and **-zar** change the spelling of the preterite **yo** form in order to preserve the same sound as the infinitive.*

**buscar**: bus**qu**é, buscaste, buscó, buscamos, buscasteis, buscaron
**llegar**: lle**gu**é, llegaste, llegó, llegamos, llegasteis, llegaron
**almorzar**: almor**c**é, almorzaste, almorzó, almorzamos, almorzasteis, almorzaron

**Llegué** al centro a las 4:00. — *I arrived downtown at 4:00.*

## Ejercicio 1

¿Qué hizo Adriana ayer por la mañana? Busque el orden más lógico.

_____ Leyó el periódico.
_____ Llegó al trabajo a las 8:30.
_____ Comió cereal con leche y fruta.
_____ Se bañó.
_____ Comió una hamburguesa.
_____ Se levantó a las 7:00.
_____ Almorzó con un colega de su trabajo.
_____ Manejó el coche al trabajo.
_____ Se preparó un desayuno pequeño.

¿Y qué hizo usted ayer por la mañana?

## Ejercicio 2

Complete los diálogos con formas de **llegar** y **leer**.

JOSÉ: ¿A qué hora _____[1] (tú) a la universidad?
CLARA: _____[2] a las ocho y media. ¿Y tú?
JOSÉ: Pilar y yo no _____[3] hasta las nueve y media porque el metro _____[4] tarde.

CLARA: ¿_____[5] el artículo sobre el viaje a Mallorca la semana pasada?
JOSÉ: Sí, lo _____[6]. (**Lo** *refers back to* **el artículo**.)
CLARA: ¿Lo _____[7] Pilar y Andrés?
JOSÉ: No sé si Andrés lo _____[8], pero lo _____[9] Pilar y yo.

---

*For more information on spelling changes in the preterite, see **Capítulo 7** in the *Cuaderno de trabajo*.

### Ejercicio 3

Éstas son las actividades de Pilar y su hermana Gloria un domingo del verano pasado en Madrid. ¿Qué oración corresponde a qué dibujo?

**a.** _____ Leyeron (por) un rato antes de apagar las luces.
**b.** _____ Caminaron desde la estación del metro hasta su apartamento.
**c.** _____ Almorzaron hamburguesas en el Wendy's de la Gran Vía.
**d.** _____ Salieron a pasear por el centro de Madrid.
**e.** _____ Vieron una película francesa.
**f.** _____ Llegaron a su apartamento a las 12:00 de la noche.
**g.** _____ Regresaron en el metro.

Ahora, piense en un domingo del verano pasado. ¿Qué actividades hicieron usted y sus amigos (o parientes)?

MODELO: Mis amigos y yo *escuchamos música y bailamos en una discoteca.*

## 7.2 Relating More about the Past (Part 1): Verbs with Irregular Preterite Forms

Some verbs have a different stem in the preterite and a slightly different set of endings.*

| | tener | estar | poder | poner | saber | hacer |
|---|---|---|---|---|---|---|
| (yo) | tuv**e** | estuv**e** | pud**e** | pus**e** | sup**e** | hic**e** |
| (tú) | tuv**iste** | estuv**iste** | pud**iste** | pus**iste** | sup**iste** | hic**iste** |
| (usted, él/ella) | tuv**o** | estuv**o** | pud**o** | pus**o** | sup**o** | hiz**o** |
| (nosotros/as) | tuv**imos** | estuv**imos** | pud**imos** | pus**imos** | sup**imos** | hic**imos** |
| (vosotros/as) | tuv**isteis** | estuv**isteis** | pud**isteis** | pus**isteis** | sup**isteis** | hic**isteis** |
| (ustedes, ellos/as) | tuv**ieron** | estuv**ieron** | pud**ieron** | pus**ieron** | sup**ieron** | hic**ieron** |

*Recognition: The **vos** forms in the preterite (regular and irregular) are identical to the **tú** forms: **vos quisiste, fuiste, hiciste.**

| | venir | querer | decir | traer | conducir | traducir |
|---|---|---|---|---|---|---|
| (yo) | vin**e** | quis**e** | dij**e** | traj**e** | conduj**e** | traduj**e** |
| (tú) | vini**ste** | quisi**ste** | dij**iste** | traj**iste** | conduj**iste** | traduj**iste** |
| (usted, él/ella) | vin**o** | quis**o** | dij**o** | traj**o** | conduj**o** | traduj**o** |
| (nosotros/as) | vini**mos** | quisi**mos** | dij**imos** | traj**imos** | conduj**imos** | traduj**imos** |
| (vosotros/as) | vini**steis** | quisi**steis** | dij**isteis** | traj**isteis** | conduj**isteis** | traduj**isteis** |
| (ustedes, ellos/as) | vini**eron** | quisi**eron** | dij**eron** | traj**eron** | conduj**eron** | traduj**eron** |

Many of the most common verbs in Spanish are irregular. Do not try to memorize each form, but refer to the chart when you write. In time, you will acquire these forms through listening and reading.

The preceding table provides the preterite forms of most common irregular verbs. Look at the table and you will notice the most important differences.

- Unlike regular preterite verb endings, the endings of the **yo** and **usted, él/ella** forms are not stressed in the last syllable.

  —¿Dónde **pusiste** mi chaqueta? —*Where did you put my jacket?*
  —La **puse** encima de la cama. —*I put it on the bed.*

  —¿Quién **vino** contigo? —*Who came with you?*
  —Nadie; **vine** solo. —*Nobody; I came alone.*

- The verb **hacer** has a spelling change from **c** to **z** in the **usted, él/ella** form.

  Ayer en el gimnasio Alberto **hizo** su tarea y yo **hice** ejercicio. *Yesterday at the gym Alberto did his homework and I exercised.*

- The verbs **conducir**, **decir**, **traducir**, and **traer** drop the **i** in the **ustedes, ellos/as** form.

  —¿Qué te **dijeron** de mí? —*What did they tell you about me?*
  —Me **dijeron** que estás locamente enamorado de Carmen. — *They told me that you are madly in love with Carmen.*

  —¿Qué **trajeron** ustedes de comer? —*What did you bring to eat?*
  —Trajimos refrescos y sandwiches. —*We brought sodas and sandwiches.*

- The verbs **dar** and **ver** take the **-er/-ir** endings, but with no written accents. The verbs **ser** and **ir** share the same stem in the past tense. Their forms are thus identical, so the meaning must be inferred from the context.

**fui** = *I went/was*
**fue** = *you (pol. sing.) went/were; he/she went/was*

| ser / ir (*to be/to go*) | | |
|---|---|---|
| (yo) | fui | *I was/went* |
| (tú) | fuiste | *you (inf. sing.) were/went* |
| (usted, él/ella) | fue | *you (pol. sing.) were/went; he/she was/went* |
| (nosotros/as) | fuimos | *we were/went* |
| (vosotros/as) | fuisteis | *you (inf. pl., Spain) were/went* |
| (ustedes, ellos/as) | fueron | *you (pl.) were/went; they were/went* |

| | |
|---|---|
| —¿Qué te **dieron**?<br>—Mi tío me **dio** dinero. | *—What did they give you?*<br>*—My uncle gave me money.* |
| —¿Adónde **fue** Luis anoche?<br>—**Fue** al cine. | *—Where did Luis go last night?*<br>*—He went to the movies.* |
| —¿Qué **fue** ese ruido?<br>—No **fue** nada. ¡Estás imaginando cosas! | *—What was that noise?*<br>*—It wasn't anything. You are imagining things!* |

## Ejercicio 4

Éstas son las actividades de ayer de algunos de los vecinos hispanos. Complete las oraciones con la forma correcta del pretérito de **ver**, **ir**, **dar**, **hacer**, **decir**, **traer**, **poner** o **venir**.

1. Ernesto Ramírez _____ una fiesta para sus amigos.
2. Dice Ernesto: « _____ más de treinta personas a mi fiesta.»
3. Dice Andrea: «Yo _____ una botella de tequila.»
4. Todos _____ que la fiesta fue fantástica.
5. Amanda _____ a Graciela hablando con su novio, Rafael.
6. Ernestito le _____ una cadena de identificación a su perro.
7. Guillermo _____ la tarea para su clase de biología.
8. Ernesto y Estela _____ al teatro.

## Ejercicio 5

Cuente lo que hicieron estas personas.

MODELO: (Soy Pilar.) Anoche fui al cine con mi hermana. Después cenamos en un restaurante y dimos un paseo por el centro. Me acosté muy tarde. →
Pilar *fue* al cine con su hermana. Después ellas *cenaron* en un restaurante y *dieron* un paseo por el centro. Pilar *se acostó* muy tarde.

1. (Soy Ricardo Sícora.) Un sábado por la mañana fui con mis hermanos Pablo y Enrique y unos amigos a una playa cerca de Ocumare a bucear. Llegamos temprano a la playa, así que descansé un rato antes de meterme al agua. Buceamos una hora y vimos muchísimos peces y animales marinos. Por la noche hicimos una fogata en la playa y cocinamos pescado en ella. Luego, toqué la guitarra y cantamos y bailamos hasta muy tarde.
2. (Soy Silvia Bustamante.) Anoche fui con mi novio Nacho Padilla a una fiesta. Llegamos a las 9:00 y cuando entré, vi a Luisa Hernández, una amiga del Instituto de Inglés, donde estudié el año pasado. La saludé y salimos al patio a charlar de los viejos amigos del Instituto. Bailé mucho con Nacho y tomé una copa de champaña. ¡Regresé a casa un poco mareada!

## Ejercicio 6

Diga qué hacen las siguientes personas generalmente, qué hicieron ayer por la tarde y qué van a hacer mañana.

MODELO: Generalmente *Adriana juega al tenis por la tarde*, pero ayer *tradujo un documento del italiano al español* y mañana *va a aprender un nuevo programa de informática.*

| | GENERALMENTE | AYER | MAÑANA |
|---|---|---|---|
| Pilar | asistir a clase | dormir toda la tarde | visitar a una amiga |
| Andrea y Pedro | almorzar con sus hijas | estar en el D.F. todo el día | ir de compras |
| Adriana | jugar al tenis por la tarde, después de salir del trabajo | traducir un documento del italiano al español | aprender un nuevo programa de informática |
| doña Lola | quedarse en casa | tomar café con sus amigas | cocinar toda la tarde |
| Carla y Rogelio | estudiar en la biblioteca | ir a la playa | lavar el carro |

## 7.3 Relating More about the Past (Part 2): Stem-Changing Verbs in the Preterite

**A.** In most cases, the vowels of stem-changing verbs do *not* change in the preterite forms. Here is a comparison of present-tense and preterite forms of the verbs **cerrar** (*to close*) and **contar** (*to tell, relate*).

**¿RECUERDA?**

You'll recall from **Gramática 4.2** that a small number of verbs have stem-vowel changes in the present-tense forms in which the spoken stress is on the stem vowel: **p*ie*nso** versus **pensar**, **d*ue*rmo** versus **dormir**. (See also **Gramática 2.3**, **3.3**, and **5.2** to review other familiar verbs with this type of stem change.)

Present:
**cierro/cierra**
**pienso/piensa**
Past:
**cerré/cerró**
**pensé/pensó**

| | cerrar | | contar | |
|---|---|---|---|---|
| | *Present* | *Past* | *Present* | *Past* |
| (yo) | cierro | cerré | cuento | conté |
| (tú) | cierras | cerraste | cuentas | contaste |
| (usted, él/ella) | cierra | cerró | cuenta | contó |
| (nosotros/as) | cerramos | cerramos | contamos | contamos |
| (vosotros/as) | cerráis | cerrasteis | contáis | contasteis |
| (ustedes, ellos/as) | cierran | cerraron | cuentan | contaron |

**B.** A few verbs, however, all in the **-ir** group, do change their stem vowel in the **usted, él/ella** and the **ustedes, ellos/as** forms of the preterite. There are two

Present:
me divierto / se divierte
duermo/duerme
Past:
me divertí / se divirtió
dormí/durmió

possible changes: **e** → **i** and **o** → **u**. The present-tense and preterite forms of the verbs **divertirse** (*to have a good time*) and **dormir** (*to sleep*) are given below.* Other common verbs with this change are **sentir** (*to feel*), **sugerir** (*to suggest*), **preferir** (*to prefer*), **mentir** (*to lie*), and **morir** (*to die*).

| | divertirse | | dormir | |
|---|---|---|---|---|
| | ***Present*** | ***Past*** | ***Present*** | ***Past*** |
| (yo) | me divierto | me divertí | duermo | dormí |
| (tú) | te diviertes | te divertiste | duermes | dormiste |
| (usted, él/ella) | se divierte | se divirtió | duerme | durmió |
| (nosotros/as) | nos divertimos | nos divertimos | dormimos | dormimos |
| (vosotros/as) | os divertís | os divertisteis | dormís | dormisteis |
| (ustedes, ellos/as) | se divierten | se divirtieron | duermen | durmieron |

Do not try to memorize all these forms, but refer to the chart when you write. In time, you will acquire the forms through listening and reading.

Yo **dormí** bien. Estela **durmió** mal. *I slept well. Estela slept poorly.*

—¿**Se divirtió** usted anoche? —*Did you have fun last night?*
—Sí, **me divertí** mucho. —*Yes, I had a great time.*

## Ejercicio 7

Complete los siguientes diálogos con la forma correcta de los verbos.

DORMIR
— ¿Cuántas horas _____[1] tú anoche?
— _____[2] solamente cinco.
— ¿Generalmente _____[3] tan pocas horas?
— No, generalmente _____[4] por lo menos siete, a veces ocho.

SENTIR(SE)
— ¿Tú te _____[5] mal ahora?
— No, me _____[6] bastante bien.
— Pero anoche te _____[7] muy mal, ¿verdad?
— Sí, anoche me _____[8] mal por un dolor de cabeza.

DIVERTIR(SE)
— ¿Te _____[9] anoche en la fiesta?
— Sí, me _____[10] muchísimo. ¿Se _____[11] tu esposa?
— No, no se _____[12] porque no le gustó la música.

MENTIR
— Tú me _____,[13] ¿verdad?
— No, no te _____.[14] Te dije la verdad.
— Pues, alguien me _____.[15]
— No fui yo.

*This same stem-vowel change also occurs in the present participle: **durmiendo** (*sleeping*), **divirtiéndose** (*having fun*).

**¿RECUERDA?**

In **Gramática 5.1** you learned that the indirect object pronouns (**me, te, le, nos, os, les**) are frequently used with verbs of informing such as **hablar, preguntar,** and **contestar.** Review that section briefly.

**Le dije que...** = *I told you (pol. sing.)/him/her that . . .*
**Me dijo que...** = *You (pol. sing.)/He/She told me that . . .*
**Le dijimos que...** = *We told you (pol. sing.)/him/her that . . .*

Remember that **dijo** is a *preterite* form, not a present-tense form.

## 7.4 Reporting the Past: Indirect Object Pronouns with *decir*

In the preterite, the verb **decir** is commonly used with indirect object pronouns to report speech.

**decir (*to say; to tell*)**

| | | |
|---|---|---|
| (yo) | dije | *I said* |
| (tú) | dijiste | *you (inf. sing.) said* |
| (usted, él/ella) | dijo | *you (pol. sing.) said; he/she said* |
| (nosotros/as) | dijimos | *we said* |
| (vosotros/as) | dijisteis | *you (inf. pl., Spain) said* |
| (ustedes, ellos/as) | dijeron | *you (pl.) said; they said* |

| | |
|---|---|
| **Le dije** que... | *I told (said to) you/him/her that . . .* |
| **Te dijimos** que... | *We told (said to) you that . . .* |
| **Me dijo** que... | *You/He/She told (said to) me that . . .* |
| **Me dijeron** que... | *You/They told (said to) me that . . .* |

Note that the phrase **Le dijo que...** has several possible meanings; interpretation depends on the context.

Le dijo que...
- *He/She told him that . . .*
- *He/She told her that . . .*
- *He/She told you that . . .*
- *You told him/her that . . .*

Don Anselmo fue a la casa de doña Rosita y **le dijo que** sus hijos van a llegar pasado mañana.

*Don Anselmo went to doña Rosita's house and told her that his children are going to arrive the day after tomorrow.*

### Ejercicio 8

Complete esta conversación telefónica usando pronombres de complemento indirecto (**me, te, le, nos, les**) y las formas correctas del pretérito del verbo **decir** (**dije, dijiste, dijo, dijimos, dijeron**).

GRACIELA: No oigo bien, Amanda. ¿Qué _____[1] _____[2]?
AMANDA: _____[3] _____[4] que no voy a estar en casa esta noche.
GRACIELA: ¡Ay, lo mismo _____[5] _____[6] tu hermano Guillermo! ¿Adónde vas?
AMANDA: Es que mi madre _____[7] _____[8] que hay una venta especial con precios muy rebajados hoy en El Palacio de Hierro.
GRACIELA: ¿Y qué _____[9] _____[10] tú a ella? ¿No _____[11] _____[12] que hoy tenemos mucha tarea?
AMANDA: Hummm... no, pero _____[13] _____[14] que tú quieres ir con nosotras. Es verdad, ¿no?
GRACIELA: Ay, sí, Amanda, sí quisiera acompañarlas, pero... ¡_____[15] _____[16] a mi papá que no voy a comprar más ropa este mes!
AMANDA: Pues, ven con nosotras pero... ¡deja tu dinero en casa!
GRACIELA: ¡Imposible!

## 7.5 Expressing *ago*: *hacer* + Time

**¿Cuánto hace que llegaste?** (*How long ago did you arrive?*)
**Hace una hora.** (*An hour ago.*)

**¿Hace cuánto tiempo que usted se graduó?** (*How long ago did you graduate?*)
**Hace 10 años.** (*Ten years ago.*)

The verb **hace** followed by an amount of time is equivalent to English expressions of time with *ago*.

| | |
|---|---|
| hace cinco minutos | *five minutes ago* |
| hace una hora | *an hour ago* |
| hace dos años | *two years ago* |

| | |
|---|---|
| —¿Cuándo salió Ricardo? | —*When did Ricardo leave?* |
| —**Hace una hora.** | —*An hour ago.* |

There are two ways to formulate the question *How long ago did . . . ?*

¿Cuánto (tiempo) hace que + *preterite*?
¿Hace cuánto (tiempo) que + *preterite*?

| | |
|---|---|
| —Srta. Durán, ¿**cuánto** (**tiempo**) **hace que** usted **fue** a México? | —*Ms. Durán, how long ago did you go to Mexico?* |
| —**Fui hace tres años.** | —*I went three years ago.* |

### Ejercicio 9

Estela está de mal humor hoy, y acusa a Ernesto de no hacer nada para ayudarla. ¿Cómo puede defenderse Ernesto?

MODELO: ESTELA: ¡Tú nunca lavas los platos en esta casa!
ERNESTO: Pero, Estela, *lavé* los platos *hace una hora*. (Pero, Estela, *los lavé hace una hora*.)

1. ¡Tú nunca limpias el baño!
2. ¡Tú nunca barres el patio!
3. ¡La alfombra está sucia porque tú nunca pasas la aspiradora!
4. El pobre perro, ¡tú nunca lo bañas!
5. Estoy cansada de comer las mismas cosas. ¡Tú nunca me llevas a ningún restaurante elegante!

### Ejercicio 10

¿Sabe usted mucho de historia? ¿Cuánto hace que... ?

MODELO: ¿Cuánto (tiempo) hace que terminó la Segunda Guerra Mundial? (1945) →
Terminó hace aproximadamente cincuenta y cinco años.

1. ¿Cuánto tiempo hace que Alejandro G. Bell inventó el teléfono? (1876)
2. ¿Cuánto tiempo hace que Gustave Eiffel construyó la Torre Eiffel? (1889)
3. ¿Cuánto hace que murió Pancho Villa? (1923)
4. ¿Cuánto tiempo hace que Colón llegó a América? (1492)
5. ¿Cuánto hace que murió Francisco Franco, el dictador de España? (1975)
6. ¿Cuánto hace que Alemania se unificó? (1990)
7. ¿Cuánto hace que los países de la antigua Unión Soviética se independizaron? (1991)

CAPÍTULO 8

# La comida

**METAS**

In **Capítulo 8** you will learn to talk about food, nutrition, shopping for and preparing food, and ordering meals in restaurants.

El Viejo San Juan, Puerto Rico

**ACTIVIDADES DE COMUNICACIÓN Y LECTURAS**


Las comidas, las bebidas y la nutrición

**Lectura** «Oda al tomate» (selecciones)

**Las palabras viven** El idioma de los aztecas

La compra y la preparación de la comida

**El mundo hispano...** su gente

**El mundo hispano...** imágenes

**Nota cultural** Algunos platillos hispanos

**Las palabras viven** ¡Estoy como agua para chocolate!

Los restaurantes

**El mundo hispano...** en los Estados Unidos

**EN RESUMEN**


**GRAMÁTICA Y EJERCICIOS**


8.1 Referring to Objects Already Mentioned: Impersonal Direct Object Pronouns **lo, la, los,** and **las**

8.2 More about Expressing Likes: The Verbs **gustar** and **encantar**

8.3 Expressing *for, from,* and *to whom:* Prepositions + Pronouns

8.4 Making Negative Statements and Questions: *No, never*

8.5 Expressing *one* or *you:* The Impersonal **se**

8.6 Using Stem-Changing Verbs like **pedir** and **servir:** Present-Tense and Preterite Forms

# Actividades de comunicación y lecturas

## Las comidas, las bebidas y la nutrición

*Lea Gramática 8.1–8.4.*

## Actividad 1. Conversación: Las comidas del día

Diga si comemos estas comidas para el desayuno, para el almuerzo o para la cena.

MODELOS: ¿Los huevos revueltos? *Los comemos para el desayuno.*

¿La sopa? *La tomamos para el almuerzo o para la cena.*

los huevos revueltos
los guisantes
las legumbres
la sopa
el pan tostado con jalea
las hamburguesas
un sándwich
el pollo frito
las enchiladas
la coliflor
los tacos
los panqueques
el cereal
los espárragos
la ensalada de lechuga
el tocino
el yogur
las chuletas de cerdo
las papas fritas
el arroz
el maíz

Ahora diga con qué frecuencia usted come estos alimentos.

MODELOS: ¿El cereal? *Nunca lo como. No me gusta.*

¿Las enchiladas? *Las como siempre en un restaurante mexicano en mi vecindario.*

## Actividad 2. Intercambios: La nutrición

¿Qué comidas son más ricas en proteína, en carbohidratos, en vitaminas? ¿Cuáles contienen más grasa? Mire los dibujos de las comidas en la página anterior. Trabajando con su compañero/a, pónganlas en uno (o más) de los cinco grupos de la tabla a continuación.

MODELO: E1: El arroz tiene muchos carbohidratos.
E2: Sí. Y las papas fritas contienen mucha grasa.

| LA PROTEÍNA | LOS CARBOHIDRATOS | EL CALCIO | LAS VITAMINAS A Y C | LA GRASA |
|---|---|---|---|---|
| | *el arroz* | | | *las papas fritas* |
| | | | | |
| | | | | |
| | | | | |
| | | | | |
| | | | | |

## LAS PALABRAS VIVEN

**VOCABULARIO ÚTIL**

| | |
|---|---|
| la guanábana | *soursop* |
| la batata | *sweet potato* |

**Algunas frutas y legumbres:** Las frutas y las legumbres reciben nombres diferentes en los países hispanos. A veces los nombres vienen del idioma indígena de cada país. Por ejemplo, las **judías verdes** son **ejotes** en México (del náhuatl, el antiguo idioma de los aztecas).

Hay frutas que no se comen en algunos sitios. La razón es que cada país tiene su propio clima y vegetación. Algunas frutas, como **la guanábana** en la región del Caribe, requieren un clima tropical y, claro, no se cultivan en países de clima frío.

La palabra para **legumbres** es **verduras** en algunos países y **hortalizas** en otros. (**Los vegetales** son plantas de cualquier tipo.) En Uruguay y Argentina **las fresas** son **frutillas**. En España, México y otros países, **la banana** es **plátano.** Y **la batata** es **camote** en México, **ñame** en los países andinos y **boniato** en Cuba. En España se le llama **patata** a **la papa** y **zumo** al **jugo de fruta**.

**Otras comidas:** La palabra más común para **sándwich** en España es **bocadillo**; en México es **la torta**. Y **el pastel** tiene varios nombres: es **bizcocho** en Puerto Rico, **queque** en Colombia y **torta** en España. Y en Cuba dicen **el cake**, que se pronuncia **quey** y a veces se escribe así también.

Para decir **helado** en México, se usa una palabra que viene del clima. Es fría, blanca y cae del cielo. ¿Sabe lo que es? Sí, en México el helado es **la nieve**. Finalmente, ¿sabe usted como se dice *junk food* en ese país? Pues... es **comida chatarra**.

### Actividad 3. Encuesta: Mis bebidas favoritas

Escoja su bebida favorita según la ocasión. Use **me gusta** o **prefiero**.

MODELO: en la mañana →
Cuando me levanto en la mañana *me gusta tomar una taza de café con leche.*

**POSIBILIDADES**

| | | |
|---|---|---|
| agua mineral | jugos naturales (de tomate, de naranja, de pera, de toronja) | refrescos |
| batidos de leche | leche | té caliente |
| café | limonada | té helado |
| cerveza | | vino |
| chocolate | | |

1. para el desayuno
2. para el almuerzo
3. en una fiesta de Año Nuevo
4. después de hacer ejercicio
5. para dormir
6. cuando hace frío
7. cuando hace calor
8. en un restaurante

## Actividad 4. Del mundo hispano: Una dieta para mejorar la salud

# Una dieta ideal

**DESAYUNO**

- jugo o porción de fruta: media toronja o una naranja entera, una porción de piña, durazno, uvas o manzanas
- Escoja uno: (a) cereal frío o caliente, (b) huevos revueltos o cocidos
- un panecillo con un poco de margarina (no use mantequilla)
- una taza de café, té (sin azúcar) o leche

**ALMUERZO**

- Seleccione uno de los grupos siguientes:
  - una ensalada de lechuga y tomate y una taza de sopa de legumbres
  - una ensalada de lechuga con trozos pequeños de queso o pollo, vinagre y muy poco aceite
  - una ensalada de fruta fresca sin azúcar
  - un sándwich de atún o una porción de pescado
- jugo de tomate, agua mineral, un refresco sin azúcar

**CENA**

- un vaso de jugo de tomate o una ensalada pequeña
- pollo horneado o pescado a la parrilla
- una papa horneada o arroz, sin mantequilla
- legumbres: bróculi, coliflor o habichuelas
- té frío sin azúcar o café sin azúcar
- una porción de fruta fresca o una porción de queso

Imagínese que usted necesita comer mejor para mejorar su salud. Aquí tiene algunas sugerencias para una dieta. Escoja los alimentos que usted va a comer mañana. Diga lo que le gusta y lo que no le gusta. ¡No coma demasiado!

## Actividad 5. Conversación: La mesa

**Parte 1.** Diga para qué sirven estos objetos de la mesa. Use las palabras y frases útiles de la próxima página.

MODELO: *El salero* sirve para *guardar la sal.*

## PALABRAS Y FRASES ÚTILES

| | | |
|---|---|---|
| las bebidas | guardar la pimienta | servir la comida |
| comer | guardar la sal | tomar café o té |
| cortar la comida | limpiarse la boca | tomar la sopa |
| cubrir la mesa | preparar la ensalada | |

**Parte 2.** Ahora, trabaje con un compañero / una compañera para decir dónde están esos objetos en el dibujo. Usen **al lado de, entre, a la derecha de, a la izquierda de, enfrente de** o **encima de.**

MODELO: E1: ¿Dónde está *el tenedor*?
E2: Está *a la izquierda del* plato.

### Actividad 6. Entrevista: La comida en casa

1. ¿Qué desayunas normalmente? ¿Qué comiste esta mañana antes de salir de tu casa?
2. ¿Qué almuerzas generalmente? ¿Qué almorzaste hoy? ¿Qué vas a almorzar mañana?
3. ¿Tomas café durante el día? ¿Lo tomas con o sin azúcar? ¿con o sin leche? ¿Cuál te gusta más, el té caliente o el café?
4. ¿Comes entre comidas? ¿Qué comes?
5. ¿Prefieres comer más al mediodía o por la noche? ¿Por qué? ¿Cenas en tu casa, generalmente? ¿Con quién(es)? ¿Qué cenan?
6. ¿Qué prefieres de postre? ¿Siempre comes postre?
7. ¿Generalmente comes mientras ves la televisión? ¿Te gustan las palomitas de maíz? ¿Les pones mantequilla o sal? ¿Qué otra cosa te gusta comer?

# «Oda al tomate» de Pablo Neruda (selecciones)

Pablo Neruda (Chile, 1904–1973) es uno de los más grandes poetas y escritores de la literatura hispana. Neruda recibió el Premio Nóbel de Literatura en 1971.[1] Entre sus muchos libros, hay varios de gran popularidad: *Veinte poemas de amor y una canción desesperada*, *Odas elementales* y sus memorias, *Confieso que he vivido*.

En *Odas elementales* Neruda dedicó una serie de odas a objetos, legumbres y otros elementos de la vida diaria. En esta colección hay poemas que describen, por ejemplo, el libro, el reloj, la cebolla y hasta el tomate.

Sí, es posible escribir un poema sobre un tomate. ¡Aquí tiene usted uno!

[1]En 1995 la poesía de Neruda se hizo aún más popular en todo el mundo con la película *Il Postino* (*The Postman*). Esta excelente película italiana narra las relaciones entre el poeta chileno y un cartero.

La calle
se llenó de tomates,
mediodía,
verano,
la luz
se parte[2]
en dos
mitades[3]
de tomate,
corre
por las calles
el jugo.
En diciembre
se desata[4]
el tomate,
invade
las cocinas,
entra por los almuerzos,
se sienta
reposado[5]
en los aparadores,[6]
entre los vasos,
las mantequilleras,[7]
los saleros azules.
Tiene
luz propia,[8]
majestad benigna[9]...
Debemos, por desgracia,[10]
asesinarlo:
se hunde
el cuchillo
en su pulpa viviente,[11]
es una roja
víscera,
un sol fresco,
profundo,
inagotable,[12]
llena las ensaladas
de Chile...

[2]se... *breaks* [3]*halves* [4]se... *breaks away* [5]calmado [6]*sideboards* [7]*butter dishes* [8]luz... *its own light* [9]buena [10]por... *unfortunately* [11]se... *the knife sinks into its living pulp* [12]*inexhaustible*

«La calle / se llenó de tomates, / mediodía, / verano... »

«Tiene / luz propia, / majestad benigna... / es... un sol fresco, / profundo,... »

## Comprensión

1. ¿En qué momento del día se describe el tomate?
2. ¿Qué estación y qué mes del año menciona el poeta? ¿Cómo se comparan con las estaciones y los meses en los Estados Unidos?
3. El poeta «personifica» el tomate, es decir, la legumbre del poema tiene atributos humanos y hace varias cosas. Mencione tres de las acciones del tomate.

## Ahora... ¡usted!

1. ¿Le gustan los tomates? ¿Qué otras legumbres o frutas le gustan? ¿Cuáles no le gustan y por qué no?
2. Normalmente, ¿qué le pone usted a una ensalada?

### Un paso más... ¡a escribir!

Escriba un breve poema sobre su legumbre favorita o la fruta que más le gusta. ¿De qué color es? ¿Qué vitaminas tiene? ¿En qué estación del año se cosecha más? ¿Por qué le gusta? Empiece con los siguientes versos de Neruda.

La calle
se llenó de...

**LAS PALABRAS VIVEN**

**VOCABULARIO ÚTIL**

| | |
|---|---|
| heredamos | *we inherited* |
| adivinar | *to guess* |

# El idioma de los aztecas

En el español que se habla en México hay muchas palabras que vienen del náhuatl. Éste es el idioma que hablaban los aztecas, habitantes de México al llegar los españoles allí en 1519.

En todo el mundo hispano hay una gran cantidad de alimentos que heredamos de los antiguos mexicanos: entre otros, *aguacatl* (**aguacate**), *xocolatl* (**chocolate**), *jitomatl* (**tomate**), *guajolotl* (**guajolote, pavo**), *ejotl* (**ejotes**) y *elotl* (**elote**).

Las siguientes palabras del náhuatl forman parte del idioma español en México y otros países: *mexica*, *coyotl*, *tomatl* y *chilli*. ¿Puede usted adivinar lo que significan esas palabras?

México, D.F.: Uno de los temas en la obra del artista mexicano Diego Rivera es el de la colonización de México.

# La compra y la preparación de la comida

*Lea Gramática 8.5.*

## Actividad 7. Definiciones: Las comidas

Combine la definición a la izquierda con un alimento a la derecha.

1. _____ Es una legumbre anaranjada que contiene vitamina A.
2. _____ Esta fruta de cáscara amarilla crece en las zonas tropicales.
3. _____ Ésta es una fruta tropical, anaranjada por dentro y verde por fuera.
4. _____ Se pone en la ensalada.
5. _____ Es blanca, como el azúcar, pero no es dulce.
6. _____ Éstas son uvas secas.
7. _____ Es un líquido dorado, muy espeso y muy dulce.
8. _____ Es una legumbre larga y verde que se usa con frecuencia en las ensaladas.
9. _____ Se cocinan por tres o cuatro horas y se sirven con tortillas; son muy populares en la cocina mexicana.
10. _____ Es un postre hecho de huevos, leche y azúcar, muy popular en los países hispanos.

a. la sal
b. los frijoles
c. el pepino
d. el flan
e. las pasas
f. el plátano
g. la zanahoria
h. el aderezo
i. la miel
j. el mango

## EL MUNDO HISPANO... su gente

***P**ara mí, una cena ideal es...*

« ... una cena sentados a la mesa y teniendo primer plato,[1] segundo plato y postre. Para la cena no me gusta nada muy pesado,[2] sino más bien ligero. Una sopa o un puré primero y una tortilla o carne después. De postre... un mousse.»
*María del Carmen Méndez Navarro, española*

« ... una pizza preparada por mí con atún y queso.»
*Joaquín Zasueta Ortiz, español*

« ... frijolitos fritos, queso, jamón, tortilla de harina o pollo con papas, con jugo de naranja.»
*Xiomara Zendejas, hondureña*

« ... arroz con frijolitos arreglados,[3] tamales (un platillo típico costarricense), puré de papas y té frío.»
*José Antonio Vásquez, costarricense*

« ... una copa de helado de vainilla, con nueces y bañado[4] de chocolate caliente (¡Mmmmmmm!).»
*Katia Capaldi, argentina*

« ... un pollo al horno con papas y verduras, con empanadas de entrada y panqueques con dulce de leche de postre.»
*Verónica Lugo, argentina*

[1]primer... *first course* [2]*heavy* [3]arroz... *rice covered with beans* [4]*drenched*

## Actividad 8. Del mundo hispano: Supermercado El Diamante

Imagínese que usted va a ir al supermercado El Diamante en Puerto Rico para hacer las compras. Estudie las dos listas y calcule el precio total de cada una.

LISTA 1

1 paquete de tocino
2 latas de sopa de legumbres
2 aguacates
3 libras de carne molida
2 libras de limones
14 onzas de avena

LISTA 2

1 libra de carne molida
1 tarro de 16 onzas de mayonesa
3 libras de cebollas amarillas
1 paquete de zanahorias
2 libras de manzanas
1 sandía de ocho libras

## EL MUNDO HISPANO... imágenes

Todos juntos a la hora de comer. Después del postre, los adultos se quedan sentados a la mesa para la «sobremesa»: conversación y café. Para muchos hispanos, la sobremesa es una parte esencial —¡y divertida!— de la comida. Es el momento de charlar y compartir[1] impresiones, ideas y gustos. ¡Muchas veces la sobremesa dura más tiempo que la comida misma!

España: la comida en familia

[1]*share*

### Actividad 9. Asociaciones: Los alimentos

En cada grupo de palabras a continuación hay una que no pertenece a la lista. Búsquela y explique por qué no pertenece.

MODELO: la salchicha, la hamburguesa, la chuleta, la pera →
*La pera* no pertenece a esta lista porque *no es carne*.

1. el apio, el pepino, la avena, los guisantes
2. el flan, el helado, las aceitunas, el pastel
3. la miel, la mazorca de maíz, la mermelada, la jalea
4. el plátano, las almejas, los camarones, la langosta
5. las nueces, el albaricoque, la piña, la toronja

**OLAFO**

### Actividad 10. Orden lógico: ¿Cómo se prepara... ?

Ponga en orden los pasos para la preparación de estas comidas.

UN SÁNDWICH DE JAMÓN Y QUESO

_____ Se cortan varias rebanadas de tomate.
_____ Se pone mayonesa y mostaza en las dos rebanadas de pan.
_____ Se corta el jamón y el queso.
_____ Se come con un refresco frío.
_____ Se sacan dos rebanadas de pan.
_____ Se le agrega la lechuga y las rebanadas de tomate.

UNA QUESADILLA MEXICANA

_____ Se saca la quesadilla de la sartén.
_____ Se dobla la tortilla.
_____ Se saca una lata de chiles y una tortilla de harina.
_____ Se pone en una sartén.
_____ Se pone el queso y un chile en un lado de la tortilla.
_____ Se tapa la sartén y se fríe la quesadilla tres minutos de cada lado.
_____ Se ralla el queso.
_____ Se sirve con salsa y se come.

## Actividad 11. Narración: Vamos a preparar chiles rellenos

Narre los pasos en la preparación de los chiles rellenos.

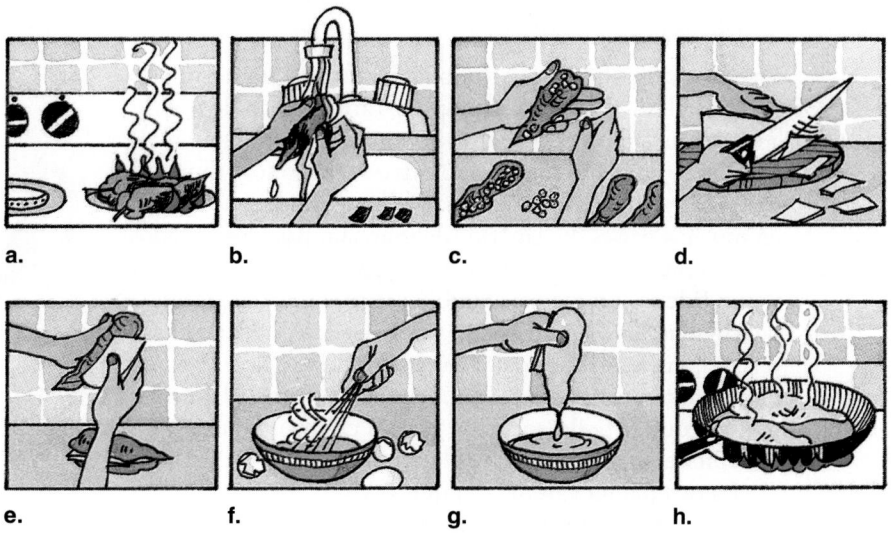


### PALABRAS ÚTILES

primero
luego
después
finalmente

## Actividad 12. Entrevista: Hacer la compra

1. ¿Quién hace la compra en tu casa?
2. ¿Se compran todos los comestibles en un supermercado o en varias tiendas pequeñas?
3. ¿Compras muchas legumbres y frutas?
4. ¿Compras muchas comidas pre-elaboradas? ¿Lees las etiquetas de las comidas para determinar si contienen colorantes o conservadores?
5. ¿Quién prepara las comidas en tu casa?
6. ¿Te gusta cocinar? ¿Qué platos sabes preparar?
7. ¿Compras mucha comida chatarra? ¿Qué compras?

NOTA CULTURAL

# Algunos platillos hispanos

**VOCABULARIO ÚTIL**

| | |
|---|---|
| ¡pruebe! | *try!* |
| la cocina | *cuisine* |
| pescado en escabeche | *fish in a marinade of oil, vinegar, and spices* |
| están de moda | *are popular* |
| los boquerones | *small sardines* |
| la ensaladilla | *potato salad* |

En esta Nota cultural se mencionan varios platillos típicos de España y América Latina. Todos son verdaderamente deliciosos. Lea las descripciones y... ¡pruebe la cocina hispana!

La cocina hispana es muy variada. Dentro de un mismo país, los platos y la manera de prepararlos varían de región a región. El **arroz con pollo** se come especialmente en el Caribe: es un plato de arroz con trozos de pollo y tomate, aceitunas y otros condimentos. Las **empanadas**, populares en muchos países de América del Sur, son pasteles rellenos de diferentes tipos de carnes. En Argentina varios platillos llevan **fideos**. En ese país también se preparan exquisitas **parrilladas**: una variedad de carnes —cerdo, cordero, ternera, salchichas— cocinadas a la parrilla. Y los peruanos tienen platillos deliciosos: entre otros, el **ají de gallina**, que es pollo cocinado en una crema de nueces, y el **cebiche**, un plato de pescado en escabeche.

La deliciosa paella es el plato más conocido de España.

La rica **paella valenciana** que se ve en la foto es el plato más conocido de España. La paella es un plato de arroz que lleva mariscos y también puede llevar pollo, chorizo y verduras. Otro platillo típico es la **tortilla española**, un tipo de *omelet* hecho de huevos, cebollas, patatas y otras legumbres. La tortilla española se sirve muchas veces como «tapa».

Ahora las **tapas** españolas están muy de moda en los Estados Unidos. Las tapas son pequeñas porciones de comida que se sirven en los bares de España; por lo general acompañan el vino o la cerveza. Las tapas pueden ser muy sencillas —**aceitunas y cacahuetes**— o platillos más elaborados, como la tortilla. Algunas de las tapas que más se comen en

En los bares, la copa de vino y la cerveza van acompañadas de una variedad de tapas: aceitunas, pescado frito, cacahuetes, patatas fritas, trozos de tortilla española y todo tipo de fiambres.

España son los **calamares**, los **boquerones fritos**, la **ensaladilla** y todo tipo de **carnes** frías o calientes.

Una de las diversiones favoritas de los españoles es «ir de tapas». Esto quiere decir que van de un lugar a otro probando una variedad de tapas. Es una oportunidad ideal para pasar tiempo con los amigos. ¡Buena conversación y rica comida!

El cebiche peruano

## Comprensión

¿Qué ingredientes se usan en estos platillos hispanos? ¡Cuidado! Algunos se usan en más de un platillo.

| | |
|---|---|
| **1.** el arroz con pollo | **a.** las aceitunas |
| **2.** la paella | **b.** los mariscos |
| **3.** la tortilla española | **c.** los huevos |
| **4.** las empanadas | **d.** las verduras |
| **5.** las tapas | **e.** las papas |
| **6.** la parrillada | **f.** la carne de cerdo |
| **7.** el cebiche | **g.** el pescado |
| **8.** el ají de gallina | **h.** la ternera |
| | **i.** las salchichas |
| | **j.** el pollo |

## Ahora... ¡usted!

1. ¿Cuáles de los platillos mencionados no conoce pero le gustaría probar? ¿Cuáles *no* le gustaría probar? Explique.
2. En algunas partes de los Estados Unidos son populares los «*tapa bars*», que en muchos casos funcionan más como restaurantes que como bares. ¿Conoce usted alguno de estos lugares? ¿Le gustan las tapas? ¿Cuáles prefiere?

### Un paso más... ¡a escribir!

Imagínese que hay una fiesta en su clase de español y que usted y su compañero/a van a planear el menú. El cocinero de un restaurante hispano cercano va a preparar todos los platillos. ¿Cuáles van a incluir ustedes? ¿Por qué? Traten de incluir otros no mencionados en la Nota cultural. ¡Hay muchos platillos en la cocina hispana!

Después, escríbanle una nota a su profesor(a) para convencerlo/la de la necesidad de incluir en la fiesta los platillos que ustedes quieren. Pueden usar el siguiente modelo.

Estimado profesor / Estimada profesora:

Gracias por permitir la fiesta en la clase. Mi compañero/a, _____, y yo pensamos que el menú debe incluir los siguientes platos: _____, _____, y _____. Seleccionamos estos platillos porque...

¡Gracias por su consideración!

Afectuosamente,

(*su firma*)

## LAS PALABRAS VIVEN

**VOCABULARIO ÚTIL**

| | |
|---|---|
| el enojo | *anger* |
| queda lista | *is ready* |
| las recetas | *recipes* |

# ¡Estoy como agua para chocolate!

En México se usa la frase coloquial **como agua para chocolate** para expresar la idea de «mucho enojo». Si una persona dice «¡Estoy como agua para chocolate!», eso quiere decir que está muy enojada (en inglés, *madder than hell*). ¡A punto de hervir como el agua!

La expresión tiene su origen en la preparación del chocolate caliente. Para hacerlo, se pone agua a calentar y cuando empieza a hervir, se le echan trozos de chocolate en barra. La rica bebida queda lista muy pronto.

La escritora mexicana Laura Esquivel usó esta frase para el título de su novela *Como agua para chocolate* (1990), donde aparecen varias recetas de la cocina de México. El libro fue adaptado después al cine, y resultó ser una película muy popular. La verdad es que el título es muy apropiado: en la novela de Esquivel se combinan los temas de la comida, el enojo y el amor apasionado.

Laura Esquivel, autora de la novela *Como agua para chocolate*.

Por tradición, el chocolate se bate a mano con un molinillo como éste.

# Los restaurantes

*Lea Gramática 8.6.*

Pedro y Andrea pidieron una ensalada, bistec al punto, papas fritas y bróculi.

El mesero les sirvió la comida.

El cocinero les preparó un platillo especial.

Andrea tomó una copa de vino tinto, pero Pedro prefirió tomar agua mineral.

Comieron con gusto.

Pagaron la cuenta con su tarjeta de crédito.

Dejaron una buena propina.

## Actividad 13. Narración: Mayín Durán sale a cenar

Lea las siguientes oraciones y póngalas en orden, según los dibujos. Luego, trabaje con un compañero / una compañera para narrar la historia.

_____ Comieron y conversaron.
_____ Pidieron la cuenta.
_____ Mayín pidió agua mineral y su amigo pidió un refresco.
_____ Mayín y su amigo pidieron la comida.
_____ Los dos pidieron postre.
_____ Pagaron la cuenta y dejaron una propina.
_____ Salieron a cenar.
_____ El mesero les sirvió la comida.
_____ Tomaron sus bebidas y conversaron, y luego el mesero les preguntó si estaban listos para pedir.
_____ Salieron a pasear.
_____ El mesero les preguntó si querían tomar algo.
_____ Leyeron el menú.

## Actividad 14. Intercambios: Restaurante Mi Casita

Con su compañero/a, lean el menú del Restaurante Mi Casita. Primero miren los precios; después escojan las comidas y bebidas que van a pedir y digan por qué las van a pedir. Sigan los modelos.

MODELOS:
E1: ¿Cuánto cuestan *los tamales de puerco*?
E2: Cuestan *$12.00 pesos*.

E1: ¿Qué vas a pedir?
E2: Me gustaría pedir *los chiles rellenos de queso*, pero voy a pedir *el chop suey porque estoy a dieta*.

E1: Voy a pedir *una hamburguesa*, porque *me fascina la comida norteamericana* (*la comida de los Estados Unidos*).

# Restaurante Mi Casita

*Rica comida mexicana e internacional a precios módicos*

**Plato del día:**
Lasaña, pan de ajo, ensalada mixta, sopa minestrone $18.50

## Antojitos mexicanos

Se sirven para el almuerzo y la cena. (Con cada uno se incluye pan o tortillas, ensalada, arroz y frijoles o sopa del día.)

| | | |
|---|---|---|
| Enchiladas (3) | verdes o rojas | $17.50 |
| Tostadas (2) | de res o de pollo | 12.50 |
| Tacos (4) | de res o de pollo | 13.00 |
| Burritos (2) | de res y/o frijoles | 9.90 |
| Chiles rellenos (2) | de carne o queso | 16.00 |
| Tamales de puerco con chile verde (3) | | 12.00 |
| Tamales dulces con almendras y pasas (3) | | 9.50 |

## Rincón internacional

| | | |
|---|---|---|
| De España: | Rica paella valenciana (mínimo tres personas) | $45.00 |
| De Perú: | Sabrosísimo cebiche | 12.00 |
| De los Estados Unidos: | Las mejores hamburguesas al sur de la frontera | 14.00 |
| De Italia: | Exquisita pizza de la casa (tamaño grande) | 45.00 |
| De China: | Delicioso y ligero chop suey de pollo | 18.60 |

## Desayuno

(Incluye pan o tortillas.)

| | |
|---|---|
| Huevos rancheros | $17.50 |
| Cereal frío | 6.30 |
| Avena | 5.00 |
| Leche (vaso) | 4.50 |
| Jugos frescos (vasito) | 5.50 |
| Fruta fresca (3 piezas) | 7.80 |

## Sopas

| | |
|---|---|
| Caldo de res con legumbres | $9.00 |
| Crema de espárragos | 8.30 |
| Crema de hongos | 7.15 |
| Minestrone | 10.50 |
| Sopa del día | 5.50 |

## Bebidas

| | |
|---|---|
| Cerveza Carta Blanca | $6.30 |
| Cerveza Tecate | 5.50 |
| Cerveza Superior | 7.00 |
| Cerveza Bohemia | 4.90 |
| Refrescos | 3.15 |
| Limonada | 4.00 |
| Té helado con limón | 2.90 |
| Tehuacán (Agua mineral) | 3.00 |
| Tehuacán de sabores | 4.65 |
| Café | 3.15 |
| Té caliente | 2.50 |
| Vino tinto (copa) | 10.50 |
| Vino blanco (copa) | 11.50 |

## Postres

| | |
|---|---|
| Arroz con leche | $6.00 |
| Flan | 8.00 |
| Helado de fresa o vainilla | 9.50 |
| Melocotón en almíbar | 5.15 |
| Mango en almíbar | 9.15 |
| Pastel (rebanada) | 7.00 |

**RECOMENDAMOS**

22 puntos **LA POSTA DEL ANGEL** Santa Clara del Mar (Mar del Plata). Reservas al (023) 602-2311/2384. Abadejo a la argelina. Inviernos, fines de semana de 12 a 05 hs. Entre $ 15 y $ 30 por persona.

18 puntos **LOS TRONCOS** Suipacha 732. Reservas al 322-1295.Parrilla. Chivito al asador. Todos los días, de 11 a 02 hs. Entre $ 17 y $ 22 por persona.

15 puntos **OVIEDO** Berutti 2602. Reservas al 83-5415. Cocina porteña y especialidades españolas. Langostinos al ajillo. Todos los días mediodía y noche. Entre $ 13 y $ 30 por persona.

16 puntos **POMODORO** Juan F. Seguí 3760. Reservas al 802-3709. Lomo Pomodoro. Todos los días mediodía y noche. Entre $ 11 (menú ejecutivo mediodía) y $ 15 (menú de la noche).

## Actividad 15. Del mundo hispano: Dónde comer en Buenos Aires

Primero lea las recomendaciones de una revista argentina que están a la izquierda. Luego conteste estas preguntas con su compañero/a.

1. De los cuatro restaurantes recomendados, ¿cuál es el mejor? ¿Cuántos puntos recibió?
2. De los restaurantes que se recomiendan en la revista, ¿cuáles son «buenos»? ¿Cuáles son «normales»? ¿Cuáles son «muy buenos»? ¿Hay alguno «excelente»?
3. ¿Cuáles son los elementos que se consideran para calificar un restaurante? ¿Cuál de todos es el más importante, en tu opinión? ¿Por qué?
4. ¿En cuál de los restaurantes es más barata la comida?
5. ¿En cuál de todos te gustaría cenar? ¿Por qué?

Ahora usen las descripciones de la revista como modelos para hablar con su compañero/a de algunos de los restaurantes de su ciudad.

**RESTAURANTES**

| 0/10 puntos | 11/15 puntos | 16/20 puntos | 21/25 puntos | 26/30 puntos |
|---|---|---|---|---|
| MALO REGULAR | NORMAL | BUENO | MUY BUENO | EXCELENTE |

**¡REÍR ES VIVIR!**

**Situaciones en el restaurante**

—¡Camarero!
—A sus órdenes, señor.
—¿Tiene algo frío?
—Sí, los pies.

—¡Mesera! ¡Señorita mesera!
—¿Sí, señor? ¿Qué pasa?
—¡En esta sopa hay una mosca!
—Ay, no se preocupe; está muerta.

## Actividad 16. Entrevista: Los restaurantes

1. ¿Qué clase de restaurante te gusta más?
2. ¿Te gusta la comida japonesa? ¿la comida china? ¿Qué otro tipo de comida internacional te gusta?
3. ¿Cuál es el restaurante más elegante cerca de tu casa? ¿Comes allí con frecuencia? ¿Te gusta la comida? ¿el ambiente? ¿Te gustan los precios? ¿Es necesario hacer una reservación?
4. ¿Conoces algún restaurante vegetariano? ¿Sirven buena comida allí?
5. ¿Cuánto consideras que se debe pagar por una comida excelente en un buen restaurante?
6. ¿Cuántas veces por semana comes fuera de casa? ¿Comes frecuentemente en algún lugar en especial? ¿Dónde?
7. ¿Vas mucho a los restaurantes de «servicio rápido»? ¿Cuál de ellos es tu favorito? ¿Por qué?
8. ¿Con quién prefieres ir a un restaurante? ¿Por qué?

## EL MUNDO HISPANO... en los Estados Unidos

Jaime Gómez es colombiano; tiene 37 años y vive en Princeton, Nueva Jersey. Jaime lleva 14 años en los Estados Unidos.

*Describa algunos platillos típicos de su país de origen. ¿Cuáles son sus favoritos? ¿Come usted esos platillos en los Estados Unidos? ¿Los prepara en su casa o los come en un restaurante?*

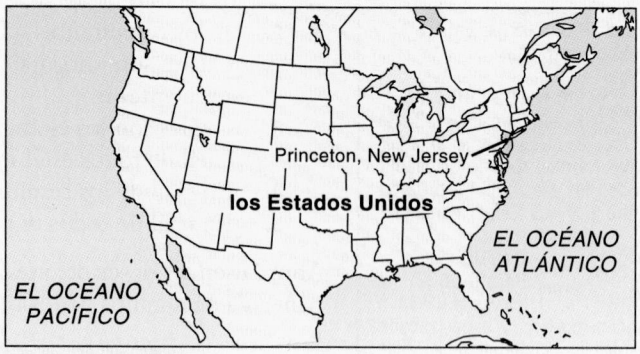


En Colombia disfrutamos de innumerables y deliciosos platos típicos; hay varios por cada región y uno para cada ocasión. Entre mis favoritos está *la bandeja paisa*, típica del departamento de Antioquía. Como su nombre lo indica, es una bandeja[1] de frijoles rojos, arroz, carne molida, huevo frito, patacón (plátano frito), chicharrón (cuero de cerdo frito) y aguacate.

Otro de mis platillos favoritos es el *ajiaco bogotano*, una sopa que se prepara con pollo, tres o cuatro clases de papas diferentes, cilantro, cebolla, alcaparras,[2] crema de leche y aguacate.

En los Estados Unidos hay algunos restaurantes latinos donde se encuentra la bandeja paisa, pero el ajiaco es más difícil de encontrar; por eso a mí me gusta prepararlos en mi casa en ocasiones especiales.

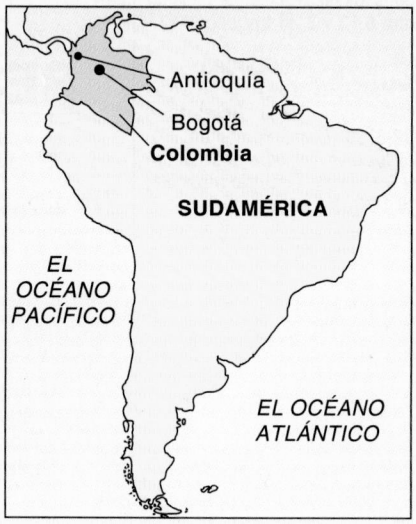


[1]*casserole* [2]*capers (plant and fruit)*

# En resumen

## De todo un poco

Cuadros de preferencias

Complete los siguientes cuadros según sus propias preferencias.

EN MI CASA SERVIMOS LAS SIGUIENTES COMIDAS CON FRECUENCIA

| COMIDAS | RAZÓN |
|---|---|
| 1. | |
| 2. | |
| 3. | |
| 4. | |
| 5. | |

ALGUNAS POSIBILIDADES
*No tiene mucha grasa.*
*Es saludable.*
*Tiene poco colesterol.*
*Nos encanta a todos.*
*Los ingredientes son baratos.*

EN MI CASA NUNCA SERVIMOS ESTAS COMIDAS

| COMIDAS | RAZÓN |
|---|---|
| 1. | |
| 2. | |
| 3. | |
| 4. | |
| 5. | |

ALGUNAS POSIBILIDADES
*Tiene mucha grasa.*
*Es muy picante.*
*Tiene mucho colesterol.*
*No nos gusta.*
*Los ingredientes cuestan mucho.*

Ahora, charle con un compañero / una compañera sobre el contenido de los cuadros.

## ¡Dígalo por escrito!

Un propósito empresarial

Trabajando con un compañero / una compañera, imagínense que van a comprar un restaurante y que necesitan un préstamo de un banco local. Escriban un plan detallado del negocio para presentárselo al banco que les va a prestar el dinero. Incluyan en el plan respuestas a las siguientes preguntas y también agreguen otra información importante. ¿Cómo se llama el restaurante? ¿Dónde está? ¿Cuántos camareros van a necesitar? ¿Van a servir tres comidas diarias o sólo el almuerzo y/o la cena? ¿Cuál es el horario del restaurante? ¡No se les olvide incluir el menú!

## VIDEOTECA

A todos les gusta comer y cenar en restaurantes... y a pocos les gusta hacer las compras. En este episodio en Sevilla, Lola se prepara para ir al mercado. Escuche bien y apunte la comida que necesita comprar. Su esposo, Manolo, le dice que no tiene que ir al mercado, que van a cenar en un restaurante. ¿Cómo es el ambiente del restaurante? ¿Qué piden de comer Manolo y Lola? En el Capítulo 8 del *Cuaderno de trabajo* hay más actividades para hacer después de ver el video.

# Vocabulario

## El desayuno — Breakfast

| | |
|---|---|
| **la avena** | oatmeal |
| **los huevos (fritos, cocidos, revueltos)** | eggs (fried, hard-boiled, scrambled) |
| **el panecillo** | roll, bun |
| **los panqueques** | pancakes |
| **el pan tostado** | toast |
| **el tocino** | bacon |

**REPASO: el cereal, el pan**

## El almuerzo y la cena — Lunch and Dinner

| | |
|---|---|
| **el caldo** | clear soup |
| **la papa al horno** | baked potato |
| **las papas fritas** | French fries |
| **el plato (platillo)** | prepared dish |
| **el queso** | cheese |
| **la salchicha** | sausage; frankfurter, hot dog |

**PALABRAS SEMEJANTES: la enchilada, la pizza, el sándwich, la sopa, la tortilla**

**REPASO: la ensalada, la hamburguesa**

## En el restaurante — In the Restaurant

| | |
|---|---|
| **el ambiente** | atmosphere |
| **la comida** | meal |
| **la cuenta** | bill, check |
| **el postre** | dessert |
| **la propina** | tip |
| **la tarjeta de crédito** | credit card |

**PALABRAS SEMEJANTES: el menú, la reservación**

**REPASO: atender (ie), la cena, cenar, la comida, la mesa, el mesero / la mesera, pagar, servir (i)**

## La carne — Meat

| | |
|---|---|
| **el ave** | poultry |
| **el bistec** | (beef)steak |
| **la carne de cerdo/puerco** | pork |
| **la carne molida** | ground beef |
| **la carne de res** | beef |
| **las chuletas (de cerdo/puerco)** | (pork) chops |
| **el hígado** | liver |
| **el jamón** | ham |
| **el pollo (frito)** | (fried) chicken |

## El pescado y los mariscos — Fish and Seafood

| | |
|---|---|
| **las almejas** | clams |
| **el atún** | tuna |
| **los camarones** | shrimp |
| **el cangrejo** | crab |
| **la langosta** | lobster |

## Las legumbres — Vegetables

| | |
|---|---|
| **el apio** | celery |
| **la calabacita** | summer squash |
| **la cebolla** | onion |
| **los frijoles** | beans |
| **los guisantes / los chícharos / las arvejas** | green peas |
| **las habichuelas / los ejotes** | green beans |
| **los hongos** | mushrooms |
| **la lechuga** | lettuce |
| **el maíz** | corn |
| **la mazorca de maíz / el elote** | ear of corn |
| **la papa** | potato |
| **el pepino** | cucumber |
| **el rábano** | radish |
| **la zanahoria** | carrot |

**PALABRAS SEMEJANTES: el bróculi, la coliflor, los espárragos, el tomate / el jitomate**

## Las frutas y las nueces — Fruits and Nuts

| | |
|---|---|
| **el aguacate** | avocado |
| **el albaricoque** | apricot |
| **las almendras** | almonds |
| **los cacahuetes** | peanuts |
| **el durazno (el melocotón)** | peach |
| **la fresa** | strawberry |
| **la manzana** | apple |
| **la nuez (las nueces)** | walnut(s) |
| **las pasas** | raisins |
| **la piña (el ananá)** | pineapple |
| **el plátano** | banana |
| **la sandía** | watermelon |
| **la toronja (el pomelo)** | grapefruit |
| **las uvas** | grapes |

**PALABRAS SEMEJANTES: la banana, el limón, el mango, el melón, la papaya, la pera**

**REPASO: la naranja (la china)**

## Los postres — Desserts

| | |
|---|---|
| **el arroz con leche** | rice pudding |
| **la crema** | cream |
| **el flan** | sweet custard |
| **las galletitas** | cookies |

**REPASO: el helado, el pastel, el yogur**

## Las bebidas — Drinks

| | |
|---|---|
| **el batido (de leche, de frutas)** | (milk, fruit) shake |
| **el jugo natural** | fresh-squeezed juice |
| **el té (caliente, frío, helado)** | (hot, cold, iced) tea |
| **el vino (blanco, tinto)** | (white, red) wine |

**PALABRAS SEMEJANTES: el agua mineral**

**REPASO: el agua, el café, la cerveza, la leche, la limonada, el refresco**

## Los condimentos, las especias y otros ingredientes
Condiments, Spices, and Other Ingredients

| | |
|---|---|
| **el aceite** | oil |
| **la aceituna** | olive |
| **el aderezo** | (salad) dressing |
| **el ajo** | garlic |
| **el almíbar** | syrup |
| **el arroz** | rice |
| **el azúcar** | sugar |
| **el conservador** | preservative |
| **la harina** | flour |
| **la jalea** | jelly |
| **la mantequilla** | butter |
| **la miel** | honey |
| **la mostaza** | mustard |
| **la pimienta** | pepper |
| **la sal** | salt |

**PALABRAS SEMEJANTES: la grasa, la margarina, la mayonesa, la mermelada, la salsa, la vainilla, el vinagre**

## La mesa y los cubiertos
Table Setting and Utensils

| | |
|---|---|
| **la azucarera** | sugar bowl |
| **la cuchara** | spoon |
| **la cucharita** | teaspoon |
| **el cucharón** | ladle |
| **el cuchillo** | knife |
| **la fuente de sopa** | soup tureen |
| **la jarra** | jug |
| **el mantel** | tablecloth |
| **el pimentero** | pepper shaker |
| **el platillo** | saucer |
| **el plato hondo** | bowl |
| **el salero** | salt shaker |
| **la servilleta** | napkin |
| **la taza** | cup; mug |
| **el tenedor** | fork |

**REPASO: el plato, el vaso**

## Las medidas y los recipientes
Measurements and Containers

| | |
|---|---|
| **la botella** | bottle |
| **la copa** | wine glass |
| **la lata** | can |
| **la libra** | pound |
| **la onza** | ounce |
| **el paquete** | package |
| **la porción** | serving |
| **la rebanada** | slice |
| **la sartén** | (frying) pan |
| **el tamaño** | size |
| **el tarro** | jar |

## Los verbos

| | |
|---|---|
| **agregar** | to add |
| **asar** | to roast |
| **batir** | to beat |
| **contener** | to contain |
| **crecer** | to grow |
| **cubrir** | to cover |
| **dejar** | to leave; to let |
| **doblar** | to fold |
| **encantar** | to delight |
| **estar a dieta** | to be on a diet |
| **freír (i) frío/fríe** | to fry |
| **incluir** | to include |
| **llenar** | to fill |
| **mejorar** | to (make) better |
| **pedir (i) pido/pide; pedí/pidió** | to ask for; to order food |
| **rallar** | to grate |
| **tapar** | to cover |

**PALABRAS SEMEJANTES: calcular, considerar, costar, determinar, fascinar, narrar**

## La descripción de la comida
Describing Food

| | |
|---|---|
| **a fuego lento** | over a low fire |
| **a la parrilla** | grilled, char-broiled |
| **al punto, cocido/a** | medium rare |
| **bien asado/a, bien cocido/a** | well-done |

| | |
|---|---|
| **crudo/a** | raw |
| **dorado/a** | golden brown |
| **dulce** | sweet |
| **espeso/a** | thick |
| **fresco/a** | fresh |
| **horneado/a** | baked |
| **ligero/a** | light |
| **maduro/a** | ripe |
| **picante** | hot (spicy) |
| **poco asado/a, poco cocido/a** | rare |
| **rico/a** | delicious |
| **saludable** | healthy |
| **seco/a** | dry |

**PALABRAS SEMEJANTES: concentrado/a, delicioso/a, excelente, exquisito/a**

## Los adjetivos

| | |
|---|---|
| **barato/a** | cheap |
| **medio/a** | half |

**PALABRAS SEMEJANTES: recomendado/a, el total, tropical, vegetariano/a**

## Los sustantivos

| | |
|---|---|
| **el agua corriente** | running water |
| **el alimento** | food; meal |
| **el antojito** | snack (*Mex.*) |
| **la cáscara** | peel |
| **la comida chatarra** | junk food (*Mex.*) |
| **la etiqueta** | label |
| **la frontera** | national border |
| **el lado** | side |
| **las palomitas de maíz** | popcorn |
| **el restaurante de servicio rápido** | fast-food restaurant |
| **la salud** | health |
| **la semilla** | seed |

**PALABRAS SEMEJANTES: el calcio, la caloría, el carbohidrato, el chocolate, el colesterol, la dieta, el error, el ingrediente, el líquido, la nutrición, la preparación, la proteína, la vitamina, la zona**

## Palabras y expresiones del texto

| | |
|---|---|
| **el paso** | step |
| **pertenecer** | to belong |
| **la razón** | reason |

**PALABRAS SEMEJANTES: el ejemplo, el elemento, el punto, la recomendación**

## Palabras y expresiones útiles

| | |
|---|---|
| **con gusto** | with pleasure |
| **demasiado** | too much |
| **ningún, ninguno/a** | none |
| **por dentro/fuera** | on the inside/outside |
| **sin** | without |

# Gramática y ejercicios

## 8.1 Referring to Objects Already Mentioned: Impersonal Direct Object Pronouns *lo*, *la*, *los*, and *las*

**lo** = *you, him, it (m.)*
**la** = *you, her, it (f.)*
**los** = *you, them (m. pl.)*
**las** = *you, them (f. pl.)*

**¿Quién preparó los frijoles?** (*Who made the beans?*)
**Papá los preparó.** (*Dad made them.*)

When referring to things already mentioned, use the Spanish object pronouns **lo** and **la**, which correspond to the English object pronoun *it:* **lo** refers to masculine words and **la** to feminine words. Spanish **los** and **las** correspond to English *them:* **los** refers to masculine words and **las** to feminine words.

| | |
|---|---|
| —¿Quién compró **el pastel**?<br>—**Lo** compró Raúl. | *—Who bought the cake?*<br>*—Raúl bought it.* |
| —¿Quién trajo **la fruta**?<br>—**La** trajo Nora. | *—Who brought the fruit?*<br>*—Nora brought it.* |
| —Luis, ¿preparaste **los tacos**?<br>—Sí, **los** preparé esta mañana. | *—Luis, did you prepare the tacos?*<br>*—Yes, I prepared them this morning.* |
| —Carmen, ¿dónde pusiste **las servilletas**?<br>—**Las** puse en la mesa. | *—Carmen, where did you put the napkins?*<br>*—I put them on the table.* |

**¿RECUERDA?**

As you saw in **Gramática 6.6**, the object pronouns **lo**, **la**, **los**, and **las** also serve as personal direct object pronouns.

| | |
|---|---|
| —¿Viste a Alberto ayer?<br>—No, no **lo** vi. | *—Did you see Al yesterday?*<br>*—No, I didn't see him.* |
| ¿La profesora Martínez? **La** vi ayer en el mercado, pero ella no me vio. | *Professor Martínez? I saw her yesterday at the market, but she didn't see me.* |

Review this section now, if necessary.

Thus the Spanish direct object pronouns **lo**, **la**, **los**, and **las** may substitute for words referring to people *or* to things. For example, **la** in the first exchange below refers to **Mónica** (*her*); in the second one it refers to **la salsa** (*it*).

| | |
|---|---|
| —¿Llamaste a **Mónica**?<br>—Sí, **la** llamé ayer. | *—Did you call Mónica?*<br>*—Yes, I called her yesterday.* |
| —Luis, ¿encontraste **la salsa**?<br>—Sí, **la** encontré en el refrigerador. | *—Luis, did you find the sauce?*<br>*—Yes, I found it in the refrigerator.* |

These pronouns take time to acquire. You will find that you will gradually come to use them in your speech as you hear and read more Spanish.

| DIRECT OBJECT PRONOUNS | |
|---|---|
| lo | *you, him, it* (*m.*) |
| la | *you, her, it* (*f.*) |
| los | *you, them* (*m. nouns* or *males* or *males and females*) |
| las | *you, them* (*f. nouns* or *females*) |

Like other pronouns, direct object pronouns are usually placed before the verb.

| | |
|---|---|
| ¿La ensalada? Ella no **la** come nunca. | *Salad? She never eats it.* |

They may, however, be attached to the end of an infinitive or present progressive form.

| | |
|---|---|
| ¿El flan? Van a preparar**lo** más tarde. | *The flan? They're going to fix it later.* |
| ¿Los huevos? Estoy batiéndo**los** ahora. | *The eggs? I'm beating them now.* |

## Ejercicio 1

Conteste con **lo, la, los** o **las** y una terminación lógica.

MODELO: —¿Cuándo bebiste el jugo de naranja?
—*Lo* bebí...
a. hace diez años.
(b.) anoche.
c. antes de levantarme.

**1.** —¿Cuándo preparaste el postre?
—_____ preparé...
**a.** en el restaurante.
**b.** ayer.
**c.** en la cocina.

**2.** —¿Dónde pusiste la carne?
—_____ puse en...
**a.** el jardín.
**b.** el supermercado.
**c.** el congelador.

**3.** —¿Dónde compraste las legumbres?
—_____ compré...
**a.** en una tienda de ropa.
**b.** en el supermercado.
**c.** en la cafetería de la escuela.

**4.** —¿Cuándo trajiste el hielo?
— _____ traje...
**a.** el año pasado.
**b.** hace diez minutos.
**c.** hace dos semanas.

**5.** —¿Dónde pusiste la mayonesa?
—_____ puse en...
**a.** la mesa.
**b.** el sofá.
**c.** el dormitorio.

**6.** —¿Cuándo preparaste las bebidas?
—_____preparé...
**a.** hace dos minutos.
**b.** para la fiesta de esta noche.
**c.** mañana por la noche.

7. —¿Dónde pusiste los vasos?
   —_____ puse en...
   a. el armario.
   b. la cómoda.
   c. el gabinete.
8. —¿Dónde compraste el pan?
   —_____ compré...
   a. esta mañana.
   b. en la panadería.
   c. en la biblioteca.
9. —¿Cuándo hiciste las tortillas?
   —_____ hice...
   a. en el fregadero.
   b. cuando me levanté.
   c. después de acostarme.
10. —¿Cuándo trajiste los tomates para la salsa?
   —_____ traje...
   a. esta mañana.
   b. hace veinte años.
   c. el mes pasado.

## Ejercicio 2

Complete estos diálogos con **lo**, **la**, **los** o **las**.

1. —¿Viste a Mónica y a Nora en la fiesta?
   —Sí, _____ vi. Las dos bailaron toda la noche.
2. —Raúl, ¿conoces a la señora Venegas?
   —No, no _____ conozco. ¿Quién es?
3. —¿Visitaron ustedes a sus parientes durante las vacaciones?
   —No, _____ visitamos hace tres semanas.
4. —Alberto, ¿conociste al profesor nuevo ayer en la reunión?
   —Sí, _____ conocí. Me parece muy simpático.
5. —Carmen, ¿es esa señora que está allí la madre de Luis?
   —No sé; no _____ conozco.

**¿RECUERDA?**

In **Gramática 1.6** you learned that the verb **gustar**, followed by an infinitive, is the most common Spanish equivalent for the English verb *to like* (*to do something*) and that **gustar** resembles the English verb phrase *to be pleasing* (*to someone*). You also learned that an indirect object pronoun (**me**, **te**, **nos**, **os**, **le**, or **les**) is used with **gustar** to identify the person to whom something is pleasing.

**A Nora le gusta** cocinar.
*Nora likes to cook.*
**Me gusta desayunar** temprano.
*I like to eat breakfast early.*

## 8.2 More about Expressing Likes: The Verbs *gustar* and *encantar*

**A. Gustar** can also be followed by a noun. If the noun is singular, use the singular form, **gusta**; if it is plural, use the plural form, **gustan**.

| | |
|---|---|
| —¿Te gusta **la sandía**? | *—Do you like watermelon?* |
| —Sí, pero me gust**an** más **las uvas**. | *—Yes, but I like grapes better.* |

The preterite forms are **gustó** (*sing.*) and **gustaron** (*pl.*).

| | |
|---|---|
| —¿Te **gustó** el helado? | *—Did you like the ice cream?* |
| —Sí, me **gustó** mucho. | *—Yes, I liked it a lot.* |
| —Nos **gustaron** mucho esas galletitas. | *—We really liked those cookies.* |

**B.** To ask who likes something, begin with **¿A quién... ?**

| | |
|---|---|
| —**¿A quién** le gusta la pizza? | —*Who likes pizza?* |
| —¡A todos nos gusta! | —*We all do!* |

To identify a specific person or persons who like(s) something, use the following pattern.

Use **gusta** if one item is being referred to; use **gustan** if more than one item is referred to.
**Me gusta el café.** (*I like coffee.*)
**Me gustan las tortillas de maíz.** (*I like corn tortillas.*)

**A** + *name* + **le(s)** + **gusta(n)**...

| | |
|---|---|
| **A Lan le gusta** leer novelas. | *Lan likes to read novels.* |
| **A Graciela** no **le gusta** la comida italiana. | *Graciela doesn't like Italian food.* |
| **A Guillermo** y **a Ernestito les gusta** mucho montar en bicicleta. | *Guillermo and Ernestito like to ride their bikes a lot.* |

**C.** To state more emphatically that someone likes something, use the preposition **a** followed by the person (noun or pronoun) and then the corresponding indirect object pronoun (**me**, **te**, **le**, **nos**, **os**, **les**) + **gusta(n)**.

| | |
|---|---|
| —**¿A Paula le gustan** las hamburguesas? | —*Does Paula like hamburgers?* |
| —**¡¿A Paula?!** No, **a ella** no **le gustan** las hamburguesas. | —*Paula?! No, she doesn't like hamburgers.* |

For emphasis, add:
**a mí**
**a ti**
**a él / a ellos**
**a ella(s)**
**a usted(es)**
**a nosotros/as**

**A mí me gusta el chocolate.** (*I like chocolate*).
**A ellas les gustan las papas fritas.** (*They like French fries.*)

The following emphatic phrases are made up of the preposition **a** followed by pronouns. Notice that these pronouns are the same as the subject pronouns, except for **mí** and **ti**.*

| | |
|---|---|
| a mí me gusta(n) | a nosotros/as nos gusta(n) |
| a ti te gusta(n) | a vosotros/as os gusta(n) |
| a usted le gusta(n) | a ustedes les gusta(n) |
| a él le gusta(n) | a ellos les gusta(n) |
| a ella le gusta(n) | a ellas les gusta(n) |

| | |
|---|---|
| Pues, **a mí me gustan** mucho todas las frutas, especialmente la papaya. | *Well, I really like all fruits, especially papaya.* |
| ¿Y de veras **a ti no te gustan** las papas fritas? | *And do you really not like French fries?* |

**D.** Emphatic short answers to questions with **gustar** are very common. Use the preposition **a** plus a pronoun or noun and the words **sí** or **no**.

| | |
|---|---|
| —¿Le gustan las sardinas? | —*Do you like sardines?* |
| —**¡A mí, no!** | —*No, I don't!* |
| —¿Les gustan los postres de chocolate? | —*Do you like chocolate desserts?* |
| —**A mí, sí**, pero **a Nora, no**. | —*I do, but Nora doesn't.* |

With **gustar:**
**a mí también** = *me too*
**a mí tampoco** = *me neither*

You can use the words **también** (*also*) and **tampoco** (*neither*) instead of **sí** and **no** in short answers.

| | |
|---|---|
| —A Pablo le gustan las fajitas. | —*Pablo likes fajitas.* |
| —Pues, **a mí también**. | —*Well, so do I.* |

*Recognition: **a vos te gusta**

| | |
|---|---|
| —Luis, a mí no me gustan mucho estos tacos. | *—Luis, I don't like these tacos very much.* |
| —**A mí tampoco.** | *—I don't either.* |

Remember to use **encanta** if referring to one item or **encantan** if more than one.
**Les encanta la comida japonesa.** (*They really like Japanese food.*)
**Nos encantan las papas fritas.** (*We adore French fries.*)

**E.** There are other Spanish verbs that function like **gustar.** One common one used to express likes and dislikes is **encantar.** (You will learn more about this kind of verb in **Gramática 10.6.**)

| | |
|---|---|
| —A mí **me encanta** el flan. | *—I adore flan.* |
| —A mí también. | *—Me too.* |
| —**Nos encantan** los mariscos que sirven en este restaurante. | *—We love the seafood they serve in this restaurant.* |
| —A nosotros también. | *—So do we.* |
| A Ernesto y a Estela **les encanta** salir a cenar. | *Ernesto and Estela love to eat dinner out.* |

The preterite forms of **encantar** are **encantó** and **encantaron**.

| | |
|---|---|
| A ella **le encantó** la cena. | *She loved the dinner.* |
| **Me encantaron** esas enchiladas. | *I really liked those enchiladas.* |

## Ejercicio 3

Complete los siguientes diálogos.

Use **me/mí** y **te/ti.**

—¿_____[1] gustan las zanahorias?
—A mí no _____[2] gustan mucho. ¿Y a _____[3]?
—A _____,[4] sí. Son muy buenas para los ojos.

Use **él/le, me/mí** y **te/ti.**

—¿A tu hermano _____[5] gusta el pollo frito?
—A _____[6] sí le gusta, pero a _____,[7] no.
—¡A _____[8] no te gusta el pollo! ¿Por qué no _____[9] gusta?
—A _____[10] sí me gusta el pollo, pero no _____[11] gusta el pollo frito.

## Ejercicio 4

Haga oraciones que describan los gustos de las personas a continuación. Use 1) una forma del verbo **encantar** (**encanta** o **encantan**); 2) el pronombre apropiado (**me**, **te**, **le**, **les** o **nos**); y 3) el nombre de una comida.

MODELO: A mi hermana *le encantan las fresas.*

**SUGERENCIAS**

| | | |
|---|---|---|
| el café | los dulces | el guacamole |
| los chiles rellenos | las fresas | las hamburguesas |
| el chocolate | los frijoles | las palomitas con mantequilla |
| la comida mexicana | la fruta | el pan |

1. A mi mejor amigo/a _____.
2. A mis padres _____.
3. A mi profesor(a) de español _____.
4. A mi novio/a (esposo/a) _____.
5. A mí _____.
6. A mi mejor amigo/a y a mí _____.

## 8.3 Expressing *for, from,* and *to whom:* Prepositions + Pronouns

**A.** As you saw in **Gramática 8.2**, pronouns often follow prepositions in Spanish.

| | | | |
|---|---|---|---|
| a mí | *to, at me* | para ella | *for her* |
| de ti, usted(es) | *of, from you* | sin nosotros/as | *without us* |
| en él | *in, on him/it* | con ellos/as | *with them* |
| | | para vosotros/as | *for you* |

| | |
|---|---|
| —¿Para quién es el regalo? ¿Es **para mí**? | —*Who is the present for? Is it for me?* |
| —No, es **para él**. | —*No, it's for him.* |
| —¿**Sin** Rogelio? No podemos ir **sin él**. | —*Without Rogelio? We can't go without him.* |
| Adriana es una magnífica empleada. Tengo mucha confianza **en ella**. | *Adriana is a great employee. I have a lot of confidence in her.* |

**B. Con** and **mí** combine to form **conmigo** (*with me*). **Con** and **ti** form **contigo** (*with you*).

**conmigo** = *with me*
**contigo** = *with you* (*inf. sing.*)

| | |
|---|---|
| —Marta, ¿quieres ir **conmigo** al teatro esta noche? | —*Marta, do you want to go to the theater with me this evening?* |
| —No, no puedo ir **contigo** esta noche. Tengo que estudiar. | —*No, I can't go with you tonight. I have to study.* |

## Ejercicio 5

Graciela le dice a Amanda para quién(es) son algunas cosas, y Amanda reacciona con sorpresa. ¿Qué dice Amanda en cada caso?

MODELO: Esta cerveza es para mi hermanito. →
¿Para *él*? ¡No lo creo! *¡Es muy pequeño!*

POSIBILIDADES

¿Para _____?
¡No lo creo!
¿Te/Le/Les gusta(n)?
¡No me/te/le/nos/les gusta(n)!
¡Es muy pequeño/a!

1. Esta comida congelada es para mi madre.
2. Este hígado es para ti.
3. Esta tequila es para Clarisa y Marisa.
4. Estos ajos son para ti y para tus amigos.
5. Esta dieta es para mi papá.
6. Este vino es para mí.
7. Estas cebollas son para la profesora de español.
8. Este jugo de naranja es para Lobo, el perro de Ernestito.

## Ejercicio 6

Complete estos diálogos con **mí**, **ti**, **él**, **conmigo** o **contigo**.

1. DIEGO: Amanda, ¿quieres ir _____[a] al Baile de los Enamorados?
   AMANDA: No, Diego, lo siento, no puedo ir _____[b] porque voy a ir con Ramón, mi novio.
2. RAFAEL: Graciela, estas rosas son para _____[a]. ¿Te gustan?
   GRACIELA: ¿Para _____[b]? ¡Ay, Rafael, muchas gracias! Me encantan.
3. AMANDA: Graciela, ¿qué piensas tú de Richard, el nuevo estudiante francés?
   GRACIELA: ¿Qué pienso de _____[a]? Pues, no lo conozco pero creo que es *muy* atractivo.
   AMANDA: Ajá... y yo voy a estudiar con _____[b] esta tarde... en mi casa.
   GRACIELA: No lo creo, Amanda! ¿Vas a estudiar con _____[c]? ¿Sola? ¿Sin _____[d]? Pues... ¡Fabuloso para _____[e] y terrible para _____[f]!

## 8.4 Making Negative Statements and Questions: *No*, *never*

| | | | |
|---|---|---|---|
| algo | *something* | nada | *nothing* |
| alguien | *somebody* | nadie | *nobody* |
| algún<br>alguno/a/os/as | *some* | ningún<br>ninguno/a (de) | *none, no one* |
| siempre | *always* | nunca (jamás) | *never* |
| también | *also* | tampoco | *neither* |

Whereas in English it is generally incorrect to have more than one negative in a sentence, in Spanish multiple negatives are frequently required.

**A.** Spanish often requires the use of multiple negatives in the same sentence.

| | |
|---|---|
| —¿Tienes algo en el horno? | —*Do you have something in the oven?* |
| —**No, no** tengo **nada**. | —*No, I don't have anything.* |
| —¿Hay alguien en la puerta? | —*Is there someone at the door?* |
| —**No, no** hay **nadie**. | —*No, there is no one.* |

| | |
|---|---|
| —Señora Silva, ¿va usted siempre al mercado los martes? | *—Mrs. Silva, do you always go to the market on Tuesdays?* |
| —**No**, **no** voy **nunca** los martes. | *—No, I don't ever (I never) go on Tuesdays.* |

**algún (alguno/a/os/as)** = *some, any*
**ningún (ninguno/a)** = *none, not any, neither*

**B. Alguno/a** corresponds to English *some* or *any*, and **ninguno/a** corresponds to English *none*, *not any*, or *neither*.

| | |
|---|---|
| —¿Hay **algunos** postres sin azúcar? | *—Are there any desserts without sugar?* |
| —No, señor, no tenemos **ningún** postre sin azúcar. | *—No, sir, we don't have any desserts without sugar.* |
| —¿Hay **alguna** sopa sin carne? | *—Are there any soups without meat?* |
| —No, no hay **ninguna**; todas tienen carne. | *—No, there aren't any; they all have meat.* |

Note that Spanish uses **ninguno/a** in the singular form.

**C. Alguno** and **ninguno** shorten to **algún** and **ningún** before masculine singular nouns.

| | |
|---|---|
| —¿Hay **algún** restaurante en esta calle? | *—Is there a restaurant on this street?* |
| —No, no hay **ningún** restaurante por aquí. | *—No, there aren't any restaurants around here.* |

**Uno/Un**, **bueno/buen**, **primero/primer,** and **tercero/tercer** follow the same rule.

| | |
|---|---|
| ¿Quieres pedir **una** copa de vino? | *Do you want to order a glass of wine?* |
| Sólo hay **un** plato mexicano en el menú. | *There is only one Mexican dish on the menu.* |
| ¡Aquí sirven **unos** mariscos exquisitos! | *They serve excellent seafood here!* |
| Esteban es un **buen** cocinero. | *Steve is a good cook.* |
| Nora y Carmen también son **buenas** cocineras. | *Nora and Carmen are also good cooks.* |
| Vamos a sentarnos en la **tercera** mesa. | *Let's sit down at the third table.* |
| El **primer** plato es la sopa. | *The first course is the soup.* |

**D. No** is not used when the negative word precedes the verb.

| | |
|---|---|
| **Nunca** como entre comidas. | *I never eat between meals.* |
| **Nadie** fue al mercado. | *Nobody went to the market.* |

**E.** Express *I* (*you*, *we* . . . ) *don't either* with a subject pronoun + **tampoco**.

| | |
|---|---|
| —Yo no quiero comer helado. | *—I don't want to eat ice cream.* |
| —**Yo tampoco.** | *—I don't either.* (*Me neither.*) |
| Yo no quiero más arroz. **Tú tampoco**, ¿verdad? | *I don't want more rice. You don't either, do you?* |

## Ejercicio 7

Conteste las siguientes preguntas de forma negativa. Use **nada**, **nadie**, **nunca** o **ninguno/a**.

MODELO: —¿Hay algo de comer en el refrigerador?
—No, no hay *nada*.

1. —¿Fue alguien al supermercado ayer?
—No, no fue _____.
2. —¿Desayunaste algo esta mañana?
—No, no comí _____.
3. —¿Siempre comes en restaurantes chinos?
—No, _____ como en ellos.
4. —¿Invitaste a alguien a cenar esta noche?
—No, no invité a _____.
5. —¿Compraste una sandía?
—No, no encontré _____ madura.
6. —¿Quieres algo de tomar?
—No gracias, no quiero _____.
7. —¿Te sirvo espinacas?
—No, gracias. ¡_____ las como!
8. —¿Por qué no invitaste a Diego y a Ramón a la fiesta?
—Los invité, pero _____ de los dos quiso venir.

## Ejercicio 8

Responda afirmativa o negativamente a lo siguiente. Venga a clase preparado/a para comentar sus respuestas con los otros compañeros de clase.

1. Me gustan las espinacas.
   a. A mí también.
   b. A mí no me gustan.
2. No me gusta comer hígado.
   a. A mí tampoco.
   b. A veces me gusta comerlo.
3. ¿Invitaste a alguien a comer la semana pasada?
   a. Sí, invité a _____ porque...
   b. No, no invité a nadie porque...
4. Prefiero el batido de chocolate al de vainilla.
   a. Yo también.
   b. No me gusta ninguno de los dos.
5. ¿Dejaste una propina la última vez que comiste en un restaurante?
   a. Sí, dejé...
   b. No, no dejé nada porque...
6. No me gusta desayunar cereal.
   a. A mí, sí. Siempre lo como.
   b. A mí tampoco. No lo como nunca.

## 8.5 Expressing *one* or *you:* The Impersonal *se*

In addition to being a reflexive pronoun (see **Gramática 4.4**), **se** is also used in "impersonal" constructions.

**Se** + third-person singular verb is used to express *one, you,* or impersonal *they.* **Se come mucho ajo en España.** (*One eats* [*They eat*] *lots of garlic in Spain.* (*Lots of garlic is eaten in Spain.*)

**Se** + third-person verb form is also used for instructions. **Primero se hierve el agua, después se le agrega la sal y luego se ponen los fideos y se cuecen por 8 minutos.** (*First you boil the water, then you add the salt, and then you put in the noodles and cook them for 8 minutes.*)

In English this structure is expressed with the impersonal *you* (*You need good film to take good pictures*), the pronoun *one* (*One should always think before acting*), the pronoun *they* (*They sell beer by the glass*), or the simple passive (*Beer is sold only by the glass here*).

| | |
|---|---|
| —¿Cómo **se dice** *tablecloth* en español? | —*How do you say* tablecloth *in Spanish?* |
| —**Se dice** «mantel». | —*You say* **mantel**. |
| Aquí **se habla** español. | *Spanish is spoken here.* (*They speak Spanish here.*) |
| Primero **se agrega** la sal y después **se mezcla** todo. | *First you add the salt and then you mix everything.* |
| No **se debe** dormir inmediatamente después de comer. | *One shouldn't* (*go to*) *sleep immediately after eating.* |

If the topic in question is plural, the verb is usually also plural.

| | |
|---|---|
| —¿**Se sirven mariscos** frescos aquí? | —*Are fresh shellfish served here?* |
| —Sí, **se preparan camarones** deliciosos y el precio es muy módico. | —*Yes, they prepare delicious shrimp, and the price is very moderate.* |

## Ejercicio 9

Complete estas oraciones con la forma **se** impersonal de los siguientes verbos: **preparar**, **poner**, **cortar**, **lavar**, **agregar**, **necesitar**, **hablar** y **batir**.

1. Para preparar un sándwich de jamón y queso, _____ el jamón y el queso en rebanadas.
2. Para alimentarse bien, _____ comer de los cuatro grupos esenciales de alimentos.
3. Primero _____ el bróculi y luego _____ en el agua a hervir.
4. En este restaurante _____ mariscos frescos y deliciosos.
5. Para hacer un buen guacamole, _____ cebolla y otros ingredientes.
6. Para hacer una tortilla española, _____ huevos y patatas.
7. ¿_____ francés en ese restaurante?
8. ¿_____ los huevos para la tortilla española?

**pedir** = *to ask for*
present: **(yo) pido, (él) pide**
past: **(yo) pedí, (él) pidió**
**servir** = *to serve*
present: **(yo) sirvo, (él) sirve**
past: **(yo) serví, (él) sirvió**
**Pedí camarones y fideos.** (*I ordered shrimp and pasta.*) **El mesero me sirvió almejas y arroz.** (*The waiter served me clams and rice.*)

## 8.6 Using Stem-Changing Verbs like *pedir* and *servir:* Present-Tense and Preterite Forms

In a few verbs like **pedir** (*to order; to ask for*) and **servir** (*to serve*), the **-e-** of the infinitive changes to **-i-** in the present tense and the preterite. In the present, all forms of **pedir** and **servir** use the stems **pid-** and **sirv-** except for the **nosotros/as** and **vosotros/as** forms and the infinitive.*†

*The **e** → **i** change also occurs in the present participles: **pidiendo** (*ordering*) and **sirviendo** (*serving*).
†Recognition: **vos pedís, servís; vos pediste, serviste**

| | pedir | servir |
|---|---|---|
| (yo) | pido | sirvo |
| (tú) | pides | sirves |
| (usted, él/ella) | pide | sirve |
| (nosotros/as) | pedimos | servimos |
| (vosotros/as) | pedís | servís |
| (ustedes, ellos/as) | piden | sirven |

In the preterite, only the **usted, él/ella** and **ustedes, ellos/as** forms use the stem with **i**.

| | pedir | servir |
|---|---|---|
| (yo) | pedí | serví |
| (tú) | pediste | serviste |
| (usted, él/ella) | pidió | sirvió |
| (nosotros/as) | pedimos | servimos |
| (vosotros/as) | pedisteis | servisteis |
| (ustedes, ellos/as) | pidieron | sirvieron |

| | |
|---|---|
| En este restaurante **sirven** excelente comida. La semana pasada me **sirvieron** una paella sabrosísima. | *They serve excellent food in this restaurant. Last week they served me a delicious paella.* |
| —Silvia, ¿qué platillo **pediste** en el Restaurante Mi Casita?<br>—**Pedí** unas enchiladas de pollo. Siempre **pido** lo mismo. | *—Silvia, what dish did you order at Mi Casita Restaurant?*<br>*—I ordered chicken enchiladas. I always order the same thing.* |

The verbs **vestirse** (*to dress*) and **seguir** (*to follow*) conform to the **e** → **i** pattern.*

| vestirse | | seguir | |
|---|---|---|---|
| ***Present*** | ***Past*** | ***Present*** | ***Past*** |
| me visto | me vestí | sigo | seguí |
| te vistes | te vestiste | sigues | seguiste |
| se viste | se vistió | sigue | siguió |
| nos vestimos | nos vestimos | seguimos | seguimos |
| os vestís | os vestisteis | seguís | seguisteis |
| se visten | se vistieron | siguen | siguieron |

*The **e** → **i** change also occurs in the present participles: **vistiendo/vistiéndose** and **siguiendo.**

| | |
|---|---|
| Raúl se **vistió** rápido anoche. | *Raúl dressed quickly last night.* |
| Estela no **siguió** la receta. | *Estela didn't follow the recipe.* |

**Reír** (*to laugh*), **sonreír** (*to smile*), and **freír** (*to fry*) also follow this pattern, except that in the third-person preterite forms one **i** is dropped: **fri-** + **-ió** → **frió**; **fri-** + **-ieron** → **frieron**.*

| freír | |
|---|---|
| ***Present*** | ***Past*** |
| frío | freí |
| fríes | freíste |
| fríe | frió |
| freímos | freímos |
| freís | freísteis |
| fríen | frieron |

| | |
|---|---|
| Doña Rosita **frió** las tortillas. | *Doña Rosita fried the tortillas.* |
| Don Eduardo **sonrió** cuando le sirvieron su platillo favorito. | *Don Eduardo smiled when they served him his favorite dish.* |

La comida mexicana es muy variada. Entre los platillos más populares se encuentran los tacos.

## Ejercicio 10

Complete estos diálogos con las formas apropiadas de **servir** o **pedir**.

PILAR: ¿Qué vas a _____[1] ahora?
CLARA: Creo que voy a _____[2] pollo asado.
PILAR: En este restaurante _____[3] muy buenos mariscos.
CLARA: Entonces voy a _____[4] camarones fritos.

JOSÉ: ¿Qué _____[5] tú en un restaurante mexicano?
PILAR: Eso depende. Si _____[6] mariscos, _____[7] un cóctel de mariscos.
JOSÉ: ¿Y si no hay mariscos?
PILAR: Entonces prefiero _____[8] un chile relleno.

PILAR: Ayer mi novio y yo fuimos a un restaurante francés muy elegante.
CLARA: ¿Qué _____[9] ustedes?
PILAR: _____[10] cóctel de mariscos, ensalada y carne de res en salsa de vino.
CLARA: Mmm. ¿Y les _____[11] postre también?
PILAR: Sí, yo _____[12] flan y mi novio _____[13] pastel de chocolate.

JOSÉ: Pilar, ¿_____[14] leche otra vez?
PILAR: No, ayer yo _____[15] una Coca-Cola y Clara _____[16] un vaso de leche.
JOSÉ: Ah sí, ya entiendo. Después ustedes _____[17] un sándwich de pollo.
PILAR: No, José. Después _____[18] un sándwich de jamón pero el mesero nos _____[19] sándwiches de pollo.
JOSÉ: ¿Y a mí también me _____[20] un sándwich de pollo?
PILAR: No, hombre. ¡Tú no fuiste con nosotros!

---

*The present participles are: **friendo, sonriendo,** and **riendo.** Recognition: Present: **vos te vestís, seguís, freís, sonreís, reís.** Preterite: **vos te vestiste, seguiste, freíste, sonreíste, reíste.**

CAPÍTULO 9

# El pasado

**METAS**

In **Capítulo 9** you will expand your ability to talk about your family. You will learn to express different kinds of memories: your habitual activities and those of others, as well as how you felt about things in the past.

Zaragoza, España

**ACTIVIDADES DE COMUNICACIÓN Y LECTURAS**


La familia y los parientes

**Las palabras viven** En México, un *cuate* es un buen amigo

**Nota cultural** Los hispanos hablan de su familia

**El mundo hispano...** imágenes

La niñez

**Lectura** ¡Así piensan los niños!

La juventud

**El mundo hispano...** su gente

**El mundo hispano...** en los Estados Unidos

**EN RESUMEN**


**GRAMÁTICA Y EJERCICIOS**


9.1 Describing Family Relationships: The Reciprocal Reflexive Verbs **parecerse** and **llevarse bien**

9.2 Saying What You Used to Do: The Imperfect Tense

9.3 Describing the Past: The Imperfect and Preterite of "State" Verbs

9.4 Saying What You Were Going to Do: The Imperfect of **ir** + **a** + Infinitive

# Actividades de comunicación y lecturas

## La familia y los parientes

*Lea Gramática 9.1.*

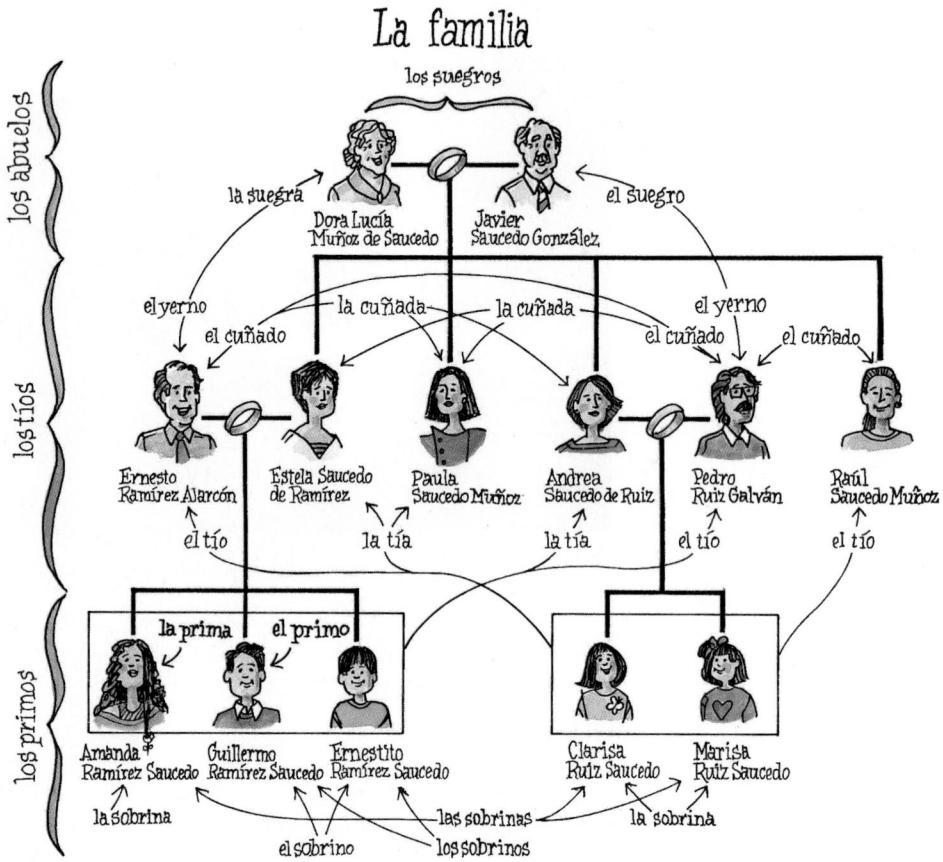


### Actividad 1. Definiciones: La familia de Raúl

Mire el dibujo de arriba y escuche las oraciones que le va a leer su profesor(a). Diga si son ciertas o falsas.

MODELO: PROF.: «La tía de Clarisa y Marisa se llama Andrea.» →
E.: Falso. Andrea es *la madre de* Clarisa y Marisa.

## Actividad 2. Intercambios: La familia de Raúl

Hágale estas preguntas a su compañero/a.

1. ¿Cómo se llaman las hermanas de Raúl?
2. ¿Cuántos sobrinos tiene Raúl? ¿Cómo se llaman?
3. ¿Tienen nueras Dora y Javier?
4. ¿Cómo se llaman los cuñados de Raúl?
5. ¿Cómo se llama el suegro de Pedro y Ernesto?
6. ¿Cómo se llaman las cuñadas de Ernesto?
7. ¿Cuántos nietos tienen Dora y Javier?
8. ¿Cómo se llaman los tíos de Clarisa y Marisa?
9. ¿Cómo se llaman los primos de Clarisa y Marisa?
10. ¿Cómo se llaman los yernos de Dora y Javier?

## Actividad 3. Descripción de dibujos: La familia de Mónica

Lea la siguiente descripción de la familia de Mónica. Basándose en el árbol genealógico, llene los espacios en blanco con los nombres o palabras apropiados.

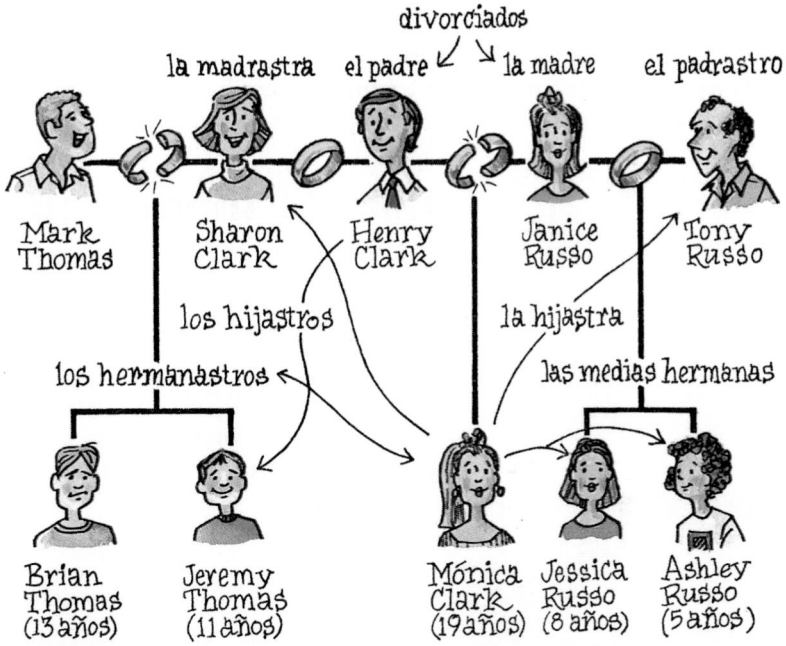


Los padres de Mónica se llaman _____ y _____ y están _____. Mónica vive con su madre y su _____, Tony. Su madre y Tony tienen dos hijas, Jessica y Ashley. Ellas son las _____ de Mónica. Jessica se parece a _____, pero Ashley se parece más a _____.

La nueva esposa de Henry Clark se llama _____. Sharon tiene dos hijos de su primer esposo; se llaman _____ y _____ y son los _____ de Mónica. Mónica no visita a sus hermanastros con frecuencia, pero se lleva bien con ellos. A Mónica le gusta hablar con Sharon, su _____, pero dice que su padrastro, Tony, no la comprende.

**LAS PALABRAS VIVEN**

**VOCABULARIO ÚTIL**

| | |
|---|---|
| el dios | *god* |
| la profecía | *prophecy* |
| señalaba | *indicated* |
| la serpiente emplumada | *feathered serpent* |

# En México, un *cuate* es un buen amigo

Entre los jóvenes mexicanos, **tener un cuate** significa lo mismo que **tener un buen amigo**. La palabra **cuate** viene del náhuatl, el idioma de los aztecas.

La llegada de Hernán Cortés a México en 1519 coincidió con la fecha que una profecía de la mitología azteca señalaba para el regreso del dios Quetzalcóatl. Quetzalcóatl les enseñó a los aztecas la agricultura, el trabajo de los metales, las artes y el calendario. Predicaba una religión de amor y resignación. Los antiguos mexicanos lo representaban como una serpiente emplumada.

En náhuatl, la palabra *coatl* significaba **serpiente**. Y también llegó a significar **gemelo**, pues Quetzalcóatl tenía un hermano idéntico a él, otro dios llamado Xolotl.

Con el tiempo y el uso diario, *coatl* se transformó en **cuate**. Hoy en día la palabra quiere decir **amigo** y **gemelo**. Pero los mexicanos la usan más que nada para referirse a un *buen* amigo.

## Actividad 4. Conversación: Las relaciones familiares

Diga a quién se parecen estas personas en su familia: usted, su hermano/a, su hijo/a, su esposo/a y su primo/a. Use **Me parezco a** y **Se parece a**.

MODELOS: Me parezco a mi abuela.

Mi hermano se parece a mi papá.

Ahora, diga con quién(es) en su familia (no) se llevan bien estas personas: usted, su padre, su hermano/a, su suegro/a y su cuñado/a. Use **(No) Me llevo bien** y **(No) Se lleva bien**.

MODELOS: Me llevo muy bien con mi padre.

Mi cuñada no se lleva bien con mi padre.

## Actividad 5. Entrevista: Mi familia y mis parientes

1. ¿Vives con tus padres o con otros parientes? ¿Cuántos años tiene tu padre? ¿Y tu madre? ¿Te llevas bien con ellos? ¿Están divorciados tus padres? ¿Tienes padrastro o madrastra? ¿Te llevas bien con él/ella?
2. ¿Te pareces más a tu padre o a tu madre? ¿Te pareces a otro pariente, por ejemplo, a un abuelo o a una tía?
3. ¿Están vivos o muertos tus abuelos? Si todavía están vivos, ¿cuántos años tienen?¿Dónde viven? ¿Los ves con frecuencia? Si están muertos, ¿cuánto tiempo hace que murieron?
4. ¿Cuántos hermanos tienes? ¿Tienes medios hermanos o medias hermanas? ¿Te pareces a ellos/as? ¿Tienes hermanastros o hermanastras? ¿Te llevas bien con ellos/as? ¿Qué cosas hacen ustedes juntos?
5. ¿Cuántos tíos tienes? ¿Dónde viven? ¿Tienes muchos primos o pocos? ¿Pasas mucho tiempo con ellos? ¿Celebras los días feriados con tus tíos y tus primos?
6. ¿Están casados tus hermanos? ¿Te llevas bien con tus cuñados? ¿Tienes sobrinos? ¿Cuántos años tienen? ¿Cómo se llaman?
7. ¿Estás casado/a? ¿Tienes hijos? ¿Cómo se llaman? ¿Cuántos años tienen?
8. ¿Están casados tus hijos? ¿Cómo es tu nuera/yerno? ¿Tienes nietos? ¿Cuántos años tienen? ¿Cómo se llaman?

NOTA CULTURAL

# Los hispanos hablan de su familia

**VOCABULARIO ÚTIL**

| | |
|---|---|
| cariño | *affection* |
| extraño | *I miss* |
| estrecha | *close* |
| recurro a | *I turn, go to* |
| se ocupa | *he takes care* |
| criarlos | *to raise them* |
| se apoyan | *support each other* |

Lea las siguientes descripciones que algunos hispanos dan de su familia. Usted va a notar que todas las familias a continuación tienen varias características en común. La más predominante es que son muy unidas.

Raúl

RAÚL SAUCEDO, estudiante mexicano de 19 años: «Mi familia es bastante grande: están mis padres, tres hermanas mayores que yo, sus esposos (dos están casadas), mis sobrinos y mis primos. Mi abuela María Eulalia también va incluida, ¡claro! (Pero ella no vive en la Ciudad de México, donde está casi toda la familia.) A veces, los domingos, nos vamos todos al Parque de Chapultepec a merendar. ¡Y cuánto nos divertimos! Ahora que vivo y estudio en Texas, los extraño mucho.»

Adriana

ADRIANA BOLINI, argentina de 35 años: «Mis padres son mis mejores amigos. Con ellos tengo una relación estrecha y sincera. Cuando estoy de viaje, los llamo por teléfono y les escribo mucho. Siempre recurro a ellos cuando necesito algún consejo.»

Rogelio

ROGELIO VARELA, estudiante puertorriqueño de 21 años: «En mi familia somos muy unidos. Cuando tengo problemas personales, prefiero hablar con mi padre, mi madre o con uno de mis hermanastros, antes que hablar con un amigo. ¿La razón?

Bueno, es que un amigo puede tratar de ayudarnos, pero nadie puede entendernos tan bien como un miembro de la familia. ¡Ésa es mi opinión!»

Susana

SUSANA YAMASAKI GONZÁLEZ, peruana de 33 años: «Tengo dos hijos: Armando de trece años y Andrés de nueve. Por el momento, los niños y yo vivimos con mis padres en Cuzco. Es que estoy divorciada, y mi ex esposo casi no se ocupa de sus hijos. La verdad, es mucho trabajo criarlos yo sola. ¡Son muy traviesos! Por suerte papá y mamá me ayudan con la crianza. Mis hijos viven en un hogar donde hay amor, donde todos nos llevamos bien. Armando y Andrés tienen los mejores abuelos del mundo.»

Rubén

RUBÉN HERNÁNDEZ ARENAS, cubano de 38 años: «Mi familia en los Estados Unidos es pequeña: mi esposa, mis padres y yo. Lamentablemente, estoy separado de varios miembros de mi familia. Vivo en Miami y tengo un hermano, dos sobrinos y varios primos que están en Cuba. De vez en cuando me comunico con ellos, pero quisiera tenerlos cerca, poder verlos. Extraño sobre todo a mis sobrinos Tatiana y Bladimir. Uno de mis sueños es reunir a toda la familia aquí algún día.»

Estas personas ofrecen una imagen realista y típica de la familia hispana. En el mundo hispano hay muchos tipos de familia; no siempre son tradicionales. Hay hogares donde el padre o la madre está ausente, o donde los abuelos crían a los nietos. Como en todas las sociedades modernas, también hay familias de padres solteros o divorciados. Pero sea cual sea el caso, la familia es una de las instituciones más fuertes y vitales de la sociedad hispana.

## Comprensión

**A.** ¿Quién habla aquí, probablemente: Rogelio (**RO**), Adriana (**A**), Raúl (**RA**), Susana (**S**) o Rubén (**RU**)?

1. _____ Mis padres son mis amigos.
2. _____ Nos gusta ir al parque los domingos.
3. _____ Tengo una familia muy unida.
4. _____ Cuando tengo un problema, hablo con mis padres.
5. _____ Extraño mucho a mis sobrinos.
6. _____ Me es difícil criar a los hijos yo sola.
7. _____ Les mando tarjetas postales y los llamo.
8. _____ Mi familia es grande.

**B.** ¿Cierto o falso? Si la oración es falsa, haga las correcciones necesarias para decir la verdad.

1. _____ La familia hispana es pequeña: normalmente la forman los padres y los hijos.
2. _____ La familia es muy importante en la sociedad hispana.
3. _____ Muchos hispanos prefieren hablar de sus problemas personales con un amigo / una amiga.
4. _____ A veces tíos y primos viven en la casa familiar.
5. _____ En el mundo hispano sólo existen familias tradicionales.

## Ahora... ¡usted!

1. ¿Quiénes forman parte de una familia norteamericana típica?
2. ¿Cómo son sus relaciones con sus padres? ¿con sus hermanos?

3. ¿Qué le gusta hacer a usted con su familia?
4. ¿Con quién(es) prefiere hablar de sus problemas? ¿Por qué?

### Un paso más... ¡a escribir!

Pregúnteles a cuatro o cinco compañeros de clase qué opina cada uno de su propia familia. Luego, escriba una composición titulada «Los estudiantes de español hablan de su familia». Use el mismo formato de la Nota cultural. ¡Y no se olvide de escribir una conclusión!

## LAS PALABRAS VIVEN

**Hablando de la familia:** La palabra **boda** se usa en todo el mundo hispano. Pero en México también se dice **casamiento** y **matrimonio**. Hay palabras de cariño para los abuelos: **tata** (abuelo) y **nana** (abuela), y los diminutivos **abuelito** y **abuelita**.

En Cuba, la palabra más usada para decir **gemelos** es **mellizos**. Y en el habla coloquial mexicana, los gemelos son **los cuates**. (Recuerde que en México un cuate es también un **buen amigo**.)

## EL MUNDO HISPANO... imágenes

Las relaciones entre los mayores y los jóvenes son íntimas y especiales. Conversan, intercambian ideas, salen a pasear. Los niños escuchan los consejos[1] de sus abuelos, y éstos disfrutan de[2] la juventud y las experiencias de sus nietos. Los abuelos a veces cuentan sus recuerdos,[3] así manteniendo viva la historia familiar.

En la foto, la abuela viste a su nietecita con un traje tradicional de la región.

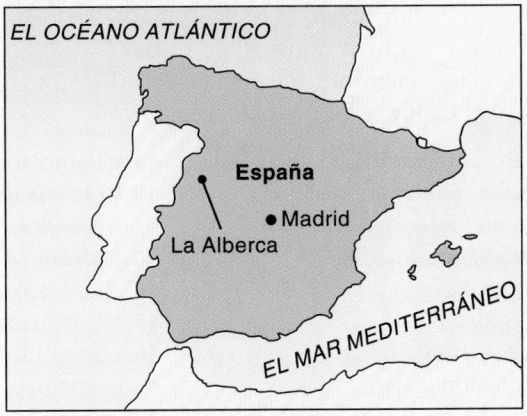


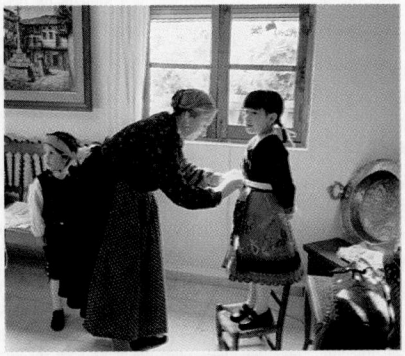

La Alberca, España

[1]*advice* [2]disfrutan... *enjoy* [3]*memories*

# La niñez

*Lea Gramática 9.2.*

Cuando Adela Martínez era niña, vivía en Guanajuato.

Mis amigas y yo jugábamos al escondite en el parque.

Leía las tiras cómicas los domingos.

Saltaba la cuerda.

Mis amigas y yo jugábamos con nuestras muñequitas en el jardín de la casa.

Mi abuela y yo preparábamos la cena.

Jugaba al bebeleche en el patio de recreo de la escuela.

## Actividad 6. Asociaciones: La niñez de algunas personas famosas

¿Qué hacían estas personas famosas en su niñez? ¿A cuál(es) de estas personas le(s) atribuye usted las actividades a continuación?

Elizabeth Taylor, actriz
Fidel Castro, primer ministro de Cuba
Marie Curie, científica francesa
Cristóbal Colón, explorador/navegante

1. Soñaba con cambiar la sociedad.
2. Pensaba mucho en la ciencia.
3. Vivía en Cuba.
4. Jugaba con muñecas.
5. Vivía en Francia.
6. Navegaba.
7. Hablaba francés.
8. Soñaba con viajar.
9. Trabajaba en el cine.
10. Leía mucho.
11. Estudiaba danza.
12. Quería descubrir «nuevos mundos».
13. Montaba a caballo.
14. Hablaba español.
15. Estudiaba los mapas.
16. Se miraba con frecuencia en el espejo.
17. Soñaba con descubrir una nueva ruta a la India.

## Actividad 7. Conversación: ¡Viva el verano!

Mire el dibujo y piense en su niñez.

¿Hacía usted las mismas cosas que los niños de los dibujos?
¿Iba al cine? ¿Con quién(es)?
¿Jugaba a la pelota? ¿Dónde?
¿Volaba un papalote? ¿Dónde?
¿Iba al zoológico? ¿Dónde? ¿Con quién(es)?
¿Paseaba en bicicleta? ¿Dónde, en el parque o en su barrio?
¿Tomaba helados? ¿Qué sabor prefería?
¿Qué otras cosas hacía durante el verano?

### ¡REÍR ES VIVIR!

**El regalo**

La señora le compró una bicicleta a su hijo, y el niño, contento, se fue a montarla.

Unos minutos después le gritó a su mamá, muy entusiasmado:

—Mira, mamá, ¡estoy montando con una mano!

La madre, preocupada, le dijo:

—¡Ten cuidado, mi niño!

El hijo no le hizo caso y exclamó:

—¡Mira, mamá, sin manos!

Al poco tiempo dijo:

—¡Con un pie!

Y una hora más tarde:

—Mira, mamá, ¡sin dientes!

## Actividad 8. Descripción de dibujos: La niñez de los amigos norteamericanos

Mire la tabla a continuación y escuche las oraciones que le lee su profesor(a). Diga si son ciertas o falsas.

Ahora, hágale preguntas a un compañero / una compañera según la tabla.

MODELO: E1: ¿Qué hacía Lan siempre de niña?
E2: *Sacaba buenas notas.*

Finalmente, hágale preguntas a su compañero/a sobre lo que él/ella hacía de niño/a.

MODELO: E1: De niño/a, ¿qué hacías después de las clases?
E2: *Jugaba con mis amiguitos.*

## LAS PALABRAS VIVEN

**VOCABULARIO ÚTIL**
andar en patineta *to skateboard*

Una de las actividades favoritas de los niños en todo el mundo es andar en patineta, que en España se dice **andar en monopatín**. A muchos niños también les gustan los juegos de video, que en México se llaman **las chispas**.

Panamá, Mar Caribe: villa de pescadores cerca de Isla Grande

**EN NUESTRO MUNDO INCREÍBLE...**

- el cerebro de un niño de siete años es casi tan grande como el de un adulto.
- los seres humanos pierden 144 huesos de la infancia a la vejez.
- se calcula que treinta y dos mil (32.000) personas en los Estados Unidos tienen más de cien años de edad.

## Actividad 9. Entrevista: La niñez

1. De niño/a, ¿vivías en una ciudad o en un pueblito?
2. ¿Qué te gustaba hacer? ¿Jugabas con muñequitas? ¿con carritos?
3. ¿Tenías perro o gato? ¿Cómo se llamaba?
4. ¿A qué escuela asistías? ¿Cómo era? ¿Recuerdas cómo se llamaba tu maestro favorito / maestra favorita? ¿Por qué era tu favorito/a?
5. ¿Qué te gustaba hacer en la escuela? ¿Qué no te gustaba hacer?
6. ¿Tenías muchos amiguitos? ¿A qué jugaban en el recreo? ¿al gato? ¿a la pelota? ¿al escondite? ¿a la rayuela (al bebeleche)?
7. ¿Qué hacías después de las clases todos los días? ¿Jugabas? ¿Estudiabas? ¿Con quién(es)?
8. ¿Hacías muchas cosas con tus padres? ¿Visitabas mucho a tus abuelos? ¿Te divertías mucho con tus hermanitos?
9. ¿Ibas al cine con frecuencia? ¿Qué películas te gustaba ver?
10. ¿Qué hacías durante el verano? ¿Salías de vacaciones? ¿Adónde? ¿Tomabas clases? ¿De qué?

# ¡Así piensan los niños!

A continuación tiene usted tres breves anécdotas de la revista española *Ser Padres*. En todas se narran experiencias humorísticas de la infancia. Léalas y... ¡recuerde el lado cómico de su niñez!

### ¡Qué diver!

María (3 años) y su amiga Patricia (5 años) estaban jugando en el jardín de nuestra casa. De pronto, María hizo una propuesta sugerente: «¿Por qué no jugamos a que tú te escondes detrás de ese árbol y yo te busco?»

(*Ana Isabel Fernández, Palma*)

**VOCABULARIO ÚTIL**

| | |
|---|---|
| diver | divertido |
| la propuesta | *proposal* |
| te escondes | *you hide* |

### Lógica infantil

Le dije a mi hija Conchita (4 años) que tenía que comer todo el arroz para hacerse grande como papá y mamá. La pequeña se quedó pensativa y después de un rato me dijo: «Mami, yo tengo que comer para hacerme grande como papá y como tú, ¿verdad?»

«¡Sí, mi niña!» exclamé, contenta de que por fin lo hubiese entendido. «Oye —prosiguió ella— ¿y vosotros para qué coméis?»

(*Conchita Palazón, Sardañola*)

**VOCABULARIO ÚTIL**

| | |
|---|---|
| hacerse grande | *become a big girl* |
| pensativa | *thoughtful* |
| un rato | *a while* |
| hubiese entendido | *she had understood* |
| prosiguió | *she continued* |

### Niña precavida

Mi hija Ana (3 años) bajó corriendo por una cuesta muy empinada. «¡Ten cuidado, que te vas a caer!» exclamé al verla correr tan alocada. «No te preocupes, mamá», respondió ella. «Voy agarrada a los tirantes!»

(*Lurdes Mejido, Badajoz*)

**VOCABULARIO ÚTIL**

| | |
|---|---|
| precavida | *cautious* |
| cuesta empinada | *steep hill* |
| ¡te vas a caer! | *you'll fall!* |
| agarrada | *hanging* |
| los tirantes | *suspenders* |

## Comprensión

1. ¿Por qué está preocupada la mamá de Ana? Según Ana, ¿por qué no necesita preocuparse su mamá?
2. ¿A qué jugaban María y Patricia?
3. Según la madre de Conchita, ¿para qué tienen que comer los niños todo lo que sus padres les sirven?
4. ¿Por qué pregunta Conchita para qué comen sus padres?
5. ¿Cuál de las tres anécdotas le parece más chistosa? ¿Por qué?

## Ahora... ¡usted!

1. ¿Recuerda algo chistoso que usted (o su hijo/a) dijo cuando tenía cuatro, cinco, seis o siete años? ¡Cuéntenoslo!
2. De niño/a, ¿a qué jugaba? ¿Con quién(es) jugaba?
3. De niño/a, ¿qué comía usted con gusto? ¿Qué no comía nunca?
4. ¿Qué hacía cuando su madre le servía algo que a usted no le gustaba? ¿Siempre servían postre en su casa?
5. ¿Comía usted en restaurantes con frecuencia? ¿Cuál era su restaurante favorito y qué pedía allí?

### Un paso más... ¡a escribir!

Usted y su compañero/a van a preparar una breve comedia en la que se presenta una experiencia cómica o interesante de la infancia. Escriban un guión y luego, ¡actúen su comedia en la clase!

# La juventud

***Lea Gramática 9.3–9.4.***

Doña Lola era una joven muy bonita.

Bailaba con su novio en las fiestas.

Estudiaba todas las noches.

En la escuela siempre sabía la lección.

Tenía muchos amigos y amigas. Iba al cine con ellos.

Conoció a su mejor amiga, Rosita, cuando las dos tenían 8 años.

Quería casarse a los 15 años, pero su papá no quiso darle permiso.

Torreón, México: La familia hispana, como lo demuestra esta familia, es generalmente grande y muy unida.

## Actividad 10. Intercambios: La juventud de los amigos hispanos

Hágale preguntas a su compañero/a sobre lo que hacían los amigos hispanos en su juventud.

MODELOS: E1: ¿Qué hacía *Ricardo después de las clases*?
E2: *Veía la televisión.*

E1: ¿Quién *iba de compras los fines de semana*?
E2: *Adriana.*

## Actividad 11. Intercambios: La escuela secundaria

Diga qué hacía usted en estas situaciones cuando era estudiante de la escuela secundaria.

1. Cuando no quería ir a la escuela,...
   a. decía: «Ay, estoy enfermo/a».
   b. iba al cine.
   c. decía: «Pero... hoy no hay clases».
   d. ¿ ?
2. Cuando mi madre no me permitía ver la televisión antes de hacer la tarea,...
   a. lloraba.
   b. hacía la tarea rápidamente.
   c. decía: «¡Pero hoy no tengo tarea!».
   d. ¿ ?

**3.** Cuando quería comprar ropa nueva y no tenía dinero,...
- **a.** le pedía dinero a mi padre (madre, abuelo,... ).
- **b.** ahorraba dinero.
- **c.** trabajaba.
- **d.** ¿ ?

**4.** Cuando quería salir con mis amigos y mi padre/madre no me daba permiso,...
- **a.** me escapaba cuando todos estaban dormidos.
- **b.** discutía con mi padre/madre.
- **c.** lloraba y gritaba.
- **d.** ¿ ?

**5.** Cuando tenía que entregarle la tarea al profesor / a la profesora y no la tenía,...
- **a.** la hacía rápidamente durante la clase.
- **b.** le decía: «Anoche no pude hacerla porque estaba enfermo/a».
- **c.** le preguntaba: «¿Teníamos tarea?».
- **d.** ¿ ?

## Y TÚ, ¿QUÉ DICES?

Yo también.
Yo no, yo...
¿De veras?
¡Qué pícaro/a!
¡No lo creo!
¡Qué mentiroso/a!
¡Qué buena idea!
¿Y nunca tuviste problemas?

MODELO: E1: Cuando mi madre no me permitía ver la televisión antes de hacer la tarea, hacía una parte y le decía: «¡Ya terminé!»
E2: ¡Qué pícaro!

## EL MUNDO HISPANO... su gente

**G**regorio Merino Díaz tiene 32 años y es chileno.

*Piense en su vida de hace cinco años. ¿Era muy diferente de su vida actual?*

Hace cinco años mi vida era algo distinta de la actual. De partida,[1] aún no estaba casado y trabajaba como profesor en dos colegios. Vivía con mi hermana mayor y su familia. Ya estaba de novio[2] pero recién empezaba a concebir[3] seriamente la posibilidad de matrimonio con mi esposa. De hecho,[4] en esa época no nos imaginábamos siquiera que tendríamos[5] una hijita tan linda como nuestra Francisquita, ni que un hijo pudiese[6] darnos tanta dicha.[7]

[1]De... *For starters* [2]estaba... *I had a serious relationship* [3]pensar en [4]De... *In fact* [5]*we would have* [6]*could* [7]alegría, felicidad

## Actividad 12. Entrevista: La escuela secundaria

1. ¿Cómo se llamaba tu escuela secundaria?
2. ¿Vivías lejos de la escuela o vivías cerca? ¿Cómo ibas a la escuela?
3. ¿Llegabas a la escuela a tiempo o llegabas tarde?
4. ¿Te quejabas de las tareas?
5. ¿Qué materia preferías? ¿Estudiabas mucho? ¿Sacabas buenas notas?
6. ¿Participabas en actividades deportivas? ¿En cuáles?
7. ¿Qué hacías después de las clases todos los días?
8. ¿Salías mucho con tus amigos? ¿Adónde iban?

## EL MUNDO HISPANO... en los Estados Unidos

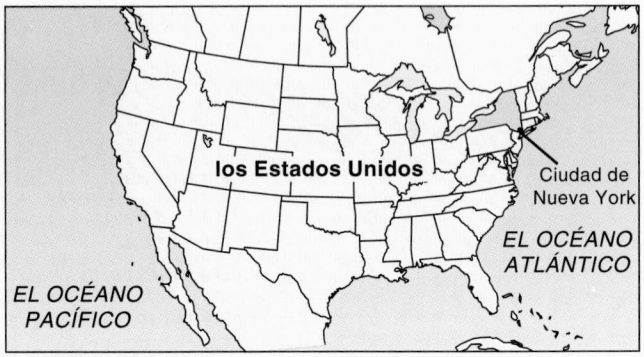


Ilia Rolón tiene 25 años y nació en Nueva York, donde vive ahora.

*Piense en los veranos de su infancia o de su juventud. ¿Cuáles eran sus actividades preferidas?*

Mi actividad preferida durante los veranos que pasaba en Puerto Rico era ir a la playa con mis primos. Recuerdo la ansiedad que sentía esperando que los adultos se alistaran para partir.[1] Al llegar, tiraba mis cosas a la arena sin mirar donde caían y corría hacia la orilla del mar para hundirme[2] bajo las olas. No me gustaba salir del agua para comer; sabía que los adultos me obligarían a[3] esperar una hora antes de entrar al agua otra vez, para prevenir calambres.[4] El agua era tibia y la arena caliente. En la noche, en mi cama, todavía podía sentir el ritmo de las olas correr por mi cuerpo.

[1]se...(*waiting for the adults*) *to get ready to go* [2]*submerge myself, plunge* [3]obligarían... *would make* [4]*cramps*

## Actividad 13. Entrevista: Los veranos

1. Cuando eras más joven, ¿dónde pasabas los veranos? ¿Viajabas solo/a o con tus padres o hermanos?
2. ¿Visitabas a tus parientes? ¿Qué hacías con ellos?
3. ¿Trabajabas? ¿Dónde? ¿Qué hacías? ¿Ganabas mucho dinero?
4. ¿Qué hacías por las tardes? ¿por las noches? ¿Practicabas algún deporte? ¿Cuál?
5. ¿Había cosas que querías hacer pero que tus padres no te permitían? ¿Recuerdas algunas? ¿Por qué no te permitían hacerlas? ¿Las hacías de todos modos?

# En resumen

## De todo un poco

Los recuerdos

¿Qué recuerdos tiene usted relacionados con su familia y con su niñez o juventud? Complete las siguientes oraciones.

MODELO: Recuerdo que para Pascua siempre *íbamos al parque a buscar huevitos.*

1. Recuerdo que en Navidad (Jánuca, Ramadán, el Año Nuevo,... ) mi abuela (madre, tío,... ) siempre...
2. Cuando era niño/a, para el Día de la Independencia (el 4 de julio) mi familia siempre...
3. Para mi cumpleaños, mis padres (tíos, primos, abuelos, hermanos,... ) siempre...
4. Todavía recuerdo que para el Día de Acción de Gracias...

Ahora, comparta sus recuerdos con un compañero / una compañera.

## ¡Dígalo por escrito!

La niñez

Piense en su niñez. ¿Qué hacía usted durante el verano cuando tenía seis, siete y ocho años? Descríbale su rutina típica a un compañero / una compañera y escuche cuando él/ella le describe sus propias actividades de los veranos de aquel entonces. En casa, escriba una composición de dos partes: una descripción detallada de sus propias actividades de verano y después una comparación de sus actividades con las de su compañero/a. ¿Eran semejantes o diferentes? ¿Por qué?

## VIDEOTECA

¿De dónde vienen sus antepasados? ¿Dónde se criaron sus abuelos? En este segmento de video los amigos de México, Diego, Lupe y Antonio, hablan de su familia. También hablan de cómo fue su niñez. Escuche bien y apunte algo sobre cada persona. Por ejemplo, ¿dónde vivieron? ¿Qué hacían de niños? Después, compare la niñez de los tres amigos con su propia niñez. ¿Fue muy diferente la suya? En el Capítulo 9 del *Cuaderno de trabajo* hay más actividades para hacer después de ver el video.

# Vocabulario

## La familia y los parientes
Family and Relatives

| | |
|---|---|
| **el cuñado / la cuñada** | brother-in-law/sister-in-law |
| **el hermanastro / la hermanastra** | stepbrother/stepsister |
| **el hijastro / la hijastra** | stepson/stepdaughter |
| **la madrastra** | stepmother |
| **el medio hermano / la media hermana** | half brother / half sister |
| **la nuera** | daughter-in-law |
| **el padrastro** | stepfather |
| **el sobrino / la sobrina** | nephew/niece |
| **los sobrinos** | nieces and nephews |
| **el suegro / la suegra** | father-in-law/mother-in-law |
| **los suegros** | in-laws |
| **el tío / la tía** | uncle/aunt |
| **el yerno** | son-in-law |

**REPASO: el abuelo (abuelito) / la abuela (abuelita), el hermano / la hermana, el hijo / la hija, la madre, el nieto / la nieta, el padre, los padres, el primo / la prima**

## Los verbos

| | |
|---|---|
| **ahorrar** | to save |
| **cambiar** | to change |
| **dar permiso** | to give permission |
| **descubrir** | to discover |
| **discutir** | to discuss; to argue |
| **entregar** | to hand in, turn in |
| **jugar (ue)** | to play |
| **a la rayuela (al bebeleche [*Mex.*])** | hopscotch |
| **al escondite** | hide-and-seek |
| **al gato** | tag |
| **con carritos, muñequitas** | with little cars, dolls |
| **llevarse bien** | to get along well |
| **parecerse** | to look like |
| **pelearse** | to fight |
| **permitir(se)** | to allow |
| **quejarse** | to complain |
| **recordar (ue)** | to remember |
| **sacar buenas/malas notas** | to get good/bad grades |
| **saltar la cuerda** | to jump rope |
| **subirse a los árboles** | to climb trees |
| **terminar** | to finish |
| **volar (ue) un papalote** (*Mex.*) | to fly a kite |

**PALABRAS SEMEJANTES: atribuir, escaparse, navegar**

## Los sustantivos

| | |
|---|---|
| **el barrio** | neighborhood |
| **la juventud** | youth |
| **la muñeca (muñequita)** | (little) doll |
| **la niñez** | childhood |
| **la pelota** | ball |
| **el pueblito** | little town |
| **el recreo** | recess, break |
| **el patio de recreo** | playground |
| **los recuerdos** | memories |
| **las relaciones familiares** | family relationships |
| **las tiras cómicas** | comic strips |

**PALABRAS SEMEJANTES: la ciencia, la danza, Europa, el explorador / la exploradora, el navegante, la pizzería, el/la primer ministro, la ruta, la sociedad, la terminal de autobuses**

## Los adjetivos

| | |
|---|---|
| **dormido/a** | asleep |
| **estar muerto/a (vivo/a)** | to be dead (alive) |
| **relacionado/a** | related |
| **sorprendido/a** | surprised |

## Palabras y expresiones útiles

| | |
|---|---|
| **¿Cómo era... ?** | What was/were . . . like? |
| **de niño/a** | as a child |
| **de todos modos** | anyway |
| **por ejemplo** | for example |
| **¡Qué mentiroso/a!** | What a liar! |
| **¡Qué pícaro/a!** | What a rascal! |
| **todavía** | still |

# Gramática y ejercicios

**¿RECUERDA?**

You have already studied some reflexive verbs (see **Gramática 4.4**) that are used to express daily routine: **levantarse, ducharse, despertarse, vestirse, afeitarse, maquillarse,** etc. Remember that reflexive verbs use a reflexive pronoun (**me**, **te**, **se**, **nos**, **os**, **se**) placed in front of the conjugated verb.

**me levanto** = *I get up*
**te bañas** = *you (inf. sing.) take a bath*
**se afeita** = *you (pol. sing.) shave; he/she shaves*
**nos vestimos** = *we get dressed*
**se acuestan** = *you (pl.)*/they *go to bed*

## 9.1 Describing Family Relationships: The Reciprocal Reflexive Verbs *parecerse* and *llevarse bien*

### Gramática ilustrada

Andrea y Paula son gemelas. Se parecen mucho (Son muy parecidas).

Susana se lleva muy bien con sus hijos.

Mónica y su padrastro no siempre se llevan bien.

Some reflexive verbs have a special meaning. One such verb is **parecerse*** (*to look like*).

**parecerse** = *to look like*
—**¿A quién te pareces?** (*Who do you look like?*)
—**Me parezco a mi hermana.** (*I look like my sister.*)

**parecerse** (***to look like***)

| | | |
|---|---|---|
| (yo) | me parezco† | *I look like* |
| (tú) | te pareces | *you (inf. sing.) look like* |
| (usted, él/ella) | se parece | *you (pol. sing.) look like; he/she looks like* |
| (nosotros/as) | nos parecemos | *we look like* |
| (vosotros/as) | os parecéis | *you (inf. pl., Spain) look like* |
| (ustedes, ellos/as) | se parecen | *you (pl.) look like; they look like* |

*Recognition: **vos te parecés**
†Don't forget to use the personal **a** with this verb. See **Gramática 6.5**.

| | |
|---|---|
| —¿**A** quién **te pareces**? | *—Who do you look like?* |
| —**Me parezco a** mi tía Lila. | *—I look like my aunt Lila.* |
| Nuestros hijos **se parecen a** mi suegro. | *Our children look like my father-in-law.* |

You may also use the adjective **parecido/a** with the verb **ser** to express resemblances.

| | |
|---|---|
| **Soy** muy **parecida** a mi madre. | *I look a lot like my mother.* |
| Guillermo y Raúl **no son** muy **parecidos**. | *Guillermo and Raul don't look very much alike.* |

**llevarse bien con** = *to get along well with*
—**¿Te llevas bien con tus hermanos?** (*Do you get along well with your siblings?*)
—**Sí, me llevo bien con todos en mi familia.** (*Yes, I get along well with everyone in my family.*)

Another reflexive verb with special meaning is **llevarse... con** (*to get along . . . with*).

| | |
|---|---|
| —¿**Con** quién **te llevas** mejor, con tu mamá o con tu papá? | *—With whom do you get along better, your mother or your father?* |
| —**Me llevo** mejor **con** mi papá. | *—I get along better with my father.* |

When used in plural form, some reflexive verbs can express reciprocal action (*to each other*). Both **parecerse** and **llevarse** can be used in this way.

Reflexive verbs are used to express reciprocal actions (*each other*).

**nos parecemos** = *we look alike* (*like each other*)
**se parecen** = *they look alike* (*like each other*)
**se llevan bien** = *they get along well* (*with each other*)

| | |
|---|---|
| Clarisa y Marisa no son gemelas, pero **se parecen** mucho. | *Clarisa and Marisa are not twins, but they look a lot alike.* |
| Mi abuela y yo **nos parecemos**. | *My grandmother and I look alike.* |
| Mi cuñada y yo **no nos llevamos** bien. | *My sister-in-law and I don't get along well.* |
| Graciela y Amanda **se llevan** muy bien; son muy buenas amigas. | *Graciela y Amanda get along very well; they are very good friends.* |

## Ejercicio 1

Use las formas apropiadas del verbo **parecerse** para completar las siguientes oraciones.

1. Ernestito _____ mucho a su padre.
2. Amanda y Guillermo son hermanos pero no _____.

   Amanda dice: «Yo _____ a papá; ¿a quién _____ tú, Guillermo?»
3. Andrea dice: «Yo _____ mucho a Paula, pero _____ menos a Raúl.»
4. Paula dice: «Sí, Andrea, tú y yo _____ mucho porque somos gemelas. Raúl _____ más a mamá.»

5. En mi familia, _____ y yo (no) _____ mucho.
6. Mi(s) hermano(s) _____ más a mi _____ que a mi _____.

## Ejercicio 2

Use las formas apropiadas del verbo **(no) llevarse** para terminar correctamente estas oraciones.

1. MÓNICA: Mis padres se divorciaron, pero ahora _____ bien.
2. SR. VO.: Lan, ¿_____ bien con tus compañeros de clase?
   LAN: Sí, papá. En la clase de la profesora Martínez todos _____ muy bien; somos buenos amigos.
3. MÓNICA: Mis hermanastros y yo _____ bien, pero yo no _____bien con mi padrastro.
4. NORA: Mis primos _____ muy bien; siempre les gusta estar juntos.
5. ESTEBAN: Raúl, ¿ahora _____ (tú) bien con las chicas?
   RAÚL: ¡Por supuesto, Esteban! Las chicas bonitas y yo _____ muy bien.

## 9.2 Saying What You Used to Do: The Imperfect Tense

The imperfect often means *used to* or *would*.
**De niña, nadaba todos los días en el verano.** (*As a child, I used to* [*would*] *swim every day in the summer.*)
**Cuando éramos jóvenes, íbamos al cine todos los sábados.** (*When we were young, we would go to the movies every Saturday.*)

**A.** The Spanish imperfect tense is used to describe actions that occurred repeatedly or habitually in the past. To express the same idea, English often uses the phrases *used to* or *would*, or just the simple past.

| | | | |
|---|---|---|---|
| ¿A qué hora **te levantabas** aquel verano? | *What time* | *did you* / *did you used to* / *would you* | *get up that summer?* |
| Siempre **me levantaba** a las 9:00. | *I always* | *got up* / *used to get up* / *would get up* | *at 9:00.* |

Imperfect endings: **-ar** verbs = **-aba**; **-er/-ir** verbs = **-ía**

**B.** There are two patterns of endings for the imperfect: for **-ar** verbs, the **-aba** endings; for **-er/-ir** verbs, the **-ía** endings.*

| | manejar | comer | vivir |
|---|---|---|---|
| (yo) | maneja**ba** | com**ía** | viv**ía** |
| (tú) | maneja**bas** | com**ías** | viv**ías** |
| (usted, él/ella) | maneja**ba** | com**ía** | viv**ía** |
| (nosotros/as) | maneja**bamos** | com**íamos** | viv**íamos** |
| (vosotros/as) | maneja**bais** | com**íais** | viv**íais** |
| (ustedes, ellos/as) | maneja**ban** | com**ían** | viv**ían** |

| | |
|---|---|
| Mis hermanos **comían** mucho cuando **visitábamos** a nuestros abuelos. | *My brothers used to eat a lot when we visited (would visit) our grandparents.* |
| —¿Qué **hacía** Raúl los domingos cuando **estaba** en la secundaria? | —*What did Raúl used to do on Sundays when he was in high school?* |
| —**Jugaba** al tenis con sus amigos. | —*He used to play tennis with his friends.* |

*Recognition: In the imperfect, the **vos** form is identical to the **tú** form: **manejabas**, **comías**, **vivías**, etc.

Only **ir**, **ser**, and **ver** are irregular in the imperfect.

**C.** Only three verbs are irregular in the imperfect.

| | ir | ser | ver |
|---|---|---|---|
| (yo) | iba | era | veía |
| (tú) | ibas | eras | veías |
| (usted, él/ella) | iba | era | veía |
| (nosotros/as) | íbamos | éramos | veíamos |
| (vosotros/as) | ibais | erais | veíais |
| (ustedes, ellos/as) | iban | eran | veían |

Te **veía** más cuando trabajabas en esta oficina.
*I used to see you more when you worked in this office.*

Cuando **era** muy joven, **íbamos** a la finca y mi padre me llevaba en su caballo.
*When I was very young, we used to go to the farm and my father would let me ride with him on his horse.*

## Ejercicio 3

¿Qué hacían estas personas de niños?

MODELO: jugar mucho al tenis / Paula → Paula *jugaba* mucho al tenis.

1. montar en bicicleta / Guillermo
2. jugar con muñecas / Amanda y yo
3. leer las tiras cómicas del periódico los domingos / Andrea
4. bañarse en el mar en Acapulco / doña Lola y doña Rosita
5. comer muchos dulces / don Eduardo
6. limpiar su recámara / Estela
7. pasar las vacaciones en Acapulco / la familia Ramírez
8. escuchar música rock / Pedro Ruiz
9. ver dibujos animados en la televisión / Ernesto
10. cuidar el jardín / el abuelo de Ernestito

## Ejercicio 4

Complete cada oración con la forma apropiada del imperfecto, y luego indique a qué dibujo corresponde.

MODELO: Ya no monta a caballo mucho, pero antes *montaba* a caballo todos los fines de semana.

**a.** _____ Ya no juegan a las cartas, pero antes _____ todas las tardes.
**b.** _____ Antes _____ a misa todos los domingos, pero ya no van mucho.
**c.** _____ De niña _____ la cuerda, pero ya nunca salta la cuerda.
**d.** _____ Ya no se pelea con sus hermanas, pero antes _____mucho con ellas.
**e.** _____ Ya no llora tanto cuando ve películas tristes, pero de adolescente _____ mucho.
**f.** _____ Cuando tenía ocho años, no _____ bien con las niñas.
**g.** _____ De niñas, _____ mucho.

## 9.3 Describing the Past: The Imperfect and Preterite of "State" Verbs

### Gramática ilustrada

Verbs of state do not express action—for example, *to want, to have.* When used in talking about the past, they are usually conjugated in the imperfect.

**A.** Some verbs express actions (*run, jump, eat*); others express states (*want, have, be, can*). In the narration of a past event, verbs describing states or ongoing conditions are usually conjugated in the imperfect tense.

| | |
|---|---|
| —Guillermo, ¿**sabías** la respuesta de la cuarta pregunta? | *—Guillermo, did you know the answer to the fourth question?* |
| —**Sabía** una parte pero no toda. | *—I knew part of it, but not all.* |
| —¿Qué **querías** hacer? | *—What did you want to do?* |
| —**Quería** ir al cine. | *—I wanted to go to the movies.* |
| —¿Por qué no **podías** ir? | *—Why couldn't you go?* |
| —Porque no **tenía** dinero. | *—Because I didn't have any money.* |

**B.** When Spanish speakers use state verbs in the preterite, they usually do so to convey that the state came to an end. English speakers often use completely different verbs to express that meaning. Compare the English equivalents of the following state verbs in the imperfect and in the preterite.

**(yo) sabía** = *I knew*
**(yo) supe** = *I found out*

**usted conocía** = *you (pol. sing.) knew*
**usted conoció** = *you (pol. sing.) met*

| IMPERFECT | | PRETERITE | |
|---|---|---|---|
| sabía | *I knew* | supe | *I found out* |
| no sabía | *I didn't know* | no supe | *I never knew* |
| conocía | *I was acquainted with* | conocí | *I met* |
| tenía | *I had* | tuve | *I had; I received* |
| quería | *I wanted* | quise | *I wanted (and tried)* |
| no quería | *I didn't want* | no quise | *I refused* |
| podía | *I was able; could* | pude | *I could (and did)* |
| no podía | *I wasn't able, couldn't* | no pude | *I (tried and) couldn't* |

| | |
|---|---|
| —¿**Supiste** lo que les pasó a Graciela y a Amanda? | *—Did you find out what happened to Graciela and Amanda?* |
| —No, no **supe** nada. ¿Qué les pasó? | *—No, I didn't find out (never heard) anything. What happened to them?* |
| —¿Por qué no **pudiste** terminar? | *—Why weren't you able to finish?* |
| —**No quise** terminar, porque me cansé mucho. | *—I didn't try to finish, because I got very tired.* |

When used to express *was/were*, **ser** and **estar** are usually in the imperfect.

**Estaba muy cansado.** (*I was very tired.*)
**Éramos amigas íntimas en la escuela secundaria.** (*We were very close friends in high school.*)

**C.** The verbs **ser** and **estar** are usually used in the imperfect; they are used in the preterite only when the state has explicitly come to an end within a specified amount of time.

| INFINITIVE | IMPERFECT | | PRETERITE | |
|---|---|---|---|---|
| ser | era | *I was* | fui | *I was* |
| estar | estaba | *I was* | estuve | *I was* |

Within a limited or specified time frame, **ser** and **estar** may be used in the preterite to express *was/were*.

**Estuvimos cinco días en Acapulco**. (*We were in Acapulco for 5 days.*)
**Mi hijo fue presidente del Club de Español por dos años**. (*My son was president of the Spanish Club for two years.*)

| | |
|---|---|
| —¿Cómo **eras** de niño? | —*What were you like as a child?* |
| —Yo **era** muy tímido. | —*I was very shy.* |
| —¿Cuánto tiempo **fuiste** presidente del club? | —*How long were you president of the club?* |
| —**Fui** presidente seis años. | —*I was president for six years.* |
| —¿Dónde **estaban** tus padres anoche? | —*Where were your parents last night?* |
| —**Estaban** con los abuelos. | —*They were with my grandparents.* |
| —¿Cuánto tiempo **estuvieron** en España? | —*How long were you in Spain?* |
| —**Estuvimos** allí de mayo a julio. | —*We were there from May to July.* |

## Ejercicio 5

Complete las oraciones según el modelo. Use el imperfecto de los verbos en letra cursiva.

MODELO: Ahora no *soy* tímido, pero de niño *era* muy tímido.

1. Ahora Guillermo *tiene* 12 años, pero cuando tú lo conociste _____ sólo 8 años.
2. Ahora *sé* muy bien las respuestas, pero esta mañana, cuando tomé el examen, no las _____.
3. Ahora *conocemos* muy bien a doña Rosita, pero hace un año no la _____.
4. Ahora Paula *es* agente de viajes, pero yo recuerdo cuando _____ secretaria.
5. Ahora Paula *está* aquí en México, pero hace una semana _____ en España.

## Ejercicio 6

Complete las siguientes oraciones con la forma apropiada del imperfecto de estos «verbos de estado»: **tener**, **querer**, **estar**, **ser**, **conocer**, **saber** y **poder**.

1. Luis _____ sólo 10 años cuando viajó a Colombia.
2. Einstein _____ un joven muy inteligente, pero sacaba malas notas.
3. Yo no _____ a tu hermano. ¡Qué guapo es!
4. (Nosotros) _____ comprar un carro nuevo pero no _____ dinero. Ahora, por fin tenemos suficiente dinero.
5. ¿Dónde _____ (tú) esta mañana?
6. Ayer almorcé a las 11:00 porque _____ mucha hambre.

Ahora, use la forma apropiada del pretérito de estos «verbos de estado»: **saber**, **tener**, **conocer**, **poder** y **querer**.

7. Ayer _____ que el hijo mayor de mi vecino es adoptado.
8. Hoy no fui a trabajar porque no dormí anoche. Toda la noche _____ un dolor de cabeza horrible.
9. ¡Qué simpático es el esposo de Andrea Ruiz! Lo _____ anoche en la fiesta.
10. Ah, sí, la fiesta de fin de año... Los Ruiz me invitaron pero yo no _____ ir. ¡A mí no me gustan las fiestas!
11. Ayer fui al parque con mis hijos; traté de patinar con ellos pero no _____. ¡Me estoy poniendo viejo!

**¿RECUERDA?**

Recall from **Gramática 1.1** that the present tense of **ir** + **a** + infinitive is used to express future actions.

Amanda, ¿**vas a llamar** a Ramón esta noche? (*Amanda, are you going to call Ramón tonight?*)

**va a** + infinitive = *he/she/you* (*pol. sing.*) *is/are going to*
**Paula va a comprar un coche**. (*Paula is going to buy a car.*)

**iba a** + infinitive = *I/he/she/you* (*pol. sing.*) *was/were going to*
**Iba a viajar por Europa pero tuve que trabajar**. (*I was going to travel through Europe but I had to work.*)

## 9.4 Saying What You Were Going to Do: The Imperfect of *ir* + *a* + Infinitive

The imperfect of **ir** (**iba, ibas, iba, íbamos, ibais, iban**) can be used in this construction to express past intentions (*was/were going to do something*).

| | |
|---|---|
| **Íbamos a esquiar** el jueves, pero ahora dicen que va a llover. | *We were going to ski on Thursday, but now they say it's going to rain.* |
| Rubén y Virginia **iban a pasar** el día en el parque, pero decidieron visitar las pirámides. | *Rubén and Virginia were going to spend the day at the park, but they decided to visit the pyramids.* |

The imperfect of **querer** and **pensar** + infinitive is similar in meaning.

| | |
|---|---|
| **Quería acampar** en las montañas este verano, pero resulta que tengo que trabajar. | *I wanted (was hoping) to go camping in the mountains this summer, but it turns out I have to work.* |
| Carmen **pensaba pasar** el verano en España, pero no ahorró suficiente dinero. | *Carmen was thinking about (was planning on) spending the summer in Spain, but she didn't save enough money.* |

### Ejercicio 7

Invente una excusa. Use **iba** + **a** + infinitivo, seguido de su excusa.

MODELO: —¿Por qué no me llamaste anoche?
—*Iba a llamarte*, pero llegué a casa muy tarde.

1. ¿Por qué no viniste en tu carro anoche?
2. ¿Por qué no trajiste flores?
3. ¿Por qué no me compraste un regalo?
4. ¿Por qué no cenaste con nosotros?
5. ¿Por qué no fuiste al «Baile de los Enamorados»?
6. ¿Por qué no me dijiste que no sabías bailar?
7. ¿Por qué no llegaste a tiempo?
8. ¿Por qué no asististe a clase ayer?

CAPÍTULO 10

# La geografía, el transporte y el medio ambiente

**METAS**

In **Capítulo 10** you will talk about places you have traveled to, including their geography and climate. You will also discuss transportation and automobile travel. Finally, you will learn about and discuss environmental issues and concerns.

Cuzco, Perú

**ACTIVIDADES DE COMUNICACIÓN Y LECTURAS**


La geografía y el clima

**Lectura** «Oda a la tormenta» (selección)

**El mundo hispano...** su gente

**El mundo hispano...** imágenes

**Lectura** Un terremoto en Chile

Los medios de transporte y el automóvil

**Lectura** Iberia, la aerolínea española

**Nota cultural** SEAT: La asistencia en la carretera

La ecología y el medio ambiente

**El mundo hispano...** en los Estados Unidos

**Lectura** La visión ideal de Costa Rica

**EN RESUMEN**


**GRAMÁTICA Y EJERCICIOS**


10.1 Saying What You Have Done: The Present Perfect

10.2 Exclaiming: **¡Qué... !, ¡Cuánto/a/os/as... !**

10.3 Expressing *by, through,* Destination, and Time: **por** and **para**

10.4 Describing Actions: Adverbs

10.5 Expressing Reactions: More Verbs like **gustar**

# Actividades de comunicación y lecturas

## La geografía y el clima

*Lea Gramática 10.1–10.2.*

¡Qué bosque tropical más húmedo!

¡Qué bonita es esta playa!

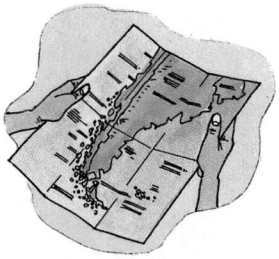

¡Cuántas islas hay en la costa de Chile!

## Actividad 1. Definiciones: La geografía

1. _____ la selva
2. _____ el río
3. _____ la montaña
4. _____ el lago
5. _____ la playa
6. _____ el desierto
7. _____ la península
8. _____ la isla
9. _____ el valle
10. _____ la bahía

a. porción de tierra rodeada completamente de agua
b. espacio entre dos montañas
c. parte de arena a la orilla del mar
d. lugar árido, a veces con mucha arena
e. porción de tierra rodeada de agua pero unida a tierra firme por un lado
f. entrada del mar en la costa, más pequeña que un golfo
g. extensión de agua rodeada de tierra
h. lugar donde llueve mucho y hay mucha vegetación
i. elevación considerable del terreno
j. corriente de agua que generalmente corre hacia el mar

## Actividad 2. Descripción de fotos: ¡Qué impresionantes son esas montañas!

Escuche la descripción que les da su profesor(a) y señale la foto correspondiente.

1. El nudo de Huascarán, Perú

2. Bariloche, Argentina

3. El Yunque, Puerto Rico

4. Cozumel, México

5. La Cordillera Vilcabamba en Perú

6. Salto del Laja, Chile

7. La playa en Cancún, México

8. San Felipe, México

9. Bariloche, Argentina

Ahora, con un compañero / una compañera, miren las demás fotos y expresen los pensamientos que se les ocurran.

**FRASES ÚTILES**

| | | |
|---|---|---|
| ¡Cuánto/a/os/as... ! | ¡Qué... ! | la vegetación |
| las olas | las estrellas | profundo/a |
| los peces coloridos | las cataratas | las flores |

## Actividad 3. Del mundo hispano: El pronóstico del tiempo

Conteste las preguntas según la información en este anuncio de un periódico de Tampico, México.

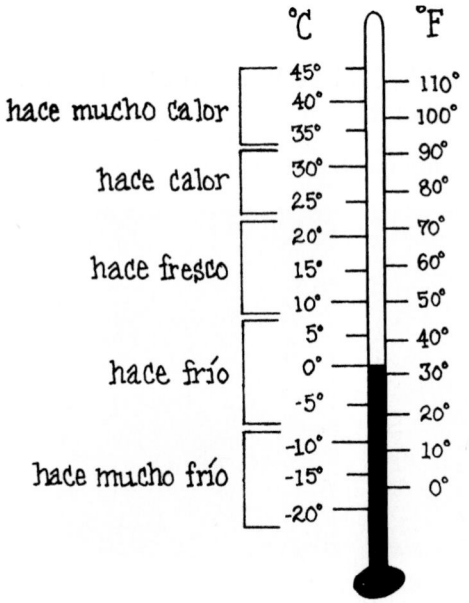


**La temperatura de la semana: Tampico**

LUNES. Se anticipa un día de calor con una temperatura máxima de 30° C (grados centígrados) y una mínima de 18° C.

MARTES. Neblina por la costa en la mañana, pero se anticipa un día de mucho calor. La temperatura máxima va a llegar a 35° C. En la noche la temperatura va a bajar a 20° C.

MIÉRCOLES. Se pronostica un día fresco, parcialmente nublado. La temperatura máxima durante el día será de 22° C y la mínima esta noche será de 14° C.

JUEVES. Un día soleado pero va a hacer más frío que ayer. Temperatura máxima de 19° C, mínima de 15° C.

1. ¿Qué día va a ser el más caluroso?
2. ¿Cuál va a ser la noche más fría?
3. ¿Va a llover esta semana?
4. ¿Qué día va a estar nublado?
5. ¿Va a haber neblina? ¿Dónde? ¿Qué día?
6. ¿Ha visto usted el pronóstico de hoy para la ciudad donde vive? ¿Qué se pronostica?

## Actividad 4. Descripción de dibujos: El tiempo

Use estas palabras para completar las oraciones a continuación: **escarcha, fresco, humedad, llovizna, neblina, nubes, rocío, tormenta, truenos** y **viento.**

1. Después de los relámpagos, casi siempre vienen los _____.
2. Si por la noche baja la temperatura puede aparecer _____ en las ventanas y en los techos.
3. Antes de una _____, las _____ cubren el sol.
4. Una lluvia ligera también se llama _____.
5. Cuando hace mucho _____, la gente pierde el sombrero.
6. En las zonas tropicales hay mucha _____.
7. Hay que manejar lentamente cuando hay mucha _____.
8. Cuando la temperatura está a 18° C, hace _____.
9. Las gotas de agua que aparecen en las plantas por la mañana son _____.

# «Oda a la tormenta» de Pablo Neruda (selección)

Usted ya tiene algunos datos importantes sobre este gran poeta chileno. Aquí incluimos otra selección de un poema suyo, de su libro *Odas elementales*. En este poema el poeta personifica la tormenta, es decir, le da las características de una persona. Dice, por ejemplo, que la tormenta tiene ojos y pelo (**cabellera**), que duerme y...

Anoche
vino
ella,
rabiosa,[1]
azul, color de noche,
roja, color de vino,
la tempestad[2]
trajo
su cabellera de agua,
ojos de frío fuego,
anoche quiso
dormir sobre la tierra.

Llegó pronto...
quería dormir
y preparó su cama,
barrió selvas, caminos,
barrió montes,[3]
lavó piedras de océano,
y entonces
como si fueran plumas[4]
removió los pinares[5]
para hacerse su cama.
Sacó relámpagos
de su saco de fuego,

[1]furiosa [2]tormenta [3]*woodlands* [4]como... *as if they were feathers* [5]*pine trees*

dejó caer truenos
como grandes barriles.[6]
De pronto
fue silencio:
una hoja
iba sola en el aire,
como un violín volante,[7]
entonces,
antes
de que llegara al suelo,[8]
tempestad, en tus manos
la tomaste...
y cuando ya creíamos
que terminaba el mundo,
entonces,
lluvia,
lluvia,
sólo
lluvia...

«Sacó relámpagos / de su saco de fuego, / dejó caer truenos... »

[6]*barrels* [7]*flying* [8]antes... *before it hit the ground*

## Comprensión

Busque en el poema...

1. dos de los colores de la tormenta.
2. cinco de las acciones que personifican la tormenta (por ejemplo, «barrió»).

## Ahora... ¡usted!

1. ¿Cree que la tormenta del poema causó mucho daño? ¿Por qué sí o por qué no? ¿Qué destruyó, probablemente?
2. ¿Ha estado usted en una tormenta fuerte alguna vez? ¿Qué pasó? ¿Qué hizo usted?
3. ¿Hay tormentas con frecuencia donde usted vive? ¿En qué estación o estaciones del año tienden a ocurrir? ¿Cómo son?

### Un paso más... ¡a escribir!

Imagínese que usted es poeta y que quiere escribir una oda para el «Concurso Pablo Neruda». Escoja un objeto de su vida diaria: puede ser una cosa que se come, un mueble, una prenda de ropa, ¡cualquier cosa! Ahora describa el objeto. ¿De qué color es? ¿Qué forma tiene? ¿Es grande o pequeño? ¿largo o corto? Personifique el objeto e imagínese un día típico en la vida de ese objeto. ¿Qué hizo? ¿Dónde estuvo? ¿Qué pasó?

## Actividad 5. Del mundo hispano: Los recursos naturales

Lea el siguiente artículo y luego trabaje con un compañero / una compañera para decir si las afirmaciones de las páginas 321–322 son ciertas o falsas. Corrijan las afirmaciones falsas con información del artículo.

# EXPEDICIONES al Mar de Cortés

**Catalogado como uno de los ecosistemas más ricos del mundo por su abundante flora y fauna, el Mar de Cortés es todo un reto para buzos profesionales y aficionados.**

Por su gran concentración y diversidad de animales y aves marinas, los especialistas afirman que el Mar de Cortés y las lagunas de Baja California —a donde llega a aparearse la ballena gris después de recorrer 10,000 kilómetros— son la versión mexicana de las islas Galápagos. En este lugar se conocen bien muchos sitios de buceo por la belleza de sus cañones y montañas submarinas; las islas rocosas y áridas contrastan con la colorida variedad de plantas y animales debajo de la superficie: nudibranquios, estrellas marinas, esponjas, anémonas y moluscos en abundancia, peces multicolores, delfines, leones marinos...

Quienes desean sumergirse en estas aguas y descubrir su extraordinaria vida marina, lo pueden hacer de junio a noviembre en expediciones organizadas que parten desde la amistosa ciudad de La Paz. Los paquetes incluyen tres inmersiones al día con tanques y pesas, experimentados maestros de buceo y tripulación, duchas de agua fresca, fácil acceso a la rampa de buceo, cubierta con área de sombra, un cocinero a bordo que prepara desayunos, comidas, refrigerios y bebidas, sistema de video VHS, hotel, transporte al aeropuerto.

## Salidas de junio a noviembre

| Precio de los paquetes: | Cabañas Los Arcos | Hotel Los Arcos |
|---|---|---|
| 3 noches, 2 días de buceo | $299 | $325 |
| 4 noches, 3 días de buceo | $399 | $460 |
| 5 noches, 4 días de buceo | $499 | $595 |
| 6 noches, 5 días de buceo | $599 | $730 |
| 7 noches, 6 días de buceo | $699 | $865 |

Todos los precios son por persona con base en ocupación doble, en dólares. Reservaciones a Expediciones Baja California al teléfono 1-800-483-7696.

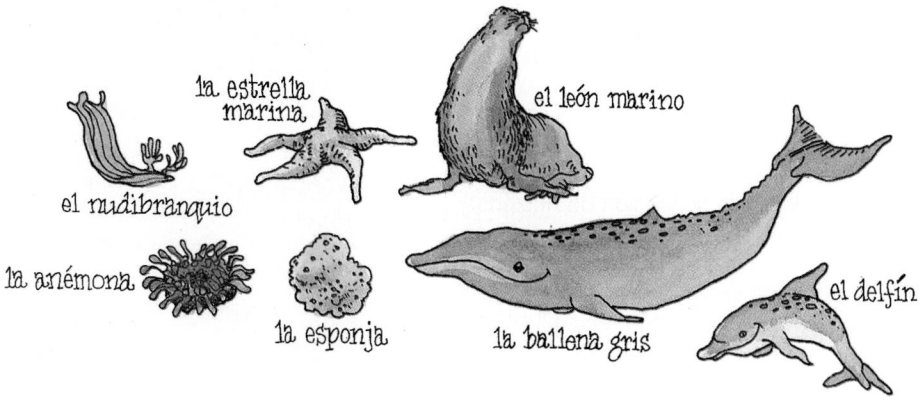


1. El Mar de Cortés se compara con las islas de Hawai.
2. Tanto en las Islas Galápagos como en el Mar de Cortés hay gran concentración y diversidad de animales y aves marinos.
3. En las lagunas de Baja California se pueden observar ballenas grises.

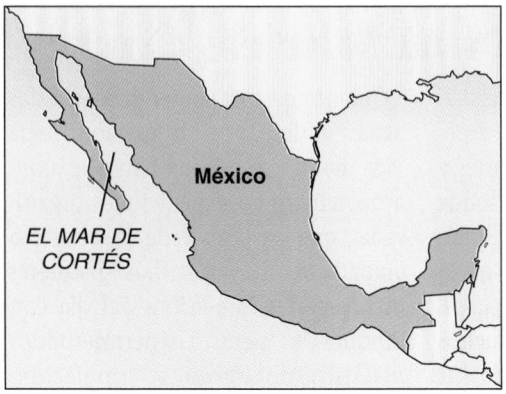


4. En este lugar hay abundancia de sitios de buceo muy bellos.
5. En el Mar de Cortés hay islas verdes y húmedas y arrecifes coloridos de muchos animales y plantas marinos.
6. Los paquetes turísticos incluyen tanques y pesas, lecciones de buceo, hotel y transporte aéreo.
7. Hay paquetes durante las cuatro estaciones del año: la primavera, el verano, el otoño y el invierno.

Ahora, hágale preguntas a su compañero/a acerca de los precios de los varios paquetes turísticos.

MODELO: E1: ¿Cuánto cuesta el paquete de 6 noches con 5 días de buceo en Cabañas Los Arcos?
E2: Cuesta *$599.00.*

## EL MUNDO HISPANO... su gente

Claudia Hernández Alarcón tiene 35 años y es española.

*¿Cómo es el clima en la ciudad donde usted vive? ¿Ha cambiado el clima últimamente? ¿De qué manera?*

En la ciudad donde vivo, que es Madrid, decimos «tres meses de invierno y nueve de infierno»[1], pero llevamos varios años que todas las estaciones son menos crudas. Apenas[2] nieva y el verano no es tan fuerte. Ya no caen esas heladas[3] que hasta los cristales de las ventanas se nos llenaban de hielo por dentro de las casas. El verano no es tan riguroso; sólo hace calor fuerte veinte días.

A mí la estación del año que más me ha gustado en mi ciudad ha sido el otoño, por el color de miel de los árboles. Los atardeceres[4] daban la sensación de dulzones[5] y más si llovía por las tardes. Pero ya los otoños no son como antes, pues se han perdido muchos bulevares con los árboles tan preciosos que tenían; en su lugar han hecho grandes avenidas para los coches.

[1]*hell* [2]*Barely* [3]*frosts* [4]*late afternoons* [5]*soft, mellow*

Parque del Retiro, Madrid: El otoño es hermoso «por el color de miel de los árboles... »

## Actividad 6. Entrevistas: Los viajes, las actividades y el tiempo

¿ADÓNDE HAS VIAJADO?

1. ¿Has pasado algún tiempo en las montañas? ¿Dónde? ¿Qué hiciste allí? ¿Te gustó? ¿Por qué?
2. ¿Vives cerca del mar? Si no, ¿cuál es el mar más cercano a donde vives? ¿Cuántas veces has ido al mar / a la playa durante los últimos seis meses? ¿Cómo estaba el agua? ¿muy fría?
3. ¿Conoces algún lago o río cerca de donde vives? ¿Cómo se llama? ¿Qué puedes hacer allí? ¿Vas con frecuencia? ¿Por qué? Explica.
4. ¿Has ido alguna vez al desierto? ¿Dónde? ¿Cuándo? ¿Qué hiciste allí?
5. ¿Has visto una selva? ¿Dónde? ¿Te gustó? ¿Por qué? Explica.

LAS ACTIVIDADES Y EL TIEMPO

1. ¿Qué te gusta hacer cuando hace calor (frío, viento, mal tiempo)?
2. ¿Qué haces cuando llueve (nieva, hace buen tiempo, hay relámpagos y truenos)?
3. ¿Has vivido en un lugar muy húmedo? ¿en un lugar muy seco? ¿Dónde? ¿Te gustó? ¿Por qué?
4. ¿Has estado alguna vez en un huracán? ¿Qué pasó? ¿Has visto un tornado alguna vez? ¿Dónde? ¿Causó daño?
5. ¿Has manejado alguna vez por la carretera en la neblina? ¿Tenías miedo? ¿Has pasado por una tormenta en avión? ¿Dónde? ¿Tuviste mucho miedo?

## EL MUNDO HISPANO... imágenes

El lago de Nicaragua está al sur del país, cerca de la frontera con Costa Rica. En Nicaragua, como en otros países del Caribe, la Navidad se asocia con la estación seca. En los países al sur de la línea ecuatorial, como Argentina, la Navidad también es una época de calor y clima veraniego.

En algunos países, como en Guatemala, hay solamente dos estaciones: la estación de las lluvias y la estación seca. En la Ciudad de Guatemala, por ejemplo, normalmente no llueve entre noviembre y abril. Por su altura —aproximadamente 1.500 metros—, hace fresco por las noches y sol durante el día. En los meses de lluvia, de mayo a octubre, puede hacer buen tiempo por la mañana y llover por una o dos horas por la tarde. Muchos llaman a Guatemala «la tierra de la eterna primavera».

El lago de Nicaragua

Tikal, Guatemala

# Un terremoto en Chile

Ésta es una noticia del periódico chileno *La Estrella*. Trata de un terremoto que no tuvo consecuencias trágicas, pero que sí asustó a muchas personas.

**VOCABULARIO ÚTIL**

| | |
|---|---|
| el sismo | *earthquake* |
| alcanzó | *attained, reached* |
| telúrico | de la tierra |
| las posteriores réplicas | *aftershocks* |
| los heridos | *wounded people* |
| las grietas | *cracks* |
| los desmoronamientos | *crumbling, breaks* |
| las desgracias | *misfortunes* |
| los derrumbes | *landslides* |

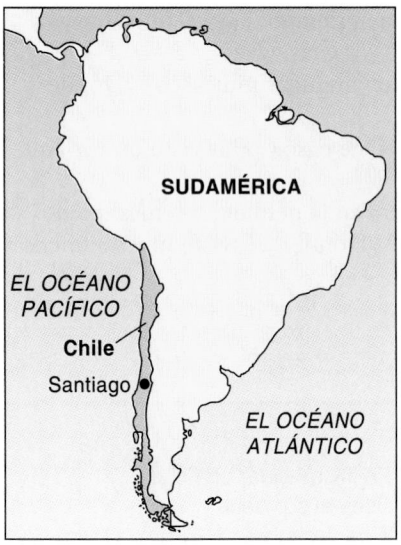


## SISMO PROVOCÓ PÁNICO EN LA TERCERA REGIÓN

COPIAPÓ, CHILE. Escenas de pánico y confusión se vivieron esta mañana en Copiapó como consecuencia de un sismo que alcanzó 6 grados en la escala de Richter. Según se informó en la Dirección Regional de Emergencia de la provincia, el temblor se registró a las 5 de la mañana con 12 minutos. En Vallenar tuvo una intensidad de 5 a 6 grados, y en Chañaral de 3 a 4.

El movimiento telúrico estuvo acompañado de fuertes ruidos subterráneos, que causaron pánico entre la población. Muchas personas abandonaron sus hogares esperando posteriores réplicas que no se produjeron. No se registraron heridos ni viviendas destruidas, aunque algunas casas antiguas resultaron con grietas o pequeños desmoronamientos.

En Vallenar, hasta este mediodía, no se tenía conocimiento de desgracias personales ni derrumbes. Tampoco había informaciones en tal sentido desde pueblos del interior. «La situación es totalmente normal», se informó.

Vecinos agregaron que «más que el movimiento, fue el gran ruido el que asustó a la gente; ¡parecía una avalancha!»

## Comprensión

Imagínese que usted es el gobernador / la gobernadora de Copiapó y que ahora tiene que mandar un informe sobre el terremoto al presidente de Chile.

1. Lugar exacto y hora del terremoto: _____
2. Grados en la escala de Richter: _____
3. ¿Hubo víctimas? _____
4. ¿Destruyó residencias? _____
5. ¿Destruyó edificios comerciales? _____
6. Describa la situación en este momento: _____

## Ahora... ¡usted!

1. Si usted ha tenido la experiencia de estar en un terremoto, descríbala. ¿Sabe cuántos puntos marcó en la escala de Richter? ¿Qué daños causó?
2. En 1985 la Ciudad de México sufrió un terremoto devastador. En 1989, en el norte de California hubo también un terremoto que causó mucho daño. Uno de los más catastróficos fue el de 1994 en Kobe, Japón. ¿Tiene usted información sobre estas catástrofes? ¿Dónde estaba y qué estaba haciendo cuando ocurrieron? ¿Estuvo presente en alguna? ¿Estuvo presente algún miembro de su familia o algún amigo?
3. ¿Cuáles son los efectos de estas catástrofes? ¿Cuál es su impacto en la comunidad donde ocurren? ¿y su impacto en el mundo?

### Un paso más... ¡a escribir!

**A.** Mencione las ciudades, los estados o las regiones de su país que se ven afectados por los siguientes fenómenos.

| FENÓMENOS | CIUDADES O ESTADOS |
|---|---|
| terremotos | _____ |
| huracanes | _____ |
| tornados | _____ |
| lluvias fuertes | _____ |
| sequías | _____ |
| nevadas | _____ |
| inundaciones | _____ |

**B.** Escriba un breve ensayo considerando las siguientes preguntas.

1. ¿Qué fenómenos naturales afectan el área donde usted vive? ¿Cómo se prepara usted para protegerse?
2. ¿Qué pasó la última vez que un fenómeno natural se manifestó donde usted vive? Narre el incidente.

# Los medios de transporte y el automóvil

*Lea Gramática 10.3–10.4.*

Se puede viajar cómodamente por avión.

Salimos ahora para España.

Los trenes en Suiza salen y llegan puntualmente.

Hicimos una gira en bicicleta por dos semanas.

Hoy salimos. Tenemos que estar en Madrid para el lunes.

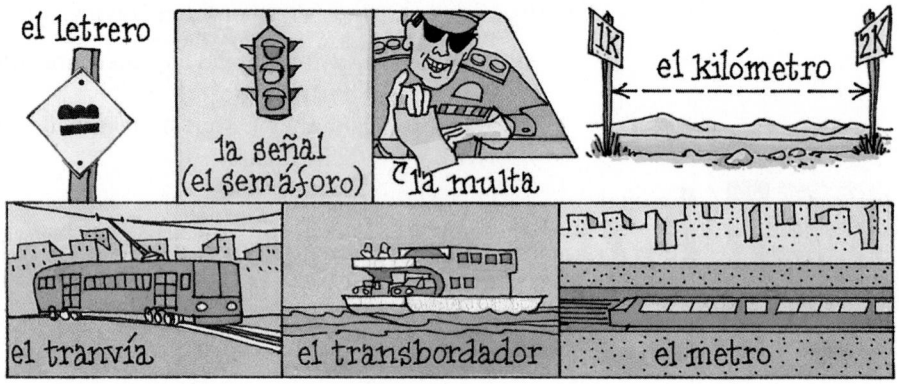

¡Qué auto más hermoso!

¡Cuánto tránsito hay hoy en la autopista!

## Actividad 7. Definiciones: El transporte

LOS MEDIOS DE TRANSPORTE

1. _____ el avión
2. _____ el tren
3. _____ el barco
4. _____ la bicicleta
5. _____ el automóvil
6. _____ el autobús

a. vehículo aéreo
b. medio de transporte personal y familiar que permite mayor independencia
c. vehículo de dos ruedas que no usa gasolina
d. vehículo de ocho ruedas que puede transportar de 30 a 80 personas
e. medio de transporte que flota en el agua
f. medio de transporte que tiene vagones y una locomotora

LAS PARTES DEL CARRO

1. _____ los frenos
2. _____ los limpiaparabrisas
3. _____ el volante
4. _____ la bocina
5. _____ la placa
6. _____ el parabrisas
7. _____ el radiador

a. Protege a los pasajeros del viento.
b. Guarda agua para enfriar el motor.
c. Se usan cuando llueve.
d. Se usan para parar el coche.
e. Se usa para manejar el coche.
f. Tiene los números para identificar el coche.
g. Se toca para llamar la atención de los peatones y otros choferes.

# Iberia, la aerolínea española

Aquí tiene un anuncio de la principal aerolínea de España. Si usted no ha viajado nunca en Iberia, ¡se la recomendamos!

**VOCABULARIO ÚTIL**

| | |
|---|---|
| cabina ancha | *wide-body aircraft* |
| sin escala | *nonstop* |
| acogedora | *welcoming* |

## Comprensión

¿Son ciertas o falsas estas afirmaciones? Si son falsas, diga por qué.

1. La cabina del avión 747 es estrecha.
2. Los vuelos a Madrid salen todos los días a las 6:10 de la tarde.
3. El 747 es ruidoso pero muy rápido.
4. Usted no puede llevar equipaje de mano a bordo.
5. A bordo del avión usted disfruta del servicio y la hospitalidad tradicionales de esta compañía.
6. La clase económica es lujosa.

## Ahora... ¡usted!

1. ¿Ha viajado usted por avión? ¿Adónde fue? ¿Le gusta usar este medio de transporte? ¿Por qué?
2. Si no ha viajado en avión, ¿le gustaría hacerlo? ¿Adónde le gustaría ir? ¿Por qué?

### Un paso más... ¡a escribir!

Describa su primer viaje en avión. ¿Cómo fue esa experiencia? ¿Adónde fue? ¿Le gustó? ¿Qué sintió? (Si no ha viajado nunca en avión, ¡imagínese la experiencia!)

## Actividad 8. Asociaciones: Cómo mantener su auto en buenas condiciones

¿Con qué frecuencia se debe hacer estas actividades relacionadas con el carro?

MODELO: Se debe *lavar el carro cada semana.*

| ACTIVIDADES DE MANTENIMIENTO | FRECUENCIA |
|---|---|
| 1. revisar la presión de las llantas | a. todos los días |
| 2. revisar el aceite | b. cada semana |
| 3. agregarle líquido al recipiente de agua para el limpiaparabrisas | c. cada mes |
| 4. revisar el acumulador | d. cada tres meses |
| 5. ponerle gasolina al tanque | e. cada seis meses |
| 6. pasar la aspiradora en el interior | f. una vez al año |
| 7. encerar el auto | g. de vez en cuando |
| 8. ¿ ? | h. ¿ ? |

NOTA CULTURAL

**VOCABULARIO ÚTIL**

| | |
|---|---|
| los talleres-rodantes | *auto repair shops on wheels* |
| veraniegas | de verano |
| cualquier | *any* |
| la mano de obra | *labor* |
| sobre ruedas | *smoothly; lit. on wheels* |

# SEAT: La asistencia en la carretera

En este anuncio se describe un servicio para las personas que viajan en coche por España.

**Si piensa hacer un viaje—**

corto o largo— no necesita preocuparse por su coche. Uno de los 250 talleres-rodantes de **SEAT** puede resolverle cualquier problema. Circulan diariamente, y sobre todo durante las vacaciones veraniegas, domingos y días festivos. Los talleres-rodantes pasan por todas las carreteras de España y reparan cualquier coche. Usted no necesita tener un **SEAT** para obtener nuestro servicio. La mano de obra es gratis…

**¡Así sus vacaciones van sobre ruedas!**

## Comprensión

Forme oraciones lógicas con las frases de ambas columnas.

1. En el servicio de SEAT no se incluye...
2. Se usa el taller-rodante cuando...
3. En todas las carreteras de España...
4. Los talleres-rodantes de SEAT reparan...
5. Hay talleres-rodantes todos los días...

a. y especialmente durante los días festivos.
b. el coche se descompone en el camino.
c. el costo de las piezas.
d. también coches de otras marcas.
e. se encuentran los talleres-rodantes de SEAT.

## Ahora... ¡usted!

1. ¿Tiene carro propio? ¿Qué hace cuando se le descompone? ¿Lo lleva a un taller de reparaciones o lo repara usted mismo/a?

2. ¿Considera que este servicio de talleres-rodantes es una buena idea? ¿Hay un servicio similar en la ciudad donde usted vive? ¿Lo ha usado? Describa el incidente. ¿Cuánto cuesta?
3. Cuando usted viaja a otras ciudades, ¿normalmente alquila un carro? ¿Por qué?

### Un paso más... ¡a escribir!

¿Ha tenido usted problemas con su coche en la carretera? ¿Qué pasó? ¿Qué hizo? ¿Lo reparó usted mismo/a? ¿Llamó a un club de automovilistas? ¡Narre su experiencia! (Si no ha tenido una experiencia personal, invente un cuento humorístico o serio sobre algún incidente en la carretera.)

## Actividad 9. Del mundo hispano: Coches pequeños

Lea este anuncio y hágale preguntas a un compañero / una compañera.

MODELO: E1: ¿Cuántas marchas tiene *el Renault 5C*?
E2: Tiene *cuatro.*

**Coches pequeños (1)**
*Hasta 1.200.000 pesetas*

| Marca y modelo | Cilindrada (c.c.) | Potencia (CV) | Velocidad máxima (km/h) | Tracción | Núm. de marchas | Combustible | Precio |
|---|---|---|---|---|---|---|---|
| Renault 4 | 1.108 | 38 | 120 | D | 4 | N | 725.215 |
| Seat Marbella L | 903 | 40 | 117 | D | 4 | N | 819.724 |
| Ford Fiesta 1.1 | 1.117 | 50 | 146 | D | 5 | S | 857.500 |
| Renault 5C | 1.108 | 38 | 135 | D | 4 | S | 909.292 |
| Opel Corsa 1.0 | 993 | 45 | 142 | D | 4 | S | 919.334 |
| Seat Ibiza Street | 903 | 44 | 132 | D | 4 | N | 936.995 |
| Volkswagen Polo Bunny | 1.043 | 40 | 143 | D | 4 | N | 960.044 |
| Fiat Uno 45S Fire | 999 | 45 | 146 | D | 4 | S | 997.500 |
| Peugeot 205 XL | 1.118 | 55 | 144 | D | 4 | S | 1.039.999 |
| Seat Ibiza 1.2 Junior | 1.193 | 63 | 154 | D | 5 | N | 1.064.715 |
| Opel Corsa Swing 1.2 | 1.196 | 55 | 153 | D | 5 | S | 1.066.984 |
| Citroën AX 14 TRS | 1.360 | 65 | 156 | D | 5 | S | 1.087.374 |
| Austin Metro 1.3 LE | 1.275 | 63 | 155 | D | 4 | S | 1.091.000 |
| Renault 5 GTL | 1.397 | 60 | 156 | D | 4 | S | 1.108.218 |
| Ford Fiesta Ghia 1.4 | 1.392 | 75 | 166 | D | 5 | S | 1.116.900 |
| Opel Corsa Swing D | 1.448 | 50 | 149 | D | 5 | G | 1.192.546 |

*N = gasolina normal; S = súper; G = gasóleo. El precio comprende IVA y transporte; ha entrado en vigor en febrero de este año y el fabricante puede haberlo modificado.*

### PREGUNTAS ÚTILES

¿Cuántas marchas (Cuántos cambios) tiene el... ?
¿Qué clase de combustible usa el... ?
¿Cuál es la velocidad máxima de un... ?
¿Cuánto cuesta un... ?

## LAS PALABRAS VIVEN

En España, **el estacionamiento** es **el aparcamiento**; en algunos países del Caribe es **el parking**. Los puertorriqueños **parquean el carro**, pero en España uno **aparca el coche**. **El carro,** a propósito, es también **el auto** y **el automóvil**.

Hay otras dos palabras para **manejar**: en España, **conducir**, y en muchas partes de América Latina, **guiar**. Una calle con mucho **tráfico** es también una calle con mucha **circulación** o **tránsito**. Y **el semáforo** puede ser **la señal de tráfico** o, entre los hispanos de los Estados Unidos, **la luz**.

Muchas personas en México viajan en **camión**, es decir, en **autobús**. El autobús es **el bus** en América Central, **la guagua** en Cuba y Puerto Rico y **el colectivo** en Argentina. Otra palabra que se usa en algunas partes es **el ómnibus**.

### AYUDA EN CARRETERA

**Ojalá que no ocurra, pero hay que estar prevenidos. En caso de avería o cualquier otro percance es útil ser socio de algún club automovilístico o asociación de ayuda al automovilista como la AMA, o ANA, que, por una cuota mensual ofrecen distintos servicios en carretera. También conviene llevar la lista de los talleres oficiales de la marca del auto que se conduzca.**

### Actividad 10. Descripción de dibujos: Los letreros de la carretera

Diga cuál es la frase u oración que corresponde a cada número.

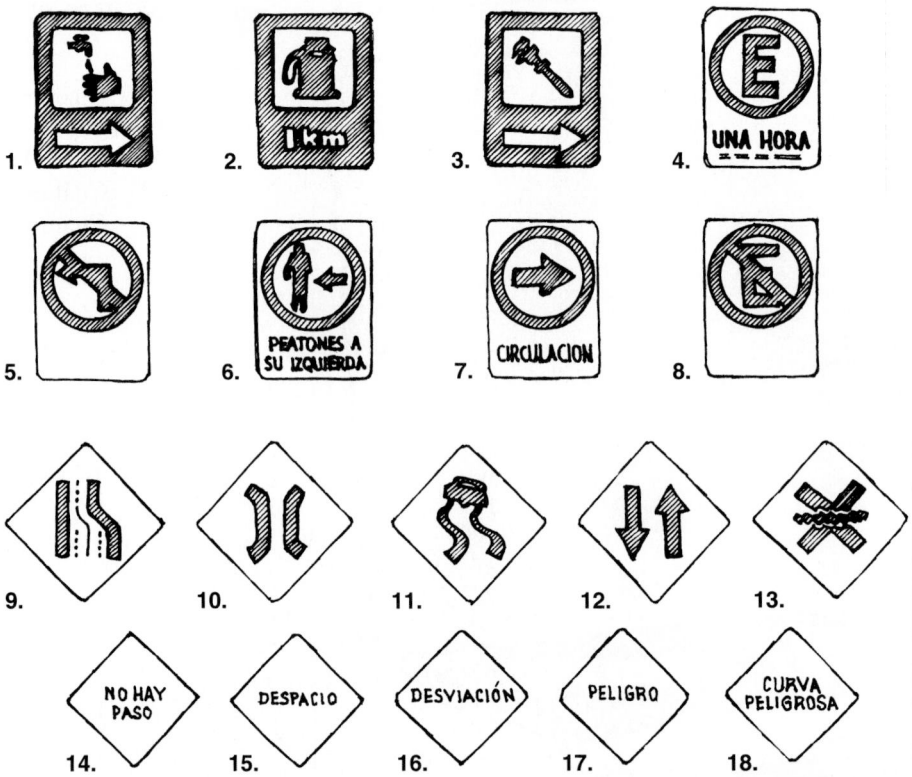


**a.** puente angosto
**b.** No doble a la izquierda.
**c.** tránsito de un solo sentido (una vía)
**d.** baños
**e.** ¡Cuidado! Puede haber personas a su izquierda.
**f.** gasolinera
**g.** mecánico
**h.** estacionamiento de una hora

**¡REÍR ES VIVIR!**

**Volando**

Un automóvil corre muy rápido por la calle. Después de seguirlo, por fin los policías lo detienen.
—¿Manejo muy rápido? pregunta el conductor.
Y uno de los policías le responde:
—No, usted vuela demasiado bajo.

**i.** tránsito de doble sentido (vía)
**j.** No se estacione.
**k.** tren
**l.** camino angosto
**m.** superficie resbalosa
**n.** prohibido el tránsito
**o.** Disminuya la velocidad porque hay una curva.
**p.** Tiene que ir por otro camino.
**q.** Disminuya la velocidad.
**r.** Tenga mucho cuidado.

## Actividad 11. Entrevistas: El transporte y los coches

EL TRANSPORTE

1. ¿Usas mucho el autobús? ¿Por qué? ¿Montas mucho en bicicleta? ¿Montabas mucho en bicicleta de niño/a? ¿Cuál es tu forma de transporte preferida?
2. De niño/a, ¿viajabas mucho en auto con tu familia? ¿Adónde iban? ¿Te gustaba hacer viajes con tu familia?
3. ¿Has viajado por tren? ¿Adónde fuiste? ¿Te gusta viajar por tren? ¿Por qué? ¿Has viajado por avión? ¿Adónde has ido? ¿Te gusta viajar por avión? ¿Crees que es peligroso viajar por avión? Explica.
4. ¿Has montado alguna vez en motocicleta? ¿Te gustó? ¿Llevas casco cuando montas en moto? ¿Crees que es peligroso montar en moto? ¿Por qué?
5. ¿Has viajado en barco? ¿Adónde fuiste? ¿Te gustó el viaje? ¿Era grande o pequeño el barco? ¿Te mareas cuando viajas por barco?

TÚ Y TU COCHE

1. ¿Tienes tu propio coche? ¿De qué marca es? ¿Cómo es tu coche? ¿Es práctico? ¿grande? ¿elegante?
2. ¿Tienes seguro? ¿De qué compañía? ¿Es muy caro? ¿Te gusta manejar? ¿Cuántas millas manejas cada día, aproximadamente?
3. ¿Has tenido un accidente en tu coche? ¿Cuánto (tiempo) hace? ¿Fue serio o sin importancia?
4. ¿Has salido de vacaciones en tu coche? ¿Cuánto (tiempo) hace? ¿Adónde fuiste? ¿Con quién fuiste? ¿Cuántas horas tuviste que manejar? ¿Te gustó?
5. ¿Le has dado «un aventón» a una persona que no conocías? ¿Tuviste miedo? ¿Por qué lo hiciste?

Monumento a la Independencia, avenida Paseo de la Reforma, Ciudad de México. En toda ciudad grande del mundo hispano, el transporte público es barato y accesible; gran parte de la población prefiere usarlo en vez de manejar. Y, claro, hay gente que simplemente camina. Muchos hispanos completan un viaje en autobús o metro con una caminata de varias cuadras para llegar a casa o al trabajo.

# La ecología y el medio ambiente

*Lea Gramática 10.5.*

A los científicos les interesa resolver el problema de la destrucción de las selvas tropicales.

A todos nos preocupa mucho el agujero en la capa de ozono.

A Esteban y a Raúl les llama mucho la atención el número de especies que están en peligro de extinción.

## Actividad 12. Asociaciones: El medio ambiente —Problemas y soluciones

¿Le preocupan los siguientes problemas ecológicos? Diga qué podemos hacer para resolverlos.

MODELO: Me preocupa *la sequía*. Creo que no debemos *desperdiciar el agua*.

PROBLEMAS ECOLÓGICOS

1. el consumo excesivo de petróleo
2. la destrucción de las selvas tropicales
3. el uso excesivo de productos plásticos
4. la destrucción del hábitat de algunas especies de animales y plantas
5. la contaminación de los ríos y los océanos
6. el agujero en la capa de ozono
7. los desperdicios de las plantas nucleares
8. la contaminación del aire en las grandes ciudades
9. la sequía; la escasez de agua
10. ¿ ?

SOLUCIONES

a. usar pesticidas no tóxicos
b. imponerles fuertes restricciones a las industrias
c. usar menos energía
d. fomentar la agricultura orgánica
e. restringir el uso de los autos
f. criar animales en los zoológicos
g. controlar la natalidad
h. crear nuevas reservas naturales
i. desarrollar otros medios de transporte
j. reducir drásticamente o eliminar la producción de carburos fluorados
k. comprar productos en envases de vidrio y participar en programas de reciclaje
l. no desperdiciar el agua
m. ¿ ?

## EL MUNDO HISPANO... en los Estados Unidos

Lety Guerrero Romero tiene 29 años y es de México, D.F. Vive ahora en Wilmington, California.

*¿Le preocupan a usted los problemas del medio ambiente y la ecología? ¿Qué hace usted para mejorar su medio ambiente?*

Este tema nos debe preocupar a todos. Debemos tomar conciencia[1] de que la Tierra es el único planeta azul que conocemos, donde sabemos que existe la vida. Pero, parece que cada día lo lastimamos[2] más. Hay que ser realistas y darnos cuenta de que cada día avanzamos con paso agigantado para destruir a la madre Naturaleza. De ella nos alimentamos y por eso vivimos. No es justo que le paguemos tan mal.[3]

Debemos colaborar cada uno de nosotros —por muy pequeña que sea la ayuda—[4] para tratar de no perjudicar[5] más este planeta. Por ejemplo, cuando vamos al parque, recoger todos los desperdicios que originamos. No desperdiciar dejando abiertas las llaves del agua, reciclar la basura. Eso a nivel del hogar. Los industriales deben de tener muchas más reglas estrictas dentro de cada área o departamento.

Nuestro pequeño planeta azul es fuerte. Pero llegará[6] un día en que ya no nos soporte más. ¡Hay que ayudarlo!

[1]tomar... *become aware* [2]lo... *we hurt it* [3]No... *It's not fair to repay it so badly.* [4]por... *no matter how small the help* [5]*damage* [6]*will arrive*

**EN NUESTRO MUNDO INCREÍBLE,...**

- ocurren dos mil setecientos temblores cada día.
- en Venezuela, hay que pasar un examen psicológico para sacar la licencia de manejar.
- las estrellas de mar no tienen cerebro.
- el pulpo tiene tres corazones.
- hay un caballo muy pequeño —¡el más pequeño del mundo!— que pesa ocho libras y mide doce pulgadas. Este caballito nació en el estado de Virginia, Estados Unidos.
- el animal que tiene la vida más larga es la tortuga gigante; ¡vive más de 150 años!
- el 98 por ciento de todos los animales y plantas que han habitado la tierra se ha extinguido.
- El dinosaurio más grande que se ha descubierto hasta el momento es el Argentinosaurio. Lo descubrió el científico Rodolfo Coria en 1995, en Patagonia. El Argentinosaurio habitó el continente sudamericano hace 100 millones de años. Este enorme dinosaurio pesaba 100 toneladas y era vegetariano.

## Actividad 13. Del mundo hispano: El «abecedario ecológico»

Lea este artículo sobre la Amazonia con su compañero/a. Luego, unan las frases para tener una lista de las ideas principales del artículo.

### ABECEDARIO ECOLÓGICO

**Amazonia:** Es una zona selvática que llega al sur de Colombia y Venezuela, a una parte del oriente peruano y a toda la zona norte de Brasil. Su área total es de 7 millones de kilómetros cuadrados, tiene 200 millones de hectáreas de flora y alberga[1] a 30 millones de especies animales. Su temperatura promedio es de 27 grados centígrados, llueve durante todo el año y está conformada[2] por densas selvas y grandes ríos, lo que le da un potencial maderero[3] e hidroéléctrico inmenso.

A pesar de esto, la flora tropical crece en terrenos relativamente infértiles, pues el 70%[4] del suelo[5] amazónico es muy pobre. La escasa cantidad de nutrientes que circula en el ecosistema se mantiene dentro de las plantas vivas. A esto se suma que el consumo maderero ha crecido 15 veces desde 1950 y para los próximos 25 años se espera una marcha de extinción animal próxima a las 100 especies por día.

Otro elemento de explotación que no ha sido controlado es el de las plantas: muchos medicamentos tienen origen en el trópico y, sin ciertas especies de la Amazonia, la industria farmacéutica no existiría. A propósito, el científico[6] brasileño Carlos Nobre asegura que «si existiera alguna cura para el cáncer, ésta se encontraría en algún lugar del Amazonas».

[1] *gives shelter to* [2] está... *is made up of* [3] potencial... *potential for lumber* [4] setenta por ciento [5] *soil* [6] *scientist*

1. La Amazonia cubre una área inmensa y...
2. La temperatura promedio es de 27° centígrados y...
3. La Amazonia tiene densas selvas y grandes ríos que...
4. El suelo de esta región es muy pobre;...
5. Dentro de los próximos veinticinco años, se espera la extinción de...
6. Según un científico brasileño, si existe una cura para el cáncer...

a. los pocos nutrientes se mantienen en las plantas vivas.
b. aproximadamente cien especies por día.
c. está entre las plantas de la Amazonia.
d. tiene 30 millones de especies de animales.
e. ofrecen mucho potencial para producir madera y energía hidroeléctrica.
f. llueve durante todo el año.

Selva amazónica en Perú

# La visión ideal de Costa Rica

**VOCABULARIO ÚTIL**

| | |
|---|---|
| rechazan | *they reject* |
| la repoblación forestal | *reforesting* |
| el Movimiento Ambiental | *Environmental Movement* |
| lanzaron | *they launched* |
| subvencionadas | *subsidized* |

En esta Lectura se discute el tema de la desaparición de los bosques. Se menciona en específico la situación de Costa Rica, un país muy rico en territorio forestal. Usted también va a descubrir aquí por qué es tan especial este país centroamericano.

Costa Rica* es un país único no sólo en el mundo hispano, sino en el mundo entero. Varios aspectos de la sociedad costarricense contribuyen a formar esta imagen especial. De partida, el país no tiene ejército, pues los ciudadanos rechazan la idea de la guerra. Pero eso no es todo. Los costarricenses también están muy conscientes de la importancia de la naturaleza. El gobierno tiene reglas estrictas con respecto al desarrollo y la construcción de viviendas y hoteles en zonas selváticas. El 40 por ciento del territorio del país está poblado de bosques. Y hay en Costa Rica uno de los sistemas más extensos de parques nacionales en todo el mundo hispano. El nombre del país es verdaderamente apropiado, pues la *costa* que da al océano Atlántico es muy *rica* en selvas tropicales.†

Playa Manuel Antonio, Costa Rica

*La población de Costa Rica es de tres millones de habitantes. El país tiene una industria estable de turismo, y exporta café, plátanos, carne, azúcar y cacao. El clima es de dos estaciones: la seca, de diciembre a abril; y la húmeda, de mayo a noviembre.

†En realidad, *Costa Rica* no se refiere a la riqueza forestal del país. Cuando los exploradores españoles llegaron a la región en el siglo XVI, le dieron el nombre porque pensaban que iban a encontrar grandes cantidades de oro allí.

Costa Rica: Parque Nacional Braulio Carillo

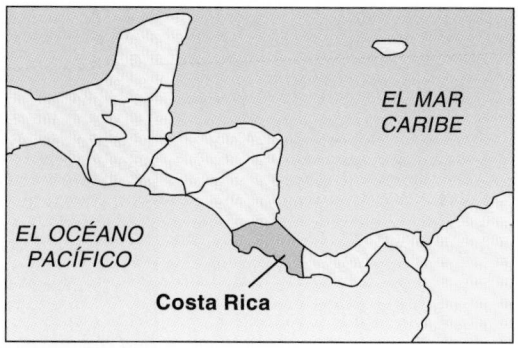

A todos los niveles de la sociedad, se nota el deseo de los costarricenses de conservar sus recursos naturales: sus especies de animales, sus bosques y selvas. De hecho, el reciente movimiento de «ecoturismo» — que propone, entre otras ideas, un tipo de turismo que no dañe el medio ambiente— comenzó en Costa Rica.

A pesar de esta visión ideal, Costa Rica ha tenido que hacer algunos sacrificios debido a presiones económicas. Hace apenas diez años, el país estaba exportando mucha madera. Como no había un plan oficial de repoblación forestal, los bosques de árboles para madera empezaron a desaparecer. Entre 1981 y 1990 Costa Rica perdió un 2 por ciento de todos sus bosques.

Por suerte, miembros del Movimiento Ambiental lanzaron una campaña para convencer al gobierno costarricense de la necesidad de sembrar árboles, y la campaña tuvo resultados muy positivos. Ahora hay varias iniciativas de repoblación forestal en Costa Rica, algunas subvencionadas por el gobierno.*

Los proyectos de repoblación forestal sufren diariamente una serie de obstáculos, no siempre económicos sino también provocados por fenómenos naturales. En 1996, por ejemplo, hubo una sequía que duró desde diciembre del año anterior hasta marzo. Inevitablemente, esta tremenda sequía afectó la siembra y el crecimiento de los árboles en regiones forestales. Pero lo importante es que los costarricenses han seguido tratando de conservar su flora y fauna. ¡Y siguen plantando árboles!

Hay pocos países como Costa Rica, con una conciencia nacional del medio ambiente, donde la gente toma en serio las cuestiones ambientales. En nuestro planeta —devastado por las guerras y por la destrucción de la naturaleza— Costa Rica representa una feliz excepción. Su visión de la Tierra es ideal.

---

*Una de las más activas es la Iniciativa de Bosques Tropicales (*Tropical Forestry Initiative, TFI*). Esta iniciativa, formada por ocho personas, tiene como propósito repoblar las selvas tropicales de Costa Rica, plantando especies de árboles indígenas a cada región.

## Comprensión

Complete las siguientes oraciones con frases de la columna a la derecha.

1. En la década de los ochenta,...
2. El Movimiento Ambiental le hizo ver al gobierno...
3. Costa Rica es un país pacífico, pues...
4. El gobierno costarricense no permite...

a. no cree en la guerra y no tiene ejército.
b. la construcción de muchos hoteles en zonas selváticas.
c. la importancia de plantar más árboles.
d. Costa Rica perdió una gran cantidad de bosques.

## Ahora... ¡usted!

1. ¿Ha estado usted en Costa Rica? Si no ha estado, ¿le gustaría visitar ese país?
2. ¿Le gustaría vivir en un país donde no haya ejército? ¿Por qué sí o por qué no? ¿Cuáles son las ventajas y desventajas de tener una fuerza militar?
3. ¿Le preocupa la cuestión de la repoblación forestal? ¿Por qué sí o por qué no? ¿Qué ideas o planes propone usted para evitar la destrucción de los bosques?

### Un paso más... ¡a escribir!

Imagínese que, por un momento fantástico, un árbol en el bosque puede hablar. ¿Qué va a decir con respecto a su vida, su medio ambiente y sus vecinos? ¿Qué va a decir sobre los seres humanos? Escriba una composición titulada «El mensaje del árbol».

# En resumen

## De todo un poco

**A.** La geografía y el clima de América Latina

Trabaje con varios compañeros para poner los nombres de los siguientes mares y océanos, las cordilleras y los ríos más importantes de América Latina en el mapa a continuación.

1. el Río Bravo
2. cuatro cordilleras:
   a. Sierra Madre Occidental
   b. Sierra Madre Oriental
   c. Sierra Madre del Sur
   d. cordillera de los Andes
3. el canal de Panamá
4. el lago Titicaca
5. el río Orinoco
6. el río Amazonas
7. el río Paraná
8. las cataratas del Iguasú
9. el océano Atlántico
10. el océano Pacífico
11. el Mar Caribe
12. el golfo de California
13. el golfo de México

Ahora, contesten estas preguntas.

1. ¿Cuál es la estación, y qué tiempo hace en México (parte del hemisferio norte) en enero? ¿Y en julio y agosto?
2. ¿Qué tiempo hace en los países de América Central (Costa Rica y Nicaragua, por ejemplo) en marzo? ¿Y en septiembre y octubre?
3. ¿Cuál es la estación, y qué tiempo hace en Argentina (parte del hemisferio sur) en enero? ¿Y en julio y agosto?
4. ¿Qué más saben ustedes del clima de América Latina? ¿Dónde lo aprendieron?

Finalmente, si algunos de ustedes han viajado por los países de habla hispana (América Latina y España), preparen un pequeño informe para sus compañeros. Incluyan la siguiente información.

en qué medio de transporte viajaron
qué países han visitado y en qué estación
qué tiempo hizo durante su viaje
cuánto (tiempo) hace que viajaron allí
qué ríos, montañas, etcétera, vieron
si vieron algo que les fascinó
si vieron algo del medio ambiente que les preocupó
dos o tres fotos de su viaje

**B.** ¡Salvemos el medio ambiente!

1. Hagan una lista de medidas que cualquier ciudadano puede tomar para reducir la cantidad de basura que produce diariamente. Compartan sus ideas con la clase.

MODELO: Uno puede llevar sus propias bolsas de lona al supermercado.

2. Digan lo que ustedes ya han hecho para proteger el medio ambiente, para reducir la cantidad de desperdicios que generan en su casa.

MODELO: Hemos usado ambos lados de las hojas de papel. Hemos reciclado el papel y el vidrio.

## ¡Dígalo por escrito!

El medio ambiente y usted

Traiga a la clase una foto o un dibujo de un problema climático o ambiental que a usted le preocupe. Explíqueles el problema a sus compañeros de clase. ¿Dónde ocurre? ¿Cuáles son las causas principales? ¿Cuáles son las consecuencias? ¿Qué se puede hacer para mitigar o resolver el problema? Después, en casa, escriba una breve composición sobre el tema, incluyendo algunos de los comentarios que sus compañeros hicieron cuando les describió el problema en clase.

## VIDEOTECA

El medio ambiente es un tema que nos preocupa a todos. En este episodio del video, Elisa Velasco, la periodista de Ecuador, escribe un artículo sobre el medio ambiente. Escuche bien mientras ella escribe. ¿Cuáles son las cosas que le molestan a Elisa? Según su artículo, ¿qué ha hecho el grupo estudiantil? Ha hecho usted algo para proteger el medio ambiente? ¿Qué ha hecho? También observe bien el sitio donde está Elisa y apunte tres cosas notables de su clima y geografía. En el Capítulo 10 del *Cuaderno de trabajo* hay más actividades para hacer después de ver el video.

# Vocabulario

## La geografía

| | |
|---|---|
| **el arrecife** | reef |
| **la bahía** | bay |
| **el bosque** | forest |
| **la catarata** | waterfall |
| **la colina** | hill |
| **la cordillera** | (mountain) range |
| **la corriente** | current (of water) |
| **la isla** | island |
| **el llano** | plain |
| **la orilla** | shore; (river)bank |
| **la selva (tropical)** | (tropical) jungle |
| **el terreno** | ground, terrain |
| **la tierra (firme)** | land |

**PALABRAS SEMEJANTES: la agricultura, la América Latina, el cañón, la costa, el desierto, la elevación, la extensión, el golfo, el océano, la península, la región, la laguna, el valle, la vegetación**

## El clima Weather

| | |
|---|---|
| **caluroso** | warm, hot |
| **el cielo** | sky |
| **la escarcha** | frost |
| **la humedad** | humidity |
| **la llovizna** | drizzle |
| **la lluvia** | rain |
| **la neblina** | fog |
| **la nube** | cloud |
| **(parcialmente) nublado** | (partially) cloudy |
| **pronosticar** | to forecast (*weather*) |
| **se pronostica...** | . . . is forecast |
| **el relámpago** | lightning |
| **el rocío** | dew |
| **soleado** | sunny |
| **la tormenta** | storm |
| **el trueno** | thunder |

**PALABRAS SEMEJANTES: el centígrado, el ciclón, húmedo, el huracán, el tornado**

**REPASO: el grado, llover (ue), la temperatura**

## Los medios de transporte
Means of Transportation

| | |
|---|---|
| **el camión** | truck |
| **el crucero** | cruise ship |
| **la lancha** | (small) boat |
| **el pasajero / la pasajera** | passenger |
| **el tránsito** | traffic |
| **el transbordador** | ferry |
| **el tranvía** | cable car; streetcar |
| **el vagón** | car (of a train) |

**PALABRAS SEMEJANTES: la locomotora, el taxi, transportar, el vehículo**

**REPASO: barco**

## El automóvil

| | |
|---|---|
| **abrocharse el cinturón de seguridad** | to fasten one's seat belt |
| **el acumulador** | battery |
| **el arranque** | ignition |
| **la autopista** | freeway |
| **los cambios** | gears |
| **el camino** | road |
| **el capó** | hood |
| **la carretera** | highway |
| **el espejo retrovisor** | rearview mirror |
| **los frenos** | brakes |
| **gastar combustible** | to use (burn) fuel |
| **el guardafangos** | fender |
| **el limpiaparabrisas** | windshield wiper |
| **la llanta (desinflada)** | (flat) tire |
| **el maletero** | trunk |
| **el parabrisas** | windshield |
| **el parachoques** | bumper |
| **el peatón / la peatona** | pedestrian |
| **la placa** | license plate |
| **la presión** | pressure |
| **el puente** | bridge |
| **la rueda** | wheel |
| **el seguro (de automóvil)** | (automobile) insurance |
| **el semáforo** | traffic light |
| **tocar la bocina** | to honk the horn |
| **el volante** | steering wheel |

**PALABRAS SEMEJANTES: el aire acondicionado, la antena, el autobús, la circulación, la gasolina, la licencia de manejar, el motor, el radiador, el tanque, la transmisión**

## Los letreros en la carretera
Road Signs

| | |
|---|---|
| **despacio** | slow |
| **desviación** | detour |

| | |
|---|---|
| **doble sentido** | two-way (street) |
| **no hay paso** | no entrance |
| **peligro** | danger |
| **la señal** | sign; signal |
| **un solo sentido** | one-way |

**PALABRA SEMEJANTE: la curva**

## La ecología y el medio ambiente
Ecology and the Environment

| | |
|---|---|
| **el agujero en la capa de ozono** | hole in the ozone layer |
| **los desperdicios (nucleares)** | (nuclear) waste |
| **el envase** | packing, packaging; bottle |
| **la madera** | wood |
| **la natalidad** | birth rate |
| **el promedio** | average |
| **el reciclaje** | recycling |
| **la sequía** | drought |
| **la superficie** | surface |
| **el vidrio** | glass (*material*) |

**PALABRAS SEMEJANTES: el carburo fluorado, la contaminación del aire, la destrucción, la energía, las especies, la extinción, el hábitat, el nutriente, el pesticida, el petróleo, la planta nuclear, la reserva, el uso**

## Los verbos

| | |
|---|---|
| **crear** | to create |
| **desarrollar** | to develop |
| **desperdiciar** | to waste |
| **disminuir** | to reduce |
| **encerar** | to wax |
| **enfriar** | to cool down |
| **hacer una gira** | to take a tour |
| **molestar** | to bother |
| **parar** | to stop |
| **preocupar** | to worry |
| **proteger** | to protect |
| **resolver (ue)** | to solve |
| **salvar** | to save |

**PALABRAS SEMEJANTES: causar, controlar, eliminar, expresar, flotar, identificar, interesar, mantener, observar, producir, reciclar, reducir, restringir**

## Los sustantivos

| | |
|---|---|
| **la ballena** | whale |
| **el buceo** | underwater swimming; diving |
| **la cantidad** | quantity |
| **el casco** | helmet |
| **el ciudadano / la ciudadana** | citizen |
| **la entrada** | entrance |
| **el esfuerzo** | effort |
| **la estrella** | star |
| **el recipiente** | container |
| **el recurso** | resource |
| **el suelo** | ground |
| **el sitio** | place |
| **la vía** | way |

**PALABRAS SEMEJANTES: la abundancia, el cáncer, la concentración, la condición, la cura, la diversidad, la industria, el potencial, el problema, la producción, el producto, la restricción, el sistema**

## Los adjetivos

| | |
|---|---|
| **aéreo/a** | pertaining to air (travel) |
| **ambos/as** | both |
| **bello/a** | beautiful |
| **cualquier(a)** | any |
| **fuerte** | strong |
| **nevado/a** | snowy |
| **pobre** | poor |
| **profundo/a** | deep |
| **resbaloso/a** | slippery |
| **rodeado/a** | surrounded |
| **tantos/as** | so many |

**PALABRAS SEMEJANTES: árido/a, colorido/a, considerable, denso/a, ecológico/a, impresionante, inmenso/a, marino/a, natural, orgánico/a, plástico/a, principal, prohibido/a, tóxico/a, turístico/a**

## Los adverbios

| | |
|---|---|
| **cómodamente** | comfortably |
| **de vez en cuando** | once in a while |
| **diariamente** | daily |
| **lentamente** | slowly |

**PALABRAS SEMEJANTES: completamente, drásticamente, puntualmente**

## Palabras y expresiones útiles

| | |
|---|---|
| **¡Cuánto/a/os/as... !** | How many . . . ! |
| **hacia** | toward |
| **¡Qué** + *noun* + **tan/más** + *adjective*! | What a + *adjective* + *noun*! |

# Gramática y ejercicios

## 10.1 Saying What You Have Done: The Present Perfect

**(Yo) he viajado a Panamá.** (*I have traveled to Panama.*)
**he** = present tense of **haber**
**viajado** = past participle of **viajar**

**Tú has visto el museo del Prado.** (*You have seen the Prado museum.*)
**has** = present tense of **haber**
**visto** = past participle of **ver**

**Ellos han ido a Europa cinco veces.** (*They have gone to Europe five times.*)
**han** = present tense of **haber**
**ido** = past participle of **ir**

**A.** The present perfect is formed with the present tense of the verb **haber*** (*to have*) followed by a form of the verb called the past participle.

| | |
|---|---|
| —¿**Han visitado** ustedes Europa? | —*Have you visited Europe?* |
| —Sí, **hemos visitado** España dos veces. | —*Yes, we've visited Spain twice.* |

**B.** The present-tense forms of **haber** are irregular.

| **haber** (***to have***) | | |
|---|---|---|
| (yo) | he | *I have* |
| (tú) | has | *you (inf. sing.) have* |
| (usted, él/ella) | ha | *you (pol. sing.) have; he/she has* |
| (nosotros/as) | hemos | *we have* |
| (vosotros/as) | habéis | *you (inf. pl., Spain) have* |
| (ustedes, ellos/as) | han | *you (pl.) have; they have* |

| | |
|---|---|
| —Ernesto, ¿**has recogido** el coche? | —*Ernesto, have you picked up the car?* |
| —No, todavía no **han llamado** del taller. | —*No, they haven't called yet from the shop.* |

**C.** The past participle is formed by adding **-ado** to the stem of **-ar** verbs and **-ido** to the stem of **-er** and **-ir** verbs.

| **-ar** | |
|---|---|
| ***Infinitive*** | ***Past Participle*** |
| hablar | hablado |
| jugar | jugado |
| preparar | preparado |

*Recognition: **vos habés**

| -er / -ir | |
|---|---|
| ***Infinitive*** | ***Past Participle*** |
| comer | comido |
| vivir | vivido |
| dormir | dormido |

| | |
|---|---|
| —¿Ya **han comprado** los señores Ruiz los boletos? | *—Have the Ruizes already bought the tickets?* |
| —No, no **han tenido** tiempo todavía. | *—No, they haven't had time yet.* |
| —Andrea, ¿**has terminado**? | *—Andrea, have you finished?* |
| —No, el agente de viajes no **ha conseguido** las reservaciones todavía. | *—No, the travel agent hasn't got the reservations yet.* |

**D.** A few verbs have irregular participles.

| | |
|---|---|
| abrir: **abierto** | *to open / opened* |
| cubrir: **cubierto** | *to cover / covered* |
| decir: **dicho** | *to say / said; to tell / told* |
| escribir: **escrito** | *to write / written* |
| hacer: **hecho** | *to do / done; to make / made* |
| morir: **muerto** | *to die / died; dead* |
| poner: **puesto** | *to put / put* |
| resolver: **resuelto** | *to solve / solved* |
| romper: **roto** | *to break / broken* |
| ver: **visto** | *to see / seen* |
| volver: **vuelto** | *to return / returned* |

The participles of verbs derived from these verbs are also irregular. For example, **describir** is derived from **escribir**.

| | |
|---|---|
| describir: **descrito** | *to describe / described* |
| devolver: **devuelto** | *to return / returned* |
| inscribir: **inscrito** | *to enroll / enrolled* |
| reponer: **repuesto** | *to put back / put back* |
| suponer: **supuesto** | *to suppose / supposed* |

| | |
|---|---|
| —Estela, ¿dónde **has puesto** mis pantalones nuevos? | *—Estela, where have you put my new pants?* |
| —Ya te **he dicho** que están encima de la cama. | *—I've already told you that they're on top of the bed.* |
| Ernesto fue a la agencia de viajes hace dos horas y todavía no **ha vuelto**. | *Ernesto went to the travel agency two hours ago and hasn't come back yet.* |

Note that **ya** (*already*) and **todavía no** (*not yet*) are adverbs commonly used with the present perfect tense.

### Ejercicio 1

Éstas son algunas de las cosas que han hecho los amigos y parientes de Estela. Complete las oraciones con **comer**, **escribir**, **ver**, **viajar**, **comprar**, **hablar**, **limpiar**, **oír**, **ir** y **pasar**.

MODELO: Mis cuñados *han ido* mucho a Puerto Vallarta porque les gustan las playas y el sol.

1. Ernesto y yo _____ la nueva película de Almodóvar cuatro veces.
2. Ramón le _____ varias cartas a Amanda.
3. Yo _____ tres veces este mes a Cuernavaca.
4. La señorita Batini _____ una casa nueva.
5. Pedro, ¿_____ en un restaurante chino últimamente?
6. Guillermo no _____ con Ernesto hoy.
7. Graciela, tú nunca _____ a España, ¿verdad?
8. Marisa y Clarisa _____ su cuarto muy bien.
9. Ernestito, ¿_____? ¡Tu padre dice que vamos a ir de vacaciones en Florida!
10. Pedro y Andrea _____ sus vacaciones en Acapulco muchas veces.

### Ejercicio 2

¿Cuántas veces ha hecho usted estas cosas? Haga preguntas y respuestas.

MODELO: bucear en el mar Caribe →
—¿Cuántas veces *has buceado* en el mar Caribe?
—Nunca *he buceado* allí. (Mi hermana y yo *hemos buceado* en el mar Caribe dos o tres veces.)

1. viajar a México
2. esquiar en un lago
3. subir a una pirámide
4. acampar en las montañas
5. alquilar un coche
6. cocinar para diez personas
7. leer tres novelas en un día
8. correr 5 kilómetros sin parar
9. decirles una mentira a sus padres
10. romper un vaso en un restaurante

## 10.2 Exclaiming: *¡Qué... !, ¡Cuánto/a/os/as... !*

**¡Qué montañas tan altas!** (*What tall mountains!*)
**¡Qué azul es el agua aquí!** (*How blue the water is here!*)

**A.** Form exclamations with **qué** using ¡**Qué** + *adjective* . . . !*

| | |
|---|---|
| ¡**Qué bonita** es la playa! | *How pretty the beach is!* |
| ¡**Qué interesante** fue ese viaje! | *What an interesting trip that was!* |

**B.** Use the pattern ¡**Qué** + *noun* + **tan/más** + *adjective*! to express *What a(n) . . . !*

| | |
|---|---|
| **¡Qué país tan grande!** | *What a large country!* |
| **¡Qué viaje más divertido!** | *What an enjoyable trip!* |

**¡Cuántas personas hay en esta playa!** (*There sure are a lot of people on this beach!* [*What a lot of people there are on this beach!*])

**C.** Use **cuánto/a/os/as** to express surprise about quantity.

| | |
|---|---|
| ¡**Cuánto** dinero tiene ese hombre! | *What a lot of money that man has!* |
| ¡No te imaginas **cuántas** horas tuvimos que esperar! | *You can't imagine how many hours we had to wait!* |

*Note that **qué** and **cuánto** take an accent mark in exclamations as well as in questions.

## Ejercicio 3

Imagínese que usted está mirando las fotos de Susana Yamasaki y sus hijos, quienes acaban de regresar de un viaje por América Latina. Exprese su sorpresa al ver estas fotos.

MODELO: las pirámides de Teotihuacán: pirámides / altas →
Las pirámides de Teotihuacán... ¡Qué pirámides tan (más) altas!

1. Bolivia: país / interesante
2. un vuelo de Quito a México, D.F.: vuelo / largo
3. los Andes: montañas / altas
4. una selva tropical en Venezuela: selva / verde
5. una playa en el Caribe: arena / blanca

## Ejercicio 4

Ahora imagínese que usted también ha hecho un viaje por España y por América Latina. Haga comentarios sobre los lugares interesantes que ha visto.

MODELO: azul / el agua del Caribe → ¡Qué azul es el agua del Caribe!

1. impresionantes / las ruinas de Machu Picchu
2. grande / el lago Titicaca
3. cosmopolita / la ciudad de Buenos Aires
4. húmeda / la selva de Ecuador
5. seco / el desierto de Atacama en Chile
6. alta / la torre de la Giralda en Sevilla
7. hermoso / el edificio del Alcázar de Segovia
8. inmenso / el parque del Retiro en Madrid
9. interesante / el Museo del Prado
10. antiguo / el acueducto de Segovia

## 10.3 Expressing *by*, *through*, Destination, and Time: *por* and *para*

**por** = movement *through* or *by*, or *means of transportation*
**para** = movement *toward a destination*
**Caminamos por la playa.** (*We walked along the beach.*)
**Fuimos por tren.** (*We went by train.*)
**Salen mañana para Cuzco.** (*They leave tomorrow for Cuzco.*)

The prepositions **por** and **para** have distinct meanings.

**A. Para** indicates movement *toward* a destination.

| | |
|---|---|
| Cuando era niño, salía **para** la escuela a las 7:30. | *When I was a kid, I used to leave for school at 7:30.* |
| Perdón, señor, ¿cuál es el tren que sale **para** Madrid? | *Excuse me, sir, which is the train that is leaving for Madrid?* |

**Por**, on the other hand, indicates motion *through* or *by* (*along*) a place.

| | |
|---|---|
| Pasamos **por** varios pueblos antes de llegar a Salamanca. | *We went through various villages before arriving in Salamanca.* |
| Por las noches caminábamos **por** la orilla del lago de Chapala. | *In the evenings we would take walks along the shore of Lake Chapala.* |

**Por** is also used to indicate means of transportation.

| | |
|---|---|
| Mis hermanos quieren viajar **por** barco, pero yo quiero ir **por** avión. | *My brothers want to travel by boat, but I want to go by plane.* |

Note the contrast in usage in the following example.

| | |
|---|---|
| Mañana salgo **para** París. Voy a viajar **por** tren. | *Tomorrow I'm leaving for Paris. I'll travel by train.* |

**por** = *length of time, during*
**para** = *deadline*
**Estuvimos en España por tres semanas.** (*We were in Spain for three weeks.*)
**Paula necesita terminar el trabajo para el lunes.** (*Paula needs to finish the job by Monday.*)

**B. Por** and **para** can also be followed by expressions of time.

1. Use **por** to indicate length of time (although you may often omit **por** in these cases). Some examples of time expressions are **por una semana, por tres meses, por un año,** and **por mucho tiempo**.

| | |
|---|---|
| Hoy tengo que trabajar en el taller (**por**) **diez horas**. | *Today I have to work in the shop for ten hours.* |

You can also use **por** to express *during*, *in*, or *at* with parts of the day: **por la mañana, por la tarde, por la noche**.

| | |
|---|---|
| Aquí **por la noche** todo el mundo sale a pasear. | *Here in (during) the evening everybody goes out for a walk.* |

2. Use **para** to indicate a deadline by which something is expected to happen.

| | |
|---|---|
| Hay que entregar el informe **para** las 10:00. | *We have to turn in the report by 10:00.* |
| La tarea es **para** el viernes. | *The homework is for (due) Friday.* |

## Ejercicio 5

Aquí tiene usted parte de una conversación entre Silvia Bustamante y su novio, Nacho Padilla. Escoja **por** o **para**.

SILVIA: Ayer trabajé _____[1] ocho horas en la terminal de autobuses.
NACHO: Yo manejé mi taxi _____[2] solamente cinco horas.
SILVIA: ¿Cuándo sales _____[3] Morelia?
NACHO: Dentro de dos días. Salgo _____[4] la mañana, y voy a viajar _____[5] tres horas.
SILVIA: ¿No vas _____[6] avión?
NACHO: ¡Claro que no! Voy _____[7] tren. Es mucho más barato.
SILVIA: ¿Cuánto tiempo piensas quedarte allí?
NACHO: ¡Una semana! Necesito recoger unos documentos importantes. Van a estar listos _____[8] el próximo viernes.

## 10.4 Describing Actions: Adverbs

**-mente** = *-ly*
**cómodamente** = *comfortably*
**calmadamente** = *calmly*

Words that describe actions are called *adverbs*. Many adverbs are formed in Spanish by adding **-mente** to the feminine or neuter form of the adjective: **rápida** (*fast*) → **rápidamente** (*quickly*); **libre** (*free*) → **libremente** (*freely*).

| | |
|---|---|
| —Amanda, ¿vas al cine **frecuentemente**? | *—Amanda, do you go to the movies frequently?* |
| —Sí, voy casi todos los fines de semana. | *—Yes, I go almost every weekend.* |

| | |
|---|---|
| En este país puedes hablar **abiertamente**. | *In this country you can talk openly.* |

## Ejercicio 6

Primero escoja el adjetivo más lógico entre **puntual**, **inmediata**, **constante**, **cómoda** y **rápida**. Luego forme un adverbio.

MODELO: (general) → *Generalmente* tomo el autobús número 73 para ir a la universidad.

1. ¡Los trenes en Japón transitan a 250 kilómetros por hora! Los pasajeros llegan _____ a su destino.
2. Me gusta viajar por tren. Me siento _____ y miro el paisaje por la ventanilla.
3. En Suiza los trenes y los autobuses llegan y salen _____.
4. ¡Nunca he visto tantos autobuses! En la estación de autobuses de Guadalajara, los autobuses llegan y salen _____.
5. Tenemos que correr; el próximo autobús sale _____.

## 10.5 Expressing Reactions: More Verbs like *gustar*

**¿RECUERDA?**

Recall from **Gramática 1.6** and **8.2** that **gustar** and **encantar** are used with indirect object pronouns.

| | |
|---|---|
| me | *to me* |
| te | *to you (inf. sing.)* |
| le | *to you (pol. sing.); to him/her* |
| nos | *to us* |
| os | *to you (inf. pl., Spain)* |
| les | *to you (pl.); to them* |

Some useful expressions:
**me interesa** = *I'm interested in*
**no me interesa** = *I'm not interested in*

**me importa** = *it matters to me*
**no me importa** = *I don't care*

**me parece que sí** = *I think so*
**me parece que no** = *I think not*

Like **gustar** and **encantar**, several other verbs also use indirect object pronouns.

| | |
|---|---|
| dar miedo *to frighten* | llamar la atención *to attract attention* |
| dar rabia *to infuriate* | molestar *to bother* |
| fascinar *to be fascinating; to love* | parecer *to seem like* |
| importar *to matter* | preocupar *to worry, be worrying* |
| interesar *to be interesting* | urgir *to be pressing, really necessary* |

The English equivalents of these verbs vary according to context.

| | |
|---|---|
| —¿Qué **te interesa**? | *—What interests you?* |
| —**Me interesa** la geografía porque **me fascina** viajar. | *—I'm interested in geography because I love to travel.* |
| El paisaje es tan lindo que no **nos importa** si llueve. | *The countryside is so pretty that it doesn't matter to us if it rains.* |
| —Susana, ¿qué **te parece** un viaje a Chile y Bolivia? | *—Susana, what do you think about a trip to Chile and Bolivia?* |
| —**Me parece** una idea fantástica. | *—It seems like a great idea to me.* |

The person whose opinion is described (**me**, **te**, **le**, **nos**, **os**, **les**) is usually mentioned first. The subject of this kind of sentence normally follows the verb. In the following sentence, *our* opinion (**nos**) is described, and the smoke (**el humo**) is the subject of the sentence. **Molesta** is singular because **el humo** is singular.

| | |
|---|---|
| **Nos** molesta **el humo**. | *The smoke bothers us.* |

If the subject that follows the verb is a singular noun or an infinitive, the verb is singular. In the following sentence, the verb is followed by an infinitive, so the verb is singular.

| | |
|---|---|
| **Me** importa **conservar** energía. | *I care about conserving energy.* |

In the next sentence, the subject (**las maletas**) is plural, so the verbs (**gustan/ parecen**) are plural.

| | |
|---|---|
| **Me** gustan **las maletas** que usted compró; **me** parecen muy prácticas. | *I like the suitcases you bought; they seem very practical to me.* |

## Ejercicio 7

Exprese su opinión usando la forma apropiada de los verbos indicados. Luego pídale su opinión a un compañero / una compañera. ¿Están ustedes de acuerdo?

MODELO: La contaminación del aire...

**a.** me _____ (molestar)
**b.** me _____ (encantar)
**c.** ¿ ? →
La contaminación del aire me *molesta.*

1. La conservación de nuestros recursos naturales...
   **a.** me _____ necesaria. (parecer)
   **b.** no me _____. (importar)
   **c.** ¿ ?
2. Los bosques y las selvas...
   **a.** me _____. (fascinar)
   **b.** no me _____. (interesar)
   **c.** ¿ ?
3. Vivir en un clima caluroso...
   **a.** me _____. (encantar)
   **b.** no me _____. (gustar)
   **c.** ¿ ?
4. El tránsito en las autopistas...
   **a.** me _____. (molestar)
   **b.** no me _____. (gustar)
   **c.** ¿ ?
5. Los ríos del mundo...
   **a.** me _____. (importar)
   **b.** no me _____. (interesar)
   **c.** ¿ ?

CAPÍTULO 11

# Los viajes

**METAS**

In **Capítulo 11** you will continue to talk about travel-related experiences: making plans, following directions, and reading maps. You will learn about travel in Spanish-speaking countries, including changing money, clearing customs, and finding lodging. You will also discover new places to visit in the Hispanic world.

Granada, España: la Alhambra

**ACTIVIDADES DE COMUNICACIÓN Y LECTURAS**


Los planes de viaje

**El mundo hispano...** su gente

Buscando sitios y usando planos

**Lectura** Una tarjeta de Clara: ¡Cuánto me gusta Madrid!

De viaje por los países hispanos

**El mundo hispano...** su gente

**Lectura** Los amigos hispanos: Planes para un viaje a México

**El mundo hispano...** imágenes

Los sitios turísticos

**El mundo hispano...** en los Estados Unidos

**EN RESUMEN**


**GRAMÁTICA Y EJERCICIOS**


11.1 Giving Instructions: Polite Commands

11.2 Softening Commands: The Present Subjunctive Following **querer** and **cuando**

11.3 Softening Commands and Expressing Future Doubt: The Present Subjunctive of Irregular Verbs

11.4 Talking about Past Actions in Progress: The Imperfect Progressive

11.5 Saying What Was Happening: The Imperfect in Contrast to the Preterite

# Actividades de comunicación y lecturas

## Los planes de viaje

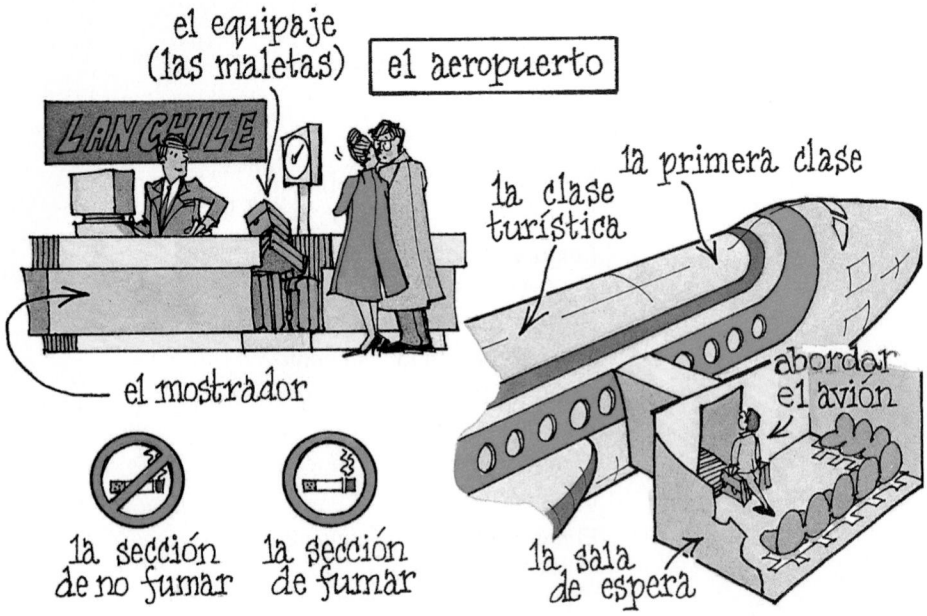

## Actividad 1. Intercambios: La agencia de viajes Salinas

MODELO: E1: ¿Cuánto cuesta el pasaje a *Costa Rica* desde Los Ángeles?
E2: Cuesta *$715.00.*

# AGENCIA DE VIAJES SALINAS

Los Ángeles, California

No haga sus reservaciones a última hora. Hágalas ahora y pase los próximos días feriados en su país natal, junto a su familia. Nosotros tenemos los precios que usted busca. Disponemos de un moderno sistema de computadoras «SABRE» para hacer sus reservaciones inmediatamente. ¡Llame ahora mismo al 850-8921 y disfrute de sus próximas vacaciones!

**Tarifas de ida y vuelta desde Los Ángeles**
(sujetas a cambios y ciertas restricciones)

| | |
|---|---|
| ARGENTINA (Buenos Aires) | $ 1,366 |
| BOLIVIA (La Paz/Cochabamba) | $ 987 |
| COLOMBIA (Bogotá) | $ 699 |
| COSTA RICA (San José) | $ 715 |
| CHILE (Santiago) | $ 1,001 |
| ECUADOR (Quito) | $ 834 |
| EL SALVADOR (San Salvador) | $ 599 |
| GUATEMALA (Guatemala) | $ 529 |
| HONDURAS (Tegucigalpa) | $ 649 |
| NICARAGUA (Managua) | $ 659 |
| PANAMÁ (Panamá) | $ 779 |
| PERÚ (Lima) | $ 954 |
| VENEZUELA (Caracas) | $ 810 |

**AGENCIA DE VIAJES SALINAS**
*¡Nombre de excelencia desde 1969!*

## EL MUNDO HISPANO... su gente

**V**erónica Lugo es una joven argentina de 20 años.

*¿Ha hecho algún viaje interesante en su vida? ¡Descríbalo!*

Hace unos años, mi mejor amiga y yo decidimos veranear en las playas de Uruguay. Trabajamos durante un año para conseguir el dinero y el permiso de nuestros padres. Finalmente, en enero partimos[1] hacia ese país. Viajamos toda una noche en colectivo y al día siguiente llegamos a Montevideo. Como estábamos las dos solas, tuvimos que hacernos cargo[2] de todo: los documentos de la aduana, el transporte de las valijas[3] y el cambio de moneda.

Por fin llegamos al camping[4] y, con la ayuda de otros chicos y chicas, armamos la carpa.[5] El lugar era hermosísimo, a dos cuadras del mar y con muchos árboles. Y estábamos con gente joven. Aunque parezca increíble, nos quedamos en ese lugar un mes, sin más lujos que[6] una carpa y las instalaciones del camping (baños, despensas,[7] agua... ). Pero teníamos todo lo que hacía falta para pasar unas vacaciones inolvidables: sol, playas, gente joven ¡y muchas ganas de divertirnos!

[1]salimos [2]hacernos... *take charge* [3]maletas (*Arg., El Salvador*) [4]*campground* [5]armamos... *we pitched the tent*
[6]sin... *with only* [7]*provisions*

## Actividad 2. Conversación: ¡Viajar es tan fácil como decir 1, 2, 3!

Ordene lógicamente estas actividades.

| | |
|---|---|
| _____ comprar los boletos | _____ hacer las maletas (empacar) |
| _____ abordar el avión | _____ comprar cheques de viajero |
| _____ comprar ropa y otras cosas | _____ ahorrar el dinero necesario |
| _____ planear el viaje | _____ hacer las reservaciones |
| _____ ir al aeropuerto | _____ sacar el pasaporte y la visa |

## Actividad 3. Intercambios: Las vacaciones ideales

Las siguientes personas quieren ir de vacaciones. Con su compañero/a, lean estas descripciones de excursiones y escojan las vacaciones perfectas para cada persona. Escriban una oración que explique su selección en cada caso. Luego, compartan su selección con la clase.

MODELOS: A _____ le(s) recomiendo la excursión a _____ porque _____.
A mí me gustaría la excursión de _____ porque _____.

Unas vacaciones de 6 noches y 7 días por las antiguas ciudades de Roma y Atenas. Excursiones al Partenón, la Catedral de San Pedro y otros lugares históricos. Alojamiento en hoteles de lujo.

**Viaje de 5 noches y 6 días para acampar en las montañas al sur de Chile. Guía experto, caminatas de 10 kilómetros diarias, alojamiento en cabañas. Todo el equipo incluido.**

CARIBE

*Viaje en crucero de 6 noches y 7 días por el Caribe. Comida internacional, música y baile todas las noches. Piscina y cancha de tenis a bordo. Excursiones a mercados y sitios turísticos en cada puerto.*

Gira de 8 noches y 9 días por la costa noreste de los Estados Unidos, incluyendo las ciudades históricas de Williamsburg, Jamestown, Boston, Baltimore y Charleston, terminando en Nueva York. Hoteles de precios módicos.

**DOS SEMANAS** —13 noches y 14 días— en moderno club de vacaciones, en la península de Yucatán. Canchas de tenis, tres piscinas de agua dulce y una de agua salada. Clases de buceo, excursiones en barco de vela, campamento para niños.

Gira de dos semanas, 13 noches y 14 días, por las capitales de Europa: Londres, Roma, París, Estocolmo, Berlín y Viena. Excursiones en cada ciudad con guías expertos. Alojamiento en hoteles de precios módicos.

Una semana, 6 noches y 7 días, en un hotel en la Playa Dominical de Costa Rica. Restaurante, bar, dos piscinas, jacuzzi, canchas de tenis.

1. Adriana Bolini: Adriana es argentina, soltera, de 35 años. Ella es mujer de negocios. Le gusta mucho viajar, y ha viajado por muchas partes de Europa.
2. Susana Yamasaki y sus hijos, Armando y Andrés (de 13 y 9 años, respectivamente): Susana es madre divorciada y trabaja de secretaria y también de guía de turistas para las ruinas de Machu Picchu. A Susana le gusta salir de vacaciones con sus hijos.
3. Dora y Javier Saucedo: Son los padres de Estela, Andrea, Paula y Raúl. Están jubilados y salen de vacaciones sólo una vez cada dos o tres años. Prefieren un viaje de lujo, con todas las comodidades.

4. Raúl Saucedo: Raúl es estudiante de ingeniería en la Universidad de Texas, en San Antonio. Es muy aventurero y le gusta viajar porque le encanta conocer a gente interesante.
5. Pilar y Clara: Clara está de visita en España por un año. Allí conoció a Pilar. Las dos son estudiantes y tienen un mes de vacaciones entre semestres.
6. Su profesor(a)
7. Usted

# Buscando sitios y usando planos

***Lea Gramática 11.1.***

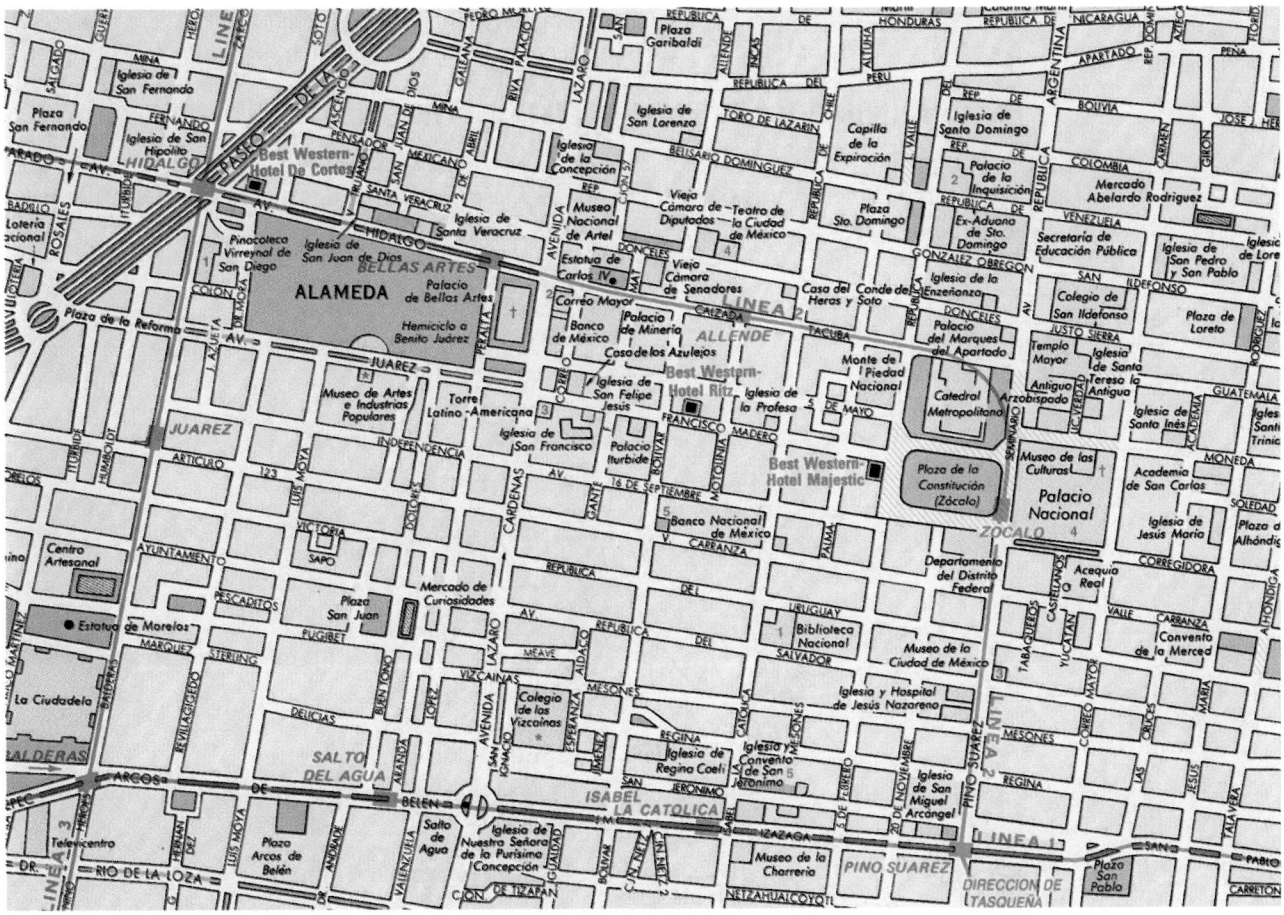


México, D.F.: Del Museo de Artes e Industrias Populares al Colegio de las Vizcaínas (los dos marcados con asterisco)

TURISTA: Perdone, ¿puede decirme cómo llegar al Colegio de las Vizcaínas?
NACHO: Sí. Mire aquí en su plano. **Salga** del museo **a la derecha** y **camine por** Juárez hasta la avenida Lázaro Cárdenas. En Lázaro Cárdenas **doble a la derecha**. Así puede ver la Torre Latinoamericana también. Si tiene tiempo, **suba**; hay una vista hermosa de la ciudad. **Camine seis cuadras por** Lázaro Cárdenas. Luego **doble a la izquierda** en Vizcaínas. El colegio está al lado derecho.
TURISTA: Muchísimas gracias, señor.
NACHO: Para servirle. Adiós.

## Cuando salga de VIAJE...

La misma atención que se pone para planear las vacaciones, se debe de tener para cuidar la casa antes de emprender el viaje. Algunos gerentes de hoteles, como Ray Schultz de Hampton Inn, recomiendan tomar estas precauciones:

- Riegue las plantas antes de irse, o pida a un vecino que lo haga por usted.
- Cierre todo, incluyendo ventanas y puertas; guarde las llaves de la casa que tenga escondidas para usar en caso de emergencia.
- Pida a un vecino que recoja su correspondencia; solicite que suspendan el envío del periódico durante su ausencia, para que parezca que hay alguien en casa.
- Verifique que los aparatos electrodomésticos estén desconectados.
- Avise a los vecinos que estará fuera y hágales saber dónde lo pueden localizar en caso de emergencia.
- Tenga suficiente comida en el refrigerador para que cuando regrese no tenga que ir de compras.
- Tire la basura para evitar los malos olores que se guardan en una casa cerrada.
- Active la contestadora telefónica.
- Deje encargadas a sus mascotas en casa de algún familiar o amigo.
- Si sus vacaciones van a ser muy largas, cubra su coche con una funda especial para evitar que se empolve. También es recomendable dejar el tanque con suficiente gasolina para usar el vehículo cuando regrese. Guarde las llaves en un lugar seguro de la casa.
- Cierre perfectamente las llaves del gas y del agua. ◑

### Actividad 4. Conversación: La Ciudad de México

Mire el plano de la página anterior y explique cómo se va de una parte del centro de la ciudad a otra. (Los números en el plano van a ayudarle a encontrar los lugares mencionados.)

MODELO: del Museo de las Culturas hasta el Palacio de Bellas Artes (los dos están marcados con un obelisco [†]) →
Después de salir del museo, tome Moneda a la izquierda y siga hasta Seminario. Doble a la derecha en Seminario y siga hasta Calzada Tacuba; doble a la izquierda. Camine ocho cuadras hasta la avenida Lázaro Cárdenas. El Palacio de Bellas Artes está en la avenida Lázaro Cárdenas.

1. de la Biblioteca Nacional a la Pinacoteca Virreinal de San Diego
2. del Palacio de la Inquisición al Correo Mayor
3. del Museo de la Ciudad de México a la Torre Latinoamericana
4. del Palacio Nacional al Teatro de la Ciudad de México
5. de la Iglesia y Convento de San Jerónimo al Banco Nacional de México

### Actividad 5. Del mundo hispano: Consejos para los viajeros

Lea el artículo de la izquierda (de la revista *Geomundo*). Luego, trabajando con un compañero / una compañera de clase, escriban otros dos o tres consejos útiles para los viajeros.

# Una tarjeta de Clara: ¡Cuánto me gusta Madrid!

Plaza de España, Madrid

En esta tarjeta, Clara habla de sus experiencias buscando sitios en Madrid. También expresa su opinión de la gente madrileña.

**VOCABULARIO ÚTIL**

| | |
|---|---|
| me he perdido | *I've gotten lost* |
| sin saber cómo | *not knowing how* |
| se me acercó | *approached me* |
| ella misma | *herself* |

Estimada profesora:

¡Cuánto me gusta Madrid! Ya conozco bien la ciudad, aunque me he perdido varias veces. Una vez tomé un autobús en la universidad para ir a la Plaza de España, y, sin saber cómo, ¡terminé en el barrio de Lavapiés! Por suerte los madrileños son muy amables; siempre ayudan a los extranjeros. Un día estaba yo buscando una calle, mirando mi plano de Madrid, y se me acercó una señora para ayudarme. ¡La señora me llevó ella misma a la calle!

Un abrazo,

Clara

Prof. Adela Martínez
Department of Foreign Languages
University of Texas at San Antonio
San Antonio, TX 78285
USA

## Comprensión

De la siguiente lista, escoja las actividades que menciona Clara en su tarjeta a la profesora Martínez.

1. Clara comió helado.
2. Fue al parque.
3. Tomó el autobús.
4. Jugó con un perro en la Plaza Mayor.
5. Recibió ayuda de una señora.

## Ahora... ¡usted!

1. ¿Conoce muy bien la ciudad donde usted vive? ¿Se ha perdido en su ciudad alguna vez? Describa qué pasó.
2. ¿Se ha perdido en otra ciudad o en otro país? ¿Le ofrecieron ayuda las personas de ese sitio? ¿Encontró el lugar que buscaba? ¿Cómo lo encontró?

### Un paso más... ¡a escribir!

Imagínese que usted está escuchando la conversación entre Clara y la amable señora madrileña que le ayudó en la calle. ¿Qué dicen? ¡Escriba el diálogo!

## LAS PALABRAS VIVEN

Si usted se pierde en un país hispano y le pregunta a alguien cómo llegar a un sitio, es muy probable que escuche la frase **siga derecho**. Si el país es México, le van a decir **derecho derecho**. Esta frase expresa la idea de que uno no debe doblar. En América Central dicen **siga recto**. Y la expresión que se escucha a veces en Costa Rica, la República Dominicana y otros países es **al fondo,** literalmente, *at the bottom*. **Ir al fondo** significa, por lo general, que uno debe caminar derecho hasta que termine la calle.

## Actividad 6. Del mundo hispano: El metro de Madrid

Dé instrucciones para ir de una estación del metro a otra. No olvide hacer los transbordos necesarios.

MODELO: De Atocha a El Carmen → Suba a un tren de la Línea 1 en Atocha, dirección Plaza de Castilla, y baje en la Estación Sol. Allí suba a un tren de la Línea 2, dirección Ventas, y baje en la Estación Ventas. En Ventas, suba a un tren de la Línea 5, dirección Canillejas, y siga hasta la primera estación. Bájese; allí es El Carmen.

1. de Tetuán a Sevilla
2. de Puente de Vallecas a Ríos Rosas
3. de Aluche a Puerta de Toledo
4. de Oporto a Portazgo
5. de Esperanza a Quintana

# De viaje por los países hispanos

*Lea Gramática 11.2–11.3.*

Cuando llegue al hotel, voy a descansar.

Cuando encuentre mi traje de baño, voy a bajar a la piscina del hotel para broncearme.

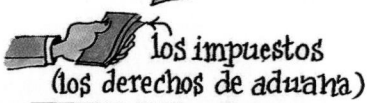


—Hummm, cámara japonesa... Tiene que pagar 12.728 pesetas de derechos.
—¡Tres veces el valor de la cámara! Pero si no es nueva, es para mi uso personal.
—Está bien, entonces. Pase usted.

—Su pasaporte, por favor.
—Aquí lo tiene.

—Quisiera cambiar cheques de viajero.
—Permítame ver su pasaporte, por favor.

—Bienvenidos al Hotel Pintor. ¿Tienen reservaciones?
—Sí, somos los señores Ruiz.
—Ah, sí, una habitación para dos con cama matrimonial, ¿verdad?

Los Ruiz se hospedaron en el Hotel Pintor por tres días. Hoy van a viajar a Segovia. Quieren que el botones recoja su equipaje.

## Actividad 7. Intercambios: Los paquetes turísticos

Mire estos paquetes turísticos ofrecidos por la aerolínea costarricense Lacsa. Después, hágale preguntas a su compañero/a.

### Barranquilla Ejecutivo

2 noches / 3 días

*Desde* **$297**

*Incluye:*

- **Boleto aéreo ida y vuelta** (sin impuestos).
- Dos noches de alojamiento con desayuno americano.
- Impuestos hoteleros.
- 3 días de Assist Card.

### Quito Ejecutivo

3 noches / 4 días

*Desde* **$478**

*Incluye:*

- **Boleto aéreo ida y vuelta** (sin impuestos).
- Traslado aeropuerto/hotel/aeropuerto.
- 3 noches de alojamiento en hotel seleccionado.
- Impuestos hoteleros.
- 4 días de Assist Card.

### Houston Ejecutivo

3 noches / 4 días

*Desde* **$495**

*Incluye:*

- **Boleto aéreo ida y vuelta** (sin impuestos).
- Traslado aeropuerto/hotel/aeropuerto.
- 3 noches de alojamiento.
- Impuestos hoteleros.
- 4 días de Assist Card.
- Vía San Salvador.

### México tradicional

4 noches / 5 días

*Desde* **$399**

*Incluye:*

- **Boleto aéreo ida y vuelta** (sin impuestos).
- Traslado aeropuerto/hotel/aeropuerto.
- 4 noches de alojamiento en hotel seleccionado.
- Impuestos hoteleros.
- Tour Basílica/Pirámides.
- 5 días de Assist Card.

### Nueva Orleáns en auto

7 días

*Desde* **$541**

*Incluye:*

- **Boleto aéreo ida y vuelta** (sin impuestos).
- Hasta 7 días de auto económico con seguros incluidos.
- Hasta 7 días de Assist Card.
- Algunas noches de alojamiento en Hotel Days Inn Canal.

### Santiago de compras

4 noches / 5 días

*Desde* **$899**

*Incluye:*

- **Boleto aéreo ida y vuelta** (sin impuestos).
- 4 noches de alojamiento en Hotel Galerías.
- Impuestos hoteleros.
- Traslado aeropuerto/hotel/aeropuerto.
- Desayuno Buffet.
- Coctel de bienvenida.
- Tour de compras.
- 5 días de Assist Card.

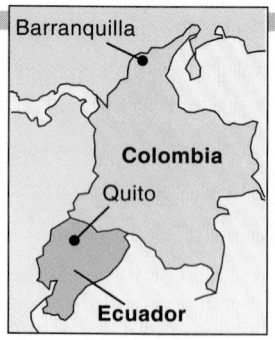


1. ¿Cuánto cuesta el paquete a Barranquilla?
2. ¿Están incluidos los impuestos de hotel en el paquete «México tradicional»?
3. ¿Está incluido un tour de compras en el paquete «Quito Ejecutivo»?
4. ¿Está incluido el seguro de auto en el paquete de Nueva Orleáns?
5. ¿Están incluidos los traslados del aeropuerto al hotel en el paquete «Houston Ejecutivo»?

6. ¿Qué más está incluido, además del alojamiento, en el paquete «Barranquilla Ejecutivo»?
7. ¿Qué incluye el paquete «Santiago de compras» además del boleto, el alojamiento y los traslados del aeropuerto al hotel?

## Actividad 8. Del mundo hispano: Hoteles y restaurantes en dos ciudades de Andalucía

# Andalucía

## Granada

### Hoteles y Restaurantes

**Hoteles:** **Alhambra Palace**. Caro. Hermoso palacio estilo morisco en la cumbre de la montaña Alhambra con magníficas vistas. Tel. 22-14-68. **Parador de San Francisco**. Caro. Está en un antiguo convento dentro de los muros de la Alhambra y es el parador más popular de España. Se requiere hacer reservación de 4 a 6 meses de anticipación. Tel. 22-14-93. **América**. Moderado. Encantador hotel dentro de los terrenos de la Alhambra. Es muy popular, reserve con anticipación. Tel. 22-74-71.

**Restaurantes:** **Baroca**. Caro. Considerado uno de los mejores de Granada. Tel. 26-50-61. **Cunini**. Caro. Muy famoso por su pescado y comida marina. Tel. 26-37-01. **Colombia**. Caro-Moderado. En la montaña de la Alhambra con elegante decorado árabe, música de guitarra y espléndidas vistas. Muy turístico, pero divertido. Tel. 22-74-33.

*De estilo morisco, el Alhambra Palace es uno de los hoteles caros de Granada, con magníficas vistas desde la cumbre de la montaña.*

## Sevilla

### Hoteles y Restaurantes

Todos los precios pueden duplicarse e incluso triplicarse durante la Semana Santa y los días que dura la Feria.

**Hoteles:** **Alfonso XIII**. De lujo. Construido en estilo morisco para la exhibición de 1929, es el hotel clásico de Sevilla lleno de belleza y encanto. Tel. 22-28-50. **Doña María**. Caro. Pequeño, con habitaciones de buen gusto amuebladas con antigüedades y piscina en el azotea con vista a la Giralda. Tel. 22-49-90. **Bécquer**. Moderado. Hotel agradable y moderno. Tel. 22-89-00. **Fernando III**. Moderado. A orillas del barrio Santa Cruz; piscina en la azotea. Tel. 21-73-07.

*Sevilla ofrece a los visitantes hoteles de lujo, como el Alfonso XIII, un edificio de estilo morisco construido en 1929 para la Exhibición Mundial.*

**Restaurantes:** **Albahaca**. Caro. Todos frecuentan este restaurante, hermosamente localizado en el corazón del viejo barrio judío; platos creativos. Tel. 22-07-14. **La Dorada**. Caro. Muy famoso por sus pescados y comida marina. Tel. 45-51-00. **Bodegón Torre del Oro**. Moderado. Atmósfera rústica, buena comida y popular entre turistas y locales. Tel. 21-31-69. **La Isla**. Moderado. Muy popular para disfrutar paella y platos de pescado. Tel. 21-26-31.

**EN NUESTRO MUNDO INCREÍBLE,...**

- visitan España más turistas al año que todas las personas que viven en ese país.
- hay un sólo lugar en América desde el cual se pueden ver el océano Atlántico y el Pacífico a la vez: desde el volcán Irazú, en Costa Rica, que está a unos 11.200 pies de altura.

EN GRANADA

1. Si usted necesita un hotel de precios módicos, ¿en dónde va a hospedarse?
2. Si quiere pasar unos días en un parador muy popular, ¿en dónde se va a hospedar?
3. Si quiere comer en un restaurante de ambiente árabe, ¿en dónde va a cenar?
4. ¿En dónde va a cenar, si tiene ganas de comer mariscos?
5. Si desea cenar en el mejor restaurante de Granada, ¿a cuál va a ir?

EN SEVILLA

1. Si desea cenar en un restaurante en el centro del barrio judío, ¿a cuál piensa ir?
2. Si busca un hotel elegante y clásico, ¿cuál va a escoger?
3. Si prefiere un hotel de precios módicos con piscina, ¿en dónde va a hospedarse?
4. Si desea comerse una buena paella, ¿en qué restaurante puede hacerlo?
5. Si quiere cenar en un restaurante de precios módicos y ambiente informal, ¿adónde va a ir?

## EL MUNDO HISPANO... su gente

Gregorio Merino Díaz es chileno y tiene 32 años. Gregorio vive con su esposa y su hija en Santiago de Chile.

*¿Qué opina usted de los estereotipos que existen de los hispanos?*

Creo que entre los norteamericanos predomina todavía el estereotipo del «latin lover», pero también el del latino flojo, sin educación, que ingresa[1] ilegalmente en los Estados Unidos y es mano de obra[2] barata.

Lamentablemente, para el común de la gente[3] de los Estados Unidos, los países de Latinoamérica son un grupo de estados que nunca podrán salir del subdesarrollo.[4] Pero existen diferencias, pues algunos países como el mío están logrando grandes avances.

[1]entra [2]mano... *labor* [3]común... *average person* [4]*underdevelopment*

# Los amigos hispanos: Planes para un viaje a México

Paula Saucedo Muñoz tiene 27 años y es gerente de una agencia de viajes en la Ciudad de México. A Paula le encanta su trabajo: le gusta ayudar a sus clientes a planear sus vacaciones, y ofrecerles información sobre los sitios turísticos de México.

En esta carta, Paula le escribe a Pilar Álvarez, su amiga española que vive en Madrid. Las amigas se han escrito muchas veces, pero no se conocen en persona. Este verano por fin van a conocerse: Pilar está planeando una visita a México.

**VOCABULARIO ÚTIL**

| | |
|---|---|
| ubicada | *located* |
| entero | *entire, whole* |
| broncearte | *to get a tan* |
| las sendas frondosas | *shaded paths* |
| mundialmente | *worldwide* |
| la obra | *art work* |
| el mármol | *marble* |
| los dramaturgos | *playwrights* |
| las conferencias | *lectures* |

Pilar Álvarez
Calle Almendras 481
Madrid, España

Querida Pilar:

¡Por fin vamos a conocernos! Sé que te va a gustar mi país. Hay tanto que ver en el Distrito Federal. Estoy preparando un itinerario para tu visita. ¡No vamos a tener un solo minuto libre! Aquí te envío algunas fotos muy bonitas y unos panfletos turísticos, para darte una idea. Pero también quiero hablarte un poquito de mi país, al que quiero mucho.

Ya sabes que la Ciudad de México es la capital más grande del mundo hispano. Los mexicanos también la llamamos «el D.F.» por el Distrito Federal. Las otras ciudades grandes de mi país son Guadalajara, Monterrey y Tijuana. También hay muchas ciudades hermosas que debes conocer, como Veracruz, un puerto en el Golfo de México, y Mérida, que está situada en la península de Yucatán. A propósito, Mérida es un centro importante de la cultura maya.

Acapulco y Puerto Vallarta son dos sitios turísticos en la costa del Pacífico, con clima tropical el año entero. Si quieres broncearte y nadar, debes ir a esas dos ciudades. (¡Y yo muy feliz te acompaño!) Hay muchas otras que conservan el aspecto colonial por su arquitectura, como Taxco, San Miguel de Allende y Guanajuato.

Uno de los lugares de la capital adonde pienso llevarte es el Parque de Chapultepec. En este parque hay dos zoológicos y muchas sendas frondosas por donde caminar. Además, uno puede visitar allí el Museo de Antropología y un castillo mundialmente famoso que data de los tiempos coloniales. Los domingos por la tarde hay conciertos gratis al aire libre en el Parque de Chapultepec.

El centro y corazón de la ciudad es el Zócalo (creo que es comparable a la Plaza Mayor de Madrid, ¿no?). En la zona del Zócalo está la catedral, que data también de los tiempos de la colonia, y el Palacio Nacional. En éste hay varios murales impresionantes de Diego Rivera.[1] Sé que te va a encantar su obra.

Aquí, en el D.F., vamos a visitar también el Palacio de Bellas Artes. Éste es un edificio de mármol blanco donde se presentan conciertos, óperas, obras de los más famosos dramaturgos del mundo, espectáculos de danza y conferencias.

Creo que esta carta se está haciendo demasiado larga, amiga mía. Antes de concluir, sólo te quiero mencionar las pirámides de Teotihuacán, que están al nordeste de la capital. Son una muestra importante de la cultura indígena.

Bueno, en mi familia todos estamos ansiosos por verte y recibirte en nuestra casa. Avísame cuando tengas tu viaje confirmado.

Abrazos de
*Paula*

[1]Diego Rivera (1886–1957) fue un pintor mexicano, famoso por sus grandes murales que narran la historia de México.

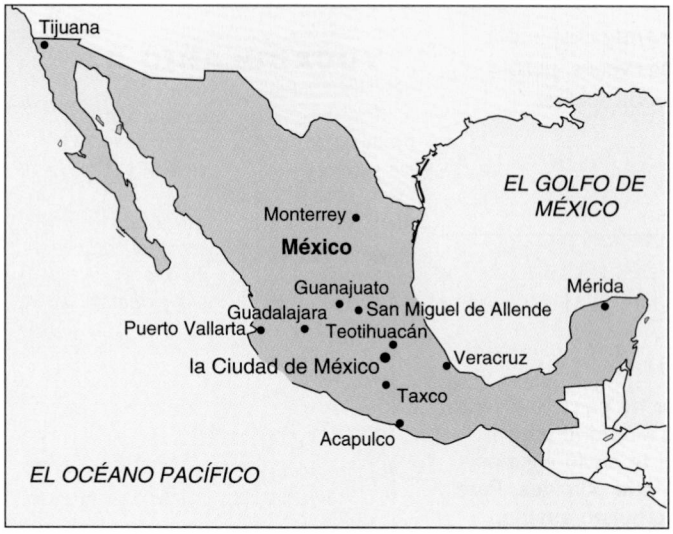

Una vista de la linda ciudad colonial de Taxco.

El Palacio de Bellas Artes, México, D.F.

Las impresionantes pirámides de Teotihuacán, México.

## Comprensión

Busque la definición correcta.

1. _____ el Palacio de Bellas Artes
2. _____ el Zócalo
3. _____ el Palacio Nacional
4. _____ Guanajuato
5. _____ Teotihuacán
6. _____ el Parque de Chapultepec
7. _____ la Ciudad de México
8. _____ Puerto Vallarta
9. _____ Veracruz
10. _____ Monterrey

a. zona en el centro de la ciudad
b. ciudad grande que también se conoce como el Distrito Federal
c. lugar al nordeste del D.F. donde están las Pirámides del Sol y de la Luna
d. una de las ciudades grandes en el norte del país
e. sitio turístico en la costa del océano Pacífico
f. edificio donde se hacen presentaciones culturales
g. ciudad y puerto en el Golfo de México
h. parque donde se ofrecen conciertos los domingos
i. ciudad que conserva su aspecto colonial
j. edificio donde se encuentran los murales de Diego Rivera

## Ahora... ¡usted!

1. ¿Ha estado en México? ¿Dónde? Describa su experiencia.
2. Mire el mapa al comienzo de esta Lectura y diga cuáles de las ciudades indicadas conoce. ¿Cuál le parece más atractiva, según la descripción de Paula? ¿Cuáles no conoce pero le gustaría visitar? ¿Por qué?

### Un paso más... ¡a escribir!

Imagínese que usted tiene un amigo hispano / una amiga hispana y que esta persona va a venir de visita a los Estados Unidos por primera vez. Escríbale una carta en que le describe los lugares que puede visitar. ¿Cuáles son los puntos de interés que usted piensa mostrarle a su visitante?

## EL MUNDO HISPANO... imágenes

La población indígena en América Latina es grande. Los indígenas mantienen vivo su pasado: muchos conservan su cultura a pesar de[1] la industrialización y las tecnologías agresivas del mundo moderno.

Los niños aprenden desde muy pequeños a hacer artesanía. Detrás de esta niña se ven los famosos bordados[2] panameños conocidos por su fino trabajo y colores brillantes.

[1]a... *in spite of* [2]*embroidery*

Este niño y su hermana son descendientes de los mayas. Están celebrando la festividad de los Reyes Magos en Tizimín, península de Yucatán, México.

Niña de la tribu Cuna en las Islas San Blas, en Panamá.

## Actividad 9. Del mundo hispano: La Barranca del Cobre en México

Lea este artículo y luego hágale las siguientes preguntas a un compañero / una compañera de clase.

### Barranca del Cobre
### Una de las maravillas naturales de México

Visitar la Barranca del Cobre es una de las grandes experiencias que puede tener un viajero en México. Localizada en la Sierra Madre Occidental de Chihuahua, en una área de más de 35,000 km², es 1.5 veces más profunda y cubre cuatro veces la extensión del Gran Cañón en Arizona. Su vegetación y fauna desde el fondo de las barrancas —que en algunas zonas llegan a tener 3,000 metros de profundidad— hasta sus sierras nevadas en invierno son tan diversas, que nunca se acaban de admirar. En la región viven dispersos más de 50,000 indios tarahumaras, que todavía conservan una cultura muy interesante.

Quienes deseen conocer esta región, considerada por muchos la octava maravilla natural del mundo, pueden hacerlo en una de las excursiónes de siete días organizadas por Ecogrupos de México. Incluyen: organizador de grupo bilingüe, seis noches de hospedaje en hotel, transportación en autobús, lanchas, tren (desde donde se tienen vistas espectaculares atravesando puentes y túneles), camionetas, entradas a los sitios de interés, caminatas guiadas por los tarahumaras, 10 alimentos y bitácora impresa con información de la región. No incluye: transportación aérea, bebidas alcohólicas, gastos extras en el hotel (teléfono, lavandería, etc.).

Adulto doble: $4,405 (579 dólares), triple: $3,607 (474 dólares), sencillo: $5,677 (746 dólares), niño $2,576 (338 dólares). Los precios no incluyen IVA. Para mayores informes y reservaciones llame al 661-9121. Fax: 663-5381.

1. ¿Dónde está la Barranca del Cobre?
2. ¿Qué tribu de indígenas vive en esta región?
3. ¿Es más grande o menos grande la Barranca del Cobre que el Gran Cañón en Arizona?
4. ¿Cómo se llama la compañía que organiza las excursiones?
5. ¿Está incluido el vuelo en el precio de la excursión?
6. ¿Es necesario saber hablar español para ir en esta excursión?
7. ¿Cuánto cuesta una habitación doble, por adulto? ¿y una habitación sencilla?

Los volcanes Popocatépetl e Iztaccíhuatl pueden verse desde la capital de México. Según la leyenda, dos jóvenes enamorados fueron convertidos en estos dos volcanes. (Vea la Lectura del Capítulo 11 del *Cuaderno de trabajo*.)

# Los sitios turísticos

*Lea Gramática 11.4–11.5.*

Pedro y Andrea hicieron las reservaciones en la Agencia Universo el 6 de junio.

Pedro y Andrea llegaron a Madrid el 2 de julio.

Pedro y Andrea dormían cuando sonó el teléfono.

**Nuevos vuelos entre Lima y Santiago**

Los viajeros de negocios pueden ahora salir por la mañana de Lima para asistir a una reunión en Santiago y estar de regreso a la hora de la cena, gracias al nuevo vuelo que ofrece United Airlines. Los vuelos que enlazan ambas ciudades operan miércoles, viernes y sábados en un Boeing 757. El vuelo 973 sale de Lima a las 8:35 a.m. y llega a Santiago a las 12:55 p.m.; el vuelo 972 sale de Santiago a las 6:00 p.m. y llega a Lima a las 8:35 p.m. El trayecto dura aproximadamente tres horas y media.

Estaban tomando un refresco en un café de la Gran Vía cuando vieron a un viejo amigo de Pedro.

A las 4:00 de la tarde Pedro y Andrea admiraban las pinturas de Goya en el Museo del Prado cuando las luces se apagaron.

## EL MUNDO HISPANO... en los Estados Unidos

**A**ntonio Galván tiene 40 años y es salvadoreño. Vive en Takoma Park, Maryland.

*¿Ha pasado usted sus vacaciones en algún sitio turístico interesante?*

Yo les recomiendo a todos —viejos y jóvenes— que vayan de vacaciones a Baja California, al lado del Golfo. ¡No se imaginan qué extraordinario es el sitio! Yo llevé a mi mujer allí para unas vacaciones de Navidad y ella no paraba de decir:[1] «¡Qué belleza!» El paisaje es un inmenso desierto lleno de flora y fauna (cuando se deja ver) que desemboca en[2] un mar de un azul profundo. La comida es para morirse del gusto:[3] mariscos a precios regalados.[4] Pero lo más agradable, creo, es la tranquilidad que da el lugar. No hay aglomeración[5] de turistas, pero sí los suficientes como para no sentirse aislado.

[1]no... *she didn't stop saying* [2]desemboca... *leads to, runs to* [3]para... *so good you could die* [4]*dirt cheap* [5]*crowds*

### Actividad 10. Descripción de dibujos: El viaje de Virginia y Rubén

Diga qué estaba pasando.

MODELO: A las 6:05 Virginia y Rubén *estaban recogiendo los boletos en la agencia de viajes.*

MODELO: Virginia y Rubén *estaban paseando por el Paseo de la Reforma cuando dos carros chocaron.*

# En resumen

**¡REÍR ES VIVIR!**

**Conversación en un hotel**
—¿Cuánto cuesta una habitación?
—En el primer piso, doscientos dólares.
—¿Y en el segundo?
—Ciento cincuenta.
—¿Y en el tercero?
—Cien.
—¿Y en el cuarto?
—No tenemos cuarto piso.
—Entonces, no me hospedo aquí.
—¿Pero por qué?
—¡Su hotel no es lo bastante alto para mí!

## De todo un poco

Dramas

Su profesor(a) va a dividir la clase en parejas, y a cada una le va a asignar uno de los siguientes escenarios para que ustedes lo preparen y lo presenten ante la clase.

1. En el aeropuerto: Usted va a salir de vacaciones con destino a Centro y Sudamérica. Acaba de llegar al aeropuerto y está en el mostrador, facturando sus maletas. Hable con el empleado / la empleada para obtener la siguiente información: la hora de salida del avión, las escalas, la hora del almuerzo, la sección de fumar, la película y la hora de llegada del avión.

2. En el banco: Un(a) turista llega al banco para cambiar cheques de viajero.

   USTED: ¿En qué puedo servirle, señor/señora?
   TURISTA: Quisiera cambiar unos cheques de viajero.
   USTED: Muy bien. ¿Cuánto quiere cambiar?
   TURISTA: Quisiera cambiar...

3. En el hotel: Usted acaba de llegar a un hotel después de manejar ocho horas. Está muy cansado/a y necesita una habitación para una noche. Dígale al empleado / a la empleada lo que usted quiere y pídale la información necesaria (el precio, etcétera). Luego, decida si quiere la habitación o no.

   EMPLEADO/A: Buenas noches, señor/señora. ¿En qué puedo servirle?
   USTED: Quisiera una habitación con...
   EMPLEADO/A: Tengo la habitación perfecta. ¿Cuál es su nombre?
   USTED: Perdón, primero quisiera verla y saber...

### ¡Dígalo por escrito!

Viajando por el mundo hispano

Imagínese que usted es agente de viajes y que su compañero/a es su cliente. Usando fotos, su propia experiencia y recomendaciones de otros clientes, trate de venderle un viaje a algún país de habla española. Después, prepare un folleto de turismo para viajeros a ese país. El folleto debe incluir fotos o dibujos, boletos, consejos y recomendaciones para turistas, mapas, hoteles, excursiones, restaurantes (incluyendo ejemplos de sus menús y precios), etcétera.

## VIDEOTECA

En este segmento de video, Elisa hace los preparativos para un viaje a las famosas islas Galápagos, que son parte de Ecuador. ¿Qué sabe usted de las islas Galápagos? Escuche bien la conversación entre Elisa y el agente de viajes. ¿Qué quiere Elisa que haga el agente? ¿Qué hicieron el agente de viajes y su esposa durante sus vacaciones en las islas? En el Capítulo 11 del *Cuaderno de trabajo* hay más actividades para hacer después de ver el video.

# Vocabulario

## Los viajes

| | |
|---|---|
| **la aduana** | customs |
| **el alojamiento** | lodging |
| **el cheque de viajero** | traveler's check |
| **los derechos de aduana** | customs duty, tax |
| **el destino** | destination |
| **el equipaje** | baggage |
| **la escala** | stopover |
| **la excursión** | tour |
| **los impuestos** | taxes |
| **las instrucciones** | directions |
| **la llegada** | arrival |
| **la maleta** | suitcase |
| **el mostrador** | counter |
| **el pasaje** | ticket |
| **la primera clase** | first class |
| **la sala de espera** | waiting room |
| **la salida** | departure, exit |
| **la vacuna** | vaccination, shot |
| **el visado (la visa)** | visa |

**PALABRAS SEMEJANTES: la clase turística, el consulado, el contrabando, la inmigración**

**REPASO: el/la agente de viajes, el plano, el seguro de automóvil**

## Los lugares y las atracciones turísticas
Places and Tourist Attractions

| | |
|---|---|
| **el correo** | post office |
| **el parador** | state (tourist) hotel |
| **la torre** | tower |

**PALABRAS SEMEJANTES: el convento, el elevador, el palacio, la ruina**

## El transporte aéreo
Air Transportation

| | |
|---|---|
| **el/la asistente de vuelo** | flight attendant |
| **el boleto** | ticket |
| **de ida y vuelta** | round-trip |
| **la sección de (no) fumar** | (no) smoking section |

| | |
|---|---|
| **el transbordo** | transfer |
| **el traslado de... a...** | transportation from . . . to . . . |

**PALABRAS SEMEJANTES: la aerolínea, el aeropuerto**

**REPASO: la agencia de viajes, el avión, el/la piloto, el vuelo**

## Los mandatos

| | |
|---|---|
| **baje (bajar)** | get off (to get off) |
| **doble (doblar)** | turn (to turn) |
| **haga (hacer)** | do; make (to do; to make) |
| **siga (seguir)** | keep going (to keep going) |
| **suba (subir)** | board (to board) |
| **tome (tomar)** | take (to take) |

## Los verbos

| | |
|---|---|
| **abordar** | to board |
| **broncearse** | to get a tan |
| **caerse** | to fall down |
| **cambiar un cheque** | to cash a check |
| **chocar (con)** | to crash, run into (*something*) |
| **cuidarse** | to take care of oneself |
| **desear** | to wish |
| **disfrutar** | to enjoy |
| **disponer de** | to have available |
| **empacar** | to pack |
| **estar de visita** | to be staying |
| **facturar (la maleta)** | to check (baggage) |
| **hacer cola** | to stand in line |
| **hacer las maletas** | to pack |
| **hacer la reservación** | to make a reservation |
| **ir de vacaciones** | to go on vacation |
| **irse** | to go away |
| **romperse** | to break |
| **sacar el pasaporte (el visado)** | to get a passport (visa) |
| **suponer** | to suppose |
| **tropezar** | to trip |

**PALABRAS SEMEJANTES: admirar, anunciar, dividir, ordenar, planear, recomendar**

**REPASO: hospedarse**

## La gente People

| | |
|---|---|
| **la camarera** | chambermaid |
| **el empleado / la empleada** | employee |
| **el/la guía de turistas** | tourist guide |
| **el viajero / la viajera** | traveler |

**PALABRAS SEMEJANTES: la tribu, el/la turista**

## Los sustantivos

| | |
|---|---|
| **el billete** | ticket |
| **el botones** | bellboy |
| **el cambio** | change (*money*) |
| **la comodidad** | comfort |
| **el consejo** | advice |
| **la contestadora telefónica** | (telephone) answering machine |
| **la cuadra** | (*street*) block |
| **el dinero en efectivo** | cash (*money*) |
| **el escenario** | scene |
| **los informes** | information |
| **el lujo** | luxury |
| **la mesita de noche** | night table |
| **la pintura** | painting |
| **la recepción** | lobby |
| **el reclamo de equipaje** | baggage claim |
| **la tarifa** | fare |
| **el valor** | value |

**PALABRAS SEMEJANTES: el ballet folclórico, la selección**

## Los adjetivos

| | |
|---|---|
| **aventurero/a** | adventurous |
| **bienvenido/a** | welcome |
| **jubilado/a** | retired |
| **sencillo/a** | simple |

**PALABRAS SEMEJANTES: informal, popular, probable**

## Palabras y expresiones útiles

| | |
|---|---|
| **además de** | besides |
| **¿Cómo se va de... a... ?** | How does one get from . . . to . . . ? |
| **en parejas** | in pairs |
| **¿En qué puedo servirle?** | How may I help you? |
| **entonces** | then |
| **junto a** | next to, near |
| **para servirle** | you are welcome |
| **perdone** | excuse me |
| **permítame** | allow me |

**PALABRAS SEMEJANTES: ¡Qué coincidencia!, respectivamente**

**REPASO: a la derecha / a la izquierda**

# Gramática y ejercicios

**¿RECUERDA?**

In **Gramática A.1** you learned that singular commands (to one person) end in **-a** or **-e**. Plural commands (to more than one person) end in **-an** or **-en**.

Polite commands:
**-ar** verbs take **-e(n)** endings: **hable** (usted), **tomen** (ustedes)
**-er/-ir** verbs take **-a(n)** endings: **coma** (usted), **escriban** (ustedes)

## 11.1 Giving Instructions: Polite Commands

**A.** Polite singular commands (a command you would make to a person you address with **usted**) are formed by changing **-ar** verb endings to **-e**; **-er** and **-ir** endings change to **-a**.

| | | |
|---|---|---|
| **-ar:** | Llev**e** el paquete. | *Take the package.* |
| **-er:** | Com**a** cereal por la mañana. | *Eat cereal in the morning.* |
| **-ir:** | Abr**a** la ventana, por favor. | *Open the window, please.* |

**B.** To give polite commands to more than one person, add **-n**.*

| | |
|---|---|
| No bail**en** más de dos horas. | *Don't dance more than two hours.* |

**C.** If a verb stem is irregular in the **yo** form of the present tense, it usually has the same irregularity in the command form: **yo pongo → ponga**.

| | |
|---|---|
| **Venga(n)** temprano, por favor. | *Come early, please.* |
| **Salga(n)** inmediatamente. | *Leave immediately.* |

Here are some common irregular commands based on the **yo** form.

| | | | | | |
|---|---|---|---|---|---|
| conozca | (conocer) | *know* | tenga | (tener) | *have* |
| diga | (decir) | *say* | traiga | (traer) | *bring* |
| haga | (hacer) | *do; make* | vea | (ver) | *see* |
| oiga | (oír) | *hear* | venga | (venir) | *come* |

| | |
|---|---|
| **Tengan** cuidado en la autopista. | *Be careful on the freeway.* |
| **Traiga** sus documentos mañana a la oficina de la aduana. | *Bring your documents tomorrow to the customs office.* |

**D.** The following irregular command forms do not match the first-person singular forms.

| | | | | | |
|---|---|---|---|---|---|
| dé | (dar) | *give* | sepa | (saber) | *know* |
| esté | (estar) | *be* | vaya | (ir) | *go* |
| sea | (ser) | *be* | | | |

| | |
|---|---|
| **Sepa** muy bien lo que quiere decir antes de hablar. | *Know well what you want to say before speaking.* |
| Si quiere reservar un asiento para diciembre, **vaya** ahora mismo a la agencia de viajes. | *If you want to reserve a seat for December, go to the travel agency right away.* |

**E.** Verbs with vowel changes in the stem show the same changes in the polite command forms.

---

*In Spain the **vosotros/as** command form is used for plural *informal* commands. See the section on **vos** and **vosotros** in the **Expansión gramatical** at the end of the *Cuaderno de trabajo*. In most of Latin America, however, the plural polite command is used to give a command to more than one person, whether one normally addresses them politely or informally.

| | | | | | |
|---|---|---|---|---|---|
| p**ie**nse | pensar (ie) | *think* | c**ie**rre | cerrar (ie) | *close* |
| d**ue**rma | dormir (ue) | *sleep* | v**ue**lva | volver (ue) | *return* |
| s**i**rva | servir (i) | *serve* | cons**i**ga | conseguir (i) | *get* |

| | |
|---|---|
| **Duerma** por lo menos ocho horas cada noche. | *Sleep at least eight hours every night.* |
| **Cierre** la maleta. | *Close the suitcase.* |
| **Sirva** los refrescos. | *Serve the refreshments.* |

**F.** Object pronouns and reflexive pronouns are attached to affirmative commands and precede negative ones.

| | |
|---|---|
| **Tráigale** café, por favor; **no le traiga** té. | *Bring her coffee, please; don't bring her tea.* |
| **Dígame** la verdad; **no me diga** que no la sabe. | *Tell me the truth; don't tell me that you don't know (it).* |
| Espere, **no lo haga** ahora; **hágalo** más tarde. | *Wait, don't do it now; do it later.* |
| **Levántese** temprano; **no se pierda** las noticias de las seis. | *Get up early; don't miss the six o'clock news.* |

## Ejercicio 1

Imagínese que usted es agente de viajes. Conteste las preguntas de sus clientes con un mandato lógico. Si es necesario, use un pronombre de complemento directo (**lo**, **la**, **los** o **las**).

MODELOS: ¿Tengo que pagar el pasaje hoy? →
Sí, *páguelo* hoy, por favor.

¿Necesito ir al consulado mañana? →
Sí, *vaya* lo más pronto posible.

1. ¿Debo hacer las reservaciones inmediatamente?
2. ¿Tengo que comprar ya los cheques de viajero?
3. ¿Tengo que traer el dinero mañana?
4. ¿Necesito recoger los pasajes la semana que viene?
5. ¿Debo llegar al aeropuerto dos horas antes de la salida de mi vuelo?
6. ¿Necesito conseguir otro pasaporte?

San Miguel de Allende, México

### Ejercicio 2

Sus primos dicen que deben hacer las siguientes cosas. Déles mandatos directos. Si es necesario, use un pronombre de complemento directo (**lo, la, los** o **las**).

MODELOS: Debemos llamar a Jorge. → ¡Buena idea! *¡Llámenlo!*
Debemos volver antes de septiembre. →
Sí, *vuelvan* antes de septiembre.

1. Debemos preparar el itinerario.
2. Debemos conseguir los pasaportes.
3. Debemos limpiar las maletas.
4. Debemos hacer las maletas esta noche.
5. Debemos dormir antes de salir.
6. Debemos salir inmediatamente.

## 11.2 Softening Commands: The Present Subjunctive Following *querer* and *cuando*

### Gramática ilustrada

Softened command: command forms after **querer que.**

**Quieren que yo termine el trabajo.** (*They want me to finish the job.*)
**Quiero que tú comas con nosotros.** (*I want you to eat with us.*)

**A.** You already know the Spanish verb forms used to give direct commands: for example, **siéntese, descanse, tome la medicina**. Rather than give a direct command, a speaker may prefer to use a "softened" expression, such as *I want you to . . .* A softened expression is used to talk about what one person wants another to do: *My parents want me to . . .*

| | |
|---|---|
| —¿Qué **quiere** el aduanero? | —*What does the customs inspector want?* |
| —**Quiere** que abramos todas las maletas. | —*He wants us to open all of our suitcases.* |

In Spanish, the verb in the clause that follows softened expressions like **quiero que...** has the same form as a command, but because these softened commands can be addressed to anyone, the second verb changes endings to indicate who is to do the action. These forms are called the *subjunctive mood.*

Quiero que { **vayamos** al museo primero.
tú **te quedes** con Adriana.
Carla nos **compre** los boletos.

*I want* { *us to go to the museum first.*
*you to stay with Adriana.*
*Carla to buy us the tickets.*

Subjunctive (command forms) also used after **cuando** when referring to the future:

**Cuando salga de viaje, voy a...** (*When I leave on my trip, I'm going to . . .*)

**B.** When the action or state described in a clause that begins with **cuando** refers to the future, the subjunctive form of the verb is also used.

| | |
|---|---|
| Vamos a facturar el equipaje **cuando revisen** el boleto. | *We are going to check in the bags when they check the ticket.* |
| Pedro va a hacer las reservaciones **cuando hable** con Andrea. | *Pedro is going to make the reservations when he speaks with Andrea.* |
| **Cuando lleguemos** a Madrid, quiero ver el Museo del Prado | *When we get to Madrid, I want to see the Prado Museum.* |

However, if the action or state described in the **cuando** clause refers to a habitual action, the present indicative is used.

| | |
|---|---|
| Mis primos **siempre** van a la costa **cuando viajan.** | *My cousins always go to the coast when they travel.* |

Present subjunctive forms = polite command forms with person/number endings: **coma, comas, coma, comamos, comáis, coman; viaje, viajes, viaje, viajemos, viajéis, viajen**

**C.** The forms of the present subjunctive are the same as the **usted** command forms plus the person/number endings: **hablar → hable + -s, -mos, -éis,* -n.** Thus, the endings contain a different vowel from the present tense (which we will call *present indicative* when we want to contrast it with the present subjunctive).

| INFINITIVE | PRESENT INDICATIVE | PRESENT SUBJUNCTIVE |
|---|---|---|
| hablar | habl**a** | habl**e** |
| comer | com**e** | com**a** |
| escribir | escrib**e** | escrib**a** |

*Note that the **vosotros/as** form drops the **-e** of the **usted** command form.

Here are the rest of the present subjunctive forms.*

| | -ar | -er | -ir |
|---|---|---|---|
| (yo) | habl**e** | com**a** | escrib**a** |
| (tú) | habl**es** | com**as** | escrib**as** |
| (usted, él/ella) | habl**e** | com**a** | escrib**a** |
| (nosotros/as) | habl**emos** | com**amos** | escrib**amos** |
| (vosotros/as) | habl**éis** | com**áis** | escrib**áis** |
| (ustedes, ellos/as) | habl**en** | com**an** | escrib**an** |

—¿Qué quiere la mesera?
—Quiere que **paguemos**† en la caja a la salida.

—*What does the waitress want?*
—*She wants us to pay at the cash register when we leave.*

**D.** Although pronouns are attached to affirmative commands (**cómalo**), they are placed before conjugated verbs. (Pronouns are also attached to infinitives and present participles.)

—¿Qué quiere nuestro agente de viajes?
—Quiere que **lo llamemos** mañana.

—*What does our travel agent want?*
—*He wants us to call him tomorrow.*

## Prohibido fumar a bordo

El aire se ha limpiado en cerca de 80% de los vuelos programados sin escala entre los Estados Unidos y destinos extranjeros, informa el Departamento de Transporte de ese país. US Air, por ejemplo, ha prohibido fumar en todos sus vuelos internacionales y American Airlines en todos sus vuelos hacia y desde Europa, el Caribe y un buen número de destinos mexicanos. United ahora prohíbe fumar en todos sus vuelos dentro de Europa y en vuelos transatlánticos (excepto entre Dulles y Milán, Italia). TWA ha prohibido fumar en todos sus vuelos hacia y desde Francia, Alemania y el Reino Unido. Continental ha prohibido fumar en sus vuelos en todo el mundo a partir del 1º de agosto. Y Delta ha quedado libre de humo desde el 1º de enero de 1995. ◑

## Ejercicio 3

Aquí tiene usted algunas recomendaciones del agente de viajes de Rubén y Virginia Hernández. Ahora Virginia está repitiéndole la información a una vecina. Use el subjuntivo en todos los casos.

MODELO: Lleguen al aeropuerto con una hora de anticipación. →
Nuestro agente de viajes quiere que *lleguemos* al aeropuerto con una hora de anticipación.

1. Recojan sus boletos pronto.
2. Escriban una lista de lo que van a necesitar.
3. No lleven demasiadas cosas en las maletas.
4. Compren cheques de viajero.
5. Coman en restaurantes buenos, no coman en la calle.
6. Lleguen al aeropuerto temprano.
7. Beban refrescos o agua mineral, no beban el agua.

## Ejercicio 4

Escoja el verbo que mejor corresponda al contexto.

---

*Recognition: **vos hablés, comás, escribás**
†See Appendix 3 and the *Cuaderno de trabajo*, **Capítulo 11**, for an explanation of spelling changes in the present subjunctive.

MODELO: Voy a darte tu boleto cuando *subamos/subimos* al avión.

1. Voy a mandarte una postal cuando *llegue/llego* al hotel.
2. Cuando *viajemos/viajamos* a Argentina, siempre nos hospedamos en el Hotel Río Plata.
3. Todos los días la asistente de vuelo sirve las bebidas cuando los pasajeros *suban/suben* al avión.
4. Voy a saber más de los mayas cuando *lea/leo* estos libros sobre su cultura.
5. José y Pilar van a pagar en la caja cuando *terminen/terminan* de cenar.

## 11.3 Softening Commands and Expressing Future Doubt: The Present Subjunctive of Irregular Verbs

The subjunctive takes a long time to acquire. You will hear it and read it extensively before you are able to produce it comfortably.

**A.** Verbs that have different stems in the **yo** forms of the present indicative have those same stems in the present subjunctive (as they do in the command forms).

| | | |
|---|---|---|
| conocer | conozco | conozca, conozcas, conozca, conozcamos, conozcáis, conozcan |
| construir | construyo | construya, construyas, construya, construyamos, construyáis, construyan |
| decir | digo | diga, digas, diga, digamos, digáis, digan |
| hacer | hago | haga, hagas, haga, hagamos, hagáis, hagan |
| oír | oigo | oiga, oigas, oiga, oigamos, oigáis, oigan |
| poner | pongo | ponga, pongas, ponga, pongamos, pongáis, pongan |
| recoger | recojo | recoja, recojas, recoja, recojamos, recojáis, recojan |
| salir | salgo | salga, salgas, salga, salgamos, salgáis, salgan |
| tener | tengo | tenga, tengas, tenga, tengamos, tengáis, tengan |
| traer | traigo | traiga, traigas, traiga, traigamos, traigáis, traigan |
| venir | vengo | venga, vengas, venga, vengamos, vengáis, vengan |
| ver | veo | vea, veas, vea, veamos, veáis, vean |

Cuando **recojamos** los boletos, le vamos a preguntar al agente si necesitamos vacunas.

*When we pick up the tickets, we'll ask the agent if we need vaccinations.*

**B.** Verbs that end in **-oy** in the **yo** form, as well as the verb **saber**, have irregular stems in the present subjunctive.*

| | | |
|---|---|---|
| dar | doy | dé, des, dé, demos, deis, den |
| estar | estoy | esté, estés, esté, estemos, estéis, estén |
| ir | voy | vaya, vayas, vaya, vayamos, vayáis, vayan |
| ser | soy | sea, seas, sea, seamos, seáis, sean |
| saber | sé | sepa, sepas, sepa, sepamos, sepáis, sepan |

*Recognition: **vos des, estés, vayás, seás, sepás**

| | |
|---|---|
| Quiero que me **des** tu nuevo número de teléfono antes de salir. | *I want you to give me your new telephone number before you leave.* |
| La profesora quiere que **sepamos** todos estos verbos para el examen. | *The professor wants us to know all these verbs for the exam.* |

Use this section as a reference; don't try to memorize all these forms!

**C.** The present subjunctive forms of stem-changing verbs are as follows.

*Group I.* Verbs with stem-vowel changes **e** → **ie** and **o** → **ue** in the present indicative keep those changes in the present subjunctive. The stems of **pensar** and **volver** always change except for the **nosotros/as** and **vosotros/as** forms.*

| INDICATIVE | SUBJUNCTIVE | INDICATIVE | SUBJUNCTIVE |
|---|---|---|---|
| pienso | piense | vuelvo | vuelva |
| piensas | pienses | vuelves | vuelvas |
| piensa | piense | vuelve | vuelva |
| **pe**nsamos | **pe**nsemos | **vo**lvemos | **vo**lvamos |
| **pe**nsáis | **pe**nséis | **vo**lvéis | **vo**lváis |
| piensan | piensen | vuelven | vuelvan |

| | |
|---|---|
| No quiero que tú **pienses** mal de mí. | *I don't want you to think badly of me.* |
| El presidente del Banco de Guadalajara quiere que sus empleados **vuelvan** al trabajo a las 2:00. | *The president of the Bank of Guadalajara wants his employees to return to work at 2:00.* |

*Group II.* Verbs like **pedir** and **servir**, whose stems show an **e** → **i** change in the present indicative (except for the **nosotros/as** and **vosotros/as** forms†), have the same stem-vowel change in *all* the present subjunctive forms.

| INDICATIVE | SUBJUNCTIVE | INDICATIVE | SUBJUNCTIVE |
|---|---|---|---|
| pido | pida | sirvo | sirva |
| pides | pidas | sirves | sirvas |
| pide | pida | sirve | sirva |
| pedimos | pidamos | servimos | sirvamos |
| pedís | pidáis | servís | sirváis |
| piden | pidan | sirven | sirvan |

**EL PARADOR DE ZAFRA**

Cuenta la historia que en un castillo de la localidad de Zafra habitó Hernán Cortés antes de partir para conquistar Méjico. Hoy, ese castillo ofrece todo el encanto de un cómodo Parador Nacional disponible para todos los que, sin sentirse héroes de grandes hazañas, están dispuestos a trasladarse hasta el siglo XV y revivir glorias pasadas. El Parador Hernán Cortés está acondicionado con todo tipo de comodidades. Destaca su restaurante especializado en platos típicos de la zona. Por su situación privilegiada, es la base

FOTOS: A. GARRIDO

perfecta para recorrer los alrededores, que ofrecen pueblos medievales de gran interés cultural. Precio: 9.000 ptas habitación doble. Parador Hernán Cortés. Zafra, Badajoz.

*Recognition: **vos pensés, volvás**
†Recognition: **vos pidás, sirvás**

| | |
|---|---|
| Papá quiere que todos **pidamos** un sándwich. | *Dad wants all of us to order a sandwich.* |
| El cocinero quiere que **se sirva** la comida a partir de las 7:00. | *The cook wants the meal to be served starting at 7:00.* |

*Group III.* Verbs like **divertirse**, which show an **e** → **ie** change in the present indicative as well as an **e** → **i** change in the preterite, and verbs like **dormir**, which show an **o** → **ue** change in the present indicative and an **o** → **u** change in the preterite, maintain *both* changes in the present subjunctive.*

| INDICATIVE | SUBJUNCTIVE | INDICATIVE | SUBJUNCTIVE |
|---|---|---|---|
| me divierto | me divierta | duermo | duerma |
| te diviertes | te diviertas | duermes | duermas |
| se divierte | se divierta | duerme | duerma |
| nos divertimos | nos divirtamos | dormimos | durmamos |
| os divertís | os divirtáis | dormís | durmáis |
| se divierten | se diviertan | duermen | duerman |

| | |
|---|---|
| Todos quieren que **nos divirtamos** mucho en el viaje. | *Everyone wants us to have a lot of fun on the trip.* |
| Quiero que **te duermas** ahora, porque el viaje mañana va a ser difícil. | *I want you to sleep now, because the trip tomorrow is going to be difficult.* |

Cuernavaca, México: uno de los impresionantes murales de Diego Rivera

## Ejercicio 5

Usted va a ir de excursión a México con un grupo de estudiantes de la clase de español. Ahora sus padres quieren saber las recomendaciones que su profesor(a) les ha hecho. Repítales la información.

MODELO: No salgan sin los boletos. →
El profesor / La profesora no quiere que nosotros *salgamos* sin los boletos.

1. Hagan las maletas dos días antes de la salida.
2. Duerman ocho horas la noche anterior a la salida.
3. Traigan ropa para ocho días.
4. Vayan directamente a la estación de autobuses.
5. Pongan el dinero en un lugar seguro.
6. Denme los pasaportes.
7. Vuelvan con buenos recuerdos del viaje.
8. No pidan comida americana en los restaurantes.
9. Diviértanse mucho.
10. Díganle «Adiós» a su familia.

*Recognition: **vos te divirtás, te durmás**

## Ejercicio 6

Primero escriba las formas apropiadas de los verbos indicados. Luego señale la frase que mejor complete cada oración.

MODELO: Mi profesora quiere que yo *me divierta* (divertirse) cuando *salga* (salir: yo) de vacaciones.

1. Mis padres quieren que los _____ (llamar: yo)...
2. Queremos que Juan, el mesero más guapo, nos _____ (servir)...
3. Quiero que _____ (oír: tú) mi nuevo disco...
4. Alberto quiere que nosotros le _____ (traer) regalos...
5. Quiero que _____ (sacar: tú) muchas fotos...

a. cuando _____ (estar: tú) en México.
b. cuando _____ (venir: tú) a visitarme.
c. cuando _____ (llegar: yo) a mi destino.
d. cuando _____ (ir: nosotros) al restaurante argentino.
e. cuando _____ (volver: nosotros) de Madrid.

## 11.4 Talking about Past Actions in Progress: The Imperfect Progressive

### Gramática ilustrada

**¿RECUERDA?**

In **Gramática 3.5** you learned how to use a present-tense form of **estar** with a present participle (the **-ando/-iendo** form of the verb) to talk about actions currently in progress. Review that section now, if necessary.

To describe an action that was taking place at some past moment, use the imperfect tense of **estar** (**estaba, estabas, estaba, estábamos, estabais, estaban**), followed by a present participle.

| | |
|---|---|
| —¿Qué **estabas haciendo** a las 4:00? | —*What were you doing at 4:00?* |
| —Creo que **estaba viendo** la televisión. | —*I think I was watching television.* |
| —Rubén, ¿qué **estabas haciendo** ayer cuando te llamé? | —*Rubén, what were you doing yesterday when I called?* |
| —¡**Durmiendo,** por supuesto! | —*Sleeping, of course!* |

## Ejercicio 7

Usando el participio del presente de **ver**, **estudiar**, **asistir**, **dormir** y **leer**, diga qué estaba haciendo y qué no estaba haciendo usted ayer.

Ayer a las 4:00 de la tarde estaba...

| | SÍ | NO |
|---|---|---|
| **1.** _____ una siesta. | ☐ | ☐ |
| **2.** _____ a una clase. | ☐ | ☐ |
| **3.** _____ la televisión. | ☐ | ☐ |
| **4.** _____ la lección de español. | ☐ | ☐ |
| **5.** _____ el periódico. | ☐ | ☐ |

Ahora diga qué estaban haciendo las siguientes personas.

**6.** Mi profesor(a) _____.
**7.** Mi mejor amigo/a _____.
**8.** Dos compañeros de clase _____.
**9.** Mis padres _____.
**10.** El presidente de los Estados Unidos _____.

## 11.5 Saying What Was Happening: The Imperfect in Contrast to the Preterite

### Gramática ilustrada

Era un día de primavera. Hacía sol y hacía un poco fresco. Pedro y Andrea estaban sentados en un café de la Gran Vía cuando de repente Pedro vio a un viejo amigo de la universidad. Pedro se levantó, corrió hacia él, lo saludó y lo invitó a tomar un refresco con él y Andrea. Los tres tomaron refrescos y charlaron.

Some review:
**preterite** = *action completed*
**imperfect** = *action went on over time in past*
**imperfect progressive** = *action was going on at a particular time in the past*

Although the imperfect and the preterite both describe past actions or states, their uses are not the same. As you know, the preterite is used with verbs of action to emphasize that a past event was completed.

| | |
|---|---|
| —¿Qué **hiciste** ayer? | *—What did you do yesterday?* |
| —**Visité** el Museo del Prado. | *—I visited the Prado Museum.* |

The imperfect, on the other hand, is chosen if the speaker wishes to emphasize that an action happened repeatedly in the past.

| | |
|---|---|
| Cuando **íbamos** de vacaciones a Acapulco, siempre **nos quedábamos** en el Hotel Condesa del Mar. | *When we were on vacation in Acapulco, we would always stay at the Condesa del Mar Hotel.* |

In **Gramática 11.4**, you learned that the imperfect progressive can be used to indicate that something was happening at a particular time in the past.

| | |
|---|---|
| —¿Qué **estabas haciendo** cuando te llamé? | *—What were you doing when I called?* |
| —**Estaba bañándome**. | *—I was taking a bath.* |

**action in progress** = *imperfect*
**interrupting action** = *preterite*

Imperfect is used for past habitual action:
**De joven, vivía en México.**
or past action in progress:
**Caminaba por la plaza cuando oí la música.**

Similarly, you can use the simple imperfect to describe an action that was in progress in the past when something else interrupted it. The interrupting action is expressed in the preterite tense.

| | |
|---|---|
| **Caminaba** por la calle cuando **vi** al agente de policía. | *I was walking down the street when I saw the policeman.* |
| **Descansaba** en mi cuarto cuando **sonó** el teléfono. | *I was resting in my room when the phone rang.* |
| **Comía** un postre cuando alguien **tocó** a la puerta. | *I was eating dessert when someone knocked at the door.* |
| **Salía** de la casa cuando me **gritó** la vecina. | *I was leaving (the house) when the neighbor yelled to me.* |
| **Llegábamos** a Madrid cuando **se descompuso** el motor. | *We were arriving in Madrid when the engine broke down.* |

## Ejercicio 8

Escriba la forma apropiada de los verbos entre paréntesis. Luego indique si eso le ha pasado a usted alguna vez.

MODELO: El profesor *hablaba* (hablar) cuando me dormí en clase.

| | SÍ | NO |
|---|---|---|
| **1.** _____ (manejar: yo) en la autopista cuando dos carros chocaron. | ☐ | ☐ |
| **2.** _____ (ver: yo) mi programa favorito cuando sonó el teléfono y no contesté. | ☐ | ☐ |
| **3.** _____ (caminar: yo) por la calle cuando vi un accidente. | ☐ | ☐ |
| **4.** Mi profesor _____ (hablar) cuando entré tarde a la clase. | ☐ | ☐ |

| | | SÍ | NO |
|---|---|---|---|
| **5.** | _____ (hacer: yo) mi tarea en la biblioteca cuando comenzó una tormenta y no pude salir por largo rato. | ☐ | ☐ |
| **6.** | _____ (bañarse: yo) cuando entró una persona desconocida. | ☐ | ☐ |

## Ejercicio 9

Pilar habla de sus vacaciones. Lea toda la historia primero y luego escoja entre el imperfecto o el pretérito según el contexto.

Cuando *era/fui*[1] niña, todos los años mi familia y yo *íbamos/fuimos*[2] a las islas Baleares. Siempre *alquilábamos/alquilamos*[3] una casa con vista al mar. De día *buceábamos/buceamos*[4] y nos *bañábamos/bañamos.*[5] De noche *salíamos/salimos*[6] a cenar a un restaurante elegante y luego *caminábamos/caminamos*[7] por la plaza.

Una tarde de verano, cuando mi hermano menor, Felipe, *tenía/tuvo*[8] ocho años, él y yo *íbamos/fuimos*[9] solos a la playa. Nuestros padres *estaban durmiendo / durmieron*[10] todavía. Mi hermanito *jugaba/jugó*[11] en el agua y yo *hablaba/hablé*[12] con unos chicos que ya *conocía/conocí*[13] de otros veranos. Después de unos minutos *miraba/miré*[14] hacia donde *jugaba/jugó*[15] mi hermanito y no lo *veía/vi.*[16] Mis amigos y yo nos *levantábamos/levantamos*[17] y *corríamos/corrimos*[18] al agua para buscarlo. No lo *encontrábamos/encontramos.*[19] Lo *buscábamos/buscamos*[20] por toda la playa y no lo *podíamos/pudimos*[21] encontrar. *Estaba/ Estuve*[22] desesperada. Por fin *regresábamos/regresamos*[23] adonde *teníamos/tuvimos*[24] las toallas... allí *estaba/estuvo*[25] sentado mi hermanito, comiendo un bocadillo. «¿Adónde *ibas/fuiste?*[26]» le *gritaba/grité.*[27] Él no me *contestaba/contestó*[28] pero yo *estaba/estuve*[29] tan contenta de verlo que no me *enojaba/enojé*[30] demasiado con él.

# Appendix 1

## VERBS

### A. Regular Verbs: Simple Tenses

| INFINITIVE<br>PRESENT PARTICIPLE<br>PAST PARTICIPLE | INDICATIVE | | | | | SUBJUNCTIVE | | IMPERATIVE |
|---|---|---|---|---|---|---|---|---|
| | PRESENT | IMPERFECT | PRETERITE | FUTURE | CONDITIONAL | PRESENT | IMPERFECT | |
| hablar<br>hablando<br>hablado | hablo<br>hablas<br>habla<br>hablamos<br>habláis<br>hablan | hablaba<br>hablabas<br>hablaba<br>hablábamos<br>hablabais<br>hablaban | hablé<br>hablaste<br>habló<br>hablamos<br>hablasteis<br>hablaron | hablaré<br>hablarás<br>hablará<br>hablaremos<br>hablaréis<br>hablarán | hablaría<br>hablarías<br>hablaría<br>hablaríamos<br>hablaríais<br>hablarían | hable<br>hables<br>hable<br>hablemos<br>habléis<br>hablen | hablara<br>hablaras<br>hablara<br>habláramos<br>hablarais<br>hablaran | habla tú,<br>no hables<br>hable Ud.<br>hablemos<br>hablad<br>hablen |
| comer<br>comiendo<br>comido | como<br>comes<br>come<br>comemos<br>coméis<br>comen | comía<br>comías<br>comía<br>comíamos<br>comíais<br>comían | comí<br>comiste<br>comió<br>comimos<br>comisteis<br>comieron | comeré<br>comerás<br>comerá<br>comeremos<br>comeréis<br>comerán | comería<br>comerías<br>comería<br>comeríamos<br>comeríais<br>comerían | coma<br>comas<br>coma<br>comamos<br>comáis<br>coman | comiera<br>comieras<br>comiera<br>comiéramos<br>comierais<br>comieran | come tú,<br>no comas<br>coma Ud.<br>comamos<br>comed<br>coman |
| vivir<br>viviendo<br>vivido | vivo<br>vives<br>vive<br>vivimos<br>vivís<br>viven | vivía<br>vivías<br>vivía<br>vivíamos<br>vivíais<br>vivían | viví<br>viviste<br>vivió<br>vivimos<br>vivisteis<br>vivieron | viviré<br>vivirás<br>vivirá<br>viviremos<br>viviréis<br>vivirán | viviría<br>vivirías<br>viviría<br>viviríamos<br>viviríais<br>vivirían | viva<br>vivas<br>viva<br>vivamos<br>viváis<br>vivan | viviera<br>vivieras<br>viviera<br>viviéramos<br>vivierais<br>vivieran | vive tú,<br>no vivas<br>viva Ud.<br>vivamos<br>vivid<br>vivan |

### B. Regular Verbs: Perfect Tenses

| INDICATIVE | | | | | | | | | | SUBJUNCTIVE | | | |
|---|---|---|---|---|---|---|---|---|---|---|---|---|---|
| PRESENT PERFECT | | PAST PERFECT | | PRETERITE PERFECT | | FUTURE PERFECT | | CONDITIONAL PERFEECT | | PRESENT PERFECT | | PAST PERFECT | |
| he<br>has<br>ha<br>hemos<br>habéis<br>han | hablado<br>comido<br>vivido | había<br>habías<br>había<br>habíamos<br>habíais<br>habían | hablado<br>comido<br>vivido | hube<br>hubiste<br>hubo<br>hubimos<br>hubisteis<br>hubieron | hablado<br>comido<br>vivido | habré<br>habrás<br>habrá<br>habremos<br>habréis<br>habrán | hablado<br>comido<br>vivido | habría<br>habrías<br>habría<br>habríamos<br>habríais<br>habrían | hablado<br>comido<br>vivido | haya<br>hayas<br>haya<br>hayamos<br>hayáis<br>hayan | hablado<br>comido<br>vivido | hubiera<br>hubieras<br>hubiera<br>hubiéramos<br>hubierais<br>hubieran | hablado<br>comido<br>vivido |

## C. Irregular Verbs

| INFINITIVE<br>PRESENT PARTICIPLE<br>PAST PARTICIPLE | INDICATIVE | | | | | SUBJUNCTIVE | | IMPERATIVE |
|---|---|---|---|---|---|---|---|---|
| | PRESENT | IMPERFECT | PRETERITE | FUTURE | CONDITIONAL | PRESENT | IMPERFECT | |
| andar<br>andando<br>andado | ando<br>andas<br>anda<br>andamos<br>andáis<br>andan | andaba<br>andabas<br>andaba<br>andábamos<br>andabais<br>andaban | anduve<br>anduviste<br>anduvo<br>anduvimos<br>anduvisteis<br>anduvieron | andaré<br>andarás<br>andará<br>andaremos<br>andaréis<br>andarán | andaría<br>andarías<br>andaría<br>andaríamos<br>andaríais<br>andarían | ande<br>andes<br>ande<br>andemos<br>andéis<br>anden | anduviera<br>anduvieras<br>anduviera<br>anduviéramos<br>anduvierais<br>anduvieran | anda tú,<br>no andes<br>ande Ud.<br>andemos<br>andad<br>anden |
| caer<br>cayendo<br>caído | caigo<br>caes<br>cae<br>caemos<br>caéis<br>caen | caía<br>caías<br>caía<br>caíamos<br>caíais<br>caían | caí<br>caíste<br>cayó<br>caímos<br>caísteis<br>cayeron | caeré<br>caerás<br>caerá<br>caeremos<br>caeréis<br>caerán | caería<br>caerías<br>caería<br>caeríamos<br>caeríais<br>caerían | caiga<br>caigas<br>caiga<br>caigamos<br>caigáis<br>caigan | cayera<br>cayeras<br>cayera<br>cayéramos<br>cayerais<br>cayeran | cae tú,<br>no caigas<br>caiga Ud.<br>caigamos<br>caed<br>caigan |
| dar<br>dando<br>dado | doy<br>das<br>da<br>damos<br>dais<br>dan | daba<br>dabas<br>daba<br>dábamos<br>dabais<br>daban | di<br>diste<br>dio<br>dimos<br>disteis<br>dieron | daré<br>darás<br>dará<br>daremos<br>daréis<br>darán | daría<br>darías<br>daría<br>daríamos<br>daríais<br>darían | dé<br>des<br>dé<br>demos<br>deis<br>den | diera<br>dieras<br>diera<br>diéramos<br>dierais<br>dieran | da tú,<br>no des<br>dé Ud.<br>demos<br>dad<br>den |
| decir<br>diciendo<br>dicho | digo<br>dices<br>dice<br>decimos<br>decís<br>dicen | decía<br>decías<br>decía<br>decíamos<br>decíais<br>decían | dije<br>dijiste<br>dijo<br>dijimos<br>dijisteis<br>dijeron | diré<br>dirás<br>dirá<br>diremos<br>diréis<br>dirán | diría<br>dirías<br>diría<br>diríamos<br>diríais<br>dirían | diga<br>digas<br>diga<br>digamos<br>digáis<br>digan | dijera<br>dijeras<br>dijera<br>dijéramos<br>dijerais<br>dijeran | di tú,<br>no digas<br>diga Ud.<br>digamos<br>decid<br>digan |
| estar<br>estando<br>estado | estoy<br>estás<br>está<br>estamos<br>estáis<br>están | estaba<br>estabas<br>estaba<br>estábamos<br>estabais<br>estaban | estuve<br>estuviste<br>estuvo<br>estuvimos<br>estuvisteis<br>estuvieron | estaré<br>estarás<br>estará<br>estaremos<br>estaréis<br>estarán | estaría<br>estarías<br>estaría<br>estaríamos<br>estaríais<br>estarían | esté<br>estés<br>esté<br>estemos<br>estéis<br>estén | estuviera<br>estuvieras<br>estuviera<br>estuviéramos<br>estuvierais<br>estuvieran | está tú,<br>no estés<br>esté Ud.<br>estemos<br>estad<br>estén |
| haber<br>habiendo<br>habido | he<br>has<br>ha<br>hemos<br>habéis<br>han | había<br>habías<br>había<br>habíamos<br>habíais<br>habían | hube<br>hubiste<br>hubo<br>hubimos<br>hubisteis<br>hubieron | habré<br>habrás<br>habrá<br>habremos<br>habréis<br>habrán | habría<br>habrías<br>habría<br>habríamos<br>habríais<br>habrían | haya<br>hayas<br>haya<br>hayamos<br>hayáis<br>hayan | hubiera<br>hubieras<br>hubiera<br>hubiéramos<br>hubierais<br>hubieran | |
| hacer<br>haciendo<br>hecho | hago<br>haces<br>hace<br>hacemos<br>hacéis<br>hacen | hacía<br>hacías<br>hacía<br>hacíamos<br>hacíais<br>hacían | hice<br>hiciste<br>hizo<br>hicimos<br>hicisteis<br>hicieron | haré<br>harás<br>hará<br>haremos<br>haréis<br>harán | haría<br>harías<br>haría<br>haríamos<br>haríais<br>harían | haga<br>hagas<br>haga<br>hagamos<br>hagáis<br>hagan | hiciera<br>hicieras<br>hiciera<br>hiciéramos<br>hicierais<br>hicieran | haz tú,<br>no hagas<br>haga Ud.<br>hagamos<br>haced<br>hagan |

## C. Irregular Verbs (continued)

| INFINITIVE<br>PRESENT PARTICIPLE<br>PAST PARTICIPLE | INDICATIVE | | | | | SUBJUNCTIVE | | IMPERATIVE |
|---|---|---|---|---|---|---|---|---|
| | PRESENT | IMPERFECT | PRETERITE | FUTURE | CONDITIONAL | PRESENT | IMPERFECT | |
| ir<br>yendo<br>ido | voy<br>vas<br>va<br>vamos<br>vais<br>van | iba<br>ibas<br>iba<br>íbamos<br>ibais<br>iban | fui<br>fuiste<br>fue<br>fuimos<br>fuisteis<br>fueron | iré<br>irás<br>irá<br>iremos<br>iréis<br>irán | iría<br>irías<br>iría<br>iríamos<br>iríais<br>irían | vaya<br>vayas<br>vaya<br>vayamos<br>vayáis<br>vayan | fuera<br>fueras<br>fuera<br>fuéramos<br>fuerais<br>fueran | ve tú,<br>no vayas<br>vaya Ud.<br>vayamos<br>id<br>vayan |
| oír<br>oyendo<br>oído | oigo<br>oyes<br>oye<br>oímos<br>oís<br>oyen | oía<br>oías<br>oía<br>oíamos<br>oíais<br>oían | oí<br>oíste<br>oyó<br>oímos<br>oísteis<br>oyeron | oiré<br>oirás<br>oirá<br>oiremos<br>oiréis<br>oirán | oiría<br>oirías<br>oiría<br>oiríamos<br>oiríais<br>oirían | oiga<br>oigas<br>oiga<br>oigamos<br>oigáis<br>oigan | oyera<br>oyeras<br>oyera<br>oyéramos<br>oyerais<br>oyeran | oye tú,<br>no oigas<br>oiga Ud.<br>oigamos<br>oíd<br>oigan |
| poder<br>pudiendo<br>podido | puedo<br>puedes<br>puede<br>podemos<br>podéis<br>pueden | podía<br>podías<br>podía<br>podíamos<br>podíais<br>podían | pude<br>pudiste<br>pudo<br>pudimos<br>pudisteis<br>pudieron | podré<br>podrás<br>podrá<br>podremos<br>podréis<br>podrán | podría<br>podrías<br>podría<br>podríamos<br>podríais<br>podrían | pueda<br>puedas<br>pueda<br>podamos<br>podáis<br>puedan | pudiera<br>pudieras<br>pudiera<br>pudiéramos<br>pudierais<br>pudieran | |
| poner<br>poniendo<br>puesto | pongo<br>pones<br>pone<br>ponemos<br>ponéis<br>ponen | ponía<br>ponías<br>ponía<br>poníamos<br>poníais<br>ponían | puse<br>pusiste<br>puso<br>pusimos<br>pusisteis<br>pusieron | pondré<br>pondrás<br>pondrá<br>pondremos<br>pondréis<br>pondrán | pondría<br>pondrías<br>pondría<br>pondríamos<br>pondríais<br>pondrían | ponga<br>pongas<br>ponga<br>pongamos<br>pongáis<br>pongan | pusiera<br>pusieras<br>pusiera<br>pusiéramos<br>pusierais<br>pusieran | pon tú,<br>no pongas<br>ponga Ud.<br>pongamos<br>poned<br>pongan |
| querer<br>queriendo<br>querido | quiero<br>quieres<br>quiere<br>queremos<br>queréis<br>quieren | quería<br>querías<br>quería<br>queríamos<br>queríais<br>querían | quise<br>quisiste<br>quiso<br>quisimos<br>quisisteis<br>quisieron | querré<br>querrás<br>querrá<br>querremos<br>querréis<br>querrán | querría<br>querrías<br>querría<br>querríamos<br>querríais<br>querrían | quiera<br>quieras<br>quiera<br>queramos<br>queráis<br>quieran | quisiera<br>quisieras<br>quisiera<br>quisiéramos<br>quisierais<br>quisieran | quiere tú,<br>no quieras<br>quiera Ud.<br>queramos<br>quered<br>quieran |
| saber<br>sabiendo<br>sabido | sé<br>sabes<br>sabe<br>sabemos<br>sabéis<br>saben | sabía<br>sabías<br>sabía<br>sabíamos<br>sabíais<br>sabían | supe<br>supiste<br>supo<br>supimos<br>supisteis<br>supieron | sabré<br>sabrás<br>sabrá<br>sabremos<br>sabréis<br>sabrán | sabría<br>sabrías<br>sabría<br>sabríamos<br>sabríais<br>sabrían | sepa<br>sepas<br>sepa<br>sepamos<br>sepáis<br>sepan | supiera<br>supieras<br>supiera<br>supiéramos<br>supierais<br>supieran | sabe tú,<br>no sepas<br>sepa Ud.<br>sepamos<br>sabed<br>sepan |
| salir<br>saliendo<br>salido | salgo<br>sales<br>sale<br>salimos<br>salís<br>salen | salía<br>salías<br>salía<br>salíamos<br>salíais<br>salían | salí<br>saliste<br>salió<br>salimos<br>salisteis<br>salieron | saldré<br>saldrás<br>saldrá<br>saldremos<br>saldréis<br>saldrán | saldría<br>saldrías<br>saldría<br>saldríamos<br>saldríais<br>saldrían | salga<br>salgas<br>salga<br>salgamos<br>salgáis<br>salgan | saliera<br>salieras<br>saliera<br>saliéramos<br>salierais<br>salieran | sal tú,<br>no salgas<br>salga Ud.<br>salgamos<br>salid<br>salgan |

## C. Irregular Verbs (continued)

| INFINITIVE<br>PRESENT PARTICIPLE<br>PAST PARTICIPLE | INDICATIVE | | | | | SUBJUNCTIVE | | IMPERATIVE |
|---|---|---|---|---|---|---|---|---|
| | PRESENT | IMPERFECT | PRETERITE | FUTURE | CONDITIONAL | PRESENT | IMPERFECT | |
| ser<br>siendo<br>sido | soy<br>eres<br>es<br>somos<br>sois<br>son | era<br>eras<br>era<br>éramos<br>erais<br>eran | fui<br>fuiste<br>fue<br>fuimos<br>fuisteis<br>fueron | seré<br>serás<br>será<br>seremos<br>seréis<br>serán | sería<br>serías<br>sería<br>seríamos<br>seríais<br>serían | sea<br>seas<br>sea<br>seamos<br>seáis<br>sean | fuera<br>fueras<br>fuera<br>fuéramos<br>fuerais<br>fueran | sé tú,<br>no seas<br>sea Ud.<br>seamos<br>sed<br>sean |
| tener<br>teniendo<br>tenido | tengo<br>tienes<br>tiene<br>tenemos<br>tenéis<br>tienen | tenía<br>tenías<br>tenía<br>teníamos<br>teníais<br>tenían | tuve<br>tuviste<br>tuvo<br>tuvimos<br>tuvisteis<br>tuvieron | tendré<br>tendrás<br>tendrá<br>tendremos<br>tendréis<br>tendrán | tendría<br>tendrías<br>tendría<br>tendríamos<br>tendríais<br>tendrían | tenga<br>tengas<br>tenga<br>tengamos<br>tengáis<br>tengan | tuviera<br>tuvieras<br>tuviera<br>tuviéramos<br>tuvierais<br>tuvieran | ten tú,<br>no tengas<br>tenga Ud.<br>tengamos<br>tened<br>tengan |
| traer<br>trayendo<br>traído | traigo<br>traes<br>trae<br>traemos<br>traéis<br>traen | traía<br>traías<br>traía<br>traíamos<br>traíais<br>traían | traje<br>trajiste<br>trajo<br>trajimos<br>trajisteis<br>trajeron | traeré<br>traerás<br>traerá<br>traeremos<br>traeréis<br>traerán | traería<br>traerías<br>traería<br>traeríamos<br>traeríais<br>traerían | traiga<br>traigas<br>traiga<br>traigamos<br>traigáis<br>traigan | trajera<br>trajeras<br>trajera<br>trajéramos<br>trajerais<br>trajeran | trae tú,<br>no traigas<br>traiga Ud.<br>traigamos<br>traed<br>traigan |
| venir<br>viniendo<br>venido | vengo<br>vienes<br>viene<br>venimos<br>venís<br>vienen | venía<br>venías<br>venía<br>veníamos<br>veníais<br>venían | vine<br>viniste<br>vino<br>vinimos<br>vinisteis<br>vinieron | vendré<br>vendrás<br>vendrá<br>vendremos<br>vendréis<br>vendrán | vendría<br>vendrías<br>vendría<br>vendríamos<br>vendríais<br>vendrían | venga<br>vengas<br>venga<br>vengamos<br>vengáis<br>vengan | viniera<br>vinieras<br>viniera<br>viniéramos<br>vinierais<br>vinieran | ven tú,<br>no vengas<br>venga Ud.<br>vengamos<br>venid<br>vengan |
| ver<br>viendo<br>visto | veo<br>ves<br>ve<br>vemos<br>veis<br>ven | veía<br>veías<br>veía<br>veíamos<br>veíais<br>veían | vi<br>viste<br>vio<br>vimos<br>visteis<br>vieron | veré<br>verás<br>verá<br>veremos<br>veréis<br>verán | vería<br>verías<br>vería<br>veríamos<br>veríais<br>verían | vea<br>veas<br>vea<br>veamos<br>veáis<br>vean | viera<br>vieras<br>viera<br>viéramos<br>vierais<br>vieran | ve tú,<br>no veas<br>vea Ud.<br>veamos<br>ved<br>vean |

## D. Stem-Changing and Spelling Change Verbs

| INFINITIVE<br>PRESENT PARTICIPLE<br>PAST PARTICIPLE | INDICATIVE | | | | | SUBJUNCTIVE | | IMPERATIVE |
|---|---|---|---|---|---|---|---|---|
| | PRESENT | IMPERFECT | PRETERITE | FUTURE | CONDITIONAL | PRESENT | IMPERFECT | |
| pensar (ie)<br>pensando<br>pensado | pienso<br>piensas<br>piensa<br>pensamos<br>pensáis<br>piensan | pensaba<br>pensabas<br>pensaba<br>pensábamos<br>pensabais<br>pensaban | pensé<br>pensaste<br>pensó<br>pensamos<br>pensasteis<br>pensaron | pensaré<br>pensarás<br>pensará<br>pensaremos<br>pensaréis<br>pensarán | pensaría<br>pensarías<br>pensaría<br>pensaríamos<br>pensaríais<br>pensarían | piense<br>pienses<br>piense<br>pensemos<br>penséis<br>piensen | pensara<br>pensaras<br>pensara<br>pensáramos<br>pensarais<br>pensaran | piensa tú,<br>no pienses<br>piense Ud.<br>pensemos<br>pensad<br>piensen |
| volver (ue)<br>volviendo<br>vuelto | vuelvo<br>vuelves<br>vuelve<br>volvemos<br>volvéis<br>vuelven | volvía<br>volvías<br>volvía<br>volvíamos<br>volvíais<br>volvían | volví<br>volviste<br>volvió<br>volvimos<br>volvisteis<br>volvieron | volveré<br>volverás<br>volverá<br>volveremos<br>volveréis<br>volverán | volvería<br>volverías<br>volvería<br>volveríamos<br>volveríais<br>volverían | vuelva<br>vuelvas<br>vuelva<br>volvamos<br>volváis<br>vuelvan | volviera<br>volvieras<br>volviera<br>volviéramos<br>volvierais<br>volvieran | vuelve tú,<br>no vuelvas<br>vuelva Ud.<br>volvamos<br>volved<br>vuelvan |

## D. Stem-Changing and Spelling Change Verbs (continued)

| INFINITIVE<br>PRESENT PARTICIPLE<br>PAST PARTICIPLE | INDICATIVE | | | | | SUBJUNCTIVE | | IMPERATIVE |
|---|---|---|---|---|---|---|---|---|
| | PRESENT | IMPERFECT | PRETERITE | FUTURE | CONDITIONAL | PRESENT | IMPERFECT | |
| dormir (ue, u)<br>durmiendo<br>dormido | duermo<br>duermes<br>duerme<br>dormimos<br>dormís<br>duermen | dormía<br>dormías<br>dormía<br>dormíamos<br>dormíais<br>dormían | dormí<br>dormiste<br>durmió<br>dormimos<br>dormisteis<br>durmieron | dormiré<br>dormirás<br>dormirá<br>dormiremos<br>dormiréis<br>dormirán | dormiría<br>dormirías<br>dormiría<br>dormiríamos<br>dormiríais<br>dormirían | duerma<br>duermas<br>duerma<br>durmamos<br>durmáis<br>duerman | durmiera<br>durmieras<br>durmiera<br>durmiéramos<br>durmierais<br>durmieran | duerme tú,<br>no duermas<br>duerma Ud.<br>durmamos<br>dormid<br>duerman |
| sentir (ie, i)<br>sintiendo<br>sentido | siento<br>sientes<br>siente<br>sentimos<br>sentís<br>sienten | sentía<br>sentías<br>sentía<br>sentíamos<br>sentíais<br>sentían | sentí<br>sentiste<br>sintió<br>sentimos<br>sentisteis<br>sintieron | sentiré<br>sentirás<br>sentirá<br>sentiremos<br>sentiréis<br>sentirán | sentiría<br>sentirías<br>sentiría<br>sentiríamos<br>sentiríais<br>sentirían | sienta<br>sientas<br>sienta<br>sintamos<br>sintáis<br>sientan | sintiera<br>sintieras<br>sintiera<br>sintiéramos<br>sintierais<br>sintieran | siente tú,<br>no sientas<br>sienta Ud.<br>sintamos<br>sentid<br>sientan |
| pedir (i, i)<br>pidiendo<br>pedido | pido<br>pides<br>pide<br>pedimos<br>pedís<br>piden | pedía<br>pedías<br>pedía<br>pedíamos<br>pedíais<br>pedían | pedí<br>pediste<br>pidió<br>pedimos<br>pedisteis<br>pidieron | pediré<br>pedirás<br>pedirá<br>pediremos<br>pediréis<br>pedirán | pediría<br>pedirías<br>pediría<br>pediríamos<br>pediríais<br>pedirían | pida<br>pidas<br>pida<br>pidamos<br>pidáis<br>pidan | pidiera<br>pidieras<br>pidiera<br>pidiéramos<br>pidierais<br>pidieran | pide tú,<br>no pidas<br>pida Ud.<br>pidamos<br>pedid<br>pidan |
| reír (i, i)<br>riendo<br>reído | río<br>ríes<br>ríe<br>reímos<br>reís<br>ríen | reía<br>reías<br>reía<br>reíamos<br>reíais<br>reían | reí<br>reíste<br>rio<br>reímos<br>reísteis<br>rieron | reiré<br>reirás<br>reirá<br>reiremos<br>reiréis<br>reirán | reiría<br>reirías<br>reiría<br>reiríamos<br>reiríais<br>reirían | ría<br>rías<br>ría<br>riamos<br>riáis<br>rían | riera<br>rieras<br>riera<br>riéramos<br>rierais<br>rieran | ríe tú,<br>no rías<br>ría Ud.<br>riamos<br>reíd<br>rían |
| seguir (i, i) (ga)<br>siguiendo<br>seguido | sigo<br>sigues<br>sigue<br>seguimos<br>seguís<br>siguen | seguía<br>seguías<br>seguía<br>seguíamos<br>seguíais<br>seguían | seguí<br>seguiste<br>siguió<br>seguimos<br>seguisteis<br>siguieron | seguiré<br>seguirás<br>seguirá<br>seguiremos<br>seguiréis<br>seguirán | seguiría<br>seguirías<br>seguiría<br>seguiríamos<br>seguiríais<br>seguirían | siga<br>sigas<br>siga<br>sigamos<br>sigáis<br>sigan | siguiera<br>siguieras<br>siguiera<br>siguiéramos<br>siguierais<br>siguieran | sigue tú,<br>no sigas<br>siga Ud.<br>sigamos<br>seguid<br>sigan |
| construir (y)<br>construyendo<br>construido | construyo<br>construyes<br>construye<br>construimos<br>construís<br>construyen | construía<br>construías<br>construía<br>construíamos<br>construíais<br>construían | construí<br>construiste<br>construyó<br>construimos<br>construisteis<br>construyeron | construiré<br>construirás<br>construirá<br>construiremos<br>construiréis<br>construirán | construiría<br>construirías<br>construiría<br>construiríamos<br>construiríais<br>construirían | construya<br>construyas<br>construya<br>construyamos<br>construyáis<br>construyan | construyera<br>construyeras<br>construyera<br>construyéramos<br>construyerais<br>construyeran | construye tú,<br>no construyas<br>construya Ud.<br>construyamos<br>construid<br>construyan |
| producir (zc)<br>produciendo<br>producido | produzco<br>produces<br>produce<br>producimos<br>producís<br>producen | producía<br>producías<br>producía<br>producíamos<br>producíais<br>producían | produje<br>produjiste<br>produjo<br>produjimos<br>produjisteis<br>produjeron | produciré<br>producirás<br>producirá<br>produciremos<br>produciréis<br>producirán | produciría<br>producirías<br>produciría<br>produciríamos<br>produciríais<br>producirían | produzca<br>produzcas<br>produzca<br>produzcamos<br>produzcáis<br>produzcan | produjera<br>produjeras<br>produjera<br>produjéramos<br>produjerais<br>produjeran | produce tú,<br>no produzcas<br>produzca Ud.<br>produzcamos<br>producid<br>produzcan |

# Appendix 2

## GRAMMAR SUMMARY TABLES

### I. Personal Pronouns

| SUBJECT | OBJECT OF PREPOSITION | REFLEXIVE | INDIRECT OBJECT | DIRECT OBJECT |
|---|---|---|---|---|
| yo | mí | me | me | me |
| tú | ti | te | te | te |
| usted | usted | se | le | lo/la |
| él | él | se | le | lo |
| ella | ella | se | le | la |
| nosotros/as | nosotros/as | nos | nos | nos |
| vosotros/as | vosotros/as | os | os | os |
| ustedes | ustedes | se | les | los/las |
| ellos | ellos | se | les | los |
| ellas | ellas | se | les | las |

### II. Possessive Adjectives and Pronouns

| ADJECTIVES | | PRONOUNS | |
|---|---|---|---|
| *my* | mi, mis | *mine* | mío/a, míos/as |
| *your (inf. sing.)* | tu, tus | *yours* | tuyo/a, tuyos/as |
| *your (pol. sing.)* | su, sus | *yours* | suyo/a, suyos/as |
| *his* | su, sus | *his* | suyo/a, suyos/as |
| *her* | su, sus | *hers* | suyo/a, suyos/as |
| *our* | nuestro/a, nuestros/as | *ours* | nuestro/a, nuestros/as |
| *your (inf. pl.)* | vuestro/a, vuestros/as | *yours* | vuestro/a, vuestros/as |
| *your (pol. pl.)* | su, sus | *yours* | suyo/a, suyos/as |
| *their* | su, sus | *theirs* | suyo/a, suyos/as |

## III. Demonstrative Adjectives and Pronouns

| MASCULINE AND FEMININE | ADJECTIVES AND PRONOUNS | NEUTER PRONOUNS |
|---|---|---|
| *this, these* | este/esta, estos/estas | esto |
| *that, those* (*not close to speaker*) | ese/esa, esos/esas | eso |
| *that, those* (*farther from speaker*) | aquel/aquella, aquellos/aquellas | aquello |

## IV. *Por / para*

| **POR** | | **PARA** | |
|---|---|---|---|
| *through, by* | por aquí | *destination* | para Madrid |
| *length of time* | por tres minutos | *time* | tres minutos para las tres |
| *during* | por la noche | *deadline* | para el viernes |
| *in place of* | Trabajo por Juan. | *recipient* | Trabajo para mi familia.<br>un regalo para ella |
| *quantity* | por dos pesos | | |
| *means* | por tren | | |

## V. Past (Preterite) and Imperfect

| PAST | | IMPERFECT | |
|---|---|---|---|
| *completed event* | comí | *event in progress* | comía |
| *completed state* | estuve | *ongoing state* | estaba |
| *completed series* | bailé,<br>canté | *"used to"* | bailaba,<br>cantaba |

# VI. Indicative and Subjunctive

| NOUN CLAUSES | | | |
|---|---|---|---|
| *Indicative* | | *Subjunctive* | |
| *assertion* | es verdad que | *possibility* | es posible que |
| *belief* | creer que | *doubt* | dudar que |
| *knowledge* | saber que | *subjective reaction* | estar contento/a de que |
| | | *volition* | querer que |

| ADJECTIVE CLAUSES | |
|---|---|
| *Indicative* | *Subjunctive* |
| *known antecedent* | *unknown antecedent* |
| Tengo un amigo que sabe… | Busco un amigo que sepa… |
| *existent antecedent* | *nonexistent antecedent* |
| Hay una persona que sabe… | No hay nadie que sepa… |

| ADVERBIAL CLAUSES: TIME | |
|---|---|
| *Indicative* | *Subjunctive* |
| cuando<br>hasta que<br>tan pronto como<br>en cuanto<br>después de que } + *habitual action* | cuando<br>hasta que<br>tan pronto como<br>en cuanto<br>después de que } + *future action* |
| Siempre cuando trabaja… | Mañana cuando trabaje… |

# Appendix 3

## Syllabication

1. The basic rule of Spanish syllabication is to make each syllable end in a vowel whenever possible.
2. When attempting to divide a word into syllables, it is easier to look for the consonants and do the following:
   a. If the word has just one consonant, it should go with the following vowel: ca-**s**a, di-**g**a, **c**a-**m**i-**n**a
   b. If there are two consonants, one will go with the first vowel and one with the second: a**l**-**c**o-hol, ca**n**-ta**n**-te, e**s**-**c**ue-**l**a, a**c**-**c**ión, i**n**-**n**o-va-ción
   c. If there are three consonants or more, the first two will remain with the first vowel and the third (etc.) will go with the following vowel: o**bs**-**tr**uc-ción, co**ns**-**c**ien-te
   d. The letter **h** always goes with the following vowel: al-co-**h**ol, pro-**hi**-bi-do
   e. The following consonant combinations are never divided: **br**-, **dr**-, **rr**-, **tr**-, **bl**-, **ll**-: a-**br**an, la-**dr**ón, bo-**rr**a-dor, con-**tr**a, ha-**bl**ar, man-te-qui-**ll**a
3. Diphthongs (vowel combinations: two weak ones or a weak one and a strong one) are not divided, unless the weak vowel has an orthographic accent. Weak vowels: **i**, **u**; strong vowels: **a**, **e**, **o**: c**iu**-dad, s**ie**-te, s**ei**s, cin-c**ue**n-ta. But: re-**ú**no, d**í**-a

## Stress

How you pronounce a specific Spanish word is determined by two basic rules of stress. Written accents to indicate stress are needed only when those rules are violated. Here are the two rules of stress.

1. For words ending in a vowel, **n**, or **s**, the natural stress falls on the next-to-last syllable. The letter **y** is not considered a vowel for stress purposes.

   Es-**te**-ban  **blan**-co  es-**cu**-chen  **ro**-ja  es-**tu**-die

2. For words ending in *any other letter*, the natural stress falls on the last syllable.

   pa-**pel**  ciu-**dad**  es-cri-**bir**  re-**loj**  es-**toy**

When these stress rules are violated by the word's accepted pronunciation, stress must be indicated with a written accent.

in-**glés** e-**léc**-tri-co es-tu-**dié** lla-ma-**rán** sim-**pá**-ti-co
**ár**-bol **Ló**-pez a-**zú**-car **hués**-ped

Note that words that are stressed on any syllable other than the last or next-to-last will always show a written accent. Particularly frequent words in this category include adjectives and adverbs ending in **-ísimo** and verb forms with pronouns attached.

gua-**pí**-si-mo es-pe-**rán**-do-te **pí**-de-se-las de-**vuél**-van-se-la

Written accents to show violations of stress rules are particularly important when diphthongs are involved. A diphthong is a combination of a weak (**i, u**) vowel and a strong (**a, e, o**) vowel (in either order), or of two weak vowels together. The two vowels are pronounced as a single sound, with one of the vowels being given slightly more emphasis than the other. In all diphthongs the strong vowel or the second of the two weak vowels receives this slightly greater stress.

*a*i: b*a*ilar i*a*: arteri*a* u*e*: vu*e*lve i*o*: vi*o*lento u*i*: cu*i*dado

When the stress in a vowel combination does not follow this rule, no diphthong exists. Instead, two separate sounds are heard, and a written accent appears over the weak vowel or the first of two weak vowels.

a-í: país ú-e: continúe í-o: frío ú-i: flúido

# Use of written accent as a diacritic

The written accent is also used to distinguish two words with similar spelling and pronunciation but different meaning.

Nine common word pairs are identical in spelling and pronunciation; the accent mark is the only distinction between them.

| | | | | | | | |
|---|---|---|---|---|---|---|---|
| **dé** | *give* | **de** | *of* | **sí** | *yes* | **si** | *if* |
| **él** | *he* | **el** | *the* | **sólo** | *only* | **solo** | *alone* |
| **más** | *more* | **mas** | *but* | **té** | *tea* | **te** | *you* |
| **mí** | *me* | **mi** | *my* | **tú** | *you* | **tu** | *your* |
| **sé** | *I know* | **se** | (*reflexive pronoun*) | | | | |

Diacritic accents are used to distinguish demonstrative adjectives from demonstrative pronouns. Although this distinction is disappearing in many parts of the Spanish-speaking world, you will find it in ***Dos mundos*** and in many other books.

| | | | |
|---|---|---|---|
| **aquellos países** | *those countries* | **aquéllos** | *those ones* |
| **esa persona** | *that person* | **ésa** | *that one* |
| **este libro** | *this book* | **éste** | *this one* |

Diacritic accents are placed over relative pronouns or adverbs that are used interrogatively or in exclamations.

| | | | |
|---|---|---|---|
| **cómo** | *how* | **como** | *as, since* |
| **dónde** | *where* | **donde** | *where* |
| **por qué** | *why* | **porque** | *because* |
| **qué** | *what* | **que** | *that* |
| **quién** | *who (interrogative pronoun)* | **quien** | *who (relative pronoun)* |
| **cuándo** | *when (interrogative pronoun)* | **cuando** | *when (relative pronoun)* |

—¿**Cómo** se llama? *What's his name?*
—No sé **cómo** se llama. *I don't know what his name is.*

**Como** es niño, tiene que acostarse temprano.
*Since he's a child, he must go to bed early.*

# Spelling changes

In general, Spanish has a far more phonetic system than many other modern languages. Most Spanish sounds correspond to just one written symbol. Those that can be written in more than one way are of two main types: those for which the sound/letter correspondence is largely arbitrary and those for which the sound/letter correspondence is determined by spelling rules.

**A.** In the case of arbitrary sound/letter correspondences, writing the sound correctly is mainly a matter of memorization. The following are some of the more common arbitrary, or *nonpatterned*, sound/letter correspondences in Spanish.

| SOUND | SPELLING | EXAMPLES |
|---|---|---|
| /b/ + *vowel* | b, v | barco, ventana |
| /y/ | y, ll, i + *vowel* | haya, amarillo, hielo |
| /s/ | s, z, c | salario, zapato, cielo, hace |
| /x/ + e, i | g, j | general, jefe<br>gitano, jinete |

Note that, although spelling of the sounds /y/ and /s/ is largely arbitrary, two patterns occur with great frequency.

1. /y/ Whenever an unstressed **i** occurs between vowels, the **i** changes to **y**.
   le**i**ó → le**y**ó  cre**i**endo → cre**y**endo  ca**i**eron → ca**y**eron
2. /s/ The sequence **ze** is rare in Spanish. Whenever a **ze** combination would occur in the plural of a noun ending in **z** or in a conjugated verb (for example, an **-e** ending on a verb stem that ends in **z**), the **z** changes to **c**.

   lu**z** → lu**c**es  vo**z** → vo**c**es  empe**z** + é → empe**c**é  ta**z**a → ta**c**ita

**B.** There are three major sets of patterned sound/letters sequences.

| SOUND | SPELLING | EXAMPLES |
|---|---|---|
| /g/ | g, gu | **g**ato, pa**gu**e |
| /k/ | c, qu | to**c**a, to**qu**e |
| /$g^w$/ | gu, gü | a**gu**a, pin**gü**ino |

1. /g/ Before the vowel sounds /a/, /o/, and /u/, and before all consonant sounds, the sound /g/ is spelled with the letter **g**.

   **g**ato **g**ordo **g**usto **g**ratis **G**loria lle**g**o

   Before the sounds /e/ and /i/, the sound /g/ is spelled with the letters **gu**.

   **gu**erra **gu**itarra lle**gu**é

2. /k/ Before the vowel sounds /a/, /o/, and /u/, and before all consonant sounds, the sound /k/ is spelled with the letter **c**.

   **c**asa **c**osa **c**urioso **c**reer **c**lub lec**c**ión to**c**o

   Before the sounds /e/ and /i/, the sound /k/ is spelled with the letters **qu**.

   **qu**eso **qu**ímica to**qu**é

3. /$g^w$/ Before the vowel sounds /a/ and /o/, the sound /$g^w$/ is spelled with the letters **gu**.

   **gu**ante anti**gu**o

   Before the vowel sounds /e/ and /i/, the sound /$g^w$/ is spelled with the letters **gü**.

   bilin**gü**e pin**gü**ino

These spelling rules are particularly important in conjugating, because a specific consonant sound in the infinitive must be maintained throughout the conjugation, despite changes in the stem vowels. It will help if you keep in mind the patterns of sound/letter correspondence, rather than attempt to conserve the spelling of the infinitive.

| | | | | | | | |
|---|---|---|---|---|---|---|---|
| /ga/ | = | **ga** | lle**g**ar | /ge/ | = | **gue** | lle**gu**e (*present subjunctive*) |
| /ga/ | = | **ga** | lle**g**ar | /ge/ | = | **gué** | lle**gu**é (*preterite*) |
| /gi/ | = | **gui** | se**gu**ir | /go/ | = | **go** | si**g**o (*present indicative*) |
| /gi/ | = | **gui** | se**gu**ir | /ga/ | = | **ga** | si**g**a (*present subjunctive*) |
| /xe/ | = | **ge** | reco**g**er | /xo/ | = | **jo** | reco**j**o (*present indicative*) |
| /xe/ | = | **ge** | reco**g**er | /xa/ | = | **ja** | reco**j**a (*present subjunctive*) |
| /$g^w$a/ | = | **gua** | averi**gu**ar | /$g^w$e/ | = | **güe** | averi**gü**e (*present subjunctive*) |
| /ka/ | = | **ka** | sa**c**ar | /ke/ | = | **qué** | sa**qu**é (*preterite*) |

# Appendix 4

## ANSWER KEY

### PASO B

**Ej. 1:** 1. b 2. b 3. a 4. a 5. b **Ej. 2:** 1. d 2. a 3. e 4. b 5. c **Ej. 3:** 1. No, no es una pizarra. Es una pared. 2. No, no es una oficina. Es un salón de clase. 3. No, no es una silla. Es un escritorio. 4. No, no es un borrador. Es un cuaderno. 5. No, no es una ventana. Es una silla. **Ej. 4:** 1. La 2. El 3. La 4. El 5. El 6. La 7. La 8. El 9. La 10. El **Ej. 5:** 1. Sí, hay libros en la mesa. 2. Sí, hay un reloj en la pared. 3. Sí, hay una profesora. 4. No, no hay un automóvil. 5. No, no hay un profesor. 6. Sí, hay papeles en los pupitres. 7. Sí, hay un bolígrafo en el pupitre de Alberto. 8. Sí, hay muchos cuadernos. 9. No, no hay una bicicleta. 10. Sí, hay una ventana. **Ej. 6:** 1. pares de zapatos. 2. perros nuevos. 3. chaquetas rojas. 4. lápices amarillos. 5. amigas norteamericanas. **Ej. 7:** 1. cuadernos pequeños. 2. gatos negros. 3. fotografías bonitas. 4. relojes bonitos. 5. libros difíciles. 6. amigos divertidos. **Ej. 8:** 1. d, i, k, n 2. b, e, i 3. g, h 4. a, k, n 5. b, e, i, m 6. h, l 7. b, e, i, o

### PASO C

**Ej. 1:** 1. tiene 2. tenemos 3. tienes 4. Tengo 5. tienen **Ej. 2:** 1. El carro es de la profesora Martínez. 2. La camisa es de Luis. 3. El perro es de Nora. 4. Los lentes son de Esteban. 5. El saco es de Alberto. 6. La bicicleta es de Carmen. **Ej. 3:** 1. su 2. sus 3. tu 4. mis 5. nuestros 6. sus; Nuestras 7. su 8. su 9. tus 10. mi **Ej. 4:** 1. tu; mi 2. tus; mis 3. Su 4. sus; nuestros **Ej. 5:** 1. Adriana Bolini tiene 35 años. 2. Carla Espinosa tiene 22 años. 3. Rubén Hernández Arenas tiene 38 años. 4. Susana Yamasaki González tiene 33 años. 5. Doña María Eulalia González de Saucedo tiene 79 años. 6. Yo tengo (¿ ?) años. **Ej. 6:** 1. Don Eduardo tiene 79 años. 2. Estela tiene 34 años. 3. Ernestito tiene 7 años. 4. Amanda tiene 13 años. 5. Doña Lola tiene 41 años. **Ej. 7:** 1. Es española. 2. Son japoneses. 3. Es alemán. 4. Son francesas. 5. Son italianas. 6. Es china. 7. Es inglés. **Ej. 8:** 1. hablan 2. habla 3. hablan 4. hablas 5. hablo; hablo **Ej. 9:** 1. habla; japonés 2. hablan español 3. hablan chino 4. Hablan inglés 5. Hablan hebreo 6. hablas ruso

### CAPÍTULO 1

**Ej. 1:** 1. mil ochocientos setenta y seis 2. mil quinientos ochenta y ocho 3. mil setecientos setenta y cinco 4. mil novecientos noventa y uno 5. dos mil 6. mil novecientos cuarenta y cinco 7. mil once 8. mil novecientos veinte y nueve (veintinueve) 9. mil seiscientos quince 10. dos mil veinte y cinco (veinticinco) **Ej. 2:** 1. a 2. b 3. a 4. a 5. a 6. a 7. a 8. a 9. b 10. b **Ej. 3:** 1. leen 2. Lees 3. lee 4. Leo 5. lee **Ej. 4:** 1. vive 2. vivimos 3. viven 4. Vivís 5. Vivo 6. Viven **Ej. 5:** 1. ¿Dónde vive Rubén Hernández? 2. ¿Qué idioma habla Susana? 3. ¿Cómo se llama Usted? 4. ¿Cuántos hijos tienen Ernesto y Estela? 5. ¿Qué eres tú? **Ej. 6:** 1. ¿Cuál es tu número de teléfono? 2. ¿Habla italiano? 3. ¿Cuándo es tu cumpleaños? 4. ¿Son sus hijas? 5. ¿Dónde viven ustedes? **Ej. 7:** 1. Son las cuatro y veinte. 2. Son las seis y cuarto. 3. Son las ocho y trece. 4. Es la una y diez. 5. Son las siete y siete. 6. Son las cinco y media. 7. Son las tres. 8. Son las dos menos once. 9. Son las doce y media. 10. Son las cinco y cuarto. **Ej. 8:** 1. te; me 2. te; me 3. les; nos **Ej. 9:** 1. le; comer 2. le; cocinar 3. les; hablar por teléfono 4. le; leer 5. le; correr 6. me; ¿ ?

### CAPÍTULO 2

**Ej. 1:** 1. vas; Voy 2. van; va; va 3. va; va; vamos 4. vas; Voy 5. vas; Voy **Ej. 2:** 1. Ernesto 2. Estela 3. No, Guillermo es el cuarto. 4. No, Amanda es la quinta. 5. Sí. 6. Ramón 7. No, es la séptima. 8. Ernesto 9. doña Lola 10. No, don Anselmo es el cuarto hombre. **Ej. 3:** 1. quiero; prefiere 2. quiere; prefiere 3. quiere; prefiero 4. quiere; prefieren 5. quiere; prefiere 6. quiere; prefiero 7. quiere; prefiere 8. quiere; prefiero 9. quieren; prefiero 10. quieren; prefiere **Ej. 4:** 1. Quiere jugar al béisbol. 2. Prefiere ver un partido de fútbol en la televisión. 3. Quieren ir de compras. 4. Preferimos leer. 5. Prefieren levantar pesas. 6. Quiere viajar. **Ej. 5:** 1. Lan va a estudiar pero prefiere charlar con amigos. 2. Carmen va a levantar pesas pero prefiere hablar por teléfono. 3. Esteban va a escribir una composición pero quiere tomar el sol en la playa. 4. Alberto va a montar a caballo pero prefiere andar en motocicleta. 5. Pablo va a hablar con la profesora pero prefiere hablar con su amiga. 6. Mi compañera va a hacer la tarea pero quiere ¿ ? 7. Yo voy a escuchar las «Actividades de comprensión» pero prefiero ¿ ? **Ej. 6:** 1. Hace sol. 2. Llueve. 3. Hace frío. 4. Hace mal tiempo. 5. Hace calor. 6. Nieva. **Ej. 7:** 1. posible 2. posible 3. imposible 4. imposible 5. imposible

## CAPÍTULO 3

**Ej. 1:** 1. estoy 2. están 3. estás 4. estamos 5. está 6. estamos 7. estás 8. está 9. están 10. estamos **Ej. 2:** 1. b 2. d 3. f 4. c 5. a 6. e **Ej. 3:** 1. escribimos 2. lleva 3. limpiamos 4. desayunan 5. lee 6. comen 7. monta 8. Hablo 9. asisten 10. escuchamos **Ej. 4:** 1. Papá, ¿tomas mucho café en el trabajo? 2. Diego, ¿juegan tus amigos y tú al béisbol? 3. Graciela y Diego, ¿tienen ustedes una computadora? 4. Raúl, ¿haces ejercicio en un gimnasio? 5. Pedro Ruiz, ¿trabajas por la noche? 6. Don Eduardo, ¿prepara usted café por la mañana? 7. Mamá, ¿cocinas por la mañana o por la tarde? 8. Clarisa, ¿ves la televisión por la noche? 9. Doña Rosita, ¿asiste usted a misa los domingos? 10. Doña Lola, ¿lava usted su ropa en casa o en una lavandería? **Ej. 5:** 1. sale; Salgo 2. juegas; juego 3. hace; hago 4. juegan; jugamos **Ej. 6:** 1. Los Ramírez son de México pero ahora están en Italia. 2. Marta es de Panamá pero ahora está en Los Ángeles. 3. Rogelio y Carla son de Puerto Rico pero ahora están en Nueva York. 4. Pilar es de España pero ahora está en Guatemala. 5. Ricardo es de Venezuela pero ahora está en España. **Ej. 7:** 1. Está leyendo. 2. Están pescando. 3. Está corriendo. 4. Está cocinando (preparando) la cena. 5. Están viendo (mirando) la televisión. 6. Está fumando. **Ej. 8:** 1. durmiendo 2. jugando 3. leyendo 4. lavando 5. tocando

## CAPÍTULO 4

**Ej. 1:** 1. vamos a la 2. van al 3. Vamos al 4. va a la 5. Voy a la 6. voy a la 7. van al 8. va a la 9. Vamos a la 10. Vas al **Ej. 2:** 1. Duermen; dormimos 2. Almuerzan; almorzamos 3. Vuelven; volvemos 4. Juegan; jugamos 5. Juegan; jugamos 6. Pierden; juegan; perdemos; jugamos 7. Prefieren; preferimos 8. Empiezan; empezamos **Ej. 3:** 1. Traigo 2. pongo 3. digo 4. oigo 5. salgo 6. vengo 7. tengo 8. Hago **Ej. 4:** 1. d 2. b 3. f 4. e 5. c 6. g 7. a **Ej. 5:** 1. No, me baño a las 6:30. 2. No, me lavo el pelo con champú. 3. No, me afeito en el baño. 8. No, me levanto tarde los domingos. 5. No, me quito la ropa en mi recámara (dormitorio). 6. No, me peino en el baño. 7. No, me maquillo en casa. 4. No, me ducho por la mañana. **Ej. 6:** 1. c 2. a 3. d 4. f 5. e 6. b **Ej. 7:** 1. ¿Están tristes Clarisa y Marisa? 2. ¿Está enojado (irritado) Ernesto? 3. ¿Están enamorados (contentos) Amanda y Ramón? 4. ¿Está ocupado Guillermo? 5. ¿Están interesados en viajar Nacho y Silvia? **Ej. 8:** 1. tiene hambre 2. tienes frío 3. Tenemos calor 4. Tengo sueño 5. tengo prisa 6. tienen sed 7. tengo miedo 8. Tengo sed **Ej. 9:** 1. f 2. e 3. g 4. a 5. b

## CAPÍTULO 5

**Ej. 1:** 1. Les 2. les 3. le 4. nos 5. me; te 6. les 7. Le; nos 8. me;te **Ej. 2:** Frame 1: me Frame 2: le Frame 3: le; me Frame 4: te Frame 5: le; nos Frame 6: nos; les **Ej. 3:** 1. sé 2. sabe 3. saben 4. Sabes 5. sabemos **Ej. 4:** 1. Puedes 2. Pueden 3. puede 4. pueden 5. Podemos **Ej. 5:** 1. Esta 2. Estos 3. Estos 4. Estas 5. Este **Ej. 6:** 1. Esas 2. Ese 3. Esa 4. Esos 5. Esos **Ej. 7:** 1. esa 2. este 3. esos 4. este 5. estas **Ej. 8:** 1. Estos 2. Aquellos 3. Esos 4. Esos 5. Aquellas 6. Estas **Ej. 9:** 1. quisiera 2. quisiéramos 3. quisieran 4. quisieras 5. quisiera **Ej. 10:** 1. le 2. les 3. le 4. me 5. nos **Ej. 11:** 1. piensa 2. piensas 3. pensamos 4. piensan 5. pienso **Ej. 12:** 1. c 2. e 3. d 4. a 5. b **Ej. 13:** 1. e 2. c 3. a 4. b 5. d **Ej. 14:** 1. Antes de preparar la comida, Estela hace la compra. (Después de hacer la compra, Estela prepara la comida.) 2. Después de limpiar la casa, Pedro y Andrea invitan a unos amigos. (Antes de invitar a unos amigos, Pedro y Andrea limpian la casa.) 3. Antes/Después de dormir una siesta, Guillermo ayuda a su papá. (Antes/Después de ayudar a su papá, Guillermo duerme una siesta.) 4. Después de correr, te bañas. (Antes de bañarte, corres.) 5. Antes de salir a bailar, nos ponemos la ropa. (Después de ponernos la ropa, salimos a bailar.) **Ej. 15:** 1. (c) ¡Vamos a preparar chocolate caliente! 2. (d) ¡Vamos a nadar en la piscina! 3. (a) ¡Vamos a hacer la compra! 4. (e) ¡Vamos a sentarnos debajo de ese árbol! 5. (b) ¡Vamos a estudiar esta noche!

## CAPÍTULO 6

**Ej. 1:** 1. El sillón pesa más que la mesa. (La mesa pesa menos que el sillón.) 2. En mi casa viven más personas que en la casa de los vecinos. (En la casa de los vecinos viven menos personas que en mi casa.) 3. La casa de los López tiene más dormitorios que la casa de los vecinos. (La casa de los vecinos tiene menos dormitorios que la casa de los López.) 4. En el patio de mis abuelos hay menos árboles que en nuestro patio. (En nuestro patio hay más árboles que en el patio de mis abuelos.) 5. En la casa de los Ruiz hay menos dormitorios que en la casa de los Ramírez. (En la casa de los Ramírez hay más dormitorios que en la casa de los Ruiz.) **Ej. 2:** (Answers may vary.) 1. Vivir en el desierto es peor que vivir en el centro de la ciudad. 2. Vivir en una casa es mejor que vivir en un apartamento. 3. Un refrigerador es el más útil de todos. 4. Armando es mayor que Irma. 5. Mi sobrino es menor que tu sobrino. 6. El Rolls Royce es el más caro de todos. **Ej. 3:** (Answers may vary.) 1. La piscina de los Lugo es tan bonita como la piscina de los Montes. 2. El edificio de la avenida Oriente no es tan alto como el edificio nuevo de la avenida del Libertador. 3. La lavandería vieja de la avenida Almendros no es tan limpia como la lavandería nueva de la calle Ebro. 4. Los condominios «San Juan» no son tan modernos como los condominios «Princesa». **Ej. 4:** 1. La sala de su casa no tiene tantas lámparas como la sala de nuestra casa. 2. La casa de los Ruiz no tiene tantos cuartos como la casa de los Ramírez. 3. La casa de al lado tiene tantos baños como la casa de mis padres. 4. El patio de don Anselmo no tiene tantas flores y plantas como el patio de doña Lola. **Ej. 5:** 1. tiene que 2. tienen que 3. tengo que 4. tenemos que 5. tienes que **Ej. 6:** 1. debe 2. debo 3. debes 4. deben 5. debemos **Ej. 7:** 1. Sí, (No, no) compré un disco compacto. 2. Sí, (No, no) comí en un restaurante. 3. Sí, (No, no) hablé por teléfono. 4. Sí, (No, no) escribí una carta. 5. Sí, (No, no) estudié por cuatro horas. 6. Sí, (No, no) abrí la ventana. 7. Sí, (No, no) visité a un amigo / una amiga. 8. Sí, (No, no) corrí por la mañana. 9. Sí, (No, no) tomé un refresco. 10. Sí, (No, no) lavé los platos. **Ej. 8:** 1. Mi madre no charló con el presidente la semana pasada. 2. El presidente de México no comió tacos en la calle ayer. 3. La profesora de español no salió con Antonio Banderas anoche. 4. No jugué al tenis con Arantxa Sánchez Vicario ayer a medianoche. 5. Fidel Castro no visitó los Estados Unidos el mes pasado. **Ej. 9:** 1. ¿Conoce usted 2. ¿Conoce usted 3. ¿Sabe usted 4. ¿Sabe usted 5. ¿Conoce usted 6. ¿Conoce usted 7. ¿Sabe usted 8. ¿Sabe usted 9. ¿Sabe usted 10. ¿Conoce usted **Ej. 10:** 1. los 2. la 3. lo 4. los 5. lo 6. lo 7. la 8. los 9. lo 10. la

## CAPÍTULO 7

**Ej. 1:** (1) Se levantó a las 7:00. (2) Se bañó. (3) Se preparó un desayuno pequeño. (4) Comió cereal con leche y fruta. (5) Leyó el periódico. (6) Manejó el coche al trabajo. (7) Llegó al trabajo a las 8:30. (8) Almorzó con una colega de su trabajo. (9) Comió una hamburguesa. **Ej. 2:** 1. llegaste 2. Llegué 3. llegamos 4. llegó 5. Leíste 6. leí 7. leyeron 8. leyó 9. leímos **Ej. 3:** a. 7 b. 5 c. 2 d. 1 e. 3 f. 6 g. 4 **Ej. 4:** 1. dio 2. Vinieron 3. traje 4. dijeron 5. vio 6. puso 7. hizo 8. fueron **Ej. 5:** 1. fue; Llegaron; descansó; meterse; Bucearon; vieron; hicieron; cocinaron; tocó; cantaron; bailaron 2. fue; Llegaron; entró; vio; estudió; saludó; salieron; Bailó; tomó; Regresó **Ej. 6:** (1) Generalmente Pilar asiste a clase, pero ayer durmió toda la tarde y mañana va a visitar a una amiga. (2) Generalmente Andrea y Pedro almuerzan con sus hijas, pero ayer estuvieron en el D.F. todo el día y mañana van a ir de compras. (3) Generalmente Adriana juega al tenis por la tarde, después de salir del trabajo, pero ayer tradujo un documento del italiano al español y mañana va a aprender un nuevo programa de informática. (4) Generalmente doña Lola se queda en casa, pero ayer tomó café con sus amigas y mañana va a cocinar toda la tarde. (5) Generalmente Carla y Rogelio estudian en la biblioteca, pero ayer fueron a la playa y mañana van a lavar el carro. **Ej. 7:** 1. dormiste 2. Dormí 3. duermes 4. duermo 5. sientes 6. siento 7. sentiste 8. sentí 9. divertiste 10. divertí 11. divirtió 12. divirtió 13. mentiste 14. mentí 15. mintió **Ej. 8:** 1. me 2. dijiste 3. Te 4. dije 5. me 6. dijo 7. me 8. dijo 9. le 10. dijiste 11. le 12. dijiste 13. le 14. dije 15. le 16. dije **Ej. 9:** (Answers may vary.) 1. Pero, Estela, limpié el baño hace dos días. (Pero, Estela, lo limpié hace dos días.) 2. Pero, Estela, barrí el patio hace tres horas. (Pero, Estela, lo barrí hace tres horas.) 3. Pero, Estela, pasé la aspiradora hace una hora. (Pero, Estela, la pasé hace una hora.) 4. Pero, Estela, bañé al perro hace tres días. (Pero, Estela, lo bañé hace tres días.) 5. Pero, Estela, te llevé a un restaurante elegante hace una semana. **Ej. 10:** (Answers are for 1997; they will vary depending on the year the book is used.) 1. Alejandro G. Bell inventó el teléfono hace ciento veintiún años. 2. Gustave Eiffel construyó la Torre Eiffel hace ciento ocho años. 3. Pancho Villa murió hace setenta y cuatro años. 4. Colón llegó a América hace quinientos cinco años. 5. Francisco Franco murió hace veintidós años. 6. Alemania se unificó hace siete años. 7. Los países de la antigua Unión Soviética se independizaron hace seis años.

## CAPÍTULO 8

**Ej. 1:** 1. Lo preparé ayer. 2. La puse en el congelador. 3. Las compré en el supermercado. 4. Lo traje hace diez minutos. 5. La puse en la mesa. 6. Las preparé hace dos minutos. 7. Los puse en el gabinete. 8. Lo compré en la panadería. 9. Las hice cuando me levanté. 10. Los traje esta mañana. **Ej. 2:** 1. las 2. la 3. los 4. lo 5. la **Ej. 3:** 1. Te 2. me 3. ti 4. mí 5. le 6. él 7. mí 8. ti 9. te 10. mí 11. me **Ej. 4:** (Answers will vary.) 1. A mi mejor amigo/a le encantan las fresas. 2. A mis padres les encanta el guacamole. 3. A mi profesor(a) de español le encanta el chocolate. 4. A mi novio/a (esposo/a) le encantan los frijoles. 5. A mí me encanta el pan. 6. A mi mejor amigo/a y a mí nos encantan los dulces. **Ej. 5:** (Answers may vary.) 1. ¿Para ella? ¡No lo creo! ¡No le gusta la comida fría! 2. ¿Para mí? ¡No lo creo! ¡No me gusta nada el hígado! 3. ¿Para ellas? ¡No lo creo! ¡Son muy pequeñas! 4. ¿Para nosotros? ¡Imposible! ¡No nos gustan! 5. ¿Para él? ¡No lo creo! ¡Tu papá es muy delgado! 6. ¿Para ti? ¡No lo creo! ¡No te gusta! 7. ¿Para ella? ¡Imposible! ¡No le gustan las cebollas! 8. ¿Para él? ¡No lo creo! ¡A él no le gusta! **Ej. 6:** 1. a. conmigo b. contigo 2. a. ti b. mí 3. a. él b. él c. él d. mí e. ti f. mí **Ej. 7:** 1. nadie 2. nada 3. nunca 4. nadie 5. ninguna 6. nada 7. Nunca 8. ninguno **Ej. 8:** (Answers will vary.) **Ej. 9:** 1. se cortan 2. se necesita 3. se lava; se pone 4. se preparan 5. se agregan 6. se necesitan 7. Se habla 8. Se baten **Ej. 10:** 1. pedir 2. pedir 3. sirven 4. pedir 5. pides 6. sirven 7. pido 8. pedir 9. pidieron 10. Pedimos 11. sirvió 12. pedí 13. pidió 14. pediste 15. pedí 16. pidió 17. pidieron 18. pedimos 19. sirvió 20. sirvió

## CAPÍTULO 9

**Ej. 1:** 1. se parece 2. se parecen; me parezco; te pareces 3. me parezco; me parezco 4. nos parecemos; se parece 5. nos parecemos 6. se parece(n) **Ej. 2:** 1. se llevan 2. te llevas; nos llevamos 3. nos llevamos; me llevo 4. se llevan 5. te llevas; nos llevamos **Ej. 3:** 1. Guillermo montaba en bicicleta. 2. Amanda y yo jugábamos con muñecas. 3. Andrea leía las tiras cómicas del periódico los domingos. 4. Doña Lola y doña Rosita se bañaban en el mar en Acapulco. 5. Don Eduardo comía muchos dulces. 6. Estela limpiaba su recámara. 7. La familia Ramírez pasaba las vacaciones en Acapulco. 8. Pedro Ruiz escuchaba música rock. 9. Ernesto veía dibujos animados en la televisión. 10. El abuelo de Ernestito cuidaba el jardín. **Ej. 4:** a. 3; jugaban b. 6; iban c. 7; saltaba d. 4; se peleaba e. 2; lloraba f. 1; se llevaba g. 5; se parecían **Ej. 5:** 1. tenía 2. sabía 3. conocíamos 4. era 5. estaba **Ej. 6:** 1. tenía 2. era 3. conocía 4. Queríamos; teníamos 5. estabas 6. tenía 7. supe 8. tuve 9. conocí 10. quise 11. pude **Ej. 7:** 1. Iba a venir, pero mi carro no arrancó. 2. Iba a traerlas, pero la tienda se cerró a las 8:00. 3. Iba a comprarte un regalo, pero no recibí mi cheque a tiempo. 4. Iba a cenar con ustedes, pero tuve que trabajar tarde. 5. Iba a ir, pero mi novio tuvo que trabajar esa noche. 6. Iba a decirte, pero no pude llamarte. 7. Iba a llegar a tiempo, pero perdí mi cartera. 8. Iba a asistir, pero no hice la tarea.

## CAPÍTULO 10

**Ej. 1:** 1. hemos visto 2. ha escrito 3. he viajado 4. ha comprado 5. has comido 6. ha hablado 7. has ido 8. han limpiado 9. has oído 10. han pasado **Ej. 2:** (Answers will vary.) 1. ¿Cuántas veces has viajado a México? He viajado a México muchas veces. 2. ¿Cuántas veces has esquiado en un lago? Nunca he esquiado en un lago. 3. ¿Cuántas veces has subido a una pirámide? He subido a una pirámide una vez en México. 4. ¿Cuántas veces has acampado en las montañas? He acampado en las montañas muchas veces. 5. ¿Cuántas veces has alquilado un coche? He alquilado un coche tres o cuatro veces. 6. ¿Cuántas veces has cocinado para diez personas? He cocinado para diez personas muchas veces. 7. ¿Cuántas veces has leído tres novelas en un día? Nunca he leído tres novelas en un día. 8. ¿Cuántas veces has corrido 5 kilómetros sin parar? He corrido 5 kilómetros sin parar una o dos veces. 9. ¿Cuántas veces les has dicho una mentira a tus padres? ¡Nunca les he dicho una mentira! 10. ¿Cuántas veces has roto un vaso en un restaurante? He roto un vaso en un restaurante dos veces. **Ej. 3:** 1. ¡Qué país tan (más) interesante! 2. ¡Qué vuelo tan (más) largo! 3. ¡Qué montañas tan (más) altas! 4. ¡Qué selva tan (más) verde! 5. ¡Qué arena tan (más) blanca! **Ej. 4:** 1. ¡Qué impresionantes son las ruinas de Machu Picchu! 2. ¡Qué grande es el lago Titicaca! 3. ¡Qué cosmopolita es la ciudad de Buenos Aires! 4. ¡Qué húmeda es la selva de Ecuador! 5. ¡Qué seco es el desierto de Atacama en Chile! 6. ¡Qué alta es la torre de la Giralda en Sevilla! 7. ¡Qué hermoso es el edificio del Alcázar de Segovia! 8. ¡Qué inmenso es el Parque del Retiro en Madrid! 9. ¡Qué interesante es el Museo del Prado! 10. ¡Qué antiguo es el acueducto de Segovia! **Ej. 5:** 1. por 2. por 3. para 4. por 5. por 6. por 7. por 8. para **Ej. 6:** 1. rápidamente 2. cómodamente 3. puntualmente 4. constantemente 5. inmediatamente **Ej. 7:** 1. a. parece b. importa 2. a. fascinan b. interesan 3. a. encanta b. gusta 4. a. molesta b. gusta 5. a. importan b. interesan

## CAPÍTULO 11

**Ej. 1:** (Answers may vary.) 1. Sí, hágalas lo más pronto posible. 2. Sí, cómprelos inmediatamente. 3. Sí, tráigalo mañana. 4. Sí, recójalos el jueves, por favor. 5. Sí, llegue dos horas antes. 6. Sí, consígalo lo más pronto posible. **Ej. 2:** 1. Sí, prepárenlo. 2. Sí, consíganlos. 3. Sí, límpienlas. 4. Sí, háganlas. 5. Sí, duerman. 6. Sí, salgan. **Ej. 3:** 1. Quiere que recojamos nuestros boletos pronto. 2. Quiere que escribamos una lista de lo que vamos a necesitar. 3. No quiere que llevemos demasiadas cosas en las maletas. 4. Quiere que compremos cheques de viajero. 5. Quiere que comamos en restaurantes buenos y que no comamos en la calle. 6. Quiere que lleguemos al aeropuerto temprano. 7. Quiere que bebamos refrescos o agua mineral y que no bebamos el agua. **Ej. 4:** 1. llegue 2. viajamos 3. suben 4. lea 5. terminen **Ej. 5:** 1. Quiere que hagamos las maletas... 2. Quiere que durmamos ocho horas... 3. Quiere que traigamos ropa... 4. Quiere que vayamos... 5. Quiere que pongamos el dinero... 6. Quiere que le demos el pasaporte. 7. Quiere que volvamos con... 8. No quiere que pidamos comida... 9. Quiere que nos divertamos mucho. 10. Quiere que le digamos «Adiós» a nuestra familia. **Ej. 6:** 1. llame; c. llegue 2. sirva; d. vayamos 3. oigas; b. vengas 4. traigamos; e. volvamos 5. saques; a. estés **Ej. 7:** 1. durmiendo 2. asistiendo 3. viendo 4. estudiando 5. leyendo (Answers will vary.) 6. estaba dando una clase. 7. estaba tomando un examen. 8. estaban comiendo. 9. estaban trabajando. 10. estaba corriendo. **Ej. 8:** 1. Manejaba 2. Veía 3. Caminaba 4. hablaba 5. Hacía 6. Me bañaba **Ej. 9:** 1. era 2. íbamos 3. alquilábamos 4. buceábamos 5. bañábamos 6. salíamos 7. caminábamos 8. tenía 9. fuimos 10. estaban durmiendo 11. jugaba 12. hablaba 13. conocía 14. miré 15. jugaba 16. vi 17. levantamos 18. corrimos 19. encontramos 20. buscamos 21. pudimos 22. Estaba 23. regresamos 24. teníamos 25. estaba 26. fuiste 27. grité 28. contestó 29. estaba 30. enojé

# Vocabulary

This Spanish-English vocabulary contains all of the words that appear in the text, with the following exceptions: (1) most identical cognates that do not appear in the chapter vocabulary lists; (2) conjugated verb forms, with the exception of certain forms of **haber** and expressions found in the chapter vocabulary lists; (3) diminutives in **-ito/a**; (4) absolute superlatives in **-ísimo/a**; and (5) some adverbs in **-mente**. Active vocabulary is indicated by the number of the chapter in which a word or given meaning is first listed (A = **Paso A**); vocabulary that is glossed in the text is not considered to be active vocabulary and is not numbered.* Only meanings that are used in this text are given.

The gender of nouns is indicated, except for masculine nouns ending in **-o** and feminine nouns ending in **-a**. Stem changes and spelling changes are indicated for verbs: **dormir** (**ue, u**); **llegar** (**gu**).

The following abbreviations are used:

| | | | |
|---|---|---|---|
| *abbrev.* | abbreviation | *m.* | masculine |
| *adj.* | adjective | *Mex.* | Mexico |
| *adv.* | adverb | *n.* | noun |
| *Arg.* | Argentina | *obj. of prep.* | object of preposition |
| *coll.* | colloquial | *pl.* | plural |
| *conj.* | conjunction | *pol.* | polite |
| *d.o.* | direct object | *poss.* | possessive |
| *f.* | feminine | *p.p.* | past participle |
| *fig.* | figurative | *prep.* | preposition |
| *Guat.* | Guatemala | *pron.* | pronoun |
| *inf.* | informal | *refl. pron.* | reflexive pronoun |
| *infin.* | infinitive | *sing.* | singular |
| *inv.* | invariable | *Sp.* | Spain |
| *i.o.* | indirect object | *sub. pron.* | subject pronoun |
| *irreg.* | irregular | | |

**Dos mundos: En breve* is derived from the Fourth Edition of ***Dos mundos,*** which has 16 regular chapters. References to the omitted chapters (12–16) still exist in this vocabulary even though the chapters do not appear in the text.

# A

**a** to; at; **a la(s)** at (*time*); **al** *contraction of* **a** + **el** to the
**abadejo** cod(fish)
**abajo** below, underneath (4)
**abandonar** to abandon
**abarrote** *m.*: **tienda de abarrotes** grocery store
**abecedario** alphabet
**abierto/a** (*p.p. of* **abrir**) open (B); opened
**abogado/a** lawyer (5)
**abolladura** dent
**abollar** to dent
**abordar** to board, get on (11)
**aborto** abortion (16)
**abrazar** (**c**) to embrace (12); **abrazarse** to hug each other (15)
**abrazo** hug
**abrelatas** *m. sing., pl.* can opener (13)
**abrigo** coat (A)
**abril** *m.* April (1)
**abrir** (*p.p.* **abierto**) to open (A)
**abrocharse (el cinturón de seguridad)** to fasten (the seatbelt) (10)
**abrumado/a** overwhelmed, oppressed
**abuelo/a** grandfather/grandmother (C); **abuelos** *pl.* grandparents
**abundancia** abundance (10)
**abundante** abundant
**aburrido/a** boring; bored (B); **¡qué aburrido!** how boring! (1)
**aburrirse** to be bored
**abusar de** to abuse (12)
**abuso** abuse (16)
**acá** here; **para acá** over here
**acabar** to finish; **acabar de** (+ *infin.*) to have just (*done something*) (13)
**acalorado/a** heated (15)
**acampar** to go camping (1)
**acariciar** to caress
**acarrear** to transport; to haul
**acceso** access
**accidente** *m.* accident (5)
**acción** *f.* action (3); **Día** (*m.*) **de Acción de Gracias** Thanksgiving Day (4)
**aceite** *m.* oil (8)
**aceituna** olive (8)
**acelerar** to accelerate
**aceptable** acceptable (16)
**aceptar** to accept (7)
**acerca de** about
**acercarse** (**qu**) (**a**) to approach, come near
**acero** steel (13)
**ácido** acid
**aclarar** to cast light on; to explain; to resolve
**acogedor(a)** cozy
**acompañar** to accompany
**acondicionado/a: aire** (*m.*) **acondicionado** air conditioning (10)
**acondicionador** *m.* conditioner (4)
**aconsejar** to give advice, advise (12)
**acorazado de combate** battleship
**acordarse** (**ue**) to remember
**acostado/a** lying down
**acostarse** (**ue**) to go to bed (4)
**acostumbrar** to be in the habit of; **acostumbrarse a** to get used to, accustomed to
**acrilán** *m.* acrylic (13)
**actitud** *f.* attitude
**activar** to activate, turn on
**actividad** *f.* activity (A)
**activista** *n. m., f.* activist (16)
**actriz** *f.* (*pl.* **actrices**) actress
**actuación** *f.* acting, performance
**actual** present-day, current (2)
**actualidad** *f.*: **en la actualidad** currently, nowadays
**actualmente** at present, nowadays
**actuar** (**actúo**) to act
**Acuario** Aquarius
**acuático/a: polo acuático** water polo; **deportes** (*m. pl.*) **acuáticos** water sports; **parques** (*m. pl.*) **acuáticos** water parks
**acudir** to go; to come (12)
**acueducto** aqueduct (11)
**acuerdo** agreement; **de acuerdo** I agree; OK; **estar de acuerdo** to agree (B); **quedar de acuerdo** to agree
**acumulado/a** accumulated
**acumulador** *m.* battery (10)
**acusado/a** *n.* accused (*person*) (5)
**acusar** to accuse
**adaptar** to adapt
**adecuado/a** adequate (12)
**adelante: de ahora en adelante** from now on; **hacia adelante** forward; **sacar adelante** to carry forward; to rear, nurture
**adelanto** advance, progress
**adelgazar** (**c**) to lose weight
**además** moreover; **además de** besides; in addition to (11)
**adentro** inside, within
**aderezo** (salad) dressing (8)
**adeudarse** to incur debt
**adictivo/a** addicting
**adiós** goodbye
**adivinar** to guess
**adivino/a** fortune-teller (15)
**adjetivo** adjective
**adjunto/a** enclosed (*in a letter*)
**administrar** to administrate
**admirador(a)** admirer
**admirar** (**a**) to admire (11)
**admitir** to admit (14)
**¿adónde?** where?
**adopción** *f.* adoption
**adoptar** to adopt
**adquirido/a** acquired
**adquirir** (**ie**) to acquire, obtain
**aduana** *sing.* customs (11); **derecho** (*sing.*) **de aduana** customs duties, taxes (11)
**aduanero/a** customs agent
**advertir** (**ie, i**) to warn, advise
**aéreo/a** pertaining to air (travel) (10)
**aerolínea** airline (11)
**aeropuerto** airport (11)
**afectar** to affect
**afeitarse** to shave (4)
**afirmación** *f.* statement
**afirmar** to affirm
**afortunadamente** fortunately
**africano/a: lenguas** (*pl.*) **africanas** African languages (C)
**afrikaans** *m. sing. a language of South Africa* (C)
**afuera** *adv.* outside; **afueras** *n. pl.* outskirts, suburb(s)
**agarrado/a a** hanging on to
**agarrador** (*m.*) **de olla** potholder
**agencia** agency; **agencia de viajes** travel agency (C)
**agente** *m., f.* agent; **agente de viajes** travel agent
**agigantado/a** gigantic, huge
**ágil** agile
**aglomeración** *f.* crowd
**agosto** August (1)
**agotado/a** exhausted; sold out
**agradable** pleasant, nice (6)
**agradecer** (**zc**) to thank
**agrario/a** *adj.* land; **reforma agraria** land reform (16)
**agregar** (**gu**) to add (8)
**agrícola** *adj. m., f.* agricultural (16)
**agua** *f.* (*but* **el agua**) water (4); **agua con sal** salt water (12); **agua corriente** running water (8); **agua mineral** mineral water
**aguacate** *m.* avocado (8)
**aguantar** to put up with, endure
**aguar** to water
**águila** *f.* (*but* **el águila**) eagle
**aguja** needle
**agujereado/a** full of holes
**agujero** hole; **agujero en la capa de ozono** hole in the ozone layer (10)
**ahí** there (4)
**ahijado/a** godson/goddaughter (15); **ahijados** *pl.* godchildren
**ahora** now (2); **ahora mismo** right now (4)
**ahorrar** to save (9)
**aire** *m.* air; **aire acondicionado** air conditioning (10); **al aire libre** outdoors (7)
**aislado/a** isolated
**ajá** aha
**ajedrez** *m.* chess
**ají** (*m.*) **de gallina** *chicken in chili sauce*
**ajiaco** *potato and chili stew*
**ajillo: al ajillo** in garlic sauce
**ajo** garlic (8)
**ajustarse** to adjust
**al** *contraction of* **a** + **el** to the; **al** (+ *infin.*) upon (*doing something*)
**ala** *f.* (*but* **el ala**) wing
**alacena** cupboard (6)
**alai: jai alai** *m.* Basque ball game
**alameda** *public walk lined with trees*
**alarmado/a** alarmed (13)
**alarmarse** to become alarmed (13)

**albahaca** basil
**albaricoque** *m.* apricot (8)
**alberca** *Mex.* swimming pool (7)
**albondigón** *m.* hamburger
**alboroto** disturbance; brawl; riot
**alcalde, alcaldesa** mayor
**alcance** *m.* scope; significance; **a su alcance** within reach
**alcancía** coin/piggy bank
**alcanfor** *m.* camphor
**alcanzar (c)** to reach (15); **no le alcanzaba** it wasn't enough (15)
**alcanzó** attained, reached
**alcaparra** caper
**alcázar** *m.* castle, fortress
**alcoba** bedroom
**aldea global** global village
**alegrarse** to be glad; **alegrarse de que** to be happy that (16)
**alegre** happy (4)
**alegría** happiness
**alejarse** to move away, leave
**alemán** *n. m.* German (language) (C)
**alemán, alemana** *n., adj.* German (C)
**Alemania** Germany (C)
**alentado/a** encouraged
**alentador(a)** encouraging
**alergia** allergy (12)
**alergista** *m., f.*: **médico/doctora alergista** allergist (12)
**alfabetización** *f.*: **campaña de alfabetización** literacy campaign (16)
**alfombra** rug; carpet (6)
**algo** something (4); **algo de comer** something to eat; **algo que hacer** something to do
**algodón** *m.* cotton (13)
**alguien** someone (6)
**algún, alguno/a** some (2); any; **algún día** someday; **alguna vez** once; ever; **algunas veces** sometimes (14); **algunos/as** some (2)
**aliado/a** *n.* ally
**alimentar** to feed; to nourish
**alimento** nourishment, food (8)
**aliviar** to alleviate
**alivio** relief
**allá** (over) there; **más allá de** beyond
**allí** there (4); **por allí** over there, around there
**alma** *f.* (*but* **el alma**) soul
**almacén** *m.* department store (4)
**almacenar** to store
**almeja** clam (8)
**almendra** almond (8)
**almíbar** *m.* syrup (8)
**almirante** *m.* admiral
**almohada** pillow (6)
**almorzar (ue) (c)** to have lunch (7)
**almuerzo** lunch (2)
**alocado/a** crazy
**alojamiento** lodging (11)
**alpaca** alpaca wool
**alquilar** to rent (6)
**alquiler** *m.* rent (6)
**alrededor de** *prep.* around (3); **alrededores** *n. m. pl.* outskirts
**altitud** *f.* altitude; height
**alto/a** tall (A); high; **alta costura** haute couture; **en voz** (*f.*) **alta** in a loud voice (15); out loud
**altura** height
**aludir a** to allude to
**aluminio** aluminum
**alumno/a** student
**alzar (c)** to raise
**ama** *f.* (*but* **el ama**) mistress (*of the house*) (14); **ama de casa** housewife (3)
**amable** kind; friendly
**amado/a** *n., adj.* beloved
**amanecer** *m.* dawn
**amante** *m., f.* lover
**amar** to love
**amarillo/a** yellow (A)
**amarrar** to fasten
**Amazonia** Amazon basin
**amazónico/a** *adj.* Amazon
**ambición** *f.* ambition
**ambiental** environmental (15); **contaminación** (*f.*) **ambiental** environmental pollution
**ambiente** *m.* environment; atmosphere (8); **medio ambiente** environment
**ambos/as** *pl.* both (10)
**amenazar (c)** to threaten
**americano/a** *adj.* American
**amigo/a** friend (A); **amigo/a íntimo/a** close friend (15); **mejor amigo/a** best friend
**amistad** *f.* friendship (15)
**amistoso/a** friendly
**amo** master (14); boss
**amor** *m.* love
**amparo** shelter
**amplio/a** ample; roomy (6)
**amueblado/a** furnished (6)
**analfabetismo** illiteracy (16)
**análisis** *m. sing., pl.* analysis; **análisis de sangre** blood test (12); **hacer análisis** to do (medical) tests
**analizar (c)** to analyze
**ananá** *m.* pineapple (8)
**anaranjado/a** orange (*color*) (A)
**ancho/a** wide
**anciano/a** elderly person
**andaluz(a)** (*m. pl.* **andaluces**) Andalusian (*from southern Spain*)
**andar** *irreg.* to walk; **¡anda!** come on!; **andar en bicicleta/motocicleta** to go for a bicycle/motorcycle ride (2); **andar en monopatín/patineta** to skateboard; **andar en velero** to go sailing (4)
**andén** *m.* train station platform
**andino/a** Andean (16)
**anécdota** anecdote, story
**anémona** sea anemone
**ángel** *m.* angel (14)
**anglicismo** Anglicism
**anglohablante** *m., f.* English-speaking person
**angosto/a** narrow
**angula** eel
**ángulo** angle
**anillo** ring (12)
**animado/a: dibujos animados** cartoons
**animal** *m.* animal; **animal doméstico** pet (5)
**anímico/a: estado anímico** mental state
**ánimo** spirit, energy; **estado de ánimo** state of mind (12)
**anoche** last night (6)
**anónimo/a** anonymous
**anotar** to write down (16)
**ansiedad** *f.* anxiety
**ansioso/a** anxious
**ante** before; faced with, in the presence of
**anteayer** day before yesterday (1)
**antepasado/a** *n.* ancestor (16)
**anterior** previous
**antes** *adv.* before; **antes (de)** *prep.* before (4); **antes de que** *conj.* before (16); **cuanto antes** as soon as possible
**anticipación** *f.*: **de anticipación** in advance
**anticiparse** to anticipate
**anticonceptivo** contraceptive (16)
**antigüedad** *f.* antiquity
**antiguo/a** old; antique (B)
**Antioquía** Antioch
**antipático/a** disagreeable (B)
**antojito** *Mex.* snack (8)
**anunciante** *m., f.* advertiser
**anunciar** to announce (11)
**anuncio** advertisement (6); **anuncio comercial** TV or radio commercial
**añadir** to add
**añejado** aged (*wine, liquor*)
**añejamiento** *n.* aging (*wine, liquor*)
**añejo** mellow, aged (*wine, liquor*)
**año** year; **Año Nuevo** New Year's Day (4); **¿cuántos años tiene(s)?** how old are you? (C); **cumplir años** to have a birthday (7); **de... años** . . . years old (B); **tener... años** to be . . . years old; **tengo... años** I'm . . . years old (C); **todo el año** all year long; **todos los años** every year
**apadrinar** to act as a godfather
**apagar (gu)** to turn off (*light*) (6)
**aparador** *m.* sideboard, buffet
**aparato** appliance (6); **aparato doméstico** appliance (13); **aparato electrodoméstico** household appliance
**aparcamiento** parking lot
**aparcar (qu)** to park
**aparearse** to mate
**aparecer (zc)** to appear
**apariencia** (outward) appearance; **en apariencia** apparently
**apartado postal** post office box
**apartamento** apartment (6); **edificio de apartamentos** apartment building

**aparte** *m.*: **punto y aparte** (write a) period and (begin a) new paragraph (*dictation*)
**apasionado/a** passionate
**apasionar** to fill with enthusiasm
**apearse** to get off, dismount
**apellido** last name (C)
**apenas** barely
**apetito** appetite
**apio** celery (8)
**aplaudir** *fig.* to commend, praise
**aplicarse (qu)** to be used
**aportar** to contribute (15)
**apoyado** supported (16)
**apoyar** to support
**apoyo** support
**apreciar** to appreciate
**aprender** to learn (4)
**aprendizaje** *n. m.* learning
**apresurarse** to hurry
**apretado/a** tight (13)
**apretar (ie)** to press; to squeeze
**aprobar (ue)** to approve (14)
**apropiado/a** appropriate (5)
**aprovecharse de** to take advantage of (16)
**aproximado/a** approximate
**aptitud** *f.* aptitude, ability (5)
**apto.** (*abbrev. for* **apartamento**) apartment
**apuntar** to point at
**apunte** *m.* note
**aquel, aquella** *adj.* that (over there) (5); *pron.* that one (over there); **en aquel entonces** at that time
**aquello** that; that thing; that fact
**aquí** here (3); **aquí mismo** right here; **por aquí** around here
**árabe** *n. m.* Arabic (language)
**árabe** *n. m., f.* Arab; *adj.* Arabic
**arándano** cranberry
**arar** to plow
**árbol** *m.* tree (2); **árbol de Navidad** Christmas tree (4); **subirse a los árboles** to climb trees (9)
**arbusto** bush (6)
**archipiélago** archipelago
**arco** arch; **arco iris** rainbow (A)
**ardilla** squirrel
**arena** sand (7); **arena movediza** quicksand
**arete** *m.* earring (A)
**argentino/a** *n., adj.* Argentinian (C)
**árido/a** arid (10)
**aritmética** arithmetic
**arma** *f.* (*but* **el arma**) arm, weapon; **arma de fuego** firearm (16); **portar armas** to bear arms (16)
**armadura** armor
**armar** to arm
**armario** closet (6)
**arqueólogo/a** archeologist
**arquitecto/a** architect
**arquitectura** architecture
**arrancar (qu)** to pull up; to snatch away; to start
**arranque** *m.* ignition (10)
**arras** *pl. coins given by a bridegroom to a bride as a symbol of his role as provider* (15)
**arrecife** *m.* reef (10)
**arreglar** to arrange; to straighten up, clean; to fix (5)
**arrestar** to place under arrest (7)
**arriba: allá arriba** up there; **arriba de** on top of (3); above; **hacia arriba** up(ward)
**arriesgar (gu)** to risk
**arrojar** to throw
**arroyo** stream, brook
**arroz** *m.* rice (8); **arroz con leche** rice pudding (8)
**arruinar** to ruin (15)
**arrullar** to lull to sleep
**arte** *m.* (*but* **las artes**) art; **artes gráficas** graphic arts; **bellas artes** fine arts; **Facultad** (*f.*) **de Bellas Artes** School of Fine Arts (3)
**arteria** artery (12)
**artesanal: feria artesanal** crafts fair
**artesanía** *sing.* crafts; craftsmanship
**artesano** craftsman
**artículo** article
**artificial: fuegos artificiales** fireworks (4)
**artista** *m., f.* artist (3)
**arveja** green pea (8)
**asado/a** roasted; **bien asado** well-done (*meat*) (8); **poco asado** rare (*meat*) (8)
**asador** *m.* barbecue (grill) (13)
**asar** to roast (8)
**ascendencia** ancestry
**ascender** to rise (*to power*)
**ascensor** *m.* elevator (6)
**asco** disgust
**asegurar** to assure; to guarantee
**asentamiento** settlement
**asesinar** to assassinate
**asesinato** murder; assassination
**asesino/a** murderer
**así** thus, so, that way, this way (5); **así es la vida** that's life (16); **así que** so (that), with the result that
**asiático/a** *n., adj.* Asian (16)
**asiento** seat
**asignar** to assign (5)
**asignatura** (school) subject
**asimismo** likewise
**asistencia** aid, assistance; attendance
**asistente** (*m., f.*) **de vuelo** flight attendant (11)
**asistir (a)** to attend (3)
**asociación** *f.* association
**asociarse** to join in partnership; to associate (16)
**asomarse** to show up, appear
**asombro** amazement; fear
**asombroso/a** astonishing
**aspecto** aspect; appearance
**aspiraciones** *f. pl.* aspiration
**aspiradora** vacuum cleaner (6); **pasar la aspiradora** to vacuum (6)
**aspirina** aspirin (12)
**astuto/a** astute, shrewd
**asumir** to assume, take on (16)
**asunto** subject, topic; matter, affair (16)
**asustado/a** scared (7)
**asustar** to scare
**atacar (qu)** to attack
**ataque** *m.* attack; **ataque del corazón** heart attack (12)
**atar** to tie (7)
**atardecer** *m.* late afternoon
**Atenas** *f.* Athens
**atención** *f.* attention; **llamar la atención a** to call attention to
**atender (ie)** to assist, take care of (12); **atender mesas** to wait on tables (5)
**aterrizar (c)** to land (*airplane*)
**atleta** *m., f.* athlete (15)
**atormentar** to torment, torture
**atraer** (*like* **traer**) to attract (16)
**atrapar** to trap (7)
**atrás** *adv.* behind
**atravesar (ie)** to cross, go across
**atreverse a** (+ *infin.*) to dare to (*do something*)
**atribuir (y)** to attribute (12)
**atropellar** to run over (*with a vehicle*) (12)
**atuendo** suit (*of clothes*), outfit
**atún** *m.* tuna (8)
**audífonos** *pl.* headphones
**aumentar** to increase (14)
**aumento** raise, increase; **aumento de sueldo/salario** raise (in pay)
**aun** even
**aún** still, yet
**aunque** although (14)
**ausencia** absence
**ausente** absent
**auto** car
**autobús** *m.* bus (3); **estación** (*f.*) **de autobuses** bus depot; **parada del autobús** bus stop (3)
**automático/a: cajero automático** automatic teller machine (ATM)
**automóvil** *m.* automobile, car (A); **seguro de automóvil** car insurance
**automovilista** *m., f.* driver
**automovilístico/a** of or related to an automobile (12)
**autónomo/a** autonomous
**autopista** freeway (10)
**autor(a)** author (16)
**autorización** *f.* authorization (16)
**autovía** highway
**¡auxilio!** help! (7)
**avance** *m.* advance
**avanzar (c)** to advance
**avda.** (*abbrev. for* **avenida**) avenue
**ave** *f.* (*but* **el ave**) bird; fowl (8)
**avena** oatmeal (8)
**avenida** avenue (3)
**aventón** *m.* ride; **dar un aventón** *Mex.* to give (*someone*) a ride (9)
**aventura** adventure (7)
**aventurero/a** adventurous (11)

**avergonzarse (güe) (c) (por)** to be ashamed (of) (16)
**avería** breakdown (*mechanical*)
**avión** *m.* (air)plane (5)
**avisar** to inform
**aviso (comercial)** notice; ad (5); **aviso clasificado** classified ad (5)
**ayer** yesterday (1)
**ayuda** help (15)
**ayudar** to help (5); **ayudarse** to help each other (14)
**azotea** flat-roofed adobe house; terraced roof
**azteca** *n. m., f.*; *adj.* Aztec (7)
**azúcar** *m.* sugar (8); **caña de azúcar** sugar cane
**azucarera** sugar bowl (8)
**azul** *n. m.*; *adj.* blue (A); **azul marino** navy blue (13)
**azulejo** glazed tile

## B

**bachillerato** bachelor's degree
**bacteriano/a** bacterial
**bahía** bay (10)
**bailador(a)** dancer
**bailar** to dance (1); **salir a bailar** to go out dancing (1)
**baile** *m.* dance (3); **salón** (*m.*) **de baile** dance hall
**bajar** to lower; to go down (2); **bajarse** to get off (11)
**bajo** *prep.* under
**bajo/a** short (*height*) (A); low; **en voz baja** in a low voice (5)
**balada** ballad
**balance** *m.* balance
**Baleares** *pl.*: **Islas Baleares** Balearic Islands
**ballena** whale (10)
**baloncesto** basketball (1)
**balonmano** handball
**banco** bank (5); bench
**banquete** *m.* feast
**bañar** to bathe (4); **bañarse** to bathe (4)
**bañera** bathtub (6)
**baño** bathroom (6); **sala de baño** bathroom (6); **traje** (*m.*) **de baño** bathing suit (7)
**bar** *m.* bar (4)
**barato/a** inexpensive, cheap (8)
**baratura** cheapness; inexpensiveness
**barba** beard (A)
**barbacoa** barbecue (*food*)
**barbitúrico** barbiturate
**barca** small boat; **pasear en barca** to take a boat ride (2)
**barco** ship (7)
**barra de pan** loaf of bread
**barranca** gully, ravine
**barrer** to sweep (6)
**barrica** large barrel; cask
**barril** *m.* barrel
**barrio** neighborhood (9); **Barrio Sésamo** Sesame Street
**basarse (en)** to be based (on) (16)
**básquetbol** *m.* basketball (1)
**basta** it's enough, sufficient; **¡basta!** enough!; **basta de** enough
**bastante** *adj.* enough, sufficient; *adv.* rather, quite
**bastón** *m.* cane
**basura** trash; **bote** (*m.*) **de la basura** trash can (6); **sacar la basura** to take out the trash (6)
**bata** robe (13)
**batalla** battle (7)
**batata** sweet potato, yam
**batería** battery
**batido de frutas** fruit shake (8); **batido de leche** milkshake (8)
**batir** to beat (8)
**bautizar (c)** to baptize (15)
**bautizo** christening ceremony, baptism (15)
**bazar** *m.* bazaar; market place
**bebé** *m., f.* baby (3)
**bebeleche** *m.*: **jugar al bebeleche** *Mex.* to play hopscotch (9)
**beber** to drink (4)
**bebida** drink
**beca** scholarship
**béisbol** *m.* baseball
**Belén** Bethlehem
**belleza** beauty; **salón** (*m.*) **de belleza** beauty parlor
**bello/a** beautiful (10); **bellas artes** fine arts; **Facultad** (*f.*) **de Bellas Artes** School of Fine Arts (3)
**bendición** *f.* blessing
**beneficio** benefit (15)
**beneficioso/a** beneficial (12)
**benigno/a** benign, kind
**berberecho** cockle
**berro** watercress
**besar** to kiss (12); **besarse** to kiss each other (15)
**beso** kiss (4); **dar un beso** to (give a) kiss (7)
**biblioteca** library (3)
**bici** *f.* bike
**bicicleta** bicycle (C); **andar/pasear en bicicleta** to go for a bicycle ride (2)
**bien** *adv.* well; **bien** + *adj.* very + *adj.*; **bien, gracias** fine, thanks; **estoy bien** I am fine (A)
**bienes** *n. m. pl.* possessions, goods
**bienestar** *m.* well-being (15); **bienestar social** social welfare (16)
**bienvenida: dar la bienvenida** to welcome (4)
**bienvenido/a** welcome (11)
**bígaro** sea-snail
**bigote** *m.* moustache (A)
**bigotillo** small moustache
**bilingüe** bilingual (5)
**billar** *m.* billiards, pool (2)
**billete** *m.* ticket (11); bill (*paper money*) (11)
**billetera** wallet (7)
**biografía** biography
**biología** biology (1)
**bisabuelo/a** great-grandfather/great-grandmother (15); **bisabuelos** *pl.* great-grandparents
**bistec** *m.* steak (8)
**bitácora** binnacle (*nautical*)
**bizcocho** sponge cake; type of pastry
**blanco/a** white (A); **espacio en blanco** blank (space) (3); **vino blanco** white wine (8)
**bloque** *m.* block (16)
**blusa** blouse (A)
**boca** mouth (B)
**bocadillo** sandwich
**boceto** sketch
**bocina** car horn; **tocar la bocina** to honk the horn (10)
**boda** wedding (4)
**bodega** grocery store
**boleto** ticket (11); **boleto de ida y vuelta** round-trip ticket (11)
**boliche** *m.* bowling (2)
**bolígrafo** ballpoint pen (A)
**bolívar** *m. monetary unit of Venezuela* (13)
**boliviano/a** *adj.* Bolivian (3)
**bolos** *pl.* bowling
**bolsa** bag; purse; sack (4); **bolsa de mano** carry-on luggage; handbag
**bolsillo** pocket (13); **calculadora de bolsillo** pocket calculator
**bombero** firefighter (5)
**boniato** sweet potato, yam
**bonito/a** pretty (A)
**boquerón** *m.* small sardine
**bordado** embroidered; *n.* embroidery
**borde** *m.* edge, border
**bordo: a bordo** on board
**borracho/a** drunk
**borrador** *m.* eraser (B)
**borrar** to erase (14)
**borrego** lamb
**bosque** *m.* forest (10)
**botas** *pl.* boots (A)
**bote** (*m.*) **de la basura** trash can (6)
**botella** bottle (8)
**botica** pharmacy, drug store
**botiquín** *m.* emergency kit
**botones** *m. sing., pl.* bellhop (11)
**boxeo** boxing
**bozo** down (*hair*) on upper lip
**bracero** farmhand, farm laborer
**brasileño/a** *adj.* Brazilian (C)
**bravo/a** angry, irate
**brazalete** *m.* bracelet
**brazo** arm (B)
**breve** *adj.* brief
**brillante** bright
**brincar (qu)** to jump up and down
**brindar** to drink a toast
**brindis** *m. sing., pl.* toast (*drink or speech*) (15)
**brisa** breeze
**bróculi** *m.* broccoli (7)
**broma: en broma** jokingly

**bromo** bromine
**broncearse** to get a tan (11)
**bronquitis** *f.* bronchitis (12)
**bruja: Día** (*m.*) **de las Brujas** Halloween (4)
**brusco/a** brusque, rough
**bruto: ingresos** (*pl.*) **brutos** gross income
**bucear** to skin-dive, scuba dive; to snorkel (3)
**buceo** underwater swimming; diving (10)
**buen, bueno/a** good (2); **¡buen viaje!** have a nice trip! (10); **buenas tardes/noches** good afternoon/evening (A); **buenos días** good morning (A); **de buenas a primeras** suddenly; **estar de buen humor** to be in a good mood (4); **hace buen tiempo** it's fine weather (1); **qué bueno que** how great that (16)
**bueno...** well . . . (C); hello (*answering phone, Mex.*)
**buey** (*m.*) **del mar** sea-cow
**bufanda** scarf (13)
**bulevar** *m.* boulevard
**bullicio** noise, hubbub
**buque** *m.* ship
**burro/a** donkey
**busca: en busca de** in search of
**buscar (qu)** to look for (5)
**búsqueda** search (16)

# C

**caballero** gentleman (13); horse rider
**caballo** horse (2); **montar a caballo** to ride a horse (2)
**cabaña** hut, cabin
**cabellera** head of hair
**caber** *irreg.* to fit (13)
**cabeza** head (B); **dolor** (*m.*) **de cabeza** headache (12)
**cabina** cabin; **cabina ancha** wide-body aircraft
**cabizbajo/a** downcast
**cabo** cape, promontory; **al cabo de** + *time expression* at the end of + *time expression*; **llevar a cabo** to carry out, fulfill
**cabrito** kid, young goat
**cacahuete** *m.* peanut (8)
**cachorro/a** puppy
**cacto** cactus
**cada** *inv.* each (A); **a cada rato** every few minutes (14); **cada día** each day; **cada semana** each/every week (6); **cada uno/a** each one; **de cada lado** on each side
**cadena** chain
**cadera** hip (12)
**caer** *irreg.* to fall; **caerle bien/mal a alguien** to make a good/bad impression on someone; **caerse** to fall down (11); **dejar caer** to let fall/drop
**café** *m.* coffee (2); café; **color café** brown (A); **tomar café** to drink coffee
**cafetera** coffee pot (6)
**cafetería** cafeteria (3)
**caja** box (13); case; cash register
**cajero/a** cashier (5); teller (*in a bank*); **cajero automático** automatic teller machine (ATM)
**cajón** *m.* drawer; crate, chest
**calabacita** squash, zucchini (8)
**calamar** *m.* squid
**calcetín** *m.* sock (13)
**calcio** calcium
**calculadora** calculator (13); **calculadora de bolsillo** pocket calculator
**calcular** to add up; to calculate
**caldo** clear soup (8)
**calefacción** *f.* heating (system)
**calendario** calendar
**calentador** *m.* heater (6)
**calentar (ie)** to warm up (6)
**calidad** *f.* quality (13)
**caliente** hot (4); **té** (*m.*) **caliente** hot tea (8)
**calificación** *f.* grade
**callado/a** quiet (6)
**callarse** to be quiet (13)
**calle** *f.* street (1)
**callejero/a: vendedor(a) callejero/a** street vendor
**calmar** to calm, quiet down
**calor** *m.* heat; **hace calor** it's hot (weather) (1); **tener calor** to be hot (4)
**caloría** calorie (7)
**caluroso/a** warm (10)
**calvo/a** bald (15)
**calzada** wide road
**calzoncillos** *pl.* men's underwear (13)
**cama** bed (3); **cama matrimonial** double bed (7); **tender la cama** to make the bed (7)
**cámara** camera; chamber
**camarera** chambermaid (11)
**camarones** *m. pl.* shrimp (8)
**cambiar** to change (9); **cambiar un cheque (dinero)** to cash a check (money) (11); **¡cómo cambia el mundo!** how the world changes! (C)
**cambio** change (11); **cambios** *pl.* gears (10); **en cambio** on the other hand
**camilla** stretcher (12)
**caminar** to walk (2)
**caminata** *n.* walk
**camino** road (10), path; journey, trip; **por el camino** on the way
**camión** *m.* truck (10)
**camioneta** van, light truck
**camisa** shirt (A)
**camiseta** T-shirt, undershirt (A)
**camisón** *m.* nightgown (13)
**camote** *m.* sweet potato
**campamento** camp
**campaña** campaign; **campaña de alfabetización** literacy campaign (16); **carpa de campaña** tent; **tienda de campaña** tent (13)
**campeón, campeona** champion
**campesino/a** peasant (16)
**camping** *m.* campground
**campo** country(side) (7)
**Canadá** *m.* Canada
**canadiense** *n., adj.* Canadian
**canailla** *type of fish*
**cáncer** *m.* cancer (10)
**cancha de tenis** tennis court (6)
**canción** *f.* song (16)
**candidato/a** candidate (16)
**cangrejo** crab (8)
**canicas** *pl.* marbles
**cansado/a** tired; **estoy un poco cansado/a** I am a bit tired (A)
**cansancio** fatigue; weariness (12)
**cansar** to make tired (12); **cansarse** to get tired (12)
**cantante** *m., f.* singer (5)
**cantar** to sing (5)
**cantarín, cantarina** fond of singing
**cantidad** *f.* quantity (10)
**cantina** bar
**canto** song
**caña de azúcar** sugar cane
**cañón** *m.* canyon (10)
**caos** *m.* chaos
**capa de ozono** ozone layer (10); **agujero en la capa de ozono** hole in the ozone layer (10)
**capacidad** *f.* capacity
**capataz** *m.* (*pl.* **capataces**) foreman
**capilla** chapel
**capital** *m.* capital (*money*) (16); *f.* capital (*city*)
**capítulo** chapter
**capó** hood (*automobile*) (10)
**capota** hood (*automobile*)
**captar** to capture
**caqui: de color caqui** khaki (13)
**cara** face (B)
**caracol** *m.* snail
**carácter** *m.* (*pl.* **caracteres**) personality, character (15)
**caracterizar (c)** to characterize (16)
**caramba** *exclamation of surprise*
**caray** *exclamation of surprise*
**carbohidrato** carbohydrate
**carbón** *m.* coal
**carburos** (*pl.*) **fluorados** fluorocarbons (10)
**cárcel** *f.* jail (16)
**carecer (zc)** to lack
**carente** *adj.* lacking
**cargo** office, position; **hacerse cargo** to take charge
**Caribe** *m.* Caribbean (3)
**caricatura** cartoon
**caridad** *f.* charity
**cariño** affection; endearment
**carmín** *m.* carmine, crimson
**carne** *f.* meat; beef; **carne de cerdo/puerco** pork (8); **carne de res** beef (8); **carne molida** ground beef (8)
**carnicería** meat market (13)
**caro/a** expensive (6)
**carpa de campaña** tent
**carpintero/a** carpenter
**carrera** career; course of study; race; **seguir una carrera** to have a career (5)

**carretera** highway (10)
**carro** car, automobile (C); **dar un paseo en carro** to go for a drive
**carta** letter; **escribir cartas** to write letters
**cartel** *m.* poster
**cartera** wallet (13)
**cartón** *m.* cardboard (13)
**casa** house (A); **ama** *f.* (*but* **el ama**) **de casa** housewife (3); **casa editorial** publishing house; **casa particular** private home (6)
**casado/a** married (C)
**casamiento** marriage
**casarse (con)** to get married (to) (7); **casarse por lo civil** to get married in a civil marriage ceremony (15)
**cáscara** rind, peel, skin (8); shell
**casco** helmet (10)
**casero/a** home-made; household
**casete** *m.* cassette
**casi** almost (1); **casi nunca** very rarely
**casimir** *m.* cashmere
**caso** case; **en caso de que** in case (15); **hacer caso** to pay attention
**castaño/a** brown (*hair; eyes*) (A)
**castellano** Spanish (language)
**castigar (gu)** to punish (14)
**castigo** punishment (14)
**castillo** castle
**casualidad** *f.* chance; coincidence
**catalizador** *m.* catalytic converter
**catarata** waterfall (10)
**catarro** cold (illness) (12)
**catedral** *f.* cathedral
**catolicismo** Catholicism
**católico/a** Catholic (16)
**catorce** fourteen (A)
**causa: a causa de** because of (15)
**causar** to cause (10)
**cavado/a** dug
**cebiche** *m. Peruvian national dish of raw fish marinated in lemon juice*
**cebolla** onion (8)
**ceja** eyebrow (12)
**celebración** *f.* celebration
**celebrar** to celebrate (4)
**celos** *pl.* jealousy; **morirse de celos** to die of jealousy
**celoso/a** jealous
**célula** cell
**cena** dinner (3)
**cenar** to have dinner (1); **cenar fuera** to go out to dinner (1)
**cenicero** ashtray
**censo** census
**centavo** cent (B); **no tener ni un centavo** to be broke (13)
**centígrado/a** *adj.* centigrade (10)
**céntrico/a** central
**centro** center; downtown (2); **centro comercial** shopping center (6)
**centroamericano/a** Central American
**cepillarse los dientes** to brush one's teeth
**cepillo** brush (13); **cepillo de dientes** toothbrush (6)
**cerca** *n.* fence (6); *adv.* near; **cerca de** *prep.* close to (3)
**cercanías** *pl.* vicinity, environs
**cercano/a** near, close by (6)
**cerdo** pork; **carne** (*f.*) **de cerdo** pork (8); **chuleta de cerdo** pork chop
**cerebro** brain (12)
**ceremonia** ceremony
**cero** zero (A)
**cerrado/a** closed (13)
**cerrar (ie)** to close (A); to turn off (*appliance*)
**cervantino/a** pertaining to Cervantes
**cerveza** beer (7)
**césped** *m.* lawn (6)
**cesta de la compra** shopping basket
**ceviche** *see* **cebiche**
**chamarra** *Mex.* jacket (13)
**champaña** *m.* champagne
**champú** *m.* shampoo
**chaqueta** jacket (A)
**charlar** to chat (2)
**chatarra** junk
**cheque** *m.* check; **cambiar un cheque** to cash a check (11); **cheque de viajero** traveler's check (11)
**chicano/a** Chicano (16)
**chícharo** green pea (8)
**chicharrón** *m.* pork crackling
**chicle** *m.* chewing gum (3)
**chico/a** *n. m., f.* young man/young woman (B); *adj.* small
**chile** *m.* chili pepper; **chile relleno** stuffed chili pepper
**Chile** *m.* Chile (2)
**chileno/a** *n., adj.* Chilean (3)
**chimenea** fireplace (6)
**china** orange (*fruit*) (7)
**chino** *n.* Chinese (language) (C)
**chino/a** *n., adj.* Chinese (C); **cobrarse a lo chino** to take a cut (*money*)
**chiquillo/a** child; *coll. Sp.* darling, beloved
**chismear** to gossip (16)
**chiste** *m.* joke
**chistoso/a** funny (12)
**chivito/a** kid, young goat
**chocar (qu)** to collide, crash; **chocar con** to crash, run into (*something*) (11)
**chocolate** *m.* chocolate; **chocolate caliente** hot chocolate
**chofer** *m., f.* driver (5)
**choque** *m.* collision, crash (12)
**chorizo** sausage
**choza** hut, shack
**chuleta** chop (8); **chuleta de cerdo** pork chop
**chuletón** *m.* large steak
**chultún** *m. subterranean chamber carved in rock*
**churrasco** barbecued meat, steak
**churrasquería** barbecue stall
**ciberespacio** cyberspace
**cibernético/a: espacio cibernético** cyberspace
**cicatriz** *f.* (*pl.* **cicatrices**) scar (12)
**ciclismo** cycling
**ciclo** cycle
**ciclón** *m.* cyclone (10)
**ciego/a** *n.* blind person; *adj.* blind
**cielo** sky (10); heaven
**cien, ciento** one hundred (C); **por ciento** percent
**ciencia** science (9); **ciencias sociales** social science (1); **ciencias políticas** political science; **Facultad** (*f.*) **de Ciencias Naturales** School of Natural Sciences (3)
**científico/a** *n.* scientist; *adj.* scientific
**cierto/a** certain (16); true
**ciervo/a** deer
**cigala** *edible crustacean*
**cigarrillo** cigarette (12)
**cigarro** cigar
**cilindrada** cylinder capacity
**cima** top, summit
**cinco** five (A); **a las cinco** at five o'clock
**cincuenta** fifty (B)
**cine** *m.* movie theater (1); **estrella de cine** movie star (15)
**cinta** tape, cassette (5); **cinta de video** video tape
**cintura** waist (12)
**cinturón** *m.* belt; **cinturón de seguridad** seat belt (10)
**circulación** *f.* circulation; traffic (10)
**circular** to circulate (12)
**ciruela** plum; **ciruela seca** prune
**cirujano/a** surgeon (12)
**cita** appointment; date (12)
**ciudad** *f.* city
**ciudadanía** citizenship (1)
**ciudadano/a** citizen (10)
**civil: casarse por lo civil** to get married in a civil marriage ceremony (15); **estado civil** marital status (1)
**civilización** *f.* civilization
**claro/a** clear; **claro** of course; **claro que no** of course not (B); **claro que sí** of course (B)
**clase** *f.* class (A); kind, type; **compañero/a de clase** classmate (A); **dar clases** to teach; **después de clases** after school; **primera clase** first class (11); **salón** (*m.*) **de clase** classroom
**clásico/a** classical
**clasificado/a: aviso clasificado** classified ad (5)
**clasificar (qu)** to classify
**clausura** closing
**clavar** to fix, fasten, nail down
**clave** *adj. inv.* key
**cliente, clienta** customer (5)
**clima** *m.* climate (2)
**climatizado/a: piscina climatizada** heated pool
**clínica** *n.* clinic (5)
**clínico/a** clinical

**clorhidrato** hydrochloride
**club** *m.* club (3); **club nocturno** nightclub (5)
**cobalto** cobalt
**cobarde** *n. m., f.* coward; *adj.* cowardly
**cobertura** coverage
**cobrar** to charge (*amount one collects*); **cobrarse a lo chino** to take a cut (*money*)
**cobre** *m.* copper
**cobro** charge (*money owed*)
**cocaína** cocaine
**coche** *m.* car, automobile (C); **coche deportivo** sports car (13)
**cochera** garage (10)
**cocido/a** cooked; **huevos cocidos** hard-boiled eggs (8); **poco cocido** rare (*meat*) (8)
**cocina** kitchen (5); stove
**cocinar** to cook (1)
**cocinero/a** cook (5)
**coctel** *m.* cocktail
**cod.** (*abbrev. for* **código**) (postal) zip code
**codo** elbow (12)
**coger** (**j**) to catch
**cognado** cognate
**coincidencia** coincidence; **¡qué coincidencia!** what a coincidence! (11)
**coincidir** to coincide (4)
**cojín** *m.* cushion, pillow (15)
**col.** (*abbrev. for* **colonia**) colony; neighborhood
**cola: hacer cola** to stand in line (11)
**colaborar** to collaborate
**colada: piña colada** *tall mixed drink of rum, cream of coconut, pineapple juice, and ice, usually mixed in a blender*
**colador** *m.* sieve
**colchón** *m.* mattress
**colección** *f.* collection
**colectivo/a** *adj.* communal; **colectivo** *n.* (*Arg., Peru*) *passenger vehicle smaller than a bus*
**colega** *m., f.* colleague
**colegio** high school (4)
**colgar** (**ue**) (**gu**) to hang (*clothes in a closet*) (6)
**coliflor** *f.* cauliflower
**colina** hill (10)
**collar** *m.* necklace; **collar de perlas** pearl necklace
**colocar** (**qu**) to place
**colombiano/a** *adj.* Colombian (3)
**colonia** colony; neighborhood; cologne (4); **colonia espacial** space colony (15)
**colonizado/a** colonized
**colonizador(a)** *n.* colonizer
**color** *m.* color; **color café** brown (A); **¿de qué color es?** what color is it? (A); **¿de qué color tiene el pelo / los ojos?** what color are your (*pol. sing.*)/his/her hair/eyes? (B); **televisor** (*m.*) **en colores** color TV set
**colorante** *m.* coloring agent
**columna** column
**comadre** *f.* very good friend (*female*); godmother; mother of one's godchild (15)
**comarca** region
**combate** *m.*: **acorazado de combate** battleship
**combinación** *f.* combination; slip (13)
**combinar** to combine
**combustible** *m.* fuel; **gastar combustible** to use gas (10)
**comedia** comedy
**comedor** *m.* dining room (6)
**comején** *m.* termite
**comentar** to comment
**comentario** comment, commentary; **hacer comentarios** to comment
**comenzar** (**ie**) (**c**) to begin; **comenzar a** (+ *infin.*) to begin to (*do something*)
**comer** to eat (2); **comerse** to eat up, finish up
**comercial** *adj.* commercial, business; **anuncio comercial** TV or radio commercial; **aviso comercial** notice; ad (5); **centro comercial** shopping center (6)
**comercio** commerce, business (16); **libre comercio** free enterprise
**comestibles** *m. pl.* food; groceries
**cometa: volar una cometa** to fly a kite (2)
**cometer** to commit (*error, crime*) (16)
**cómico/a** comical; **tiras cómicas** comic strips (9)
**comida** food (4, 8); meal; lunch
**comisión** *f.* commission
**como** as; as a; like; since (6); **como si nada** as if nothing were wrong; **tal y como** exactly the same as; **tan... como** as . . . as (6); **tan pronto como** as soon as (15); **tanto(s)/tanta(s)... como** as many . . . as (6)
**cómo no** *interj.* of course
**¿cómo?** how?; what?; **¿cómo era... ?** what were you (*pol. sing.*) / was he/she/it like? (8); **¿cómo eres (tú)?** what are you (*inf. sing.*) like? (B); **¿cómo es usted/él/ella?** what are you (*pol. sing.*) / is he/she like? (B); **¿cómo está usted?** how are you (*pol. sing.*)? (A); **¿cómo estás (tú)?** how are you (*inf. sing.*)? (B); **¿cómo se llama?** what is his/her name? (A); **¿cómo se llama usted? / ¿cómo te llamas?** what is your name? (A); **¿cómo son ustedes/ellos/ellas?** what are you (*pol. pl.*) /they like? (B)
**cómoda** chest of drawers (6)
**cómodamente** *adv.* comfortably (10)
**comodidad** *f.* comfort (11)
**cómodo/a** comfortable (13)
**compacto: reproductor** (*m.*) **para discos compactos** CD player (1)
**compadre** *m.* very good friend (*male*); godfather; father of one's godchild (15)
**compañero/a** companion; **compañero/a de clase** classmate (A)
**compañía** company (5)
**comparación** *f.* comparison (6)
**comparar** to compare (3)
**compartir** to share (6)
**compatriota** *m., f.* fellow countryman/countrywoman, fellow citizen
**competencia** competition
**competir** to compete
**complacer** (**zc**) to please
**complejo** *n.* complex; **complejo turístico** tourist resort
**complemento: pronombre** (*m.*) **de complemento directo/indirecto** direct/indirect object pronoun
**completar** to complete (7)
**completo/a** complete; **jornada completa** full-time (5); **por completo** totally
**comportamiento** behavior (14)
**composición** *f.* composition
**compra** purchase; grocery shopping; **cesta de la compra** shopping basket; **hacer las compras** to go grocery shopping (6); **ir de compras** to go shopping (1)
**comprar** to buy (4)
**comprender** to understand (5); **comprenderse** to understand each other (14)
**comprensión** *f.* comprehension, understanding
**comprometerse a** (+ *infin.*) to pledge oneself, promise to (*do something*)
**comprometido/a: estar comprometido/a** to be engaged (15)
**compromiso** engagement
**compuesto** compound (*chemical*)
**computación** *f.* computation; calculation
**computación móvil** portable computing
**computador(a)** computer
**común** common (16); **el común de la gente** the majority of the people
**comunicación** *f.* communication (A)
**comunicar** (**qu**) to communicate; **comunicarse** to communicate with each other
**comunidad** *f.* community (16)
**comunista** *n. m., f.*; *adj.* communist (16)
**con** with (A); **con tal (de) que** provided that; as long as (16)
**concebir** (**i, i**) to conceive
**concentrado/a** concentrated
**concierto** concert; **entradas para un concierto** tickets for a concert
**concluir** (**y**) to conclude
**concurso** contest
**conde, condesa** count/countess
**condición** *f.* condition (10)
**condicional** conditional
**condimento** condiment
**condominio** condominium
**conducir** (**zc**) (**j**) to drive
**conducta** conduct, behavior
**conductor(a)** driver (16)
**conectar** to connect (16)
**confeccionar** to make, prepare
**conferencia** conference (15); lecture
**conferencista** *m., f.* conference speaker, lecturer
**confesar** (**ie**) to confess

**confianza** confidence; **de confianza** confidential
**conformarse** to make do
**confrontar** to confront
**confuso/a** confused
**congelador** *m.* freezer (6)
**congelar** to freeze
**congestionado/a** congested (12)
**congreso** congress
**conjunto** group
**conmigo** with me (4)
**conmovedor(a)** *adj.* moving
**conocedor(a)** *n., adj.* expert
**conocer (zc)** to meet (6); to know (6); **dar a conocer** to make known
**conocimiento** knowledge
**conquistador(a)** conqueror (16)
**conquistar** to conquer (16)
**consciente** conscious; aware; **ser consciente de** to be aware of
**consecuencia** consequence (15)
**conseguir (i, i) (g)** to obtain, get (15)
**consejo** advice (11)
**consenso** consensus
**consentimiento** consent
**conservación** *f.* preservation
**conservador(a)** *n.* preservative (8); *adj.* conservative (B)
**conservar** to preserve; to maintain (14)
**considerar** to consider
**consistir en** to consist of (15)
**constitución** *f.* constitution (16)
**construcción** *f.* construction (13)
**construir (y)** to build (16)
**consulado** consulate (11)
**consulta** consultation, office visit
**consultar con** to consult (12)
**consultorio** doctor's office (5)
**consumidor(a)** consumer
**consumo** consumption (9)
**contador(a)** accountant (5)
**contaduría** notary's office
**contagiarse de** to catch (*a disease*)
**contagio** spreading (*of disease*)
**contaminación** *f.* pollution; **contaminación ambiental** environmental pollution
**contar (ue)** to count; to tell, narrate (7)
**contener** (*like* **tener**) to contain (8)
**contenido** *sing.* contents
**contento/a** happy (4); **estar contento/a de que** to be happy that
**contestación** *f.* answer, reply
**contestadora telefónica** answering machine (11)
**contestar** to answer (C)
**contigo** *inf. sing.* with you (14)
**continuación: a continuación** next, following
**continuo/a** continual
**contra** against (12); **estar en contra de** to be against (15)
**contracción** *f.* contraction (12)
**contraer** (*like* **traer**) to contract
**contratista** *m., f.* contractor
**contribuir (y)** to contribute (15)
**control** *m.* control; **control de la natalidad** birth control (16)
**controvertible** controversial
**convencer (z)** to convince
**convenir** (*like* **venir**) to suit; to be convenient
**converger (convergir) (j)** to converge
**conversación** *f.* conversation
**conversar** to converse, talk, chat (2)
**convertir (ie, i)** to change; **convertirse en** to become
**convivir** to live together (harmoniously); to coexist
**coordinador(a)** coordinator
**coordinar** to coordinate
**copa** (wine)glass (8)
**corazón** *m.* heart (12); **ataque** (*m.*) **del corazón** heart attack (12)
**corbata** tie (*clothing*) (A)
**cordero** lamb
**cordillera** mountain range (10)
**corral** *m.* yard; stockyard, pen (13)
**corrección** *f.* correction
**corredor** *m.* corridor
**corregir (i, i) (j)** to correct
**correo** mail; post office (11); **correo electrónico** e-mail (15); **mandar por correo** to send by mail
**correr** to run (2); **correr riesgo** to run a risk
**correspondencia** correspondence
**corresponder** to correspond (4)
**correspondiente** corresponding (4)
**corrida de toros** bullfight
**corriente** *f.* current (10); **agua corriente** running water (8)
**corsé** *m.* corset
**cortar** to cut (5); **cortarse el pelo** to cut one's hair, have one's hair cut
**corte** *f.* court; *m.* cutting; cut, fit (*of clothing*) (13)
**cortésmente** courteously
**cortina** curtain (6)
**corto/a** short (*in length*) (A)
**cosa** thing (B)
**cosecha** crop, harvest
**coser** to sew (2)
**cosmopolita** *adj. m., f.* cosmopolitan
**cosmos** *m. sing., pl.* universe; world
**costa** coast (10); **a costa de** at the expense of
**costado** *n.* side (12)
**costar (ue)** to cost; **¿cuánto cuesta(n)... ?** how much is/are . . . ? (B); **cuesta(n)...** it costs (they cost) . . . (B)
**costarricense** *n., adj.* Costa Rican (3)
**costilla** rib (12)
**costo** cost
**costumbre** *f.* habit, custom (16)
**costura: alta costura** haute couture
**cotidiano/a** *adj.* daily
**cotillear** *coll.* to gossip (16)
**creación** *f.* creation
**crear** to create (10)
**crecer (zc)** to grow, grow up (8)
**crecimiento** growth
**crédito** credit; **tarjeta de crédito** credit card (8)
**creencia** belief
**creer (y)** to believe; to think (5); **creo que no** I don't think so (16); **creo que sí** I think so (16); I should think so!; **(no) creer que** to (not) believe that (16); **no lo creo** I don't believe it (1); **no lo puedo creer** I can't believe it (16); **ya lo creo** of course
**crema** cream (8)
**criada** (live-in) maid
**criado** servant
**crianza** upbringing (14)
**criar(se)** to bring up (be brought up); to grow up (15); to raise (*cattle*)
**crimen** *m.* crime
**criollo/a** Creole; *Born in Latin America of European parents*
**crisis** *f. sing., pl.* crisis (16)
**cristal** *m.* pane of glass
**cristiano/a** Christian
**crítica** criticism
**criticar (qu)** to criticize
**crítico/a** critical
**cronológico/a** chronological
**crucero** cruise ship; cruise (10)
**cruda** hangover
**crudo/a** *adj.* raw (8); severe, harsh (*weather*)
**cruz** *f.* (*pl.* **cruces**) cross; **la Cruz Roja** Red Cross (11)
**cruzar (c)** to cross (7)
**cuaderno** notebook (B)
**cuadra** stable; block (*street*) (11)
**cuadrado/a** squared
**cuadro** box, square (4); picture (*on the wall*) (6); **de cuadros** checkered, plaid (13)
**¿cuál?** what?, which? (C); **¿cuál(es)?** which (ones)?; **¿cuál es su nombre?** what is your name? (A)
**cualidad** *f.* quality (15)
**cualquier(a)** any (10)
**cuando** when (4); **de vez en cuando** once in a while (10)
**¿cuándo?** when?
**¿cuánto/a?** how much?; how long?; **¿cuánto cuesta(n)... ?** how much is/are . . . ? (B); **cuánto hace que** + *present... ?* how long have/has . . . ? (9); **¿cuánto tiempo hace que... ?** how long has it been since . . . ? (7); **¿cuánto vale?** how much is it? (13)
**cuanto: en cuanto** as soon as (15); **en cuanto a** as for, as regards; **unos/as cuantos/as** a few
**¿cuántos/as?** how many?; **¿cuanto/a/s... ?** how many . . . ? (10); **¿cuántos/as (hay)?** how many (are there)? (A); **¿cuántos años tiene(s)?** how old are you? (C)
**cuarenta** forty (B)
**cuarto** room; bedroom; **y/menos cuarto** quarter past/to (*time*) (1)
**cuarto/a** fourth (2)

**cuartucho** hovel; small room
**cuate/a** twin; buddy
**cuatro** four (A)
**cuatrocientos/as** four hundred
**cubano/a** *n., adj.* Cuban (3)
**cubanoamericano/a** *adj.* Cuban American
**cubierto/a** (*p.p. of* **cubrir**) covered
**cubismo** cubism
**cubrir** (*p.p. of* **cubierto**) to cover (8)
**cuchara** spoon (8)
**cucharita** teaspoon (8)
**cucharón** *m.* ladle (8)
**cuchillo** knife (8)
**cuello** neck (B); **cuello en V / en pico** V-neck collar (13)
**cuenco** bowl
**cuenta** bill, check (8); **darse cuenta (de)** to realize; **tomar en cuenta** to take into account
**cuento** short story
**cuerda: saltar la cuerda** to jump rope (9)
**cuero** leather (13)
**cuerpo** body (B)
**cuestión** *f.* question, issue, matter
**cuestionar** to question
**cuidado** care; **con cuidado** with care, carefully (7); **¡cuidado!** (be) careful!; **cuidado médico** medical care; **tener cuidado** to be careful
**cuidar (de)** to take care (of) (5); **cuidarse** to take care of oneself (11)
**culata** butt (*gun*)
**culpa** fault, blame; **tener la culpa** to be to blame, be guilty (12)
**culpabilidad** *f.* guilt
**cultivarse** to be cultivated
**cultivo** cultivation
**culto** educated; cultured (16)
**cultura** culture (16)
**culturismo** body-building
**cumbre** *f.* summit
**cumpleaños** *m. sing., pl.* birthday (1); **feliz cumpleaños** happy birthday (1)
**cumplir (con)** to fulfill, carry out (16); **cumplir años** to have a birthday (7)
**cuñado/a** brother-in-law/sister-in-law (9)
**cuota** quota
**cupón** *m.* coupon
**cura** *f.* cure (10); *m.* priest (*Catholic*) (15)
**curar** to cure; **curarse de** to cure oneself, be cured of (16)
**curiosidad** curiosity
**curioso/a** curious
**curita** adhesive bandage (12)
**curso** course (4)
**curtido/a** tanned (*leather*)
**curva** curve (10)
**cuyo/a** whose (16)

# D

**dálmata** *adj. m., f.*: **perro dálmata** dalmatian (dog)
**dama** lady (13)
**damas** *pl.* checkers
**danza** dance (9)
**dañar** to damage
**dañino/a** harmful
**daño** damage; **hacer daño** to harm
**dar** *irreg.* to give (6); **da lo mismo** it doesn't matter; **dar a conocer** to make known; **dar como resultado** to result in; **dar la bienvenida** to welcome (4); **dar miedo** to frighten; **dar muchas vueltas** to go back and forth; **dar permiso** to give permission (9); **dar rabia** to anger, enrage; **dar risa** to make laugh; **dar un aventón** *Mex.* to give (*someone*) a ride; **dar un beso** to (give a) kiss (7); **dar un paseo** to take a walk (4); **dar un paseo en carro** to go for a drive; **dar un paso** to take a step; **dar una fiesta** to give a party (2); **dar vueltas** to go around; **darle la mano a alguien** to shake someone's hand; **darle risa a alguien** to make someone laugh; **darle una vuelta a alguien** to take someone for a walk; **darle vergüenza a uno** to be ashamed; **darse cuenta (de)** to realize; **darse la mano** to shake hands with each other (15); **darse por vencido** to give up
**datar de** to date from
**datos** *pl.* data; **datos personales** personal data
**de** *prep.* of; from (A); by; **del, de la** of the (A)
**debajo de** under (3)
**deber** *n. m.* duty
**deber** *v.* to owe; **deber** (+ *infin.*) should, ought to (*do something*) (3); **debía de ser** it should be
**debido a** due to (16)
**década** decade
**decidir** to decide (12)
**décimo/a** tenth (2)
**decir** *irreg.* to say, tell (1); **es decir** that is to say; **¡no me digas!** you don't say!; **querer decir** to mean; **y tú, ¿qué dices?** and you? (what do you say?) (1)
**decisión** *f.* decision (15); **tomar una decisión** to make a decision
**declaración** *f.* declaration; statement (7)
**declarar** to declare (16); **declarar la huelga** to go on strike
**decorado** *n.* decor
**decorado/a** *adj.* decorated (6)
**decretar** to decree
**dedicar (qu)** to dedicate
**dedo** finger (12)
**deducir (zc) (j)** to deduct
**defenderse (ie)** to defend oneself
**defensa** defense (16)
**definición** *f.* definition
**definir** to define (16)
**dejar** to leave (7); to abandon; to allow; **déjame en paz** leave me alone; **dejar** (+ *infin.*) to allow (*someone*) to (*do something*) (14); **dejar caer** to let fall/drop; **dejar de** (+ *infin.*) to stop (*doing something*) (12); **dejar que** (+ *subjunctive*) to allow someone to (*do something*) (14); **se lo(s)/la(s) dejo en...** I'll let you have it (them) for . . .
**del** (*contraction of* **de** + **el**) of the (1); from the
**delante de** in front of
**delfín** *m.* dolphin
**delfinario** dolphin tank
**delgado/a** thin (A)
**delicioso/a** delicious
**delincuencia** delinquency
**delito** crime, offense
**demanda** demand; request
**demandar** to demand; to ask (for)
**demás: lo demás** the rest; **los/las demás** the rest, others (7)
**demasiado** *adv.* too much (8)
**demasiado/a** *adj.* too much; **demasiados/as** *pl.* too many
**democracia** democracy
**democrático/a** democratic (6)
**demostrar (ue)** to demonstrate (16)
**demostrativo: pronombre** (*m.*) **demostrativo** demonstrative pronoun
**denso/a** dense (10)
**dental: hilo dental** dental floss
**dentista** *m., f.* dentist
**dentro** inside; **dentro de** inside; within (15); **por dentro** on the inside (8)
**departamento** *Mex.* apartment (6); province
**dependencia** room
**depender de** to depend on (15)
**dependiente, dependienta** clerk, salesperson (5)
**deporte** *m.* sport; **practicar un deporte** to play a sport (2)
**deportista** *n. m., f.* sportsman/sportswoman; *adj. m., f.* athletic (B)
**deportivo/a** *adj.* sporting, sport related (2); **coche** (*m.*) **deportivo** sports car; **ropa** (*sing.*) **deportiva** sports clothes (1)
**depósito** deposit
**deprimido/a** depressed (4)
**derecha** *n.* right hand, right side; **a/de la derecha** to/from the right (3)
**derecho** *n.* right (*legal*); law; straight ahead; **de derecho** by right; **derecho** (*sing.*) **de aduana** customs duties, taxes (11); **Facultad** (*f.*) **de Derecho** School of Law (3)
**derecho/a** *adj.* right; right-hand
**derivarse (de)** to derive (from)
**derramar** to spill
**derrocar (qu)** to overthrow
**derrotar** to defeat (16)
**derrumbe** *m.* landslide
**desafortunadamente** unfortunately
**desagradable** unpleasant (5)
**desagradar** to displease; to bother; to upset
**desahogadamente** comfortably
**desamparado/a** homeless person (14)
**desanimarse** to become discouraged
**desaparecer (zc)** to disappear

**desaparición** disappearance
**desarmarse** to fall to pieces
**desarrollar** to develop (10)
**desarrollo** development (16); **en vías de desarrollo** *adj.* developing
**desastre** *m.* disaster (6); **¡qué desastre!** what a mess! (16)
**desatarse** to be let loose
**desayunar** to have breakfast (2)
**desayuno** breakfast (4)
**descansar** to rest (2)
**descanso** rest; break (2)
**descender (ie)** to descend
**descendiente** *m., f.* descendant
**descenso** descent
**descomponerse** (*like* **poner**) to break down (12)
**desconectar** to disconnect
**descongestionante** *m.* decongestant (12)
**desconocido/a** *n.* stranger (14); *adj.* unknown
**describir** (*p.p.* **descrito**) to describe
**descripción** *f.* description (A)
**descrito/a** (*p.p. of* **describir**) described
**descubierto/a** (*p.p. of* **descubrir**) discovered
**descubridor(a)** discoverer (16)
**descubrimiento** discovery
**descubrir** (*p.p.* **descubierto**) to discover (9)
**desde** *prep.* from (3); **desde la(s)... hasta la(s)...** from . . . to . . . (*time*) (4); **desde que** *conj.* since
**desear** to desire, wish (11)
**desecho** waste
**desembocar (qu) en** to flow into
**desempacar (qu)** to unpack
**desempleado/a** *adj.* unemployed (16)
**desempleo** unemployment; **tasa del desempleo** unemployment rate (16)
**desempolvar** to dust (6)
**desentenderse (ie)** to feign ignorance
**deseo** desire, wish (2)
**deseoso/a** desirous
**desequilibrio** instability
**desesperación** *f.* desperation
**desesperado/a** desperate (7)
**desgracia** misfortune; **por desgracia** unfortunately
**desgraciadamente** unfortunately
**deshacerse** (*like* **hacer**) **de** to get rid of
**deshidratación** *f.* dehydration
**desierto** desert (10)
**desilusión** *f.* disillusion
**desinflado/a** flat, deflated; **llanta desinflada** flat tire (10)
**deslizar (c)** to slip out
**desmayarse** to faint (12)
**desmentir (ie, i)** to deny
**desmoronamiento** crumbling, decaying
**desocupado/a** vacant, unoccupied
**desordenado/a** *n.* disorderly person; *adj.* disorderly, disarranged
**despacio** *adv.* slowly (10)
**despedirse (i, i)** to say goodbye
**despegar (gu)** to take off (*airplane*)
**despejar** to clear up; to clear (*weather*)
**despensas** *pl.* provisions
**desperdiciar** to waste (10)
**desperdicios** *pl.* waste; **desperdicios** (*pl.*) **nucleares** nuclear waste (10)
**despertador** *m.* alarm clock
**despertar (ie)** to wake; **despertarse** to wake up (4)
**despierto/a** awake; awakened
**desplazar (c)** to displace; to move; to transport
**después** *adv.* after (2); **después de** *prep.* after (4); **después de clases** after school; **después de que** *conj.* after (14); **poco después** a bit later (7)
**destacarse (qu)** to stand out
**destapar** to decongest; to unplug
**destino** destination (11); destiny
**destrucción** *f.* destruction (10)
**destruir (y)** to destroy (16)
**desventaja** disadvantage (15)
**desviación** *f.* detour (10)
**detallado/a** detailed
**detalle** *m.* detail (15)
**detección** *f.* detection (16)
**detectar** to detect
**detector** (*m.*) **de metales** metal detector
**detener** (*like* **tener**) to detain; to stop (16); **detenerse** to stop oneself (12); to linger
**determinación** *f.* determination
**detestar** to hate
**detrás de** behind (3)
**deuda** debt; **deuda externa** foreign debt (16)
**devaluación** *f.* devaluation
**devastador(a)** devastating
**devolver (ue)** (*p.p.* **devuelto**) to return (*something*) (13)
**devuelto/a** (*p.p. of* **devolver**) returned (*something*)
**día** *m.* day; **buenos días** *pl.* good morning (A); **cada día** each day; **de día** by day; **Día de Acción de Gracias** Thanksgiving Day (4); **día de fiesta** holiday; **Día de la Independencia** Independence Day (4); **Día de la Madre** Mother's Day (4); **Día de la Raza/Hispanidad** *a celebration of Hispanic identity held on October 12;* **Día de los Enamorados** Valentine's Day (4); **Día de los Muertos** All Souls' Day (4); **Día de los Reyes Magos** Epiphany, Jan. 6th (*lit.* Day of the Magi) (4); **Día de Todos los Santos** All Saints' Day (4); **Día del Padre** Father's Day (4); **día del santo** saint's day (4); **día feriado** holiday; **día festivo** holiday; **en el día a día** in day-to-day life; **hoy (en) día** nowadays; **todo el día** all day long; **todos los días** every day (4)
**diablo** devil
**diálogo** dialogue (A)
**diamante** *m.* diamond (13)
**diariamente** daily (10)
**diario/a** daily (3)
**dibujar** to draw (5)
**dibujo** drawing (B)
**diccionario** dictionary (B)
**dicho** *n.* saying
**dicho/a** (*p.p. of* **decir**) said
**diciembre** *m.* December (1)
**dictador(a)** dictator (16)
**dictadura** dictatorship
**diecinueve** nineteen (A)
**dieciocho** eighteen (A)
**dieciséis** sixteen (A)
**diecisiete** seventeen (A)
**diente** *m.* tooth (11); **cepillarse los dientes** to brush one's teeth; **cepillo de dientes** toothbrush (6); **lavarse los dientes** to brush one's teeth (4); **pasta de dientes** toothpaste
**dieta: estar a dieta** to be on a diet (8)
**dietético/a** *adj.* diet
**diez** ten (A)
**diferencia** difference
**difícil** difficult (B)
**dificultad** *f.* difficulty (16)
**dilema** *m.* dilemma
**diminutivo** diminutive (e.g., **-ito/a**)
**dinastía** dynasty
**dinero** money (5); **cambiar dinero** to change/exchange money; **dinero en efectivo** cash (*money*) (11); **ganar dinero** to earn money
**dinosaurio** dinosaur
**dios** *m.* god; **Dios** God
**diplomático/a** diplomat (16)
**diputación** *f.* delegation; committee
**dirección** *f.* direction; address (1)
**directamente** directly
**director(a)** (school) principal (6)
**dirigente** *adj.* ruling
**dirigir (j)** to direct (15)
**discernir (ie)** to discern
**disco** record (3); **poner discos** to play records (3); **reproductor** (*m.*) **para discos compactos** CD player (1)
**discoteca** discotheque (4)
**disculpar** to excuse, pardon; **disculpe** excuse me (7)
**discusión** *f.* discussion
**discutir** to discuss; to argue (9)
**diseñar** to draw; to design
**diseño** design
**disfrutar** to enjoy (11)
**disminución** *f.* reduction
**disminuir (y)** to diminish, reduce (10); **disminuir la velocidad** to reduce speed
**disolvente** *m.* solvent
**disperso/a** dispersed
**disponer** (*like* **poner**) **de** to have (*at one's disposal*) (11)
**disponible** available
**dispuesto/a** willing; **estar dispuesto/a a** to be willing to (15)
**distancia** distance

**distinto/a** different (14)
**distracción** *f.* distraction
**distraerse** (*like* **traer**) to distract oneself
**distraído/a** distracted
**distribuir** (**y**) to distribute
**distrito** district
**disuelto/a** dissolved
**diversidad** *f.* diversity
**diversión** *f.* entertainment (6)
**diverso** diverse
**divertido/a** fun (B); **¡qué divertido!** how fun! (1)
**divertirse** (**ie, i**) to have fun (4)
**dividir** to divide (11)
**divisa** motto
**división** *f.* division
**divorciado/a** divorced (C)
**divorciarse** to divorce
**divorcio** divorce (16)
**doblar** to turn (11); to fold (6)
**doble sentido** two-way (street) (10)
**doce** twelve (A)
**doctor(a)** doctor (B)
**dólar** *m.* dollar (B)
**dolencia** ache, pain; ailment (12)
**doler** (**ue**) to hurt, ache (12)
**dolor** *m.* pain (12); **dolor de cabeza** headache (12)
**doloroso/a** painful (12)
**doméstico/a** domestic; **animal** (*m.*) **doméstico** pet (5); **aparato doméstico** appliance (13); **empleado/a doméstico/a** servant (6)
**domicilio** address
**dominar** to dominate
**domingo** Sunday (1); **Domingo de Pascua** Easter Sunday (4)
**dominicano/a** of the Dominican Republic (3); **República Dominicana** Dominican Republic (3)
**dominio** power; authority
**dominó** *m. sing.* dominoes
**don** *m. title of respect used with a man's first name* (A)
**donde** where
**¿dónde?** where? (3); **¿de dónde es usted / eres tú?** where are you from? (3)
**dondequiera: por dondequiera** everywhere
**doña** *title of respect used with a woman's first name* (A)
**dorado/a** golden brown (8)
**dormido/a** asleep (9); **quedarse dormido/a** to fall asleep
**dormir** (**ue, u**) to sleep (1, 4); **dormir todo el día** to sleep all day (1); **dormir una siesta** to take a nap; **dormirse** to fall asleep (4)
**dormitorio** bedroom (6)
**dos** two (A); **los/las dos** both
**doscientos/as** two hundred
**drama** *m.* drama, play
**dramaturgo/a** playwright
**drástico/a** drastic
**droga** drug (12)
**drogadicción** *f.* drug addiction (12)
**drogadicto/a** drug addict (16)
**ducha** shower (6)
**ducharse** to shower (3)
**duda: sin duda** without a doubt
**dudar** to doubt; (**no**) **dudar que** to (not) doubt that (16)
**dudoso/a** doubtful; **es dudoso que** it is doubtful that (16)
**dueño/a** owner
**dulce** *adj.* sweet (8); *n. m. pl.* candy (14)
**dulcería** candy store (13)
**dulzón, dulzona** sickly sweet; *coll.* cloying
**dúo** duo, duet
**duque** *m.* duke
**durante** during (1)
**durar** to last
**durazno** peach (8)
**durísimo/a** very severe

## E

**e** and (*used instead of* **y** *before words beginning with* **i** *or* **hi**)
**ebola** *f.* ebola (*type of virus*)
**echar** to throw, cast; **echar a correr** to break into a run; **echarse a** (+ *infin.*) to begin (*doing something*); **echar de menos** to miss someone or something; **echarse de menos** to miss each other
**ecogrupo** *m.* ecology group, group of ecologists
**ecología** ecology
**ecológico/a** ecological (10)
**economía** economy
**económico/a** economic
**ecosistema** *m.* ecosystem
**ecoturismo** ecotourism
**ecuatorial: línea ecuatorial** equator
**ecuatoriano/a** Ecuadoran (3)
**ecuestre** *m.* horseback riding
**edad** *f.* age (C); **edad límite** maximum age; **mayor de edad** of age, adult; **menor de edad** minor; (legally) under age (16); **¿qué edad tiene(s)?** how old are you? (C)
**edificio** building (3); **edificio de apartamentos** apartment building
**edo.** (*abbrev. for* **estado**) state
**educación** *f.* education (14); **educación sexual** sex education (16)
**educar** (**qu**) to educate
**educativo/a** educational (16)
**EE.UU.** (*abbrev. for* **Estados Unidos**) United States
**efectivo: dinero en efectivo** cash (*money*) (11)
**efecto** effect; **poner en efecto** to carry out; **surtir efecto** to work, have the desired effect
**eficacia** effectiveness
**eficaz** (*pl.* **eficaces**) effective (16)
**eficiente** efficient
**egipcio/a** Egyptian (C)
**Egipto** Egypt (C)
**egoísta** selfish (14)
**ejecutivo/a** *adj.* executive
**ejemplo** example; **por ejemplo** for example (9)
**ejercer** (**z**) to exercise
**ejercicio** exercise; **hacer ejercicio** to exercise (1)
**ejercitarse** to exercise
**ejército** army (16)
**ejote** *m.* green bean (8)
**el** *m. definite article* the (A); **el lunes** on Monday
**él** *sub. pron.* he; *obj. of prep.* him (B)
**elaborar** to manufacture, produce
**elástico** elastic (13)
**elección** *f.* election
**electricidad** *f.* electricity (15)
**eléctrico/a** electrical; **rasuradora eléctrica** electric razor (4)
**electrodoméstico: aparato electrodoméstico** household appliance
**electrónico: correo electrónico** e-mail (15)
**elegir** (**i, i**) (**j**) to elect
**elevación** *f.* elevation (10)
**eliminar** to eliminate (10)
**ella** *sub. pron.* she; *obj. of prep.* her (B)
**ellos/as** *sub. pron.* they; *obj. of prep.* them (B)
**elote** ear of corn (8)
**embajada** embassy
**embajador(a)** ambassador (16)
**embarazada** pregnant (14); **quedar embarazada** to become pregnant
**embarazo** pregnancy
**embarcarse** (**qu**) to embark (*on an enterprise*)
**embargo: sin embargo** however (7)
**embellecimiento** embellishment
**emblema** *m.* emblem
**emborracharse** to get drunk
**embriagante** *adj.* intoxicating
**emergencia** emergency (12); **sala de emergencias** emergency room (12)
**emigrante** *m., f.* emigrant
**emigrar** to emigrate (15)
**emisión** *f.* emission
**emisora** radio station (3)
**emoción** *f.* emotion
**emocionante** *adj.* exciting; moving
**empacar** (**qu**) to pack (11)
**empanada** turnover pie or pastry
**emparejar** to match
**empeorar** to worsen (15)
**emperador** emperor (7)
**emperatriz** empress (7)
**empezar** (**ie**) (**c**) to begin (2); **empezar a** (+ *infin.*) to begin to (*do something*)
**empinado/a** steep
**empleado/a** employee (11); **empleado/a doméstico/a** servant (6)
**emplear** to use; to employ
**empleo** job (5)
**emplumado/a** feathered
**empobrecimiento** impoverishment
**empolvarse** to get dusty

**emprendedor** enterprising
**emprender** to undertake, take on
**empresa** company, firm (15)
**empresario/a** manager
**en** in; on (A); at
**en seguida** immediately
**enamorado/a (de)** in love (with) (4)
**enamorados** *pl.* sweethearts; **Día** (*m.*) **de los Enamorados** Valentine's Day (4)
**encabezar (c)** to head, lead
**encaje** *m.* lacework
**encantado/a** delighted, pleased (*to meet someone*) (6)
**encantador** *adj.* delightful
**encantar** to delight, charm (8); **me encanta que** I love it when
**encarcelar** to imprison, jail
**encargarse (gu)** to be in charge
**encarnar** to represent; to embody
**encender (ie)** to turn on; to set on fire; **encender la luz** to turn on the light (6)
**encerar** to wax (10)
**encerrar (ie)** to shut in; to lock up
**enchilada** *rolled tortilla filled with meat and topped with cheese and sauce, cooked in an oven*
**encías** *pl.* gums (*anatomy*) (12)
**enciclopedia** encyclopedia
**encima de** on top of (3)
**encomienda** *Indian village granted to Spanish colonist by royal decree*
**encontrar (ue)** to find (3); to meet; **encontrarse con** to meet; to run into
**encuentro** encounter; meeting
**encuesta** survey (4)
**endurecer (zc)** to harden
**enemigo/a** enemy
**energía** energy (10); **fuente** (*f.*) **de energía** energy source (16)
**enérgico/a** energetic
**enero** January (1)
**énfasis** *m. sing., pl.* emphasis; stress
**enfatizar (c)** to emphasize
**enfermarse** to get sick (12)
**enfermedad** *f.* illness; disease; **enfermedad venérea** sexually transmitted disease
**enfermero/a** *n.* nurse (5)
**enfermo/a** *n.* sick person; *adj.* sick (4)
**enfrentar** to face; to confront; to meet, encounter (16); **enfrentarse con** to face
**enfrente** *adv.* in front; **de enfrente** in front; **enfrente de** in front of (3)
**enfriar (enfrío)** to cool off (10)
**engañar** to deceive
**engaño** deceit
**engordar** to get fat
**enjuagar (gu)** to rinse
**enlace** *m.* link; bond; union, marriage (15)
**enlazar (c)** to link, connect
**enmendar (ie)** to amend; to reform
**enojado/a** angry (4)
**enojar: hacer enojar** to make angry, anger; **enojarse** to get angry (12)
**enorme** enormous (13)
**enriquecer (zc)** to enrich; **enriquecerse** to get rich
**enrollar** to roll up
**ensabanar** to cover
**ensalada** salad (3)
**ensaladilla** potato salad
**ensayista** *m., f.* essayist
**ensayo** essay
**enseñanza** teaching (16)
**enseñar** to teach (5); to show (14)
**entablar** to strike up (*correspondence*)
**entender (ie)** to understand; **no entendí bien** I didn't quite understand (1)
**enterarse** to find out
**entero/a** whole (7)
**enterrado/a** buried
**entonces** then (11); **en aquel entonces** at that time
**entorno** environment, surroundings
**entrada** entrance (10); ticket (1); **de entrada** as an entrée (*meal*); **entradas para un concierto** tickets for a concert (1)
**entrar (en)** to enter; **entrar al trabajo** to start work (5); **entrar en vigor** to go into effect
**entre** between, among (3); **entre paréntesis** in parentheses; **entre semana** on weekdays, during the week (14)
**entregar (gu)** to hand in (9); to turn over
**entrenamiento** training; coaching
**entrenar(se)** to train
**entretener** (*like* **tener**) to amuse
**entretenimiento** entertainment, amusement
**entrevista** interview (B)
**entrevistar** to interview
**entristecer (zc)** to sadden; **entristecerse** to become sad (12)
**entusiasmado/a** excited
**entusiasmo** enthusiasm
**entusiasta** *adj. m., f.* enthusiastic (B)
**envase** *m.* packing, packaging; bottle (10)
**enviar (envío)** to send (6)
**envidia** envy; **¡qué envidia!** how I envy you! (7)
**envío** shipping
**envolver (ue)** (*p.p.* **envuelto**) to wrap (13)
**enyesado/a** in a cast (12)
**epidemia** epidemic
**episodio** episode (12)
**época** era, age (16)
**equilibrar** to balance
**equipaje** *m.* baggage (11); **exceso de equipaje** excess baggage; **reclamo de equipaje** baggage claim (11)
**equipamiento** equipment
**equipo** equipment; gear; (sports) team (1); **equipo de música** stereo (1)
**equitativamente** equitably
**equivaler** *irreg.* to be equivalent
**equivocarse (qu)** to make a mistake
**era** era, age
**escabeche** *m. marinade of oil, vinegar, herbs, and spices (to preserve fish)*
**escala** scale; stopover (11); **sin escala** nonstop (flight)
**escalar montañas** to go mountain climbing (5)
**escalera** stairway, stairs (6)
**escaparse** to escape, run away (12)
**escarcha** frost (10)
**escasez** *f.* (*pl.* **escaseces**) scarcity; shortage (14)
**escaso/a** scarce; scant; limited
**escena** scene (12)
**esclavo/a** slave (16)
**escoba** broom (6)
**escobilla** brush
**escocés, escocesa** *adj.* Scotch
**escoger (j)** to choose (4)
**escolar** of or pertaining to school
**esconder** to hide
**escondite** *m.* hiding place; **jugar al escondite** to play hide-and-seek (9)
**escopeta** shotgun
**Escorpión** *m.* Scorpio
**escribir** (*p.p.* **escrito**) to write; **¿cómo se escribe...?** how do you spell . . . ? (1); **escribir a máquina** to type (5); **escribir cartas** to write letters (1)
**escrito/a** (*p.p. of* **escribir**) written
**escritor(a)** writer (13)
**escritorio** desk (B)
**escritura** *n.* writing
**escuchar** to listen (to) (1)
**escuela** school (4); **escuela primaria** grade school; **escuela secundaria** high school (7)
**escultura** sculpture
**ese, esa** *pron.* that (one); *adj.* that (3)
**esencial** essential
**esfuerzo** effort (10)
**esgrima** fencing
**eso** that, that thing, that fact; **a eso de** (+ *time*) around (*specific time*); **por eso** for that reason
**esos/as** *pron.* those (ones); *adj.* those
**espacial** *adj.* space; **colonia espacial** space colony (15)
**espacio** space; **espacio en blanco** blank (space) (3)
**espada** sword; **entre la espada y la pared** between a rock and a hard place
**espaguetis** *m. pl.* spaghetti
**espalda** back (B)
**España** Spain (C)
**español** *n. m.* Spanish (language) (A); **español** (*m.*) **mocho** broken Spanish
**español(a)** *n.* Spaniard; *adj.* Spanish (C)
**espárragos** *pl.* asparagus
**especial** special
**especialidad** *f.* specialty; major (*field of study*) (2)
**especialista** *m., f.* specialist
**especializado/a** specialized
**especialmente** especially (4)
**especie** *f. sing.* species (10)

**específico/a** specific
**espectacular** spectacular
**espectáculo** spectacle; show; performance
**especulación** *f.* speculation
**espejo** mirror (6); **espejo retrovisor** rearview mirror (10)
**espera: sala de espera** waiting room (11)
**esperanza** hope
**esperar** to hope; to wait for (3); **esperar... de...** to expect (*something*) from (*somebody*)
**espeso/a** thick (8)
**espinacas** *pl.* spinach
**espíritu** *m.* spirit
**espléndido/a** splendid
**esponja** sponge
**esponjoso/a** spongy
**espontáneo/a** spontaneous
**esposo/a** husband/wife (C)
**esqueleto** skeleton (12)
**esquí** *m.* skiing (1); ski
**esquiar (esquío)** to ski (2)
**esquina** corner
**estabilidad** *f.* stability
**estabilizar (c)** to stabilize (16)
**estable** *adj.* stable
**establecer (zc)** to establish
**establo** *n.* stable (13)
**estación** *f.* station (3); season (*weather*); **estación de autobuses** bus depot
**estacionamiento** parking lot (3)
**estacionar** to park (7)
**estadio** stadium (1)
**estado** state (3); **estado civil** marital status (1); **estado de ánimo** state of mind (12); **Estados Unidos** United States (C); **golpe** (*m.*) **de estado** *coup d'état*, overthrow of the government (16)
**estadounidense** *n. m., f.* United States citizen; *adj.* of, from, or pertaining to the United States
**estallar** to break out; to flare up
**estancia** stay
**estante** *m.* shelf (6)
**estar** *irreg.* to be (7); **¿cómo está usted?** how are you (*pol. sing.*)? (A); **¿cómo estás (tú)?** how are you (*inf. sing.*)? (B); **estar a dieta** to be on a diet (8); **estar a favor de / en contra de** to be for/against (15); **estar comprometido/a** to be engaged (15); **estar de acuerdo** to agree; **estar de buen/mal humor** to be in a good/bad mood (4); **estar de moda** to be in style; **estar de pie/sentado** to be standing/seated, sitting down; **estar dispuesto/a a** to be willing to (15); **estar listo/a** to be ready (5); **estoy bien/regular** I am fine/OK (A); **estoy un poco cansado/a** I am a bit tired (A)
**estatal** *adj.* state
**estatua** statue (6)
**estatura** height (B); **estatura mediana** medium height (B)
**este, esta** *pron.* this (one); *adj.* this (5); **esta noche** tonight, this night (1); **este...** um . . . (*pause in speech*)
**estereotípico/a** stereotypical
**estereotipo** stereotype (2)
**estilo** style (13)
**estimado/a** dear; esteemed (14); **Estimado/a (Profesor/a)** Dear (Professor)
**estimarse** to be estimated
**estimulante** stimulating
**estimular** to stimulate; to encourage
**estímulo** stimulus
**estirar la pata** *coll.* to kick the bucket, die
**estireno** styrene
**esto** this, this thing, this matter (3)
**Estocolmo** Stockholm
**estómago** stomach (B); **dolor de estómago** stomach ache (12)
**estornudar** to sneeze (12)
**estornudo** sneeze (12)
**estos/as** *pron.* these (ones); *adj.* these
**estrategia** strategy
**estrecho/a** narrow; tight (13)
**estrella** star (10); **estrella de cine** movie star (15)
**estrellarse** to crash
**estremecer (zc)** to shake, tremble
**estreno** premiere, first performance
**estrés** *m.* stress
**estudiante** *m., f.* student (A)
**estudiantil** *adj.* student (16); **residencia estudiantil** university dorm (5)
**estudiar** to study (2)
**estudio** study; *pl.* studies, schooling (15)
**estudioso/a** studious
**estufa** stove (6)
**estupendo/a** stupendous
**eterno/a** eternal
**etiqueta** etiquette; tag, label (8)
**étnico/a** ethnic (16)
**Europa** Europe (9)
**europeo/a** European (2)
**eutanasia** euthanasia (16)
**evaluación** *f.* evaluation
**evangelizar (c)** to evangelize
**evitar** to avoid (12)
**exactamente** exactly (15)
**examen** *m.* (*pl.* **exámenes**) test
**examinar** to examine (5)
**excedente** *m.* excess, surplus
**exceder** to exceed, surpass
**excelencia** excellency
**excepción** *f.* exception
**exceso** excess; **exceso de equipaje** excess baggage; **exceso de velocidad** speeding (7)
**excursión** *f.* excursion (11); **hacer excursiones** to go on outings
**exhibirse** to be exhibited
**exigir (j)** to demand
**existente** existing
**existir** to exist
**éxito** success; **con éxito** successfully; **tener éxito** to be successful
**experiencia** experience
**experimentado/a** experienced
**experimentar** to test, try out
**experto/a** *n., adj.* expert (15)
**explicación** *f.* explanation
**explicar (qu)** to explain (5)
**explorar** to explore
**explosión** *f.* explosion
**explotador(a)** exploiter
**explotar** to exploit
**exponerse** (*like* **poner**) to open oneself up; to expose oneself
**exportación** *f.* export (16)
**exportar** to export (13)
**exposición** *f.* exhibition (16)
**expresar** to express (10)
**expresión** *f.* expression
**expresivo/a** expressive
**expulsar** to expel
**exquisito/a** exquisite
**extender (ie)** to extend
**extensión** *f.* extension (10)
**extenso/a** extensive
**exterior** *adj.* foreign; exterior
**externo/a: deuda externa** foreign debt (16)
**extinción** *f.* extinction (10)
**extinguir (g)** to extinguish
**extirpar** to remove (*surgically*)
**extranjero/a** *n.* foreigner; *n. m.* abroad; *adj.* foreign (15)
**extrañar** to miss, long for
**extraño/a** *adj.* strange (3); *n. m.* stranger
**extrovertido/a** *n.* extrovert; *adj.* extroverted (B)

## F

**fábrica** factory (5)
**fabricación** making, manufacture (13)
**fabricado/a a mano** made by hand
**fabricante** *m.* manufacturer
**fabuloso/a** fabulous
**fácil** easy (B)
**facilidad** *f.* facility; ease
**facilitar** to facilitate (16)
**fácilmente** easily (12)
**factura** invoice, bill
**facturar** to check (baggage) (11)
**facultad** *f.* school (*of a university*); **Facultad de Bellas Artes** School of Fine Arts (3); **Facultad de Ciencias Naturales** School of Natural Sciences (3); **Facultad de Derecho** School of Law (3); **Facultad de Filosofía y Letras** School of Humanities (3); **Facultad de Medicina** School of Medicine (3)
**faja** waist band
**fajita** *a dish served in Mexican-style restaurants in the United States made of grilled meat, onions, and green peppers rolled in a tortilla*
**falangista** *n. m., f.* Falangist, partisan of Spain's dictator Franco
**falda** skirt (A)
**fallecer (zc)** to die
**fallido/a** unsuccessful; failed

**falso/a** false
**falta: hacer falta** to be necessary
**faltar** to be missing, lacking; to be absent
**fama** fame
**familia** family
**familiar** *n. m., f.* member of the family; *adj.* family; **relaciones** (*pl.*) **familiares** family relationships (9)
**famoso/a** famous (A)
**farmacéutico/a** pharmacist (12)
**farmacia** pharmacy (4)
**fascinante** fascinating
**fascinar** to fascinate
**fase** *f.* phase
**favor: estar a favor de** to be for (15); **favor de** (+ *infin.*) please (*do something*); (5) **por favor** please (1)
**favorecer (zc)** to favor (16)
**favorito/a** favorite
**fe** *f.* faith
**febrero** February (1)
**fecha** date; **fecha de nacimiento** date of birth (1)
**felicidad** *f.* happiness (15); *pl.* congratulations (1)
**felicitar** to congratulate
**feliz** (*pl.* **felices**) happy (1); **feliz cumpleaños** happy birthday (1)
**femenino/a** feminine (15)
**fenómeno** phenomenon
**feo/a** ugly (A)
**feria** fair; **feria artesanal** crafts fair
**feriado: día** (*m.*) **feriado** holiday (3)
**ferrocarril** *m.* railway (16)
**festividad** *f.* celebration, holiday
**festivo: día** (*m.*) **festivo** holiday
**fiambre** *m.* cold cut
**fibra** fiber
**ficción** *f.*: **ciencia ficción** science fiction (15)
**fidelidad** *f.* faithfulness
**fideos** *pl.* noodles, pasta
**fiebre** *f.* fever (12)
**fiel** faithful
**fierro** iron
**fiesta** party; **dar una fiesta** to give a party (2); **día** (*m.*) **de fiesta** holiday; **hacer una fiesta** to have a party; **ir a fiestas** to go to parties (1)
**fiestón** *m.* large party
**figura** figure
**figurar** to calculate
**fijo/a** fixed
**fila** line, row
**filosofía** philosophy; **Facultad** (*f.*) **de Filosofía y Letras** School of Humanities (3)
**filosófico/a** philosophical (B)
**fin** *m.* end (4); purpose, goal; **a fines** (*pl.*) **de** at the end of; **en fin** in short, in brief; **fin de semana** weekend (1); **ponerle fin a** to put an end to (16); **por fin** finally (12)
**final** *n. m.* end; *adj.* final; **al final** in the end; **al final de** at the end of (14)
**finalmente** finally (2)
**finanzas** *pl.* finances
**finca** farm (16)
**fino/a** fine; of good quality (13)
**firma** signature (1)
**firmar** to sign (7)
**firme** solid
**fiscal** *m., f.* public prosecutor
**físico/a** physical (A)
**flan** *m.* sweet custard (8)
**flojo/a** lazy
**flor** *f.* flower (2)
**florero** flower vase (12)
**flotante** *adj.* floating
**flotar** to float (10)
**flujo** flow
**fluorado: carburos fluorados** fluorocarbons
**fogata** bonfire
**folleto** brochure
**fomentar** to foster, encourage
**fondo** fund (15); **plato de fondo** main dish
**forestal** pertaining to forests; **masa forestal** forest
**forma** form (12)
**formación** *f.* formation (16)
**formalidad** *f.* formality
**formar** to form (16)
**formatear** to format
**fornido/a** well-built
**forzar (ue) (c)** to force
**foto** *f.* photo; **sacar fotos** to take pictures (1)
**fotocopia** photocopy
**fotografía** photography; picture (5)
**fotógrafo/a** photographer (13)
**fracaso** failure (15)
**fractura** fracture, break
**fracturarse** to fracture, break
**fragmento** excerpt
**francés** *n. m.* French (language) (C)
**francés, francesa** *n., adj.* French (C); **despedirse a la francesa** to leave without saying goodbye
**Francia** France (C)
**frase** *f.* sentence, phrase (C)
**fraude** *m.* fraud (16)
**frazada** blanket
**frecuencia** frequency; **con frecuencia** frequently (2)
**frecuentemente** frequently (12)
**fregadero** kitchen sink (6)
**freír (frío) (i, i)** to fry (8)
**freno** brake (10)
**frente** *m.* front; *f.* forehead (12); **en frente de** in front of; **frente a** *prep.* facing, opposite
**fresa** strawberry (8)
**fresco/a** fresh (8); cool; **hace fresco** it's cool (weather) (1)
**frigorífero** refrigerator
**frigorífico** refrigerator
**frijol** *m.* bean (8)
**frío/a** cold; **hace frío** it's cold (weather) (1); **té** (*m.*) **frío** cold tea (8); **tener frío** to be cold (4)
**frito/a** (*p.p. of* **freír**) fried; **huevos fritos** fried eggs (8); **papas fritas** French fries (8); **pollo frito** fried chicken (8)
**frondoso: sendas** (*pl.*) **frondosas** shaded paths
**frontera** border, frontier (8)
**frotar** to rub
**fruta** fruit; **batido de frutas** fruit shake (8)
**frutal** *adj.* fruit
**frutería** fruit store (13)
**frutilla** strawberry
**fuego** fire; **a fuego lento** over a low fire (8); **arma** *f.* (*but* **el arma**) **de fuego** firearm (16); **fuegos artificiales** fireworks (11)
**fuente** *f.* source; fountain (4); **fuente de energía** energy source (16); **fuente de sopa** soup tureen (8)
**fuera** out, outside (5); **cenar fuera** to go out to dinner (1); **por fuera** on the outside (8)
**fuerte** strong (10)
**fuertemente** strongly
**fuerza** strength
**fumar** to smoke (3); **sección** (*f.*) **de (no) fumar** (no) smoking section (11)
**función** *f.* function (12)
**funcionar** to function
**fundación** *f.* foundation
**fundado/a** founded (16)
**fundamentos** *pl.* fundamentals
**fundar** to found
**furioso/a** furious
**fusilar** to shoot, execute by firing squad
**fútbol** *m.* soccer (1); **fútbol americano** football (1)
**futuro** *n.* future
**futuro/a** *adj.* future

## G

**gabardina** gabardine (*type of cloth*)
**gabinete** *m.* cabinet (*government*); cabinet (6); cupboard
**Gales** *m. sing.* Wales
**gallego/a** from or characteristic of Galicia (*northern region of Spain*)
**galleta** biscuit; cracker; cookie
**galletita** cookie (8)
**gallina** hen; fowl
**galón** *m.* gallon
**galope** *m.*: **al galope** at a gallop
**galvanizar (c)** to galvanize; to electroplate
**gamba** prawn
**ganadero/a** *adj.* cattle-raising
**ganado** cattle; **pasto de ganado** cattle grazing
**ganador(a)** winner (16)
**ganancias** *pl.* earnings
**ganar** to earn; to win (7); **ganar dinero** to earn money (5)
**ganas** *pl.*: **tener ganas de** (+ *infin.*) to feel like (*doing something*) (5)
**ganga** bargain (13); **¡qué ganga!** what a bargain! (13)
**garaje** *m.* garage; **venta de garaje** garage sale

**garantizar (c)** to guarantee
**garganta** throat (12)
**gárgaras** *pl.*: **hacer gárgaras** to gargle (12)
**garúa** drizzle
**garza** heron
**gasolinera** gas station (6)
**gastar** to spend (*money*) (13); to consume; **gastar combustible** to use gas (10)
**gasto** expense (16)
**gato/a** cat (A); **jugar al gato** to play tag (9)
**gaveta** drawer (6)
**gemelo/a** twin (C)
**Géminis** *m. sing.* Gemini
**gene** *m.* gene (16)
**generación** *f.* generation
**general** *adj.* general; **en general** in general (2); **por lo general** in general
**generalmente** generally (3)
**generar** to generate
**género** gender
**generoso/a** generous (B)
**gente** *f. sing.* people (3)
**geografía** geography
**geográfico/a** geographical (16)
**geoturismo** *tourism of natural areas and parks*
**gerente** *m., f.* manager (5)
**gestación** *f.* gestation
**gesto** gesture
**gigante** *adj.* giant
**gimnasia: hacer gimnasia** to do gymnastics
**gimnasio** gymnasium (3)
**gira** tour; **hacer una gira** to take a tour (10)
**girar** to spin around
**giro postal** money order
**gitano/a** gypsy
**glicerina** glycerine
**globo** globe (12)
**glosario** glossary
**gobernador(a)** governor (14)
**gobernante** *m., f.* ruler
**gobernar (ie)** to govern (16)
**gobierno** government (16)
**gol** *m.* goal (*sports*)
**golf** *m.* golf (15)
**golfo** gulf (10)
**golpe** *m.* blow, hit; **golpe de estado** *coup d'état* (16); **golpe militar** military coup
**golpear(se)** to hit (oneself) (12)
**goma** rubber (13)
**gordo/a** *adj.* fat (A); **premio gordo** grand prize (15)
**gorra** cap (13)
**gorro** party hat
**gota** drop; **gotas para la nariz** nose drops (12)
**goteo nasal** nasal drip
**gozar (c) de** to enjoy (15)
**grabación** *n. f.* recording
**grabadora** tape recorder
**grabar** to record
**gracias** thank you (A); **Día** (*m.*) **de Acción de Gracias** Thanksgiving Day (4); **gracias a** thanks to; **muchas gracias** thank you very much
**grado** degree (2)
**graduación** *f.* graduation (5)
**graduarse** to graduate (5)
**gráfico** *n.* chart; diagram
**gráfico/a** *adj.* graphic
**gragea** sprinkle (*colored candy granule used for decorating cakes*); pill
**grama** grass
**gramática** grammar (A)
**gran, grande** big, large (B); great; **en gran parte** to a large degree; **de gran valor** of great value (14)
**grano** grain
**grasa** *n.* fat
**gratificador(a)** gratifying, pleasurable
**gratis** *inv.* free (*of charge*)
**gratuito/a** free (*of charge*) (16)
**grave** serious
**Grecia** Greece
**griego/a** *n.* Greek; *adj.* Grecian (16)
**grieta** crack, fissure
**grifo** faucet
**gringo/a** *coll.* foreigner
**gripa** *Mex.* flu
**gripe** *f.* flu (12)
**gris** gray (A)
**gritar** to yell, shout, scream (4); **gritarse** to yell at each other
**grito** shout, scream (7)
**grueso/a** thick
**gruñón, gruñona** grumpy
**grupo** group
**guacamayo** macaw
**guacamole** *m. dip or sauce made of avocados*
**guagua** *Cuba, Puerto Rico* bus
**guanábana** custard apple
**guante** *m.* glove (13)
**guapo/a** good-looking (A)
**guaraní** *m.* Guaraní (*indigenous language of Paraguay*); Paraguayan currency (13)
**guardabarros** *m. sing., pl.* fender
**guardafangos** *m. sing., pl.* fender (10)
**guardar** to keep; to save; **guardar ropa** to put away clothes (6)
**guardería (infantil)** childcare center (16)
**guardia** *m., f.* guard
**guatemalteco/a** *adj.* Guatemalan (3)
**guayabera** *embroidered shirt of light material worn in tropical climates* (13)
**guerra** war (15); **Segunda Guerra Mundial** Second World War
**guerrero** soldier
**guerrillero/a** guerrilla (16)
**guía** guide(book) (4)
**guiar (guío)** to guide
**guión** *m.* script
**guisante** *m.* pea (8)
**guitarra** guitar
**gustar** to be pleasing; **a mí (sí/no) me gusta...** I (do/don't) like to . . . (1); **le gusta...** you (*pol. sing.*) like to . . . ; he/she likes to . . . (1); **les gusta...** you (*pl.*) like to . . . they like to . . . (1); **(no) me gusta...** I (don't) like to . . . (1); **¿qué le gusta hacer?** what do you (*pol. sing.*) like to do?; what does he/she like to do? (1); **¿qué te gusta hacer?** what do you (*inf. sing.*) like to do? (1); **te gusta...** you (*inf. sing.*) like to . . . (1)
**gusto** taste (14); pleasure, delight; **con gusto** with pleasure; **mucho gusto** pleased to meet you (A); **¡qué gusto!** what a pleasure! (15)

# H

**ha habido** (*infin.* **haber**) there has/have been (13)
**Habana: La Habana** Havana
**haber** *irreg.* (*infin. of* **hay**) to have (*auxiliary*); to be; to exist (12)
**había** (*infin.* **haber**) there was/there were
**habichuela** green bean (8)
**habilidad** *f.* ability; skill
**habitación** *f.* room (6)
**habitado/a** inhabited (16)
**habitante** *m., f.* inhabitant (16)
**habitar** to inhabit (16)
**hábito** habit (12)
**hablar** to speak, talk; **hablar por teléfono** to speak on the phone (A)
**habrá** (*infin.* **haber**) there will be
**habría** (*infin.* **haber**) there would be
**Habsburgo** Hapsburg
**hacendado/a** property owner (16)
**hacer** *irreg.* (*p.p.* **hecho**) to do; to make (1); **¿cuántas millas hace por...?** how many miles per . . . do you get?; **¿cuánto hace que** + *present*? how long have/has . . . ?; **¿cuánto tiempo hace que...?** how long has it been since . . . ? (7); **hace** + *time* (*time*) . . . ago (7); **hace** + *time* + **que** + *present* (I) have been (*doing something*) for + *time*; **hace buen/mal tiempo** it's fine/bad weather (2); **hace calor/fresco/frío/sol/viento** it's hot/cool/cold/sunny/windy (weather) (2); **hacer análisis** to do (medical) tests; **hacer caso** to pay attention; **hacer cola** to stand in line (11); **hacer comentarios** to comment; **hacer daño** to harm; **hacer ejercicio** to exercise (1); **hacer el papel de** to play the role of (6); **hacer enojar** to make angry, anger; **hacer erupción** to erupt; **hacer excursiones** to go on outings; **hacer falta** to be necessary; **hacer gárgaras** to gargle (12); **hacer las compras** to go grocery shopping (6); **hacer las maletas** to pack (11); **hacer preguntas** to ask questions (5); **hacer ruido** to make noise; **hacer transbordo** to change (*trains, etc.*); **hacer una fiesta** to have a party; **hacer una gira** to take a tour (10); **hacer una limpieza** to clean; **hacer viajes** to take trips, travel; **hacerse** to become; to pretend, feign to be; **hacerse cargo** to take charge; **hacerse socio** to become a member (15); **¿qué le**

**gusta hacer?** what do you (*pol. sing.*) like to do?; what does he/she like to do? (1); **¿qué te gusta hacer?** what do you (*inf. sing.*) like to do? (1); **¿qué tiempo hace?** what is the weather like? (2); **se me está haciendo tarde** it's getting late
**hacia** toward (10); **hacia adelante** forward
**hada: cuento de hadas** fairy tale
**hallar** to find
**hambre** *f.* (*but* **el hambre**) hunger; **pasar hambre** to go hungry; **tener hambre** to be hungry (4)
**hambruna** famine
**hamburguesa** hamburger
**harapiento/a** ragged; unkempt
**harina** flour (8)
**hasta** *prep.* up to, until (3); *adv.* even; **desde la(s)... hasta la(s)...** from . . . to . . . (*time*) (4); **hasta la fecha** up to now; **hasta luego** see you later (A); **hasta mañana** see you tomorrow; **hasta que** *conj.* until (15)
**hay** there is, there are; **¿cuántos/as hay?** how many are there? (A); **hay que** one has to (6); **no hay paso** no entrance (10)
**hazaña** deed, achievement
**hebreo** Hebrew (language) (C)
**hechizar (c)** to bewitch; to charm; to fascinate
**hecho** *n.* fact; event (7); **de hecho** in fact
**hecho/a** (*p.p. of* **hacer**) made; **de qué está hecho/a?** what is it (made) of? (13); **hecho/a a mano** handmade (13)
**hectárea** hectare (*2.471 acres*)
**helada** frost; freezing weather
**heladera** refrigerator (10)
**heladería** ice cream parlor (13)
**helado** ice cream (C)
**helado/a** frozen; **té** (*m.*) **helado** iced tea (7)
**hembra** female
**hemisferio** hemisphere
**heredar** to inherit
**herida** wound (12)
**herido/a** *n.* wounded person (12); *adj.* wounded
**hermanastro/a** stepbrother/stepsister (9)
**hermano/a** brother/sister (B)
**hermoso/a** beautiful (4)
**héroe** *m.* hero (5)
**heroico/a** heroic (7)
**heroína** heroin; heroine (5)
**herramienta** tool (13)
**hervir (ie, i)** to boil
**hielo** ice; **patinar en el hielo** to ice skate (1)
**hierba** grass
**hierro** iron (13)
**hígado** liver (8)
**hijastro/a** stepson/stepdaughter (9)
**hijo/a** son/daughter (C); **hijo/a único/a** only child (14); **hijos** *pl.* children (sons, sons and daughters) (C)
**hilo** linen (13); **hilo dental** dental floss
**hinchado/a** swollen (12)
**hipotético/a** hypothetical (15)
**hispánico/a** Hispanic
**hispanidad** *f.* Hispanic identity; Hispanic world
**hispano/a** Hispanic
**Hispanoamérica** Spanish America (15)
**hispanohablante** *m., f.* Spanish speaker
**histérico/a** hysterical (16)
**historia** story; history
**historial** (*m.*) **clínico** medical history (12)
**histórico/a** historical (7)
**historieta** short story, anecdote
**hnos.** (*abbrev. for* **hermanos**) brothers
**hogar** *m.* home (15)
**hoja** leaf (2)
**hola** hi (B)
**holgado/a** loose; comfortable
**hombre** *m.* man (A)
**hombro** shoulder (B)
**homicidio** homicide (16)
**hondo: plato hondo** soup plate, bowl (8)
**hondureño/a** *adj.* Honduran (3)
**honestidad** *f.* honesty
**hongo** mushroom (8)
**honrado/a** honorable, honest
**hora** hour; time; **¿a qué hora (es)...?** at what time (is) . . . ? (1); **a última hora** at the last minute; **¿qué hora es?** what time is it?; **¿qué hora tiene?** what time do you (*pol. sing.*) have? (1); **¡ya era hora!** it was about time! (16)
**horario** schedule
**horneado/a** baked (8)
**horno** oven (6); **horno de microondas** microwave oven (6)
**horóscopo** horoscope
**hortaliza** *Mex.* vegetable garden
**hospedaje** *m.* lodging
**hospedarse** to stay (7)
**hospital** *m.* hospital (3)
**hospitalidad** *f.* hospitality
**hotel** *m.* hotel (4)
**hotelero/a** *adj.* hotel
**hoy** today (1); **hoy (en) día** nowadays
**huelga** (labor) strike (16); **declarar la huelga** to go on strike
**huelguista** *m., f.* striker
**huérfano/a** orphan
**hueso** bone (12)
**huésped(a)** guest
**huevo** egg; **huevos cocidos** hard-boiled eggs (8); **huevos rancheros** *eggs, usually fried or poached, topped with a spicy tomato sauce and sometimes served on a fried corn tortilla;* **huevos revueltos** scrambled eggs (8)
**huir** to escape, run away (16)
**humanidad** *f.* humanity
**humanitario/a** humanitarian (16)
**humano/a** *n., adj.* human (B); **ser** (*m.*) **humano** human being (15)
**humedad** *f.* humidity (10)
**humedecido/a** damp, moist
**húmedo/a** humid (10)
**humilde** humble
**humo** smoke
**humor** *m.* humor; mood; **estar de buen/mal humor** to be in a good/bad mood (4); **ponerse de buen/mal humor** to get into a good/bad mood; **sentido del humor** sense of humor (14)
**humorístico/a** humoristic
**hundirse** to sink
**huracán** *m.* hurricane (10)

# I

**ida: boleto de ida y vuelta** round-trip ticket (11)
**idea: ¡qué buena idea!** what a good idea! (2)
**idealista** *adj. m., f.* idealistic (B)
**idéntico/a** identical
**identificación** *f.* identification (A)
**identificar (qu)** to identify (10)
**ideología** ideology
**idioma** *m.* language
**iglesia** church (4)
**ignorar** to ignore
**igual** equal
**igualdad** *f.* equality
**igualmente** *interjection* same here (A)
**ilegal** illegal (16)
**ileso/a** uninjured
**iluminador/a** illuminating
**ilustración** *f.* illustration
**ilustrar** to illustrate
**imagen** *f.* image
**imaginario/a** imaginary (16)
**imaginarse** to imagine (6)
**impaciencia** impatience
**impaciente** impatient
**impartir** to impart, give (*instruction*)
**impedir (i, i)** to prevent
**imperio** empire (16)
**implicación** *f.* implication
**implicar (qu)** to implicate; to involve; to imply
**imponerse** (*like* **ponerse**) to dominate, impose one's authority (16)
**importación** *f.* importing, importation; **de importación** imported
**importado/a** imported (13)
**importancia** importance (14)
**importante** important
**importar** to matter, be important; **¿qué me importa a mí?** I don't care! (16)
**imposible** impossible (14)
**imprenta** printing shop
**impresión** *f.* impression (16)
**impresionante** impressive (10)
**impresionar** to impress
**impresionista** *n. m., f.* Impressionist
**impreso/a** printed
**impresora** printer (15)
**imprimir** to print
**impuesto** tax (11)
**impulsado/a** make run, runs (*batteries*)
**impune** *adj.* unpunished

**inagotable** inexhaustible
**inaudito/a** unheard of; unprecedented
**inca** *n. m., f.* Inca; *adj.* Incan (16)
**incaico/a** Incan
**incansable** indefatigable
**incendio** fire (5); **alarma de incendio** fire alarm
**incivilizado/a** uncivilized
**inclinar** to bow, bend; **inclinarse** to bow; to lean
**incluir (y)** to include (8)
**incluso** *adv.* even; including
**incómodo/a** uncomfortable
**incondicional** unconditional (15)
**inconsciente** unconscious (12)
**incontenible** unstoppable
**incorporar** to incorporate
**increíble** unbelievable
**incrementar** to increase
**indeciso/a** indecisive; hesitant
**independencia** independence; **Día** (*m.*) **de la Independencia** Independence Day (4)
**independiente** independent
**indeseado/a** unwanted
**indicación** *f.* indication
**indicar (qu)** to indicate
**índice** (*m.*) **de natalidad** birthrate
**indígena** *n. m., f.*; *adj.* Indian; indigenous, native (7)
**indio/a** *n.* Indian (16)
**indirecto: pronombre** (*m.*) **de complemento indirecto** indirect object pronoun
**indiscreto/a** indiscreet (7)
**indispensable** essential
**individuo** person, individual
**indocumentado/a** illegal, without papers
**índole** *f.* nature
**indudable** doubtless
**industria** industry (10)
**industrial: obrero/a industrial** industrial worker (5)
**industrialización** *f.* industrialization
**industrializado/a** industrialized
**inesperado/a** unexpected
**inestable** unstable
**infancia** infancy; childhood
**infante** *m.*: **jardín** (*m.*) **de infantes** kindergarten
**infantil** *adj.* infant; child's; children's; **guardería infantil** childcare center (16)
**infarto** heart attack
**infección** *f.* infection (12)
**infectado/a** infected
**infierno** hell
**infinito/a** infinite
**influencia** influence
**influir (y)** to influence (14)
**información** *f.* information
**informar** to inform
**informática** data processing (2)
**informe** *m.* report; (*pl.*) information (7)
**ingeniería** engineering (2)
**ingeniero/a** engineer (5)
**ingerir (ie, i)** to swallow; to ingest
**Inglaterra** England (C)
**inglés** *n. m.* English (language) (C)
**inglés, inglesa** *n., adj.* English (C)
**ingrediente** *m.* ingredient
**ingresar (en)** to enter
**ingresos** *pl.* income
**iniciar** to initiate (16)
**iniciativa** initiative
**ininterrumpidamente** uninterruptedly; continuously
**injusto/a** unfair
**inmediato/a** immediate (16)
**inmejorable** unsurpassable
**inmenso/a** immense (10)
**inmersión** *f.* dive
**inmigración** *f.* immigration (11)
**inmigrante** *m., f.* immigrant (16)
**inmobiliario/a** *adj.* real-estate; property
**inmortalizado/a** immortalized
**inmunodeficiencia** immunodeficiency
**inodoro** toilet (6); **taza del inodoro** toilet bowl (6)
**inolvidable** unforgettable
**inquisición** *f.* inquisition
**inscribir(se)** (*p.p.* **inscrito**) to enroll (oneself) (16)
**inscrito/a** (*p.p. of* **inscribir**) registered, enrolled
**inseguro/a** unsure
**inseminación** (*f.*) **artificial** artificial insemination
**insistir** to insist (16)
**inspeccionar** to inspect
**inspector(a)** inspector
**instalación** *f.* installation
**instalar** to install; **instalarse** to settle; to establish oneself
**instante** *m.* moment
**instintivamente** instinctively
**institución** *f.* institution
**instrucción** *f.* instruction (11)
**instruir (y)** to instruct
**insultarse** to insult each other
**intacto/a** intact
**integración** *f.* integration
**intelecto** intellect
**inteligencia** intelligence (15)
**inteligente** intelligent (B)
**intensidad** *f.* intensity
**intensivo/a** intensive
**intentar** to try; **intentar** (+ *infin.*) to try to (*do something*)
**intento** attempt
**interacción** *f.* interaction
**intercambiar** to exchange (15)
**intercambio** *n.* exchange
**interés** *m.* interest
**interesante** interesting (B); **¡qué interesante!** how interesting! (1)
**interesar** to interest, be interested in (10); **le interesa** you (*pol. sing.*) are interested; he/she is interested; **me interesa** I am interested
**interferir (ie, i)** to interfere
**interior** *m., adj.* interior, inside; **ropa interior** underwear (13)
**internacional** international
**internado/a** hospitalized (12)
**internar** to admit, put into (*a hospital*) (12)
**interno/a** internal
**interrogar (gu)** to interrogate
**interrumpir** to interrupt
**intervención** *f.* intervention
**intervenir** (*like* **venir**) to intervene (16)
**íntimo/a** close, intimate; **amigo/a intimo/a** close friend (15)
**intranquilidad** worry; uneasiness; anxiety
**introvertido/a** introverted (B)
**intuitivo/a** intuitive
**inundación** *f.* flood
**invadir** to overrun; to invade
**invasión** *f.* invasion
**invernar** to hibernate
**inversión** *f.* investment
**inversionista** *m., f.* investor
**investigación** *f.* research (15)
**invierno** winter (1)
**invitación** *f.* invitation
**invitado/a** guest
**involucrado/a** involved
**inyección** *f.* injection (12)
**ir** *irreg.* to go (1); **¿cómo se va de... a...?** how does one get from . . . to . . . ?; **ir a** (+ *infin.*) to be going to (*do something*); **ir a fiestas** to go to parties (1); **ir de compras** to go shopping (1); **ir de vacaciones** to go on vacation (11); **ir + -ndo** to be in the process of (*doing something*); **irse** to go away, get away (11); **que te/le vaya bien** may it go well for you; **vamos a** (+ *infin.*) let's (*do something*); **vamos a ver** let's see; **ya voy** I'm coming
**iraní** (*pl.* **iraníes**) *n.* Iranian person (16)
**iris: arco iris** rainbow
**Irlanda** Ireland
**irlandés, irlandesa** *n.* Irishman/Irishwoman; *adj.* Irish (16)
**irreverente** irreverent; disrespectful
**irritado/a** irritated
**irrompible** unbreakable
**isla** island (10)
**israelí** *n. m., f.*; *adj.* (*pl.* **israelíes**) Israeli
**istmeño/a** Panamanian
**istmo** isthmus (16)
**Italia** Italy (C)
**italiano** *n.* Italian (language) (C)
**italiano/a** *n., adj.* Italian (C)
**izquierda** *n.* left hand; left-hand side; **a/de la izquierda** to/from (on) the left (3)
**izquierdo/a** *adj.* left, left-hand

## J

**jabón** *m.* soap (4)
**jadeo** *n.* panting; gasping
**jai alai** *m. Basque ball game*
**jalar** *Mex.* to pull (14)

**jalea** jelly (8)
**jamás** never; **más que jamás** more than ever
**jamón** *m.* ham (8)
**Jánuca** *m.* Hanukkah (4)
**Japón** *m.* Japan (C)
**japonés** *m.* Japanese (language) (C)
**japonés, japonesa** *n., adj.* Japanese (C)
**jarabe** *m.* **(para la tos)** (cough) syrup (12)
**jardín** *m.* garden (2); yard; **jardín de infantes** kindergarten
**jardinería** gardening
**jarra** pitcher, jug (8)
**jeans** *m. pl.* (blue) jeans (15)
**jefe, jefa** boss, chief (14)
**jonrón** *m.* home run
**jornada** day's work; **jornada completa** full-time (5); **media jornada** part-time (5)
**jorobado** *n. m.* hunchback
**joven** *n. m., f.* youth; *adj.* young (A)
**joya** jewel (13); *pl.* jewelry
**joyería** jewelry store (13)
**jubilarse** to retire (15)
**judía verde** green bean
**judío/a** *n.* Jew; *adj.* Jewish (16); **Pascua Judía** Passover (4)
**juego** game (1); **Juegos Olímpicos** Olympic Games
**jueves** *m. sing., pl.* Thursday (1)
**juez** *m., f.* (*pl.* **jueces**) judge (5)
**jugador(a)** player
**jugar (ue) (gu)** to play (1); **jugar a la rayuela** to play hopscotch (9); **jugar al** + *sport* to play (*a sport*); **jugar al bebeleche** *Mex.* to play hopscotch (9); **jugar al escondite** to play hide-and-seek (9); **jugar al gato** to play tag (9)
**jugarreta** dirty trick
**jugo** juice; **jugo natural** fresh-squeezed juice (8)
**juguete** *m.* toy (4)
**julio** July (1)
**junio** June (1)
**juntar** to join
**junto a** *prep.* next to (11)
**juntos/as** *pl.* together (3)
**jurar** to swear
**justamente** *adv.* just, exactly
**justificar (qu)** to justify
**justo/a** fair (16)
**juventud** *f.* youth (9)

## K

**kaki** *m.* khaki
**kayac** *m.* kayak
**kg.** (*abbrev. for* **kilogramo**) kilogram, kilo
**kilo** kilogram, kilo
**kilómetro** kilometer (7)
**kínder** *m.* kindergarten
**km.** (*abbrev. for* **kilómetro**) kilometer

## L

**la** *definite article f.* the (A); *d.o.* her, it, you (*pol. sing.*)
**labio** lip (12)
**labor** *f.* labor, work
**laboral: horas laborales** working hours
**laborar** to work
**laboratorio** laboratory
**lacio/a** straight (*hair*) (A)
**lacón** *m.* shoulder of pork
**ladera** hillside, slope (*of a mountain*)
**lado** side (8); **al lado de** next to, to the side (3); **de al lado** next door; **de cada lado** on each side; **por todos lados** on all sides
**ladrador(a)** *adj.* barking (*dog*)
**ladrar** to bark (3)
**ladrillo** brick (13)
**ladrón, ladrona** thief (7)
**lago** lake (2)
**lágrima** tear
**laguna** pool; lagoon (10)
**lamentablemente** unfortunately
**lámpara** lamp (6)
**lana** wool (13)
**lancha** boat (10)
**langosta** lobster (8)
**langostino** prawn, crayfish
**lanzar (c)** to launch; to fire
**lápiz** *m.* (*pl.* **lápices**) pencil (A)
**lapsus** *m. sing., pl.* lapse; mistake
**largo/a** long (A)
**las** *definite article f. pl.* the (A); *d.o. f. pl.* them, you (*pol. pl.*)
**lasaña** lasagna
**lástima** compassion; shame; **¡qué lástima!** what a pity! (4); **¡qué lástima que... !** what a pity that . . . !
**lastimar** to harm, injure; to pity
**lata** can (8)
**latino/a** *n., adj.* Latin (16)
**Latinoamérica** Latin America
**latinoamericano/a** Latin American
**latón** *m.* brass
**lavable** washable
**lavabo** bathroom sink (6)
**lavadora** washing machine (6)
**lavandería** laundromat (3)
**lavaplatos** *m. sing., pl.* dishwasher (6)
**lavar** to wash (2); **lavarse el pelo** to wash one's hair (4); **lavarse los dientes** to brush one's teeth (4)
**lazo** lasso, lariat; tie (15)
**le** *i.o.* to/for him, her, it, you (*pol. sing.*)
**lealtad** *f.* loyalty (15)
**lección** *f.* lesson (3)
**leche** *f.* milk (4); **arroz** (*m.*) **con leche** rice pudding (8); **batido de leche** milk shake (8)
**lechón** *m.* piglet
**lechuga** lettuce (8)
**lector(a)** reader
**lectura** *n.* reading (1)
**leer (y)** to read (1); **leer el periódico** to read the newspaper (1)
**legalización** *f.* legalization (16)
**legalizar (c)** to legalize
**legislador/a** legislator (16)
**legislatura** legislature
**legumbre** *f.* vegetable
**lejano/a** distant, remote
**lejos** *adv.* far away; **lejos de** *prep.* far away from (3)
**lengua** tongue; language (12); **lengua materna** mother tongue (16); **lenguas africanas** African languages (C)
**lenguaje** *m.* language
**lentamente** slowly (10)
**lentes** *m. pl.* (eye)glasses (A)
**lento/a** slow; **a fuego lento** over a low fire (8)
**leño: al leño** spit-roasted (*over a wood fire*)
**león, leona** lion/lioness
**les** *i.o.* to/for them, you (*pol. pl.*)
**lesión** *f.* injury
**letra** letter (*of the alphabet*); *pl.* literature; **Facultad** (*f.*) **de Filosofía y Letras** School of Humanities (3)
**letrero** sign
**leucemia** leukemia
**levantar** to lift, raise up; **levantar pesas** to lift weights (2); **levantarse** to get up (4)
**ley** *f.* law (16)
**leyenda** legend
**liberado/a** liberated, freed
**libertad** *f.* liberty, freedom (16)
**libertador(a)** liberator (16)
**libra** pound (8); **Libra** Libra
**libre** free (*to act*) (16); available (4); **al aire** (*m.*) **libre** outdoors (7); **mercado libre** free market (16); **tiempo libre** free time (2)
**librería** bookstore (3)
**libreto** film script
**libro** book (A)
**licencia de manejar** driver's license (10)
**licenciado/a** lawyer (16)
**licenciatura** university degree
**lícito/a** legal
**licor** *m.* liquor
**licuadora** blender (13)
**líder** *m.* leader (16)
**liderazgo** leadership
**liga** league
**ligero/a** light (*not heavy*) (8)
**limitar** to limit (14)
**límite** *m.*: **edad** (*f.*) **límite** maximum age
**limón** *m.* lemon
**limonada** lemonade
**limpiaparabrisas** *m. sing., pl.* windshield wiper (10)
**limpiar** to clean (2)
**limpieza** cleaning; **hacer una limpieza** to clean
**limpio/a** clean (7)
**lindo/a** pretty (7)
**línea** line; **en línea** on line (15); **línea ecuatorial** equator
**lino** linen (13)
**líquido** liquid
**lista** list

**listo/a** ready, prepared; **estar listo/a** to be ready (5); **ser listo/a** to be smart, clever
**literatura** literature
**litio** lithium
**litoral** coast
**litro** liter
**llamada** (telephone) call (4)
**llamar** to call (4); **¿cómo se llama?** what is his/her name? (A); **¿cómo se llama usted? / ¿cómo te llamas?** what is your name? (A); **llamar la atención (a)** to call, attract attention (to); **llamar por teléfono** to phone (4); **llamarse** to be called, named; **me llamo...** my name is . . . (A); **se llama...** his/her name is . . . (A)
**llano** *n.* plain (10)
**llanta** tire; **llanta desinflada** flat tire (10)
**llanto** *n.* weeping, crying
**llave** *n. f.* key (12)
**llegada** arrival (11)
**llegar (gu)** to arrive (2); **llegar a ser** to become (16); **llegar a tiempo** to arrive/be on time (5); **llegar al poder** to attain power (16); **llegar tarde** to arrive/be late (5)
**llenar** to fill (8)
**lleno/a** full (16)
**llevar** to wear (A); to take (*someone or something somewhere*) (D); to carry; **llevar** + *time* + **-ndo** to have been (*doing something*) for + *time;* **llevar a cabo** to carry out, perform; **llevarse** to carry off, take away (13); **llevarse bien** to get along well (9); **me lo/la llevo** I'll take (*buy*) it (12)
**llorar** to cry (3)
**llover (ue)** to rain (2)
**llovizna** drizzle (10)
**lluvia** rain (10)
**lo** *d.o. m.* him, it, you (*pol. sing.*); **lo** + *adj.* the + *adj.* part, thing, that which is + *adj.*; **lo que** that which, what (7); **lo siento** I'm sorry
**lobo** wolf
**local** *m.* place; premises
**localidad** *f.* location; locality
**localizar (c)** to locate
**loción** *f.* lotion
**loco/a** *n.* crazy person; *adj.* crazy; **volverse loco/a** to go crazy (12)
**locomoción** *f.* locomotion; public transportation
**locomotora** locomotive (10)
**lodo** mud
**lógico/a** logical
**lograr** to achieve, attain (15); **lograr** (+ *infin.*) to manage to (*do something*), succeed in (*doing something*)
**logro** achievement
**loma** hill
**lomo** back; loin
**lona** canvas
**Londres** *m. sing.* London (C)
**los** *definite article m. pl.* the (A); *d.o.* them, you (*pol. pl.*)
**lote** *m.* share, portion (13)
**lotería** lottery (15)
**lucha** fight, struggle
**luchar** to fight, struggle; **luchar por** to fight for (16)
**lucrativo/a** lucrative; profitable
**luego** then (C); **desde luego** of course; **hasta luego** see you later (A); **luego de** after
**lugar** *m.* place; **lugar de nacimiento** place of birth (1); **tener lugar** to take place (15)
**lujo** luxury (11); **de lujo** deluxe
**lujoso/a** luxurious
**luna** moon (7); **luna de miel** honeymoon (15)
**lunar** *m.*: **de lunares** polka-dotted (13)
**lunes** *m. sing., pl.* Monday (1)
**luz** *f.* (*pl.* **luces**) light (B); electricity; **apagar la luz** to turn off the light (6); **encender la luz** to turn on the light (6); **prender la luz** to turn on the light (6)

# M

**machismo** male pride
**machista** *adj. m., f.* chauvinistic
**macho** *n.* male
**madera** wood (10)
**maderero/a** *adj.* relating to wood or timber
**madrastra** stepmother (9)
**madre** *f.* mother (C); **Día** (*m.*) **de la Madre** Mother's Day (4)
**madrileño/a** resident of Madrid
**madrina** godmother (15)
**madrugada** dawn
**madrugar (gu)** to get up early
**madurar** to mature
**maduro/a** mature; ripe (8)
**maestro/a** *n.* teacher (5); *adj.* masterly, expert; **obra maestra** masterpiece
**mágico/a** *adj.* magic
**magistral: conferencia magistral** professorial lecture
**magnífico/a** magnificent; great
**Mago: Día** (*m.*) **de los Reyes Magos** Epiphany, Jan. 6th (*lit.* Day of the Magi) (4)
**magullado/a** bruised
**mahometano/a** *n.* Muslim
**maíz** *m.* corn (8); **mazorca de maíz** ear of corn (8); **palomitas** (*pl.*) **de maíz** popcorn (8)
**majestad** *f.* majesty
**mal** *n. m.* evil; *adv.* badly
**mal, malo/a** *adj.* bad (6); **estar de mal humor** to be in a bad mood (4)
**maldición** *f.* curse
**malentendido** *n.* misunderstanding
**malestar** *m.* discomfort, malaise, indisposition (12)
**maleta** suitcase (11); **facturar la maleta** to check baggage (11); **hacer las maletas** to pack (11)
**maletero** trunk of a car (10)
**maltrato** mistreatment, abuse
**mamá** mother (B)
**mancha** stain
**manchar** to stain
**mandado** errand; job
**mandar** to send (16); to order, command; **mandar a buscar** to have (*someone*) look for; **mandar por correo** to send by mail
**mandarina** mandarin orange
**mandato** command (A)
**manejar** to drive (2); **licencia de manejar** driver's license (10)
**manera** manner, way (6); **de esta manera** in this way; **de manera que** so that (16); in such a way that; **manera de pensar** way of thinking
**manga** sleeve (13)
**manguera** hose
**manifestar (ie)** to manifest
**mano** *f.* hand (B); **a mano** by hand; **bolsa de mano** carry-on luggage; handbag (10); **con las manos en la masa** red-handed, in the act; **darse la mano** to shake hands with each other (15); **equipaje** (*m.*) **de mano** hand luggage, carry-on luggage; **hecho/a a mano** handmade (13); **mano de obra** manual labor
**mansión** *f.* mansion
**manta** blanket
**mantel** *m.* tablecloth (8)
**mantener** (*like* **tener**) to maintain (10); **mantenerse** to keep oneself (12)
**mantenimiento** maintenance
**mantequilla** butter (8)
**mantequillera** butter dish
**manzana** apple (8)
**mañana** *n.* morning; tomorrow (1); *adv.* **de/por la mañana** in the morning (1); **hasta mañana** see you tomorrow; **mañana por la mañana** tomorrow morning; **pasado mañana** day after tomorrow (1)
**mapa** *m.* map
**maquillaje** *m.* makeup
**maquillarse** to put on makeup (4)
**máquina** machine; **escribir a máquina** to type (4)
**maquinaria** machinery
**mar** *m., f.* sea, ocean (2); **nivel** (*m.*) **del mar** sea level (16)
**maravilla** wonder, marvel; **¡qué maravilla!** how marvelous! (16)
**maravilloso/a** marvelous
**marca** brand (4)
**marcado/a** strong, pronounced
**marcar (qu)** to indicate, show; to dial (*telephone*)
**marcha** march; speed (gear)
**mareado/a** dizzy (12); nauseated
**marearse** to get sea-/carsick, dizzy
**mareo** dizziness, nausea (12)
**mariachi** *m.* (*Mex.*) *band; type of music with trumpets, guitars, and marimba*
**marido** husband

**marino/a** sea (10); **azul** (*m.*) **marino** navy blue (13); **estrella marina** star fish; **león marino/a** *adj.* marine, sea; **león marino** (*m.*) sea lion
**mariposa** butterfly (10)
**mariscada** seafood dish
**marisco** shellfish, seafood
**mármol** *m.* marble
**martes** *m. sing., pl.* Tuesday (1)
**martillo** hammer (13)
**marzo** March (1)
**más** more (B); **el/la más** + *adj.* the most . . . , the ___-est (6); **más de** + *number* more than + *number;* **más o menos** more or less; **más que (de)** more than (2); **más tarde** later (6); **más vale** (+ *infin.*) it is better to (*do something*)
**masa: con las manos en la masa** red-handed, in the act
**mascarada** masquerade
**mascota** mascot (14)
**masivo/a** large-scale
**masticar (qu)** to chew (3)
**matar** to kill (15)
**matemáticas** *pl.* mathematics
**materia** subject (*school*) (8); **materia prima** raw material (13)
**materializar (c)** to materialize
**maternidad** *f.* maternity
**materno/a** maternal; **lengua materna** mother tongue
**matrícula** registration (14)
**matricular(se)** to enroll
**matrimonial: cama matrimonial** double bed (6)
**matrimonio** matrimony, marriage; couple (15)
**mausoleo** mausoleum
**máximo/a** maximum; high, highest (*temperature*)
**maya** *n. m., f.; adj.* Maya(n)
**mayo** May (1)
**mayonesa** mayonnaise
**mayor** *adj.* older (C); oldest; major, main; greater; **la mayor parte** the majority; **mayor de edad** adult, person of legal age; **mayores** *m. pl.* adults
**mayoría** majority (6)
**mazmorra** dungeon
**mazorca de maíz** ear of corn
**me** *d.o.* me; *i.o.* to/for me; *refl. pron.* myself
**mecánico/a** *n.* mechanic (5); *adj.* mechanical
**mecedora** rocking chair (13)
**medalla** medal
**mediado: a mediados de** in the middle of; **desde mediados** (*pl.*) **de** since the middle of
**mediano/a** medium (*length*) (A); average; **estatura mediana** medium height (B)
**medianoche** *f.* midnight (1)
**mediante** by means of, through (15)
**medias** *pl.* nylons, stockings (13); *Caribbean* socks
**medicamento** medicine
**medicina** medicine; **Facultad** (*f.*) **de Medicina** School of Medicine (3)
**médico** *n.* doctor (5); *adj.* medical; **cuidado médico** medical care; **receta médica** medical prescription (12); **seguro médico** health insurance (12)
**medida** *sing.* means, measure; **a medida que** as, at the same time as
**medio** *n. sing.* means; middle; **en medio de** in the middle of (3); **medio ambiente** environment; **medios de comunicación** means of communication; mass media; **medios de producción** means of production; **número medio** median; **por el medio** in half; **por medio de** by means of (15)
**medio/a** *adj.* half (8); middle; **es la una y media** it's one-thirty (half past one) (1); **media jornada** part-time (5); **número medio** median
**mediodía** *m.* noon, midday (1)
**medir (i, i)** to measure
**Mediterráneo** *n.* Mediterranean (Sea)
**mediterráneo/a** *adj.* Mediterranean
**medula (médula): hasta la medula** to the core
**mejilla** cheek (12)
**mejor** better (B); best (6); **mejor amigo/a** best friend (6); **es mejor que...** (+ *subjunctive*) it is better that . . . (14)
**mejorar** to improve (8)
**mella** dent
**mellizo/a** *n., adj.* twin
**melocotón** *m.* peach (8)
**melón** *m.* melon
**memoria** memory
**mencionar** to mention
**menor** younger (C); youngest; **menor** (*m.*) **de edad** minor; (legally) under age (16)
**menos** less (1); least; **a menos que** unless (16); **echarse de menos** to miss each other; **más o menos** more or less; **menos que (de)** less than (6); **por lo menos** at least
**mensaje** *m.* message (15)
**mensual** monthly
**mente** *f.* mind; **ten en mente** keep (*inf. sing.*) in mind
**mentir (ie, i)** to lie
**mentira** lie (7)
**mentiroso/a** liar; **¡qué mentiroso/a!** what a liar! (9)
**menú** *m.* menu
**menudo/a** small; insignificant; **a menudo** often (6)
**mercado** market (4); **mercado libre** free market (16); **sacar al mercado** to put (*a new product*) on the market; **salir al mercado** to appear on the market
**mercadotecnia** marketing
**mercancía** merchandise
**merecer(se) (zc)** to deserve
**merendar (ie)** to have a snack; **merendar en el parque** to have a picnic in the park (2)
**merengue** *m. popular dance/music of the Dominican Republic*
**merluza** hake (*type of fish*)
**mermelada** marmalade
**mero/a** pure, simple; **la mera verdad** the simple truth
**mes** *m.* month; **¿en qué mes nació?** in what month were you (*pol. sing.*) (was he/she) born?
**mesa** table (B); **atender mesas** to wait on tables
**mesero/a** waiter/waitress (5)
**meseta** plateau (16)
**mesita** coffee table (6); **mesita de noche** night table (11)
**meta** goal (14)
**meter** to put; **meterse** to get into, enter
**método** method
**metro** subway (3); meter
**metrón** evening primrose
**mexicano/a** Mexican
**México** Mexico
**mexicoamericano/a** Mexican American
**mezcla** mixture
**mezclilla** denim (13)
**mi** *poss.* my (A)
**mí** *obj. of prep.* me; **¿a mí qué?** what is it to me? (15)
**miau** *m.* meow
**microbio** germ
**microondas** *pl.*: **horno de microondas** microwave oven (6)
**microplaqueta** microchip
**miedo** fear; **dar miedo** to frighten; **tener miedo** to be afraid (4)
**miel** *f.* honey (8); **luna de miel** honeymoon (15)
**miembro** member
**mientras** meanwhile (3); **mientras más... más...** the more . . . the more . . . ; **mientras que** while; **mientras tanto** in the meanwhile
**miércoles** *m. sing., pl.* Wednesday (1)
**migratorio/a: trabajador(a)** (*m.*)**/obrero/a migratorio/a** migrant worker
**mil** thousand, one thousand (13)
**milagrosamente** miraculously
**militar** *n. m.* soldier; *adj.* military (16)
**milla** mile (6); **¿cuántas millas hace por...** ? how many miles per . . . do you get?
**millón** *m.* million (13)
**millonario/a** millionaire
**mineral** *adj.*: **agua** (*f. but* **el agua**) **mineral** mineral water
**minifalda** miniskirt
**mínimo** *n.* minimum
**mínimo/a** *adj.* minimum; **mínima** low, lowest (*temperature*)
**ministro** minister; **primer ministro** prime minister

**minoritario/a** minority; **grupos minoritarios** minorities
**minuta** breaded cutlet
**mío/a** *poss.* my, (of) mine
**mirar** to look at (3), watch
**misa** Mass (2)
**mismo** *adv.* right; **ahora mismo** right now (2); **aquí mismo** right here
**mismo/a** *pron.* same (one); *adj.* same; self (11); **da lo mismo** it doesn't matter; **el/la mismo/a** the same (5); **sí mismo/a** oneself; **tú mismo/a (usted mismo/a)** yourself (11); **uno/a mismo/a** oneself (14)
**misterio** mystery
**misterioso/a** mysterious
**mitad** *f.* half
**mito** myth
**mitología** mythology
**mixto/a** mixed
**mochila** backpack (B)
**mocho: español** (*m.*) **mocho** broken Spanish
**moda** fashion (13); **de moda** fashionable (13); **estar de moda** to be in fashion; **ponerse de moda** to become fashionable
**moderado/a** moderate (16)
**módico/a** affordable (4)
**modificado/a** modified
**modismo** idiom
**modo** way, manner; **de modo que** so that (16); **de otro modo** in a different way; **de todos modos** anyway (9); **ni modo** oh well; tough! (16)
**mojar** to dip; to wet (7)
**molestar** to bother (10); **me molesta que** it bothers me when
**molestia** bother; discomfort
**molesto/a** upset (12)
**molido/a: carne** (*f.*) **molida** ground beef (8)
**molinillo** whisk, beater
**molusco** mollusk
**momia** mummy
**monarca** *m., f.* monarch
**monasterio** monastery
**moneda** currency; coin
**monja** nun
**mono/a** monkey
**monógamo/a** monogamous
**monolingüe** monolingual
**monolingüismo** monolingualism
**monopatín** *m.* skateboard
**montaña** mountain (2)
**montañoso/a** mountainous
**montar a caballo** to ride a horse (2); **montar en bicicleta** to ride a bike; **montar en motocicleta** to ride a motorcycle
**monte** *m.* mount, mountain
**morado/a** purple (A)
**moraleja** moral, lesson
**mordedor(a)** *adj.* biting
**morder (ue)** to bite
**moreno/a** brown-skinned, dark-skinned (A)
**morir(se) (ue, u)** (*p.p.* **muerto**) to die (15); **morirse de celos** to die of jealousy
**morisco/a** Moorish
**moro/a: hay moros en la costa** watch out!
**mosca** fly
**Moscú** *f.* Moscow (C)
**mostaza** mustard (8)
**mostrador** *m.* counter (11)
**mostrar (ue)** to show (13)
**motivo** motive, reason
**moto** *f.* motorcycle
**motocicleta** motorcycle; **andar/montar en motocicleta** to ride a motorcycle (2)
**motor** *m.* motor, engine (10)
**movedizo/a: arena movediza** quicksand
**mover (ue)** to move
**móvil: computación móvil** portable computing
**movimiento** movement (12)
**mts.** (*abbrev. for* **metros**) meters (*unit of measurement*)
**muchacho/a** boy/girl; young man / young woman (A)
**muchedumbre** *f.* crowd
**muchísimo** very much
**mucho** *adv.* a lot; much (B)
**mucho/a** *adj.* much; *pl.* many; **muchas gracias** thank you very much; **muchas veces** many times (5); **mucho gusto** pleased to meet you (A); **tener mucha hambre** to be very hungry (3)
**mudanza** *n.* move, moving
**mudarse** to move (to another home) (15)
**mueble** *m.* piece of furniture; *pl.* furniture (5); **sacudir los muebles** to dust (5)
**muela** molar (tooth) (12)
**muerte** *f.* death; **pena de muerte** death penalty (16)
**muerto/a** *n.* dead person; *adj.* dead (C); *p.p. of* **morir** died; **Día** (*m.*) **de los Muertos** All Souls' Day (4)
**mujer** *f.* woman (A)
**mula** mule
**mulato/a** mulatto (*person of mixed African and European ancestry*)
**muleta** crutch (12)
**multa** fine; traffic ticket (7)
**mundial** *adj.* of or pertaining to the world (16); **red mundial** Internet (2); **Segunda Guerra Mundial** Second World War
**mundialmente** worldwide
**mundo** world (B); **¡cómo cambia el mundo!** how the world changes! (C); **Tercer Mundo** Third World
**muñeca** wrist (12); doll (9)
**muñequita** little doll (9)
**muralista** *m., f.* muralist
**muralla** wall; rampart
**muro** wall
**musculación** bodybuilding
**músculo** muscle (12)
**museo** museum (4)
**música** music; **equipo de música** stereo (1)
**músico/a** musician
**muslo** thigh (12)
**musulmán, musulmana** *n., adj.* Moslem (16)
**mutuamente** mutally
**muy** very (B); **muy bien** very well, very good

# N

**nacer (zc)** to be born (2); **¿en qué mes nació?** in what month were you (*pol. sing.*) (was he/she) born?; **recién nacido/a** newborn (15)
**nacimiento** birth; **fecha de nacimiento** date of birth; **lugar** (*m.*) **de nacimiento** place of birth
**nación** *f.* nation
**nacional** national
**nacionalidad** *f.* nationality
**nacionalización** *f.* nationalization (16)
**nada** nothing (C); **como si nada** as if nothing were wrong
**nadador(a)** swimmer
**nadar** to swim (1)
**nadie** no one, nobody, not anybody
**nado** *n.* swimming
**nalga** buttock (12)
**nana** grandma
**naranja** orange (*fruit*) (A)
**nariz** *f.* (*pl.* **narices**) nose (B); **nariz tapada** stuffy nose (12)
**narrar** to narrate
**nasal: goteo nasal** nasal drip
**natación** *f.* swimming (4)
**natal** *adj.* native
**natalidad** *f.* birthrate; birth (10); **control** (*m.*) **de la natalidad** birth control (16); **índice** (*m.*)**/tasa de natalidad** birthrate
**natural: jugo natural** fresh-squeezed juice (8); **recurso natural** natural resource (16)
**naturaleza** nature (16)
**náusea: tener náuseas** *pl.* to be nauseated (12)
**navaja** (razor)blade (4)
**navegante** *m., f.* navigator (9)
**navegar (gu)** to sail (9)
**Navidad** *f.* Christmas (4); **árbol** (*m.*) **de Navidad** (3)
**navío** ship
**neblina** fog (10)
**nebulización** *f.* spray
**necesario/a** necessary (6)
**necesidad** *f.* necessity
**necesitado/a** needy (16)
**necesitar** to need (5); **necesitar** (+ *infin.*) to need to (*do something*) (5); **se necesita** is needed
**nécora** small crab
**negar(se) (ie) (gu)** to deny; **negarse a** (+ *infin.*) to refuse to (*do something*)
**negociante** *m., f.* businessman/businesswoman (16)
**negocio** business (15); **hombre/mujer de negocios** businessman/businesswoman (3); **viaje** (*m.*) **de negocios** business trip

**negrilla** boldface
**negro** *n.* black
**negro/a** *n.* African-American; *adj.* black (A)
**nene, nena** baby, infant
**nervio** nerve (12)
**nervioso/a** nervous (B)
**nevada** snowfall
**nevado** snowy (10)
**nevar (ie)** to snow (2)
**ni** neither; nor; even; **ni modo** oh well; tough! (16); **ni... ni** neither . . . nor; **¡ni pensarlo!** don't even think of it!; no way! (4); **ni siquiera** not even
**nicaragüense** *adj. m., f.* Nicaraguan (3)
**nido** nest
**nieto/a** grandson/granddaughter (C); **nietos** *pl.* grandchildren
**nieve** *f.* snow
**nimio/a** trivial, insignificant
**ningún, ninguno/a** none, not any (8)
**niñera** babysitter (14)
**niñez** *f.* childhood (9)
**niño/a** boy/girl (B); child; **de niño** as a child (9)
**nivel** *m.* level (15); **nivel del mar** sea level (16)
**no** no; not (A)
**Nóbel: Premio Nóbel** Nobel Prize (16)
**noche** *f.* night; **buenas noches** good evening; good night (A); **de noche** at night (10); **esta noche** tonight, this night (2); **por la noche** in the evening, at night (1); **salir de noche** to go out at night (3)
**Nochebuena** Christmas Eve (4)
**Nochevieja** New Year's Eve (4)
**nocturno/a** nighttime; **club** (*m.*) **nocturno** nightclub (5)
**nodo** node
**nombrado/a** named (16)
**nombrar** to name (1)
**nombre** *m.* name; **¿cuál es su nombre?** what is your name? (*pol. sing.*) (A); **mi nombre es...** my name is . . . (A)
**nordeste** *m.* northeast
**noreste** *m.* northeast
**normalidad** *f.* normalcy, normality
**normalmente** normally
**norte** *m.* north
**Norteamérica** North America
**norteamericano/a** North American (C)
**nos** *d.o.* us; *i.o.* to/for us; *refl. pron.* ourselves
**nosotros/as** *sub. pron.* we (B); *obj. of prep.* us
**nota** note; grade (*academic*) (4); **sacar buenas/malas notas** to get good/bad grades (5)
**notar** to note, notice
**noticia(s)** news (16)
**noticiero** newscast
**novecientos/as** nine hundred
**novela** novel; **novela policíaca** detective novel
**novelista** *m., f.* novelist
**noveno/a** ninth (2)
**noventa** ninety (C)
**noviazgo** courtship (15)
**noviembre** *m.* November (1)
**novio/a** boyfriend/girlfriend (3); fiancé(e); groom/bride (15)
**nube** *f.* cloud (10)
**nublado/a** cloudy (10); **parcialmente nublado** partly cloudy (10)
**nuclear** nuclear; **desperdicios** (*pl.*) **nucleares** nuclear waste (10)
**nudibranquio** nudibranch (*type of mollusk*)
**nudo** knot
**nuera** daughter-in-law (9)
**nuestro/a** *poss.* our
**nueve** nine (A)
**nuevo/a** new (A); **Año Nuevo** New Year's Day (4); **de nuevo** again
**nuez** *f.* (*pl.* **nueces**) nut (8)
**numeración** *f.* numbering
**numérico/a** numerical
**número** number; **número medio** median
**numeroso/a** numerous (15)
**nunca** never (3); **casi nunca** very rarely
**nutriente** *m.* nutrient (10)

# O

**o** or
**objetivo** objective
**objeto** object (6)
**obligación** *f.* obligation
**obligar (gu)** to oblige
**obra** work (16); **mano** (*f.*) **de obra** manual labor; **obra maestra** masterpiece
**obrero/a (industrial)** (industrial) worker (5)
**obsequio: de obsequio** free, complimentary
**observador(a)** observant
**observar** to observe, watch (10)
**obstante: no obstante** nevertheless, however
**obtener** (*like* **tener**) to obtain, get (5)
**obviamente** obviously
**ocasión** *f.* occasion
**occidental** western (16)
**océano** ocean (10)
**ochenta** eighty (C)
**ocho** eight (A)
**ochocientos/as** eight hundred
**ocio** leisure time
**octavo/a** eighth (2)
**octubre** *m.* October (1)
**ocupación** *f.* occupation
**ocupado/a** busy (4)
**ocupar** to occupy; **ocuparse** to be busy
**ocurrencia: ¡qué ocurrencia!** what a silly idea! (4)
**ocurrir** to occur
**oda** ode
**oeste** *m.* west (16)
**ofender** to offend
**oficina** office (B)
**oficio** job, profession; trade
**ofrecer (zc)** to offer (2)
**oído** (inner) ear (12)
**oír** *irreg.* to hear (7); **oye...** hey . . .
**ojalá (que)** I hope (that)
**ojo** eye (A); **¿de qué color tiene los ojos?** what color are your (*pol. sing.*)/his/her eyes? (B)
**ola** wave (*ocean*) (7)
**oler** *irreg.* to smell (12)
**olfato** sense of smell
**Olimpiadas** *pl.* Olympics (7)
**Olímpico/a: Juegos Olímpicos** Olympic Games
**olla** pot
**olor** *m.* odor
**olvidar(se)** to forget (12)
**ómnibus** *m.* bus
**once** eleven (A)
**onda: estar en onda** to be "in," current
**onza** ounce (8)
**opción** *f.* option
**ópera** opera (16)
**operación** *f.* operation
**operador(a)** operator
**operar (a)** to operate (on) (12)
**opinar** to think, believe (15)
**opinión** *f.* opinion
**oponerse a** (*like* **ponerse**) to oppose (16)
**oportunidad** *f.* opportunity, chance (15)
**oposición** *f.* opposition
**optimista** *n. m., f.* optimist; *adj.* optimistic
**opuesto/a** opposite
**oración** *f.* sentence (4)
**oratoria** public speaking; debate
**orden** *m.* order (*chronological*); *f.* order, command (14); **poner en orden** to order, put in order
**ordenado/a** tidy
**ordenador** *m. Sp.* computer
**ordenar** to arrange, put in order (11)
**ordinal: número ordinal** ordinal number
**oreja** (outer) ear (B)
**orgánico/a** organic (10)
**organización** *f.* organization
**organizar (c)** to organize (1)
**órgano** organ (11)
**orgulloso/a** proud (15)
**oriente** *m.* east (16)
**origen** *m.* origin
**originar** to cause
**orilla** bank, shore (10)
**oro** gold (13)
**orquesta** orchestra
**os** *d.o.* (*Sp.*) you (*inf. pl.*); *i.o.* (*Sp.*) to/for you (*inf. pl.*); *refl. pron.* (*Sp.*) yourselves (*inf. pl.*)
**oscilar** to fluctuate
**oscuro/a** dark
**oso** bear (7)
**ostra** oyster
**otoño** autumn (1)
**otro/a** other; another (B); **de otro modo** in a different way; **otra vez** again (5); **por otra parte** on the other hand
**oveja** sheep

**oxígeno** oxygen
**ozono: capa de ozono** ozone layer (10); **agujero en la capa de ozono** hole in the ozone layer (10)

# P

**paciencia** patience
**paciente** *n. m., f.; adj.* patient (4)
**pacífico/a** peaceful
**padecer (zc)** to suffer (from) (12)
**padrastro** stepfather (9)
**padre** *m.* father (C); priest; *pl.* parents (C); **Día** (*m.*) **del Padre** Father's Day (4)
**padrino** godfather (15); *pl.* godparents
**paella** *Valencian (Spain) rice dish with meat, fish, or seafood and vegetables*
**pagar (gu)** to pay (7)
**página** page (A)
**pago** payment
**país** *m.* country; **país natal** native country
**paisaje** *m.* countryside
**pájaro** bird (3)
**pala** shovel (13)
**palabra** word (3); **libertad** (*f.*) **de palabra** freedom of speech
**palacio** palace (7)
**paletilla** shoulder blade
**palidecer (zc)** to turn pale
**palma** palm (*botanical*)
**palmera** palm tree (7)
**palmo a palmo** inch by inch
**palomitas** (*pl.*) **de maíz** popcorn (8)
**palpable** palpable; tangible; concrete
**pampa** pampa, prairie; **La Pampa** *region of Argentina*
**pan** *m.* bread (8); **barra de pan** loaf of bread (12); **llamar al pan pan y al vino vino** to call a spade a spade; **pan tostado** toast (8)
**pana** corduroy (13)
**panadería** bakery (4)
**Panamá** *m.* Panama (3)
**panameño/a** *n., adj.* Panamanian (3)
**pandilla** gang (16)
**panecillo** roll, bun (8)
**panfleto** pamphlet
**pánico** panic
**panorámico/a** panoramic
**panqueque** *m.* pancake (8)
**pantaletas** *pl.* women's underpants (13)
**pantalón, pantalones** *m. sing., pl.* pants (A); **pantalones cortos** shorts (A); **pantalones vaqueros** jeans (2)
**panteón** *m.* mausoleum, graveyard
**pantimedias** *pl.* nylons, pantyhose (13)
**pantorrilla** calf (*of leg*) (12)
**pantufla** slipper
**paño** cloth
**pañuelo** handkerchief
**papa** potato (8); **papas fritas** French fries (8); **puré** (*m.*) **de papas** mashed potatoes
**papá** *m.* papa, dad (B)
**papalote** *m. Mex.* paper kite; **volar un papalote** to fly a kite (9)
**papel** *m.* paper (B); role; **hacer el papel de** to play the role of (6)
**papelería** stationery store (4)
**papelero/a** relating to paper
**paperas** *pl.* mumps (12)
**paquete** *m.* package (8)
**par** *m.* pair (13)
**para** for; in order to (1); **para que** in order that (15); **¿para qué sirve?** what is it used for? (6)
**parabrisas** *m. sing., pl.* windshield (10)
**paracetamol** *m.* acetaminophen (*non-aspirin pain reliever*)
**parachoques** *m. sing., pl.* bumper (10)
**parada del autobús** bus stop (3)
**parador** *m.* inn (11)
**paraestatal** semi-official; public
**paraguas** *m. sing., pl.* umbrella (13)
**Paraguay** *m.* Paraguay (3)
**paraguayo/a** *n., adj.* Paraguayan (3)
**paralizado/a** paralyzed
**parar** to stop (10)
**parcialmente** partially; **parcialmente nublado** partly cloudy (10)
**parecer (zc)** to look; seem; **parecerle (a uno)** to seem (to one) (6); **parecerse** to look alike (like each other) (9); **¿qué te/ le parece...?** what do you think of . . . ?
**parecido/a: bien parecido** good-looking (15)
**pared** *f.* wall (B)
**pareja** couple; **en parejas** in pairs (11)
**paréntesis** *m. sing., pl.*: **entre paréntesis** in parentheses
**pariente, parienta** relative (4)
**París** *m.* Paris
**parque** *m.* park (2); **merendar en el parque** to have a picnic in the park (2)
**parra** (grape)vine
**párrafo** paragraph
**parrilla: a la parrilla** grilled, charbroiled (8)
**parrillada** grilled meat
**parroquia** parish
**parte** *f.* part; **las partes del cuerpo** parts of the body (12); **por otra parte** on the other hand; **por todas partes** everywhere
**Partenón** *m.* Parthenon
**participación** *f.* participation
**participar** to participate
**particular** particular; private; **casa particular** private home (6)
**partida** departure
**partidario/a** supporter, advocate
**partido** party (*political*); game, match (1); **ver un partido de...** to watch a game of . . . (1)
**partir** to leave; to divide; **a partir de** + *time* starting from + *time*
**párvulo: escuela de párvulos** kindergarten
**pasa** raisin (8)
**pasado** *n.* past (5)
**pasado/a** *adj.* past, last; **la semana pasada** last week (6); **pasado mañana** day after tomorrow (3)
**pasaje** *m.* passage; fare, ticket (11)
**pasajero/a** passenger (10)
**pasaporte** *m.* passport; **sacar el pasaporte** to get a passport (11)
**pasar** to pass; to happen; to come in; to spend (*time*); **pasar hambre** to go hungry; **pasar la aspiradora** to vacuum (6); **pasar por** to go through; **pasar tiempo** to spend time (2); **pasarlo bien/mal** to have a good/bad time; **¿qué pasa?** what's going on? (7); **¿qué pasó?** what happened? (7); **¿qué te/le pasa?** what's the matter with you?
**pasatiempo** pastime (2)
**Pascua** Easter; **Domingo de Pascua** Easter Sunday (4); *pl.* Easter; **felices Pascuas** Merry Christmas (*regional*); **Pascua Judía** Passover (4)
**pasear** to go for a walk; to take a ride; **pasear en barca** to take a boat ride (2); **pasear en bicicleta** to go for a bicycle ride
**paseo** walk, stroll; **dar un paseo** to take a walk (4); **dar un paseo en carro** to go for a drive
**pasión** *f.* passion
**paso** step (8); **dar un paso** to take a step; **de paso** incidently; **no hay paso** no entrance (9); **paso a paso** step by step
**pasta de dientes** toothpaste
**pastel** *m.* cake (4)
**pasto de ganado** cattle grazing
**pastor** *m.* shepherd
**pata: estirar la pata** *coll.* to kick the bucket, die
**patacón** *m.* fried banana
**patata** *Sp.* potato
**paterno/a** paternal
**patinaje** *m.* skating
**patinar** to skate; **patinar en el hielo** to ice-skate (1)
**patineta: andar en patineta** to skateboard
**patio** patio; **patio de recreo** schoolyard (9)
**pato** duck
**patria** country, homeland, native land (16)
**patriota** *m., f.* patriot (16)
**paulatino/a** slow, gradual
**pavo** turkey
**payaso** clown
**paz** *f.* (*pl.* **paces**) peace (15); **déjame en paz** leave me alone
**peatón, peatona** *n.* pedestrian (10)
**pecho** chest (12); breast
**pedagogía** pedagogy; education
**pediatría** *sing.* pediatrics
**pedir (i, i)** to ask for, request (8); **pedir permiso** to ask for permission (4); **pedir(se) perdón** to apologize (to each other)
**pegado/a** close together
**pegar (gu)** to hit, strike; **pegarse un susto** to get a shock
**peinarse** to comb one's hair (4)
**Pekín** *m.* Beijing (C)

**peladura** *n.* peel, peeling
**pelea** fight
**pelear** to fight; **pelearse** to fight with each other (9)
**película** movie (2); **rollo de película** roll of film (13)
**peligro** danger (10)
**peligroso/a** dangerous (5)
**pelo** hair (A); **cortarse el pelo** to cut one's hair, have one's hair cut; **¿de qué color tiene el pelo?** what color is your (*pol. sing.*)/his/her hair? (B); **lavarse el pelo** to wash one's hair (4); **secarse el pelo** to dry one's hair (4)
**pelota** ball (9)
**peluquería** beauty parlor (5)
**peluquero/a** hairdresser (5)
**peluquín** *m.* hairpiece
**pena de muerte** death penalty (16)
**pendiente** *n. f.* slope, incline; *adj.* hanging
**pensamiento** thought
**pensar (ie)** to think (5); **¡ni pensarlo!** don't even think about it!; no way! (4); **pensar** (+ *infin.*) to plan to (*do something*) (5); **pensar en** to think about (*something/someone*) (5); **pensar que** to think that (16); **pensarlo** to think about it
**pensativo/a** thoughtful
**peor** worse (6); worst (6)
**pepino** cucumber (8)
**pequeño/a** small (B)
**pera** pear
**percance** *m.* mishap, misfortune
**percibir** to perceive
**perder (ie)** to lose; **perderse** to get lost (12)
**perdón** *m.* pardon; *interj.* pardon/excuse me (C); **pedir(se) perdón** to apologize (to each other)
**perdonar** to excuse
**perezoso/a** lazy (B)
**perfeccionar** to perfect
**perfil** *m.* profile
**perfume: ponerse perfume** to put on perfume (4)
**perico** parakeet
**periódicamente** periodically
**periódico** newspaper; **leer el periódico** to read the newspaper (1)
**periodista** *m., f.* journalist
**período** period
**periquito** parakeet; little parrot (14)
**perjudicar (qu)** to damage, harm
**perla** pearl
**permanecer (zc)** to remain
**permiso** permission; **dar permiso** to give permission (9); **pedir permiso** to ask for permission (4)
**permitir** to allow (9); **permitirse** to be allowed (9)
**pero** but (C)
**perro/a** dog (A)
**persecución** *f.* persecution (16)
**perseguir (i, i) (g)** to pursue; to persecute
**persona** person
**personaje** *m.* character (*fictional*)
**personal: datos** (*pl.*) **personales** personal data
**personalidad** *f.* personality (14)
**personalmente** personally; in person (4)
**personificar (qu)** to personify
**pertenecer (zc)** to belong (8)
**Perú** *m.* Peru (3)
**peruano/a** *n., adj.* Peruvian (3)
**pesa: levantar pesas** to lift weights (2)
**pesado/a** heavy
**pesar** *v.* to weigh; **a pesar de** (*prep.*) in spite of
**pescado** fish (*caught*)
**pescador(a)** *m., f.* fisherman
**pescar (qu)** to fish (1)
**pesebre** *m.* manger; Nativity scene
**peseta** *monetary unit of Spain* (4)
**pesimista** *n. m., f.* pessimist; *adj.* pessimistic
**peso** *monetary unit of Mexico, Colombia, Cuba, etc.*; weight (1)
**pestaña** eyelash (12)
**pesticida** *m.* pesticide (10)
**petróleo** petroleum; oil (10)
**pez** *m.* (*pl.* **peces**) fish (*live*) (3)
**pibe, piba** *Arg.* child
**picante** spicy (8)
**pícaro/a** *n.* rogue, scoundrel; *adj.* scheming, mischievous; **¡qué pícaro/a!** what a rascal! (9)
**picazón** *f.* itch, itching (12)
**pico: cuello en V / en pico** V-neck collar (13); **sombrero de tres picos** three-cornered hat
**pie** *m.* foot (B); *pl.* feet (B); **(estar) de pie** (to be) standing; **ponerse de pie** to stand up
**piedra** stone (13)
**piel** *f.* skin; leather (13)
**pierna** leg (B)
**pieza** piece (7)
**pijama** *m. sing.* pajamas
**píldora** pill (12)
**pileta** *Arg.* swimming pool
**pilotear** to fly (*plane*)
**piloto** *m., f.* pilot (5)
**pimentero** pepper shaker (8)
**pimienta** pepper (8)
**pinacoteca** art gallery
**pinar** *m.* pine grove
**pinta** look, appearance
**pintar** to paint (5)
**pintor(a)** painter (10)
**pintoresco/a** picturesque (16)
**pintura** painting (11)
**piña** pineapple (8); **piña colada** *tall mixed drink of rum, cream of coconut, pineapple juice, and ice, usually mixed in a blender*
**pirámide** *f.* pyramid (7)
**Pirineos** *pl.* Pyrenees
**piscina** swimming pool (1)
**Piscis** *m. sing., pl.* Pisces
**piso** floor (B); *Sp.* apartment
**pista** hint
**pizarra** (chalk)board (B)
**placa** license plate (10)
**placer** *n. m.* pleasure
**plan** *m.* plan (5)
**plancha** iron
**planchar** to iron (3)
**planear** to plan (11)
**planeta** *m.* planet
**planificar (qu)** to plan
**plano** plan, diagram; map (of a room or city) (3)
**planta** plant (A)
**plantar** to plant
**plasmar** to create
**plástico** plastic (10)
**plata** silver (13)
**plataforma** platform
**plátano** banana (8)
**platillo** dish (*food*) (8); saucer (8)
**plato** plate (6); culinary dish (8); **plato hondo** bowl (8)
**playa** beach (1)
**playera** *Mex.* T-shirt (13)
**pleno/a** full
**plomero/a** plumber (5)
**pluma** feather; *Mex.* pen (B)
**población** *f.* population
**poblador(a)** settler; colonist; inhabitant
**poblar (ue)** to populate
**pobre** *n. m., f.* poor person; *adj.* poor (10)
**pobreza** poverty (16)
**poco/a** little; *pl.* few; **dentro de poco** within a short time; **poco a poco** little by little; **poco asado** rare (*meat*) (8); **poco cocido** rare (*meat*) (8); **poco después** a bit later (7); **un poco** a little
**poder** *n. m.* power; **llegar al poder** to attain power
**poder** *v. irreg.* to be able; **poder** (+ *infin.*) to be able to (*do something*) (5)
**poderoso/a** powerful
**poema** *m.* poem
**poesía** poetry
**poeta** *m.* poet (16)
**polen** *m.* pollen
**policía** *m., f.* police officer (5); *f.* police force (7)
**policíaco/a** *adj.* police; **novela policíaca** detective novel
**polideportivo** sports complex
**poliéster** *m.* polyester (13)
**política** *sing.* politics; policy (16)
**político/a** *n.* politician; *adj.* political; **ciencias** (*pl.*) **políticas** political science
**politizado/a** politicized
**pollera** *Arg., Uruguay* skirt
**pollo** chicken (8); **pollo frito** fried chicken (8)
**Polonia** Poland (16)
**polonio** polonium (*chemical element*)
**polvo** dust (6)
**pomelo** grapefruit (8)

**poncho** poncho
**poner** *irreg.* to put, place (4); to put on; to put up; to show (*film*); **poner discos compactos** to play CDs (3); **poner en efecto** to carry out; **poner en orden** to order, put in order; **ponerle fin a** to end, put an end to (16); **ponerse** + *adj.* to get, become + *adj.*; **ponerse a** (+ *infin.*) to begin to (*do something*); **ponerse de buen/mal humor** to get into a good/bad mood; **ponerse de moda** to become fashionable; **ponerse de pie** to stand up; **ponerse la ropa** to put on clothes (4); **ponerse perfume** to put on perfume (4); **ponerse rojo/a** to blush (7)
**por** by; through; because of; for; per; around, about; on; because of, on account of; **darse por vencido** to give up; **por aquí** around here; **por ciento** percent; **por completo** totally; **¿por cuánto?** for how much?; **por dentro** on the inside (8); **por dondequiera** everywhere; **por ejemplo** for example (9); **por el medio** in half; **por eso** that's why; **por favor** please (1); **por fin** finally (12); **por fuera** on the outside (8); **por la mañana/tarde/noche** in the morning/afternoon/evening/at night (1); **por lo general** in general; **por lo menos** at least; **por lo tanto** therefore; **por supuesto** of course; **por último** finally, lastly (2)
**porcelana** porcelain
**porcentaje** *m.* percentage
**porción** *f.* serving (8)
**¿por qué?** why? (2); **¿por qué no?** why not?
**porque** because (5)
**portal** *m.* porch; doorway
**portar** to carry; **portar armas** to bear arms (16); **portarse** to behave
**portátil** portable
**portazgo** toll, tollbooth
**porteño/a** of or from Buenos Aires
**portero eléctrico** *intercom with automatic door-opener*
**portugués** *m.* Portuguese (*language*) (C)
**portugués, portuguesa** *n., adj.* Portuguese (C)
**porvenir** *m.* future
**posada** inn
**poseer** (**y**) to possess
**posesivo/a** possessive
**posibilidad** *f.* possibility (5)
**posponer** (*like* **poner**) to postpone
**postal: apartado postal** post office box number; **giro postal** money order; **tarjeta postal** postcard
**posterior** *adj.* rear; **réplicas posteriores** aftershocks
**postre** *m.* dessert (8); **de postre** for dessert
**potable** potable, drinkable
**potencia** power, force
**potencial** *n. m.* potential (10)
**potro** colt
**p.p.m.** (*abbrev. for* **palabras por minuto**) words per minute
**pqte.** (*abbrev. for* **paquete**) package
**práctica** practice
**practicar** (**qu**) to play (*sport*); to practice (2); **practicar un deporte** to play a sport (2)
**práctico/a** practical (B)
**precavido/a** cautious
**precio** price (4)
**precioso/a** precious (13)
**precisamente** exactly (12)
**precolombino/a** pre-Colombian
**preconcebido/a** preconceived
**predicar** (**qu**) to preach
**predominar** to predominate
**preferible** preferable
**preferido/a** favorite (3)
**preferir** (**ie, i**) to prefer (2)
**pregunta** *n.* question (A); **hacer preguntas** to ask questions (5)
**preguntar** to ask (questions) (5); **pregúntele a...** ask . . .
**prejuicio** prejudice (16)
**prematuro/a** premature
**premio** prize (15); premium; **premio gordo** grand prize (15); **Premio Nóbel** Nobel Prize (16)
**prenda de ropa/vestir** garment
**prender** (**la luz**) to turn on (the light) (6)
**prensa** press; **libertad** (*f.*) **de prensa** freedom of the press
**prensador** *m.* press
**preocupación** *f.* worry
**preocupado/a** worried (4)
**preocupar** to worry (10); **me preocupa que** it worries me that
**preparación** *f.* preparation
**preparar** to prepare (3)
**preparativos** *pl.* preparations
**preparatoria** *n.* prep school; high school (2)
**preparatorio/a** *adj.* preparatory
**presencia** presence
**presenciar** to witness, be present at
**presentación** *f.* presentation; introduction (5)
**presentar** to present; to introduce (A)
**presente** *n. m.; adj.* present
**preservar** to preserve
**presidencia** presidency
**presidente, presidenta** president
**presión** *f.* pressure (10)
**presionar** to pressure
**préstamo** loan (16)
**prestar** to lend (14)
**prestigio** prestige
**presupuesto** budget (14)
**pretender** to pretend; to claim
**pretérito** preterite
**prevenido/a** prepared, ready
**prevenir** (*like* **venir**) to prevent; **más vale prevenir** it is better to be prepared
**preventivo/a** preventive
**prima: materia prima** raw material (13)
**primaria: (escuela) primaria** elementary school
**primavera** spring (1)
**primer, primero/a** first (2); **de buenas a primeras** suddenly; **por primera vez** for the first time (8); **primera clase** first class (11)
**primo/a** cousin (C)
**princesa** princess (C)
**príncipe** *m.* prince (C)
**principio** beginning; principle; **para principios de** by the beginning of
**prioridad** *f.* priority (16)
**prisa: tener prisa** to be in a hurry (4)
**privado/a** private (14)
**privilegiado/a** privileged, favored
**probador** *m.* fitting room
**probar(se)** (**ue**) to try (out); to prove; to taste; to try on (13)
**problema** *m.* problem (10)
**procedente** *adj.* coming, originating
**procesador** (*m.*) **de palabras** word processor (15)
**procesador(a)** *adj.* processing
**proceso** process; trial
**prodigioso/a** excellent, wondrous
**producción** *f.* production (10)
**producir** (**zc**) (**j**) to produce (10)
**profecía** prophecy
**profesión** *f.* profession
**profesor(a)** professor (A)
**profundidad** *f.* depth
**profundo/a** deep (10)
**programa** *m.* program
**programador(a)** programmer (5)
**programar** to schedule; to plan
**progresar** to make progress; to progress
**progreso** progress (16)
**prohibir** (**prohíbo**) to prohibit (14)
**prolongar** (**gu**) to prolong
**promedio** average (10)
**prometer** to promise (16)
**promover** (**ue**) to promote; to advance, further
**promulgar** (**gu**) to proclaim; to put into effect
**pronombre** *m.* pronoun; **pronombre de complemento directo/indirecto** direct/indirect object pronoun
**pronosticar** (**qu**) to forecast (10)
**pronóstico del tiempo** weather forecast (2)
**pronto** soon (7); **de pronto** suddenly (4); **lo más pronto posible** as soon as possible; **tan pronto como** as soon as (15)
**pronunciar** to pronounce
**propagar** (**gu**) to propagate
**propiedad** *f.*: **título de propiedad** deed (15)
**propietario/a** owner, proprietor (16)
**propina** tip (*for a service*) (8)
**propio/a** own (6); typical, characteristic
**proponer** (*like* **poner**) to propose
**proporcionar** to furnish, provide
**propósito** purpose
**propuesto/a** (*p.p. of* **proponer**) proposed

**proseguir (i, i) (g)** to continue
**prosperidad** *f.* prosperity
**próspero/a** prosperous
**protagonista** *m., f.* protagonist
**proteger (j)** to protect (10)
**protesta** protest
**proveedor(a)** provider, supplier
**proveer (y)** to provide
**provenir** (*like* **venir**) to originate
**provincia** province, region
**provocar (qu)** to provoke
**próximo/a** next (2); **la próxima semana** next week (4)
**proyectar** to project
**proyecto** project; plan (14)
**prueba** test
**psicología** psychology
**psicólogo/a** psychologist (12)
**psiquiatra** *m., f.* psychiatrist (12)
**ptas.** (*abbrev. for* **pesetas**) *monetary unit of Spain*
**publicación** *f.* publication (16)
**publicar (qu)** to publish
**público/a** *adj.* public; **salud** (*f.*) **pública** public health (16)
**pueblito** little town (9)
**pueblo** town (6); people
**puente** *m.* bridge (10)
**puerco** pork; **carne** (*f.*) **de puerco** pork (8)
**puerta** door (A)
**puerto** (sea)port
**puertorriqueño/a** *n., adj.* Puerto Rican (3)
**pues...** well . . . (1)
**puesta del sol** sunset
**puesto** *n.* job; stand, booth
**puesto/a** (*p.p. of* **poner**) put, placed; turned on (12); **puesto a punto** adjusted, regulated; **tengo una falda puesta** I have a skirt on, I'm wearing a skirt
**pulga** flea
**pulgada** inch
**pulgar** thumb (12)
**pulmón** *m.* lung (12)
**pulmonía** pneumonia (12)
**pulpa** pulp, flesh
**pulpería** grocery store
**pulpo** octopus
**pulsera** bracelet
**pulso** pulse (12)
**puntaje** *m.* score
**puntiagudo/a** *adj.* pointed
**punto** point; period; **al punto** medium rare (*meat*) (8); **puesto/a a punto** adjusted; regulated; **punto de vista** point of view; **punto y aparte** (write a) period and (begin a) new paragraph (*dictation*)
**puntual** punctual
**pupitre** *m.* student's desk (A)
**puré** (*m.*) **de papas** mashed potatoes
**pureza** purity
**puro/a** pure (16)

## Q

**que** that, which; than; **lo que** that which, what (6); **más/menos que** more/less than (6); **ya que** since
**¿qué...?** what . . . ? (B); **¿de qué está hecho/a?** what is it (made) of? (13); **¿qué tal?** how's it going?; how are you? (6); **¿qué tal si...?** how about if . . . ?; **¡qué va!** no way! (16)
**quechua** *m.* Quechua (*language*) (*indigenous to Peru, Bolivia, etc.*)
**quedar(se)** to remain, stay; to get left behind (12); to fit; to be, be situated; to be, get; **no quedar más remedio** to not have any other choice; **quedar embarazada** to become pregnant; **quedar de acuerdo** to agree; **quedarle apretado/suelto** to fit tightly/loosely (13); **quedarle bien/mal** to look nice/bad on one (13); **quedarle grande/pequeño** to be too big/small (13); **quedarse dormido** to fall asleep; **quedarse en casa** to stay home (4)
**quehacer** *m.* chore
**quejarse** to complain (9)
**quemadura** burn (12)
**quemar** to burn (7)
**queque** *m.* bun, cake (*Colombia*)
**querer** *irreg.* to want (1); to love; **querer decir** to mean; **quererse** to love each other (15)
**querido/a** *n.* dear; *adj.* dear; beloved; **ser** (*m.*) **querido** loved one (15)
**quesadilla** (*Mex., Honduras*) *cornmeal or tortilla pie filled with cheese*
**queso** cheese (8)
**quetzal** *m. monetary unit of Guatemala* (13)
**quien(es)** who, whom
**¿quién(es)?** who?, whom? (A); **¿de quién es/son...?** whose is/are . . . ? (C); **¿quién es? / ¿quiénes son?** who is it? / who are they? (A)
**química** chemistry (2)
**químico/a** *adj.* chemical
**quince** fifteen (A)
**quinceañera** fifteenth-birthday party
**quinientos/as** five hundred
**quinto/a** fifth (2)
**quintuplicar (qu)** to quintuple
**quiosco** kiosk
**quitamanchas** *m. sing., pl.* stain remover
**quitar(se)** to remove; **quitarse la ropa** to take off clothes (4)
**quizá(s)** perhaps

## R

**rábano** radish (8)
**rabia: dar rabia** to anger, enrage
**rabioso/a** furious
**racimo** cluster, bunch
**ración** *f.* portion, helping
**racista** *adj. m., f.* racist
**radiador** *m.* radiator (10)
**radio** *m.* radio (*receiver*); *f.* radio (*broadcasting*); **radiocassette (portátil)** (portable) radio cassette player (13); **radio despertador** alarm clock radio (13)
**radiografía** X-ray
**raíz** *f.* (*pl.* **raíces**) root
**rallar** to grate (8)
**ramo** cut branch; bouquet; piece (*fig.*)
**rancheros: huevos rancheros** *eggs, usually fried or poached, topped with a spicy tomato sauce and sometimes served on a fried corn tortilla*
**rape** *m.* anglerfish
**rápidamente** fast, rapidly (4)
**rapidez** *f.* rapidity; **con rapidez** rapidly
**rápido** *adv.* fast; quickly
**rápido/a** *adj.* rapid, fast, quick (4)
**raqueta** racket
**ráquetbol** *m.* racketball
**raro/a** strange
**rascar (qu)** to scratch
**rasgo** trait, characteristic
**Rastro** *Madrid flea market* (13)
**rasuradora eléctrica** electric razor (4)
**rato** a while (7); little while, short time; **a cada rato** every few minutes (14)
**ratón** *m.* mouse
**raya: de rayas** striped (13)
**rayo** ray
**rayuela** hopscotch; **jugar a la rayuela** to play hopscotch (9)
**raza** race (16)
**razón** *f.* reason (8); **con razón** with good reason; **sea cual sea la razón** whatever the reason may be; **tener razón** to be right (14)
**reacción** *f.* reaction (16)
**reaccionar** to react
**real** real; royal
**realidad** *f.* reality
**realizar (c)** to attain, achieve; to carry out; to realize (15)
**reata** riata, lariat (*rope used to tie horses or mules in single file*)
**rebajado/a** reduced (*price*) (13)
**rebajar** to reduce a price (13)
**rebanada** slice (8)
**recaída** relapse; setback
**recámara** *Mex.* bedroom (6)
**recepción** *f.* reception; lobby (11)
**recepcionista** *m., f.* receptionist (B)
**receta** recipe; medical prescription (12); **surtir una receta** to fill a prescription (12)
**recetar** to prescribe (12)
**rechazar (c)** to reject
**recibir** to receive (2)
**reciclaje** *m.* recycling (10)
**reciclar** to recycle (10)
**recién** recently; **recién nacido/a** newborn (15)
**reciente** recent (16)
**recipiente** *m.* container (10)

**recíproco/a** reciprocal
**reclamo** claim; **reclamo de equipaje** baggage claim (11)
**recoger (j)** to pick up (3)
**recomendación** *f.* recommendation
**recomendar (ie)** to recommend (11)
**reconciliarse** to become reconciled
**reconocer (zc)** to recognize
**reconstrucción** *f.* reconstruction
**reconstruir (y)** to reconstruct
**recordar (ue)** to remember (9)
**recorrer** to tour, travel across
**recortar** to cut out
**recreo** recess (9); **patio de recreo** schoolyard (9); **sala de recreo** recreation room (13)
**recto/a** straight (13)
**rectoría** office of the president (rector) of a university (3)
**recuerdo** souvenir; *pl.* memories (9)
**recuperar** to recuperate, get back
**recurrir (a)** to appeal (to)
**recurso** resource (10); **recurso natural** natural resource (16)
**red** *f.* network; **red mundial** Internet (2)
**reducción** *f.* reduction (16)
**reducir (zc) (j)** to reduce (10)
**reelegir (i, i) (j)** to reelect
**referirse (ie, i) a** to refer to (16)
**reflejar** to reflect
**reflexión** *f.* reflection
**reflexionar** to reflect on, think about
**reforma agraria** land reform (16)
**reformar** to reform
**reforzar (ue) (c)** to reinforce
**refrán** *m.* proverb
**refrescar (qu)** to cool; to refresh
**refresco** soft drink (3)
**refrigerador** *m.* refrigerator (6)
**refrigerio** snack
**refugio** refuge, shelter
**regalado/a: a precios regalados** inexpensively priced, "given away"
**regalar** to give as a gift
**regalo** gift (4)
**regaño** scolding (14)
**regar (ie) (gu)** to water (6)
**regatear** to bargain (13); **a regatear** let's bargain
**regateo** *n.* bargaining (13)
**régimen** *m.* (*pl.* **regímenes**) regime; diet (16)
**región** *f.* region (10)
**registrar** to register
**regla** rule (12)
**regresar** to return (3)
**regreso: de regreso** *adj.* return
**regulado/a** adjusted, calibrated
**regular** fair, so-so; **estoy regular** I am OK (A)
**reina** queen
**Reino Unido** United Kingdom
**reír(se) (río) (i, i)** to laugh
**relación** *f.* relationship; **relaciones** (*pl.*) **familiares** family relationships (9)
**relacionado/a** related (9)
**relacionar** to relate
**relajador(a)** *adj.* relaxing
**relajarse** to relax
**relámpago** lightning (10)
**relato** account, story
**religión** *f.* religion
**religioso/a** religious (B)
**relleno** *n.* filling
**relleno/a** *adj.* stuffed; **chile** (*m.*) **relleno** stuffed chili pepper
**reloj** *m.* watch (A); clock
**remedio** remedy; **no quedar más remedio** to not have any other choice
**remesa** shipment
**remo** *n.* rowing
**remoto/a** remote
**remover (ue)** to remove
**renacer (zc)** to be reborn
**rendir (i, i) tributo** to pay tribute
**renovado/a** remodeled (13)
**renovar (ue)** to renovate
**renunciar** to renounce
**reparación** *f.*: **taller** (*m.*) **de reparación** garage (5)
**reparar** to repair, fix (2)
**repartir** to divide; to distribute
**repaso** review
**repente: de repente** suddenly
**repetir (i, i)** to repeat
**repisa** shelf
**repleto/a de** replete with, full of
**réplica** replica, copy
**repoblación** (*f.*) **forestal** reforesting
**repoblar (ue)** to reforest
**reponer** (*like* **poner**) to put back
**reportaje** *m.* report (3)
**reportero/a** reporter (15)
**reposado/a** calm, peaceful
**reposar** to lie; to remain
**repositorio** repository
**repostería** cake shop
**representante** *m., f.* representative
**representar** to represent
**represión** *f.* repression
**represivo/a** repressive (16)
**reproducir (zc) (j)** to reproduce
**reproductor** (*m.*) **para discos compactos** CD player (1)
**república** republic (16); **República de Sudáfrica** South Africa (C); **República Dominicana** Dominican Republic (2)
**republicano/a** Republican
**repuesto/a** (*p.p. of* **reponer**) replaced; **de repuesto** replacement (*part*)
**requerir (ie, i)** to require (16)
**requisito** *n.* prerequisite; requirement (5)
**res** *f.* head of cattle; beast; **carne** (*f.*) **de res** beef (8)
**resbaloso/a** slippery (10)
**rescatado/a** rescued
**reseña** review (15); description
**reservación** *f.* reservation
**reservar** to reserve
**resfriado** *n.* cold (*illness*) (12)
**resfriado/a: estar resfriado/a** to have a cold (12)
**resfriarse** to catch a cold (12)
**resfrío** cold (*illness*) (12)
**residencia** residence; **residencia estudiantil** university dorm (5)
**residencial** residential
**residir** to reside
**resolver (ue)** (*p.p.* **resuelto**) to solve (10)
**respaldo: de respaldo** back-up
**respecto: al respecto** about the matter; **con respecto a** with respect to (15); **respecto a** with respect to
**respetar** to respect
**respeto** respect (16)
**respirar** to breathe (12)
**responder** to respond, answer (14)
**responsabilidad** *f.* responsibility
**responsable** responsible (6)
**respuesta** answer (2)
**restante** *m.* remainder
**restaurante** *m.* restaurant
**resto** rest; *pl.* remains (14)
**restricción** *f.* restriction (10)
**restringir (j)** to restrict (10)
**resuelto/a** (*p.p. of* **resolver**) resolved, solved
**resultado** result (14); **dar como resultado** to result in
**resultante** resulting, consequent
**resultar** to turn out, result
**resumen** *m.*: **en resumen** in short, in conclusion (B)
**retirarse** to pull out, pull back
**retornable: no retornable** non-returnable
**retraso** backwardness, underdevelopment
**retrovisor(a): espejo retrovisor** rearview mirror (10)
**reunión** *f.* meeting (3)
**reunirse** to get together (4)
**revisar** to check (3)
**revista** magazine (2)
**revivir** to relive
**revolución** *f.* revolution (16)
**revuelto/a: huevos revueltos** scrambled eggs (8)
**rey** *m.* king; **Día** (*m.*) **de los Reyes Magos** Epiphany, Jan. 6th (*lit.* Day of the Magi) (4)
**rezar (c)** to pray (4)
**rico/a** rich; delicious (6, 8)
**ridículo/a** ridiculous
**riesgo** risk (14); **correr riesgo** to run a risk
**riguroso/a** severe, harsh
**rincón** *m.* corner
**riñón** *m.* kidney (12)
**río** river (2)
**riqueza** *sing.* riches, wealth
**rítmico/a** rhythmic; **gimnasia rítmica** eurhythmics

**ritmo** rhythm
**rizado/a** curly (A)
**robar** to rob, steal (7)
**roble** *m.* oak
**robot** *m.* robot (B)
**roca** rock
**rocío** dew (10)
**rock** *m.* rock music
**rocoso/a** rocky
**rodante** *adj.* rolling
**rodeado/a** surrounded (10)
**rodear** to surround
**rodilla** knee (12)
**rogar (ue) (gu)** to beg (14)
**roído/a** (*p.p. of* **roer**) gnawed
**rojo/a** red (A); **ponerse rojo/a** to blush (7)
**rol** *m.* role
**rollo** roll; **rollo de película** roll of film (13)
**romano/a** Roman
**romántico/a** romantic
**romper(se)** to break (11)
**ron** *m.* rum
**ronda** night watch or patrol; beat (*of a police officer*)
**ronquera** hoarseness
**ropa** *sing.* clothes, clothing; **guardar ropa** to put away clothes (6); **ponerse la ropa** to put on clothes (4); **quitarse la ropa** to take off clothes (4); **ropa deportiva** sport clothes (1); **ropa interior** underwear (13)
**rosa** rose (A)
**rosado/a** pink (A)
**roto/a** (*p.p. of* **romper**) broken
**rubio/a** blond(e) (A)
**rueda** wheel (10)
**ruido** noise (14); **hacer ruido** to make noise
**ruidoso/a** noisy
**ruinas** *pl.* ruins (11)
**rumbo** direction
**rumor** *m.* rumor
**ruso** Russian (language) (C)
**ruso/a** *n., adj.* Russian (C)
**rústico/a** rustic
**ruta** route (9)
**rutina** routine

## S

**sábado** Saturday (1)
**sábana** sheet
**saber** *irreg.* to know (4); to find out about; **saber** (+ *infin.*) to know how to (*do something*) (5); **ya lo sé** I already know it; **(yo) sé** I know (1)
**sabiduría** wisdom
**sabor** *m.* flavor, taste; **de sabores** flavored
**saborear** to savor
**sabroso/a** delicious, tasty
**sacar (qu)** to take out; to get, receive (*grade*); **sacar adelante** to carry forward; **sacar al mercado** to put (*a new product*) on the market; **sacar buenas/malas notas** to get good/bad grades (5); **sacar fotos** to take pictures (1); **sacar el pasaporte (la visa)** to get a passport (visa) (11); **sacar la basura** to take out the trash (6)
**saco** bag; jacket, sport coat (A)
**sacrificar (qu)** to sacrifice
**sacrificio** sacrifice
**sacudir** to dust; to shake off (14)
**Sagitario** Sagittarius
**sagrado/a** sacred, holy
**sal** *f.* salt (8); **agua** (*f. but* **el agua**) **con sal** salt water (12)
**sala** room; living room (6); **sala de baño** bathroom (6); **sala de emergencias** emergency room (12); **sala de espera** waiting room (11); **sala de recreo** recreation room (13); **sala de urgencias** emergency room (12)
**salado/a** *adj.* salt, salted
**salario** salary; **aumento de salario** raise
**salchicha** sausage, frankfurter, hot dog
**salero** saltshaker (8)
**salida** departure; exit (11)
**salir** *irreg.* to leave; to go out; **salir a** (+ *infin.*) to go or come out to (*do something*); **salir a bailar** to go out dancing (1); **salir al mercado** to appear on the market; **salir de noche** to go out at night (3); **salir de vacaciones** to go on vacation (3); **salir del trabajo** to get off work
**salón** *m.* room; **salón de baile** dance hall; **salón de belleza** beauty parlor; **salón de clase** classroom
**salsa** salsa (*music*); sauce
**saltar** to jump; to jump up; **saltar la cuerda** to jump rope (9)
**salud** *f.* health (8); **¡salud!** bless you! (*after a person sneezes*); to your health! (12); **salud pública** public health
**saludable** healthy (8)
**saludar** to greet, say hello (7); **saludarse** to greet each other
**saludo** greeting (A)
**salvadoreño/a** *n., adj.* Salvadoran (3)
**salvaje** wild, savage
**salvar** to save (*from danger*) (10)
**salvo** except
**san, santo/a** saint; **día** (*m.*) **del santo** saint's day (3); **Día** (*m.*) **de Todos los Santos** All Saints' Day (3); **Semana Santa** Holy Week (4)
**sandalia** sandal
**sandía** watermelon (8)
**sándwich** *m.* sandwich
**sangre** *f.* blood (12); **análisis** (*m.*) **de sangre** blood test (12)
**sangriento/a** bloody
**sano/a** healthy
**sarampión** *m. sing.* measles (12)
**sartén** *f.* (frying) pan (8)
**satélite** *m.* satellite
**satisfacción** *f.* satisfaction (15)
**satisfacer** (*like* **hacer**) to satisfy
**se (impersonal)** one; *refl. pron.* herself, himself, itself, themselves, yourself (*pol. sing.*) yourselves (*pol. pl.*)
**sea cual sea** whatever it might be
**secador** (*m.*) **de pelo** hair dryer
**secadora** dryer (6); **secadora de pelo** hair dryer
**secar (qu)** to dry; **secarse** to dry off, dry oneself (4); **secarse el pelo** to dry one's hair (4)
**sección** (*f.*) **de (no) fumar** (no) smoking section (11)
**seco/a** dry (8); **ciruela seca** prune
**secretario/a** secretary (B)
**secuencia** sequence (7)
**secundaria: (escuela) secundaria** high school (7)
**sed** *f.* thirst; **tener sed** to be thirsty (4)
**seda** silk (13)
**seguida: en seguida** immediately (14)
**seguir (i, i) (g)** to follow (3); to continue; **seguir + -ndo** to go on (*doing something*) (13); **seguir una carrera** to have a career (5)
**según** according to (C)
**segundo** *n.* second; *adv.* secondly
**segundo/a** *adj.* second (2)
**seguridad** *f.* safety; **cinturón** (*m.*) **de seguridad** seatbelt (10); **con toda seguridad** with absolute certainty
**seguro** *n.* insurance (10); **seguro de auto(móvil) / seguro automovilístico** car insurance (10); **seguro médico** health insurance (12)
**seguro/a** *adj.* sure; safe
**seis** six (A)
**seiscientos/as** six hundred
**selección** *f.* selection, choice (11)
**seleccionar** to select, choose (16)
**selva** jungle; **selva tropical** tropical jungle
**selvático/a** *adj.* jungle
**semáforo** signal; traffic light (10)
**semana** week; **a la semana** per week; **cada semana** each/every week (6); **entre semana** on weekdays, during the week (14); **fin** (*m.*) **de semana** weekend (1); **la semana pasada** last week (6); **la próxima semana** next week (4); **Semana Santa** Holy Week (4); **... veces a la / por semana** . . . times a week (4)
**sembradío** land prepared for sowing
**sembrar (ie)** to sow
**semejante** similar (A)
**semestre** *m.* semester
**semilla** seed (8)
**seminario** seminar
**senador(a)** senator (14)
**sencillo/a** simple (11)
**sendas** (*pl.*) **frondosas** shaded paths
**sensación** *f.* sensation
**sensatez** *f.* sense, sensibleness; **Sensatez y sentimiento** *Sense and Sensibility*
**sensible** sensitive (16)
**sentado/a** seated; **(estar) sentado** (to be) seated, sitting down

**sentarse (ie)** to sit down
**sentido** sense; **doble sentido** two-way (*street*) (10); **sentido del humor** sense of humor (14); **un solo sentido** one-way (*street*) (10)
**sentimiento** *n.* feeling; **Sensatez y sentimiento** *Sense and Sensibility*
**sentir(se) (ie, i)** to feel (7); **lo siento** I'm sorry
**señal** *f.* sign; signal (10)
**señalar** to indicate, show; to point out (12)
**señor (Sr.)** *m.* man; Mr. (A); **los señores...** Mr. and Mrs. . . .
**señora (Sra.)** woman; Mrs., Ms. (A)
**señorita (Srta.)** young woman; Miss (A)
**separar** to separate; **separarse** to resign; to get separated
**septentrional** northern
**septiembre** *m.* September (1)
**séptimo/a** seventh (2)
**sequía** drought (10)
**ser** *n. m.* being; **ser humano** human being (15); **ser querido** loved one (15)
**ser** *v. irreg.* to be (2); **a no ser que** unless; **¿cómo eres (tú)?** what are you (*inf. sing.*) like? (B); **¿cómo es usted/él/ella?** what are you (*pol. sing.*) / is he/she like? (B); **¿cómo son ustedes/ellos/ellas?** what are you (*pol. pl.*)/they like? (B); **¿de qué es?** what is it (made) of?; **¿de quién es/son...?** whose is/are . . . ? (C); **llegar a ser** to become; **o sea** that is; **¿quién es? / ¿quiénes son?** who is it? / who are they? (A); **sea cual sea la razón** whatever the reason may be; **ser consciente de** to be aware of; **ser listo/a** to be smart, clever
**serie** *f. sing.* series
**serigrafiado/a** silk-screened
**serio/a** serious (6)
**serpiente** *f.* serpent
**servicio** service
**servilleta** napkin (8)
**servir (i, i)** to serve (5); **¿en qué puedo servirle?** may I help you? (*pol. sing.*) (11); **¿para qué sirve?** what is it used for? (6); **para servirle** at your (*pol. sing.*) service (11)
**Sésamo: Barrio Sésamo** Sesame Street
**sesenta** sixty (B)
**sesión** *f.* meeting; conference (15)
**setecientos/as** seven hundred
**setenta** seventy (C)
**sexenio** period of six years
**sexo** sex
**sexto/a** sixth (2)
**sexual: educación** (*f.*) **sexual** sex education (16); **violación** (*f.*) **sexual** rape (16)
**si** if (8)
**sí** yes (A)
**sí: en sí** in itself; **sí mismo/a** oneself
**SIDA** *m. sing.* (*abbrev. for* **síndrome de inmunodeficiencia adquirida**) AIDS (12)
**sidra** cider
**siembra** *n.* sowing
**siempre** always (2)
**sierra** mountain range (16)
**siesta: dormir una siesta** to take a nap; **tomar una siesta** to take a nap (2)
**siete** seven (A)
**sigla** acronym
**siglo** century (7)
**significado** meaning
**significar (qu)** to mean
**significativo/a** significant
**signo** sign
**siguiente** following, next (2)
**silbar** to hiss
**silencio** silence
**silla** chair (B)
**sillón** *m.* easy chair (6)
**silueta** figure
**símbolo** symbol (15)
**simpático/a** friendly, nice (B)
**sin** without (8); **sin duda** without a doubt; **sin embargo** however (7); **sin que** *conj.* without (16)
**sincero/a** sincere
**sincronizado/a** synchronized
**sindicalista** *adj. m., f.* of or related to a trade union
**sindicato** labor union (16)
**síndrome** *m.* syndrome
**sino** but (rather)
**síntesis** *f. sing., pl.* synthesis
**síntoma** *m.* symptom (12)
**siquiera** even; **ni siquiera** not even
**sismo** earthquake
**sistema** *m.* system (10)
**sitio** place, location (10)
**situación** *f.* situation
**situado/a** located (16)
**sobrante** *adj.* leftover, remaining
**sobras** *pl.* leftovers
**sobre** on, on top of; above; about (1); **sobre todo** above all, especially
**sobremesa** after-dinner conversation
**sobrepoblación** overpopulation
**sobresalir** (*like* **salir**) to stand out
**sobresaltarse** to be startled
**sobreviviente** *m., f.* survivor
**sobrevivir** to survive
**sobrino/a** nephew/niece (9)
**social: bienestar** (*m.*) **social** (social) welfare (16); **trabajador(a) social** social worker (5)
**socialista** *n. m., f. adj.* socialist (16)
**sociedad** *f.* society (9)
**socio/a** member
**sociología** sociology
**socorro** help (12)
**sofá** *m.* sofa (6)
**sofocado/a** suffocated
**sol** *m.* sun; *monetary unit of Peru* (13); **de sol a sol** from sunup to sundown; **hace sol** it's sunny (weather) (1); **tomar el sol** to sunbathe (2)
**solamente** *adv.* only (2)
**soldado** soldier
**soleado/a** sunny (10)
**soledad** *f.* solitude (16)
**soler (ue)** (+ *infin.*) to be accustomed to (*doing something*)
**solicitar** to request
**sólido/a** solid (16)
**sólo** *adv.* only (C)
**solo/a** alone (2); **un solo sentido** one-way (*street*) (10)
**solomillo** sirloin
**soltero/a** single (*unmarried*) (C)
**solución** *f.* solution
**sombra** shadow; shade
**sombrero** hat (A)
**sonar (ue)** to ring, go off (*alarm clock*) (7)
**sonido** sound (12)
**sonoro/a** sonorous
**sonreír (sonrío) (i, i)** to smile
**sonrisa** smile
**soñar (ue) con** to dream about (4)
**sopa** soup
**soportar** to stand, endure, put up with
**Sor** *f.* Sister (*used before the name of a nun*)
**Sorbona** Sorbonne (*university in Paris*)
**sorprender** to surprise
**sorpresa** surprise
**sos** (*Arg.*) *form of* **ser** *that goes with* **vos (tú eres, vos sos)**
**sospechar** to suspect (14)
**sostén** *m.* bra (13)
**sostener** (*like* **tener**) to hold up, support
**Sr.: señor** *m.* Mr. (A)
**Sra.: señora** *f.* Mrs., Ms. (A)
**Srta.: señorita** *f.* Miss (B)
**su** *poss.* his, her (B); its, their, your (*pol. sing., pl.*)
**suave** soft
**subdesarrollo** underdevelopment
**subir** to rise; to go up (7); **subir a** to board (*train, plane, bus*); **subirse a los árboles** to climb trees (9)
**subjuntivo** subjunctive (14)
**sublevarse** to rise up, revolt
**subsede** *f.* secondary venue
**subterráneo/a** subterranean
**subvencionado/a** subsidized
**subyacente** underlying
**subyugar (gu)** to subjugate
**suceder** to happen
**sucio/a** dirty
**sucursal** *f.* branch office
**Sudáfrica: República de Sudáfrica** South Africa (C)
**sudafricano/a** *n., adj.* South African (C)
**Sudamérica** South America (3)
**sudar** to sweat
**sudor** *m.* sweat
**sueco/a** *n.* Swede; *adj.* Swedish; **hacerse el sueco** to play dumb; to pretend not to hear or understand
**suegro/a** father-in-law/mother-in-law (9)
**suela** sole (*shoe*)

**sueldo** salary (5)
**suelo** floor; ground (10)
**suelto/a** loose (13)
**sueño** dream; **tener sueño** to be sleepy (4)
**suerte** *f.* luck; lot, fate
**suéter** *m.* sweater (A)
**sufrir** to suffer
**sugerencia** suggestion (5)
**sugerente** *adj.* thought-provoking; full of suggestions
**sugerir (ie, i)** to suggest (14)
**suicidio** suicide (16)
**Suiza** Switzerland
**sujetar** to hold (13)
**sujeto** *n.* subject
**sujeto/a** (*adj.*) **a** subject to
**suma** sum
**sumar** to add up
**sumergirse (j)** to dive; to submerge
**sumido/a** sunken
**suministrar** to provide, supply
**sumiso/a** submissive
**¡súper!** great! (16)
**superficie** *f.* surface (10)
**supermercado** supermarket (4)
**superpoblación** *f.* overpopulation
**supervisar** to supervise
**supervisor(a)** supervisor (5)
**suponer** (*like* **poner**) to suppose (11)
**supuestamente** supposedly
**supuesto/a** (*p.p. of* **suponer**) supposed; **por supuesto** of course
**sur** *m.* south
**surco** furrow
**sureño/a** southern
**surgir (j)** to arise
**suroeste** *m.* southwest
**surrealista** *adj. m., f.* surrealistic (16)
**surtir** to fill (*prescription*) (12); **surtir efecto** to work, have the desired effect; **surtir (una receta)** to fill (a prescription) (12)
**suscribirse** (*p.p.* **suscrito**) to subscribe
**suspender** to suspend, dismiss
**suspiro** sigh
**sustantivo** noun
**susto** scare, fright; **pegarse un susto** to get a shock
**susurrar** to whisper
**suyo/a** *poss.* your, of yours (*pol. sing., pl.*); his, of his; her, of hers

# T

**tabaco** tobacco (3)
**tabla** table (graph), chart (2)
**tacaño/a** stingy (B)
**taciturno/a** taciturn; silent; moody
**taco** (*Mex.*) *rolled or folded tortilla filled with meat and beans* (7)
**tacón** *m.* heel (*shoe*); **zapatos de tacón alto** high-heeled shoes (13)
**tacto** sense of touch
**tal** such, such a; **con tal (de) que** provided that (15); **¿qué tal?** how's it going?; how are you? (5); **¿qué tal si...?** how about if . . . ?; **tal vez** perhaps (15); **tal y como** exactly the same as
**talla** size; **¿qué talla usa?** what size do you wear? (13)
**taller** (*m.*) **de reparación** (mechanic's) garage (5)
**tamal** *m. Mex.* tamale (*dish of minced meat and red peppers rolled in cornmeal wrapped in corn husks or banana leaves*)
**tamaño** size (8)
**también** also (B); **a mí también me gusta...** I like to . . . also (1)
**tampoco** neither, not either (4); **a mí tampoco me gusta...** I don't like to . . . either (1)
**tan** so (10); **tan... como** as . . . as (6); **tan pronto como** as soon as (15)
**tanque** *m.* tank (10)
**tanto** *adv.* so much; as much; **mientras tanto** in the meanwhile; **por lo tanto** therefore; **tanto como** as much as
**tanto/a** *adj.* so much; such, such a; *pl.* so many; **tanto(s)/tanta(s)... como** as many . . . as (6); **¡tanto tiempo sin verte!** I haven't seen you (*inf. sing.*) in ages! (6)
**tapado/a** stuffed up, congested (12)
**tapar** to cover (8)
**tapas** *pl.* hors d'oeuvres
**tapizado/a** upholstered
**taquilla** box office
**taquillero/a** *adj.* box office hit
**tardar** (*time*) **en** (+ *infin.*) to take (*time*) to (*do something*); **¿cuánto tiempo tarda(s) en...?** how long does it take you to . . . ? (4)
**tarde** *n. f.* afternoon; *adv.* late (4); **buenas tardes** good afternoon (A); **de/por la tarde** in the afternoon (1); **llegar tarde** to arrive/be late (4); **más tarde** later (2); **toda la tarde** all afternoon long
**tarea** homework (3); task
**tarifa** rate, price, fare (11)
**tarjeta** card; **tarjeta de crédito** credit card (8); **tarjeta postal** postcard
**tarro** jar (8)
**tarta** pastry
**tasa** rate, level; **tasa del desempleo** unemployment rate (16)
**tasca** *coll.* bar, tavern
**tata** granddad
**Tauro** Taurus
**tauromaquia** art and technique of bullfighting
**taxi** *m.* taxi (10)
**taza** cup, mug (8); **taza del inodoro** toilet bowl (6)
**te** *d.o.* you (*inf. sing.*); *i.o.* to/for you (*inf. sing.*); *refl. pron.* yourself (*inf. sing.*)
**té** *m.* tea (2); **té caliente/frío/helado** hot/cold/iced tea (8); **té con hielo** iced tea
**teatro** theater (3)
**techo** roof (B)
**tecla** key (*of a typewriter keypad, etc.*)
**teclado** keyboard
**técnico/a** *n.* technician; *adj.* technical
**tecnificarse (qu)** to become more technological
**tehuacán** *m. Mex.* mineral water
**tejido** fabric
**tel.** (*abbrev. for* **teléfono**) telephone
**tela** cloth, material (13)
**tele** *f.* television
**telecomunicación** *f. sing.* telecommunications
**telefónico/a** *adj.* telephone
**teléfono** telephone; **hablar por teléfono** to speak on the phone (A); **llamar por teléfono** to phone; **por teléfono** on the telephone, by telephone (A)
**telégrafo** telegraph
**telenovela** soap opera; **ver una telenovela** to watch a soap opera (1)
**televisión** *f.* television; **ver la televisión** to watch television (1)
**televisor** *m.* TV set (5); **televisor en colores** color TV set
**telúrico/a** terrestrial
**tema** *m.* theme, topic
**temblor** *m.* tremor; earthquake
**tempestad** *f.* storm
**temporada** season (*sports*) (2)
**temprano** early (4)
**tenaz** (*pl.* **tenaces**) tenacious
**tender (ie)** to extend; **tender a** (+ *infin.*) to tend to, have a tendency to (*do something*); **tender la cama** to make the bed (7)
**tenedor** *m.* fork (8)
**tener** *irreg.* to have (C, B); **¿cuántos años tiene(s)?** how old are you? (C); **¿de qué color tiene los ojos?** what color are your (*pol. sing.*)/his/her eyes? (B); **no tener razón** to be wrong; **¿qué edad tiene(s)?** how old are you? (C); **¿qué hora tiene?** what time do you (*pol. sing.*) have?; **tener... años** to be . . . years old; **tener calor/frío/hambre/miedo/sed/sueño** to be hot/cold/hungry/afraid/thirsty/sleepy (4); **tener contagio** to be infected; **tener cuidado** to be careful; **tener de todo** to be well-stocked (13); **tener en vista** to have in mind; **tener éxito** to be successful; **tener ganas de** (+ *infin.*) to feel like (*doing something*) (5); **tener interés en** to be interested in; **tener la culpa** to be to blame, be guilty (12); **tener lugar** to take place (15); **tener náuseas** to be nauseated (12); **tener prisa** to be in a hurry (4); **tener que** (+ *infin.*) to have to (*do something*) (5); **tener razón** to be right (14); **tengo... años** I'm . . . years old (C)
**tenis** *m.* tennis; **cancha de tenis** tennis court (6); **zapato de tenis** tennis shoe (A)
**tenista** *m., f.* tennis player
**Tenochtitlán** *Aztec capital* (16)
**tentación** temptation

**teoría** theory
**terapeuta** *m., f.* therapist (5)
**tercer, tercero/a** third (2); **Tercer Mundo** Third World (16)
**terciopelo** velvet (12)
**terminación** *f.* ending
**terminar** to finish (9)
**término** term (15)
**ternera** veal
**terraza** terrace
**terremoto** earthquake
**terreno** ground, terrain (10)
**territorio** territory (16)
**testarudo/a** obstinate, stubborn
**testigo** *m., f.* witness (12)
**tetera** teapot (6)
**ti** *obj. of prep.* you (*inf. sing.*)
**tibio/a** lukewarm, tepid
**tiempo** time; weather (1); **a tiempo** on time; **¿cuánto tiempo hace que... ?** how long has it been since . . . ? (7); **llegar a tiempo** to arrive/be on time (5); **pasar tiempo** to spend time (2); **pronóstico del tiempo** weather forecast (2); **¿qué tiempo hace?** what is the weather like? (2); **¡tanto tiempo sin verte!** I haven't seen you (*inf. sing.*) in ages!; **tiempo libre** free time (2)
**tienda** store (3); **tienda de campaña** tent (13)
**tierra** earth; land (10)
**tijeras** *pl.* scissors (13)
**timbre** *m.* doorbell
**tímido/a** timid (B)
**tinta** ink
**tinto/a: vino tinto** red wine (8)
**tintorería** *sing.* dry cleaners
**tío/a** uncle/aunt (9)
**típico/a** typical (3)
**tipo** type (4); *coll.* guy, character; **todo tipo de** all kinds of
**tirantes** *m. pl.* suspenders
**tirar** to throw
**tiras** (*pl.*) **cómicas** comic strips (9)
**tirita** adhesive bandage
**titular** to title, entitle
**título** title (4); **título de propiedad** deed (15)
**tiza** chalk (B)
**toalla** towel (6)
**tobillo** ankle (12)
**tocacintas** *m. sing., pl.* tape player
**tocador** *m.* dresser (6)
**tocar** (**qu**) to touch; to play (*musical instrument*) (3); **tocar a la puerta** to knock; **tocar la bocina** to honk the horn (10)
**tocino** bacon (8)
**todavía** still, yet (9)
**todo/a** all; every
**todo/a** *adj.* all, all of; **con toda seguridad** with absolute certainty; **de todos modos** anyway (9); **por todas partes** everywhere; **tener de todo** to be well-stocked (13); **toda la vida** one's whole life (14); **todo el día** all day long; **todo tipo de** all kinds of; **todos los días** every day (4)
**Tokio** Tokyo
**tomar** to take; to drink; to eat; **tomar café** to drink coffee; **tomar el sol** to sunbathe (2); **tomar en cuenta** to take into account; **tomar la decisión** to make the decision; **tomar una siesta** to take a nap (2)
**tomate** *m.* tomato
**tonelada** ton
**tono** tone
**tonto/a** *n.* fool; *adj.* silly, foolish; dumb, not too smart (B)
**toque** *m.* touch
**torcido/a** twisted, sprained (12)
**torero(a)** bullfighter
**tormenta** storm (10)
**toro** bull; **corrida de toros** bullfight
**toronja** grapefruit (8)
**torre** *f.* tower (11)
**torta** cake; *Mex.* sandwich
**tortilla** (*Mex.*) *thin cake made of cornmeal or flour;* **tortilla española** *Spanish omelette made of eggs, potatoes, and onions*
**tortuga** tortoise (14)
**tos** *f.* cough (12)
**toser** to cough (12)
**tostada** (*Mex.*) *dish with beans, meat, lettuce, etc. on a crisp, fried tortilla*
**tostado/a: pan** (*m.*) **tostado** *Sp.* toast (8)
**tostador** *m.* toaster (6)
**totalitario/a** totalitarian
**tóxico/a** toxic (10)
**trabajador(a)** *n.* worker (5); *adj.* hard-working (B)
**trabajar** to work (1)
**trabajo** work (3); job; **entrar al trabajo** to start work (5); **salir del trabajo** to get off work
**trabajólico/a** workaholic (16)
**tradición** *f.* tradition
**tradicional** traditional
**traducción** *f.* translation
**traducir** (**zc**) (**j**) to translate
**traer** *irreg.* to bring (4); **traer dinero** to be carrying money (13)
**traficar** (**qu**) to traffic, deal (*drugs*)
**tráfico** traffic
**tragarse** (**gu**) to swallow
**trágico/a** tragic
**traje** *m.* suit (A); **traje de baño** swimsuit (7)
**trampa** trick
**tranquilamente** peacefully (6)
**tranquilidad** *f.* tranquility, calm
**tranquilo/a** calm, peaceful (12)
**transbordador** *m.* ferry (10)
**transbordo** transfer (11); **hacer transbordo** to change (*trains, etc.*)
**transformar** to transform
**transitar** to travel
**tránsito** traffic (10)
**translúcido/a** translucent (13)
**transmisión** *f.* transmission (10)
**transmitir** to transmit
**transportar** to transport (10)
**transporte** *m.* transportation (6)
**tranvía** *m.* cable car (10)
**trapo** rag
**tras** *prep.* after
**trascender** (**ie**) to transcend
**trasladarse** to move
**traslado** transfer (11)
**trastes** *m. pl.* leftovers
**tratado** treaty
**tratamiento** treatment (12)
**tratar** to treat; to deal with; **tratar de** (+ *infin.*) to try to (*do something*) (5); **tratarse de** to be about (*something*) (16)
**trato** agreement
**través: a través de** through, by means of
**travesura** prank
**trayecto** trip
**trazar** (**c**) to trace
**trece** thirteen (A)
**treinta** thirty (A)
**treinta y dos** thirty-two (A)
**treinta y uno** thirty-one (A)
**tremendo/a** tremendous
**tren** *m.* train (2)
**tres** three (A)
**trescientos/as** three hundred
**tribu** *f.* tribe (11)
**tributo** tribute
**trigo** wheat
**trimestre** *m.* trimester; quarter
**triplicarse** (**qu**) to triple
**tripulación** *f.* crew
**triste** sad (4)
**tristeza** sadness
**triunfador(a)** *adj.* winning
**triunfo** triumph
**trompeta** trumpet
**tronco** trunk; stem, stalk
**tropezar** (**ie**) (**c**) to trip, stumble (11)
**tropical** *adj.* tropical; **selva tropical** tropical jungle
**trópico** tropic
**trotar** to jog (3)
**trozo** piece, chunk
**trueno** thunder (10)
**tu** *poss.* your (*inf. sing.*) (B)
**tú** *sub. pron.* you (*inf. sing.*) (B); **y tú, ¿qué dices?** and you? what do you say? (B)
**tuberculosis** *f.* tuberculosis
**tubería** *sing.* pipes
**tufillo** *coll.* odor
**túnel** *m.* tunnel
**turbio/a** cloudy (*liquid*)
**turismo** tourism
**turista** *n. m., f.* tourist (11)
**turístico/a** *adj.* tourist (10); **complejo turístico** tourist resort
**turrón** *m.* nougat
**tuyo/a** *poss.* your, of yours (*inf. sing.*)

## U

**u** or (*used instead of* **o** *before words beginning with* **o** *or* **ho**)

**ubicado/a** located (16)
**ubicar (qu)** to place, put; to locate
**Ud.: usted** *sub. pron.* you (*pol. sing.*); *obj. of prep.* you (*pol. sing.*)
**Uds.: ustedes** *sub. pron.* you (*pol. pl.*); *obj. of prep.* you (*pol. pl.*)
**últimamente** lately
**último/a** last (6); latest; **a última hora** at the last minute; **la última vez** the last time (6); **por última vez** for the last time; **por último** finally, lastly (2)
**un, uno/a** *indefinite article* a, an; one (A); *pl.* some
**único/a** *adj.* only; unique; **lo único** the only thing
**unidad** *f.* unit
**unido/a** united; attached; **Estados Unidos** United States (C)
**unificar (qu)** to unify
**unir** to unite, join
**universidad** *f.* university
**universitario/a** of or pertaining to the university (14)
**uña** fingernail (12)
**urbano/a** urban
**urbe** *f.* large city
**urgencia** emergency
**urgir (j)** to be pressing, be really necessary
**uruguayo/a** *n., adj.* Uruguayan (3)
**usar** to use (3); **¿qué talla usa?** what size do you wear? (13)
**uso** use (10)
**usted (Ud., Vd.)** *sub. pron.* you (*pol. sing.*) (B); *obj of prep.* you (*pol. sing.*); **¿y usted?** and you (*pol. sing.*)? (A)
**ustedes (Uds., Vds.)** *sub. pron.* you (*pol. pl.*) (B); *obj. of prep.* you (*pol. pl.*)
**usurero/a** profiteer, moneylender
**utensilio** utensil (6)
**útil** useful
**utilidad** *f.* utility
**utilización** *f.* use, utilization
**utilizar (c)** to utilize, use (13)
**uva** grape (8)

## V

**vaca** cow
**vacaciones** *f. pl.* vacation; **ir de vacaciones** to go on vacation (11); **salir de vacaciones** to go on vacation (3)
**vacío/a** empty
**vacuna** vaccination (11)
**vago/a** bum
**vagón** *m.* car (*train*) (10)
**vainilla** vanilla
**valenciano/a** *adj.* from Valencia (*Spain*)
**valer** *irreg.* to be worth; to cost (13); **¿cuánto vale?** how much is it? (13); **más vale** (+ *infin.*) it is better to (*do something*); **valerse de** to make use of, avail oneself of
**valiente** *n. m., f.* brave person; *adj.* brave
**valija** suitcase
**valioso/a** valuable (12)
**valle** *m.* valley (10)
**valor** *m.* value; cost (11)
**valorar** to value (15)
**vampiresa** femme fatale
**vanidad** *f.* vanity
**vapor** *m.* steam
**vaquero/a** cowboy/cowgirl; **pantalones** (*m. pl.*) **vaqueros** jeans (2)
**variar (varío)** to vary
**varicela** chicken pox (12)
**variedad** *f.* variety
**varios/as** *pl.* several (3)
**varón** *m.* male
**vasco/a** *adj.* Basque
**vasija** container
**vaso** (drinking) glass (4)
**vasto/a** vast, huge
**Vd.: usted** *sub. pron.* you (*pol. sing.*); *obj. of prep.* you (*pol. sing.*)
**Vds.: ustedes** *sub. pron.* you (*pol. pl.*); *obj. of prep.* you (*pol. pl.*)
**vecindad** *f.* neighborhood
**vecindario** neighborhood
**vecino/a** neighbor (B)
**vegetación** *f.* vegetation (10)
**vegetal** *m.* vegetable; plant
**vehículo** vehicle (10)
**veinte** twenty (A)
**veinticinco** twenty-five (A)
**veinticuatro** twenty-four (A)
**veintidós** twenty-two (A)
**veintinueve** twenty-nine (A)
**veintiocho** twenty-eight (A)
**veintiséis** twenty-six (A)
**veintisiete** twenty-seven (A)
**veintitrés** twenty-three (A)
**veintiuno** twenty-one (A)
**vejez** *f.* old age
**vela** *n.* sailing
**velación** *f.* wake, vigil
**velero** sailboat; **andar en velero** to go sailing (4)
**velocidad** *f.* speed; **disminuir la velocidad** to reduce speed (13); **exceso de velocidad** speeding (7)
**vena** vein (12)
**vencer (z)** to conquer
**vencido/a: darse por vencido/a** to give up
**vendaje** *m.* bandage (12)
**vendedor(a)** salesperson, seller (13)
**vender** to sell (13)
**venéreo/a: enfermedad** (*f.*) **venérea** sexually transmitted disease
**venezolano/a** *adj.* Venezuelan (3)
**venir** *irreg.* to come (4)
**venta** sale (13); **de venta** for sale (9); **venta de garaje/zaguán** garage sale
**ventaja** advantage (15)
**ventana** window (B)
**ventanilla** window (*car, train, etc.*)
**ventilación** *f.* ventilation
**ventilador** *m.* (electric) fan (6)
**ventricular** *adj.* ventricular
**ver** *irreg.* to see (1); to watch; **a ver** let's see (13); **nos vemos** we'll be seeing each other; see you (2); **¡tanto tiempo sin verte!** I haven't seen you (*inf. sing.*) in ages! (6); **vamos a ver** let's see; **ver la televisión** to watch television (1); **ver una telenovela** to watch a soap opera (1); **ver un partido de...** to watch a game of . . . (1); **verse** to see oneself; to look, appear
**veranear** to spend the summer
**veraniego/a** *adj.* summer, summer-like
**verano** summer (1)
**veras** *pl.*: **¿de veras?** really? (4)
**verbo** verb
**verdad** *f.* truth (6); **de verdad** truly, really; **es verdad** that's right (true); it's true (B); **la mera verdad** the simple truth; **¿verdad?** right?, isn't it? (2)
**verdadero/a** true, truthful
**verde** green (A)
**verduras** *pl.* (green) vegetables
**vergüenza: darle vergüenza a uno** to be ashamed
**verificar (qu)** to check
**versátil** versatile
**versión** *f.* version
**verso** verse, rhyme
**vestido** dress (A)
**vestir (i, i)** to dress; **vestirse** to get dressed (7)
**veterinario/a** veterinarian (12)
**vez** *f.* (*pl.* **veces**) time; **a la vez** at the same time (5); **a veces** sometimes (C); **alguna vez** once; ever; **algunas veces** sometimes (14); **de vez en cuando** once in a while (10); **dos veces** twice; **en vez de** instead of; **la última vez** the last time (6); **muchas veces** many times (5); **otra vez** again (5); **por primera vez** for the first time (8); **por última vez** for the last time; **tal vez** perhaps (15); **una vez** once (8); **... veces a la / por semana** . . . times a week (4)
**vía** road; way (10); **en vías de desarrollo** developing
**viajar** to travel (C)
**viaje** *m.* trip; **agencia de viajes** travel agency (C); **agente** (*m., f.*) **de viajes** travel agent; **¡buen viaje!** have a nice trip! (10); **hacer viajes** to take trips, travel; **viaje de negocios** business trip
**viajero/a** traveler (11); **cheque** (*m.*) **de viajero** traveler's check (11)
**vicio** vice, bad habit (12)
**víctima** *m., f.* victim
**vida** life (3); **así es la vida** that's life (15); **toda la vida** one's whole life (14)
**videocasetera** videocassette player (13)
**videocentro** video store (4)
**videoteca** film (video) library
**vidrio** glass (*material*) (10)
**viejo/a** *n.* old person; *adj.* old (A)
**viento** wind; **hace viento** it's windy (1)
**viernes** *m. sing., pl.* Friday (1)

**vigencia: entrar en vigencia** to take effect
**vigilar** to keep en eye on; to watch (out) for
**VIH** *m.* (*abbrev. for* **virus** [*m.*] **de la inmunodeficiencia humana**) HIV (12)
**villancico** Christmas carol
**vinagre** *m.* vinegar
**vino** wine (8); **llamar al pan pan y al vino vino** to call a spade a spade; **vino blanco/tinto** white/red wine (8)
**viña** vineyard
**violación** *f.* violation; **violación sexual** rape (16)
**violar** to rape
**violencia** violence (16)
**violento/a** violent
**violeta** *adj. m., f.* violet
**violín** *m.* violin (5)
**Virgen** *f.* Virgin (Mary)
**virreinal** viceregal
**virreinato** viceroyalty
**virus** *m. sing., pl.* virus
**visa** visa (11); **sacar el visado** to get a visa (11)
**visado** visa (11)
**víscera** viscera
**visionario/a** *n.* visionary
**visita** visit; **de visita** visiting
**visitante** *m., f.* visitor
**visitar** to visit
**vislumbrar** to glimpse, catch a glimpse of
**vista** view (6); **punto de vista** point of view; **tener en vista** to have in mind
**visto/a** (*p.p. of* **ver**) seen, viewed
**viudo/a** widower/widow (C)
**vivienda** housing (15)
**vivir** to live (1); **viva...** long live . . .
**vivo/a** alive (8)
**vocabulario** vocabulary
**vocero/a** spokesperson (16)
**volante** *m.* steering wheel (10)
**volar (ue)** to fly (9); **volar una cometa / un papalote** *Mex.* to fly a kite (2, 9)
**volcán** *m.* volcano
**voleibol** *m.* volleyball
**voltio** volt
**voluntad** *f.* will, desire
**volver (ue)** (*p.p.* **vuelto**) to return (4); **volverse** to turn into, become (14); **volverse loco/a** to go crazy (12)
**vos** *sub. pron.* (*Arg., Guat., etc.*) you (*inf. sing.*)
**vosotros/as** *sub. pron.* (*Sp.*) you (*inf. pl.*); *obj. of prep.* (*Sp.*) you (*inf. pl.*)
**votar** to vote (16)
**voz** *f.* (*pl.* **voces**) voice (14); **en voz alta/baja** in a loud/low voice (5)
**vuelo** flight (7); **asistente** (*m., f.*) **de vuelo** flight attendant (11)
**vuelta** *n.* turn; **boleto de ida y vuelta** round-trip ticket (11); **dar muchas vueltas** to go back and forth; **dar vueltas** to go around; **darle una vuelta a alguien** to look in on someone (*invalid or hospital patient*); **una vuelta más** another time around
**vuelto/a** (*p.p. of* **volver**) returned
**vuestro/a** *poss.* (*Sp.*) your (*inf. pl.*), of yours (*inf. pl.*)

## X

**xenofobia** xenophobia
**xilometazolina** zylometazolin

## Y

**y** and (A); plus
**ya** already (5); now; **ya era hora** it was about time (16); **ya lo creo** of course; **ya lo sé** I already know it; **ya no** no longer; **ya que** since; **ya voy** I'm coming
**yerno** son-in-law (9)
**yo** *sub. pron.* I (B)
**yogur** *m.* yogurt

## Z

**zaguán** *m.*: **venta de zaguán** garage sale
**zanahoria** carrot (8)
**zapatería** shoe store (4)
**zapatilla** slipper (13)
**zapato (de tenis)** (tennis) shoe (A); **zapatos de tacón alto** high-heeled shoes (13)
**zar** *m.* czar (16)
**zócalo** *Mex.* plaza, town square
**zoológico** zoo (7)
**zumbido** *n.* buzzing
**zumo** juice

# Index

This index is divided into two parts. "Grammar" covers grammar, structure, and usage; "Topics" lists cultural and vocabulary topics treated in the text. Topics appear as groups; they are not cross-referenced. Any abbreviations in the index are identical to those used in the end vocabulary.

## GRAMMAR


**a**, + **el**, 153
  + infinitive, 97
  + noun or pronoun, to specify indirect object, 183–184, 280–281
accent marks. *See also* Appendix 3
  with interrogatives and exclamations, 346
adjectives, agreement of, 13–15, 30–32, 44–48, 187–188
  defined, 13–15
  demonstrative, 187–188
  descriptive, 4, 9, 21, 24, 96
  forms of, 13–15, 30
  irregular comparative forms of, 217
  listed, 96
  meaning after **ser** and **estar**, 144, 160, 162
  nominalization (used as nouns)
  of nationality, 38–39, 41, 47–48, 113, 121
  ordinal, 83, 96, 98
  past participle used as, 144
  position of, 13–15
  possessive (stressed). *See* Appendix 2
  possessive (unstressed), 44–46. *See also* Appendix 2
  regular comparative forms of, 216–217
adverbial clauses with subjunctive, 374–376. *See also* Appendix 2
adverbs, defined, 348
  ending in **-mente**, 348
  of time, 208, 215, 221, 229. *See also* Appendix 2
affirmative words, 283–284
age, expressing, 37, 46
*ago* (with **hacer**), 235, 252
agreement, of adjectives, 13–15, 30–32, 44–48, 187–188
  of articles, 13–15, 27–29
  of nouns, 13–15, 27–29
  of possessive adjectives, 44–46
  of subject and verb, 14, 26–27, 124–125
**al**, 153
alphabet, Spanish, 70–71
**andar** (*irreg.*). *See* Appendix 1
apocopation, 98, 284
**-ar** verbs, commands, 372
  imperfect, 309. *See also* Appendix 1
  past (preterite), 207, 220–221, 227, 230–231, 243–245, 344. *See also* Appendix 1
  present, 14, 48–49, 124. *See also* Appendix 1
  subjunctive, 374–376. *See also* Appendix 1
articles, definite, 13–15, 217
  indefinite, 13–14, 27–29
  plural, 15, 30–31

**caer** (*irreg.*). *See* Appendix 1
cardinal numbers, 6, 10, 19, 37, 54–55, 69
**comer**. *See* Appendix 1
commands (imperative), defined, 11
  formal (polite; **usted**, **ustedes**), 2, 8, 11
  of stem-changing verbs, 372–373
  placement of object pronouns with, 373
  softened, 374–379
  **vosotros/as**, 376. *See also* Appendix 1
comparisons, of equality, 218
  of inequality, 216–217
  of irregular adjectives, 217
  of nouns, 216–218
  of regular adjectives, 216–218
conditional, forms. *See* Appendix 1
  uses of, 176
conjugate, defined, 48
conjunctions, of time, 352, 377–379
  use of subjunctive after, 352, 377–379
**conmigo**, **contigo**, 282
**conocer (zc)**, 222–223, 312, 372, 377
  uses of, 222–223, 312
  versus **saber**, 222–223
**construir (y)**, 377. *See also* Appendix 1
contractions, **al**, 153
  **del**, 43
**cuando**, subjunctive after, 377
**cuánto**, **¿cuántos/as?**, in exclamations, 327, 346
  to ask *how long . . . ?*, 327
**dar** (*irreg.*), 247, 377. *See also* Appendix 1
dates, expressing, 51–52
days of the week, 67
**de**, + **el**, 43
  + infinitive, 191
  + noun, 191
  to express origin, 113–114, 128–129
  to show possession, 35, 43
  used with prepositions, 191
  with **salir**, 127
**deber**, uses of, 202, 215, 219, 334
**decir** (*irreg.*), 156, 247, 345, 372, 377. *See also* Appendix 1
  to report speech, 184, 251
  with indirect object pronouns, 164, 184, 251
definite articles, forms of, 13–15
  use and omission of, 13–15, 217
**del**, 43
demonstrative adjectives, 187–188. *See also* Appendix 2
describing, 4, 21, 24
descriptive adjectives, 4, 9, 13–15, 21, 24, 96
desires, expressed with **querer**, 86, 99, 378

direct object, 223–224, 277–278
direct object pronouns, impersonal, 277–278
  personal, 223–224, 277–278
  placement of, 223–224, 278, 373. *See also* Pronouns
**dormir (ue, u)**, 155, 249–250, 345, 373, 379. *See also* Appendix 1
double negative, 283–284

endings, personal, commands, 372
  defined, 14
  for regular **-ar** verbs, 14, 48–49, 124, 309, 372, 375–376
  for regular **-er** verbs, 71–72, 124–125, 309, 372, 375–376
  for regular **-ir** verbs, 71–72, 124–125, 309, 372, 375–376. *See also* Appendix 1
equality, comparisons of, 218
**-er** and **-ir** verbs, commands, 372
  imperfect, 309. *See also* Appendix 1
  past (preterite), 207, 220–221, 227, 230–231, 243–245. *See also* Appendix 1
  present tense, 71–72, 124–125. *See also* Appendix 1
  subjunctive, 375–376. *See also* Appendix 1
**escribir**, 345, 375–376
**estar** (*irreg.*), 123, 246, 312–313, 372, 377, 380. *See also* Appendix 1
  + adjective to describe physical and mental states, 144, 160, 312–313
  + adjective versus **ser** + adjective, 160, 162
  + present participle (**-ndo**; actions in progress), 116–117, 130, 380
  to express location, 123, 128–129, 153–154
  uses of, 116–117, 123, 130, 144, 153–154, 162, 380
  versus **ser**, 128–129, 160, 162
exclamations, 327, 346

feminine nouns, 13–15, 27–29, 31–32
formal commands, 2, 8, 11, 372–373
future, forms of. *See* Appendix 1
  informal (**ir** + **a** infinitive), 79, 97, 176, 314
  subjunctive used to express, 352, 377–379

gender, of nouns and adjectives, 13–15, 27–29, 31–32, 47–48
generalizations (impersonal expressions), with **se**, 285–286
greetings, 7, 9, 17–18
**gustar**, 279–281
  + infinitive, 60, 75–76, 189–190, 280–281
  using, 60, 75–76, 189–190, 279–281
  verbs like, 349
  with indirect object pronouns, 76, 183, 280, 349
**gustaría**, 189–190

**haber** (*irreg.*). *See* Appendix 1
  as an auxiliary verb, 344–345
  **hay que**, 202, 215, 219
habitual actions, indicative versus subjunctive for, 375
  in the past (imperfect) tense, 296, 301, 309–310
  in the present tense, 375
**hablar**. *See* Appendix 1
**hacer** (*irreg.*), 90–91, 101, 127, 156, 247, 345, 377. *See also* Appendix 1
  idioms with, 90–91, 101, 235, 252
  in time expressions, 235, 252, 327, 343
  to describe weather, 90–91, 101, 162
**hay**, 29
**hay que**, 202, 215, 219

identification, with **ser**, 12–13
idioms, with **hacer**, 90–91, 101, 235, 252
  with **tener**, 37, 46, 145, 161–162, 176, 189–190
imperatives. *See* Commands
imperfect indicative tense, versus past (preterite), 301, 367, 381–382. *See also* Appendix 2
  forms of, 309–310. *See also* Appendix 1
  uses of, 296, 301, 309, 314, 380–382
imperfect subjunctive. *See* Past subjunctive
impersonal **se**, 285–286
indefinite and negative words, 261, 283–284
indefinite and nonexistent antecedents. *See* Appendix 2
indefinite articles, 13–14, 27–29
indicative, versus subjunctive, 375–376. *See also* Appendix 2
  in adjective clauses. *See* Appendix 2
  to express habitual activities, 375
indirect object pronouns, forms of, 164, 183–184, 251
  placement of, 164, 183–184, 373, 377
  with **decir**, 164, 183–184, 251
  with **gustar**, 76, 183, 189–190, 280, 349
  with verbs of informing, 183–184, 251. *See also* Pronouns
indirect object verbs, 183–184, 251
inequality, comparisons of, 216–217
infinitives. *See also* Appendix 1
  after prepositions, 97, 191
  and indirect object pronouns, 184
  and reflexive pronouns, 157–158
  as verb complement, 97
  defined, 48–49
  with **gustar**, 60, 75–76, 189–190, 280–281
  with **ir** + **a** to express future time, 79, 97, 176, 314
  with **querer** and **preferir**, 86, 99
  with verbs of obligation and duty, 202, 215, 219
information questions, 3, 8–9, 12, 42, 46, 280
informing, verbs of, 183–184, 251
interrogatives. *See* Questions
**ir** (*irreg.*), 247, 310, 314, 373, 377. *See also* Appendix 1
  + **a** + infinitive, 79, 97, 176, 314
  **a(l)**, **a la**, to express movement toward, 153
  uses of, 79, 97, 153, 176
**-ir** and **-er** verbs, commands, 372
  imperfect. *See* Appendix 1
  past (preterite), 207–208, 220–221, 227, 230–231, 241, 243–245. *See also* Appendix 1
  present tense, 71–72, 124–125. *See also* Appendix 1
  subjunctive, 375–376. *See also* Appendix 1
irregular verbs. *See* Appendix 1

**jugar (ue)**, 128, 155, 344
  + **al** + sport, 128

**le/les** as direct object pronouns, 224
*let's* (**vamos a**), 192
location, expressed by **estar en**, 123, 128–129, 153–154
  expressed by **ir** + **a(l)**, 153
  of people and things, with **estar**, 123, 128–129, 153–154

masculine nouns, 13–15, 27–29, 31–32
**-mente**, 348
mood, defined, 377
nationality, adjectives of, 38–39, 41, 47–48, 113, 121
negation, of sentences, 13, 283–284
  words for, 261, 283–284
negative, double, 283–284
neuter demonstratives. *See* Appendix 2
**no**, 13, 284
nouns, comparison of, 216–218
  direct object, 277
  following **gustar**, 279–281, 349
  gender of, 13–15, 27–29
  indirect object, 183–184
  plural of, 15, 30–31
number. *See* Agreement

numbers, cardinal, 6, 10, 19, 37, 54–55, 69
ordinal, 83, 96, 98
years, how to read, 69

obligation and duty, verbs expressing, 202, 215, 219–220
**oír** (*irreg.*), 156, 372, 377. *See also* Appendix 1
order. *See* Word order
ordinal numbers, 83, 96, 98
origin, and nationality, 38–39, 41, 113–114, 121, 128–129
expressed by **ser de**, 113–114, 128–129
orthographic changes. *See* Spelling changes
**os**, 349

**para** versus **por**, 325–326, 347–348. *See also* Appendix 2
participles, past, 344–345
present, 116–117, 130, 184. *See also* Appendix 1
past participle, forms of, 344–345. *See also* Appendix 1
used as adjective, 144
with **estar**, 144, 160
with **haber**, to form perfect tenses, 344–345. *See also* Appendix 1
past perfect indicative. *See* Appendix 1
past perfect subjunctive. *See* Subjunctive; Appendix 1
past progressive, 380
past subjunctive, formation of. *See* Appendix 1
**pedir (i, i)**, 268, 286–287. *See also* Appendix 1
**pensar (ie)**, 154, 176, 189–190, 249, 314, 373, 378. *See also* Appendix 1
uses, 189–190
with infinitive and **de**, **en**, **que**, 189–190
present perfect indicative, 344–345
present perfect subjunctive. *See* Appendix 1
personal (subject) pronouns, 12–14, 26–27, 48–49, 280, 282
pluperfect (past perfect) indicative. *See* Appendix 1
pluperfect subjunctive. *See* Subjunctive; Appendix 1
plural, adjectives, 15, 31–32, 44–46
nouns, 15, 30–31
of **tú** and **usted**, 25–26
**poder (ue, u)** (*irreg.*), 168, 186, 246, 312. *See also* Appendix 1
uses of, 168, 186
polite commands, 2, 8, 11, 372–373
polite requests and statements with past subjunctive, 176, 189–190
**poner(se)** (*irreg.*), 156, 246, 345, 377. *See also* Appendix 1
**por** versus **para**, 325–326, 347–348. *See also* Appendix 2
position. *See* Word order
possession, with **de**, 35, 43
with possessive adjectives, 44–46. *See also* Appendix 2
with **ser de**, 35, 43
with **tener**, 35, 43
possessive adjectives, agreement of, 44–46
unstressed, 44–46. *See also* Appendix 2
possessive pronouns. *See* Appendix 2
**preferir (ie)**, 86, 99, 154, 249–250
with infinitive, 86, 99
prepositions, followed by infinitives, 97, 191
followed by nouns or subject pronouns, 280, 282
of location and time, 104, 120, 191
present participle, and indirect object pronouns, 184
and reflexive pronouns, 158–159
formation (regular and irregular), 130
of **-ir** stem-changing verbs, 249–250, 286
with **estar** (progressive), 116–117, 130, 380
with stem changes, 130, 249–250, 286. *See also* Appendix 1
present perfect indicative, 344–345. *See also* Appendix 1
present perfect subjunctive. *See* Subjunctive
present progressive, 116–117, 130
present subjunctive, forms of, 374–379
meaning of, 377
of stem-changing verbs, 378–379. *See also* Subjunctive; Appendix 1
used to express future, 352, 374–376
present tense, of **-ar** verbs, 14, 48–49, 124. *See also* Appendix 1
of **-er** and **-ir** verbs, 71–72, 124–125. *See also* Appendix 1
of regular verbs, 14. *See also* Appendix 1
of stem-changing verbs, 99, 128, 154–155, 249–250. *See also* Appendix 1
to express habitual actions, 375
preterite (past), versus imperfect, 301, 367, 381–382. *See also* Appendix 2
irregular forms of, 241, 246–247
meaning of, 381
question-and-answer patterns in, 207
regular forms of, 207, 220–221, 227, 230–231, 243–245
stem-vowel changes in, 245, 249–250. *See also* Appendix 1
uses of, 207, 227
**vos** forms, 246
**producir (zc)**. *See* Appendix 1
progressive forms (with **estar**), past (with imperfect), 380
present, 116–117, 130
pronouns, as object of preposition, 280, 282
direct object, 223–224, 277–278
indirect object, 164, 183–184, 251
object. *See also* Direct object pronouns; Indirect object pronouns
personal (subject), 12–14, 26–27, 48–49, 280, 282
placement of (summary), 376
reflexive, 157–159
subject, 12–14, 26–27, 48–49, 280, 282. *See also* Appendix 2
with commands, 373

**que**, + infinitive, 219
**¿qué?**, in questions, 346
to express reactions, 327, 346
**querer (ie)** (*irreg.*), 86, 99, 154, 247, 312, 314. *See also* Appendix 1
uses, 374
questions, information, 3, 8–9, 12, 42, 46, 280
**quisiera**, 176, 189–190

radical-changing verbs. *See* Stem-changing verbs
reciprocal pronouns and verbs, 307–308
redundant pronoun construction, 280
reflexive, and daily routine, 142, 157–159
pronouns, 157–159. *See also* Appendix 2
to express reciprocal action, 308
verbs, 142, 157–159
regular verbs. *See* **-ar**, **-er**, **-ir** verbs; Appendix 1
**reír (i, i)**, 288. *See also* Appendix 1

**saber** (*irreg.*), 168, 186, 222–223, 246, 312, 373, 377. *See also* Appendix 1
to express ability, 168, 186, 222–223
uses of, 168, 186, 222–223, 312
versus **conocer**, 222–223
**salir** (*irreg.*), 127, 156, 207, 227, 372, 377. *See also* Appendix 1
**se**, impersonal (*one*; passive), 285–286
reflexive pronoun, 142, 157–159
**seguir (i, i) (ga)**, 287. *See also* Appendix 1

*-self/-selves*, 157–159
**sentir (ie, i)**, 249–250. *See also* Appendix 1
sequence of events, words and expressions to show, 191, 208, 229
**ser** (*irreg.*), 12–13, 25–27, 247–248, 310, 373, 377. *See also* Appendix 1
  to describe characteristics, 21, 160
  to identify people and things, 12–13, 129
  to tell time, 74–75
  uses of, 12–14, 25–27, 35, 43, 74–75, 128–129, 160, 312–313
  versus **estar**, 128–129, 160
  with adjectives, 14, 21, 129, 160
  with **de** (origin, possession), 35, 43, 113–114, 128–129
shortened forms. *See* Apocopation
softened requests, and statements with past subjunctive, 176, 189–190
spelling changes. *See also* Appendix 3
  in formal commands, 373
  in past (preterite), 245
  in present subjunctive, 378–379
  verbs with. *See also* Appendix 1
state-of-being verbs in the past, 311–313
states (physical and mental), description of, 144, 151
  expressed by **estar** + adjective, 144, 151, 160, 162
  expressed by **tener** + noun, 145, 151, 161–162, 176, 189–190
  past, expressed by imperfect, 311–313
stem-changing verbs, in polite commands, 373
  in present participles, 250
  in the past (preterite), 245, 249–250
  in the present subjunctive, 378–379
  in the present tense, 99, 128, 154–155, 249
  verbs like **pedir**, 286–288, 378. *See also* Appendix 1
stem-vowel changes. *See* Stem-changing verbs
stress. *See* Appendix 3
**su(s)**, agreement of, 44–46
subject pronouns, agreement of, 12–14, 26–27, 124–125
  as objects of prepositions, 280, 282
  forms of, 12, 26–27. *See also* Pronouns; Appendix 2
  omission of, 13–14, 26–27, 48–49, 124
  use of, 12–14, 26–27, 124–125, 280, 282
subjunctive, concept of, 375
  following **cuando**, 352, 374–375
  in adjective clauses. *See* Appendix 2
  in adverbial (time) clauses, 374–375. *See also* Appendix 2
  present, 375–376, 377–379
  present perfect. *See* Appendix 1
  summary of uses. *See* Appendix 2
  used after expressions of influence (requests), 375–376
  used after nonexistent and indefinite antecedents. *See* Appendix 2
  versus indicative, 375–376. *See also* Appendix 2
  with object pronouns, 376
syllabication. *See* Appendix 3

telling time, 57, 67, 74–75, 95
**tener** (*irreg.*), 14, 35, 43, 156, 246, 312, 372, 377. *See also* Appendix 1
  idioms with, 37, 46, 145, 161–162, 176, 189–190
  + noun, to describe states, 145, 151, 161–162, 176, 312
  + **que**, to express obligation, 202, 215, 219
  to express possession, 35, 43
time of day (telling time), 57, 67, 74–75, 95
**traer** (*irreg.*), 156, 246–247, 372. *See also* Appendix 1
**tú**, versus **usted**, 17, 25–26, 45–46
**un(o/a)**, 13–14, 98
**usted(es)**, commands, 2, 8, 11, 372–373
  versus **tú**, 17, 25–26, 45–46

**vámonos, vamos a**, 192
**venir** (*irreg.*), 156, 246–247, 372, 377. *See also* Appendix 1
**ver** (*irreg.*), 207, 247, 310, 345, 372, 377. *See also* Appendix 1
verbs. *See* Commands; Subjunctive; Individual tenses; Appendices 1 and 2
verbs of reporting, 183–184, 251
**vivir**. *See* Appendix 1
**volver(se) (ue)** (*irreg.*), 155, 345, 373, 378. *See also* Appendix 1
**vos**, in South and Central America, 246
**vosotros/as**. *See* Appendix 1
  commands. *See* Appendix 1
**vuestro/a**, 44–45. *See also* Appendix 1

word order, in negative sentences, 13, 283–284
  of adjectives, 13–15
  of object pronouns, 164, 373
  of perfect tenses, 344–345
*would*, in polite requests, 176, 189–190
written accent mark, 12, 346

years, how to read, 69

## TOPICS

Culture, general
  agriculture, in Peru, 210
  careers and professional life, 178–179
  celebrations and holidays, 137–141
  cities, in Hispanic countries, 200–202
  climate
    Guatemala, 323
    Madrid, 322
  Colombia, food in, 272
  Costa Rica, ecology, 337–338
    towns in, 201–202
  Ecuador, Incan culture in, 239
  education, Hispanic system of, 175
  English terms used in Spanish, 167
  evening activities, 79, 89
  family life and relationships, 293–295, 303
  food and meals, 262, 264, 266–267, 272
  greetings, 7, 9
  Guatemala
    climate, 323
    Mayan ruins (Tikal), 323
  hello and goodbye, 7, 9
  Hispanics in the U.S., 115
  hobbies, 56, 89
  housing, 200–201
  introductions, 211
  jai alai, 62
  leisure activities, 56, 63–64, 89, 92, 296, 353
  Martí, José, 147
  meals and food, 262, 264, 266–267, 272
  Mexico
    Aztec language in, 260
    Guanajuato, 110–112
  Mexico City, tourism in, 362–364
  months and seasons, 51–52
  movies and moviegoing, 135
  Neruda, Pablo, 258–259, 319–320
  Panamá, Indian population of, 365
  Perú
    agriculture in, 210
    Machu Picchu, 237–238
  physical appearance, 21
  **la plaza**, 89, 92
  professional life and careers, 178–179
  religious life, 127, 137, 139–140
  schedule, 107
  social life, 89, 92

Spain
Madrid, 106, 136, 322, 356
**el Prado**, 136
Spanish terms used in English, 167
sports, 62–64
**las tapas**, 266
time of day, 57, 67, 209
**tú** versus **usted**, 17, 25–26, 45–46
Uruguay, beaches in, 353
**usted** versus **tú**, 17, 25–26, 45–46

Vocabulary
abilities (**saber** and **poder**), 168, 181, 186
academic subjects, 82, 95
addresses and phone numbers, 54–55, 67
affirmative and negative words, 283–284
airport and air travel, 325, 328, 342
body, parts of the, 20, 23
buildings, office and apartment, 198
campus locations, 120–121
cars and driving, 326–327, 332, 333, 342
celebrations and holidays, 51, 137, 150–151
cities, 40, 42
city streets, 105, 121, 133, 150, 214
classes and university life, 82, 95, 105, 120–121
classroom activities, 181
classroom expressions, 2–3, 8–10, 18, 22
climate, weather, and geography, 316, 342
clothing and accessories, 5, 9
colors, 5, 9
commands, 2, 8, 371
comparisons, 215
containers and measurements, 275
countries, 38–39, 41, 113, 121
daily schedule, 107, 142, 151, 158, 202, 214
dates and seasons, 51–52
days of the week, 67
description, 4, 9, 21, 24, 96
desires and wishes, 182
directions, 355, 371
ecology and the environment, 334, 343
education, 82, 95
everyday life, 107, 142, 151, 202, 214
family and relatives, 34, 41, 290, 306
food and drink, 254, 256, 261, 269, 274–275
frequency, 215
furniture and appliances, 194–196, 213–214
geographical terms, 38–40, 113, 121, 316, 342
greetings and leave-takings, 7, 9
hobbies, 56, 60
hotels, 359
house, features and rooms of a, 194, 198, 213–214
housework/domestic tasks, 202, 214
immigration, 359
introductions, 3, 211
languages, 38–39, 42
leisure/weekend activities, 56, 60, 67–68, 79
likes and dislikes (**gustar**), 60, 279–281
locations, 104–105, 120–121, 133, 150
measurements and containers, 275
mental and physical states, 151
months and seasons, 51–52, 67
nationalities, 38–39, 41, 113, 121
nature, 241
necessity, expressions of, 202, 215, 219–220
negative and affirmative words, 283–284
numbers, 6, 10, 19, 37, 54–55, 69, 96
obligations and duties, 202, 215, 219–220
ordinal numbers, 83, 96
people, 9, 23, 42
personal data, 54–55, 67
personal possessions, 195–196
personality descriptions, 21, 24
physical and mental states, 144, 151
physical descriptions, 4, 9, 21, 24, 96
plans, expressing personal, 176, 182, 189–190
preferences, expressing, 60, 86, 99
prepositions, 104, 120
questions, 3, 8–9, 12, 42, 46, 280
relationships, 211
road trips and signs, 326–327, 343
rooms of a house, 194, 198, 213–214
schedule, daily, 107, 142, 151, 158, 202, 214
shopping, 133
sports and leisure, 60, 62, 67–68, 79
states, physical and mental, 144, 151
subjects, academic, 82, 95
time, telling, 57, 67, 95
time expressions, 80, 95, 151, 182, 191, 208, 215, 221, 306
travel, 325–327, 342–343, 352, 358–359, 367, 370–371
university, 82, 95, 104–105, 120–121
weather, 90–91, 95
work/employment, 171–172, 181, 371

# About the Authors

**Tracy D. Terrell** (*late*) received his Ph.D. in Spanish Linguistics from the University of Texas at Austin and published extensively in the areas of Spanish dialectology, specializing in the sociolinguistics of Caribbean Spanish. Professor Terrell's publications on second-language acquisition and on the Natural Approach are widely known in the United States and abroad.

**Magdalena Andrade** received her first B.A. in Spanish/French and a second B.A. in English from San Diego University. After teaching in the Calexico Unified School District Bilingual Program for several years, she taught elementary and intermediate Spanish at both San Diego State and the University of California, Irvine, where she also taught Spanish for Spanish Speakers and Humanities Core Courses. Upon receiving her Ph.D. from the University of California, Irvine, she continued to teach there for several years.

**Jeanne Egasse** received her B.A. and M.A. in Spanish linguistics from the University of California, Irvine. She has taught foreign language methodology courses and supervised foreign language and ESL teachers in training at the University of California, Irvine. Currently, she is an instructor of Spanish and coordinates the Spanish Language Program at Irvine Valley College. In addition, Ms. Egasse leads children's literature circles and read-aloud sessions at a local public school. She also serves as a consultant for local schools and universities on implementing the Natural Approach in the language classroom.

**Elías Miguel Muñoz** is a Cuban-American poet and prose writer. He has a Ph.D. in Spanish from the University of California, Irvine, and has taught language and literature at the university level. He is co-author, with Tracy D. Terrell, of the *¡Bravo!* series for high school. He is also the author of *Viajes fantásticos* and *Ladrón de la mente*, titles in the Storyteller's Series of Spanish readers, which he created in collaboration with Stephen Krashen. Other published works include two books of literary criticism, three novels, as well as two poetry collections. Dr. Muñoz has written for the theater and has contributed to numerous anthologies of U.S. Latino literature. He has recently completed his fourth novel, *Brand New Memory*.

**Photo credits: Page 1** © Robert Frerck/Odyssey/Chicago; **4** © Peter Menzel; **8** © Bernard Wolf/Monkmeyer; **16** © Robert Frerck/Odyssey/Chicago; **33** © Bob Daemmrich/Stock Boston; **39** © Michael Grecco/Stock Boston; **39** © Clive Brunskill/Allsport USA; **50** © Chip & Rosa María de la Cueva Peterson; **56** © Owen Franken/Stock Boston; **56** © SuperStock; **62** © Allsport USA; **63** © Polly Hodge; **75** Museum of Modern Art, New York/A.K.G., Berlin/SuperStock/© 1998 Demart Pro Arte®, Geneva/Artists Rights Society (ARS), New York; **78** © Robert Frerck/Tony Stone Images; **84** © Stuart Cohen/Comstock; **89** © Peter Menzel; **89** © Bob Daemmrich/Stock Boston; **92** © Macduff Everton/The Image Works; **93** © Ulrike Welsch; **103** © Bob Daemmrich/Stock Boston; **106** © Beryl Goldberg; **112** © M. Algaze/The Image Works; **114** © Robert Fried/Stock Boston; **114** © Peter Menzel; **115** © Beryl Goldberg; **118** © SuperStock; **132** © Bob Daemmrich/ Stock Boston; **135** © Paul Conklin/PhotoEdit; **136** © Beryl Goldberg; **139** © Ulrike Welsch; **140** © Kal Muller/Woodfin Camp & Associates; **140** © Suzanne Murphy-Larronde/D. Donne Bryant Stock; **140** © Piko/Agencia Comesaña; **141** © David Simson/ Stock Boston; **144** © David Young-Wolff/PhotoEdit; **147** © Paul Conklin/PhotoEdit; **163** © Ulrike Welsch; **171** © SuperStock; **175** © Ulrike Welsch; **175** © Ulrike Welsch; **175** © David Young-Wolff/PhotoEdit; **177** © Paul Conklin/Monkmeyer; **193** © Peter Menzel; **200** © Oliver Benn/Tony Stone Images; **200** © Peter Menzel; **201** © Peter Menzel; **205** © Cron/Monkmeyer; **210** © Robert Frerck/Odyssey/Chicago; **201** © SuperStock; **226** © Robert Frerck/Tony Stone Images; **230** © Robert Frerck/Odyssey/ Chicago; **232** (clockwise from top center) © Robert Frerck/Odyssey/Chicago; Ramon Surroca i Nouvilas; © Peter Menzel; © Peter Menzel; Chip & Rosa María de la Cueva Peterson; © Jim Pickerel/Tony Stone Images; **234** © D. Donne Bryant; **238** © Robert Frerck/ Odyssey/ Chicago; **238** © Andy Jillings/Tony Stone Images; **239** © Suzanne Murphy-Larronde/D. Donne Bryant Stock; **253** © Robert Frerck/Odyssey/Chicago; **259** © Peter Menzel; **259** © Phyllis Picardi/Stock Boston; **260** © Stuart Cohen/Reproduction authorized by El Instituto Nacional de Bellas Artes y Literatura; **264** © Robert Frerck/ Odyssey/ Chicago; **266** © Stuart Cohen/Comstock; **266** © Robert Frerck/Odyssey/Chicago; **267** © Beryl Goldberg; **268** Jerry Bauer, 1995; **268** Jeff Shaw; **272** © SuperStock; **288** © Olivier Rebbot/Stock Boston; **289** © Jack Fields/Photo Researchers, Inc.; **292** © H. Huntly Hersch/D. Donne Bryant Stock; **292** © D. Donne Bryant Stock; **295** © Joseph Nettis/Photo Researchers, Inc.; **299** © Robert Frerck/Odyssey/Chicago; **301** © Chip & Rosa María de la Cueva Peterson; **303** © David Young-Wolff/PhotoEdit; **304** © SuperStock; **315** © SuperStock; **317** © Alpamayo/D. Donne Bryant; **317** © Thomas R. Fletcher/Stock Boston; **317** © Steven Krous/Stock Boston; **317** © Ulrike Welsch; **317** © Roberto Bunge/D. Donne Bryant; **317** © SuperStock; **317** © Dave Bartruff/Stock Boston; **317** © Hans Wendler/The Image Bank; **317** © Catherine Noren/Stock Boston; **320** © SuperStock; **321** Jeff Rotman; **321** Jeff Rotman; **322** © Chip & Rosa María de la Cueva Peterson; **322** © Alpamayo John Phelan/D. Donne Bryant; **323** © Chip & Rosa María de la Cueva Peterson; **323** © Rob Crandall/Stock Boston; **333** © Cameramann/The Image Works; **335** © SuperStock; **337** © J. Oetzel/Comstock; **337** © D. Donne Bryant; **338** © Will & Deni McIntyre/Photo Researchers, Inc. **351** © Robert Frerck/Woodfin Camp & Assoc.; **353** © Chip & Rosa María de la Cueva Peterson; **356** © Dave Bartruff/Stock Boston; **361** © SuperStock; **361** © Michael J. Howe/SuperStock; **362** © David Young-Wolff/PhotoEdit; **364** © Beryl Goldberg; **364** © Beryl Goldberg; **364** © SuperStock; **365** © Robert Frerck/Odyssey/ Chicago; **365** © Anna E. Zuckerman/PhotoEdit; **366** © Stuart Cohen/Comstock; **368** © D. Donne Bryant; **373** © Mike Yamashita/ Woodfin Camp & Assoc.; **379** © Chip & Rosa María de la Cueva Peterson/Reproduction authorized by El Instituto Nacional de Bellas Artes y Literatura

**Realia credits: Page 37** *Cambio16*; **59** *Guía del Ocio*; **70** Reprinted with permission of the United States Olympic Committee; **76** Reprinted with permission of Dunlop-Slazenge, Inc.; **88** Reprinted with permission of *El Semanal*; **109** King Features Syndicate; **139** © Quino/Quipos; **173** © Quino/Quipos; **196** © Quino/Quipos; **235** *Muy Interesante*; **255** Reprinted with permission of General Mills; **264** King Features Syndicate; **271** *Noticias de la Semana*; **296** Pilar Gomez, *Semana*; **297** *Tedi*, Editorial Armonia; **328** Reprinted with permission of Iberia Airlines of Spain; **329** © Robert Bosch GmbH; **331** Tribuna de la Actualidad; **332** *Ser Padres Hoy*; **355** © AAA, reproduced by permission; **356** *Geomundo*; **361** *Geomundo*; **366** *Geomundo*; **367** *Geomundo*; **369** *Geomundo*; **376** *Geomundo*; **378** *Biba*, Editorial América Ibérica

**Literary credits: Pages 319-320** "Oda a la tormenta," © Pablo Neruda, 1954 y Fundación Pablo Neruda

# El mundo hispano a su alcance

## Argentina

| | |
|---|---|
| población | 34.700.000 |
| capital | Buenos Aires |
| moneda | el peso |
| idiomas | el español, el italiano |
| alfabetización | 95% |
| exportación principal | cereales |
| agricultura | caña de azúcar, trigo, ganadería |

## Bolivia

| | |
|---|---|
| población | 7.200.000 |
| capitales | La Paz y Sucre |
| moneda | el peso boliviano |
| idiomas | el español, el aimará, el quechua |
| alfabetización | 78% |
| exportación principal | gas natural |
| agricultura | café, caña de azúcar, papa |

## Brasil

| | |
|---|---|
| población | 162.700.000 |
| capital | Brasilia |
| moneda | la cruzada (o cruzeiro) |
| idiomas | el portugués, el alemán, el japonés |
| alfabetización | 81% |
| exportación principal | metales |
| agricultura | café, soya, caña de azúcar |

## Colombia

| | |
|---|---|
| población | 36.800.000 |
| capital | Bogotá |
| moneda | el peso |
| idiomas | el español, el chibcha, el arauaco |
| alfabetización | 91,3% |
| exportación principal | café |
| agricultura | café, plátano, flores |

## Costa Rica

| | |
|---|---|
| población | 3.500.000 |
| capital | San José |
| moneda | el colón |
| idiomas | el español, el inglés-criollo |
| alfabetización | 93% |
| exportación principal | café |
| agricultura | café, plátano, maíz, arroz |

## Cuba

| | |
|---|---|
| población | 11.000.000 |
| capital | La Habana |
| moneda | el peso |
| idioma | el español |
| alfabetización | 94% |
| exportación principal | azúcar |
| agricultura | caña de azúcar, arroz, café |

## Chile

| | |
|---|---|
| población | 14.300.000 |
| capital | Santiago |
| moneda | el peso |
| idiomas | el español, el mapuche |
| alfabetización | 94% |
| exportación principal | metales |
| agricultura | frutas, trigo, cebada |

## Ecuador

| | |
|---|---|
| población | 11.500.000 |
| capital | Quito |
| moneda | el sucre |
| idiomas | el español, el quechua |
| alfabetización | 92% |
| exportación principal | petróleo |
| agricultura | plátano, café, algodón, caña de azúcar |

## España

| | |
|---|---|
| población | 39.000.000 |
| capital | Madrid |
| moneda | la peseta |
| idiomas | el español, el catalán, el gallego, el vascuence |
| alfabetización | 97% |
| exportación principal | equipos de transporte |
| agricultura | trigo, cebada, remolacha azucarera |

## Guatemala

| | |
|---|---|
| población | 11.300.000 |
| capital | Ciudad de Guatemala |
| moneda | el quetzal |
| idiomas | el español, varios idiomas mayas |
| alfabetización | 55% |
| exportación principal | café |
| agricultura | café, plátano, caña de azúcar, maíz |